THE FINANCIAL REVOLUTION
IN ENGLAND

1. Charles Montague, 1st Earl of Halifax, Chancellor of the Exchequer 1694–9, First Lord of the Treasury 1697–9, 1714–15

The Financial Revolution in England

A STUDY IN THE DEVELOPMENT OF PUBLIC CREDIT

1688–1756

P. G. M. DICKSON

FELLOW OF ST CATHERINE'S COLLEGE, OXFORD

MACMILLAN

LONDON · MELBOURNE · TORONTO

ST MARTIN'S PRESS

NEW YORK

1967

MACMILLAN AND COMPANY LIMITED
Little Essex Street London WC 2
also Bombay Calcutta Madras Melbourne

THE MACMILLAN COMPANY OF CANADA LIMITED
70 Bond Street Toronto 2

ST MARTIN'S PRESS INC
175 Fifth Avenue New York NY 10010

Library of Congress Catalog Card Number:
67–12509

PRINTED IN GREAT BRITAIN

UXORI

DILECTISSIMAE

Contents

IV. *Government Short-term Borrowing*

V. *The Market in Securities*

Illustrations

ACKNOWLEDGEMENTS

Grateful thanks are due to the following for permission to reproduce paintings and documents belonging to them: the Bank of England for nos. 1, 2, 3 and 10; the British Museum for nos. 8 and 9; the Gemeente Archief, Amsterdam, for nos. 6 and 7; the Goldsmiths' Library, London University, for no. 4; the Public Record Office for nos. 5 and 11; and the Stock Exchange Library for no. 12.

A 2

D.F.R.

Tables

Unless otherwise stated, all sums in the text and tables are rounded to the nearest £

CHART

Dates, spelling, citations

UNTIL 1752 England began the year for most purposes on 25 March, and used the Julian calendar, which until 1700 was ten, and after 1700 eleven, days behind the Gregorian calendar used by many European countries. Dates given in the text and footnotes are Julian ones (Old Style, abbreviated O.S.) unless stated as Gregorian or New Style (N.S.). The year, however, is assumed to start on 1 January. Thus what contemporaries wrote as 1 February 1739 is transcribed as 1 February 1740.

Quotations in the text and footnotes reproduce as far as possible the spelling and punctuation of the sources from which they are taken. The full titles of books and articles cited by the authors' names only or in shortened form can be found in the Bibliography. The authors of pamphlets have been stated when traceable; when not, only the titles of the pamphlets are given, without 'Anon.' in front of them.

Since the completion of this book the records of the East India Company formerly in the Bank of England Record Office (for a list, see the Bibliography) have been removed to the India Office Library.

Abbreviations

Add. MSS.	British Museum Additional Manuscripts
AHR	*American Historical Review*
A.N.	Archives Nationales, Paris
Archief Brants	Gemeente Archief, Amsterdam, archive of the Brants family
BIHR	*Bulletin of the Institute of Historical Research*
B.M.	British Museum
BPP	*British Parliamentary Papers*
Cal. T. Bks., Papers	*Calendar of Treasury Books, Papers*
D. Ct. Bk.	Directors' Court Minute Book
DNB	*Dictionary of National Biography*
Econ. H.R.	*Economic History Review*
EHR	*English Historical Review*
G. Ct. Bk.	General Court Minute Book
Gent. Mag.	*Gentleman's Magazine*
HCJ	*House of Commons Journals*
HLJ	*House of Lords Journals*
H.L.R.O.	House of Lords Record Office
H.M.C.	Historical Manuscripts Commission
J. Ec. Hist.	*Journal of Economic History*
J. Mod. Hist.	*Journal of Modern History*
N.S.	New Style (see note on dates)
O.S.	Old Style (see note on dates)
Parl. Hist.	*Cobbett's Parliamentary History of England*
P.R.O.	Public Record Office
TRHS	*Transactions of the Royal Historical Society*

Preface and Acknowledgements

THIS study began more than a decade ago as an inquiry into the amount of foreign investment in English government securities in the eighteenth century, a subject raised by Professor C. H. Wilson in his pioneering work on Anglo-Dutch commerce and finance published in 1941. As work progressed, however, it became clear that foreign investment could not usefully be assessed without reconstructing in detail the system of government borrowing of which it formed part. In an ideal world the ensuing investigation, which was necessarily long and complex, would no doubt have been conducted by a team of researchers who would scrupulously have checked each other's results. In its absence, I have tried to work to as narrow a margin of error as possible. The book has been taken up and laid aside as other commitments dictated. It was largely written in 1964 and earlier this year, partly during sabbatical leave granted to me for this and another project.

The amount of detail in the text reflects, unapologetically, my belief that insufficient is as yet known about the eighteenth century, in England or Europe, to bear the weight of generalization with which historians have normally loaded it, and which only detailed monographs can modify and render more supportable. The title reflects a further belief: that the smooth, even flow of history, interrupted at long intervals by sharp, short political upheavals, is a myth invented by historians; that the life of nations, as of individuals, proceeds in jerks (to adapt Clapham's description of the Quantum Theory); and that there are periods of accelerated development in both which can without distortion of language be called revolutionary, even though they have nothing to do with tumbrils or barricades. Lastly, the use of 'England' and 'English' throughout the book is deliberate. English historians' perennial ignorance of Irish and Scottish developments, and of the reaction of these developments on English ones, cannot, respectably, be redeemed by substituting 'British' for 'English' and then continuing to ignore Ireland and Scotland. In fact, in this period, the contribution of the Scottish revenue to Westminster was negligible, and Ireland's exchequer remained separate from England's until 1817, but it would be interesting to know more than is at present known about the Scottish and Irish financial systems, and the local interests tied to them.

It is a pleasant task to record my gratitude to those whose help and counsel have made this book possible. In the first place, to Dr. L. S. Sutherland, Principal of Lady Margaret Hall, Oxford, for her constant support and encouragement, acute criticism, and generous help with sources and with transcripts of particular materials. Second, to Professor A. H. John, of the London School of Economics and Political Science, for transcripts of material, and for many helpful and original suggestions about problems involved in the inquiry. Third, to the Governor and Company of the Bank of England, without whose generous permission to use their very extensive records the book could not have been written. Mr. J. A. Giuseppi and Mr. R. A. Woods, successively Archivists to the Bank, have been unfailingly helpful in arranging for me to see this material and in answering numerous inquiries. I should also like to thank the Warden and Fellows of Nuffield College, Oxford, who elected me to a Studentship and then to a Research Fellowship in the period 1953–6; the Houblon–Norman Fund of the Bank of England, whose Trustees gave me a grant for research in London and Amsterdam in 1961; and the University of Oxford for making a grant towards the expense of typing the manuscript.

The early stage of my researches benefited greatly from discussions with Dr. J. E. D. Binney, Mrs. A. C. Carter of the London School of Economics, Dr. C. D. Chandaman, Dr. A. Farnsworth, and Professor J. G. Sperling. I am indebted to Dr. Binney, Dr. Chandaman and Professor Sperling for allowing me to read their doctoral theses. Professor Earl J. Hamilton kindly gave me permission to use some of his data about borrowing and loan-rates in Amsterdam. For permission to use material, or for help in interpreting it, I am also indebted to Mr. C. D. Baker, Secretary of the Royal Exchange Assurance; Mr. J. D. Bannister, Secretary of the London Assurance; Mr. Giles Barber; Miss M. B. C. Canney, Goldsmiths' Library, University of London; Mr. Donovan Dawe, Guildhall Library; Mr. J. A. C. Greenwood, General Manager of the Sun Alliance & London Insurance Group; Professor H. J. Habakkuk; the Earl of Harrowby; Mr. L. G. Hart, Departmental Records Officer of Post Office Records, St. Martin's-le-Grand; Dr. Simon Hart of the Gemeente Archief, Amsterdam, whose friendly help guided me through the shoals of Dutch source material; and Mr. G. H. Penney, Librarian of the Stock Exchange Library, London. Mr. C. G. Randolph, formerly Chairman of the Sun Insurance Office and Managing Director of Glyn, Mills & Co., kindly gave permission for me to inspect the records of Child's Bank, and Mr. S. W. Shelton, Archivist of Glyn, Mills & Co., helped me in using them. Mr. G. A. Webb, Sub-Librarian of the Codrington Library, Oxford, has responded with unfailing good humour to my unsparing demands on his time. My debt to the resources and staffs of the Bodleian Library, British Museum, Corporation of London Records Office, House of Lords Record Office, Institute of Historical Research and Public Record Office will be extensively apparent from the text. My thanks are due also to Mrs. P. W. Jayakar, who has typed and re-typed a difficult manuscript with speed and accuracy. I acknowledge a fraction of my debt to my wife for her patience and help by dedicating the book to her.

St. Catherine's College, Oxford   P. G. M. DICKSON
December 1965

'Methought I returned to the Great Hall, [of the Bank of England] . . . but to my Surprize, instead of the Company that I left there, I saw towards the upper end of the Hall, a beautiful Virgin seated on a Throne of Gold. Her Name (as they told me) was *Publick Credit.* The Walls . . . were hung with many Acts of Parliament written in Golden Letters. At the Upper end of the Hall was the *Magna Charta*, with the Act of Uniformity on the right Hand, and the Act of Toleration on the left. At the Lower end of the Hall was the Act of Settlement, which was placed full in the Eye of the Virgin that sat upon the Throne. Both the Sides of the Hall were covered with such Acts of Parliament as had been made for the Establishment of Publick Funds. The Lady seemed to set an unspeakable value upon these several Pieces of Furniture, insomuch that she often refreshed her Eye with them, and often smiled with a Secret Pleasure, as she looked upon them; but, at the same time, showed a very particular Uneasiness, if she saw any thing approaching that might hurt them. . . .

'Behind the Throne was a prodigious Heap of Bags of Money . . . The Floor, on her right Hand and on her left, was covered with vast Sums of Gold that rose up in Pyramids on either side of her : But this I did not so much wonder at, when I heard, upon Enquiry, that she had the same virtue in her Touch, which the Poets tell us a *Lydian* King was formerly possess'd of ; and that she could convert whatever she pleas'd into that precious Metal.'

JOSEPH ADDISON,
The Spectator, No. 3, 3 March 1711

PART ONE

The Scope
of the Problem

I

The Financial Revolution

As the war clouds of the terrible middle decades of the seventeenth century rolled away from Europe, a new generation of statesmen and thinkers, weary of their predecessors' ideological battles, turned their attention to the problems of administrative and economic reconstruction. For Louis XIV of France, Leopold I of Austria, Frederick William of Prussia, Charles II of England, and their advisers, the problems involved, which were basically those of efficient government and the increase of national wealth, were as urgent and complex as similar ones are proving for the emerging states of the twentieth century. The questions of political assent, administrative control, and the elimination of corruption on the one hand, and on the other of such issues as the supply of skilled labour, the level of wages, the supply and price of raw materials, the volume of investment in particular industries, and the pattern of foreign trade, were peculiarly difficult for an age only beginning to apply systematic analysis to its problems. But the tone of government and society was optimistic, and rulers assumed that the problems could be solved. They reasoned like Leopold, Duke of Lorraine, who in 1700 established 500 official distilleries, intending by means of commerce and manufactures to ' restore our states ravaged by the long wars with which they have been afflicted for seventy years'.[1]

In England, the generation which welcomed back its exiled king in May 1660 was keenly interested in these problems, and in the new sciences of physics and mathematics which it connected with them. It was the age of the Royal Society (1662). It was the age of William Petty (born 1623), Robert Boyle (1627), Josiah Child (1630), John Locke and Christopher Wren

---

[1] Paris, A[rchives] N[ationales], G 7/722, undated (1706?); proposal of Sieur Marchal for establishing brandy distilleries, attaching a proclamation of 1701 by the Duke of Lorraine. The passage referred to runs as follows: 'Entre les moyens qui Nous ont été proposés pour rétablir nos États désolés par les longues guerres dont ils ont été affligez depuis soixante & dix ans, le commerce nous a paru un des plus considérables, & Nous avons creu ne pouvoir le faire mieux réussir qu'en établissant par tout des Ouvriers & Manufacturiers de toutes espèces.'

(both 1632), the economist and founder of fire-insurance Nicholas Barbon and the historian Thomas Rymer (both 1641), Isaac Newton (1642), the statistician Gregory King (1648), the economist Charles Davenant and the astronomer Edmund Halley (both 1656). It was an age, too, of expanding commerce to the new 'plantations' in the West Indies and North America, and of a restless spirit of technical innovation among the merchants and traders of the City of London, anxious to wrest the crown of economic superiority from the Dutch, whose successful wooing of 'the fair Mistress Trade' had made them the commercial masters of the world.

The English writers of the period renewed with zest the economic debate begun before the civil wars by Mun, Roberts, and Misselden. Their programme was essentially a practical one, a programme of growth, though in formulating it they gave precision for the first time to some of the technical concepts of economics.[1] Their model was Dutch society, whose organization seemed to them as intelligent and dynamic as American society was to seem to many European economists of the twentieth century. The first Earl of Shaftesbury (who was to die in exile in Amsterdam) argued that religious toleration, for which the Dutch were famous, would give England major practical benefits. It would keep at home industrious artisans whom persecution might have driven out, and attract skilled labour from countries whose rulers were less enlightened. At the same time, registration of title to estates would attract wealthy families to settle in England.[2] Sir Josiah Child argued for more general commercial education, and for equal division of estates so that merchants would no longer be left

to wrastle with the world in their youth, with inconsiderable assistance of fortune, as most of our youngest Sons of Gentlemen in England are, who are bound Apprentices to Merchants.[3]

Other writers suggested that mercantile law should be codified, and administered by special courts so as to speed up the resolution of commercial disputes. Yarranton argued that internal communication should be improved by deepening harbours and rivers.[4] This would create employment for the poor, who should also be helped by a network of 'lumber houses' to give them cheap

---

[1] Cf. William Letwin, *The Origins of Scientific Economics* (1963).

[2] See his memorandum of 1669 in Christie, *Life of Shaftesbury* (1871, 2 vols.), vol. ii, app. i.

[3] J[osiah] C[hild], *Brief Observations concerning Trade and Interest of Money* 1668), p. 3.

[4] Andrew Yarranton, *England's Improvement by Sea and Land. To Out-do the Dutch without Fighting* (1677).

credit.[1] In 1685 Sir Robert Southwell outlined a further scheme for a network of canals centring on London.[2]

Credit facilities in general, most writers agreed, were defective, and must be improved if dear finance was not to put England at a disadvantage to Holland, with its cheap money. Child thought interest could be lowered by reducing the legal maximum rate and also by establishing banks,

> which are of so immense advantage to them [the Dutch], that some not without good grounds have estimated the profit of them to the Publick to amount to at least one million of pounds sterling per annum.[3]

Yarranton thought the Dutch 'Publick Bank' [the Bank of Amsterdam, established in 1609]

> the great Sinews of Trade, the Credit thereof making Paper go in Trade equal with Ready Money yea better in many parts of the World than Money.[4]

His own remedy for encouraging the creation of banks in England was (like Shaftesbury) to introduce registration of land titles, which would make loans charged on land swift and secure like those in Holland, where such registers had long existed.[5] The *raison d'être* of this proposal was, according to him, that capitalists lent money to bankers who invested it in mortgages, from which they had great trouble in disinvesting. (In effect they were borrowing short and lending long.)[6] Acceleration of land transfer would therefore stimulate credit, banking, and trade generally. Banks would be set up at Bristol, Exeter, Hull, [King's] Lynn and, above all, London:

> If it shall please God once to raise a Bank in London of six hundred thousand pounds Fund and Anchorage, out of such a Bank will sprout out many Lumber houses and smaller Banks, to quicken trade. And certainly then the Moneys will be lent at four in the hundred.[7]

---

[1] Ibid. Yarranton meant well-regulated loan funds for the poor (Lombard Houses) on the lines of the Italian *Monti di Pietà*.

[2] T. S. Willan, *River Navigation in England, 1600–1750* (1936), p. 12.

[3] Child, op. cit., p. 5. [4] Yarranton, op. cit., p. 7.

[5] Ibid., pp. 7 ff. He complained that the new houses built since the Great Fire of London in 1666 ought all to have been put on a register. He also asserted that Scottish land, which was registered, was at twenty-four years' purchase whereas Irish land, unregistered, was at eight years' purchase. This was a disingenuous argument, in view of Ireland's greater poverty.

[6] Ibid., pp. 17–21. 'Of late years the monied Men in England sent their moneys into Lombard-street, and there received a Note from a Goldsmiths Boy, which was all they had to show for their Moneys.' The goldsmiths invested this money in mortgages. For evidence that mortgage loans were not always for long terms see below, p. 441.

[7] Ibid., p. 23.

Similarly, a writer of 1697 wanted to see the establishment at the Guildhall of a General National Office of Credit which would have branches in the wards of the City and in market towns and power to issue paper money as directed by the Treasury.[1] Besides these plans for internal credit there were others for a marine-insurance corporation (1661) and for the creation of fire-insurance offices; the latter were first successfully established in London in the 1680s.[2] These and similar proposals of the writers, projectors, and statesmen of the period 1660–88 were intelligent and, with some exceptions, mutually consistent. They envisaged a liberal society without legal barriers to the advance of the individual (at least the Protestant individual); the improvement of agriculture and communictations; and, almost above all, improving credit and insurance by creating a network of banking and insurance services, centring on London, which would stimulate investment in domestic and foreign trade. The implied philosophy behind this was that wealth was good and could be earned by talent and hard work, and that, given intelligent government planning and encouragement, individuals seeking their own good would create wealth and prosperity in a competitive world for their country as a whole.

In several important respects the proposals of the later Stuart period were realized during the sixty years after the political revolution of 1688. Substantial toleration of religious dissent had been obtained by the 1720s. Commercial education, though far from general, was fostered by the growth of specialized academies for practical studies.[3] There were several schemes for Land Banks in the 1690s. Though none succeeded in England, several were established in America (where many seventeenth-century dreams were realized) and continued to do business until the 1760s.[4] Registration of land

[1] *Proposals to Supply His Majesty with Twelve or Fourteen Millions of Money* (1697).

[2] P. G. M. Dickson, *The Sun Insurance Office 1710–1960* (1960), ch. 1. It was hoped that the marine-insurance office (which in fact came to nothing) would become 'the insurance office for Europe' (ibid., p. 3). Cf. Schoppens & Edwards in London to Simon Bevel in Haarlem, 13 May 1720 — 'if the new insurance office for ships [the reference is either to the London Assurance or to the Royal Exchange Assurance] succeeds all Europe will insure in London.' (Archief Brants, 1649.)

[3] Nicholas Hans, *New Trends in Education in the Eighteenth Century* (1951).

[4] For the English schemes see W. R. Scott, *Joint Stock Companies*, iii. 246–53, and J. K. Horsefield, *British Monetary Experiments 1650–1710* (1960), pp. 156–217. The American banks are described by T. Thayer, 'The Land-Bank System in the American Colonies', *J. Ec. Hist.* xiii (1953), 145. The American banks at first issued paper against mortgages of land, but in the war of 1756–63 grossly over-issued; in 1764 the English Government forbade the use of paper money as legal tender in all the American colonies.

titles was introduced into Ireland, Middlesex and Yorkshire in 1704–9.[1] The practice of merchants was adopted into common law and equity under Hardwicke and Mansfield. Private debts became assignable in equity, and the public debts statutorily transferable by an easy method of registration.[2] A good deal of capital and ingenuity was devoted both to agricultural improvements and to the deepening of harbours and rivers.[3] The Bank of England was established in 1694, and other banks grew up round it, at first in London and after the mid-eighteenth century in the provinces as well. Fire-insurance facilities in both London and the provinces increased rapidly after the establishment of the Sun Fire Office in 1710, and two marine-insurance corporations, the London Assurance and Royal Exchange Assurance, were set up in 1720. By the 1750s the rate of interest, measured by the yield on Consols, was down to 3%. Meanwhile foreign trade, particularly to the Americas, had rapidly expanded. By the eve of the Seven Years War London was already the leading world centre of foreign trade, dealings in jewels and gold, provision of insurance cover, and the flotation of public loans.[4]

Cutting across, and profoundly influencing, this process of building up the infrastructure of the Industrial Revolution, however, was a force whose power, duration, and importance the Restoration economists did not foresee — war. England was at war for twenty-nine of the sixty-six years between 1688 and the outbreak of the great struggle with France in 1756.[5] These wars, moreover, were waged on a scale and with a ferocity of which the country had no previous experience. Their basic cause was the bitter rivalry between France and England for influence in Europe and for colonial markets. Both sides tended to regard this struggle as one to contain the other's power. As the English commissioners negotiating for a union with Scotland in December 1702 explained to their Scottish colleagues:

[1] 2 & 3 Anne, c. 4 (1703), and 6 Anne, c. 20 (1707), West Riding; 6 Anne, c. 62 (1707), East Riding; 7 Anne, c. 20 (1708), Middlesex; 6 Anne, c. 2 (I), created a Public Register Office for Ireland in Dublin.

[2] See below, p. 460.

[3] T. S. Willan, op. cit.; A. H. John, 'The Course of Agricultural Change, 1660–1760' in L. S. Pressnell (ed.), *Studies in the Industrial Revolution presented to T. S. Ashton* (1960).

[4] Cf. the preamble to 6 Geo. II, c. 7 (1733), which established free import and export of diamonds and precious stones. It explained that England had now become 'a great Mart for Diamonds' and that jewels were sent there to be finished. Cf. also the summary in English of Dr. Gedalia Yogev's unpublished Ph.D. thesis (Hebrew University of Jerusalem, 1962), 'The Economic Activity of the Anglo-Jewish Patriciate in the eighteenth century international trade'.

[5] Counting only the major wars of 1689–97, 1702–13, and 1739–48, and ignoring minor wars such as those of 1718–21 and 1726–8.

the sayd [English Government] debts have been contracted by a long War entered into more particularly for the Preservation of England & the dominions thereunto belonging, yet that Scotland has tasted of the Benefits which have accrued to Great Brittain in general from the Opposition that has been made to the Growth and Power of France.[1]

Frenchmen, meanwhile, thought of their country as encircled by foes, and complained that since 1679 the Allies had always disposed of a third more troops and ships than France.[2] But the real cause of conflict was that both England and France were growing in wealth and ambition, and that both increasingly regarded overseas trade as the true key to prosperity and power. The view taken of colonies was that they were property yielding returns, much like a gentleman's estate. As the English Commissioners for Union remarked:

... the Plantations are the Property of English Men; and that this Trade is of so great a consequence & so beneficial as not to be communicated, as is Proposed, till all other Particulars which shall be thought necessary in this union be adjusted.[3]

Branches of trade were thought of in the same monopolistic terms; thus in 1709 Cazier was complaining that his plan of 1693 approved by Colbert de Croissy for robbing the English and Dutch of the Smyrna trade had been shelved by the Ministry.[4] When Chatham stated that trade was England's last entrenchment, which she must defend or perish, he was stating an eighteenth-century commonplace.

In this long conflict, which was only finally decided in England's favour on the hard-fought field of Waterloo, victory might confidently have been expected by the French, whose resources in population, natural wealth, and military organization were far greater than those of England. Throughout the period, indeed, many Englishmen anticipated such a victory.[5] The bogy of French power was a reality a century before Napoleon. The Victory Column at Blenheim Palace, and Thornhill's ceiling for the new Painted Hall at Greenwich, depicting Louis XIV trampled underfoot, were signs of national relief as well as national pride. Yet it was England, not France,

---

[1] B.M., Harl. MS. 4959, Minutes of the Union Commissioners 1702-3, f. 21, 16 December 1702.

[2] A.N. G 7/722, undated *mémoire* of Sieur Cazier enclosed with a letter dated 4 October 1706 (N.S.).

[3] Minutes of the Union Commissioners, loc. cit.

[4] A.N., loc. cit., undated letter of Sieur Cazier endorsed 23 July 1709 (N.S.).

[5] See below, pp. 22-23.

which was the more consistently successful, despite the inferiority of its resources for most of the period. The causes of this success were partly extraneous. The cessation of the bitter Anglo-Dutch rivalry of the seventeenth century not only removed a drain on England's strength, but added to it in the wars of 1689–1713 an army of over 100,000 men, and a fleet which was the third largest in Europe, even if its numbers later declined.[1] In the Seven Years War, when the Dutch were neutral, Prussia was an even more powerful friend. England's other allies before 1756, particularly Austria-Hungary, were also important. It is significant that the country reached its most serious position in the eighteenth century when abandoned by all its possible allies during the American War of Independence. In the struggle against Napoleon, England's early industrialization was the most important cause of victory, but it is doubtful whether, despite the boasts of John Bull, he could have won alone.

Alliances were therefore important. They were almost certainly more important than other causes of English superiority alleged at the time and since, ranging from supposedly greater English naval and military skill through the virtues of Protestantism to the merits of roast beef and leather shoes, in ascending order of implausibility. More important even than alliances, however, was the system of public borrowing developed in the first half of the period, which enabled England to spend on war out of all proportion to its tax revenue, and thus to throw into the struggle with France and its allies the decisive margin of ships and men without which the reresources previously committed might have been committed in vain. De Pinto's opinion, for instance, was that the capture of Havana in 1762, which astonished Europe, would not have been possible if one-third fewer ships and troops had been assigned to the task.[2] Table 1 shows that the proportion of Government expenditure financed by public borrowing described a rising curve from 31% in the War of the Spanish Succession to 37% in the Seven Years War and a peak of 40% in the American War of Independence. It then declined sharply owing to the introduction of the income tax in 1799. By the close of the Napoleonic Wars the National Debt thus created

[1] In December 1693 the Dutch were said to have 92,540 men under arms and a further 15,000 raising (HCJ xi. 24). For Dutch quotas in Flanders, ibid. xvii. 40–43. The Dutch navy had 106 ships of twenty guns or more in 1700, but only 49 in 1741 (J. C. de Jonge, *Geschiedenis van het Nederlandsche Zeewezen* (Zwolle, 1869, 5 vols.), iv. 775–6, and *Lists of Men of War* (Soc. for Nautical Research, Occasional Publications (C.U.P., 1938)), pt. iv.

[2] [Isaac de Pinto], *Traité de la Circulation et du Crédit* (Amsterdam, 1771), pp. 66–67. This work was partly written in 1761.

amounted to over £670m. which the addition of the separately accounted Irish debt brought to nearly £770m.[1]

TABLE I

English War Expenditure and Public Borrowing 1688–1815

1 Years (each inclusive)	2 Total expenditure	3 Total income	4 Balance raised by loans	5 Col. (4) as % of Col. (2)
	£	£	£	%
1688–97*	49,320,145	32,766,754	16,553,391	33·6
1702–13	93,644,560	64,239,477	29,405,083	31·4
1739–48	95,628,159	65,903,964	29,724,195	31·1
1756–63	160,573,366	100,555,123	60,018,243	37·4
1776–83	236,462,689	141,902,620	94,560,069	39·9
1793–1815	1,657,854,518	1,217,556,439	440,298,079	26·6
TOTALS	2,293,483,437	1,622,924,377	670,559,060	33·3

Source: BPP (1868–9), xxxv (Return of Public Income and Expenditure from 1688), 1193. For this Return see Bibliography, p. 549. Revenue figures were recorded net of collection costs until 1801, see below, p. 10.

* The Exchequer year began at Michaelmas, so part of the sums for 1688–9 are for the months before war was declared in May 1689.

Given the country's relative poverty and lack of bureaucratic organization over the greater part of the period, direct and indirect taxes could never have been imposed to an extent sufficient to make such expenditure possible. Taxation, partly imposed to pay the interest on state loans, was heavy enough as it was. Within a generation of the political revolution of 1688, which had occurred as much as anything owing to the country's fear of military power, nearly two hundred thousand men were under arms and the gentlemen of England were paying away a fifth of their incomes in Land Tax, besides heavy local taxes.[2] Other expedients to finance war which might have been

[1] BPP (1890–1), xlviii. Report of the Commissioners of the National Debt, 1786–1890, pp. 583–5. The Irish debt at the close of 1815 was £72·2m. administered in England and a further £25·1m. administered in Ireland. Added to the £670·5m. English debt this made £767·8m.

[2] For complaints about the level of taxation in the War of the Spanish Succession see below, pp. 25–27.

tried (and were, by other powers), such as inflation of the currency or writing off accumulated debts, were by definition self-defeating in anything except the short run. It is a fair generalization, therefore, that the wealth of the nation in this embryonic stage of its development could only be tapped with maximum effect for war purposes by a well-organized system of long-term government borrowing, whose existence would compensate for the inadequacies of taxation, and enable taxes to be kept lower than they would otherwise have been. A badly organized system of borrowing, on the other hand, would deliver the state into the hands of financial cliques, discredit it in the eyes of its citizens, and necessitate further tightening of the screws of taxation. This was what happened in eighteenth-century France, and there is no reason to doubt that the fiscal incompetence of the French monarchy was the main reason for its ultimate collapse.

The new system of English public borrowing was complete in its essentials by the eve of the Seven Years War, at whose close de Pinto wrote:

L'exactitude scrupuleuse & inviolable avec laquelle ces intérêts ont toujours été payés, & l'idée qu'on a de l'assurance Parlementaire, ont établi le crédit de l'Angleterre, au point de faire des emprunts qui ont surpris et étonné l'Europe.[1]

Like most favourable commentators, de Pinto was primarily impressed by the sheer scale of military and naval success which England's new financial system had made possible. In retrospect the system was important for somewhat different reasons. First, the wars of 1739–63 were crucial, not so much for national prestige, however much this was boosted, as for the decisive increase in export demand resulting from the preservation and extension of the North American and West Indian markets. Conversely, if these markets had fallen to the French, English economic development must have been retarded. Internally, the rise of public borrowing in the first half of the eighteenth century was important because it created a whole range of securities in which mercantile and financial houses could safely invest, and from which they could easily disinvest. The new partnership banks, the new insurance offices, the trading companies, the busy merchants, brokers, and jobbers of the City of London, unexpectedly found at their disposal facilities for investment far more varied and flexible than land alone, cast by Yarranton for this role, could ever have provided.[2] Without these facilities, it is at least arguable that the City's complex structure of services could not have been built up by the mid-eighteenth century, for there was no industrial sector whose bonds

---

[1] De Pinto, op. cit., pp. 41–42.   [2] For Yarranton's views see above, p. 5.

could be used for the same purpose. Delay in the emergence of the City as a financial centre would, like failure to hold existing overseas markets and win new ones, have put back England's industrialization, and thus changed the course of European history.

Because of its importance both in financing the capture of empire and in stimulating the growth of the internal capital market, the origins of the system of public borrowing which Chatham and Newcastle used to such effect therefore deserve careful study. The rise of this system in the six decades before the Seven Years War was rapid enough, and important enough in both its main and secondary effects, to deserve the name of the Financial Revolution. Its effects on the country's life, social attitudes, and historical development resemble on a smaller scale those of the Industrial Revolution which followed it, and which it arguably helped to make possible. Yet the subject has been virtually neglected by historians, for whom the first half of the eighteenth century is usually ground to be covered at a conventionally rapid pace. This book is a study of the main features of the new system in its formative period: the development of long- and short-term borrowing, the relations between the Treasury and the City, the development of a market in securities, and the sources of the capital invested in public loans. Many of the technical reasons for the Government's success, and some of the pitfalls which it avoided or successfully climbed out of, emerge from this analysis. But there was a further and more general condition of the development of successful public borrowing, which this preliminary chapter may usefully end by discussing. This was the creation of stable and efficient government, a task of whose difficulty in an economically backward country, with a largely illiterate population, the mid-twentieth century is perhaps better aware than Victorian historians were.

The English statesmen and administrators of the decades that followed the political revolution of 1688 were in some respects very lucky. The economic tensions of the century 1560–1660 had greatly lessened, and those of the century after 1760 were still in the future. The price level, a vital factor in the well-being of the poor, was stable or falling for the greater part of the period 1688–1756, and population was growing much more slowly than it did in the Elizabethan and early Stuart period and after 1760. The stability of the price level is one of a number of indications that there was a good deal of slack in the economy up to the 1760s. Thus the government was able to borrow for up to a third of its overall requirements in war time without competing with the capital requirements of the private sector, and without any significant effect on prices; it is arguable that its activities even stimulated economic growth.[1] (In fully-employed modern economies by contrast, a tax revenue deficit of 5% or more is usually reckoned to have inflationary consequences.) Meanwhile foreign trade, particularly to the Americas, was expanding. There can be little doubt that this relatively favourable economic background was an important cause of the success of the new Hanoverian dynasty. At the same time, the tone of public opinion was sensible, pragmatic, and optimistic, and a majority of the politically conscious nation must have felt that Pope's dictum, 'whate'er is best administered, is best' was at least half true. The bitter religious quarrels of the previous century could no longer flourish in this atmosphere; those of the later eighteenth century, partly fanned by economic discontent, lay in the future. Administratively this permitted a decentralisation in local government which previous and subsequent periods, more troubled by economic difficulties, found impracticable. At the same time the physical isolation of the most backward areas of government in Ireland and the Highlands of Scotland made it possible to ignore the misery of their inhabitants, or to subject them to military rule, without arousing public outcry.

These were largely fortuitous aids to effective government. But the statesmen and administrators of the period also had real and difficult achievements to their credit. First, Parliament became a real focus for the major interests within the country, and enabled political leadership to be endorsed by the political nation. At the beginning of the period this seemed unlikely to happen, and many must have thought that Parliament would go the way of the Polish Diet. That it did not was partly due to the general cooling of the political atmosphere after George I's accession, partly to the lengthening of Parliament's life with the Septennial Act of 1716, but above all to the skilful handling of the relations between the executive (in many ways an executive with growing powers) and Parliament under Walpole and the Pelhams, which set the tone of parliamentary management for a century to come. Anyone with experience of the difficulties involved in reconciling efficient executive action with the consent of a representative body, with its collective irresponsibility and obtuseness as well as its collective fairness and common sense, must admire this achievement. Second, the union with Scotland in 1707 greatly strengthened the powers of government in London; the problems of Irish government, to become so important by the 1770s, were still relatively dormant. At the same time the tone of English society, partly owing to governmental action or inaction, was kept reasonably liberal.

[1] Cf. Thomas Tooke, *History of Prices*, vol. i (1838) and A. H. John, 'War and the English Economy, 1700–1763', *Econ. H.R.*, New Series, vii (1954–5), 329.

The principle of careers open to talent was preserved in the law, the administrative offices, the navy, and, to a lesser extent, the army, provided the aspirant was willing to profess at least token allegiance to the Established Church. Even in the Church there was never the monopoly of high office by aristocrats common elsewhere in Europe. Outside the professions religious barriers were not important, and it was common form that industrious apprentices were free to rise by their own efforts to become City magnates, or, as a future generation was to experience, captains of industry. Lastly, the development of a relatively free Press in the first half of the eighteenth century meant that public issues were publicly debated, and not merely settled behind closed doors, and that the management of public opinion became of concern and importance for all administrations.

The essentially practical and successful character of English government in this period may be contrasted with that of France. At the close of the seventeenth century many observers must have thought that French government, based on central autocracy acting through provincial intendants, and fettered only by the supposedly historic powers of the *parlements* and provincial assemblies, was the most efficient in Europe. Compared to it, the political squabbling and frequent elections in England must have seemed as effete (and as unpropitious for economic and military success) as capitalist Governments seemed to admirers of Soviet Russia in the 1930s. Yet the French administration was to find its system rigid and unadaptable in the storms of the eighteenth century. It lacked a great representative body like the English Parliament where the political nation's consent to necessary measures could be obtained in advance. Failing this, policy had to be driven through by obtaining consent region by region, and in the critical reforming era of the 1780s these local and partial bodies repeatedly and correctly refused to endorse measures which they felt required the assent of the nation as a whole. The history of the States General summoned in 1789 was to show that a national representative body could not easily be imposed on the country by a stroke of the pen. Had France possessed an effective Parliament — which amounts to supposing that her structure of government could have been quite different — the legal and fiscal injustices of eighteenth-century French society would have been difficult to sustain, political reform could have been introduced piecemeal, and the monarchy might have developed a system of public borrowing as impressive as its neighbour's, and equally able to tap the capital resources of Europe. Had it done so, the universal monarchy feared by contemporary Englishmen might have become a harsh reality.

2

The Contemporary Debate

I

THE Financial Revolution generated a prolonged discussion of its political, social, and economic consequences.[1] A minority view (but only a minority view) throughout the period was that it was advantageous to England. Thus it was pointed out in 1695 that the foundation of the Bank of England had sharply reduced the discount on government tallies, and enabled the state to borrow more cheaply.[2] Following the same line of thought in 1707 Nathaniel Tench, a director and former Governor of the Bank claimed that by discounting bills it had increased the flow of trade, and that its 'ingraftment' of defective tallies in 1697 had saved the country from disaster.[3] Bishop Berkeley noted in 1735:

Query whether the credit of the public funds be not a mine of gold to England? And whether any step that should lessen this credit ought not to be dreaded? Whether such credit be not the principal advantage that England hath over France? I may add, over every other country in Europe?[4]

In 1737 it was explained that the

profess'd End . . . of the Institution of the Bank of England was, that both the Public and private Persons, should be supplied with Money on more easy Terms, or that no such Advantages should be made of the Public, or private Men's Necessities for the future,

and how this establishment was certain to

[1] William Kennedy, *English Taxation, 1640–1799* (1913), is still a very interesting survey of contemporary opinions, but it almost wholly neglects the subject of government borrowing.

[2] *Angliae Tutamen: or, the Safety of England. By a Person of Honour* (1695), pp. 5–6. Tallies were a form of Exchequer receipt, see below, p. 350.

[3] *A Defence of the Bank of England* (1707). The ingraftment is described below, p. 353.

[4] George Berkeley, Bishop of Cloyne, *The Querist* (1735), *Works*, ed. A. C. Fraser, iii (1871), 374.

reduce the Interest of Money to Three per Cent. in a few Years, without any Law to inforce it, in like manner as it is in all other Countries where Banks were establish'd.[1]

Another writer in the same year observed that

There can't be a stronger Proof of that high Esteem which the People of England, and neighbouring Nations also, entertain for our glorious Constitution, than the immense Credit our Legislature has found in borrowing of Money. It is not probable that the greatest absolute Monarch could, in his most extensive Dominions, raise by voluntary Contributions, a Loan of fifty Millions of Money. And yet France, Turkey, Persia, India and China, severally yield much larger annual Revenues than Great-Britain.[2]

The explanation was that in these states the security for public loans 'would be as the Breath in a Man's Nostrils'.[3] Sir John Barnard was arguing in Parliament at this time that public credit had become stronger than private credit.[4] This was indeed a far cry from the dangerous days of the 1690s to which Tench had earlier referred. In 1747 the government's capacity to borrow heavily at the end of an expensive war was contrasted with the exhausted financial resources of France.[5] In the following year it was claimed that since the National Debt and national credit were closely connected, the redemption of the debt would lead to 'such losses and Inconveniences . . . as wou'd greatly diminish the Riches of our Country'.[6] Thomas Mortimer, in a lyrical passage written in 1769 for the seventh edition of his treatise on stock-jobbing, referred to English public credit as this 'standing miracle in politics, which at once astonishes and over-awes the states of Europe'.[7] Shortly afterwards Isaac de Pinto developed at length the thesis that Great Britain's superior public credit was one of the major reasons for her defeat of France and Spain in the Seven Years War.[8]

---

[1] *Considerations upon a Proposal for Lowering the Interest of all the Redeemable National Debts to Three per Cent. per Ann.* (1737), pp. 8–9.

[2] *A Speech Without-Doors, Addressed to the National Creditors for the Redeemables at 4l. per Cent.* (1737), p. 1.

[3] Ibid., p. 2.

[4] Debate of 28 March 1737, *Parl. Hist.* x. 123.

[5] *Gent. Mag.* (1747), p. 528.

[6] *An Essay upon Publick Credit in a Letter to a Friend* (1748), p. 10.

[7] Thomas Mortimer, *Every Man his own Broker* (7th ed., 1769), p. 156.

[8] [Isaac de Pinto], *Traité de la Circulation et du Crédit* (Amsterdam, 1771).

II

In the main, however, public reactions to the Financial Revolution were as hostile as they were later to be to the Industrial Revolution. The first line of criticism was political. It alleged that the National Debt had been created to meet not an economic need, the need for greater revenue, but a political need: to secure for the political settlement of 1689 the support of the powerful groups concerned in Government loans. The case was sketched by Burnet and Davenant.[1] The latter's Modern Whig observes:

'Tis true, we have run the Nation over Head and Ears in debt by our Fonds, and new Devices, but mark what a Dependance upon our Noble Friends, this way of raising Mony has occasion'd. Who is it sticks to 'em but those who are concern'd in Tallies and the new Stocks?[2]

Swift developed the theme, particularly in his *History of the Four Last Years of the Queen* written in 1713 though not published until 1758. He explained that

National Debts secured upon Parliamentary Funds of Interest, were things unknown in England before the last Revolution under the Prince of Orange.[3]

The new style of finance was introduced by Gilbert Burnet, Bishop of Salisbury, from Holland, partly to keep taxes lower than they would otherwise have been, partly to enable 'artful Men in Office and Credit' to 'raise vast Wealth for themselves ... who were to be the Managers and Directors of it'.[4] But there was another and more urgent motive. It was argued that

Whoever were Lenders to the Government, would by the surest Principle be obliged to support it. Besides, the Men of Estates could not be persuaded without Time and Difficulty to have those Taxes laid on their Lands, which Custom hath since made so familiar; and it was the Business of such as were then in Power to cultivate a money'd Interest; because the Gentry of the Kingdom did not very much relish those New Notions in Government, to which the King, who had imbibed his Politics in his own Country, was thought to give too much way.[5]

---

[1] Burnet, *History of his own Time* (1823 ed.), iv. 63, 66–67, 72; Charles Davenant, *The True Picture of a Modern Whig* (1701).

[2] Davenant, op. cit., p. 26.   [3] Swift, *Works*, ed. H. Davis, vii (Oxford, 1951), p. 68.
[4] Ibid., p. 69.   [5] Ibid., pp. 68–69.

The Dutch conception that it 'was for the Interest of the Publick to be in Debt' might, Swift argued, be valid in Holland, but was hardly so in England, whose society and politics were quite different.[1]

The idea that the National Debt was a political trick persisted. In April 1737 the *Craftsman* observed how much it affected him

to hear it publickly avow'd 'that it is necessary to continue the Debts of the Nation, as the best Security of the Protestant Religion, and the present, royal Family on the Throne.'[2]

As a pamphleteer put it in the same year:

There was a Time, when lending Money to the Publick, was understood as an undoubted Proof, that the Lender was a Friend to the late Revolution.[3]

Bolingbroke, in his *Reflections on the Present State of the Nation*, written in 1749, worked the thesis up into a form which, as taken up by Disraeli, particularly in *Sybil* (1845), became a standard Tory myth about the post-Revolution period. Bolingbroke contended that

When King William entered, immediately after the revolution on this great scene of action; the unincumbered condition of this nation . . . was such that he might have been supported in it . . . by a land-tax, by the excise on malt, and by some additional subsidies, all of which would have been raised within the year. A scheme of this kind was prepared and offered . . . but it was rejected for a reason that appeared plausible in political refinement, and has proved most pernicious in its consequences. It was said that a new government, established against the ancient principles and actual engagements of many, could not be so effectually secured any way, as it would be if the private fortunes of great numbers were made to depend on the preservation of it; and that this could not be done unless they were induced to lend their money to the public, and to accept securities under the present establishment. Thus the method of funding and the trade of stock-jobbing began. Thus were great companies created, the pretended servants, but in many respects the real masters of every administration.[4]

Bolingbroke's last point, about the sinister influence of the monied companies, dates back as a line of argument at least to the 1690s. Thus it was thought in 1699 that a reduction of the nation's debts would

set Bounds to the Bank from engrossing the mony Credit and Trade into the hands of that Body pernicious to the general Affairs of the Realm.[5]

---

[1] Ibid.   [2] *The Country Journal or the Craftsman*, 9 April 1737.

[3] *A Speech Without-Doors Addressed to the National Creditors at 4l. per Cent.* (1737), p. 21.

[4] Bolingbroke, *Some reflections on the present State of the Nation* [dated 1749], in *Works* (1754), iii. 151.

[5] Add. MS. 20721, revenue accounts 1685–1699, f. 61.

This was at the close of a decade in which monopolies in foreign trade had been subject to constant and not unsuccessful attack.[1] Criticism of the political influence which the Bank derived from its monopoly powers continued. In 1705 an opponent hinted at its capacity to become a monopoly lender to government and to overawe government and Parliament.[2] In 1707 another writer complained that the Bank and New East India Company had interlocking directorates, whose joint power gave the companies a sinister control of City and Parliamentary elections.[3] In 1710–11 the contention that 'they that have the Money, must have the Management' was the ground for the belief of Godolphin's supporters that Harley's new Ministry would founder on the opposition of the monied interest.[4] Analogous fears were expressed in 1720 about the power which the proposed increase in the capital of the South Sea Company would put in the hands of its directors. 'What man can foresee', asked James Milner in April 1720,

the dismal consequences that may happen to this Nation from a Body of Men with Forty Three Millions and a half Capital. . . . What may not Men do with such a Mass of Treasure? May they not give the Nation the greatest Convulsions they ever struggled with?[5]

The events of the year returned an unequivocal answer to this question and confirmed public fears of corporate power. In 1737 the contention (partly due to the relative success of the South Sea scheme of 1720) that it was actually of more advantage to the public to owe its debts to one company rather than several companies or a mass of individual creditors was indignantly repudiated by Sir Robert Walpole. He argued that

If the whole debt we now owe were in the hands of any one company, it would be in the power of that company to distress the public whenever they had a mind; whereas, while that debt is in the hands of several companies, if one should resolve to distress, the others would probably resolve to support, and by that means the public can never be in danger of being distressed by either.[6]

---

[1] G. L. Cherry, 'The Development of the English Free-Trade Movement in Parliament, 1689–1702', *J. Mod. Hist.* xxv (ii) (1953), 103.

[2] *Remarks upon the Bank of England* (1705).

[3] *The Reasons of the Decay of Trade and Private Credit . . . By a Merchant of London* (1707), pp. 16, 28–29.

[4] See below, p. 64.

[5] [James Milner], *A visit to the South-Sea Company and the Bank* (1720), second letter, April 1720, p. 26.

[6] *Parl. Hist.* x. 54, 11 March 1737.

D.F.R.

He added that, given such multiple ownership, a company which refused 'to comply with any reasonable proposition that may be offered' could always be coerced by the Treasury. This anticipated Pelham's tactics in the conversion of 1749. But Walpole overlooked the fact that to many critics of the City divided company power was no more agreeable than monopoly company power. Moreover, he partly gave away his case by going on to say that

> though in most sorts of trade, an exclusive privilege may be of bad consequence, I am nevertheless of opinion, that with respect to the Banking trade, and the trade to the East-Indies, neither the one nor the other can be carried on with such success, or in such an extensive manner, by private adventurers, as by a public company with such an exclusive privilege as our present companies have; and in this opinion I am supported by the example of our neighbours the Dutch, who, I believe, understand trade as well as most of their neighbours.[1]

This defence of monopoly showed the cloven hoof, despite the economically fashionable appeal to Dutch practices. The case against company power and directoral influence was still strong enough in 1749 for Bolingbroke to describe the companies as 'the real masters of every administration' and their directors as 'the principal men in our great companies, who, born to serve and obey, have been bred to command even government itself'.[2]

It was possible to argue in this way that the development of the National Debt had led to a shift in the centre of gravity of government towards the private sector, but it was also possible to argue that the growth of taxation accompanying the rise of public borrowing had greatly increased the power of the state. Pulteney pointed out in 1734 that the drafting of parliamentary Money bills had virtually become the province of skilled civil servants: 'the Gentlemen of the Revenue . . . have lately taken upon them a sort of exclusive Authority to draw and present all Money-Bills to the House.'[3] Similarly, the *Craftsman* referred in 1737 to 'the revenue, to which such a sacred Regard is paid, upon all Occasions'.[4] Pulteney also argued that the long wars had created a large and expensive Civil Service, and that

> This Multiplicity of civil Officers is not only a Burthen to the Kingdom, as they are so many unprofitable Members of the Commonwealth, and live, like Drones, on the Labour of the industrious Hive; but by the Power of favouring or harassing the trading Part of the Kingdom, according to the Inclinations of their Superiors, they are become formidable to our Liberties.[5]

---

[1] Ibid., 55.   [2] Bolingbroke, *Works* (1754), iii. 151.
[3] William Pulteney, *An Enquiry into the Conduct of our Domestick Affairs* (1734), p. 8.
[4] *The Country Journal or the Craftsman*, 19 February 1737.
[5] Pulteney, op. cit., p. 13.

This was one reason why the 'Craftsman's Catholicon' in 1737 included 'the Redemption of all burthensome Duties'.[1]

This argument shaded into the larger question of the need to free the nation of its debts. Most contemporaries would have agreed with a writer of 1737 that

so long as the Nation labours under so great a load of Debt, it is impossible it should maintain its Honour and Rights, with the same vigour as formerly.[2]

The problem was how to put this sentiment into effect. Since the earliest government long-term loans were in the form of annuities, the debts could be treated as self-liquidating. As early as 1711, however, Defoe was arguing that the terms settled were so long that the debts were in fact perpetual, and that in future all loans should be redeemable.[3] The flaw in this was that it omitted to discuss how the debts so created were to be paid. This was exposed by the massive increase of the redeemable debt, without provision for its repayment, between 1710 and 1713. The proposals made by Asgill and Leigh shortly after the war to pay it off by creating Exchequer Bills with legal currency for a run of years were no more convincing than a scheme of 1743 to vest all waste lands in Great Britain and Ireland in the Crown, to be leased to pay part of the National Debt.[4] The creation of the Sinking Fund in 1717 offered a more practical solution, given added plausibility by the conversion of the greater part of the existing annuities for terms of years into redeemable South Sea stock in 1720. The failure of the Fund to answer its expected purpose quickly enough, however (partly because of its diversion to other uses), led eventually to a return to the idea that, since annuities were self-liquidating, it would be better, even if their annual interest was high, to change both existing and future loans to this basis. This idea seems to have first been sketched by Sir Richard Steele in 1720[5]. Similar proposals of a rather more sophisticated kind were brought forward by Sir John Barnard in Parliament in 1737 and by an anonymous projector in the *Gentleman's Magazine* in November 1749. But they were implausible at this stage, in view of the hostility of the state's creditors and the City, and the imminence of new wars and new borrowing. They were successfully revived in the very different conditions of the Napoleonic Wars. In the meantime,

[1] *The Country Journal or the Craftsman*, loc. cit.
[2] *Reasons against Lowering the Interest of the Redeemable National Debt* (1737), p. 2.
[3] Daniel Defoe, *A Review of the State of the British Nation*, 8 February 1711.
[4] John Asgill, *An Abstract of the Publick Funds* (1715); Edward Leigh, *An Essay upon Credit* (1715); *An Essay or a Method to pay the National Debts* (1744).
[5] Sir Richard Steele, *A Nation a Family* (1720).

plans to reduce the interest on the Debt acted as a partial substitute.[1]

These discussions of the nation's liabilities took place against a background of fears about France's capacity to pay off her debts quicker than England and once more 'give the law to all Europe'. Defoe, commenting in 1711 on the high proportion of English government debts in the form of long annuities which would not run off for nearly a century, added:

> The French King is not thus, he will recover himself, gather Strength, lessen his Debt, and lay up Money; a few Years of Peace will recover him, restore his Loss, and make him the same Powerful immensely Rich Prince that he was before.[2]

Not long after the peace of 1713 John Law's 'system' gave point to these anxieties. Lord Stair, the English Ambassador in Paris, wrote in 1719 to Secretary Craggs in London that Law's financial legerdemain looked like clearing off the French Government's debts, and that Law

> pretended he will set France higher than ever she was before, and put her in a condition to give the law to all Europe. . . . He said publickly the other day at his own table . . . that there was but one great kingdom in Europe and one great town; and that was France and Paris.[3]

The collapse of the System, and Law's own disappearance from the public scene, did not seriously allay English fears. A pamphleteer of 1726 urged England to cultivate her North American colonies and to

> have a vigilant eye on France, who has made great Encroachments since our first Settlements there, and watches an Opportunity to divest us of our Properties in that Part of the World.[4]

France's improved financial situation under Fleury, it was argued, increased the risk of aggression. Pulteney noted in 1729 that the French

> rise apace from that low Condition to which they were reduced. . . . Their Incumbrances are either cleared, or thrown into such a Form as to sit easy upon them, and almost deserve to lose that name.[5]

---

[1] For Barnard's reduction proposals in 1737 see below, p. 212. He was still pushing his scheme to convert Government stock into annuities in the 1750s (Newcastle Papers, Add. MS. 33038, f. 359, 'A Proposal for converting three p. ct. Annuities [i.e. government stock] into Annuities for lives or for the term of 31 years. Recd. from Sir John Barnard, July 31st 1754.').

[2] Daniel Defoe, *A Review of the State of the British Nation*, 8 February 1711.

[3] Stair to Craggs, 9 September 1719 (N.S.), Lord Hardwicke (ed.), *Miscellaneous State Papers* (2 vols., 1778), ii. 593.

[4] Erasmus Philips, *The State of the Nation, in Respect to her Commerce, Debts and Money* (1726), p. 10.

[5] [William Pulteney], *Some Considerations on the National Debts* (1729), p. 82.

Bolingbroke argued later that the Peace of Utrecht left France 'too power-ful, no matter by whose fault, as I am ready to admit that she was', and under Walpole 'France grew frugal, she made the debts she could not pay sit more lightly on her, she raised her credit, and she extended her commerce. ... In short, her strength increased and ours diminished.'[1] French com-petition in the Americas and the Mediterranean led Sir John Barnard in 1737 to declare that France was now a more serious commercial rival than Holland.[2] A pamphleteer writing in 1750 assessed the relative financial positions of England and France as follows:

France is at present as much incumbered with Debts as we are, and that Nation which first eases itself of it's Burthen will be enabled to give the Law to the other, and to the rest of Europe. Sorry I am to say, that, by the Regulation of the French Revenue, such a Proportion is set apart for the Payment of their Debts, that, in the space of fifteen Years, they will have discharged thirty Millions Sterling. Unless we can therefore in some Measure keep Pace with them in the Reduction of our Debt, we shall be necessitated to accept the Law from them; and be no longer able to oppose their Attempts for universal Monarchy.[3]

Similar fears survived the Seven Years War. Lord Northumberland, entrusted in 1765 to act as the king's go-between with the Duke of Cum-berland, observed gloomily to the latter that he

much lamented both the King's situation and that of his affairs; that with such an administration nothing great could be done; that they lived from day to day, whilst France was restoring their finances, paying off their debt, and putting their naval force again in condition. That, therefore, if ever it pleased France to begin with us, they would find us in the same exhausted state that had obliged us to grant them the favourable terms of peace they had obtained from us.[4]

This conversation took place in a stable at Newmarket, appropriately enough for a century of horseflesh and political jobbery, and was as biased as the opinions of Pulteney or Bolingbroke previously referred to. The fox-hunting gentlemen of England may not have been so apprehensive of French fiscal skill as they appeared when using the issue as a stick with which to beat Ministers. Nevertheless, it is as well to remember that the *prépondérance anglaise* in this period was less evident and less predestined to contemporary observers than it has seemed to posterity.

---

[1] *Works* (1754), iii. 146, 153, 155.
[2] *Parl. Hist.* x. 80.
[3] *The Necessity of Lowering Interest and Continuing Taxes* (1750), pp. 9–10.
[4] Lord Albemarle (ed.), *Memoirs of the Marquis of Rockingham* (2 vols., 1852), i. 188.

III

Besides these mainly political arguments about the development of government borrowing there were others which concentrated on its social and economic consequences. These were thought particularly serious for the landed interest, owing to the implicit eighteenth-century assumption that it had special virtues denied to other members of society.

Soon after the political revolution of 1688 it was claimed that war taxes weighed unfairly on land and that

it cannot be, but they must of necessity fall very much, if the whole Burthen of Rates and Taxes should continue to be laid upon them, as hitherto it has been; for who, that hath Money by him, will have a mind to be concern'd with Land which is liable to so many Incumbrances and Charges, when he can better dispose of it, and more to his Advantage, without being subject to pay any Rates or Taxes, or to be troubled with any such casual Expenses or Charges whatsoever ?[1]

The author argued that one way of keeping up the price of land, since it varied inversely with the rate of interest, would be to reduce the latter to four per cent. He optimistically asserted that monied men, threatened with this reduction, would agree to pay a tax of 2% on what they lent. He also proposed a $33\frac{1}{3}$% tax on marine insurance profits, perhaps on the strength of Sir Dudley North's assertion that premiums were currently 36%.[2]

The connection between the price of land and the rate of interest was restated in 1694 by John Briscoe in his able and bitter attack on the new finance, *A Discourse on the Late Funds of the Million-Act*.[3] He suggested that few contemporaries had seriously reflected on the implications of the new methods of borrowing.

I doubt few have entered into the Account of it; but whoever lives but a few Years, will find them (if some other Methods are not taken to prevent it) like a Canker, which will eat up the Gentlemen's Estates in Land, and beggar the Trading Part of the Nation, and bring all the Subjects in England to be the Monied Men's Vassalls.[4]

---

[1] *A Plain and Easie Way for the Speedy Raising of Money. . . . By a Divine of the Church of England* (November 1691), pp. 9–10.

[2] [Sir Dudley North], *Discourses upon Trade* (1691), p. 7.

[3] John Briscoe, *A Discourse on the Late Funds of the Million-Act* (1694). The Million Act was the Tontine and Life Annuity loan of 1693, discussed below, pp. 53 and 254.

[4] Briscoe, op. cit., p. viii.

Land would fall to twelve to fourteen years' purchase, because the taxes charged on it to service Government loans would lessen its attraction, while demand for it would slacken as landed men came to appreciate the superiority of Government securities as an investment.

> They can not have 4*l*. per Cent. per Annum for their Money [in Land] when [sc. whereas] they can buy a perpetual Rent-Charge on the Crown (as in the Bank of England) which will bring them in above 8*l*. per Cent. per Annum, clear of all Taxes.[1]

As the projector of a land bank, Briscoe had an axe to grind, but his line of attack was developed by other writers. An author of 1705, ignoring both the restrictions in the Bank's charter and economic logic, argued that the Bank might become a monopolist of land and drastically reduce its price. 'How far this may affect all the landed Men of England', he observed, 'is what seems to call for their very serious and timely consideration.'[2] Their consideration was also thoughtfully called for in 1707 in a pamphlet that emphasized the close connection between good trade, abundant money, low interest, and high land prices. 'Trade to Land', it was argued, 'is like the Soul to the Body, the latter without being animated by the former, would be inactive and insignificant.'[3] New taxes on trade also fell on land. First, they raised the cost of living for landowners. Second, by causing trade to decay they increased unemployment and hence the Poor Rate, which was already in some places 'near as burdensome as the Land Tax'.[4] The double imposition was among the causes why 'so many Estates are every Day found crouded in our publick Papers to be sold'.[5]

Other writers insisted on the obstacles that the development of government borrowing had put in the way of landowners who wanted to borrow on mortgage. In 1707 and again in 1710 opponents of the Bank of England repeated the argument, devised by Briscoe and others in the 1690s, that the high yields on Bank stock and Exchequer tallies had diverted capital away from land and trade into stock-jobbing, and thus driven up the rate of interest

---

[1] Ibid., p. 24.

[2] *Remarks upon the Bank of England. By a Merchant of London and a true Lover of our Constitution* (1705), p. 25.

[3] *Reasons Against Charging Trade with Annuities* (1707), p. 3.

[4] Ibid., p. 4.

[5] Ibid. Fielding, writing in 1742, makes Peter Pounce argue similarly that 'the greatest fault in our constitution is the provision made for the poor. . . . Sir, I have not an estate which does not contribute almost as much again to the poor as to the land tax.' *Joseph Andrews*, bk. III, ch. 13.

on mortgages.[1] It was also pointed out that even if the Bank were prepared to lend to landowners at 5% the offer would be refused because of the publicity of such loans 'when public Registers have been rejected upon that very Account'.[2]

During the four last years of the queen the note of incipient class-hatred on which these writers played was developed by St. John and Swift into a savage and brilliant onslaught on the monied men. Arguing in the Commons in favour of the Landed Property Qualification Bill on 20 December 1710, St. John alleged that

we might see a time when the money'd men might bid fair to keep out of that house all the landed men, and he had heard of Societys of them that joint'd Stocks to bring in members, and such a thing might be an Administration within an Administration, a juncto; and these mony'd men might arise to such a pitch of assurance as to oppose the Crown and advise in matters that did not belong to them.[3]

This thinly-veiled reference to the Bank's recent attempt to persuade the queen not to dismiss Lord Godolphin was particularly appealing to a Tory Parliament whose members, like Sir John Packington, desired an end to the war to prevent monied and military men becoming 'lords of us who have lands'.[4]

Swift's argument was longer, and equally bitter. The land paid taxes to endow a *rentier* class,

the Style of Men at Ease, who lay the heavy Burthens upon others, which they will not touch with one of their Fingers. I have known some People such ill Computers, as to imagine the many Millions in Stocks and Annuities, are so much real Wealth in the Nation; whereas every Farthing of it is entirely lost to us, scattered in Holland, Germany and Spain; and the Landed-Men, who now pay the Interest, must at last pay the Principal.[5]

Two years later Swift described how

a new Estate and Property sprung up in the hands of Mortgagees, to whom every House and Foot of Land in England paid a Rent Charge free of all Taxes and Defalcations. . . . so that the Gentlemen of Estates were in effect but Tenants to

---

[1] *Reasons Offer'd against the Continuance of the Bank. In a Letter to a Member of Parliament* (1707); *A Letter to a Person of Quality, Relating to the Bank of England* (1710).

[2] *Reasons Offer'd . . .* , p. 13. For land registers see above, pp. 5, 7.

[3] J. J. Cartwright (ed.), *Wentworth Papers, 1705–1739* (1882), p. 167.

[4] *Parl. Hist.* vi. 932, Sir John Packington's speech 15 December 1710. For the Bank's action see below, p. 64.

[5] Swift, *The Conduct of the Allies* (1711), in *Works*, ed. H. Davis (1951), vi. 59.

these New Landlords; many of whom were able in time to force the Election of Burroughs out of the hands of those who had been the old Proprietors and Inhabitants. This was arrived to such a Height, that a very few Years more of War and Funds would have clearly cast the Balance on the Money'd Side.[1]

Swift admitted that he was 'not very well versed either in the Style or Matter' of financial affairs,[2] but the fears upon which he played were clearly real enough, and were not merely the product of the last years of a war of unprecedented cost during which party passions had run high. In the pamphlet debates about the Excise scheme of 1733 similar arguments were restated and elaborated. War finance and its aftermath had burdened the landowner with heavy direct taxes.

Let People cast their Eyes for Five and Forty years backward, and compute what the Landed Men have payed to the Support of this Government; no less than Sixty Millions of Money have been payed by the Land-Tax into the Exchequer since the Revolution.[3]

The landowner had also to pay indirect taxes, poor rates, and tithes, and, despite these burdens, to maintain his station in his county and educate and endow his children.[4] Further, the very forces that depressed the landed interest were creating a new parvenu class,

a Set of brocaded Tradesmen cloathed in Purple and Fine Linnen, and faring sumptuously every Day, raising to themselves immense Wealth, so as to marry their Daughters to the first Rank, and leave their Sons such Estates as to enable them to live to the same Degree.[5]

Yet it was the landed interest that was the true one:

The Landed Gentlemen, Yeomen and Farmers, whose Substance is fix'd in this particular part of the Globe, are to be esteemed the most settled Inhabitants and the Bulk of the Nation.[6]

Or, as Bolingbroke put it in 1749:

---

[1] Swift, *The History of the Four Last Years of the Queen* (written 1713, published 1758), in *Works*, ed. H. Davis, vi. 70.

[2] Ibid., p. 71.

[3] *The Reply of a Member of Parliament to the Mayor of his Corporation* (1733), p. 37.

[4] *An Appeal to the Landholders concerning the Reasonableness and General Benefit of an Excise upon Tobacco and Wine* (1733). In *The Duty and Office of a Land-Steward* (Dublin, 1731) Edward Laurence assumes that tenants pay the Church, Poor, and Police rates, the landlord paying the Land Tax (p. 62).

[5] *The Landed Interest consider'd . . . by a Yeoman of Kent* (1733), p. 35.

[6] Ibid., p. 27.

the landed men are the true owners of our political vessel, the moneyd men as such, are no more than passengers in it.[1]

Joseph Danvers, M.P. for Bramber, put the case succinctly and bitterly in a speech in Parliament in 1733.

The Landed Gentlemen bore the greatest Share of the late War; by that they had been loaded with many heavy taxes; by that were all those Funds created out of which the Plumb Men of the City of London have made most of their Estates, by which they are enabled to deck their Wives in Velvet and rich Brocades, while poor Country Gentlemen are hardly able to afford their Wives a Gown of Lindsey Woolsey.[2]

Danvers and other squires must have felt that war finance, by depressing their class and elevating the monied interest, had made a mockery of the triumph of Liberty and Property in 1688.

The argument for tax relief for landowners was also involved in proposals for reduction of the interest on the National Debt. Sir Nathaniel Gould contended in 1726 that a reduction to 3% was possible, but by lessening the income of the government's creditors would depress demand and hence wages and prices, including the price of land.[3] This rather implausible argument was repeated in 1737 by the opponents of Sir John Barnard's proposal to reduce the interest on South Sea annuities to 3%, although one writer added the cautious rider that the price of land would fall, 'at least [in] all the Counties within an hundred Miles of London'.[4] But the contrary view that a lower rate of interest would, among its other benefits, raise the price of land, increase rents, and enable taxes to be cut had greater appeal to landed men. Barnard himself pointed out in 1746 that new government loans must be raised at a low rate of interest, since if they were not,

It likewise raises the Rate of Interest between private Persons; and also lowers the Value of Land; so that the whole Community suffers thereby.[5]

[1] Bolingbroke, *Some Reflections on the Present State of the Nation* (written 1749), in *Works* (1754), iii. 151.

[2] *Gent. Mag.* (1733), p. 450, report of a debate of 21 February 1733 on the application of the Sinking Fund. Cf. the views of William Allen, a Pembrokeshire gentleman, in 1734, below p. 476.

[3] Sir Nathaniel Gould, *An Essay on the Publick Debts of this Kingdom* (1726).

[4] *A Speech Without-Doors addressed to the National Creditors . . . at 4l. per Cent.* (1737), p. 30.

[5] Sir John Barnard, *A Defence of several Proposals for Raising of Three Millions for the Service of the Government for the year 1746* (1746), postscript.

It was generally considered that the landed interest, swayed by reasoning of this kind, supported Pelham's conversion of the National Debt to a 3% basis in 1749. 'Tis no wonder', complained one writer opposed to the reduction of interest,

that the House of Commons should approve the Scheme in general, because as the Members that compose that honourable Body are principally Landholders, the Reduction of Interest will be to their advantage.[1]

IV

The economic effects of government borrowing on the landed interest were discussed primarily in terms of social prejudice. The diversion of savings into government stock, for example, was resented because it was thought to affect the price of land, and hence the social position of landowners, rather than because it deprived them of risk capital for improvements, as might have been argued. On the other hand, the effects of the Financial Revolution on trade were discussed in largely economic terms, for trade was increasingly accepted as the motor that drove the whole economy.

The argument that government finance acted as a magnet attracting capital away from trade soon made its appearance in the 1690s. (Houghton's point that the real cause of the diversion of capital was the war's obstruction of foreign commerce tended to be conveniently ignored.)[2] The shift of investment might only be in the short run. In 1692, for example, the author of *The Clothiers Complaint*, denouncing the rise of the Blackwell Hall factors as intermediaries between the clothier and the merchant over the previous thirty years, alleged that the long credit (up to fifteen months) that clothiers now had to allow the factors and merchants put idle capital into the latter's hands, 'and no Citizen but understands the value of Money, Seven per Cent. to the Exchequer, or otherwise'.[3] The shift might, however, be permanent. Briscoe in 1694 asserted that traders had now become financiers instead:

[1] *Annotations on a Late Pamphlet Intituled Considerations on the Proposal for reducing the Interest on the National Debt* (1750), pp. 13–14.

[2] For Houghton's view see below, p. 486.

[3] *The Clothiers Complaint: or, Reasons for Passing the Bill Against the Blackwell-Hall Factors* (1692), p. 16.

now almost their whole Discourse is of Lottery-Tickets, Annuities, Bank-Bills, &c. and in contriving how they may draw their Money out of Trade, to put it upon some of these late Funds.[1]

He met the objection that 'a great part of the Money was advanced by such who had plenty of Money and did not imploy it in Trade, and not by Tradesmen' by agreeing 'that very many Traders paid in large sums of Money from 100 to 10,000*l*. apiece' but arguing that these capitalists would otherwise have lent to small traders at reasonable rates.[2]

The argument was elaborated by a writer of 1707. He claimed that five-sixths of the trade of the nation was carried on by men of £500 or £1,000 capital, who could secure credit for five times their own worth from the great traders and in turn allowed a long payment time to exporting merchants. This structure was now distorted, for the big traders, preferring to invest in Bank bills and East India bonds, pressed their own debtors and created a general stringency of credit.[3] This was accentuated by seasonal fluctuations in the demand for money. In the winter of 1706-7, for example, the Bank of England had given out bills bearing interest at a time when the East India Company wanted bullion for export, the Hamburg and Virginia fleets needed funds to pay customs dues, and Supply loans were being raised at the Exchequer.[4] In the same year another writer complained that the Bank was a money-monopolist diverting capital from trade, and that all the talk in the Exchange was now of Bank stock and tallies 'as if that was the grand and only Commerce of the Nation, and the Promoting any other not worth a serious thought'.[5] If monied men were not able to secure such high yields on government stock, repeated a pamphleteer of 1710, they would invest their capital in trade, to the nation's benefit.[6]

In the 1720s and 1730s, when low yields on government stock had robbed these arguments of some of their plausibility, the thesis was developed that government borrowing affected trade not so much by starving it of capital as by burdening it with taxes imposed to pay interest on the National Debt. The idea was most fully elaborated in the pamphlet debate of 1737, in and outside Parliament, about Barnard's proposal to reduce govern-

---

[1] John Briscoe, *A Discourse on the Late Funds of the Million-Act* (1694), p. 20.
[2] Ibid., pp. 22-23.
[3] *The Reasons of the Decay of Trade and Private Credit. By a Merchant of London* (1707), pp. 14 ff.
[4] Ibid., pp. 5-6.
[5] *Reasons Offer'd against the Continuance of the Bank* (1707), p. 10.
[6] *A Letter to a Person of Quality, Relating to the Bank of England* (1710), p. 3.

ment stock to 3%.[1] Supporters of the reduction claimed that it would enable taxes to be cut. Low interest rates and a low level of taxation would cheapen raw materials and the cost of living, and thus lessen production costs. Sir John Barnard specifically argued that wages determined prices, and the cost of food determined wages. The implication of this neo-Ricardian argument was that a reduction of taxes would enable wages to be cut back, a conclusion that the advocates of low interest were less coy about drawing than the Anti-Corn-Law League a hundred years later. They added, however, that the consequent stimulus to foreign trade would increase the level of domestic employment.

Their opponents were unable to deny that a reduction of the National Debt and therefore of taxes was desirable, but emphasized the necessity of dealing honourably with the national creditors, raised doubts whether the yield on government securities was a satisfactory indication of the rate of interest, and suggested that a reduction would harm trade by cutting home demand. These difficulties would be increased by massive selling of government stock by foreigners, who were computed to hold a quarter of the National Debt. In reply, it was said that the interests of a small group must give way to the good of the majority. Second, as English stockholders normally reinvested most of their dividends, the fall in public demand would be negligible. Lastly, the amount of government stock owned abroad was exaggerated. And the Dutch, the biggest foreign owners, would in any case not sell on a reduction of interest, since rates of interest in Holland were so low they could not profitably invest there. Even if they did all decide to sell, market prices would collapse and the exchange would move heavily against them.

Dutch reactions to Pelham's reduction of interest from 4% to 3½% (1749–50) were perhaps less clear-cut than they should have been if these arguments were right, though in the end most Dutch holders of English Government securities agreed to it.[2] The reduction itself was not accompanied by any extensive re-examination of principles; the main arguments had all been previously rehearsed. The government's creditors were advised to agree to it on the grounds that it was self-evidently necessary. Opponents of the measure complained that they were being treated unfairly, that interest rates were in fact higher than 4%, and that other means of reducing expenditure could be adopted. The great increase in the annual charge of the National Debt, however, made these arguments less plausible than they had

[1] *Parl. Hist.* x. 74 ff., and the pamphlets of 1737 listed in the Bibliography.
[2] For Dutch hesitations see below, pp. 234 n. and 238.

been in 1737, and it was easy to treat them as the factious discontent of an upstart minority of monied men 'who as such are the very Drones of a Society, and live upon the Labour of the industrious Merchant, Trader and Manufacturer'.[1] Indeed, the burden of new taxes, which the reduction only partly alleviated, gave added force to the argument that the National Debt hampered England's foreign trade. A writer of 1753 restated the familiar points that the taxes imposed to service Government borrowing drove up the price of necessities and hence the level of wages, so that the country was 'undersold in the foreign market'. A reduction in the volume of the debt would, by releasing capital for trade and industry, enable England to employ her poor and 'undersel all the world abroad'.[2]

The Financial Revolution was thus said to have affected land and trade in similar ways. Capital had been diverted from both into government loans; this had affected the price of land and the rate of investment in trade. It had also made borrowing by both landowners and merchants more expensive, because they had to compete with the attractive yields on government stock. This argument was less plausible after these yields began to fall from 1713; it was to reappear later in the century. Lastly, the indirect taxes imposed to pay interest on Government loans were said to have affected merchants by raising the price of labour and raw materials, so that English manufacturers were undersold in foreign markets, the poor insufficiently employed, and the poor rate kept unnecessarily high; and to have affected landowners by sharply increasing their general costs at a time when direct taxation was heavier for them, even in peace-time, than it had been before 1688.

V

Finally, it is worth noting that while few aspects of the Financial Revolution were of greater political and economic utility than the development of a market in securities in London, none united contemporary opinion more against it.[3] It was denounced as inherently wicked and against the public interest. The phrase 'stock-jobbing', freely used to denote every kind of

---

[1] *A Copy of a Letter wrote to a Member of Parliament* (1750), p. 8.

[2] [Patrick Murray, Lord Elibank,], *An Inquiry into the Original and Consequences of the Publick Debt* (Edinburgh, 1753), pp. 11–12.

[3] The rise of the Stock Exchange is discussed in Chap. 20, below.

activity in the market, had clear overtones of self-interest and corruption. An anthology of comments by contemporaries would be remarkably uniform, indeed monotonous, in its tone, and uninformative about how the market actually worked. Some examples are sufficient. Defoe in his *Essay upon Projects* (1697) described how public companies began with those established for the Indian and American trades.

Here began the forming of publick Joint-Stocks, which, together with the East-India African, and Hudson's-Bay Companies, before establish'd, begot a New Trade, which we call by a new Name, Stock-Jobbing, which was at first only the simple Occasional Transferring of Interest and Shares from one to another . . . but by the Industry of the Exchange-Brokers, who got the business into their hands, it became a Trade; and one perhaps manag'd with the greatest Intriegue, Artifice, and Trick, that ever any thing that appear'd with a face of Honesty could be handl'd with.[1]

In 1701 Defoe followed this up with his *The Villainy of Stock-Jobbers detected*. In 1705, in *The Consolidator*, he grudgingly conceded that 'by chance some honester Men than usual are got in among them',[2] but the general tone of public comment remained abusive. The South Sea Bubble confirmed the darkest contemporary suspicions of Exchange Alley. Even before the Bubble burst, pamphleteers were arguing that it merely encouraged stockjobbing, which was a public evil and should be suppressed.[3] The techniques of the market put power into the hands of sharpers:

That Trade that is drove by the giving of Money for their refusal, or the Putt of Stocks for stated times . . . [puts it] in the Power of a sett of Jobbers to raise or sink Stock as they please.[4]

The Bill of 1733 and the Act of 1734 against jobbing were, understandably in this climate, entitled 'against the infamous Practice of Stockjobbing'; a further draft of 1746 referred to the Act of 1734 as making

many wholesome provisions . . . to prevent that wicked and detestable Practice; which have been found, by Experience, to be of great Utility to the Publick.[5]

---

[1] Daniel Defoe, *An Essay upon Projects* (1697), pp. 29–30.

[2] Daniel Defoe, *The Consolidator: or, Memoirs of sundry transactions from the world in the moon* (1705), p. 258.

[3] *An Examination and Explanation of the South Sea Company's Scheme* (17 February 1720).

[4] [James Milner], *A visit to the South-Sea Company and the Bank* (1720), 1st letter, March 1720.

[5] B.M. Collection of Parliamentary Papers, 1731–1800, i, no. 27 (1746). For this Bill and the measures of 1733–4 see below, pp. 507, 519.

Hostility was reinforced by racial prejudice. This was focused by the rise of Samson Gideon as financial adviser to Henry Pelham in the 1740s, which seems genuinely to have shocked contemporaries.[1] Aware that many jobbers were Jews, they found it convenient to treat them as though they all were. Thus Mr. Trueblue, an engaging country gentleman with minimal intelligence (and an undefinable provincial accent), is taken in 1753 to Jonathan's to see the jobbers, who are described as 'a Number of Jews circumcised and uncircumcised' and whose leader, Caiphas, is fairly clearly Gideon himself. Mr. Trueblue laments that England should be drained of her wealth by such leeches, and describes to his friend how he used to discuss with Lord Turncoat 'the true Interest of Great Britain' and 'Old England without Taxes' until they were both ready to cry. Turncoat had subsequently gone over to the Ministry.[2] In similar vein 'Mr. Town's' *The Connoisseur* published early in 1754 a letter from a Jew describing his purchases in Italy. The second item

is 'the Triumph of Gideon'. This I intended, if a late project in favour of our brethren had not miscarried, to have been hung up in St. Stephen's Chapel, as a memorial of our victory over the Uncircumcised.[3]

The controversy about the Jewish Naturalization Act of 1753, to which this refers, had provincial repercussions, for in April 1754 Mr. Town's cousin Mr. Village described the country town he was staying in as

divided into two parties, who are distinguish'd by the appellation of Christians and Jews. The Jews, it seems, are those, who are in the interest of a nobleman who gave his vote for passing the Jew-bill, and are held in abomination by the Christians.[4]

On the eve of the great struggle with France, the 'Powerful immensely Rich' kingdom which the Financial Revolution had been initiated to curb, this mixture of financial retrogression and racial hostility obviously still appealed to members of sophisticated society as a diagnosis of ills and a programme for reform.

---

[1] For Samson Gideon's activities see below, esp. pp. 222–8 and 230–6.

[2] 'Charles Ranger' (pseudonym for A. Murphy), *The Grays Inn Journal*, no. 6, 3 November 1753.

[3] *The Connoisseur. By Mr. Town, Critic and Censor-General*, no. 2, 7 February 1754.

[4] Ibid., no. 13, 25 April 1754. The Act, simplifying naturalization procedure for foreign-born Jews, had to be repealed almost at once owing to the clamour against it. See the study of this episode by T. W. Perry, *Public Opinion, Propaganda and Politics in Eighteenth-Century England* (Harvard, 1962).

VI

Such were the main reactions of contemporaries to the rapid changes in public and private finance in the six decades after 1688. They were essentially ones of alarm and disapproval. They were based on fear of dislocation of the social order by the rise of new economic interests, and dislike of commercial and financial manipulation of all kinds, and had roots going back into the Middle Ages. They were to be much in evidence again during the early stages of industrialism, which also seemed to threaten 'traditional' society. Neither alarm nor disapproval was precise; indeed each put a premium on blurring or misstating facts in order to make a case. Neither was truly historical though both depended on appeals to a largely unhistorical past. But neither can be disregarded, for they are evidence of strong if muddled reactions to events. The remainder of this book, by examining the structure and development of the Financial Revolution, provides some evidence of the extent to which they were justified.

PART TWO

Government
Long-term Borrowing

3

The Earliest Phase of
the National Debt 1688–1714

WHEN William of Orange landed at Torbay in November 1688 bringing with him — as contemporaries alleged — the secret of running the state over head and ears in debt, English government borrowing of different kinds already had a long and tangled history dating back to the Plantagenets. For most of this period its reputation had been unsavoury. To start with, the very idea of lending money was suspect. As late as the seventeenth century borrowing tended to be regarded as an index of necessity, and lenders as those who took advantage of necessity. This was the line of thought behind the prohibition of usury until the sixteenth century, and the subsequent establishment of maximum rates of interest for loans between private persons.[1] These statutes did not bind the Crown, which was free to offer whatever interest its creditors demanded. But this in turn seemed shocking to contemporaries, who thought that the state was being drained by leeches. There were also more specific reasons for the uncertain reputation of public borrowing. Although its form changed considerably between the war loans of Edward III and those of the Commonwealth, it had certain common characteristics. First, the Crown seems always to have been acting in haste and therefore at a disadvantage. Money had to be found, and found quickly. This explains why, secondly, interest was always stiff and frequently exorbitant. Third, and following from this, the Crown always had great difficulty in paying the interest, which had often to be funded in the principal, thus creating a growing snowball of debt. Lastly, no clear distinction was drawn between short-term debts and long-term ones. Public loans were shadowed by the

---

[1] Acts of 1487 and 1495 forbidding usury completely were relaxed in 1546 by an Act allowing maximum interest of 10%, but were reimposed in 1552. In 1571 the maximum rate of 10% was restored. It was lowered to 8% in 1623, 6% in 1651 (confirmed in 1660) and 5% in 1714. The maximum rate under the seventeenth-century Acts was not to be exceeded 'upon any contract . . . for loan of any monies', but this was held not to bind the Crown. For discussion of the pre-1571 position see R. H. Tawney's introduction to his edition (1925) of Thomas Wilson's *A Discourse upon Usury* (1572).

lenders' expectation of early repayment. This was the natural result of the absence of an effective market in which lenders could sell their claim on the state for a capital sum. It was therefore impossible to divide borrowing into anticipation pure and simple, regularly paid back from incoming revenue, and long-term borrowing in which the state would undertake to repay the principal with interest over a number of years. Failing this basic distinction, it was no wonder that subtler gradations, like ranking short-term debts in order for repayment, could not be introduced. Thus English government borrowing down to the seventeenth century tended to be a hotchpotch, with creditors either pressing for payment or running up claims against the state at compound interest. The only way out of the quagmire was the sale of royal land or, as in the 1650s, satisfying public creditors by giving them forfeited estates in Ireland or elsewhere.

These characteristics of public borrowing were not confined to England. They probably obtained everywhere in Europe for much of the period. Nor were they confined to public loans. Many a sixteenth- or seventeenth-century nobleman, paying 10% on his debts, and paying off old debts with new ones until the accumulated principal swallowed up his estate, would have recognized his case as that of the government in miniature. Merchants, too, though usually more prudent both in the scale of their needs and in keeping accounts than kings and nobles, also borrowed and repaid on an essentially short-term basis. This general picture in both the public and private sectors is presumably explained by a relative scarcity of funds available for long-term as distinct from short-term loans, and by the fact that commercial activity was geared to the short run, and placed a high value on liquidity of assets so that capital could be switched readily from one occupation to another.

By the middle of the seventeenth century there are signs that this picture was changing, both for the state and for individuals. English private finance began to shift to a longer-term basis with the development of the joint-stock company and the strictly-settled landed estate. The crucial factor in joint-stock companies was the right (and possibility) of selling shares, for this enabled the company to continue, without constantly repaying its capital, while its shareholders had both income (dividends) and capital liquidity. These advantages were not at first recognized, and several of the early joint-stock ventures were wound up after each voyage. Gradually, however, they became apparent and accepted. The strictly settled estate, which was important from the 1650s, was more difficult to alienate and therefore encouraged the growth of charges on its revenue. For it was now primarily by mortgage, rather than by sale of part of the land, that capital sums for children's portions or for investment could most easily be obtained. At the same time, strict settlement must have encouraged the formulation of longer-term plans for agricultural improvement, and hence have increased the revenue against which mortgage loans could be charged.

Besides these two developments there was a growing interest in insurance to lessen the hazards of shipwreck, fire, and premature death. Marine and fire insurance developed empirically. The theoretical work needed to lay the foundations of modern actuarial science (and hence life assurance) was begun by Pascal, Fermat, and Huyghens in the 1650s, and continued over the next hundred years by de Wit (1671), Halley (1693), van der Burch (1702), de Moivre (1725), and Simpson (1742). Small-scale facilities for all three kinds of cover were available in London by the 1690s.[1] At the same time in the United Provinces private investors were using tontine loans as a speculative form of life cover. A group would subscribe a capital sum, which was then invested in East India shares or other securities. The income would be paid *pro rata* to each beneficiary as long as a named person (his *nominee*) lived. As each nominee died the surviving beneficiaries drew a larger income, until one drew the whole. Since the beneficiaries would normally also be the nominees, it was possible in this way to give a child a certain annuity with a chance of its increasing. The basic idea is usually attributed to Lorenzo Tonti (1630–95), an Italian financial adviser to Cardinal Mazarin. Tonti intended his scheme to be for state loans, and drafted a plan for one in 1653, but it made no provision for dividing nominees into classes according to age and never got off paper. The Dutch adapted his plan not only to private insurance but to municipal finance. In 1670 Kampen and Groningen in the United Provinces both floated tontine loans. Middelburg and Delft followed suit in 1671 and 1673.[2] A proposal to raise a loan for the City of London on a similar basis, with the nominees classified according to age, was drafted in 1674, no doubt owing to the Dutch examples, and printed by order of the Corporation.[3] By the time that these developments were taking place in private and municipal finance, the governments of both France and the United Provinces had already developed reasonably viable systems of long-

---

[1] Dickson, *Sun Insurance Office*, chs. 1 and 6.

[2] M. van Haaften, *Elementaire Levensverzekerings-wiskunde*, ii (Groningen and Batavia, 1947), paras. 146–9, draws on the scattered Dutch literature. For Tonti and the early French tontines see A. Vührer, *Histoire de la dette publique en France* (2 vols., Paris 1886).

[3] *Proposals for Subscriptions of Money &c.* (1674), Goldsmiths' Library, London University.

term borrowing, which enabled the state to tap the capital resources that existing taxation could not reach. Loans were of various kinds, but were mostly annuities for lives or for terms of years.[1] In 1689 the French government belatedly took up Tonti's suggestions by successfully floating a survivorship loan of 14m. livres, with the nominees divided into 14 classes, the interest ranging from 5% to 12% according to age.

The English government at this stage had no system of long-term borrowing to match those of its neighbours, and still had to rely on sales of Crown lands and rents to cover revenue deficits. Its financial position (and hence its credit rating) had nevertheless improved in many ways since the earlier seventeenth century. The introduction from Dutch precedents of an effective tax on internal consumption, the excise of 1643, which was retained at the Restoration, and the experience of direct taxation during the Commonwealth, helped to put the revenue on a sounder basis after 1660 and thus provide a surer fund for government borrowing. It was in this period (1660–88) that a system of short-term anticipation of direct taxes was evolved which was carried over virtually without change into the eighteenth century.[2] At the same time, the drastic price-inflation of the early Stuart period levelled off after the middle of the seventeenth century, so that Crown income was no longer constantly eroded in real terms. At first the sources of revenue settled on the Crown in 1660 — mainly customs and excise duties and crown lands — failed to yield the £1·2m. expected from them, even with the addition of the unpopular hearth tax in 1662. The heavy costs of the second Dutch War were, however, covered, or partly covered, by direct taxes, so that the combined ordinary and extraordinary (i.e. war) revenue amounted in 1665 and 1666 to over £2m. From the end of the war in 1667 extraordinary revenue declined sharply but ordinary revenue increased, reaching a level of £1·3m. to £1·4m. for the rest of Charles II's reign, and, with the new taxes imposed at the beginning of his brother's, a peak of nearly £2m. in 1687, which direct taxes brought up to just over the £2m. mark. This increase in revenue yields was due partly to increased internal and external trade, and partly to better administration, in particular the ending of farming in the Customs (1671) and the Excise (1683).[3] By 1688, therefore, Stuart revenues, though grossly inferior to those

---

[1] Vührer, op. cit.; D. Houtzager, *Hollands Lijf-en Losrentleningen voór 1672* (Schiedam, 1950).

[2] See below, p. 341.

[3] This section is based on the careful analysis in Dr. C. D. Chandaman's unpublished doctoral thesis 'The English Public Revenue (1660–1688)' (London, 1954). Dr. Chanda-

of France, computed by Gregory King as over £10m., were in better shape than they had ever been, which must have given James II as much false confidence as Bishop Juxon's careful husbanding of resources had given Charles I. It is ironic that the two occasions in the seventeenth century when Stuart finances reached a zenith were immediately followed by political disaster.

These improvements in the revenue should have strengthened the Crown's position as a borrower in much the same way that a landowner with increased rents normally found it easier to mortgage his estates. Looking only at the anticipation of direct and indirect taxes there is little doubt that this was so, and that the arrangements made between 1660 and 1688 were a good deal more satisfactory than those under James I and Charles I.[1] But there was a flaw in the picture. The Stop of the Exchequer in 1672, though less injurious to government credit than the cries of the victims at the time and the assertions of Whig propagandists after 1688 suggest, was undoubtedly a severe blow to Charles II's financial prestige. The circumstances in which the Stop occurred were as follows. In 1665, at the height of the Dutch war, a new method of authorizing payments was introduced at the Exchequer. The new Orders of Payment (as they were called) were of three kinds. The first was an Order to repay a lender his principal with interest when the tax in anticipation of which he had lent was collected. The second was an Order entitling a supplier of government goods to payment. The third was an Order entitling any government creditor to payment, for instance for wages or salary due.[2] Orders were serially numbered and were paid 'in course', that is in order of priority. They were assignable by endorsement. Clarendon attributes the idea to Sir George Downing, who hoped to turn the Exchequer into a bank, no doubt in anticipation of the Bank of Amster-

man exposes in a masterly way the errors and omissions in Dr. W. A. Shaw's *Introductions* to the *Calendar of Treasury Books* (H.M.S.O., 1904–61) on which historians have previously relied. Dr. Chandaman's detailed figures for revenue, expenditure, and public borrowing are worked out from the Exchequer records and differ in important respects from those given by Shaw. For the *Cal. T. Bks.* series see also Bibliography below.

[1] Chandaman, op. cit. Cf. also below, p. 342. For the pre-1640 position see Robert Ashton, *The Crown and the Money Market, 1603–1640* (Clarendon Press, Oxford, 1960).

[2] Orders were first made out by authority of 17 Ch. II, c. 1 (1665). The whole of this section is based on Chandaman, op. cit., pp. 43 ff., 513 ff., and 554–81. Cf. also R. D. Richards, *The Early History of Banking in England* (1929), ch. iii, and 'The Stop of the Exchequer', *Econ. Hist.* ii (1929–30), 45. W. A. Shaw, 'The Beginnings of the National Debt'. in *Historical Essays*, ed. T. F. Tout and J. Tait (1907), which takes the Stop as the first funding of government loans, is not illuminating.

D.F.R.

C

dam, which he must have known well.[1] The development of the Order experiment certainly shows this line of thought being followed out. Orders were at first charged only on the direct taxes imposed to finance the war. In the Exchequer year 1667–8, however, the third type of Order of Payment began to be charged on the revenue in general in increasing amounts and in small denominations. This was asking for trouble. For while the Orders charged on direct taxes had a certain revenue earmarked to pay them, and were therefore not really instruments of credit, but only of anticipation, the Orders charged on the revenue in general had not, and were therefore genuine instruments of credit, like bank-notes. And like bank-notes they depended for their success on their holders' willingness to refrain from asking for their money back, at least all at once. This crucial condition was absent, and in January 1672 the Crown had to declare a moratorium on £1,173,353 of these Orders. (The Orders charged on direct taxes were specifically excluded from the Stop.) The Crown undertook to pay 6% interest until it could repay the principal. Interest was in fact paid fairly regularly until 1680 but then fell more and more into arrears; by 1688 payment was just being made for 1683.[2] The most important holders of Orders were London bankers, hence the rather misleading collective title of 'the Bankers' Debt' given to the whole principal.[3] After a protracted lawsuit in the 1690s, which centred, surprisingly, not on a successor government's obligation to honour its predecessor's debts, but on whether the bankers' assignees could enforce their rights, the Crown settled the claim against it by funding the sum due at 3% with accrued interest from Christmas 1705. It amounted to £1,328,526. The 'Bankers' Annuities' created in this way were administered by the Exchequer and had a steady if slow turnover.[4] They were redeemable by the government on payment of half their principal, and in 1717 half was duly exchanged for 5% government stock, which was in turn exchanged for South Sea stock in 1720.[5]

The 'shutting-up of the Exchequer' was thus a partial repudiation of part of the Crown's debts rather than an outright declaration of bankruptcy. In the end the royal creditors were paid ten shillings in the pound with interest. Meanwhile, other sectors of credit — loans in anticipation of customs, excise,

---

[1] *The Life of Edward, Lord Clarendon, written by himself* (Oxford, 1829), iii. 12 ff. Downing was English Resident at The Hague between 1657 and 1665.

[2] Chandaman, op. cit. 513 ff.

[3] The names of the principal creditors are given in Richards, *Early History of Banking*, ch. iii.

[4] See below, p. 466.   [5] See below, p. 86, and App. B.

and direct taxes — continued to function smoothly. By French standards there was nothing very shocking about the whole incident. But credit is a delicate plant, and after 1672 there was always a question-mark against Charles's financial reputation. In particular the royal creditors must have reflected that had their loans been 'on parliamentary security', instead of being backed only by the Crown's promises, they would not have been repudiated. At a technical level the Stop showed that plans to charge bills against the revenue must be more carefully laid, and must include adequate reserves for payment. These lessons were duly noted by the statesmen of the 1690s, who were determined that government credit should never again be 'as the Breath in a Man's Nostrils'.[1]

By 1688 private and public finance both in England and abroad had therefore developed and improved and had already moved on to a longer-term basis. A contradictory trend was the addiction of contemporaries to gambling on a massive scale. It was an age of wagers on the lives of private and public men, the chances of war, and the occurrence of natural events, as well as the issue of a horse-race, the fall of dice, the turn of a card.[2] This helps to explain the keen public interest in lotteries. Thus in August 1693 Thomas Neale, Groom Porter to the Court Master of the Mint and planner of the Seven Dials estate, advertised a lottery of £25,000 in 10s. tickets with 250 prizes, modelled on the Venetian lottery of the previous year. Eleven London goldsmiths were to act as receivers.[3] In January 1694 another advertisement announced the sale of £1,500 worth of furniture by a lottery with no fewer than 12,000 half-crown tickets.[4] In February 1694, £2,500 worth of plate and jewels were advertised to be disposed of by the same method; six goldsmiths were to act as receivers.[5] A further lottery sale occurred in April.[6]

This was the background against which the advisers of William and Mary began to study how to finance England's contribution to the war to contain the power of the Sun King. The finances of the state had, with reservations,

[1] For this phrase see above, p. 16.   [2] Cf. below, p. 491.

[3] John Houghton, F.R.S., *A Collection for Improvement of Husbandry and Trade*, 18 August 1693. The goldsmiths were William Atwell, Sir Francis Child, John Coggs, Sir Stephen Evance, Joseph Fells, Richard Hoare, John Johnson, Richard Lassells, John Sweetaple, William Shepherd and Thomas Williams.

[4] Ibid., 5 January 1694.

[5] Ibid., 9 February 1694. The goldsmiths were Peter Luparte, 'upper end Lombard Street'; James Marmcon, Fleet Street; Moses Sicklemore, St. Margaret's Hill, Southwark; John Smith, Norfolk Street, Strand; John Spackman, 'Near Northumberland House'; and Joseph Wilson, Fleet Street.

[6] Ibid., 6 April 1694.

improved in important respects since 1660, but they were still essentially on a short-term basis. There was a restless spirit of economic innovation in England, particularly in London. This was due partly to the stimulus given to active men by the expansion of commerce to distant quarters of the globe, partly to an appetite for gambling fostered by the hard and uncertain conditions of life itself. At the same time in France, Holland, and Italy, experience, assisted by a developing study of actuarial science, was generating greater confidence in the handling of private insurance, municipal finance, and long-term government borrowing. It remained to be seen how the architects of the new English state would draw on this mixed inheritance.

II

The immediate result of England's entry into the war against France in 1689 was to make public expenditure increase between two and three times. Before 1688 it had been under £2m. a year. Between 1689 and 1702 it was between £5m. and £6m. a year, as the Treasury noted in the books which it now started to keep to record income and expenditure — England being the first major European Power to take this elementary step.[1] If the machinery of long-term borrowing evolved by the 1740s had already been in existence there would have been little difficulty in financing most of this increase by public loans at reasonable rates of interest. As it was, both the government and Parliament made serious mistakes which ran the new state into crisis.

There were several causes of this mishandling of the situation. In the first

[1] The Treasury Annual Account Books are abstracted in the *Calendar of Treasury Books* from 1689 to 1718. Their contents were used by H. W. Chisholm to give balanced accounts of public revenue and expenditure from 1689 to 1867, *BPP* (1868-9), xxxv. Cf. also Sir John Sinclair, *History of the Public Revenue of the British Empire* (3rd ed., 1804), iii, app. iv, 'A General Abstract of the Receipts and issues of the Public Revenue . . . from the 5th of November 1688 to the 25th of March 1702', evidently from a manuscript source, and B.M. Add. MS. 20721, revenue accounts 1685-99, a manuscript volume perhaps drawn up by the Parliamentary Commission of Accounts. The revenue was recorded at the Exchequer net of collection costs until 1801. In 1732 collection costs were estimated as £398,212, which would have been just over 6% of the gross revenue, Add. MS. 17477, ff. 118-19. For a detailed discussion of this problem see J. E. D. Binney, *British Public Finance and Administration 1774-92* (Oxford, Clarendon Press, 1958), esp. app. v.

place, the political situation was unstable and difficult. Parliament, thanks to the war's demands for finance rather than to constitutional theory, had won its claims to sit annually as a partner in government, but had not learned responsibility or self-discipline. The executive, highly dependent on an auto-cratic king whose true interests were outside England, was uncertain of its position as against the Crown, potential rivals for office, and above all Parliament, which can seldom have been more difficult to manage. The success of the change of dynasty, with all that it implied, hung for some years in the balance, and few observers rated its chances of success very highly. A second discouraging factor was the Commons' obstinate unwillingness to acknowledge that the war would be long and expensive, and that its cost must be spread. They insisted instead on trying to finance it by short-term loans. To compound confusion, the yield of the new taxes imposed to service these loans was often overestimated. In consequence, in 1697 and 1702 over £7m. short-term debts had to be extended to later dates of payment[1]. Thirdly, despite the growth of foreign trade and financial expertise under Charles II and James II, there was before the 1690s little or no experience of large and sophisticated financial projects, either in Whitehall or in the City of London. The City's corporate memories of Whitehall were in any case unpleasant, and discouraged co-operation. It remembered the Exclusion Crisis, the trial of Shaftesbury, the execution of Russell and Sydney, and the loss of its own charter in 1683.[2]

It is perhaps not surprising in these circumstances that government long-term borrowing during King William's War was expensive, small in its relative amount, and tentative and experimental in form. It covered no more than £6·9m. of a total government expenditure of over £72m. between 1688 and 1702, while Customs yielded £13·2m., Excise £13·6m. and the new Land Taxes £19·2m.[3] The annual charge for £6·9m. raised was £575,676, an average rate of interest of 8·3%. This is partly a notional figure, since the lottery of 1697 was a failure and only financial desperation made the Treasury use the tickets as cash. On the other hand the life annuities were expected to lapse fairly soon, so an artificially generous return could be allowed on them. None the less, the state was borrowing well above the legal maximum for

[1] For the crisis in short-term borrowing see below, pp. 343 ff.

[2] The City had no formal charter of incorporation as many other cities and boroughs had. 'Charter' in the text is shorthand for London's 'liberties, privileges, and franchise' forfeited by *quo warranto* in 1683 and regranted, in terms giving the Crown strict control. In 1689 the *quo warranto* proceedings were annulled and the former position was restored.

[3] Expenditure, and revenue yields, from Sinclair's manuscript, see above, p. 46 n. 1.

TABLE 2

Government Long-term Borrowing, 1693–8

No.	Date of royal assent to Loan Act	Sum raised £	Interest %	Fund on which interest charged	Administration of loan
1	26 January 1693	108,100	10 until midsummer 1700, then 7.	Additional excise on beer and vinegar, and on imported beer, cider, and brandy, for 99 years from 25 January 1693.	A tontine loan (see text). It was hoped to raise £1m. The interest would be divided among the contributors until, by deaths, one took all.
2	Same Act as (1)	773,394	14	Same fund as (1).	This and (3) were single-life annuities to complete the £1m. contemplated by (1).
3	8 February 1694	118,506	14	Same fund as (1).	
4	23 March 1694	1,000,000	14	Duties on (a) imported salt, 1694–7, (b) half of new duties on beer, vinegar, cider, and brandy, 1697–1711. This fund was expected to yield £140,000 p.a. for 16 years. Duties were administered by the Excise.	A lottery of 100,000 £10 tickets. After the draw holders were given so much a year for 16 years. The sum varied from £1,000 p.a. for the largest prizes to £1 p.a. for blanks. After 16 years all payments were to cease.

5	24 April 1694	1,200,000	8	(a) Additional customs, 1694–8; (b) five-sevenths of *second* half of new duties in (b) above.	If half the sum of £1·2m. was lent by 1 August 1694, the subscribers were to be incorporated as the *Bank of England*. The state could repay the £1·2m. borrowed on one year's notice after 1706.
6	Same Act as (5)	300,000	10, 12, and 14	The other two-sevenths of the fund in (b) above.	Annuities for one, two, and three lives, at respectively 14%, 12%, and 10%. The sums raised were £107,848 on one life, £170,917 on two, and £21,235 on three.
7	16 April 1697	1,400,000	6·3	(a) Excise of 6d. a bushel on malt; (b) duties on rum, cider, and perry, 1697–9.	A lottery of 140,000 £10 tickets. Only 1,763 tickets were in fact sold. The rest were used by the Exchequer as cash. £657,850 were paid and cancelled by 1702, the rest between 1702 and 1711.
8	5 July 1698	2,000,000	8	(a) Additional excise duties on imported and home-produced salt from 1699 in perpetuity; (b) duties on vellum, parchment, and paper in perpetuity.	The subscribers were incorporated later in the year as the *New East India Company*.

£6,900,000

Source: Loan Acts and *BPP* (1898), lii.

private individuals of 6%. Furthermore, it had had to concede substantial privileges to the new Bank of England and East India Company to get a rate as low as 8%. And even so two of the loans floated, in 1693 and 1697 were outright failures. The fact that Parliament guaranteed all these loans made them 'debts of the nation' or 'national debts', and both Englishmen and foreigners were quick to realize that this change from merely royal security was extremely important.[1] In the short run, however, it was equally important that no amount of promising could guarantee that loans would be filled. Further, the tontine, at least, tied up parts of the revenue for a century ahead, a method soon applied to other loans as well.

The first consideration at parliamentary level of long-term borrowing to raise part of the annual supplies occurred on 12 January 1692, when the House of Commons appointed a committee of ten to 'receive Proposals for raising a Sum of Money towards the carrying on the War against France upon a Fund of perpetual Interest'.[2] The idea of a 'fund of Credit' had by now been generally accepted for a number of years. It meant no more at this stage than that a securely-settled revenue could be anticipated by borrowing. Thus in his speech of 21 October 1678 the Lord Chancellor had stated that 'the Poll Bill . . . was made a Fund of Credit for Three Hundred Thousand Pounds', in other words that £300,000 was being borrowed in anticipation of the tax's collection.[3] Similarly, in the debates on the royal revenue in March 1690 it seems to have been generally accepted that once a revenue was fixed it would at once become a 'fund of credit' for loans.[4] The word 'fund' itself had overtones, like 'bank', of a physical store of wealth, funds however being earmarked for a particular use. What was new in the in-

---

[1] The usage 'debts of the Nation', as in Walpole's pamphlet of 1712, *The Debts of the Nation Stated and Considered in four Papers*, seems to have changed after the peace of 1713 to 'the publick Debts', then to 'the National Debts', and finally, in the 1730s, to 'the National Debt', though there are variations; see the list of pamphlets in the Bibliography. By the mid-eighteenth century 'the Funds' was, for obvious reasons, acceptable shorthand for 'Government stock'. The phrase 'the funded Debt', however, seems to date from a later period.

[2] *HCJ*, x. 620–1. Clapham, *Bank of England*, i. 15, incorrectly dates the appointment of the committee 'early in 1693'. Cf. the list of pamphlets and other proposals for paper credit from 1690 onwards in J. K. Horsefield, *British Monetary Experiments, 1650–1710* (1960), p. 116.

[3] *HLJ*, xiii. 294 (21 October 1678).

[4] Grey's *Debates* quoted in W. A. Shaw, *Introduction* to *Cal. T. Bks.* ix (i), pp. lxix–lxx. Scott, *The Constitution and Finance of . . . Joint Stock Companies to 1720* (Cambridge, 1910–12), i, ch. xx, confines his discussion of the 'fund of credit' to its use by the new companies to which the state owed money.

struction to the committee of 1692 was the word 'perpetual': though what was really meant was 'long-term'. The committee reported back on 18 January 1692 that it had considered two proposals. The first was from 'Six or Seven' of those concerned in the Bankers' Debt. They had suggested doubling their stake (this had clear echoes of the 'doubling' of army debts in the 1640s) in return for a guaranteed income of 6 % on the whole debt. This was an ingenious way of persuading the state to settle Charles II's obligations, but it was not followed up, because some of the other bankers evidently feared the scheme might prejudice 'the Judgement they expected to have in the Exchequer for their Debt'.[1] The second proposal was from William Paterson, the persistent Scot who, with Michael Godfrey, drew up the plans for the Bank of England in 1693–4, and was prominent in the ill-fated Darien Company in 1695.[2] His plan envisaged raising £1m. in 'Bills of Property' at a 'yearly rent' of £65,000, of which £5,000 was to be for management and the rest for payment of interest at 6%. A further £200,000 was to be raised in specie to support the bills. The phrase 'yearly rent', obviously a translation of the Dutch *jaarlike rente* or annual interest, showed that Paterson had been studying the Dutch precedents. But the committee disliked his proposal that the Bills should have legal currency, and turned the whole plan down.[3] It told Paterson, however,

That they would receive any proposal for advancing One million upon a perpetual Fund of Interest to be in the Nature of a Purchase; where they might assign their Interest, as they please, to any who consented thereunto.[4]

With this somewhat Delphic instruction it ended its inquiries for the time being. What it evidently envisaged was a plan to raise a capital sum the in-

[1] *HCJ*, x. 631–2. For the Bankers' Debt see above, p. 44. The Exchequer judgement in fact rejected the bankers' claims.

[2] William Paterson (1658–1719) was the son of a Dumfries-shire farmer. He travelled in Holland and (probably) America, then settled as a merchant in London. Several drafts of his dated about 1691 for raising money by creating bills charged on taxes, fee, farm rents, etc., are reproduced from a manuscript collection, made by the Chancellor of the Exchequer Charles Montague and now in the Advocates' Library in Edinburgh, by Saxe Bannister, *The Writings of William Paterson* (2 vols., 1858), vol. ii, pp. vii ff. See also G. P. Insh, *The Company of Scotland* (New York, 1932), for Paterson's part in the Darien Company. For his share in establishing the Bank of England in 1694 see below, p. 55.

[3] Paterson's scheme as set out in the *Commons Journal* is far from clear. The version of it stated above is an expansion of the phrase 'the Summe of ready Money being only Two Hundred Thousand Pounds proposed to circulate a Million it was refused', in *An Account of the Transactions of Mr. William Paterson in Relation to the Bank of England* (1695), B.M. 8223.e.7.

[4] *HCJ*, x. 631–2.

C2

terest on which would be guaranteed by Parliament. Those who lent it were to be able to assign their right to the interest to a third party. This outline obviously derived from the tontine and annuity loans floated in Holland and France, and it cannot be coincidence that when the Commons again considered long-term borrowing a few months later the scheme endorsed was a loan by a tontine and life annuities. It is worth pausing for a moment at this stage to ask why the Commons was canvassing private individuals at all instead of making up its own mind on the basis of official information. The answer seems to be that the revenue departments were as yet too small and too inexperienced in these matters to give the guidance they were able to provide by the mid-eighteenth century, while the private sector teemed with enthusiastic projectors anxious to convince Parliament of the soundness of their ideas. Thus, according to Davenant, Thomas Neale devised the scheme for the Million Lottery of 1694 from Venetian precedents, while Foot Onslow was behind the plan for the tax on leather, Paterson and Godfrey behind the Bank of England, Sir John Foch behind the Capitation Tax, and Mordecai Abbot behind the creation of Exchequer bills.[1] Similarly, John Kynvin petitioned the Treasury Board in the early 1690s to be allowed to manage the duty on parchment and paper, the plan for which he had helped James Isaakson draw up and lay before Parliament. He added that he knew how the similar duty was collected in Spain.[2] Again, in 1717 the Treasury paid Thomas Herbert £200 for drafting proposals for a tax on soap in 1709, which had been presented to Parliament in 1711.[3] Grateful government acceptance of individual initiatives in taxation was in fact probably common form throughout Europe for most of the eighteenth century.

It seems probable, therefore, though there is no direct evidence, that Paterson was the author of the proposal for a tontine loan which the Commons accepted in December 1692. The House had voted the supplies for the coming year on 10 December 1692. On 15 December the Committee of Ways and Means, discussing how they were to be raised, appointed a sub-committee of five to draft a bill for a tontine loan of £1m. Three of the five had been on the committee which had negotiated with Paterson in January.[4] The Bill passed quickly through both Houses and received the royal assent

---

[1] Charles Davenant, *The True Picture of a Modern Whig* (1701), p. 25. Neale had used the Venetian lottery as a precedent for a private lottery in 1693; see above, p. 45.

[2] *Cal. T. Papers*, xvii. 335, dated 1693-4.

[3] *Cal. T. Bks.* xxxi (ii) (1717), p. 307, 18 May 1717.

[4] The members of the drafting committee were the Attorney-General, the Solicitor-General, Sir Thomas Clarges, Paul Foley, and Sir Christopher Musgrave. The last three had been members of the earlier committee.

on 26 January 1693.[1] Subscriptions to the loan began on 3 February.[2] Its terms were as follows. A sum of £1m. was to be lent to the government at an interest of 10% until midsummer 1700 and 7% thereafter. This interest was secured on new excise duties settled for ninety-nine years from 25 January 1693 — the period chosen was presumably a straight adoption of the term common in conveyances of land. The interest was to be paid to each contributor *pro rata* and tax-free during his own life or the life of someone he named (his *nominee*) until only seven nominees were left. It would then abate as each remaining nominee died. No provision was made for dividing nominees by age groups, as had been done in the French tontine of 1689, so the scheme offered a very attractive return — provided a young nominee went on living.[3] The omission may have been a deliberate attempt to coax the investing public into the novel experiment of government long-term borrowing. But Parliament sensibly recognized that it must have a safety net. The Act provided that if the £1m. wanted had not been lent on a tontine basis by 1 May 1693, the rest could be taken up by the sale of 14% single-life annuities.[4] These, too, like all subsequent government loans until the introduction of income tax, were to be tax-free. A contributor's interest in both the tontine and the life annuities could be assigned to a third party.[5]

Both these offers were generous, but the second was the more appealing of the two. It gave contributors a straightforward opportunity of a high yield for their own lives. Compared with this the tontine, though offering the possibility of getting more, must have seemed too complicated. The distribution of subscriptions between the two parts of the loan reflected this. At first £377,600 was lent on the tontine, but between 1 May and 29 September 1693 many of these contributors changed to a life annuity instead, as the Act allowed them to do. When the accounts were made up, £773,394 had been lent on life annuities and only £108,100 on the tontine.[6] This was in any case £118,506 short of the £1m. hoped for. In February 1694 a further life-annuity loan was floated at 14% to raise the small balance.[7] In April 1694 Parliament authorized another loan of £300,000 on annuities for

---

[1] 4 Wm. and M. c. 3.   [2] See below, p. 254.

[3] For the origins of tontine loans see above, p. 41.

[4] The annuities were described in the Act as 'the Annuity Rent or Payment', a further example of Dutch influence; cf. above, p. 51.

[5] Transfer arrangements are discussed below, Ch. 18.

[6] The sum originally lent on the tontine is shown in *Cal. T. Bks.* x (i), p. 326, 11 September 1693; the sums finally lent on the tontine and life annuities in 5 Wm. and M. c. 5, and *BPP*, lii (1898), 275.

[7] 5 Wm. and M. c. 5; see above, p. 48, Table 2.

one, two, or three lives.[1] This was the last on life annuities until 1704.

Most of the long-term borrowing for 1694 was by different means. In March Parliament authorized a lottery of £1m. with £10 tickets, the holders of which were to receive interest at varying rates for sixteen years.[2] Like the tontine and the life annuities, lotteries had both Dutch and French precedents, and they were already being used in London for private sales.[3] It at once proved very popular. It tapped the general rage for gambling, and was almost at once adapted to meagre purses by ticket-office keepers who bought up batches of tickets and then sold 'shares' in them for as little as a few shillings each. Later, more sophisticated practices like 'hiring' and 'insuring' tickets were developed.[4] In the harsh and uncertain conditions of eighteenth-century life the state lottery was a perennial way of escape into wealth and leisure — if only in the imagination.[5] Mortimer asserted in the 1760s that it attracted more subscribers than any other form of government loan.[6] It was only knocked on the head in 1826. By this date both the social and moral climate had drastically changed, and there was a strong case for arguing that lotteries had become a public nuisance.[7]

In April 1694, a month after passing the Bill for the Million Lottery, Parliament assented to a very different project whose consequences were to be as far-reaching as the prior decision to create a National Debt. This was the establishment of the Bank of England. Loans were invited for a total of £1,200,000, the remainder to make up £1·5m. being raised by life annuities.[8] If half the sum of £1·2m. promised were lent to the state at 8% by 1 August 1694, the subscribers were to be incorporated under the Great Seal as 'the Governor and Company of the Banke of England'. The plan for the bank was evidently drawn up by William Paterson and Michael Godfrey, both of

---

[1] 5 & 6 Wm. and M. c. 20; see Table 2.

[2] Wm. and M. c. 7; see Table 2.

[3] See above, p. 45. C. L. Ewen, *Lotteries and Sweepstakes in the British Isles* (1932) is a much more accurate and systematic overall account than J. Ashton, *A History of English Lotteries* (1893). Cf. also J. Cohen, 'The Element of Lottery in British Government Bonds, 1694–1919', *Economica*, xx (1953), p. 237.

[4] For division, hiring, and insuring of lottery tickets see below, pp. 497, 506.

[5] Public fancy was kept alive by titbits such as the following from the *London Journal* of 14–21 May 1720: 'We hear that Mr. Wanley, the Goldsmith, who 'tis said got so many great Prizes in the last Lottery, has left off his Business, and is retired to his fine New House at Tottenham.' Cf. the episode of the fortunate lottery ticket in Fielding, *Joseph Andrews* (1742), bk. iii, ch. 3.

[6] Thomas Mortimer, *Every man his own Broker* (5th ed., 1762), p. 69.

[7] Cf. *BPP* (1890–91), xlviii. 688 ff., for analysis of the abuses.

[8] See above p. 49. The Act authorizing both loans was 5 & 6 Wm. and M. c. 20.

whom became directors, in consultation with the Treasury Commissioner Charles Montague who from May 1694 was Chancellor of the Exchequer though there had been frequent plans for banks of one sort or another since the 1650s.[1] Paterson himself had been trying to interest the Government in a scheme for a bank since 1691.[2] The subscription, opened on 21 June 1694, was filled with almost contemptuous ease in ten days, the king and queen heading the lists.[3] The new bank's charter was sealed on 27 July in Lord Somers's new residence, Powis House in Lincoln's Inn Fields.[4] Lord Powis, a Roman Catholic, had been one of James II's closest supporters, and after 1688 his property was forfeited to the Crown. His house looked out across Lincoln's Inn Fields to the site of the scaffold where Lord Russell had been executed for treason to Charles II in 1683.[5] Russell's leader, Shaftesbury, had fled to Amsterdam and died there in January 1683. Two years earlier, in 1681, Shaftesbury had been acquitted of high treason by a London jury 'worth a million of money'. Its members included John Houblon and Michael Godfrey — the first Governor and Deputy Governor of the Bank of England in 1694 — both of whom were members of the mercantile community in the City whose close liaison with Shaftesbury, and hostility to the Court, led to the forfeiture of the City's charter in the same year that Shaftesbury and Russell died.[6] This was exactly the kind of background of

[1] R. D. Richards, *The Early History of Banking in England*, ch. iv; J. K. Horsefield, *British Monetary Experiments, 1650–1710*. Charles Montagu, or Montague as he himself spelled his name (1661–1715), was Commissioner of the Treasury from March 1692 to 30 April 1694, when he succeeded Richard Hampden as Chancellor of the Exchequer. He became First Lord of the Treasury on 1 May 1697, but resigned both offices in 1699. He was later created Baron Halifax, and then Earl of Halifax, and was again First Lord 1714–15.

[2] According to *An Account of the Transactions of Mr. William Paterson in Relation to the Bank of England*, see above, p. 51 n. 3; this is the most useful contemporary account of Paterson's part in the establishment of the Bank of England.

[3] See below, p. 254. Three-fifths was payable in 1694. The remainder was called up in 1697 (one-fifth) and 1707 (one-fifth).

[4] The official history of the Bank of England by Sir J. H. Clapham, *The Bank of England: a History* (2 vols., 1944) supersedes previous works, though it is not Clapham at his best. W. Marston Acres, *The Bank of England from within* (2 vols., 1931) and his biographical notes on the directors of the Bank of England, *Notes and Queries*, vol. 179 (1940), are valuable supplementary sources of information. In *Notes and Queries*, 3 February 1951, Acres published a few corrections to his earlier list.

[5] Powis House, subsequently Newcastle House (1705–71), has been occupied by the solicitors' firm of Farrer & Co. since 1790.

[6] Cf. Margaret Priestley, 'London Merchants and Opposition Politics in Charles II's Reign', *BIHR* xxix (1956), 205. There is no good published account of City politics and society in the period 1683–94.

republicanism, treason, and Dutch connections that contemporaries expected plans for a national bank to have. 'Where there is a Bank', commented
Harington in 1658, 'ten to one there is a Commonwealth.'[1] A few years
later Sir Richard Ford was solemnly explaining to Pepys and other listeners
how a bank was all very well in Holland but in England would be incom-
patible with monarchy.[2] Yarranton's care in refuting this argument in the
1670s shows how plausible it seemed.[3] It was therefore more than a coincidence that the foundation of a national bank in England followed the over-
throw of James II in 1688, and the effective establishment of parliamentary government — under a Dutch monarch. It was precisely the
absence of trust in (and control over) the royal revenues before this date that
had caused the numerous projects for a bank under Charles II and James II
to come to nothing. The ceremony in Powis House was thus a neat and
ironical summary of many trends in recent history.

The Bank of England at once began to make substantial cash advances to
the government, over and above its original loan. These were insufficient,
however, to check the rapid deterioration of state credit in 1695-6, due as
much as anything to unrealistic reliance on short-dated borrowing. Deficiencies mounted, Exchequer tallies were quoted at increasing discounts,
and the foreign exchanges moved against London. Early in 1697 over £5m.
of short-term debts due for redemption had to be extended to later dates of
payment. Without the help of the Bank of England in this operation the
government would have faced financial disaster. As it was England was able
to conclude peace in September 1697 with an enemy as exhausted as herself,
and to take a breathing-space.[4] It is possible, though far from certain, that an
attempt to borrow substantial sums for long terms in the mid-1690s might
have checked this crisis before it developed. As it was, the Treasury contented itself in 1695 and 1696 with offering the single-life annuitants of
1693-4 the chance of converting them into annuities for terms of years on
payment of additional capital sums of between four and a half and five years'

[1] James Harington, 'The Prerogative of Popular Government', in *Works*, ed. J. Toland
(1737), p. 247.

[2] Pepys, *Diary*, 17 August 1666.

[3] For Yarranton's plans for a bank see above, p. 5. Hutchinson's contention in the
parliamentary debate on the Civil List in 1690 that if the revenue was given 'to a good
Prince he may be thrifty and may have a Bank and may presume upon it to destroy our
liberties' (*Cal. T. Bks.* ix (i) (1689–92)), lxix, seems to refer to a store of money rather than
a bank in the technical sense.

[4] For a detailed consideration see below, Chs. 13 and 14. The Bank's early advances to
the state are discussed in Ch. 17.

purchase. It provided that if an annuitant did not want to pay, a third party might buy the reversion, i.e. the right to payment once the annuitant died. The terms of years extended to 1792. The opportunity to make the extra payment was again offered in 1697, 1698, and 1700. In return for this further mortgaging of the public revenue until the end of the eighteenth century the Exchequer netted £581,975. In 1702, £5,842 p.a. was still available for sale: the life-tenants had died and no one had bought the reversions. This amount was therefore sold and realized a further £87,630.[1] These long annuities — subsequently called 'the Fourteen Per Cents' — foreshadowed the massive creation of annuities to finance the War of the Spanish Succession.

In April 1697 the virtually complete failure of the Malt Lottery loan showed how desperate a financial crisis the government had stumbled into.[2] With the settlement of most of the outstanding debts in the same month, however, and the coming of peace in September, credit rapidly recovered and the scheme for a New East India Company in rivalry to the Old Company was successfully floated in the summer of 1698. The company lent £2m. to the Exchequer, starting with a downpayment of one-tenth.[3] Like the Bank of England the new company was able to use the state's debt to it as a 'fund of credit', in other words a certain income against which notes or bonds could be charged. From 1709 the New and Old Companies were run together as the United East India Company, having in 1708 made the state a further loan of £1·2m. for the extension of their charter to 1728.[4]

III

The first measures taken to create a system of government long-term borrowing were thus marked by haste, carelessness, and episodic failure — even if in comparison with the management of short-term finance they were shiningly successful. But such mistakes and errors of judgement were perhaps

[1] The seven Conversion Acts were 6 & 7 Wm. and M. c. 5 (1695), 7 & 8 Wm. III, c. 2 (1696), 8 & 9 Wm. III, c. 21 (1697), 9 Wm. III, cc. 5 and 24 (1698), 11 Wm. III, c. 3 (1700) and 1 Anne, stat. 2, c. 5 (1702). (The money obtained must almost have been absorbed by the salaries of the parliamentary draftsmen.) For the Million Bank's purchases of reversionary annuities under these Acts see below, p. 270.

[2] For this loan see above, p. 49, Table 2.   [3] 9 Wm. III, c. 44.

[4] The complicated finances of the Old and New East India Companies are fully discussed by Scott, op. cit. ii. 128–89.

inevitable in a trial period. Some valuable lessons had been learned: about the connections between long- and short-dated finance, about consultation with the City of London, about the importance of foreign confidence in sterling, about the relative popularity of different kinds of loans. Above all, a national bank had been established which quickly showed that in the quality of its management it could challenge comparison with the Bank of Amsterdam, hitherto the cynosure of European eyes. It provided a point of growing importance around which the developing machine of government finance could turn.

The ability and patriotism of the bourgeois directors of the Bank were a sharp contrast to the quarrelling cliques of aristocracy and gentry disputing control of the state in Whitehall and Westminster. But here too the situation was on the point of changing for the better. This was partly because of a change in the direction of financial affairs. Macaulay and many later writers have treated Charles Montague who was Chancellor of the Exchequer from 1694 to 1699 as a financial wizard because of his connection with the origins of the National Debt and the Bank of England, and his work on the recoinage of 1696.[1] This is uncritical. Montague was certainly enthusiastic, and interested in financial matters, and he backed the Bank from the start against its rivals and detractors. But he did not really carry enough weight to dominate the very difficult and unstable political and financial situation. His period of office was fertile in projects; Montague himself was a kind of super-projector. But it was also marked by mistakes, and at least one serious financial crisis, for which he must carry some of the blame. The death of William III and the creation of Sidney Godolphin as Lord Treasurer in 1702 marked the beginning of new and much more successful management of government finance as a whole. In addition, the political situation, however anarchic by the standards of the mid-eighteenth century, was markedly more stable under Anne than under William III, partly because able Ministers could now count on getting their own way instead of being obliged to obey royal commands. Parliament, too, was at one in its devotion to the last of the Stuarts, if on nothing else. At the official level, moreover, William Lowndes, who had been made Secretary to the Treasury in April 1695, was beginning to get a grip on his department, and to exert the influence which over a quarter-century of office was to become one of the stabilizing factors in the financial history of the period.[2]

[1] For which see below, p. 349.

[2] For William Lowndes (1652–1724) see *DNB* and D. M. Clark, 'The Office of Secretary to the Treasury in the Eighteenth Century', *AHR*, xlii (1936–7), p. 22. Lowndes died in

Godolphin managed the national finances with great care and skill. The problems involved at a short-term level were not only anticipation of tax revenue and simplification of the structure of taxes, but the remittance for payment of the troops abroad of sums up to £3m., with all the formidable difficulties of trade balance and exchange rates that this involved.[1] He worked in close touch with the Bank of England and the mercantile community in the City, and rapidly won their confidence as a financier of great ability. This enabled him to handle the problem of long-term borrowing with comparative ease between 1704 and 1708, despite the size of the amounts raised. He was helped by a run of good harvests which kept corn prices low and political tensions down, as well as by the increasing public confidence generated by Marlborough's victories at Blenheim (1704), Ramillies (1706) and Oudenarde (1708); correspondingly, French credit, weakened by repeated military failure, steadily declined. Including the £187,689 received for converting life into long annuities (loan 1, Table 3) the total raised was £8,191,427. The strategy of these loans was simple, if disputable. They were all raised by the sale of long annuities and were all administered by the Exchequer.[2] They were serviced by raiding the Civil List (in 1704) and by continuing the periods for which existing interest funds were settled. This, as Swift complained in 1713, enabled Godolphin to refrain from new taxation only by tying up further parts of the revenue for the rest of the century.[3] Rates of interest were kept well below the level of the previous reign, yet the evidence is that the loans were eagerly filled.[4] Given the unprecedented expense, running at between £8m. and £9m. a year, in which England was involved in its struggle with France, this strategy, which had the merits of simplicity and success, was probably correct. But it

January 1724 and was succeeded by John Scrope (?1662–1752) who served until April 1752; cf. below, p. 220. For most of the period there was a second-string joint-secretary as well. Both Lowndes and Scrope exercised great influence, though it is impossible to document it except at occasional points. Scrope's longevity is astonishing; he began his career in the service of the Duke of Monmouth and died, in harness, only two years before Henry Pelham.

[1] None of the published lives of Godolphin throws much light on his work. By far the best unpublished study is J. G. Sperling, 'Godolphin and the Organization of Public Credit, 1702 to 1710', Cambridge University Ph.D. thesis, 1955. Ch. iv of this thesis discusses the foreign remittances. For Godolphin's work on short-term finance see below, p. 360.

[2] For methods of subscription see below, Ch. 4.

[3] Swift, *History of the Four Last Years of the Queen* (written 1713, published 1758), in *Works*, ed. H. Davis, vii, 70–71.

[4] See below, p. 361.

TABLE 3

Government Long-term Borrowing, 1704–8

No.	Date of royal assent to Loan Act	Sum raised £	Interest* %	Fund on which interest charged	Administration of loan
1	24 February 1704	1,382,976	6·6	£3,700 a week from the Crown's hereditary excise.	(i) £1,018,868 was raised by the sale of annuities for 99 years from 25 March 1704. (ii) The balance was raised by the sale of annuities for one, two, and three lives. Under 3 Anne, c. 2 (1704), the single-life annuities were converted into 99-year annuities on payment of a further £187,689.
2	16 January 1705	690,000	6·6	Surplus of the fund in (1), calculated as £46,599 a year.	Annuities for 99 years from 25 December 1705.
3	16 February 1706	2,855,762	6·4	(a) One-third customs (1704) continued for 98 years from 1707. (b) Duty on coals (1697) continued from 1708 to 1710. (c) Million Lottery fund (see Table 2, p. 48) continued from 1713 for 99 years.	Annuities for 99 years from 25 March 1706.

4	27 March 1707	1,155,000	6·25	(a) Surpluses of funds settled for five loans of 1690s. (b) Duties on sweeps, low wines,† hawkers and pedlars, vellum and parchment continued for 99 years from 1707–1710.	Annuities for 99 years from 25 March 1707.
5	13 February 1708	640,000	6·25	(a) Surplus of fund for (4). (b) Additions of one or two years to terms for which funds settled for (4). (c) Tontine excise (see Table 2, p. 48) settled for a further 15 years, i.e. to 1807.	Annuities for 99 years from 25 March 1708.
6	11 March 1708	1,280,000	6·25	Ad valorem 2½% customs continued for 96 years from 1712.	Annuities for 99 years from 24 June 1708.

£8,003,738

Source: Loan Acts and *BPP* (1898), lii.

* The annuities were sold at 15, 15½, or 16 years' purchase. This was equivalent to 6·6%, 6·4%, and 6·25% respectively. The annuities were for such long terms that the return on them can be treated as though they were perpetual.

† Weak spirits.

added a further £527,000 a year to the existing burden of long annuities, making their total annual charge nearly £667,000. This could not be lessened without the proprietors' consent, and there was no obvious reason why they should consent. Nor would the payments fall in until the early 1800s. This was to prove one of the war's most difficult financial legacies.

In 1708 and 1709 Godolphin supplemented the sums borrowed from the public by loans from the East India Company and the Bank of England. The latter also agreed to fund £1·7m. Exchequer bills.[1] By this date the financial horizon, hitherto clear, was becoming stormy. Dissatisfaction with the length of the war and its cost in blood and money was growing. It was fanned by the bitter winter of 1708–9 and the bad harvests and high prices of the following summer and brought to a peak by the failure of the peace negotiations at The Hague in August 1709, followed by the bloody battle of Malplaquet in September. Short-dated government bills, particularly those of the Navy and Victualling Boards, had greatly increased in volume and started to be quoted at accelerating discounts.[2] In 1709, as Bishop Nicolson of Carlisle noted in a letter to his colleague William Wake, the annual supplies had reached an unprecedented level.[3] Nicolson thought the Union with Scotland in 1707 had given England the strength for this. Godolphin, sitting nearer to the centre of power, must have wondered if the effort could be renewed. It is significant that in 1710 he completely changed his tactics for long-term loans. He reintroduced a lottery, the first since the fiasco of 1697, and coupled with it a sale of annuities for a shorter term than before, thirty-two years, but a much higher rate of interest, 9%.[4] The Bank of England acted — for the first time — as receiver for both loans. In April Godolphin followed up these public loans by borrowing £150,000 from the rich Canton of Berne.[5]

With the exception of the loan of 1706 these were the largest sums Godolphin had ever raised. They were also the last. A political crisis had for some months been superimposed on the economic crisis. On 8 August 1710 Godolphin was summarily dismissed from office, despite an ill-judged attempt

[1] For the East India Company's loan of £1·2m. in 1708 see above, p. 57. For the negotiations with the Bank of England in 1709 see below, p. 373.

[2] For a fuller discussion of the crisis see p. 361.

[3] Add. MS. 6116, f. 12, Nicolson to Wake, 21 April 1709.

[4] E. Baasch, *Holländische Wirtschaftsgeschichte* (Jena, 1927), p. 191, mentions Dutch annuities for a similar term. It was repeated in the lottery loans of 1711–14 (see below). The reasons for its adoption are not clear.

[5] *Cal. T. Bks.* xxiv (ii) (1710), p. 243, 19 April 1710. The tallies pledged as security for this loan were exchanged for South Sea stock in 1711.

TABLE 4

Government Long-term Borrowing in 1710

No.	Date of royal assent to Loan Act	Sum raised £	Interest %	Fund on which interest charged	Administration of loan
1	18 January 1710	1,500,000	9*	Customs duties on coals continued for 32 years from 1710. (See Table 3, p. 60.)	A lottery of 100,000 £10 tickets. Holders of blanks were to receive 14s. p.a. for 32 years, holders of prizes varying amounts for the same period.
2	13 March 1710	900,000	9†	(a) Additional excise on beer, cider, etc., for 32 years from 1710. (b) Additional customs on imported pepper, raisins, nutmeg, cinnamon, clover, snuff for 32 years from 1710.	Annuities for 32 years from 29 September 1710. The sum of £9 p.a. was paid for each £100 subscribed.
		£2,400,000			

Source: Loan Acts and *BPP* (1898), lii.

* The annual issues for the lottery were £135,000 or 9% on the principal lent.
† Similarly, the annual issues were £81,000.

by the directors of the Bank of England in June to convince the Queen that such a step would be disastrous to public credit — an indication of how highly the City rated him.[1] A new Tory Ministry came in under Robert Harley and Henry St. John, determined to end the war and if possible to break the politicians who had run it so far. Harley became Chancellor of the Exchequer on 10 August 1710, and was made Lord Treasurer on 29 May 1711. He faced a difficult political and financial situation for the solution of which the rash cries of his extremist supporters offered little guidance.[2] In 1710 and 1711 his opponents freely circulated the opinion that in view of the hostility to his Ministry of the financial interests entrenched in the City, especially in the Bank of England, he stood little chance of financial success, and since 'they that have the Money, must have the Management', of political success either.[3] In particular he had to face the urgent and complex question of the debt of the Navy. The creditors of the Navy and Ordnance Boards, including London finance houses who had discounted bills for contractors, were owed over £4m. and applied increasing pressure on the Treasury for payment in the winter of 1710–11.[4] Harley turned to his own advisers in the City to see what could be done. He received proposals from John Blunt, a scrivener who was secretary to the Sword Blade Bank, from

---

[1] Clapham, *The Bank of England: a History*, i. 74. The background to this intervention was the Bank's anxiety about its financial position in the economic crisis of 1709–10. On 20 April 1710 the directors had appointed a special subcommittee 'to consider the State of the Bank', to which Justus Beck was added on 6 July 1710. On 20 July it reported drawing on Holland to strengthen the Bank's position. Between 29 December 1709 and 26 January 1710 the Bank refused to discount Exchequer tallies except for the government. It also, in January 1710, put up its rate of discount on foreign bills to 6%. On at least one occasion in the same period it refused Lord Treasurer Godolphin a loan, though reversing its view the next day. Bank D. Ct. Bk. F., ff. 43–78, December 1709–August 1710.

[2] One of the first discoveries the new House of Commons thought it had made was that £35·3m. public money was still 'to be accounted for'. (Report of Commons committee appointed 13 January 1711 to examine how far government paymasters had passed their accounts, *HCJ* xvi. 611, 24 April 1711). The discovery turned out to be based on misunderstanding of Exchequer techniques. In fact, only £4·3m. was not accounted for, largely because the local paymasters with the forces in Spain and elsewhere had not had time to transmit their papers to London. The remainder of the 'missing 35 millions' was before the Auditors, but not yet formally passed. Robert Walpole, explaining this in his pamphlet *A State of the Five and Thirty Millions* (1711), states (p. 1) that 'in every Coffee-house and Ale-house in some Countries [Counties] I may hear it with confidence asserted . . . that Thirty five Millions were lost to the Publick during the late Administration'.

[3] [Daniel Defoe], *Eleven Opinions about Mr. H—y with Observations* (1711), a pamphlet Harley commissioned to support the Ministry.

[4] For the Navy debt see below, p. 403.

George Caswall, one of the partners in the same bank, and from Sir Ambrose Crowley, one of the biggest contractors with the Navy Board. Their substance evidently was that the Navy and other creditors should be incorporated, the state's debts to them being cancelled in return for an equivalent amount of stock.[1] If this were carried through, commented Caswall, it would 'much promote the retreiving Publick Credit and give great honour to those in the Administration who shall apeare Zealous for its Execution'.

A similar solution — perhaps emanating from the same source — had been put forward some years earlier for the Army debts left over from the 1690s, but had been rejected.[2] Their common ancestor was the Bank of England's agreement with the government in 1697 to 'ingraft' deficient Exchequer tallies into its capital.[3] Harley was no doubt aware of both precedents. He was also aware that he had little freedom of action. He could not pay off the floating debt in cash, and could produce no alternative to the Blunt–Caswall plan. He therefore decided to give it legislative effect and see whether it would succeed. Its details, as spelled out in the statute incorporating it, which received the royal assent on 12 June 1711, showed that John Blunt had aimed high — as he was to do again in 1720.[4] The government's short-term creditors, holding debts of nearly £9m., were to be incorporated under the Great Seal as 'the Governor and Company of Merchants of Great Britain Trading to the South Seas and other parts of America and for encouraging the Fishery'.[5] This meant in fact the trade with South America: the company was to have a monopoly of trade with the east coast from the River Orinoco to Tierra del Fuego, and of the whole

---

[1] B.M. Portland Loan 29/28, George Caswall to Harley, 6 October 1710. This letter, which refers to the proposals without spelling them out, is reproduced in J. G. Sperling, *The South Sea Company. An Historical Essay and Bibliographical Finding List* (Publ. 17, Kress Library of Business and Economics, Boston, 1962). Dr. Sperling's essay is by far the best printed account of the early years of the South Sea Company. Elizabeth Donnan, 'The Early Days of the South Sea Company, 1711–1718', *J. Econ. and Bus. Hist.* ii (1929–30), 419, throws no light on the company's origins or finances.

[2] See below, p. 394.   [3] See below, p. 353.

[4] The statute was 9 Anne, c. 15. For Blunt's role in the South Sea Bubble see Ch. 5.

[5] Not 'the Fishing', as Scott says in his account of the company. The company was in theory to accumulate a fund of 1% for each £100 stock to promote the Atlantic fishing trade. The Government retained control of the company by nominating the first board of directors, Harley becoming governor. This was the only clause of the Bill on which a division occurred — the Whigs hoping for elections which they would win. The Government won the division by 110 to 29. See J. G. Sperling, 'The Division of 25 May 1711, on an Amendment to the South Sea Bill', *Hist. J.*, vol. 2 (1961), 191.

of the west coast.[1] What was not clear was how this trade was ever to be carried on, in view of Spain's notorious determination to exclude foreigners from it.[2]

The choice of this rich region, which had gripped Englishmen's imaginations since the mid-sixteenth century, was a deliberate attempt to placate the government's creditors with the lure of high profits. It was also, historically, the last of many English attempts since Elizabeth's reign to penetrate the Spanish-American trade by force or licence. Like them it was to fail, and the real opening-up of what proved to be a rich market indeed had to wait for the political independence of the Spanish colonies in the nineteenth century.[3] There is a third factor to be considered. The company's establishment coincided with plans for an Anglo-Dutch expedition to attack the Spanish West Indies (August–December 1710) and an actual though unsuccessful English expedition against Quebec (August 1711). It can therefore be regarded as part of a three-pronged drive for empire in the New World, though there is little doubt that in fact this grand design was three-quarters bluff, intended to assist Harley's peace negotiations.[4] The South Sea Company certainly proved a tame lion. The idea was at first sold to the general public that Spain would concede four fortified ports on the American mainland, which could be used as bases for the company's trade. When the government gave up this claim in October 1711, under Franco-Spanish pressure, the company itself formed plans to seize a town or towns by force, and actually appointed a date, 26 June 1712, for the expedition to set out. As Dr. Sperling says, this was no more than a flight of fancy.[5] The English government was already committed to making peace, and in March 1713 signed at Madrid a treaty defining the new company's trading rights. The

---

[1] Excluding, however, Portuguese territory, to which all English merchants were to have access — if they could get it. Surinam, owned by the Dutch, was also excluded from the monopoly.

[2] The new company, unlike the Bank of England and the East India Company, had no term set for the expiry of its charter. This concession was made to it in a subsequent Act, 10 Anne, c. 30 (1712).

[3] Though already by the 1780s, according to Arthur Young, English woollens had a large sale in South America. This was presumably via Old Spain. The organization and volume of English trade to Spanish America between 1750 and 1830 still await a historian.

[4] Dr. Sperling, op. cit., pp. 9–10, convincingly rejects the 'imperial' interpretation of the company's origins given by W. T. Morgan, 'The Origins of the South Sea Company', *Pol. Sci. Q.* xliv (1929), 16, and 'The South Sea Company and the Canadian Expedition in the reign of Queen Anne', *Hisp. Am. Hist. R.* viii (1928), 143.

[5] Sperling, op. cit., p. 18. This section is based on Dr. Sperling's very interesting account.

claim for fortified towns — which alone might have made the rest of the agreement enforceable — was abandoned. Unfortified factories (trading-posts) were to be established instead.[1] The company was given permission to send a 500-ton ship once a year to trade at the fairs of Cartagena or Veracruz. Supply ships of 150 tons could be sent to victual the factories. The King of Spain was to receive 28% of all trading profits. In addition, the company was assigned for a thirty-year term the *Asiento de Negros*, the contract to supply New Spain with African slaves. This had been in Dutch hands from 1685 to 1702, but currently belonged to the French. The company was to deliver annually 4,800 slaves of specified condition. They were to pay tax on 4,000 of these, and, in addition, 10% of their profits to the King of Spain. Combined with his 28% on the trade with the fairs this was a respectable cut. In November 1713 the final draft of the agreement was found to include a $22\frac{1}{2}\%$ share of trading profits for Queen Anne as well. Under pressure she ceded this back to the company in June 1714, a month before her death.[2]

This was the unsatisfactory framework within which the new company's trade operated. It is not surprising that it yielded meagre returns and in-creasing difficulties. Brief Anglo-Spanish hostilities in Europe on two occasions (1718, 1726) gave Spain the excuse to confiscate entirely the company's effects in the New World, and in 1739 the two countries went to war to settle the trading issue by the sword. By this date internal changes had gravely weakened the company, and at the peace of 1748 it agreed to be paid off by Spain, and abandon its trade.[3] Part of the explanation for its original ineffectiveness was the weakness of its capital structure, to which we must now return. The company's original capital was entirely fictitious, consisting of the debts to be exchanged for South Sea stock. These were listed by the Act authorizing the company's creation as shown in Table 5. These debts had been incurred partly before and partly after 1702. The Navy debt (1) included the part of it already in existence in 1702 (£1,722,679), while the sums in (2) were all for old obligations of the 1690s. Provision was made ((3) and (6)) for debts created since Michaelmas 1710, that is, since the change of Ministry. Walpole asserted in 1712 that the debts

[1] Factories were established at Buenos Aires, Porto Bello, Panama, Cartagena, Santiago de Cuba, Havana, and Veracruz.

[2] Sperling, op. cit., p. 19.

[3] For the company's compensation by Spain and abandonment of its trade see below, p. 240. For detailed studies of the history of the company's trade see Sperling, op. cit., and J. O. McLachlan, *Trade and Peace with Old Spain, 1667–1750* (Cambridge, 1940).

TABLE 5

Debts to be exchanged for South Sea Company stock, 1711

Category	Type of debt	Sub-total £	Total £
1	(a) Debt of the Navy and Victualling to Michaelmas 1710	5,130,539	
	(b) Ordnance to same date . . .	154,325	
	(c) Transport office to same date . .	424,791	5,709,655
2	(a) Outstanding Army and Transport Debentures issued before 1702, principal £987,157, interest to Michaelmas 1710 £31,500	1,018,657	
	(b) Deficiency of Coal Duties charged to repay short-term loans of 1697 and 1702 .	12,025	
	(c) Arrears of subsidy due to Elector of Hanover for war of 1689–97	9,375	1,040,057
3	(a) Navy, Ordnance, and Transport debts, 29 September–25 December 1710. Also arrears of interest on Army and Transport Debentures in same period . . .	378,859	
	(b) Interest on such part of the debt as carried it, 25 December 1710–25 March 1711 .	85,000	463,859
4	Principal and interest of short-term loans charged on 8 Anne, c. 13 (1710), with interest to 25 March 1711 . . .	..	1,371,428
5	Sum for current Supply	..	500,000
6	Interest on the whole debt, 25 March–25 December 1711	..	386,325
			£9,471,324

Source: 9 Anne, c. 15, amounts regrouped; [Robert Walpole], *The Debts of the Nation Stated and Consider'd in four Papers* (1712), J. J. Grellier, *History of the National Debt* (1810).

incurred before Michaelmas 1702 and after Michaelmas 1710 were together greater than those created in the period 1702–10.[1] Careful provision was made for interest. The tallies of loan on the sixth General Mortgage of 1710 (4), were largely in the hands of the departmental paymasters and the fund on which they were struck was not clear from previous incumbrances until 1 August 1716.[2] By securing their exchange for South Sea stock the Treasury became free to settle these duties from 1716 in perpetuity to help pay interest on the company's capital. At the same time the duties under the Candle Act of 1710, which were to expire on 1 May 1715, and were already charged with tallies of loan, were continued in perpetuity from 1715 to form the other part of the South Sea fund, once these tallies were discharged.[3] Until these somewhat remote funds took effect, the annual interest payable, computed as £568,280 with a further £8,000 p.a. for management, was to be paid quarterly to the company by the Treasurer of the Navy from unappropriated monies in his hands, in other words from the current supply. Lastly (5) a sum of half a million in stock was arbitrarily created for the government's own use.

The exact amount of the new company's capital depended on the extent to which these debts were offered for exchange, though the Act seems to have made no provision for alternative payment. The task of taking the subscriptions was formidable, and occupied the company's attention for more than two years.[4] By the end of July 1711 £3,405,560 had already been subscribed.[5] The commissions for taking subscriptions were renewed in

[1] Walpole, *Debts of the Nation* (see sources for Table 5), pp. 52–54. He computed the debts incurred before 1702 as £2,897,530, those incurred from 1702 to Michaelmas 1710 as £3,864,151, and those incurred since Michaelmas 1710 as £2,721,613.

[2] *Cal. T. Bks.* xxiv (ii), 244–5, shows that the £1,296,552 authorized to be borrowed on security of 8 Anne, c. 13, was issued in tallies of fictitious loan to the departments. J. Postlethwayt, *History of the Public Revenue* (1759), p. 71, says that £1,103,755 of this amount was subscribed into the South Sea Company. The duties on which the tallies were charged were settled from 1714 to 1716 by 7 Anne, c. 8, the fifth General Mortgage, in April 1709. For the General Mortgage Acts and the use of tallies of fictitious loan see below, Ch. 13. £150,000 of the tallies charged on the sixth General Mortgage were security for the Canton of Berne's loan in 1710, for which see p. 62 above.

[3] The Candle Act was 8 Anne, c. 6. £500,000 was lent on it in 1710, largely in the form of tallies of fictitious loan issued to the departments (P.R.O. E 401/2595). The sum of £346,793 still outstanding in 1717 was funded in 4% stock; see below, p. 87.

[4] The process can be followed in the company's first two Directors' Court Minute Books, Add. MSS. 25494, 25495. Special ledgers and forms for subscribers were devised, Add. MS. 25494, ff. 20–24.

[5] Add. MS. 25494, f. 7.

1711, 1712, and 1713.[1] By Christmas 1713, when the books were finally closed, the total had risen to £9,177,968, a figure rather smaller than that envisaged by the South Sea Act of 1711, and on which the company was to receive annually from the Government £550,678 for interest and £8,000 for management.[2] Although in July 1712 the South Sea General Court was thanking the Lord Treasurer for his 'great Care of the Company and Punctuall Payment of the Annuity',[3] this punctuality unfortunately did not last. At midsummer 1715, for instance, interest was half a year in arrears. These fluctuations, and the necessarily slow progress made in starting a trade to Spanish America, caused the company serious financial embarrassment. In 1712, 1713, and 1714 proprietors were given the option of receiving their dividends in bonds instead of cash.[4] At midsummer 1715 they were offered no choice, but were required to take bonds.[5] In 1716 the midsummer and Christmas dividends were both paid in stock.[6] Fortunately the latter was now at par. The securities funded in 1711–13, though at a discount, had been exchanged for stock at par. Thus *A.B.* in 1711 could buy a £1,000 Navy bill at 30% discount for £666 13s. 4d. and exchange it for £1,000 South Sea stock. But the discount was immediately transferred to the stock, whose market price remained in the 70s throughout 1712. Although by the end of 1713 it had risen to 94, it only reached and stayed at par at the end of 1716.[7]

These prices reflected among other things the Government's use of stock to pay creditors and as security for loans. Of the company's capital of £9,177,968, a sum of £2,371,402 had been subscribed 'for the use of the Publick'.[8] This included the General Mortgage tallies of 1710 subscribed by the departmental paymasters in 1711, and the £500,000 stock created for the Government's own use by the South Sea Act. The Treasury repeatedly drew on this balance for payments and as security for advances to departments in the period 1712–15.[9] It was not a popular practice. Thus in

---

[1] The first commission was 27 June 1711. The three others were 4 March 1712, 12 February 1713, and 22 September 1713, Add. MS. 25498, f. 17. The Company's charter, dated 8 September 1711, permitted subscriptions to be taken until Christmas 1711; this was perhaps a sixth, supplementary, commission.

[2] Add. MS. 25495, f. 132.

[3] Add. MS. 25494, f. 109, South Sea D. Ct. Bk., 16 July 1712. The company also paid the Secretary to the Treasury, William Lowndes, £215 in gold (ibid., f. 108).

[4] Add. MSS. 25494, f. 101; 25495, f. 70; 25496, f. 3.

[5] Add. MS. 25496, f. 58.   [6] Ibid., f. 118.

[7] The stock reached par in May 1715, but only temporarily.   [8] Add MS. 25494, f. 91.

[9] See for example Add. MS. 25494, f. 48, and *Cal. T. Bks.* xxvi (ii), 1712, index, under 'South Sea Company Stock'.

May 1713 the Bank of England's General Court asked that no Act of the current session of Parliament should oblige the Bank to make loans on security of South Sea stock.[1] The amount of it in government hands increased by £238,000 in 1715, but by 1716 the Treasury only had £170,000 to be disposed of.[2] In the following year (1717) the South Sea fund became free from its incumbrances and was confirmed by Parliament, which also enacted that its deficiencies would in future be paid from the General Fund.[3] By this date, too, some progress had been made in starting a trade to Spanish America. The company's early difficulties seemed for a brief moment to have been overcome. The frenzy and confusion of the South Sea Bubble, and the long and tangled train of diplomatic negotiations with Spain over the American trade, mercifully lay concealed in the future.

The establishment of the South Sea Company got rid of the floating debt, with the grudging acquiescence of the financial community in the City. It did nothing to solve the problems of anticipation of annual taxes and of long-term loans for supply, particularly urgent since the war had now reached its maximum level of expense. The Tory back-benchers, who had probably hoped that they now had a rival interest in the City to the Bank of England, saw with dismay that the company had its work cut out to function at all, and that the Bank's support was as necessary for Harley as it had been for Godolphin. Luckily for Harley it was also forthcoming. Thanks to this, he was able to create new Exchequer bills on a massive scale to cover short-term supply, and to use the Bank as receiver in three of the four very large lottery loans floated in 1711 and 1712 to cover the revenue deficit.[4] The Bank also acted as receiver in the smaller lotteries of 1713 and 1714. The fact that Edward Gibbon, one of Harley's City advisers, was made receiver, together with a number of his associates, for the second lottery of 1711, the scheme for which was drafted by John Blunt, whose cousin Charles Blunt acted as paymaster, is therefore perhaps less significant than it seems.[5] It was

[1] Bank G. Ct. Bk. ii, ff. 103–4, 5 May 1713.

[2] Add. MS. 25496, f. 108, South Sea D. Ct. Bk., 13 April 1716. The Treasury tried to persuade the company to accept £93,000 of this stock as payment of the interest due on its capital at Lady Day and to buy the rest. The company at first agreed to this, but in the end refused (ibid., ff. 108–12).

[3] 3 Geo. I, c. 8; for this fund see below, p. 86.

[4] For the Exchequer bills see below, p. 375.

[5] Blunt's authorship of the lottery scheme is stated in N. Tindal, *The History of England by Mr. Rapin de Thoyras continued* . . . (4 vols., 1745), iv, part 1, sect. 2, p. 200 n. Charles Blunt was either nephew or cousin of John Blunt. He committed suicide in 1720; see below, p. 495.

TABLE 6

Government lottery loans, 1711–12

No.	Date of royal assent to Loan Act	Sum raised £	Additional liability incurred £	Total liability £	Funds on which payment of interest and principal charged	Administration of loan
1	6 March 1711	1,500,000	428,870	1,928,570	(a) Customs duties for 32 years from 1711. (b) Further coal duties from 1710 for 32 years. (c) Duties on home and imported candles for 32 years from 1711. (d) Further miscellaneous duties for 32 years.	A lottery of 150,000 £10 tickets, the scheme of prizes being so drawn that the government undertook to repay £1,928,570. Until it did so holders of prizes and blanks were to have 6% interest.
2	12 June 1711	2,000,000	602,200	2,602,200	(a) Licences on hackney coaches and chairs for 32 years. (b) Duties on parchment and paper, playing-cards, hides, and leather for 32 years. (c) Duties on Irish salt imported.	A lottery of 20,000 £100 tickets. These were divided into five classes, the prizes being slightly different in each. The government obliged itself (as above) to repay £2,602,200, and to pay 6% meanwhile.

3	22 May 1712	1,800,000	541,740	2,341,740	Duties of customs and excise for 32 years on painted linens, soap, silk, paper, pasteboard, and books.	A lottery of 180,000 £10 tickets. The government obliged itself to repay £2,341,740. Other arrangements as in (1).
4	21 June 1712	1,800,000	541,990	2,341,990	Duties for 32 years on coffee, tea, gilt and silver wire, hides and skins, vellum, parchment, cards, dice and starch, drugs, and insurance policies.	A lottery of 18,000 £100 tickets. These were divided into six classes, the prizes being slightly different in each. The government obliged itself to repay £2,341,990. Other arrangements as in (1).
		£7,100,000	2,114,800	9,214,500		

Source: Loan Acts and *BPP* (1898), lii.

not so much an attempt to cut out the Bank as to cut in Harley's cronies on one deal in order to keep them out of others and keep some of their loyalty.

The schemes of the lotteries of 1711–12 were so drafted that a liability was incurred greater than the sums lent: in effect the loans were floated at a discount. If the state had obliged itself to pay all the ticket-holders at once, this ingenuity would have defeated its own ends. Instead, as in 1694 and 1710 the Treasury engaged to pay interest at nearly 8%, and added the further bait that it would within thirty-two years pay the principal as well. In fact it was only able to repay small amounts of the principal, most of which had to be funded in 5% stock in 1717.[1] At the time, however, the unrealistic generosity of the terms offered made the lotteries highly popular, 'and indeed', commented Tindal later, 'this method has never yet failed of raising a speedy supply'.[2] To the Treasury's unmistakable relief the first, which must have served as a model for the next three, was over-subscribed.[3] Many investors were turned away, and the Whigs, as a Tory pamphleteer sarcastically observed, were seen 'like the Israelitish Army, running and treading on the Heels of one another, to . . . crowd that Money they had resolved to keep so close into the New Fund.'[4]

Nonetheless, contemporaries must have been aware that these lotteries, however justified by the necessity of the hour, were scraping the barrel of taxation. The funds settled to pay principal and interest were of absurd complexity and seemed almost a parody of the Whig taxes against which the squirearchy had long protested. Yet they proved insufficient to make the payments they were intended for. Fortunately for Ministers the conclusion of peace in 1713 made it possible to reduce the scale of long-term borrowing. In 1713 the only long-term loan was a lottery of £500,000 to discharge the debts of the Civil List. Interest at 4% was charged on the Crown revenues, and the principal was also to be repaid within thirty-two years.[5] An additional

[1] See below, p. 84. The Treasury paid 6% on the nominal capital of the lottery, which was larger than the sums actually lent. The real interest rate was 7·8%.

[2] Tindal, loc. cit.

[3] *Cal. T. Bks.* xxv, p. 25, 13 March 1711. Nathaniel Gould, Deputy Governor of the Bank, reports that the lottery has been over-subscribed by 29,000 tickets; what is to be done? The Treasury, after consulting the Law Officers, returns an evasive reply the same day, ibid.

[4] *Eleven Opinions about M. H — y with Observations*, p. 42. Cf. H.M.C. *Kenyon MSS.*, p. 446, Sir Roger Bradshaigh to George Kenyon, 24 March 1711, on the impossibility of 'outsiders' obtaining a share of this subscription.

[5] 12 Anne, c. 11.

liability of £133,010 was incurred, making the capital sum repayable £633,010. In 1714 a similar loan was floated for the public service. The lottery raised £1.4m., which the additional liability made £1,876,400, again repayable within thirty-two years.[1] Further duties were laid on soap, paper, linen, silks, calicoes, parchment, and coals to pay interest and principal.

[1] 13 Anne, c. 18.

4

Problems of Administration
and Reform 1693-1719

I

THE second part of this chapter describes the financial situation on the morrow of the Treaty of Utrecht, and the reforms then undertaken to clear or simplify the nation's debts. Before coming to this, however, it is worth looking at the administration of the loans of 1693–1714 described in the previous chapter. All the loans for life and long annuities were received at the Exchequer. The subscriber was given a tally of receipt and a paper Standing Order, which was assignable, for the future payment of the annuity.[1] Both the initial payment and collection of the tally appear to have been frequently entrusted to agents, many of whom were London goldsmiths. Of 1,257 known contributors to the tontine loan of 1693, for example, 536 made their payments by an agent. Six London goldsmiths alone acted in this way for seventy-two persons.[2] A register survives for the annuity loans of 1708–10 showing delivery of tallies to lenders, or, more frequently, their agents, who included many well-known goldsmith bankers.[3] Before 1704 the money subscribable had evidently to be paid in as one sum. In 1704 payment by instalments of one-third was introduced. A separate tally was given

---

[1] Tallies were notched wooden sticks used by the Exchequer as receipts; see below, p. 350, for a fuller discussion. Procedure for subscriptions appears clearly from the loan Acts. No Standing Orders for long-term loans appear to have survived for this period. They were probably similar in form to those for short-term loans, for which see Plate 8. There are examples of the receipts which annuitants gave on receiving their half-yearly payment in Add. MS. 34195, ff. 129–49, and P.R.O. E 404/520.

[2] The six goldsmiths were Adrian Courtney, Whitfield Hayter, Richard Hoare, Thomas Johnson, Edward Mompesson, and Richard Smith. For subscriptions to the Tontine see below, p. 253 and Plate 5.

[3] P.R.O. E 407/166.

for each instalment and a Standing Order when they were completed.[1] This made it possible, though inconvenient, to transfer to a third person by deed a subscription which had not been fully paid.[2] The dealings in scrip characteristic of the war loans of the 1740s and later years were thus indistinctly foreshadowed, though a real increase in this type of speculation depended on the removal of loans from the slow and cumbersome machinery of the Exchequer of Receipt, a change only effected after 1714.

The technique of subscription in lottery loans was necessarily different and more complex. It can be followed in the nine state lotteries of 1694–1714, all of which had similar features.[3] First, Managers of the lottery were appointed under the Great Seal. Their task was to supervise the receivers, who were appointed by the Treasury to sell the lottery tickets, pay the money into the Exchequer, and give the Managers an account of it, and of the tickets sold, at the close of a stated period. One or more duplicates were kept of each ticket sold. The draw, which was publicly announced, took place at Guildhall. The Managers took duplicates of the tickets from a sealed box and compared them aloud with an identical number of tickets, previously divided into prizes and blanks, deposited in a second sealed box. The Managers afterwards printed a list of the winning tickets and their holders, and returned the original list of prize-winners to the Exchequer.[4]

Certain changes were made between 1694 and 1714. The price of tickets varied. Normally it was £10, but in the two Class lotteries of 1711 and 1712 it was £100. Beginning with the first lottery of 1711, subscriptions for tickets were, like those for annuities, made payable in instalments. Instalments subsequent to the first were endorsed on the ticket by the receiver. The schemes of prizes and blanks also varied. The maximum prize offered was as high as £20,000 in three of the lotteries of 1711–14 and as low as £1,000 in 1697. Later, £10,000 seems to have become a normal maximum, though

---

[1] 2 & 3 Anne, c. 3. Under Anne, c. 48 (1708), subscribers could borrow instalments subsequent to the first from the Exchequer at 4%. This anticipated the Bank of England's regular practice from the 1720s of making loans to enable subscribers to complete their payments (Bank General Ledgers).

[2] 3 & 4 Anne, c. 14 (1704), showed the difficulties that could arise: John Holland and Stephen Leacroft of London, who had separately paid in one-third on two annuities, assigned the latter, by two separate deeds, to Samuel Cooke of Plymouth. Cooke failed to pay the second call, owing to sickness, and was thus liable to forfeit. The Act gave him relief.

[3] Cf. also C. L. Ewen, *Lotteries and Sweepstakes in the British Isles.*

[4] P.R.O. E 401/2599 and 2600, books for two of the lotteries of 1711 and 1712, appear to be the only surviving examples.

£20,000 was again sometimes offered.[1] Payment of tickets might consist of a stated amount each year for a term of years, as in the lotteries of 1694 and 1710. An alternative was to promise to pay the principal within thirty-two years and interest meanwhile, as in the lotteries of 1711–14. In 1697 no term was set for payment.

Lastly, changes were made in the method of paying prizes and blanks. Before 1711 the holder of a ticket was obliged to exchange it after the draw for a series of payment slips. Each time he was paid he had to present one of these at the Exchequer, which kept a duplicate. A third copy was lodged at a Transfer Office in the Exchequer, so that if *A.B.* proposed to transfer to *C.D.* his payment slip for six years ahead *C.D.* could verify his title there.[2] This was both dangerous and inconvenient, and in 1711 Harley, apparently as the result of criticism by Lord Halifax, introduced instead a Standing Order of payment for each ticket-holder, similar to those used for long annuities.[3]

Early subscriptions were therefore made at the Exchequer of Receipt or by the purchase of lottery tickets. Despite the introduction of subscriptions by instalments and of surer ways of paying lottery tickets, however, the Exchequer's medieval processes were not really suited to this type of business. Rapid transfer of partly paid subscriptions was virtually impossible, and assignment of the Standing Orders received when instalments were completed was slow and complicated. The Exchequer, moreover, was never certain who its creditors were at any one time.[4] And the loan-subscriptions thrust on it obliged it to create offices for the payment of annuities and the transfer of lottery tickets just at a time when the growing size and complexity of government revenue was straining to the limit the existing

---

[1] See the table of prizes in Ewen, op. cit., p. 163.

[2] The form of tickets and payments slips are set out in the Lottery Acts of 1694, 1697, and 1710.

[3] 9 Anne, c. 6. For Halifax's criticisms see H.M.C., *Portland MSS.* iv. 658, Halifax to Harley, 11 February 1711: 'There is one further improvement that I will offer to your better judgment. I believe the smallness of the tickets, and the great number of them, which people are obliged to keep for the several payments that are to be made, are very troublesome; they are apt to be lost or mislaid: for every blank they have 32, and for every benefit 64 little pieces of paper so easily scattered about that they are obliged often to have recourse to Parliament for clauses to renew them that have been lost or destroyed. Now in this new lottery . . . might not there be a method established, for giving out orders for their re-payment in the course in which they are drawn; these orders would be more easily kept, assigned, and transferred, and consequently of more value, but this is submitted to you.'

[4] See below, p. 458.

machinery of receipt, account, and audit.[1] The problem could perhaps have been solved by creating a Department of State to receive subscriptions to loans, register subsequent transfers, and pay interest to the lenders. A simpler and more obvious solution was to entrust this business to the Bank of England, which had already acted as receiver in six of the seven state lotteries of 1710–14, and, thanks to its management of Exchequer bills and loans on security of departmental tallies, had acquired a central position in short-term finance. The change was made gradually after 1714, and was virtually complete by the 1740s, as will be shown later.

II

We must now return to the financial situation that faced George I's new ministers in 1714. After the long wars, England's reckoning, like that of every major power engaged, was formidable. The War of the Spanish Succession had added to the long-term debts already incurred £34·9m.: £8·2m. in long annuities, £2·4m. in short annuities, £11·7m. in lotteries, £1·6m. for loans by the Bank of England and East India Company, and a further £10·9m. of short-term debts funded by the Bank in 1709 and the South Sea Company in 1711. This was more than a third of total government expenditure.[2] Omitting Tontine and life annuities of about £45,000 a year, the structure of the National Debt at Michaelmas 1714 was as shown in Table 7.

The average rate of interest was just over 6%, but this conceals the fact that interest on the long annuities was nearly 7%, and was payable until the 1790s or longer. Besides these funded debts there were lesser, but more important, floating ones, notably over £4·5m. in Exchequer bills. In addition, debts of uncertain amount were due for arrears of army pay and foreign subsidies.[3]

---

[1] The expansion of Exchequer staff owing to the increases in taxes and loans can be followed in the successive editions of Chamberlayne's *Angliae* (later *Magnae Britanniae*) *Notitia*. At least two annuity offices and a lottery transfer office had been created by 1714.

[2] Total government expenditure was £99m. including the year 1714 (excluded in Table 1, p. 10 above). The figures in the text assume the capital value of the annuities to be the same as the sums paid for them. The exact figures are: long annuities £8,191,427; short annuities £2,400,000; lotteries, 1711–14, £11,723,910; lent by Bank of England, 1709, £400,000; by United East India Company, 1708, £1,200,000; funded by Bank, 1709, £1,775,028; by South Sea Company, 1711–13, £9,177,968; a total of £34,868,333.

[3] See below, Chs. 14 and 15.

TABLE 7

The National Debt at 29 September 1714

Group	Category of debt	Sub-total £	Total £	Annual charge £
1.	*Irredeemable debts*			
	(a) Long annuities of £666,566 a year, capitalized at market value of 15 years' purchase.	9,998,490		
	(b) Short annuities of £216,000 a year, capitalized at market value of 11¾ years' purchase.	2,538,000		
			12,536,490	882,566
2.	*Redeemable debts*			
	(i) *Managed at the Exchequer*			
	(a) *Lottery loans:*			
	First lottery, 1711	1,928,570		
	Second lottery, 1711	2,602,200		
	First lottery, 1712	2,341,740		
	Second lottery, 1712	2,341,990		
	Civil List lottery, 1713	633,010		
	Lottery, 1714	1,876,400		
		11,723,910		
	Less sums discharged, 1711–14	320,648		
			11,403,262	684,196
	(b) *Bankers' Annuities (1705)*		664,263*	39,856
	(ii) *Owed to corporations*			
	(a) to Bank of England	3,375,028	..	202,512
	(b) to East India Comp.	3,200,000	..	160,000
	(c) to South Sea Comp.	9,177,968		
			15,752,996	550,678
			£40,357,011	£2,519,808

Source: Tables in preceding text and *BPP* (1898), lii. Prices for annuities from J. Castaing, *The Course of the Exchange, and other things,* for which see below, p. 488.

* The Banker's Debt could be redeemed for this sum, which was half the full debt. Interest was meanwhile paid on the whole debt. See above, p. 44.

Further, the structure of the revenue, thanks to the creation of numerous funds for payment of interest, had become so complex as to be intelligible only to experts. This was a considerable discouragement to foreign trade.[1]

After Shrewsbury's dramatic creation in 1714 as Lord Treasurer of England to foil Bolingbroke's ambitions, the Treasury went into commission, as befitted the more sober reign of a German king, and has stayed in commission ever since. The new commissioners, headed by Charles Montague, now Earl of Halifax and at the end of his life, faced a series of problems of graduated urgency. They must reduce the outstanding volume of Exchequer bills. They must ascertain the debts due to the army. If market rates of interest fell, they must see whether the charge of the redeemable National Debt could not be lowered and a fund settled to repay its principal. If all this were done the most difficult question of all could be tackled: how to persuade the holders of long and short annuities to surrender them for redeemable stock so that this, too, could be paid off. Lord Carlisle, who succeeded Halifax on the latter's death in May 1715, was, according to a later pamphleteer, 'as desirious to pay off the National Debt as any man since, and had actually formed Designs for this Purpose'.[2] During his short tenure of office he certainly took a number of very useful steps. In June 1715 he framed a plan to settle the large arrears of interest due to the South Sea Company.[3] Negotiations with the company continued until August, when an agreed Bill was introduced into Parliament. The substance of the measure was that the company's capital was to increase from midsummer 1715 by £822,032 to a round £10m. The increase comprised £275,339 arrears on the old capital of £9,177,968, a half year's interest, £300,000, on the new capital of £10m., and £238,693 stock, for use by the Treasurer of the Navy, to make up a round sum.[4] In August 1715 Carlisle asked the Bank of England to handle the year's supply loan of £910,000. The directors agreed to do this provided the stock created could be 'transferred in like form

---

[1] See introduction to William Edgar, *Vectigalium Systema* (1714). In 1720 the Exchequer Receipt Books contain 68 revenue accounts, the greater part of which were funds for various loans (P.R.O. E 401/2044). In 1732 there were 71 accounts (Add. MS. 17477, ff. 118–20).

[2] [William Pulteney], *Some Considerations on the National Debts* (1729), p. 66. Charles Howard, sixth Earl of Carlisle, was First Lord of the Treasury from 23 May to 10 October 1715, when Robert Walpole succeeded him.

[3] Add. MS. 25496, f. 41, South Sea D. Ct. Bk., 14 June 1715. The causes of the arrears are discussed above, pp. 70 ff.

[4] Ibid., f. 71, 28 September 1715 (transfer of stock to company), and 1 Geo. I, st. 2, c. 21, royal assent 21 September 1715.

with Bank stock'.[1] The Treasury solemnly assented. This was the first long-term loan administered by the Bank, which applied to it the methods of ledger double-entry and simple transfer that it had already worked out for its own stock. Although the loan itself was under-subscribed owing to the Jacobite rebellion, its importance as a step towards the virtually complete control of government long-term borrowing which the Bank had established by the 1740s can hardly be overestimated.[2] A further point is that the Bank was not in future to be dissolved until this, and subsequent debts which it managed, were paid off. Its charter thus became a less and less exact indication of how long its privileges would last.

In the same month in which he reached agreement with the Bank of England, Carlisle saw through Parliament the Act creating an 'Aggregate Fund' into which seven hitherto separate sets of customs and excise duties were to be paid and from which miscellaneous charges were to be met.[3] Both the revenue of the fund and the disbursements from it were uncertain. But it was an important first move towards the simplification of the revenue structure, which Walpole was to carry much further two years later. Lastly, in September 1715, commissioners were appointed to determine what debts were due to the army.[4]

Carlisle had therefore made some financial headway by October 1715 when Robert Walpole, then aged thirty-nine, succeeded him as First Lord of the Treasury. But important problems remained. The bulk of the redeemable National Debt still carried interest at over 6%, though the legal maximum for private individuals had been reduced to 5% in 1714 and the

[1] *Cal. T. Bks.* xxix. 284 (2 August 1715). The loan was subsequently increased, by a second Act of Parliament, by £169,000, because it was thought the money could be raised at 5% instead of 6% as at first authorized. The Bank administered this second loan as well. Its allowance for management was to be £450 p.a. As the Bank came to manage more and more new government loans this figure was standardised as an allowance of £450 per million on stock transferred at the Bank. This remained constant until 1798.

[2] For the Bank's later position see below, p. 382, and for its methods of transfer, p. 460. When the loan of £910,000 closed on 29 September 1715, only £451,800 had been submitted in cash. The balance was created in the name of the Navy Treasurer, who was able to sell the stock over a period of eighteen months to two years (ledger for this loan, Bank of England Record Office).

[3] See Table 8. The Aggregate Fund was established by 1 Geo. I, stat. 2, c. 12. The royal assent to the Act was given on 30 August 1715. There were precedents of a kind in 8 & 9 Wm. III, c. 20 (1697), and 6 Anne, c. 2 (1707), both of which had settled various duties as 'the General Fund' to pay interest and principal on debts.

[4] 1 Geo. I, stat. 2, c. 24, royal assent 21 September 1715. For the commission's report see below, p. 397.

TABLE 8

Charges to be met from the Aggregate Fund, 1715

No.	Charge
1	Interest on Exchequer bills at 2*d*. per cent.*
2	Circulation allowance to Bank of England of 3% on Exchequer bills outstanding.*
3	Additional annual allowance of £53,000 to Bank of England for Exchequer bills, conceded in 1711 and 1713.*
4	Interest of £54,600 for the loan of £910,000, 1715.
5	Any deficiencies of the funds settled in 1694 and 1709 to pay interest on the capital of the Bank of England.
6	An annual sum of £270,999 to redeem the principal of Exchequer bills.

Source : 1 Geo. I, stat. 2, c. 12.
* For these bills and allowances see below, p. 374.

trend of market yields was in the same direction.[1] The principal of the lotteries of 1710–12 was clearly never going to be paid from the funds settled for the purpose. It looked as though over a million pounds would be payable for Army debts. Lastly, the delicate question of the irredeemable annuities had not been touched. Walpole must have studied these problems closely in the year after he took up office; in September 1716 he wrote to Stanhope 'I am now very busy in projecting and forming a scheme for paying the debts of the nation'.[2] As he put it later:

The Circumstances of Time, high Credit, and low Price of Money, led those, whose particular Province and Business it was, to consider of proper Means to make Use of that favourable Opportunity, that the Publick might share in the common Advantage of the flourishing State of publick Credit.[3]

The Government's creditors, in other words, were to be asked to 'accept of the common Rate of Interest upon good Security', which was lower than the rate they were then receiving.[4] As in 1749, success would depend on the co-operation of the great monied companies, and they were therefore brought closely into the preliminary discussions. 'It cannot be doubted', says Walpole,

[1] Cf. below, pp. 373 ff.
[2] Coxe, *Walpole*, ii. 95, Walpole to Stanhope, 28 September 1716.
[3] [Sir Robert Walpole], *Some Considerations concerning the Publick Funds* (1735), p. 11.
[4] Ibid.

D 2

but many Conferences and Considerations were had upon this extensive Question, among the monied Men, and Money-Corporations, in order to bring the Scheme to Maturity, before it should be laid before the Parliament.[1]

The conferences are not recorded in the minute books of the Bank or South Sea Company.[2] But there is little doubt that they were an important cause of the broad scope and relative success of Walpole's proposals.

The King's Speech on 20 February 1717 recommended to the Commons the reduction of the 'Debts of the Nation'.[3] A Committee of the Whole House was ordered to consider the problem, and on 23 March its chairman, William Farrer, reported fourteen resolutions at which it had arrived under Walpole's guidance.[4] The measures envisaged were as follows. The redeemable part of the National Debt, including the debts due to the South Sea Company and the Bank of England, were to be reduced to 5% or to be repaid. The duties settled to pay the lotteries of 1711–12 were to be perpetuated and run together as one fund. The ticket-holders were to be offered the choice of a reduction to 5% or repayment of their principal. The Crown was empowered to borrow to pay dissentients. The Exchequer bills charged on the Aggregate Fund were to be circulated at a lower rate of interest. The long and short annuitants were to be offered the choice of exchanging their terms of years for redeemable stock. Finally, the savings effected by the reduction were to be devoted to the discharge of the principal of the debt.[5]

---

[1] Walpole, *Considerations*, p. 13. In his dialogue *An Inquiry into the state of the Union ... by the Wednesday's Club in Friday Street*, published in Jan. 1717 (Bannister, *Writings of William Paterson*, vol. ii) the veteran projector William Paterson discussed the public debts and the possibility of reducing all of them, including the annuities, to 4%, and repaying them over twenty-two years. Bannister (ii, p. lxvii) claims from a pamphlet of 1717 that Walpole commissioned Paterson to make these calculations, and that Paterson was thus the true author of the Sinking Fund.

[2] The East India Company's debt had been at 5% since 1708 and was therefore not included in the reduction scheme.

[3] *HCJ* xviii. 474.

[4] Ibid., pp. 512–13. An attempt to sound the feelings of the monied men by floating a short-term loan at 4%, a rate 1% lower than the usual one, had meanwhile failed. The resolution to raise £600,000 at 4% was debated on 5 March 1717, (*Parl. Hist.* vii. 424). On 8 March Lechmere, the Solicitor-General, reported to the House that only £45,000 had been subscribed to the loan, a failure which Walpole attributed to the machinations of jobbers (ibid. 425–6).

[5] *HCJ* loc. cit. The comprehensive nature of these proposals is ignored by Coxe, whose account is nonsensical (*Walpole*, i. 108–9), by Scott, op. cit. iii, 298, and by Dr. Plumb, *Sir Robert Walpole. The Making of A Statesman* (1956), p. 247.

Only part of this very extensive plan, which aimed at resolving all the state's outstanding financial problems at one swoop, was put into practice, owing to Walpole's quarrel with Stanhope and resignation in mid-April 1717.[1] On 10 April, just after his resignation, Walpole introduced a Bill for part of the resolutions, but it was repeatedly postponed, and then shelved.[2] On 6 June the new administration ordered three new Bills, the terms of which the Committee of Ways and Means had previously negotiated with the two monied companies.[3] The Bills were presented to the House by the senior Treasury Secretary, William Lowndes, who must have been doing his homework on the issues involved for at least eighteen months, and passed without a division, receiving the royal assent on 17 July 1717. They were obviously based on Walpole's previous proposals. But they made one very important change of policy by dealing only with the redeemable debts and omitting any reference to the annuities for terms of years — the most onerous charge on the revenue.[4] In view of the probable difficulty of persuading the annuitants to let the government off the hook this was probably a wise change, which gave the rest of the plan a better chance. The problem of the annuities was only taken up again, in very different circumstances, in 1719–20.

The first of the three conversion Acts dealt with the lotteries of 1711–12 and created a General Fund and a Sinking Fund. The second and third covered the debts due from the Bank of England and the South Sea Company.[5] Under the first Act the outstanding principal of the lotteries of 1711–1712 and half that of the Bankers' Annuities of 1705 were to be exchanged for (i.e. funded in) 5% stock managed by the Bank of England. The sums involved were £8,875,703 for the lotteries and £658,635 for the Bankers'

---

[1] Lord Stanhope succeeded Walpole as First Lord of the Treasury on 15 April 1717. He ceded the post to Sunderland on 21 March 1718, John Aislabie, then Treasurer of the Navy, becoming Chancellor of the Exchequer.

[2] *HCJ* xviii. 541, 548, 560, 564, 566, 576.

[3] Ibid. 566, 24 May 1717, report from the Committee.

[4] Dr. Plumb, loc. cit., following N. Brisco, *The Economic Policy of Robert Walpole* (New York, 1907), pp. 30–40, states that 'one or two minor alterations' were made in Walpole's plan, but it is clear that it was in fact cut in half. For Solicitor-General Lechmere's hostility to any offer to the annuitants see *Parl. Hist.* vii. 426. The author of *An Argument To shew the Disadvantage From obliging the South-Sea Company To fix what Capital Stock They will give for the Annuities* (1720), p. 13, appears to be referring to this episode when he says that the annuitants have already in the present reign obstructed a plan for paying off the National Debt.

[5] 3 Geo. I, cc. 7, 8, and 9.

annuities, a total of £9,534,358.[1] The other two Acts arranged for contingent finance of £4·5m. from the other two companies to repay dissentients, but there were only six, so these loans were not needed.[2] The Bank's staff, working round the clock, received the public creditors' Exchequer Orders and credited them with 5% stock in six large new ledgers.[3] The interest was to be paid from the duties previously settled for each loan. These duties, however, were now to be run together as a 'General yearly fund' computed to amount to £724,849. Its deficiencies were to be provided by Parliament. This was just as well, since in future it was as regularly in deficit as the Aggregate Fund was in surplus, as Walpole's opponents gleefully noted later.[4] Its surpluses, together with those of the Aggregate Fund and South Sea Fund, were to be paid into a Sinking Fund to discharge

the principal and interest of such national Debts and Incumbrances as were incurred before the 25th day of December 1716 in such manner as shall be directed or appointed by any future Acts of Parliament and to or for none other use, intent, or purpose, whatsoever.[5]

This new fund thus had an uncertain revenue, and objects which Parliament could in future modify. Nor were trustees appointed to administer it. In all these respects it differed from Pitt's Sinking Fund of 1786, and as it was the only free fund at the government's disposal, Ministers were to be constantly tempted to raid it for current supply or to charge new loans on its revenues.[6]

The second part of the 1717 conversion dealt with the debts due to the Bank of England and the South Sea Company. The Bank of England

---

[1] The principal of the 1711–12 lotteries by 1717 was £8,762,625; the additional balance funded was arrears of interest. The Bankers' Annuities of 1705 (see above, p. 44) were redeemable on payment of half their principal. Half should have been £664,263, but evidently some Orders had never been made out; *Cal. T. Bks.* xxxii. 129–33, 8 January 1718.

[2] The names of the six dissentients, who controlled five accounts with a total of £471 stock, are given by Walpole in his pamphlet *Some Considerations concerning the Publick Funds*, p. 20 n.

[3] P.R.O. T 1/242, Treasury In Letters, 1720; the Bank claimed that its staff worked 'for at least six months . . . till 10, 11, and 12 a Clock at night and on holydays'. The ledgers are in the Bank of England Record Office.

[4] [William Pulteney] *Some Considerations on the National Debts* (1729), p. 65. The deficiencies were, however, only book-keeping ones, since the charges on the fund were less than anticipated. For annual tables of Sinking Fund revenue see *BPP* (1868–9), xxxv. 682 ff.

[5] 3 Geo. I, c. 7, s. 37. Cf. below, p. 211, for later conflicting interpretations of what this meant.

[6] Cf. below, p. 207.

received payment from the state from four distinct interest funds. The first provided an annual £100,000 on £1,200,000 which the Bank had lent in 1694 and £400,000 which it had lent in 1709. This interest, which was at 6%, could not be reduced until 1732. Second, the Bank received annually £106,502 representing 6% interest on £1,775,028 Exchequer bills which it had funded in 1709. Third, it received £136,830 as an allowance (at 3%) for circulating £4,561,025 Exchequer bills. Lastly, it received additional circulation allowances, settled in 1711 and 1713, which could not be reduced until the principal of bills outstanding was only £1·9m.[1] The Treasury agreed with the Bank that the second of these charges, £106,502, should be reduced at midsummer 1718 to 5% or £88,751.[2] The Exchequer bill liability was separated into two. The Bank agreed to fund £2m. bills at 5% from Christmas 1717 and to give up the extra circulation allowances, even though the bills outstanding were still more than £1·9m. Further, the state reduced the interest it allowed on the bills to 1·5% (a penny a day). The agreement with the South Sea Company was similar, though less complex. The state was to pay interest on its £10m. capital at 5% instead of 6% after midsummer 1718. The company, however, succeeded in securing the concession that the Bank had failed to obtain — that this should not be further reduced for a period of five years. Together, the Acts of 1717 reduced the floating debt to a reasonable size, cleared off the lottery payment Orders of 1711–12, grouped a large part of the tangled revenue into distinct funds, and established a Sinking Fund for reduction of the National Debt. They also lowered its annual charge by £325,876, a reduction of about 13%, less than the reductions of 1727–30 and 1750, but a welcome boon to the state. The market reacted optimistically to the conversion's success, most holders of stock probably reasoning like Sir James Bateman, who told Lord Stanhope that 'he was glad this resolution had been taken; because, tho' his interest diminished, he should think his principal more secure than ever'.[3] By the end of 1717 government 5% stock was quoted at four points above par.

The Treasury rounded off these complicated arrangements by funding £946,929 floating debts between July and December 1717 in 4% stock managed by the Bank of England, and funding £1·6m. debentures made out

[1] For details of the Exchequer bill arrangements see below, p. 374.

[2] For the Bank's discussions with the Treasury see Bank D. Ct. Bk. G, ff. 186, 191, 15 May and 4 June 1717, and G. Ct. Bk. ii, ff. 134–7, 15 and 17 May 1717. The Bank tried in vain to make the Treasury pay the 5% for five years.

[3] As reported by Bolingbroke, *Works*, iii (1754), 169–70.

for arrears of army pay and foreign subsidies in a similar 4% stock in the following year.[1] A small sum of £110,313 due to the Treasurer of the Navy in 1718 was handled in the same way.[2] The interest of all three stocks was charged on the General Fund of 1717.

The measures taken between 1715 and 1719 had solved all the main problems left over from the war except the thorniest one: the high (and virtually perpetual) interest payable to the annuitants for terms of years. Before anything could be done about this, the annuitants would have to be persuaded to exchange their annuities for redeemable stock at an agreed capitalization. This was what Walpole had evidently intended in 1717. The Treasury must therefore have been making the first move in the same direction (only two years after Walpole's scheme had been dropped) when in January 1719 it laid before the directors of the South Sea Company a proposal that the holders of 1710 lottery Orders (which ran for a period of thirty-two years) should exchange them for South Sea stock.[3] The company's capital and the interest the government paid on it would increase in proportion. The Treasury's calculation was that the £135,000 a year payable on these Orders should be capitalized at a market price of eleven and a half years' purchase to give £1,552,500. To this, £168,750 was to be added for one and a quarter year's arrears of interest due to the company. Finally, the latter was to lend the Exchequer £778,750. This would bring the increase in the state's debt to it to a round £2·5m. If less were exchanged, the other amounts were to diminish in proportion.[4]

When the subscription, which was held in the spring and early summer of 1719, was completed, it was found that only £94,330 of the Orders, about

---

[1] The sum of £946,929 largely consisted of unpaid loans of 1711 (£346,793) and 1716 (£509,127), though there were also unpaid bills drawn for the Quebec expedition of 1711. The tallies of loan were largely in the hands of departmental paymasters. For the army debentures see below, p. 397.

[2] The new Navy Treasurer, Richard Hampden, had paid the South Sea Company £139,958 for a deficiency on its fund at midsummer 1718. He had been repaid £29,645; the £110,313 was the balance. The Land Tax Act for 1719, 5 Geo. I, c. 1 (12 December 1718), authorized this to be raised by loans. The Treasury in fact created tallies of fictitious loan for this amount, which Hampden exchanged for 4% stock at the Bank on 3 February 1719. On 5 February 1719 he transferred the stock to Thomas Hawes, a senior Navy Board officer, who sold it to various purchasers by March 1720; ledger for this stock, Bank of England Record Office.

[3] Add. MS. 25498, ff. 86–87, South Sea D. Ct. Bk., 27 January 1719.

[4] Ibid. Besides the loan from the South Sea Company, the Government raised £1m. in 1719 by two lotteries of equal amounts, the first managed by the Bank and the second by the Exchequer.

two-thirds of the whole, had been subscribed.[1] The company's nominal capital therefore increased by £1,746,844 to £11,746,844. It had to place £1,084,790 of the increase to the accounts of the new stockholders, together with a further £117,912 for arrears of interest. This left £544,142 to be paid to the Exchequer. It was obtained by selling £520,000 of the new stock at 114 in July 1719. The subscription, payable in fifths, was fully met by December 1719, realizing £592,800.[2] As the company already had claims against the state for £193,582 it only had to pay over £350,560 of this, leaving itself a handsome profit of £242,240 on the whole operation.[3] Further, as it had sold only £520,000 stock it still had £24,000-odd in hand.[4] The fact that the agent used for this successful conjuring trick was the South Sea Company, with whom the new Chancellor of the Exchequer John Aislabie had been in fairly close contact for some years (he had previously, as Navy Treasurer, had to pay the interest on its capital), is strong presumptive evidence that this was a pilot-project for the much larger operation of the same kind which the company undertook in the following year. This was to be known to posterity as the South Sea Bubble.

[1] 5 Geo. I, c. 19. For the total subscribed see Add. MS. 25498, f. 132, 5 August 1719.

[2] Add. MS. 25498, f. 124, South Sea D. Ct. Bk., 25 June 1719; none to subscribe less than £500 or more than £5,000. The books were to be open on 2 July 1719 only. For the issue price of 114 see ibid., f. 125, 1 July 1719; for the filling of the subscription, ibid., 2 July 1719.

[3] Ibid., f. 132, 5 August 1719, for the set-off allowed by the Treasury because of arrears of interest due to the company.

[4] Cf. below, p. 110.

5

The South Sea Bubble (I)

I

By 1720 the new English state initiated so precariously in 1688 could congratulate itself on immense achievements. In the long wars of 1689–1713 it had led and partly paid for the successful resistance to Louis XIV's last and most costly attempt to expand the power of France in Europe. It had carried through the Union with Scotland. It had broken the legitimate succession to the English throne, excluded the Stuarts from it, and forced the Bourbons to recognize this exclusion. The pro-Stuart risings of 1715 and 1719 had been brushed aside. Civil and religious liberty had been effectively established, and all this had encouraged considerable investment and innovation in domestic finance and foreign trade. If England on the eve of the 'never-to-be-forgot or forgiven South-Sea Scheme'[1] was bolder and more confident than ever before, it was because of her successes, and not from mere bravura.[2]

[1] [Sir Robert Walpole] *Some Considerations concerning the Publick Funds*, p. 31.

[2] Previous discussions of the South Sea Bubble include those by Adam Anderson, *An Historical and Chronological Deduction of the Origin of Commerce* (2 vols., 1764; 4 vols., 1787–9); Sir John Sinclair, *The History of the Public Revenue of the British Empire* (3 vols., 1785–90); William Coxe, *Memoirs of . . . Sir Robert Walpole* (3 vols., 1798); J. J. Grellier, *The History of the National Debt* (1810); Lord Mahon, *History of England . . . 1713–1783*, vol. ii (1837); W. Michael, 'Der Südseeschwindel vom Jahre 1720, *Vierteljahrschrift für Sozial- und Wirtschaftsgeschichte*, vol. vi (1908), p. 549; idem, *Englische Geschichte im achtzehnten Jahrhundert*, iii (1934), ch. 3; M. Bouniatian, *Studien zur Theorie und Geschichte der Wirtschaftskrisen* (2 vols., Munich, 1908), vol. ii, *Geschichte der Handelskrisen in England 1640-1840*; W. R. Scott, *The Constitution and Finance of . . . Joint Stock Companies to 1720* (3 vols., Camb. 1910–12); Lewis Melville, *The South Sea Bubble* (1921); C. B. Realey, *The Early Opposition to Sir Robert Walpole* (Lawrence, Kansas 1931); Viscount Erleigh, *The South Sea Bubble* (1933); J. H. Plumb, *Sir Robert Walpole. The Making of a Statesman* (1956); Virginia Cowles, *The Great Swindle: the story of the South Sea Bubble* (1960), and J. P. Carswell, *The South Sea Bubble* (1960). Anderson was a South Sea Company clerk at the time of the Bubble and was familiar with the problems involved. Subsequent writers have drawn on him, with or without acknowledgement. Scott's very full account from printed sources has become standard, though it contains a number of mistakes. Mr. Carswell's very interesting recent study is perhaps stronger on personalities

But success creates its own problems. The same forces which encouraged greater tolerance about religion and politics, and greater confidence in handling intricate issues of public and private finance, also encouraged speculation, belief that wealth was the only real criterion of worth, and relative indifference to the means by which wealth was obtained. This was partly what Dr. Johnson meant when he said later that Whiggism was the negation of all principles. Above all, perhaps, the very success with which England had ridden out the storms of war and acquired, in contrast to France, the reputation of immense skill and reliability in matters of finance, had encouraged myopia about the economic limits to financial projects, and disregard of the country's relatively limited and recent experience in handling them. The failure of many private companies since 1688 and the doubtful success of several government taxes and loans were conveniently forgotten. Before the end of 1720 they were to be bitterly remembered.

The initial stimulus to the South Sea Company's proposals in 1719 about the National Debt came from France, where since 1716 the star of John Law, the Scottish exile and exponent of monetary reform, had been steadily rising. Law's 'system', established with Court favour in the teeth of bitter opposition from the financial establishment in Paris, centred on the union of three monopolies: a note-issuing central bank with provincial branches, the Banque Royale, December 1718; a universal trading company, the Compagnie des Indes, May 1719;[1] and the lease of the greater part of the collection of indirect taxes, the General Farms, in August 1719. Law aimed in the longer run at stimulating the French economy by providing liberal finance for domestic investment and foreign trade. In the shorter run he had a different and politically more exciting motive. He hoped to pay off the whole of the French government's debts by encouraging the holders to exchange them for the rapidly appreciating shares of the India Company. New shares would be created as required. This part of the plan was successfully launched in October 1719.[2] The English Ambassador at Paris, Lord Stair, nervously

than on the financial details. None of these accounts is satisfactory on the financial reconstruction which followed the Bubble.

[1] This company was popularly though inaccurately called the 'Mississippi Company', the slang name for the *Compagnie d' Occident* ceded to Law in September 1717.

[2] Law's 'system' is described in E. Levasseur, *Recherches historiques sur le système de Law* (Paris, 1854); there is a convenient summary in Lavisse, *Histoire de la France*, VIII (1908), ii. 21 ff. Cf. also the stimulating discussion by H. Lüthy, *La Banque Protestante en France. I. Dispersion et Regroupement (1685-1730)* (1959), ch. iii. J. Vilain, 'Heurs et malheurs de la spéculation (1716-1722)', *Revue d'histoire moderne et contemporaine*, vol. 4 (1957), 121, and J. van Klaveren, 'Rue de Quincampoix und Exchange Alley. Die

reported to his government in the previous month that Law openly declared he would put France in a position to give the law to all Europe, and concluded his dispatch by urging the necessity 'in the mean time, to exert ourselves with all imaginable vigour, to find some immediate relief from the pressure of our public debt'.[1]

Since the end of the war in 1713 successive English Ministries had done much to lessen the burden of the debts contracted during it. In particular, short-term debts had been largely cleared by turning them into long-term Government stock, and the interest on all long-term debts, with the exception of the annuities for lives and terms of years, had been reduced to 5% in 1717.[2] The exception, however, was important. The government's debts fell into four main categories: short-dated ones such as Exchequer and Navy bills; government stock at 4% and 5% which could be repaid at a year's notice; the debts owed to the Bank, the East India Company, and the South Sea Company, which could also be redeemed on giving sufficient notice; and the annuities for lives and for terms of years. The annuities for single lives, originally created under William III and Anne, had largely been voluntarily converted into long annuities by 1720, and those for two and three lives, amounting to about £45,000 p.a., were not included in the South Sea scheme.

The long annuities, which yielded their holders nearly 7% on the original capital lent, were due to run out between 1792 and 1807. The short annuities, which yielded 9%, were due to expire in 1742.[3] Contemporaries called both types Irredeemables, since the Government could not, without the annuitants' consent, terminate or reduce the annuities. And there was naturally no reason for the annuitants to consent. If the government unilaterally terminated or reduced its payments — as French kings had often done — it would break faith with its creditors and imperil all future loans. It could, of course, offer the annuitants a capital sum, in cash or new stock, in lieu of their annuities. But for this to be attractive enough to be accepted the government would have to offer terms so disadvantageous to itself that even after the exchange it would be paying as high an interest as before. This was presumably why the inclusion of such an offer in the great conversion

Spekulationsjahre 1719 und 1720 in Frankreich und England', *Vierteljahrschrift für Sozial- und Wirtschaftsgeschichte*, vol. 48 (1961), 329, are two recent articles on aspects of the problem.

[1] Stair to Secretary Craggs, 9 September 1719, *Miscellaneous State Papers*, ed. Hardwicke (2 vols., 1778), ii. 594. For Law's boasts about French power see above, p. 22.

[2] For details see the preceding chapter.

[3] For the rates at which the original loans were made see above, p. 48.

TABLE 9

Government Long-term Debts at Michaelmas 1719
(excluding life annuities)

		£	£
1) *Owed to companies*			
(a) Bank of England		3,375,028	
(b) East India Company		3,200,000	
(c) South Sea Company		11,746,844	
			18,321,872
(2) *Redeemable Government stock*			16,546,202
(3) *Annuities for terms of years*			
(a) Long annuities, £666,566 p.a., at 20 years' purchase*		13,331,322	
(b) Short annuities, £121,669 p.a., at 14 years' purchase*		1,703,366	
			15,034,688
			49,902,762

Source : BPP (1898), lii. For details of (2) and (3) see below, App. B.
* The market price.

plan of 1717 was in the end discarded.[1] Something more than a flat exchange was needed to induce the annuitants to move on terms advantageous to the Exchequer. The bait which was dangled before them in 1720 was capital appreciation. They were offered in exchange for their annuities not money, nor Government stock, but new South Sea Company stock, the value of which was rapidly increasing. Two-thirds of them were to swallow the bait.

II

By the autumn of 1719 the South Sea Company had for nearly a year been cut off by war with Spain from its trade with the New World.[2] The outlook for it was unpromising. Its trade to Spanish America, of which such high hopes had been entertained, seemed likely, in the face of natural obstacles and Spanish intransigence, to be a liability rather than an asset. It was

[1] See above, p. 85.   [2] War had been declared on 28 December 1718.

certainly not to be compared with the rich markets which the East India Company was able to tap. At home, the company had no alternative basis for expansion such as the banking monopoly on which the Bank of England's prosperity was founded, or the rapidly growing fire-insurance business which was to make the fortunes of the new Sun Fire Office. John Law's Compagnie des Indes had too many sources of wealth to be able to exploit any of them properly; the South Sea Company had too few. But it could perhaps find a way out of its dilemma by securing Government backing for a scheme to ease the burden of the National Debt. If it could initiate and carry through a proposal of this kind, it could win great profit and great prestige. The government, alarmed by Law's success in the same direction, was favourably disposed to listen to such proposals; while some members of it, particularly John Aislabie, the Chancellor of the Exchequer, and the elder James Craggs, the joint Postmaster-General,[1] had for some years had fairly close contacts with the leading South Sea directors. In the confident, indeed strident, atmosphere of 1719 the viability of the South Sea Company's proposals and the moral and political implications of its influence with members of the government of the day were unlikely to be too closely examined. A tidal wave of speculation and company flotation, initiated in Paris, was already beginning to rise in all the leading commercial centres of Europe.[2] It was against this background that the comedy of the 'South Sea Scheme', so quickly to develop into farce, then tragedy, was begun.

Neither the Treasury Board minutes nor those of the South Sea Company refer to the latter's proposals until the middle of January 1720.[3] It seems likely from Aislabie's later statements, however, that the matter had been discussed between members of the Government and the leading South Sea directors in the summer and autumn of 1719.[4] In November 1719 one of

[1] The other Postmaster was Lord Cornwallis. An Act of 1710 made it obligatory for one holder of the office to sit in the Lords.

[2] See below, pp. 137 ff.

[3] The South Sea Directors' Court Minutes for 1718–20 are in Add. MS. 25,498. The Treasury Board Minutes for March 1718 to April 1722 are in P.R.O. T 29/24 (i) and (ii). From 23 July 1719 to 5 February 1720 the Treasury Board met thirty-nine times. Sunderland, the First Lord, attended only eight meetings; Aislabie, the Chancellor of the Exchequer, only missed one. Sunderland was frequently absent from meetings even in the critical period November 1720 to April 1721. This must have put Aislabie in virtual control of the Treasury.

[4] The only evidence about the genesis of the company's proposals is *The Secret History of the South Sea Scheme*, published under John Toland's name but written by one of the South Sea directors, evidently in 1721, and the speeches made in Parliament by Aislabie on 19 and 20 July 1721 against the Bill to confiscate part of his estate; *Parl. Hist.* x. 863–92.

these directors, John Blunt, having failed to gain access to Lord Sunderland, presented to Lord Stanhope a plan to incorporate the whole of the National Debt, including the debts owed to the Bank of England and the East India Company, into the South Sea Company. The details of this proposal are not known, but it must have followed the same lines as the scheme later accepted. Blunt's argument was that John Law had copied the South Sea conversion of lottery tickets in 1719; he would now outdo Law.[1] Stanhope was cool, and referred Blunt to the Chancellor of the Exchequer, John Aislabie, who may well have had a hand in drawing up the proposal in the first place. Sunderland was evidently by-passed.

The project had come into doubtful hands. Aislabie was described later by Arthur Onslow as

a man of good understanding . . . and very capable of business; but dark, and of a cunning that rendered him suspected and low in all men's opinion. . . . He was much set upon increasing his fortune and did that.[2]

He brought into the discussions with the company his colleague the elder James Craggs, who was joint Postmaster-General, and William Clayton, one of the Treasury commissioners. The chief South Sea representatives were Blunt himself, Sir George Caswall, who was not a director but was an old ally of Blunt and a director of the Sword Blade Bank, with which the company kept part of its cash, Francis Hawes, a South Sea director, and the company's cashier, Robert Knight.[3] Craggs, according to Onslow and, later, Shelburne, was able but unscrupulous.[4] He was, says Onslow, 'diligent close and unwearied in business . . . restrained by no scruples of conscience, by no danger or toil'.[5] Robert Surman, the company's deputy cashier, told the Parliamentary committee of inquiry in 1721 that

The Toland pamphlet is included in des Maizeaux (ed.), *The Miscellaneous Works of Mr. John Toland* (2 vols., 1747), i. 404. References to the pamphlet below are to this edition. Dr. Plumb's statement (*Walpole*, i. 297), that negotiations between the company and the Government began in November 1718 is presumably a slip for November 1719.

[1] *Secret History*, pp. 406–8. The pamphlet mentions no one by name. Sunderland is referred to as 'the prime Minister', Stanhope as 'one of the Secretaries of State, who had been at the head of the Treasury'.

[2] H.M.C., *14th Rep.*, app. ix, *Onslow MSS.*, p. 510. Cf. K. Darwin, 'John Aislabie 1670–1742', *Yorks. Arch. J.* xxxvii (1950), 262.

[3] *Parl. Hist.* x. 883, and Sir Theodore Janssen's statements to the Committee of Secrecy on 20 and 26 January 1721, *The Reports of the Honourable the Committee of Secrecy . . . exactly set forth. By A[rchibald] H[utcheson]*, undated [1721], p. iii. For the South Sea Company's directors and servants see below, pp. 112 f.

[4] H.M.C., *Onslow MSS.*, p. 511; Fitzmaurice, *Shelburne* (1912), i. 31.

[5] *Onslow MSS.*, loc. cit.

during the time that the Proposals of the South Sea Company and the Bill thereto relating, were depending in Parliament, he observed the said Mr. Craggs more frequently with Mr. Knight than any Body else; and believes he influenced Mr. Knight in many things relating to Stock, and Subscriptions.[1]

News of the negotiations leaked into the London Press early in 1720. On 2 January 1720 the *St. James's Weekly Journal* reported that

We hear the South-Sea Company have in a manner agreed with the Treasury for taking into their Capital the Annuities of 99 Years; and that the East-India Company have laid a Proposal before the Treasury for taking in the Annuities of 9 per Cent. per Ann. given in the Year 1710. Both which Contracts will be very advantageous to the Government, and beneficial to both Companies.[2]

London gossip was less respectful. 'The town says', wrote Thomas Brodrick, M.P. for Stockbridge, to his brother Lord Midleton on 24 January 1720,

the bargaine with the South Sea Company was agreed att his [Attorney-General Lechmere's] chambers, between Mr. Aislaby, sir George Caswell, and three or four other South Sea-men; since which, they say Mr. Aislaby has bought 27,000*l.* stock.[3]

The newspaper report about the East India Company seems to have been unfounded; in December 1720 the company claimed that 'their Adventurers . . . no ways contributed to the late Unhappy Circumstances'.[4] The rumour about Aislabie was true. His broker Matthew Wymondesold bought £20,000 stock for him on 30 January 1720, a further £10,000 on 10 February, and £20,000 more on 1 March. By the end of June the purchases totalled £77,000. All was quickly sold for the rise.[5] Aislabie was also buying Bank of England stock on a large scale in December 1719, which he sold at a profit in 1720.[6] And shortly afterwards he was involved in, and benefited by, the massive bribery which helped secure parliamentary approval for the South Sea Company's proposals. The company's plans had thus already secured important backing by the time they were first officially clarified in its Directors' Court Minutes on 21 January 1720.[7]

---

[1] *HCJ* xix. 520, 3rd Report of the Committee of Secrecy, 21 April 1721.

[2] *St. James's Weekly Journal*, 2 January 1720.   [3] Coxe, *Walpole*, ii. 183.

[4] East India G. Ct. Bk. i, f. 217, 22 December 1720.

[5] *HCJ* xix. 440 shows Wymondesold's account for Aislabie, who sold out rather too quickly, netting only £146,420. There are manuscript notes of Wymondesold's deposition in London Univ. MS. 89, f. 68, subf. 2, 1 February 1721.

[6] Bank stock ledger L for 1720, f. 5467, shows Aislabie's account (Bank of England Record Office). He bought £10,000 Bank stock from Sir George Caswall on 4 and 9 December 1719. He sold £6,000 of this on 7 January 1720 and the rest on 14 April 1720.

[7] For the company's bribery see below, p. 110.

On this date the Sub-Governor of the company, Sir John Fellowes, laid before the court 'A Paper which was handed to him from the Rt. Honble. the Chancellor of the Exchequer'.[1] The intention to 'take in' the debts owed to the Bank of England and the East India Company had by this stage been abandoned, a prudent modification, since the two companies would undoubtedly have resisted strongly.[2] The proposal followed the same line as the conversion of part of the Irredeemables into South Sea stock in April 1719, but it was extended to cover the Redeemable debts, with the exception of those owed to the two other monied companies.[3] The South Sea Company was to offer the holders of the Irredeemables and Redeemables new South Sea stock in exchange for their securities. For the privilege of making this offer, the company was to pay the government £1·5m. and, in addition, two years' purchase of all the Irredeemables exchanged. The maximum on this head would be £1,578,752, making the total payment to the state £3,078,752.[4] From the government's standpoint, however, the *raison d'être* of the scheme was not so much expectation of this premium but the hope that the annuitants would agree to take a lump sum in new South Sea stock in exchange for their annuities. For in this way the obstinate problem of the Irredeemables would at last be solved. The state would owe the South Sea Company an additional debt equal to the government securities exchanged for new South Sea stock. But it would pay interest on this at a lower rate, and, above all, could repay it when it had the means to do so. These implications of the company's first proposals were not spelled out in its minutes, but there is no doubt that they were perfectly well understood by those versed in financial affairs. As Robert Walpole, with his usual capacity to reduce complicated financial problems to essentials, put it in December 1720, the aim of the South Sea scheme was

to consult the landed and trading interest of the nation, by lessening its incumbrances and public debts, and putting them in a method of being paid off in a few years; which could not have been done, unless a way had been found to make the Annuities for long terms redeemable; which had been happily effected by the South-Sea Scheme, without a breach of parliamentary faith.[5]

The time-table of operations must have been precisely agreed between the

---

[1] Add. MS. 25498, f. 155, South Sea D. Ct. Bk. 21 January 1720.

[2] Their charters could not be terminated until the government had repaid its debts to them.

[3] For the conversion of 1719 see above, p. 88.

[4] Add. MS. 25498, ff. 155 f. See below, Appendix A.

[5] *Parl. Hist.* vii. 690, 20 December 1720.

government and the company, for the next day Aislabie, speaking in a Committee of the Whole House of Commons,

in pretty general terms, opened the South Sea company's scheme, of a proposal for putting the national debt in such a way of payment, as might effect it in the shortest time possible: this he gave us to understand, would bee 25 years.[1]

The younger James Craggs, perhaps briefed by his father, and certainly with Stair's urgings to repay England's debts in mind, spoke in support.[2] He said he assumed that all agreed the company might make its proposal. The members of the administration interested in the scheme obviously hoped to win this first position by a *coup de main*, counting on the attractiveness of any government proposal to relieve the nation of its debts, and perhaps also on the difficulty many independent members must have had in understanding the issues involved. Its hopes were disappointed. After a lengthy pause, Thomas Brodrick, our reporter of the debate, declared that

the first gentleman who spoake, seemed . . . to recommend the scheme nott onely in opposition, but even exclusively to all others, . . .

and suggested that proposals should be made by 'every other company, nay any other society of men'.[3] The House agreed that other proposals should be made. The government — and the company — had lost the first round. 'Our great men', wrote Brodrick to his brother, 'lookt as if thunderstruck, and one of them in particular, turned as pale as my cravate.'[4]

Although this asserted the principle of open tender, only the Bank of England, and perhaps the East India Company, had the financial resources to make an alternative and better offer. The East India Company made no move, but the Bank acted at once. At this date eight of its directors and two of its ex-directors were M.P.s.[5] Some of them must have been present at the debate on 22 January and at once alerted their Court of Directors, for on 23 January 1720 the latter resolved to propose to the General Court summoned for the 25th:

[1] Coxe, *Walpole*, ii. 181, Thomas Brodrick to his brother Lord Midleton, 24 January 1720. Brodrick dates the debate simply 'Friday'; this must have been 22 January, as 1720 was a leap year.

[2] Ibid. For Stair's warnings see above, p. 91.   [3] Coxe, op. cit. ii. 182.   [4] Ibid.

[5] Robert Bristow, Sir John Cope, Josiah Diston, Nathaniel Gould, Sir Gilbert Heathcote, John Rudge, Sir Thomas Scawen (the Deputy Governor), and Sir John Ward were the eight directors who were M.P.s in 1720; Richard Chiswell and Humphrey Morice, both M.P.s, were elected directors in 1718 and again in 1720, but from April 1719 to April 1720 were ineligible since only two-thirds of those chosen in one year could be re-elected the next. John Hanger, the Governor of the Bank, was not an M.P. in 1720.

That it may be for the Service of the Bank to make a Proposal to the Honble. the House of Commons upon their taking into Consideration that part of His Majesties Speech which relates to the Publick Debts.[1]

When the General Court met it gave full powers to the directors. The latter asked their own Committee of Treasury to draft a proposal, since the General Court ignored the suggestion that it should nominate members to join in the task. The draft proposal with some amendments was placed before the adjourned General Court on 27 January 1720. The Court empowered a committee of directors to fill up the blanks left for the amounts offered and to dispatch the proposal to the House of Commons. It was submitted to the Committee of the Whole House on the same day.[2] The General Court had thus virtually abdicated responsibility, and placed its interests blindly in the hands of its directors; fortunately for the Bank their offer was not accepted. The General Court of the South Sea Company acted in the same way. It met on 27 January 1720 at Merchant Taylors' Hall and gave its directors discretion to fill up the blanks in the company's new proposal, which was at once hurried to the House of Commons.[3] This reckless haste on the part of both companies' stockholders did not prevent them being extremely abusive about their directors later in the year. Thanks to the race between the Bank and the South Sea Company, the Committee of the Whole House thus received on the same day two tenders, each of which seemed to promise great benefits for the state.[4] It was reported in the Press that the committee had considered the South Sea Company's scheme

for taking in Annuities and other Government Securities into their Capital, upon which several Speeches were made in the House on that Behalf: On the other hand, Mr. Gould, Mr. Eyles, and Humphrey Morris, Esq, Directors of the Bank of England, made excellent Speeches on their Part.[5]

At this stage Aislabie evidently consulted Blunt about sharing the scheme between the two companies, but received the reply 'No, Sir, we will never divide the child.'[6]

[1] Bank of England D. Ct. Bk. H, f. 109, 23 January 1720.

[2] Ibid., ff. 109–13 and Bank G. Ct. Bk. ii, ff. 155–7. For the terms offered see below, Appendix A.

[3] Add. MS. 25498, ff. 158–61, South Sea D. Ct. Bk., 27 January 1720. There are no surviving minutes for South Sea General Courts until January 1721.

[4] See below, Appendix A.

[5] *Whitehall Evening Post*, 26–28 January 1720. Francis Eyles was a South Sea director, not a Bank director. Humphrey Morice was not a Bank director in 1720; see above, p. 98, n. 5.

[6] *Parl. Hist.* vii. 884, Aislabie's speech on 20 July 1721.

The House of Commons, hoping for still higher gains, gave both sides leave to amend their offers. On 1 February 1720, after approval by complaisant General Courts, the two new proposals were returned to the Committee of the Whole House.[1] After a warm debate, in which Aislabie supported the South Sea Company and Walpole the Bank of England, the committee decided to recommend the adoption of the South Sea proposal.[2] On the next day, 2 February 1720, the House of Commons agreed to this recommendation without dividing.[3] The South Sea directors meanwhile thanked their Sub-Governor and Deputy-Governor for 'their great Care, Secrecy, and Prudence' in managing the proposal.[4] Its terms showed how high the failure to carry Parliament at the first attack had raised the stakes in the game of financial poker now begun. The company engaged to pay the state £4m. for the privilege of making an offer to the government creditors. It also engaged to pay four and a half years' purchase on all the annuities exchanged for new South Sea stock by 1 March 1722 and, in addition, one year's purchase on any long annuities not exchanged by that date. The maximum payable was £7,567,503.[5] On 16 February 1720, perhaps as a calculated offset to this increase in the premium asked, the Commons resolved to lend the company £1m. in Exchequer bills; these were handed over early in June.[6]

As a result of 'setting the nation up to auction', as Aislabie later put it, the possible gains to the state had thus increased from a maximum of £3m. to a maximum of £7·5m. within a fortnight.[7] This was thought a fine achievement. 'Whoever had heard', wrote Thomas Brodrick to his brother on 2 February 1720,

how highly the first scheme was applauded, how earnestly recommended for our acceptance, and how very near it was to bee soe, would stand amased, that ever the publique (in any instance) should be soe fortunate as to more than double the summe intended for them; butt thus it has for once happened.[8]

---

[1] Bank D. Ct. Bk. H, f. 30, 1 February 1720 (a committee of four directors appointed to amend the proposal, after the session of the General Court); Add. MS. 25498, ff. 162–7, South Sea D. Ct. Bk., 29 January and 2 February 1720. For the revised terms offered see below, Appendix A.

[2] Parl. Hist. vii. 640.   [3] Ibid. and HCJ xix. 248.

[4] Add. MS. 25498, f. 165, South Sea D. Ct. Bk., 2 February 1720.

[5] See below, Appendix A. The South Sea Act incorporating the company's proposals is discussed below, pp. 103–5.

[6] The bills were to be lent to the company at 5%. See below, p. 141, for the use to which they were put.

[7] Aislabie's phrase is in his speech of 20 July 1721; Parl. Hist. vii. 884.

[8] Coxe, Walpole, ii. 185, Thomas Brodrick to Lord Midleton, 2 February 1720.

Brodrick was no doubt thinking that his own intervention on 22 January 1720 had set the auction going. The majority in Parliament clearly shared his opinion that an advantageous bargain had been struck. Cooler reflection might have prompted different conclusions. The South Sea Company had not made its original offer from altruism, but for profit and power. The more it had to pay the state, the less profit it could keep for itself, unless it could weight the terms of the proposed exchange markedly against the government's creditors.[1] If, for example, the whole £31m. of subscribable debts were exchanged for £15·5m. new South Sea stock valued at 200, the South Sea Company would be entitled to increase its nominal capital by £31m., but would only be obliged to assign £15·5m. of this to the public creditors. It could sell the other £15·5m. at the highest possible price. Its profit would come from the difference between the proceeds of this sale and the sum payable to the government. Thus the larger the sum payable to the Exchequer, the higher the market price of stock had to be for the company to get the same profit. Unfortunately, the increased size of the premium payable to the Exchequer was by no means the only motive for the South Sea directors to push up the market price of stock. For the ratio of exchange was not defined in advance. If, therefore, prices could be got up to 300, 400, or over, and the government's creditors agreed to an exchange at this level, the amount of the new stock that the company could sell for its own account would steadily increase. For example, if the whole £31m. of subscribable debts were exchanged for only £7·75m. new South Sea stock valued at 400, the company, which would as before be entitled to increase its capital by £31m., could sell the remaining £23·25m. stock in a rising market. Conversely, if the price of South Sea stock remained too low, the whole scheme would be in danger of foundering. For the government's creditors would not agree to a disadvantageous exchange unless they had the prospect of reselling on a rising market. And even if they did the company would not be able to sell the surplus stock to any advantage. Everything depended, therefore, on the 'rise of the stocks'.

These dangers were partly foreseen as soon as the details of the proposals were published. In February 1720 it was pointed out that the company's profit, over and above the £7·5m. due to the government, would depend on a rise in the price of its stock. Since its trade did not justify such a rise, the scheme put a premium on stock-jobbing.[2] In March, Archibald Hutcheson, M.P. for Hastings and a consistent opponent of the scheme, asked whether

[1] The debts available for exchange are set out in Appendix B, below.
[2] *An Examination and Explanation of the South-Sea Company's Scheme for taking in the Publick Debts* (17 February 1720).

If the Truth be, as I verily believe it is, that there is no real Foundation for the present, much less for the further expected, high Price of South-Sea Stock, and that the Frenzy which now reigns, can be of no long Continuance . . . is not the Duty of a British Senate to take all necessary Precautions, to prevent the Ruin of many Thousands of Families?[1]

Another pamphlet, written either in February or March 1720, favoured the Bank of England's proposals, and cast doubts on the South Sea Company's ability to fulfil its contract unless it was able to drive up the price of its stock.[2] The newspaper *The Theatre* computed in its issue of 29 March–2 April 1720 that South Sea stock, currently at over 200, was not intrinsically worth more than 140, while on 2 April *The Weekly Journal* included an elaborate calculation of the losses to which the scheme would lead. But the tide of speculation was already swelling to a flood, and few paid attention to these warning voices. As Aislabie later put it, from the time the market started to rise,

it became difficult to govern it; and let those gentlemen that opened the flood-gates wonder at the deluge that ensued as much as they please, it was not in one man's power, or in the power of the whole administration, to stop it, considering how the world was borne away by the torrent.[3]

The Bill incorporating the South Sea Company's proposals was read for the first time on 17 March 1720.[4] On 21 March it was committed by 201 votes to 131.[5] On the 23rd there was a warm debate on a motion that the company should define in advance the amount of new stock it would give the government creditors in exchange for their stock and annuities.[6] Had this course of action, which the Bank of England had been willing to follow in its own proposals, been adopted, the worst features of the subsequent speculation might have been avoided. The company's supporters preferred to take the view that it would make the whole scheme impracticable.[7] In

[1] [Archibald Hutcheson], *Some Calculations Relating to the Proposals made by the South-Sea Company* (1720), p. 8, preface dated 31 March 1720. Hutcheson was later a member of the Commons' Committee of Secrecy appointed to inquire into the Bubble; see below, p. 171.

[2] [John Trenchard], *A Comparison between the Proposals of the Bank and the South-Sea Company* (1720).

[3] *Parl. Hist.* vii. 885, speech of 20 July 1721.   [4] *HCJ* xix. 304.

[5] Ibid. 315. On 19 March accounts of the Irredeemables and Redeemables, ordered on the 18th, were presented to the House; ibid. 305, 312–14.

[6] Ibid. 317.

[7] *An Argument to shew the Disadvantage That would Accrue to the Publick, From obliging the South-Sea Company To fix what Capital Stock They will give for the Annuities* (1720).

the debate, Nathaniel Gould, Mr. Pitt, Sir Richard Steele, and Horatio and Robert Walpole supported the motion, and John Aislabie, Sir Joseph Jekyll, Thomas Pelham, and William Yonge attacked it.[1] It was finally defeated by 244 votes to 140.[2] On the same day petitions from the merchants of London and from the Corporation of Liverpool asking that the South Sea Company should be restricted to the trade first granted it, lest it should 'oppress all private Merchants in any Branch of Trade', were ordered to lie on the table.[3] On 2 April 1720 the amended Bill was read for a third time, passed by 172 votes to 55, and sent to the House of Lords.[4] It was read there a first and second time on 4 April, and committed on 5 April by 83 votes to 17. Lord Cowper, Lord North and Grey, and the Duke of Wharton were the Bill's chief critics; they and eight others of the minority entered a Protest.[5] On 7 April the Bill was read a third time and received the royal assent the same day.[6] Its merits and demerits had by this stage been debated at some length both inside and outside Parliament. Attendance in the Commons had been 332 (out of a total membership of 558) on 21 March, and 384 in the important debate of 23 March, falling off to 227 at the third reading. These figures denoted considerable interest by contemporary standards. It is worth noting, on the other hand, that the *Commons Journals* give the impression that while this measure, soon to disturb the peace of three kingdoms, was being passed, the House was more concerned with the campaign of the weavers against imported Indian calicoes, which was just reaching a violent climax.[7]

The South Sea Act (6 Geo. I, c. 4) was drafted by a parliamentary committee under the direction of the senior Treasury Secretary, William Lowndes, M.P. for St. Mawes. Certain South Sea directors were asked to assist the committee.[8] The Act had ninety-eight sections and took up thirty-

---

[1] *Parl. Hist.* vii. 644–5. It is not known which of the four Pitts in the House Mr. Pitt was.

[2] *HCJ* xix. 317. *Parl. Hist.* (loc. cit.) says 144 to 140.   [3] *HCJ* xix. 317.   [4] Ibid. 327–8.

[5] *HLJ* xxi. 288, 290. The Lords who protested were Aylesford, Bingley, Boyle, Castleton, Cowper, Haversham, Maynard, North and Grey, Warrington, Westmorland, and Wharton.

[6] Ibid. 294, 296.

[7] *HCJ* xix, index under 'Accounts' and 'Calicoes', nearly ninety entries; 'South Sea Company' (ibid. under 'Supply') has only half this number of references. For the weavers' campaign see below, p. 137.

[8] Add. MS. 25498, f. 167, South Sea D. Ct. Bk., 2 February 1720, appointment of the two governors and eleven directors, with a quorum of four, to take care of the company's interest in the Bill. For their co-operation with Lowndes's committee, see ibid., f. 172, 24 February and 14 March 1720. The minutes of the South Sea directors' committee are in H.L.R.O. Parchment Coll., South Sea Company papers, Box 167.

five pages in the printed statutes. It can be divided into three parts. The first consisted of a detailed examination of the debts affected. These were stated to be £666,821 p.a. long annuities, £127,260 p.a. short annuities (the two together comprising the Irredeemables), and £16,546,482 Redeemable stock.[1] The Exchequer life annuities and the debts owed to the Bank of England and East India Company were excluded from the Act. The next section gave the South Sea Company powers to 'take in, either by Purchase or Subscriptions' the debts previously described. As far as the Irredeemables were concerned, this was to be done 'without any Compulsion on any of the said Proprietors . . . at such Price . . . as shall be agreed' between them and the company. The Redeemables were to be subscribed (exchanged for new South Sea stock) or discharged in cash, at the owners' option. The Bank and Exchequer were to prepare schedules of the public creditors' names and the amounts they owned and send them to the South Sea Company. Early in May the Treasury named the latter's directors to be the managers for the scheme; this effectively put supervision of it in the hands of those who stood to gain most from its execution.[2]

The third part of the Act covered the terms of the bargain. The company was to be entitled to increase its nominal capital by £2,000 for each £100 p.a. long annuity exchanged for new South Sea stock and by £1,400 for each £100 p.a. short annuity exchanged.[3] (These were the ruling market prices for long and short annuities respectively.) The increase for Redeemables was to be £100 for each £100 exchanged or paid off in cash. Since the total of the debts subscribable, if the annuities were capitalized at these prices, was £31·5m., if all were exchanged or paid off the company's nominal capital, and the debt owed to it by the government, would both increase by this amount. The government agreed to pay interest on the increased debt partly at 5% and partly at 4% until midsummer 1727. From then on the whole debt due to the company was to be reduced to a flat 4%. On its part, the company agreed to pay its premium, now increased from £4m. to £4,156,306, at the four quarter-days of 1721.[4] It was also to pay four and a half years' purchase on *all* Irredeemables exchanged, and one year's purchase

[1] These figures were based on the accounts submitted to Parliament on 18 March 1720, above p. 102, n. 5. They were later slightly modified; see below, Appendix B.

[2] The Treasury Commission naming the directors as Managers was dated 6 May 1720; *Parl. Hist.* vii. 698.

[3] For details see below, Appendix A.

[4] The increase in the premium was probably due to the fact that the company had originally overestimated the amount of the Irredeemables (on which it was to pay four and a half years' purchase, as above), so less could be expected on this head.

on all *long* annuities *not* exchanged by 1 March 1722; these variable payments were to be made at the four quarter-days of 1722. Finally, the
company assumed a liability to circulate up to £1m. Exchequer bills gratis
to midsummer 1727. These were the same bills which the state had promised
to lend the company — and which it in turn intended to lend to its proprietors in order to increase the demand for South Sea stock. This acquisition
of the Bank of England's Exchequer bill contract must have seemed at the
time another triumph which the company could chalk up against Threadneedle Street. But the contract, like the rest of the proposals, was to be
signally mishandled.[1]

III

After the South Sea scheme ignominiously collapsed, there were frequent
insinuations that Parliament had only approved it because Members had a
personal interest in its success, or because they were the docile tools of a
corrupt Ministry. Another interpretation of their complaisance in face of
the scheme's obvious dangers was that they were not competent to handle
such complex matters at all. As a pamphleteer later observed,

the gentlemen who compose the lower house of parliament are most of them
descended from antient families, and live on their patrimonial estates. They are
unacquainted with figures and calculations in matters of so complicated a nature as
the present accumulation of public debts.[2]

The social structure of the House of Commons which passed the South
Sea Act, and the investments of Members of both Houses during the Bubble,
show that though there was a grain of truth in these charges, none of them
can be accepted without serious reservations. Allowing for the usual difficulties of classification, the number of placemen in the Commons at the
beginning of 1720, appears to have been 122.[3] This 'Treasury interest' was

[1] For the lending-out of the Exchequer bills see below, p. 141; for the company's
neglect of its contract see below, p. 380. The Exchequer bill contract returned to the Bank
of England in 1722.

[2] *A Dispassionate Remonstrance of the Nature ... of the Laws ... for the Reduction of
Interest* (1751), p. 8.

[3] This section is based on *The British Representative* (1734), and R. Beatson, *Political
Index* (2 vols., 1788); *Chronological Register of the British Parliament* (3 vols., 1807). As none
of these gives the exact dates at which offices were assumed and relinquished, the figures in
the text have an element of uncertainty.

not a reliable and united band of voters. Only about half its members were among the 140 M.P.s still sitting in January 1720 who had voted for the Stanhope–Sunderland administration in both the critical divisions of 1719, the repeal of the Occasional Conformity Act, and the Peerage Bill.[1] Some of its members were among the 162 M.P.s still sitting in January 1720 who had voted against the administration on both these measures. Ministers, unable to rely on a hard core of voters to anything like the same extent as their modern successors, counted for support in critical divisions on the Scottish M.P.s and on the 'independent' Members, who normally regarded it as their duty to support the Crown. The Opposition was probably equally indeterminate in composition. Unfortunately no lists survive for the two divisions in March 1720 when first 131, then 140, M.P.s opposed the South Sea Bill. It is therefore not possible to say how many of these opponents belonged to the group of 162 Members sitting in January 1720 who had opposed the administration on the two key Bills of 1719.

To what extent were Members unskilled in business affairs? From what sort of social background did they come? At the end of January 1720, when Parliament began to discuss the South Sea Company's proposals, sixteen M.P.s were Irish peers, thirty-eight were the sons or brothers of English peers, nine were sons of Irish or Scots peers, and 104 were baronets. There was also a considerable number of independent country gentlemen, perhaps as many as 100. In addition to this landed interest in the House, however, there was a substantial minority of Members drawn from trade, finance, and the professions. There were fifty-eight merchants or financiers, including eight directors of the Bank of England, nine East India directors, and four South Sea directors.[2] This representation of the monied companies seems to have caused a good deal of latent irritation, and in February 1721 advantage was taken of the South Sea Company's collapse to move that in future

---

[1] The two votes were in January 1719 (Conformity) and December 1719 (Peerage). The division lists are printed in R. Chandler, *History and Proceedings of the House of Commons* (1742), viii, appendix.

[2] The Bank: Robert Bristow, Sir John Cope, Josiah Diston, Nathaniel Gould, Sir Gilbert Heathcote, John Rudge, Sir Thomas Scawen, Sir John Ward. There were also two ex-directors; see above, p. 98, n. 5. The East India Company: William Aislabie (brother of the Chancellor of the Exchequer), Sir Matthew Decker, Sir John Eyles, Sir Richard Gough, Edward Harrison, Thomas Heath, John Heathcote, Joseph Herne, and Samuel Shepheard (directors elected April 1719; Boyer's *Political State*, xvii. 445). The South Sea Company: Sir Robert Chaplin, Bart., Francis Eyles, Sir Theodore Janssen, Bart., Jacob Sawbridge (see below, pp. 112 ff.). Arthur Ingram, M.P., was only the namesake of the South Sea director Arthur Ingram of York Buildings.

2. Sir John Houblon, first Governor of the Bank of England

3. William Lowndes, Secretary to the Treasury 1695–1724

directors of all three companies should be debarred not merely from sitting in, but also from voting for, Parliament. It is indicative of the temper of the time that the motion was defeated by fewer than fifty votes in a crowded House.[1] Besides the financial and commercial interests in the House at the beginning of 1720, there were at least thirty-nine practising lawyers, thirty-three Army officers and five naval officers.[2] The Commons in 1720 was thus less connected with the peerage, and less weighted with monied and professional men, than it was to become by the close of the Seven Years War, and in this still showed traces of the 'independent' Parliaments of Charles II's reign, but it contained a substantial minority of businessmen and lawyers used to unravelling complex financial and commercial problems. A number of Members, largely coinciding with this business and professional group, were already holders of government securities by 1720; so was a much smaller minority in the House of Lords.[3]

Whether well qualified by previous experience or not, Members of both Houses of Parliament were active participants during 1720 in the issues and loans made by the South Sea Company.[4] The records from which their activities can be traced are not free from suspicion but are the only ones available. Including amongst peers a handful of Irish and Scottish peers not sitting in Parliament, the figures seem to have been as shown in Table 10.

Those involved came from all political groups and social backgrounds. Eighteen M.P.s appear in all four subscriptions and the loan; one of these was the prominent Tory Sir John Hynde Cotton. Most members of the government took the plunge, including Aislabie, Argyll, both Craggs, Hampden the Navy Treasurer, Stanhope, Townshend,

---

[1] *HCJ* xix. 422. The voting was 211 to 164.

[2] Taking lawyers' names from the (incomplete) printed records of the Inns of Court and omitting eleven further names which are doubtful. In view of Professor Walcott's estimate that sixty-two lawyers sat in the Parliament of 1701, the estimate of thirty-nine for 1720 may be too low (R. Walcott, *English Politics in the Early Eighteenth Century* (Oxford, 1956), pp. 168 ff.). Eight of the army officers were governors and two were Admiralty Commissioners. These are included in the total of 122 placemen.

[3] See below, p. 280.

[4] The subscriptions and loans are discussed below, pp. 123 ff. The figures for M.P.s and peers involved in the Bubble are usually given as 462 and 122 (e.g. by Scott, op. cit. iii. 332). These derive from a pamphlet published in 1722, *Index Rerum et Vocabulorum for the use of the Freeholders of Counties and Freemen of Corporations*. The writer had evidently only used the books for the second and third subscriptions and for the loan. His estimate for peers is therefore too low. His estimate for M.P.s is too high, as it includes relatives who were not Members.

E

TABLE 10

Members of Parliament and peers whose names are in the books for the South Sea Company loan and subscriptions in 1720

	1st money subscription		2nd money subscription		3rd money subscription	
	Nos.	£	Nos.	£	Nos.	£
M.P.s	128	292,700	190	225,200	352	572,700
Peers*	58	168,000	73	127,500	119	222,500
	186	460,700	263	352,700	471	795,200

	4th Money subscription		Loan		Total	
	Nos.	£	Nos.	£	Net Nos.	£
M.P.s	76	48,500	132	1,133,545	401	2,272,645
Peers*	56	28,500	64	685,715	177	1,232,215
	132	77,000	196	1,819,260	578	3,504,860

Source: South Sea Company copy subscription books and loan register, H.L.R.O. Parchment Coll., B 57–63, and South Sea Company Papers, Box 167. It appears from the reports of the parliamentary Committee of Secrecy in 1721 that the lists are far from perfect and that the company falsely inserted or excluded many names.

* Includes a few Irish and Scottish peers not sitting in Parliament.

and Walpole.[1] None of them, however, appears in the company's loan register.

In interpreting these figures, several points must be borne in mind. Ministers came into the subscriptions because they were included in the government lists, and were probably expected to subscribe; presumably this is why Townshend and Walpole, who only rejoined the government in June 1720, were not in the first two subscriptions held in April.[2] Valuation

[1] Argyll and Stanhope were thought not to be 'in the stocks'; Drummond to D. Pulteney, 24 November 1720, cit. Coxe, *Walpole*, ii. 197.

[2] For the lists by which subscriptions were filled up see below, p. 126.

TABLE II

Members of the government involved in South Sea subscriptions in 1720

	Subscriptions					
Name	*First* £	*Second* £	*Third* £	*Fourth* £	*Total* £	*Valued at* £900
John Aislabie	4,000	5,000	4,000	..	13,000	117,000
Duke of Argyll	4,000	2,000	2,000	500	8,500	76,500
James Craggs, Sen.	4,000	..	2,000	..	6,000	54,000
James Craggs, Jr.	4,000	5,000	2,000	..	11,000	99,000
Richard Hampden	3,000	2,000	3,000	500	8,500	76,500
Lord Stanhope	4,000	4,000	2,000	..	10,000	90,000
Lord Sunderland	4,000	5,000	4,000	..	13,000	117,000
Lord Townshend	..	..	2,000	500	2,500	22,500
Robert Walpole	..	..	2,000	..	2,000	18,000

Source : See Table 10.

of the stock held at a top market price makes it seem more valuable than it was, since this price did not rule for long, and safe buyers prepared to pay cash down must have been the exception rather than the rule. Further, all subscriptions were only fractionally paid up by the autumn of 1720, so that holders would have been subject to further calls over a long period. As against all this is the likelihood (the matter was never examined) that Ministers sold their scrip at advanced prices as soon as they got it. Moreover, their speculation may not have been limited to the company's subscriptions. At least one Minister, the great John Hampden's great-grandson Richard, who was Treasurer of the Navy, used official balances for speculation in South Sea stock and had to be sold up in the mid-1720s. Several Masters in Chancery used suitors' funds for the same purpose.[1] It is worth noting one point in conclusion. Walpole was frequently accused of supporting the Bank of England because he had large holdings of its stock. In February 1722 he told the House of Commons that this rumour was quite untrue, and that he had 'for a long time' held not a penny of Bank stock. He added that he owned considerable amounts of South Sea stock.[2] The stock ledgers show that this

[1] For Hampden's case and the Chancery Masters see below, pp. 173, 292.
[2] *Parl. Hist.* vii. 965.

statement, disappointingly for his opponents, was true. In 1712 he had sold £1,000 Bank stock bought in 1711. After this he held no Bank stock until his death in 1745. At midsummer 1723, on the other hand, he held £14,237 South Sea stock, part of which he later sold.[1]

In one way or another, Members of both Houses thus became extensively involved in South Sea speculation, and probably burned their fingers in doing so. This partly accounts for the fury of Parliament against the South Sea Company and its directors in 1721, and makes Walpole's achievement in blocking a complete recision of the whole scheme even more impressive.[2] But the passions aroused were not due merely to the knowledge that Ministers, like Members, had bought and sold stock and subscriptions. The Commons' Committee of Secrecy appointed in January 1721 discovered at once that the South Sea Company had ensured support while its Bill was passing through Parliament by the 'sale' of £574,500 South Sea stock to potential supporters at favourable prices. This stock was fictitious, 'the Company having at that time, in their own Right, only a small Quantity of Stock not exceeding Twenty-five thousand Pounds or Thirty Thousand Pounds at the most'.[3] It was disposed of by the cashier Knight and a directors' committee consisting of the Sub- and Deputy Governor, Blunt, Chester, Gibbon, and Houlditch.[4] According to Gibbon,

Mr. Knight said, He was to take upon himself the transacting that Stock; and the Persons to whom it was to be delivered, were to be accountable for the Price; But he was to transact this on the behalf of the Company; and the Persons who were to have it, might either have it transferred to them, or take the Difference.[5]

Gibbon meant that the recipients could choose to be paid the difference between the price at which they had 'received' the stock and the later market price if prices rose. As Sir Theodore Janssen told the Committee, the gossip in 'the Town' was that the bargains were to be good if stock rose, and void

[1] Bank of England Record Office, ledgers for Bank stock and South Sea Old Annuities. His holding of the latter was finally cleared in July 1732. The disposal of the other half of his South Sea holding in 1723 cannot be traced, as the ledgers for South Sea stock do not survive. (For the division into stock and annuities in 1723 see below, p. 181.)

[2] See below, p. 168.

[3] HCJ xix. 426, First Report of the Committee of Secrecy. The Committee returned to the subject in their Sixth Report, ibid. 568 ff. The episode is examined in detail in Scott, iii. 331–46.

[4] HCJ xix. 426.

[5] HCJ xix. 573, Sixth Report of the Committee of Secrecy.

if it fell.[1] No date was set for delivery of the stock 'sold', so that, as the committee reported,

> if the Price of Stock had fallen as might be expected if the Scheme had miscarried, no Loss could have been sustained by them [the 'buyers']; but if the Price of Stock should advance, as it actually did by the Success of the Scheme, the Difference by the advanced Price was to be made good to the pretended Purchasers: And accordingly, the Account of such Stock was made up, and adjusted with Mr. Knight; and the Money arising by the Difference of the Price, between the Times of such taking in, or holding, the Stock, and the making such Adjustments, was paid ... out of the Company's Cash to the pretended Purchasers.[2]

The names of these purchasers were left blank in the company's cash-book, but under examination it appeared that those accommodated included Sunderland, Aislabie, the elder Craggs, Charles Stanhope the junior Treasury Secretary (no one, presumably, dared to try to bribe the senior Secretary, Lowndes), and the king's reigning mistresses, the Duchess of Kendall and the Countess of Platen.[3] As to the others, the committee was only able to obtain cryptic hints. Knight, it was reported to them, 'used to keep an Account of the Stock thus disposed in a particular Book of his own'.[4] The recipients were 'Names not proper to be known to a great many', 'Persons of Distinction', 'Forty or Fifty of the Company's best Friends'.[5] Knight himself admitted that he 'did not think it proper to enter the Names of the Members of Parliament who had any Part of this Stock, in the Cash-book', but added that 'such Members did not know it was the Company's Stock'.[6] An inconclusive investigation which the Committee of Secrecy made in June 1721 into the purchases of twenty-eight M.P.s and five peers seems to confirm this.[7] Knight himself, 'only to avoid the Weight of the Enquiry, which I found too heavy for me', fled to the Austrian Netherlands on 21 January 1721.[8] The government in Vienna was able to block the English Parliament's angry demands for his extradition by relying on the statute of *Joyeuse Entrée* which Charles V had conceded to Brabant; they

---

[1] *The Reports of the Honourable the Committee of Secrecy ... exactly set forth. By A[rchibald] H[utcheson]*, n.d. [1721], p. iii, examination of Sir Theodore Janssen, 20 and 26 January 1721.

[2] *HCJ* xix. 426.   [3] Ibid. 425 ff.   [4] Ibid. 428.
[5] Ibid. 426–7.   [6] Ibid. 432.   [7] Ibid. 568–78.

[8] Knight's letter to the South Sea Company containing the phrase in the text is copied in the South Sea D. Ct. Bk. for 23 January 1721, Add. MS. 25499, f. 154. It is printed in *Parl. Hist.* vii. 707n. Parliament learned of Knight's 'withdrawal' on 23 January; *HCJ* xix. 406.

said they could not infringe it without risk of popular disturbance.[1] The real reason, however, according to Arthur Onslow, was that Sunderland had arranged, or at least connived at, Knight's flight, and had paid the acting Governor of the Netherlands, the Marquis de Prié, £50,000 from the Civil List to keep him safely.[2] Whether or not this was true, Ministers must have been very glad he was out of the way. There is no reason to think he was exaggerating when he declared that 'if he should disclose all he knew, it would open such a Scene as the World would be surprised at'.[3]

IV

During the winter and spring of 1720–1 when popular fury against the South Sea Company was at its height, and the Commons' Committee of Secrecy was exposing the doubtful background of the scheme's acceptance, no names or penalties were thought too severe for the South Sea directors, and these harsh judgements have become the judgements of history. Closer investigation shows that they cannot be accepted without considerable qualification. The Sub- and Deputy Governor and twenty-nine directors of the South Sea Company at the beginning of 1720 were for the most part men of wealth, substance, and reputation, with widespread business interests.[4] Some

---

[1] The letters and reports about Knight's possible extradition are in *HCJ* xix. 484 ff., 496 ff., 500–1, 509–12, 538–40.

[2] Onslow makes this statement 'on undoubted authority', H.M.C., *14th Rep.*, app. ix, *Onslow MSS.*, 507. The Governor-General of the Netherlands, Prince Eugène, lived in Vienna, corresponding with his deputy de Prié in Brussels. This was as well for Sunderland, for de Prié, an Italian, had the reputation of being bribable; Eugène of being incorruptible.

[3] *HCJ* xix. 436. For Knight's influence cf. below, p. 120; for his return to England in 1743 see below, p. 189.

[4] The Sub-Governor was Sir John Fellowes, the Deputy Governor Charles Joye. The directors were William Astell, Sir Lambert Blackwell, Bart., John Blunt, Sir Robert Chaplin, Bart., Sir William Chapman, Robert Chester, Stephen Child, Peter Delaporte, James Edmundson, Francis Eyles, Edward Gibbon, John Gore, Sir William Hamond, Francis Hawes, Richard Horsey, Richard Houlditch, Arthur Ingram, Sir Jacob Jacobsen, Sir Theodore Janssen, Bart., Sir John Lambert, Bart., Sir Harcourt Master, William Morley, Ambrose Page, Hugh Raymond, Samuel Reade, Jr., Thomas Reynolds, Jacob Sawbridge, William Tillard, and John Turner. The company's Governor was George I. The two previous Governors were Robert Harley, Earl of Oxford (1711–14), and Frederick, Prince of Wales (1714–18). The vacancy in the directorate created when the

were already very rich. The richest, Sir Theodore Janssen, was a Huguenot immigrant of burgher descent and a merchant prince of international standing. He had been a director of the Bank of England three times between 1694 and 1719. He said later that his estate was £300,000 long before the Bubble, 'which I thought enough; and therefore took no measures to increase it'.[1] Sir Lambert Blackwell had acquired land valued at over £40,000 before 1720. William Astell, Sir Robert Chaplin, Edward Gibbon (the historian's grandfather), Francis Hawes, and Richard Houlditch were also considerable landowners. The majority had more moderate fortunes, although in view of the fact that their estates when sold realized over £2m. the South Sea clerk Adam Anderson was understating when he wrote later that

the inventory of all their estates, exclusive of antecedent settlements, did not much exceed a million of money; which among so many persons was, on an average, little more than thirty thousand pounds each.[2]

Socially, the directors were a mixed bunch, with manners varying from those of the cosmopolitan Janssen or Sir Lambert Blackwell, General Lambert's grandson, described as affecting 'much the Gentleman in his Dress, and the Minister in his Conversation',[3] to the thrusting coarseness of John Blunt, a principal architect of the South Sea scheme, as he had been

---

director Charles Joye became Deputy Governor in 1719 was not filled, hence there were only twenty-nine instead of thirty directors in 1720 (Add. MS. 25498, f. 101). The company in 1720 had thirty servants at South Sea House, of whom the most important were the cashier, Robert Knight, his deputy Robert Surman, and the accountant John Grigsby. (This figure excludes doorkeepers, etc.).

[1] *The Case of Sir Theodore Janssen*, n.d. [probably 1721], Bank of England Museum, no. 497. Biographical information in this section is drawn from Beaven's *Aldermen of London*, Chamberlayne's *Mag. Brit. Notitia*, G.E.C.'s *Complete Baronetage*, F. G. Hilton Price's *Handbook of London Bankers*, Shaw's *Knights of England* and *Letters of Denization*, the inventories of the directors' estates printed by order of Parliament in 1721, the catalogues of the sales of these estates in the Bodleian Library, and the indexes of the stock ledgers in the Bank of England Record Office. The inventories are valuable but very confused in their form. Cf. also the biographical notes in J. P. Carswell's *The South Sea Bubble*, app.

[2] Adam Anderson, *An Historical and Chronological Deduction of the Origin of Commerce* (1787 ed.), iii. 123. For the sales of the directors' estates in the 1720s see below, p. 187. The gross sale value of the directors' estates was just under £3m. From this nearly £700,000 must be deducted for debts, etc., leaving net assets of over £2m.

[3] *Memoirs of the Secret Services of John Macky, Esq.* (Roxburghe Club, 1895), p. 98.

of the company itself; he was the son of a prosperous Baptist shoemaker in Rochester.[1] Most of the directors were from London backgrounds. Thus Sir Robert Chaplin, Sir William Chapman, and Stephen Child were all sons of former Lord Mayors of London, while Francis Eyles and John Gore were both members of well-known City families.[2] Eyles was a relative, perhaps the nephew, of the tough Sir John Eyles who was put in as Sub-Governor in 1721 to restore the shaken South Sea Company to equilibrium.[3] Edward Gibbon's father, Matthew, was a linen-draper in Leadenhall Street, whose widow continued his business.[4] Some directors were of foreign extraction. Sir Theodore Janssen has already been mentioned. Peter Delaporte was probably a relative of James Delaporte, son of Isaack Delaporte of Caen, who was naturalized in 1660. Sir John Lambert (1666–1723) was the son of a merchant in the Île de Rhé, had been educated a Protestant in England, but married a French wife.[5] Sir Jacob Jacobsen, the son of Heinrich Jacobsen of Hamburg, was naturalized in 1685 at the instance of his uncle Theodore Jacobsen, a childless London merchant who promised to bring him up as a good Protestant and leave him the bulk of his fortune. Whether born in London or not, the directors, almost to a man, had made their living and their reputations there. Their advance in this harsh world can partly be followed from the alphabet (index) books to the Bank stock ledgers for the period 1694–1720. Of the governors and twenty-nine directors twenty-eight held Bank stock before 1720, as well as three of the company's servants. All are given London addresses. Ten are initially described as 'merchant' or 'gent.', but later as 'esquire'; nine others had moved up from 'merchant' or 'esquire' to 'knight' or 'baronet'.[6] The directors

---

[1] For Blunt's contribution to the company's establishment in 1711 see above, p. 64.

[2] The three Lord Mayors were Sir Francis Chaplin (Lord Mayor 1677–8), Sir John Chapman (1688–9), and Sir Francis Child (1698–9). John Gore's brother William, of Tring, Herts., was elected an M.P. in 1713, 1722, and 1734, though not sitting in 1720. He is probably the same William Gore who was a director of the Royal African Company during 1723–7. Another brother, Charles, was elected M.P. in 1722, 1734, 1736, and 1747.

[3] See p. 177 below.

[4] Indexes to *Cal. T. Bks.* 1685–92, under 'Matthew and Hester Gibbon'.

[5] G.E.C., *Complete Baronetage*. His wife was Madeleine, daughter of Benjamin Beuzelin of Rouen, perhaps related to Francis Beuzelin, a big holder of East India stock in Anne's reign and later an African Company director; see index under 'Beuzelin'.

[6] Bank of England Record Office, ledgers for Bank stock. The three directors not included are Delaporte, Gore, and Turner; though it is likely Turner held stock, he cannot be certainly identified. The servants were Robert Knight, John Grigsby, and Robert Surman. For directors' titles and offices see below, p. 117.

married (if they married — Fellowes, for instance, was a bachelor) in the circles they had been born in or moved into. Thus Sir Lambert Blackwell married the daughter of the rich merchant Sir Joseph Herne. Sir Robert Chaplin married a granddaughter of another merchant prince, Sir James Bateman. Blunt married as his second wife the widow of his South Sea colleague Stephen Child's former partner Benjamin Tudman. Sir William Chapman's son and heir John later (1736) married Rachel, the daughter of the South Sea director James Edmundson.

The laconic description 'merchant' against most of the directors' names in the Bank stock alphabets conceals widespread business activities.[1] For example, William Astell was a Russia merchant dealing in spices, hemp, tallow, and other products, with firms in Amsterdam, Archangel, Barbados, Boston, Carolina, Leghorn, and St. Petersburg. Sir William Chapman and William Morley were both Spanish merchants; the former's accounts were with firms in Barcelona, Cadiz, the Canaries, Jamaica, Lisbon, Málaga, Nantes, Tenerife, and (by consignment) 'New Spain'. Edward Gibbon had accounts with houses in Amsterdam, Genoa, Leghorn, Lisbon, Marseilles, Paris, and Venice. A minority of the directors were not merchants. Sir Robert Chaplin was a Bencher of the Inner Temple. Stephen Child and Jacob Sawbridge were both goldsmith bankers. The former, a son of Sir Francis Child, a leading Tory banker of the previous reign, was in partnership with Benjamin Tudman in a banking business at the Crown in Lombard Street from 1708 to 1712 (when Tudman died), then from 1712 to 1718 with other partners.[2] Sawbridge was a partner in the Sword Blade Bank with which the South Sea Company kept part of its cash.[3] One of the company's servants, Robert Surman, was also a goldsmith banker. He had been a clerk in the Sword Blade Bank until 1718, when he was brought into the South Sea Company as deputy cashier, but he evidently continued in business as a goldsmith both then and later.[4] Besides these, the director John Turner may

---

[1] This section is largely based on the directors' printed inventories (see above, p. 113, n. 1). 'Russia merchant', 'Spanish merchant', etc., were contemporary labels to describe merchants trading to those areas.

[2] F. G. Hilton Price, *London Bankers*, pp. 32, 178.

[3] R. D. Richards, 'The Bank of England and the South Sea Company', *Econ. Hist.* ii (1930–3), p. 348. The Sword Blade partnership was Sir George Caswall, Elias Turner, and Jacob Sawbridge; in 1720 Sir John Blunt's son Henry and Robert Knight's nephew Robinson Knight were admitted as copartners (*HCJ* xix. 430).

[4] He is described as a clerk in the Sword Blade Bank in *HCJ* xix. 431. In the Bank stock alphabet he appears as 'Sword Blade Office, goldsmith'. For his subsequent career see below, p. 189.

E 2   D.F.R.

have been a partner in the firm of Turner, Marke & Co., and was perhaps related to Elias Turner, Sir George Caswall's partner in the Sword Blade Bank. John Blunt was by profession a scrivener, though he had evidently deserted his calling for the lucrative arts of share-pushing and company promotion. In the summer of 1720 he was at the height of his career, advising Ministers on making London a free port, and being rewarded by the king with a baronetcy for his part in the South Sea scheme.[1] James Edmundson, one of the poorest of the directors, had bought the office of purser for life on H.M.S. *Royal Anne*. Ambrose Page was a brewer at Stratford-le-Bow. Hugh Raymond, of Marine Square, Goodman's Fields, had connections with the East India Company and may have been a marine underwriter. Thomas Reynolds was chairman of the Navy Victualling Commissioners. The Sub-Governor, Fellowes, was evidently a marine underwriter as well as a general merchant, for in 1718–20 he invested over £16,000 in bottomry bonds. Grigsby, the company's accountant, was a member of the Merchant Taylors' Company and had been a Sworn Broker in 1708–12. He was related to Sir John Blunt, suffered from gout, had soaring social ambitions, and was 'vulgarly reputed to have studied the black art'.[2] Robert Knight, a prime mover of the South Sea scheme, was a descendant of the family of Knight of Barrells near Henley-in-Arden[3] and a member of the Grocers' Company; he had been the company's cashier since its establishment.

The statutory ban on interlocking of directorates between the three monied companies did not apply to smaller concerns, and several South Sea directors either already had other directorates by 1720 or acquired them during the Bubble.[4] Jacob Sawbridge, besides being a partner in the Sword Blade Bank, was a director of the Million Bank; another director of this bank was Thomas Hawes, a close relative, perhaps the brother, of the South Sea director Francis Hawes.[5] Three other South Sea directors, Sir William Chapman, Sir Jacob Jacobsen, and Colonel Hugh Raymond, were closely involved in 1719–20 in plans to establish a corporation for marine insurance, and when these plans matured at midsummer 1720, with the creation of the

---

[1] For his scheme for a free port see *Applebee's Original Weekly Journal*, 6 August 1720. For his baronetcy see below, p. 117.

[2] *Secret History of the South Sea Scheme*, p. 407; Corporation of London Records Office, Brokers' admissions 1708–1801.

[3] J. P. Carswell, *The South Sea Bubble*, p. 62.

[4] The ban was imposed in 1710 by 9 Anne, cc. 7 (Bank of England and East India Company) and 15, s. 47 (South Sea Company, Bank, and East India Company).

[5] See below, p. 276, for the Million Bank's activity in 1720.

London Assurance, Chapman and Jacobsen were appointed the first governors, and Raymond was made a director.[1] In August Jacobsen was also elected
to the Court of Assistants of the English Copper Company.[2]

A number of directors had been connected with government service or
offices, and some some still were. Thus Sir Lambert Blackwell had been
English Envoy to Genoa, Tuscany, and Venice between 1699 and 1705
and English Consul at Leghorn from 1690 to 1696.[3] Sir Theodore Janssen
and Sir John Lambert were important exchange contractors for the govern-
ment in the War of the Spanish Succession.[4] Edward Gibbon, a former East
India director, was Paymaster of the Train of Artillery in Flanders in
William III's reign, and evidently continued to contract with the Board of
Ordnance under Anne. In 1711 he was a receiver of the state lottery.[5]
Francis Hawes had been cashier to Sir Thomas Littleton, the Navy
Treasurer, from 1699 to 1710. In 1720 he was joint Customs cashier, an
office to which he had been appointed in June 1716.[6] Richard Houlditch
was collector of four revenue duties,[7] and Sir Harcourt Master was Receiver-
General of the Land Tax for London, Westminster, and Middlesex,[8] while
Thomas Reynolds, as already mentioned, was chairman of the Navy
Victualling Commissioners. For these and other services five members of
the court had been created baronets by 1720 and four others had been
knighted.[9] In June 1720 John Blunt and Sir William Chapman were also

---

[1] Boyer, *Political State*, xx (1720), 459. Two members of the court of the rival Royal
Exchange Assurance, elected the same day, Charles Goodfellow and Richard Lockwood,
were business associates of the South Sea directors William Astell and Edward Gibbon. In
1726 Lockwood was a director of the Royal African Company.

[2] *The Evening Post*, 11–13 August 1720.

[3] D. B. Horn, *English Diplomatic Representatives, 1689–1789* (Camden Soc. Publcns.,
xlvi, 1932), pp. 73, 78, 82.

[4] Indexes to *Cal. T. Bks.* 1702–13, and Sperling, ch. iv.

[5] Indexes to *Cal. T. Bks.* 1689 ff. For his receivership in the lottery see above, p. 71.

[6] For his post as cashier to Littleton see *HCJ* xix. 9. For his appointment as Customs
cashier see *Cal. T. Papers*, 1714–19, p. 261, 20 June 1716. The other cashier then was
evidently Horace Walpole Sen. On 18 July 1717, Walpole was replaced by Anthony
Lechmere; *Cal. T. Bks.* xxxi. 375. Hawes kept his revenue account at the Bank of England;
see below, p. 389.

[7] P.R.O. E 401/2044, Receipt Book (Pells) 1719–20.

[8] As appears from his inventory.

[9] Sir Lambert Blackwell (Bart., 16 July 1718); Sir Robert Chaplin (Bart., 19 September
1715); Sir John Fellowes (Bart., January 1719); Sir Theodore Janssen (Bart. 11 March
1715); Sir John Lambert (Bart., 6 February 1711). Sir William Chapman and Sir Harcourt
Master were knighted in 1714, Sir William Hamond in 1717, Sir Jacob Jacobsen in
1718.

made baronets, presumably for their respective parts in the South Sea scheme and the new London Assurance.[1] Some directors also held local offices. In December 1719 Sir Lambert Blackwell became Sheriff of Norfolk, and at least as early as May 1720 four directors — Ingram, Master, Page, and Raymond — were London J.P.s.[2] Only one director, Sir Harcourt Master, was (and continued to be) an Alderman of London. Lastly, four members of the court, Chaplin, Eyles, Janssen, and Sawbridge, were Members of Parliament.[3]

This was the group, 'many of [whom] had the best of characters till that infatuation',[4] which presided over the launching, then the wreck, of the South Sea scheme. In the diversity of their background, characters, and business interests they were probably representative of the mercantile oligarchy that dominated City life. Like most boards of directors at the time, not excluding the Bank of England, the South Sea board contained varieties not only of wealth but of honesty and ability. Contemporaries insisted that the initiation and subsequent management of the South Sea scheme were not the work of the whole court but of a group of directors within it who kept their colleagues in the dark. The *Secret History of the South-Sea Scheme*, written in 1721 by one of the 'innocent' directors, insists that Blunt and his cronies on the Board bamboozled the Sub-Governor Fellowes, who did not really understand the whole affair, hamstrung the important Committee of Treasury, and managed all the important decisions behind the backs of the remaining directors, who were treated with contumely, and exposed to Blunt's neo-Biblical oratory (this was presumably his Baptist ancestry coming out); he declared, for instance, that 'The greatest thing in the world is referred to you. All the mony of Europe will center amongst you. All the nations of the earth will bring you tribute.'[5] It was because of these differences between members of the court that Parliament in 1721 punished some directors much more heavily than others, and that the 'Junto of Managers' is the collective villain of Anderson's history of the Bubble. Who composed this inner ring of 'South Sea men'? Examination of the appointments to six important South Sea directors' committees in 1720 shows that eight directors

[1] The Act creating the London Assurance and Royal Exchange Assurance obliged each to pay £300,000 towards the debts of the Civil List.

[2] Boyer, *Pol. State*, xviii. 567 for Blackwell; the *Weekly Journal*, 14 May 1720, for a list of London J.P.s.

[3] Respectively for Great Grimsby, Devizes, Yarmouth (I. o. W.), and Cricklade.

[4] Anderson, *Origin of Commerce* (1787 ed.), iii. 123.

[5] *Secret History*, p. 443. For this pamphlet see above, p. 94, n. 4.

were nominated either five or six times and nine not at all.[1] The names occurring most frequently were those of Robert Chester and Richard Houlditch (six times) and the two governors, Blunt, Chapman, and John Gore (five times). Those not named at all were Blackwell, Child, Delaporte, Edmundson, Hamond, Ingram, Page, Reade, and Turner. It is probably significant that five of these — Delaporte, Edmundson, Hamond, Ingram, and Turner — were among those most lightly punished in 1721. The inference that those most nominated were the governing clique is confirmed by the Committee of Secrecy's discovery in 1721 that the governors, Blunt, Gibbon (appointed to four committees), Chester, and Houlditch had control of the £574,500 fictitious stock used for bribes.[2] The severity of Francis Hawes's initial punishment indicates that he should be added to the inner ring.[3] The *Secret History's* list of the 'Cabinet Council' which ran the scheme, and was dominated by Sir John Blunt, seems to be Fellowes, Joye, Blunt, Chester, Gibbon, Hawes, Houlditch, and Sawbridge, aided by Knight, and Blunt's crony the accountant John Grigsby.[4] There is no reason to doubt the universal contemporary belief that the leader of this inner group was neither Fellowes nor Joye but Blunt himself, whose baronetcy in June 1720 put the official seal on his position as the doyen of the South Sea scheme.[5]

It seems clear, therefore, both that there was an inner ring of directors, and that several others were 'innocent', as Anderson claimed. This is not surprising, for active, passive, and wavering groups are found in most corporate bodies. But it is worth making some qualifications. Innocence might simply mean absence. Thus William Astell was away in the country for most of 1720. But this was not in order to dissociate himself from his colleagues' activities. He was recovering from the shock of the fire in

[1] The committees were as follows: (i) 22 January 1720, to frame the company's proposals for the House of Commons; (ii) 2 February 1720, to look after the company's interest in the Bill incorporating these proposals; (iii) 27 July 1720, to consider a 'rights issue' of stock; (iv) 24 September 1720, to devise relief for the annuitants; (v) 18 October 1720, to take care of the company's loans and bonds; (vi) 13 December 1720, to prepare for Parliament an account of all the company's proceedings under the South Sea Act. The names are in the D. Ct. Bks. under these dates (Add. MS. 25498, ff. 158, 167; 25499, ff. 34, 55, 64, 84).

[2] *HCJ* xix. 426, First Report of the Committee of Secrecy.

[3] He was at first allowed only £31 from his estate. This was later modified to £5,000; see below, p. 187. He served on three committees.

[4] *Secret History*, p. 411. The pamphlet gives only the first letters of the names.

[5] Compare the amusing description in the *Secret History*, p. 431, of Blunt and his family at Tunbridge Wells in July 1720 boasting of 'our Scheme'.

January which had burned down his house in Austin Friars and killed his wife and three children. In August he was sufficiently recovered to haggle with Lord Bristol over the sale of land.[1] In September he was nominated to a South Sea committee. At a more general level, it must be allowed that despite the attempts of the author of the *Secret History* to maintain that there was nothing the 'innocent' directors could do to check the actions of the Junto, the line between inactivity and connivance at illicit practices is finely drawn. As the Committee of Secrecy put it,

upon the Examination of the Directors, it doth not appear to your Committee, that any one of them protested against or declared any Publick Dissent from any of the said Proceedings. And it appears, that all of them took their Shares and Proportions of the Subscriptions which were allotted for the respective Directors to dispose of.[2]

Scott ridicules the attempts of the directors to cast a major share of the blame on their cashier, Robert Knight.[3] Contemporaries were less certain. The Committee of Secrecy ended its last report in June 1721 with the statement that

your Committee find themselves under a Necessity of closing their Inquiry . . . by reason of the Absence of Mr. Knight, who appears to have been principally, and in many Instances solely entrusted in the Execution of this black and destructive South Sea Scheme.[4]

Sir Theodore Janssen alleged that Knight, who was evidently working in close touch with his deputy Surman, had virtually complete control over the loans the company made in 1720, directors applying to him if they wished to borrow for themselves or their friends.[5] Evidence given to the Committee of Secrecy tends to confirm this.[6] It must be remembered that senior company officers at this time had considerable power, and might be as well off as their masters. When in 1737 James Johnson married the widow of Daniel Wescomb, formerly Secretary of the South Sea Company, she brought with her a fortune of £30,000.[7] The eldest daughter of Thomas Maddockes, the

---

[1] The fire is reported in the *Post-Boy*, 7–9 January 1720. His wife, son, and two daughters were killed. He was said to have lost £20,000 (*Weekly Journal*, 16 January 1720). In August 1720 he recovered £4,200 from the Union Fire Office (ibid., 27 August 1720). For his dealings with Lord Bristol see below, p. 147. In his inventory Astell pleaded that his absence from London absolved him from responsibility.

[2] *HCJ* xix. 433, First Report of the Committee of Secrecy.

[3] Scott, op. cit. iii. 335.   [4] *HCJ* xix. 596, 16 June 1721.

[5] *The Case of Sir Theodore Janssen*, n.d. [probably 1721], Bank of England Museum, no. 497.

[6] See particularly the First and Fourth Reports, *HCJ* xix. 425 ff., 555 ff.

[7] *Gent. Mag.*, January 1737, under 'Marriages'.

chief cashier of the Bank of England, had a portion of £10,000 on her marriage in 1739.[1] Robert Knight's princely estate, valued at over £260,000 in 1721, shows that in exceptional circumstances a sharp company officer could climb very high.[2] There seems good reason to believe that, together with Blunt and the politicians Aislabie and the elder Craggs, he played a large part in devising and managing the South Sea scheme.

[1] Ibid., February 1739.   [2] For Knight's estate see below, p. 187.

6

The South Sea Bubble (II)

I

T H E last chapter described how the South Sea Company's scheme originated, and was accepted by the government and Parliament, and some of the personal factors influencing these events. The present chapter is concerned in the first place with the exchanges of government debts for new South Sea stock in 1720 and the company's issue for sale of part of the new stock remaining after these exchanges; and then with the frantic rise in the market price of all securities which formed a background to them. It concludes with the shattering of the market in the late summer of 1720, which made drastic measures of financial relief and reconstruction inevitable. These measures in turn, and the slow climb back to financial and social stability, are discussed in Chapters 7 and 8.

At this point it may be as well to recapitulate the nature of the South Sea Company's proposals about the National Debt, which were essentially simple. Their key idea was that the holders of annuities for terms of years, which the government could not buy out or reduce to a lower rate unless the holders consented, should voluntarily exchange them, at a price to be agreed, for a capital sum in the form of new South Sea stock. The government debt to the company would increase at a predetermined ratio with these exchanges. The Treasury could subsequently either repay these debts (and cancel the stock) or reduce the interest on them.[1] But though the underlying idea of the scheme was simple, its execution became extremely complicated. This was for four main reasons. First, the scheme, illogically, was extended to cover the redeemable government debts (government ordinary stock, largely managed at the Bank of England). Second, instead of first exchanging the annuities and then calculating the amount of new stock left over for sale, the South Sea Company made its first two capital issues in April 1720 before the 'annuitants' subscriptions' had taken place. Further, the exchanges of government securities for new South Sea stock took place not at one date but

---

[1] For sample calculations see above, p. 101.

at three different dates, at each of which different amounts were 'subscribed' (i.e. exchanged). Thirdly, as will be seen in the next chapter, the terms offered to both the former government creditors and the buyers of new stock were twice altered in 1720–1, once by the company and then by the Government. Lastly, all these operations took place against a background of frenzied speculation in old and new South Sea stock and scrip, existing market securities, and the shares of a wave of newly floated companies.

II

The timing of the South Sea Company's operations in 1720 is shown in Table 12.

Quite apart from the muddled contemporary use of 'subscription' to denote both the government creditors' registration of their debts for exchange and the listing of names of those prepared to buy new stock, the mixture of two types of operation is confusing. Logically, (2), (4), and (6) to (9) inclusive should have preceded (1), (3), (5), and (10). Logic, however, was elbowed aside by expediency. The company wanted to market its new stock while prices were rising; the same consideration made it defer the second exchange of government debts until the market was at its height in August, so as to weight the terms of the exchange more heavily against the government's creditors. The remainder of this section examines first, the sale of new South Sea stock (the Money Subscriptions), and then the more complex question of the exchanges of debts in April, July, and August, which made these sales possible.

The terms of the four Money Subscriptions are shown in Table 13.

The rising curve of amounts and prices corresponded to the rise of the market, which the directors were doing their best to encourage.[1] The amount of stock issued was perhaps not excessive, even though greater than was at first contemplated. The true extravagance came in the price of the last two subscriptions and the length of the payment periods needed to make this price acceptable. Stock at a lower price paid for more quickly would have been a more realistic offer. As it was, the market was flooded with South Sea scrip (subscription receipts) which changed hands at ever increasing prices as the price of stock itself soared.[2]

[1] See below, p. 141.   [2] See below, Table 17.

TABLE 12

The timing of the South Sea Company's operations in 1720

No.	Date	Type of Operation
	1720	
1	14 April	First 'Money Subscription'. Issue of £2,250,000 South Sea stock at a price of 300.
2	28 April	'Subscription' (i.e. registration for exchange) of about two-thirds of the long and short government annuities at South Sea House.
3	29 April	Second 'Money Subscription'. Issue of £1,500,000 South Sea stock at a price of 400.
4	19 May	Terms of exchange announced for the annuitants who 'subscribed' on 28 April. One week given for them to decide.
5	17 June	Third 'Money Subscription'. Issue of £5m. South Sea stock at a price of 1,000.
6	23 June	Formal notification to the South Sea managers (i.e. the directors themselves) of the amount of annuities subscribed for exchange on 28 April.
7	14 July	Subscription (i.e. registration for exchange) at South Sea House of the greater part of the redeemable government debts managed by the Bank of England.
8	4 August	Subscription (i.e. registration for exchange) of part of the remainder of the annuities, i.e. those not subscribed on 28 April; and of redeemable debts managed by the Exchequer.
9	12 August	Terms of exchange announced for those who 'subscribed' on 12 August.
10	24 August	Fourth 'Money Subscription'. Issue of £1,250,000 South Sea stock at a price of 1,000.
11	15 and 17 October	Formal notification to the South Sea managers of sums of redeemable stock, and of annuities, subscribed on 14 July and 4 August.

Source : Copies of the preambles to the subscriptions of debts and subscriptions for sale of new South Sea stock in H.L.R.O. Parchment Coll., South Sea Company papers, Box 167. Existing histories of the Bubble assign various dates to these operations, partly because they all ignore the fact that both subscriptions of debts took place in two stages. Scott (iii. 320–3, 354–9) dates the last three Money Subscriptions 30 April, 15 June, and 12 August, and the subscriptions of debts 19 May, 4 August and 12 August.

TABLE 13

Money Subscriptions (issues of stock) made by the South Sea Company in 1720

No.	Date	Issue price	Amount of stock proposed to be issued	Amount of stock actually issued	Cash payable on subscription or later	Cash payable to company if all calls met
	1720		£	£	£	£
1	14 April	300	2,000,000	2,250,000	One-fifth down: balance in eight calls at two-monthly intervals. Last call 14 August 1721.	6,750,000
2	29 April	400	1,000,000	1,500,000	One-tenth down: balance in nine calls at three- or four-monthly intervals. Last call 14 December 1722.	6,000,000
3	17 June	1,000	No limit set	5,000,000	One-tenth down: balance in nine calls at six-monthly intervals. Last call 2 January 1725.	50,000,000
4	24 August	1,000	1,000,000	1,250,000	One-fifth down: balance in four calls at nine-monthly intervals. Last call 25 September 1723.	12,500,000
				£10,000,000		£75,250,000

Source: For amounts issued see Table 12. For amounts proposed to be issued (but exceeded) see Add. MS. 25499, ff. 8, 12, 25, and 41, South Sea D. Ct. Bk., 13 April, 28 April, 15 June, and 23 August 1720. The first four calls on the second subscription were at four-monthly intervals, the rest three-monthly; calls on the third subscription were on 2 January and 2 July each year, and so on.

Partly because of the easy terms of payment, which encouraged sub-scribers to believe that they could pass the buck to someone else long before they themselves had to pay up, the company had no difficulty at all in filling each subscription. The second and third, and probably the first also, were completed from 'lists' put in by directors and members of the Government. In the fourth, however, it was ordered 'that no director or other Person do bring in any List'.[1] In the second subscription each director had £26,000 and the governors the remainder. In the third each director was supposed to have £54,000.[2] In practice each had on average over £72,000, for the twenty-nine lists totalled £2,099,000.[3] Five directors brought in lists for over £100,000: Chester (£117,000), Blunt (£198,400), Master (£110,000), and Janssen (£139,500). The sub-governor's list was for £587,500 and the deputy governor's for £389,200. In addition there were extensive Govern-ment lists: Aislabie's for £75,300, the younger Craggs's for £691,500, Charles Stanhope's for £49,700, and Sunderland's for £167,000.[4] The total of directors', governors', and Government lists was no less than £4,059,100 — over four-fifths of the subscription. Many of the M.P.s who subscribed came in in this way. Craggs's list, for instance, contained 153 M.P.s. (Sunderland's was markedly less political — thirty-five of the eighty-eight names on it were women.) Only a handful of names were those of foreigners. (They included Count Starhemberg, the great Austrian financial expert (£2,000).) The near-monopoly imposed explains why a Dutch merchant in London wrote to a correspondent in Amsterdam that the subscriptions are 'taken up in advance by courtiers'.[5] The Committee of Secrecy was able to show later that the increase in the intended amount of the first two sub-scriptions was due to pressure by interested parties. More damningly, it showed that subscriptions for the issues in June and August had been with-drawn when the price fell; thus their amount was initially reported to Parliament in 1721 as £4·4m. and £1·2m., instead of £5m. and £1·25m.[6]

The pressure to subscribe seems to have been intense, even in the last subscription, when prospects were clouding. The first was reported to have

[1] Add. MS. 25499, f. 42, South Sea D. Ct. Bk., 23 August 1720.

[2] *HCJ* xix. 434, First Report of the Committee of Secrecy.

[3] H.L.R.O. Parchment Coll., South Sea Company papers, Box 167, copies of directors', governors', and government lists.

[4] Ibid. The Committee of Secrecy (*HCJ*, loc. cit.) stated Craggs's list as £695,000.

[5] 'Besproken by de hovelingen', Peter Crellius in London to David Leeuw in Amster-dam, letters evidently dated 30 April and 2 May 1720, quoted in F. Ph. Groeneveld, *De Economische Crisis van het Jaar 1720* (Groningen and Batavia, 1940), p. 138.

[6] *HCJ* xix. 433–4, First Report of the Committee of Secrecy.

been filled 'in an Hour's Time',[1] and the second and third 'in a few Hours',[2] while at the fourth 'there was such great crowding of People, that by one of the Clock the Subscriptions were compleated'.[3] In the huge third subscription the company 'had Money enough paid in for near Eight millions', and had to abate each subscription proportionately.[4] The directors were evidently constantly badgered about new issues of stock. Adam Anderson says that he

remembers distinctly, that further on in this summer, a certain director (Mr. Ed...n, long since dead) being asked by a gentleman at Garraway's coffee-house, whether the report was true, that the court of directors soon intended to open their third subscription at one thousand per cent? Mr. E — facetiously replied, 'Truly gentlemen seem to strive to talk us into some such price, whether we will or no.'[5]

The directors questioned in 1721 about their reasons for holding the third and fourth subscriptions expanded Edmundson's excuse. They said that they were exposed to

solicitations from Persons of all Ranks to open a Third Money Subscription ... [so] considering ... that by denying or delaying such voluntary Subscriptions, pressed with so much Eagerness, they would have been very much blamed by all the Proprietors [they] took in the 3rd Money-Subscription at £1000 per Cent.[6]

That this was not all special pleading is confirmed by the surviving copies of the subscription books.[7] Their evidence is admittedly defective, since the company made many alterations in 1720–1 in desperate attempts to cover its tracks. But they show a distinct proportionate increase in the number of those involved in the last two subscriptions, and a corresponding decrease in the average sum subscribed, which cannot be due simply to cooking the books. Thus, in the fourth subscription there were about 2,500 names, compared with about 1,500 in the first subscription, which was for nearly twice the amount of stock. The directors certainly resolved not once but four times — on 28 April, 13 May, 20 July, and 24 August — not to take further subscriptions. Whether this was more than face-saving and implied a genuine conflict between what some directors wanted and what others wanted, or between what the court wanted and the public wanted, cannot, however, be determined. Despite the resolutions, three further subscriptions

[1] *Weekly Journal*, 16 April 1720.
[2] Abel Boyer, *Political State of Great Britain* (1720), xix. 450; *Weekly Journal*, 18 June 1720.
[3] *Weekly Journal*, 27 August 1720.   [4] *HCJ* xix. 434.
[5] Anderson, *Origin of Commerce* (1787 ed.), iii. 96.   [6] *HCJ* xix. 404.
[7] H.L.R.O., Parchment Coll., B 57–63.

were held. Further, on 27 July the court appointed a committee to consider yet another subscription, confined to existing holders of stock. This plan was only abandoned on 8 September 1720.[1]

One further complication must be noted: no receipts for the third and fourth subscriptions were ever delivered. The reasons for this are illuminating. On 27 July 1720 the directors ordered the delivery of third subscription receipts to those who wanted them.[2] None was evidently delivered, however, for on 20 September 1720 the rich financier John Hopkins attended a committee of the directors' court and

in the name of himself and Several Others with whom he was Concerned, demanded that the Receipts for the 3d. Subscription may be delivered out in the same manner and Form and on the same Foot on which they were subscribed; Lest any alteration might be deem'd a Vacating the Bargains made about them or render them disputable.[3]

The directors ordered their solicitor to take counsel's opinion.[4] Presumably in consequence of this opinion the sub-governor explained to the General Court on 30 September 1720 that the receipts for the last two subscriptions would have to be delivered at 1,000, but would at once be exchangeable for others at 400 (the level to which the issue price was going to be reduced).[5] This decision, however, cannot have been carried out, for in the next General Court, on 23 December 1720, Sir George Caswall argued for the delivery of receipts. He declared that many had sold their subscriptions 'and that the Persons who had paid for them, rely'd solely on the Honour of those they had contracted with'.[6] A contemporary estimated that one-sixth of the

---

[1] Add. MS. 25499, ff. 33–34, 44, 48, South Sea D. Ct. Bk., 27 July, 25 August and 8 September 1720. The subscription was to be for 20% of the existing capital. The General Court on 8 September 1720 resolved that it should not be held.

[2] Add. MS. 25499, f. 32. These receipts were to be in multiples of £1,000 only. In the Bodleian Library (Firth b. 18 (54)) there is a third subscription receipt, for £300, to Joseph Safford, a South Sea Co. clerk, signed by the cashier Robert Knight. Presumably receipts were made out for various sums but never delivered. Safford's indorsement would have conveyed the title to the subscriber, *HCJ* xix. 436.

[3] Add. MS. 25499, f. 54, South Sea D.Ct. Bk., 20 September 1720. Hopkins is referred to only as 'Mr. Hopkins'; it is a fair presumption that he was John Hopkins of Old Broad Street, later a purchaser of forfeited South Sea estates, see below, p. 188.

[4] Add. MS. 25499, f. 54.

[5] Ibid., agenda for the General Court. For the alteration of the issue price see the next chapter.

[6] *The Proceedings of the Directors of the South-Sea Company* (1721), p. 77. This pamphlet collects the newspaper reports of the debates in the General Courts of the monied companies in the autumn and winter of 1720.

third subscription had at once been sold for cash;[1] Caswall and Hopkins were therefore the spokesmen of powerful interests. On the other hand, those who had agreed to take scrip at 1,000 must have been more than willing to use non-delivery of receipts as an excuse for vacating their bargains. Their view evidently prevailed, for the directors promised that no receipts would be delivered without the consent of a General Court.[2] Although the new South Sea directors in 1721 were still uncertain whether receipts could be insisted on none were ever delivered, and bargains stipulating their receipt became void because performance was not possible.[3]

III

The directors of 1720 had decided to set the ball rolling with the Money Subscriptions, while logically they should have started with the exchanges of debts. Their confidence in reversing the order was due, first, to the knowledge that they could legally increase their capital without any limit, provided they applied part of the proceeds to paying off the government's creditors; second, to their wish to take the exchanges in stages, rather than spoiling the market by taking them all at once.[4] A third motive was, of course, their wish to cash as quickly as possible the cheque which the Government had handed them without waiting to see if there were funds to meet it. In any case, their experience with the first exchange of debts in April showed that they were unlikely to have much trouble from the public creditors at this stage.

[1] *A True State of the Contracts Relating to the Third Money-Subscription* (1721), p. 9. London Univ. MS. 89 contains several contracts made by Aislabie's son-in-law Edmund Waller to deliver third subscription receipts 'as soon as the Receiptts shall be delivered out by the said Company'. In return Waller received premiums which were either certain or depended on the amount paid up on the scrip at delivery.

[2] Add. MS. 25499, f. 96.

[3] Add. MS. 25544, f. 6, South Sea G. Ct. Bk., 9 March 1721. For annulling of bargains see below, p. 191.

[4] Scott, iii. 308, 316, thought the company's capital could only be increased in proportion to the debts exchanged for South Sea stock and that the early capital issues were therefore illegal. But as Professor Heckscher points out, under ss. 48 and 52 of the South Sea Act the company was empowered to increase its capital without limit to raise funds (E. Heckscher, 'A Note on South Sea Finance', *J. Econ. and Bus. Hist.* iii (1930-1), 321.)

At first, it was widely suggested that the company could only profit by exchanging the redeemable debts (ordinary stock, mainly administered by the Bank of England) and would therefore prefer to pay the fine stipulated in the Act and ignore the annuitants completely.[1] James Milner in March 1720 depicted 'the Lady of the South Sea' as having at her feet 'the poor Annuitants in Mourning, petitioning to be admitted Sharers in the glorious Harvest: But she spurned them from her with these Words, *No long Annuities.*'[2] In April the directors recommended to the General Court that the sums realised by the first Money Subscription should be used to pay off part of the Redeemables.[3] But this plan was soon abandoned. As the directors explained to the General Court in September, they had thought

of applying part of the Sums raised by these Money Subscriptions, towards paying off the Redeemable Debts: But the Generality of the Proprietors not only of the Redeemable Debts, but also of the long Annuities, 9 p. Cents and Tickets of Lottery 1710 ... appearing desirious to have Stock in the Company for those debts, and annuities etc; Your Court of Directors, being willing to comply with their Desires, and believing it to be for the Common Interest of the Company, did open Subscriptions for admitting part of the said Redeemable debts annuities etc. into the Stock of the Company.[4]

To have ignored the annuitants completely would certainly have been a flagrantly dishonest interpretation of the penalty clause in the South Sea Act, and would have brought prompt action even from a Government as committed to the company as Sunderland's was. There was probably also pressure from the annuitants to subscribe, for the company's attempts to limit the amounts taken in proved a failure, as is shown below.

The subscription was ordered for 28 April 1720, and the company nominated four of its servants to handle the paper work.[5] The annuitants or their attorneys attended at South Sea House in Broad Street, bringing their title documents with them. If these were not brought they were to be surrendered by 7 May — later extended to 25 May.[6] The annuitants entered their

---

[1] The company was to pay the government one year's purchase on all long (not short) annuities *not* subscribed, see above, p. 105. If none had been subscribed they would therefore have had to pay £666,566.

[2] [James Milner], *A visit to the South-Sea Company and the Bank* (March 1720), p. 9.

[3] Add. MS. 25499, ff. 9–10, South Sea D. Ct. Bk., 21 April 1720, statement to be presented to the General Court.

[4] Ibid., f. 47, 8 September, 1720.

[5] Add. MS. 25499, f. 12. The servants were Robert Knight, the cashier; John Grigsby, the accountant; Daniel Wescomb, the secretary; and Rupert Clarke, the solicitor.

[6] Ibid., ff. 11, 14, 16, 18.

names and the annual amounts they received into books headed by a preamble
— which most of them did not bother to read.[1] The preamble empowered
three South Sea clerks, Joseph Safford, Thomas Knapp and Samuel Whit-
tingham, to subscribe 'for us and in our Names into the Capital Stock of the
[company] the Several Yearly Sums with or against our Names at such
Times and upon such Terms and Conditions as the said Company shall
appoint'.[2] It is clear from this that the annuitants had most imprudently
delivered themselves bound into the company's power, had it cared to take
advantage of them. But it chose instead, when it announced the terms of
the exchange on 19 May 1720, to give the annuitants until 25 May to dissent.
It is not known that any did.[3]

The second stage of this subscription, deferring until later discussion of
the terms of the exchange, was the three South Sea clerks' formal presenta-
tion to the South Sea managers on 23 June of the amounts involved. The
accounts they delivered entered in adjoining columns the amount of each
creditor's annuity, the amount by which, in proportion, the company's
capital was to be increased, and the sums in new South Sea stock and bonds
that the company was allowing him.[4] The amounts involved in this first
exchange, and the sums to which the company had tried to limit them, are
shown in Table 14.

The annuitants may have thought (as was later alleged) that they were
legally obliged to subscribe.[5] Their hope, in any case, was to get hold of the
new South Sea stock allowed them and to sell it in the booming market. This
hope the company cynically frustrated. It had no intention of spoiling the
market by flooding it with new stock, and it was not until 30 December
1720 that it ordered 'that Mr. Lockyer do carry to the Credit of each

[1] *The Pangs of Credit . . . By an Orphan Annuitant* (1722), p. 27. The habit of signing
documents without reading them is so widespread that given the crush of subscribers this
statement seems plausible.

[2] Copies of the preambles, H.L.R.O. Parchment Coll. South Sea Company papers, Box
167, with some words omitted.

[3] Add MS. 25499, f. 18, South Sea D. Ct. Bk., 19 May 1720.

[4] Copy preamble and first three entries (H.L.R.O., loc. cit.). The books themselves
(which would give complete lists of all the creditors who came into the scheme) have
unfortunately not survived. The company's capital was to increase by the 'Parliament
Price' as the preamble puts it, i.e. 20 years' purchase for long, and 14 years' purchase for
short annuities, see above, p. 104.

[5] *Gent. Mag.*, November 1749, 'A Letter from a Gentleman in Town to his Friend in
the Country': 'I am not at all surprised that you, who in 1720 (under the apprehension of
being obliged to do so) wrote your annuities into South-Sea stock . . . should now be
greatly alarmed,' etc.

TABLE 14

*Amounts involved in the first exchange of long and
short annuities for new South Sea stock, 28 April 1720*

(1)	(2)	(3)	(4)
Type of security	Total per annum	Total per annum for which South Sea Company proposed to allow subscriptions	Amounts per annum actually subscribed
	£	£	£
Long annuities	666,566	about 200,000	427,849
9%s (1710)	81,000	about 30,000	48,132
Lottery annuities (1710)	40,669	about 15,000	15,994

Source: For col. 2 see Appendix B; for col. 3, Add. MS. 25499, f. 11,
South Sea D. Ct. Bk., 28 April 1720; for col. 4, H.L.R.O. Parchment Coll., South Sea Company papers, Box 167, An 'Abstract
of what Publick Debts . . . have been subscribed.'

Proprietor's General Account in the Books of this Company Stock for all the
Several Subscriptions of the Public Debts.'[1] The supplementary amounts
allowed in South Sea bonds and in cash, on the other hand, were presumably
given out at once, because they would increase demand for the existing
stock.[2]

Had the public creditors not involved in the subscription in April known
that this delay would be applied to them in their turn, they might have thought
twice about coming in too. As it was, when the company decided in July
1720 to proceed further with exchanges of debts, the pattern set in April
was repeated. The company this time proposed to 'take in' £6m. of the
£13·3m. ordinary government stock transferred at the Bank of England,
which formed the major part of the redeemable debt.[3] The amount subscribed on 14 July was £11,240,145, nearly twice that intended.[4] The
Weekly Journal reported that

[1] Add. MS. 25499, f. 102, South Sea D. Ct. Bk., 30 December 1720.

[2] For these amounts see below, p. 135.

[3] Ibid., f. 29, 8 July 1720. The nominal capital of the six stocks transferred at the Bank
was £13,274,892. The total redeemable debt was £16·5m.

[4] H.L.R.O. Parchment Coll. South Sea Company papers, Box 167, 'An Abstract of
what Publick Debts . . . have been Subscribed' shows this sum as £11,240,425; the error
of £280 was corrected by 3 Geo. II, c. 16.

On Thursday the South Sea Company opened their Books at their House in Broad-street to take in Subscriptions of Lottery Annuities of 4 and 5 per Cent. and took in the Sum of Six Millions before they closed them. The People came thither in great Numbers, and great Crowding there was to subscribe.[1]

The method employed was the same as in April, except that the stock-holders had no title documents to deliver up. They entered their names and the amounts they owned under a similar preamble empowering the three South Sea clerks to subscribe them into the company on such terms as it should decide.[2] The South Sea managers returned schedules of the amounts subscribed to the Bank of England, which wrote off the sums in its stock ledgers.[3] On 4 August the directors decided to make a third (and as it turned out, final) exchange. This was to cover the annuities not exchanged in April, and the second category of redeemable debts, those managed at the Exchequer.[4] Once more the directors tried to limit the amounts to be 'taken in'. Once more the misguided enthusiasm of the public creditors defeated their intentions, as is shown in Table 15.

Procedure was the same as in April and July. But when the company's terms for those who had subscribed in July and August were finally announced on 12 August 1720, no option to dissent was allowed, as it had been to those who subscribed in April. The formal accounts of both the last subscriptions were presented to the South Sea managers on 15 and 17 October 1720.[5]

The public creditors had thus taken up the South Sea Company's offers with a blind enthusiasm reminiscent of the Gadarene swine. They had not agreed on terms in advance, yet throughout 1720 they had no more than the expectation of actually possessing South Sea stock. It is not the least curious feature of the whole scheme that among those who acted so rashly were powerful institutions like the Bank of England and the Million Bank, who subscribed sums running into six figures; while many of the other stock-

---

[1] *The Weekly Journal or Saturday's Post*, 16 July 1720.

[2] Copy preamble, H.L.R.O., Parchment Coll., South Sea Company papers, Box 167.

[3] Ledgers for these stocks, Bank of England Record Office. The only surviving schedules of subscriptions are for the 5%s of 1715 and the 4%s of 1717 (ibid.). Secretary Craggs wrote to Lord Stanhope on 15 July that 'the crowd of those that possess the redeemable annuities is so great that the bank, who are obliged to take them in, has been forced to set tables with clerks in the streets'; Coxe, *Walpole*, ii. 189. This misconception has re-appeared in most histories of the Bubble, e.g. Scott, op. cit. iii. 323. The South Sea Company was taking subscriptions: the Bank was writing the amounts subscribed off its own ledgers.

[4] Add. MS. 25499, f. 33, South Sea D. Ct. Bk., 27 July 1720.

[5] Copy preamble to this account, H.L.R.O., Parchment Coll. loc. cit.

TABLE 15

*Amounts involved in the third exchange of Government
securities for new South Sea stock, 4 August 1720*

(1) *Type of Security†*	(2) *Total per annum or nominal capital* £	(3) *Total for which South Sea Company proposed to allow subscriptions* £	(4) *Amounts actually subscribed* £
(a) Long annuities	238,717 p.a.*	120,000 p.a.	107,544 p.a.
(b) Lottery annuities 1710	24,675 p.a.*	13,000 p.a.	18,368 p.a.
(c) 9% annuities 1710	32,868 p.a.*	15,000 p.a.	14,841 p.a.
(d) Lottery 1713	563,300	300,000	464,990
(e) Lottery 1714 (Prizes)	652,020	300,000	538,720
(f) Lottery 1714 (Blanks)	1,055,990	500,000	865,250
(g) Lotteries 1719	1,000,000	500,000	876,305

Source: For col. 2 see Appendix B, for col. 3 Add. MS. 25499, f. 33, South Sea D. Ct. Bk.,
27 July 1720, for col. 4 H.L.R.O. Parchment Coll. South Sea Company papers,
Box 167, 'An Abstract of what Publick Debts . . . have been subscribed.'
* Amounts still unsubscribed after the exchange in April.
† (a) to (f) managed at the Exchequer, (g) managed half at the Exchequer, half at the
Bank of England.

holders were individuals of wealth, power and presumably sound judgement.[1]
As a result of their gullibility, 80% of the long and short annuities (the
Irredeemables) and 85% of Government ordinary stock (the Redeemables)
were converted into South Sea stock.[2] The company's nominal capital
increased by over £26m., on which the Government was to pay interest
partly at 5% and partly at 4% until midsummer 1727, then entirely at 4%.
Despite bitter pressure on the part of the disappointed public creditors in the
winter of 1720–1, the exchanges were not rescinded, so, as Walpole pointed
out the scheme was successful in its basic aim of altering the structure of
the National Debt, whatever sound and fury accompanied it.[3]

The terms which the public creditors had bound themselves to accept
show that the whole exchange of debts was a confidence trick entirely

[1] The public creditors in 1720 are discussed below, pp. 270 ff.
[2] For details see Appendix B.
[3] For Walpole's statement see above, p. 97.

TABLE 16

Conditions on which Government securities were exchanged for new South Sea stock in 1720

Type of security	First set of terms, announced 19 May 1720 after subscription of 28 April					Second set of terms, announced 12 August 1720 after subscriptions of 14 July and 4 August				
	Stock at 375	Value	Bonds and cash	Total sum nominally received	As years' purchase	Stock at 800	Value	Bonds and cash	Total sum nominally received	As years' purchase
	£	£	£	£		£	£	£	£	
(1) Long annuities, for each £100 p.a.	700	2,625	575	3,200	32	400	3,200	400	3,600	36
(2) 14 per cents, for each £98 p.a.	700	2,625	511	3,136	32	420	3,360	168	3,528	36
(3) 9 per cents (1710), for each £90 p.a.	350	1,312·5	217·5	1,530	17	200	1,600	..	1,600	$17\frac{7}{9}$
(4) Lottery prizes (1710), for each £100 p.a.	400	1,500	200	1,700		200	1,600	150	1,750	$17\frac{1}{2}$
(5) Lottery blanks (1710), for each £98 p.a.	350	1,312·5	353·5	1,666	17	210	1,680	35	1,715	$17\frac{1}{2}$
(6) Redeemables, for £105 stock	..	..	..	..	..	12·5	100	..	100	..

Source: Add. MS. 25499, ff. 17–18 and 39. South Sea D. Ct. Bk., 19 May and 12 August 1720. The reason why the company broke up the amounts is not known. By inference (2) was allowed more than (1) because the annuities expired slightly earlier; (6) was presumably an attempt to weight the exchange even more heavily against the stockholders.

dependent on the rise in the market price of South Sea stock. At the date of the first exchange this price was between 370 and 380. At the date of the second it was about 900.

The really severe terms were those announced on 12 August, which mostly affected holders of Redeemables. It was their plight alone which was later relieved by the company and Parliament; the terms of April remained un-altered.[1] When it put the accounts together, the company found that, thanks to the rise in the market price of its stock, it had been able to persuade holders of £26m. of the £31m. subscribable debts to exchange them for South Sea stock so over-valued that they only obtained £8·5m. of it. Even this amount was lower than a straight exchange would have produced, since the company deliberately made part of the exchange in about £3m. of its own bonds. The remainder (£17·5m.) of the £26m. by which the company became entitled to increase its nominal capital was available for sale. It was shown above that even before these accounts were available £10m. stock was in fact issued for a theoretical price of over £75m.[2] This state of affairs was tolerable as long as the price of South Sea stock remained high, but no longer. As soon as the price broke the public creditors were bound to raise a storm of complaint. If the company had been less greedy, it would not have driven bargains whose inequity would so soon become apparent, and which were then bound to be altered at its expense. But, like everyone else, it was borne along on a roaring flood of speculation, which it had helped to create, and which even in strong-holds of capitalism like the Bank of England was to drive sound judgement and long views to one side.

[1] See below, p. 176.

[2] Above, pp. 125 ff. 'An Account of what Stock has been made out pursuant to Agreements made with the Subscribers to ye South Sea Companys Capital Stock and at what time' (H.L.R.O., Parchment Coll., South Sea Company papers, Box 167) shows that £8,515,919 had been allotted to the public creditors by the end of 1720. Since the company was entitled to increase its capital by £26,055,359 its initial profit in stock was £17,539,440. From this, however, over £1m. must be deducted for the midsummer dividend, which was paid in stock (below p. 141). By the end of 1720, owing to these and perhaps other payments, the company only held £15,743,500 stock, nearly all of which was subsequently distributed to the public creditors and Money Subscribers, see below p. 184. The company issued £3,223,850 bonds in 1720 according to 'An Account of what sums . . . have been taken up on account of the S.S. Co.' (H.L.R.O., Parchment Coll. loc. cit.), and £3,630,000 according to its Register of Bonds (Add. MS. 25580). Some of these were allotted to borrowers from the company (see below, p. 144) but more to the public creditors. Cf. Scott's independent computation (op. cit. iii. 358–9), that the company allotted the public creditors £3,133,757 in bonds and cash in 1720. For the annual volume of South Sea bonds see Appendix C.

IV

By the autumn of 1719 the tempo of business activity in the City of London was visibly accelerating. In October 1719 a syndicate headed by a company promoter, Case Billingsley, took over the moribund York Buildings Company in order to use it to buy Scottish estates forfeited in 1715 and 1719. These were to become 'a fund for granting annuities for life, and for assuring lives'.[1] At the same time new companies were being floated, particularly in insurance and fishing. Their nominal capital was generally large, but subscribers were not wanting. In December 1719, for instance, it was reported that the books of 'the Grand Fishery lately projected at London' had been specially reopened to allow Mr. Dickson, an eminent merchant in Edinburgh, and his friends, to subscribe £200,000.[2]

These projects were partly due, like those of the early 1690s, to dissatisfaction with the current profits of overseas trade, reinforced by uncertainty about domestic industry. War had severed the South Sea Company from its Spanish-American trade. Fears were rife that the woollen interest was decaying, owing to French competition in the Levant and, particularly, the importation of calico by the East India Company. Two newspapers, *The Weaver* and *The Manufacturer*, were started at the end of 1719 to argue the case for weavers' protection.[3] The weavers themselves took more direct action. In London and Bristol during the spring and summer of 1720 they attacked women wearing calico and tore the clothes from their backs.[4] In May the weavers at Norwich threatened to pull down the house of a South Sea director, Sir Lambert Blackwell, who had recently been appointed Sheriff of Norfolk. He prudently declared that he supported their cause.[5] The weavers' violence was so pervasive that a special Act was passed in the spring making it punishable after midsummer by death. In July a weaver was executed.[6]

---

[1] *Reps. from Committees of the House of Commons* (15 vols., 1803), vol. i, report on the company made in 1733.

[2] *St. James's Post*, 30 December 1719–1 January 1720.

[3] *The British Merchant*, founded at the same date, supported the case for free trade.

[4] *The London Journal*, 20–27 February 1720, and 11–18 June 1720; *The Flying Post*, 30 April–3 May 1720; *Applebee's Original Weekly Journal*, 16 July 1720 (incidents at Bristol).

[5] *The London Journal*, 7–14 May 1720.

[6] 6 Geo. I, c. 23 (1720), 'An Act for the further preventing Robbery, Burglary and other Felonies and for the more effectual Transportation of Felons.' The weaver's execution is reported in *The London Journal*, 16–23 July 1720.

But the London projects were also due to a far more positive cause, the speculative fever emanating from Paris, which was soon to affect all the major cities of Europe. Profits made in Law's 'Bubble' were already beginning to have multiple effects. It was reported from Geneva in December 1719 that

everything in our Town has a pleasing Aspect at this Time, on account of the considerable fortunes which several of the Inhabitants have made in the Mississippi Trade. This Humour prevails so much here, that even the houses begin to be stockjobbed.[1]

In the same month a despatch from Vienna informed English readers that

A Company is establishing here for carrying on the trade to the Eastern Countries, for which the Emperor has subscribed 100,000 Florins, and several of the Ministers and Courtiers have subscribed considerable sums.[2]

It was added that the Turks were willing to participate. Meanwhile, the Senate of Venice was raising a fund of 2m. ducats at 3% for unspecified purposes.[3] Shortly afterwards brisk dealings began at Hamburg in the shares of projected insurance companies, though the plans for these soon foundered on the opposition of the magistrates.[4]

It was against this background of international projecting that the first rumours of the South Sea Company's scheme were reported early in January 1720.[5] By the end of February the rise of South Sea stock, even though Parliament had not yet passed the Bill incorporating the company's proposals, was sufficiently marked for it to be reported that a duke and a baronet had made £50,000 each by stock-jobbing, while eight to ten citizens had been bankrupted.[6] The duke was subsequently identified as the Duke of Chandos. A month later a Jew stock-jobber was said to have lost £100,000 in 'puts' since speculation began.[7] This was not surprising, since prices were rising so quickly that those who sold forward were liable to be overtaken by the market, as Table 17 shows.

---

[1] *St. James's Evening Post*, 31 December 1719–2 January 1720, report from Geneva dated 16 December 1719 (N.S.).

[2] *St. James's Weekly Journal*, 2 January 1720.

[3] *The St. James's Post*, 1–4 January 1720.

[4] C. Amsinck, 'Die ersten hamburgischen Assekuranz Compagnien und der Aktienhandel im Jahre 1720', *Zeitschr. des Vereins für Hamburgische Geschichte*, ix (1894), 465.

[5] See above, p. 96.

[6] *The London Journal*, 20–27 February 1720.

[7] *Whitehall Evening Post*, 24–26 March 1720. For 'puts' as a means of selling forward, see below, p. 491.

Friday. Sept 23ᵈ 1720.

At a meeting of the Comittee of the Directors of the Bank of England, & a Comittee of the Directors of ye South-Sea-Company &c.

That the Fonds of the Bank of England of 2,000,000ᵇ & of 1,775,000ᵇ making together 3,775,000ᵇ or thereabouts, redeemable by Parliement upon a year's notice, be subscribed into the Stock of the South-Sea-Company, for wᶜʰ the Bank shall be intitled to such Shares in the Capital Stock of ye South-Sea-Company, as ye sᵈ Fonds will produce, The Stock being valued at 400ᵇ pr Cᵗ. The Bank to be intitled to receive ye Dividend of midsumer last of 10 pr Cᵗ in Stock, & all other Profits arising from that time; The South-Sea-Company to be intitled to the Annuity due from ye said Fonds of 3,775,000ᵇ from & after michaelmas day next.

4. The 'Bank Contract' of September 1720, in Robert Walpole's handwriting

TABLE 17

Fortnightly prices* of South Sea and other securities, and exchange on Amsterdam, 1720

Date	Price of Bar Gold	Exchange on Amsterdam	South Sea stock	South Sea subscriptions			Bank stock	East India stock	African Coy. stock
				1	2	3			
1720	£ s. d.				d = *discount*				
1 Jan.	3.18.0	35.6	128	..	..	..	150	200	24
15 Jan.	3.18.0	35.9	134¼	..	..	..	152	204	26
1 Feb.	3.18.0	35.6	131	..	..	..	157	207	25
16 Feb.	3.18.0	35.5	187	..	..	..	148	216	26
1 Mar.	3.18.0	35.4	170	..	..	..	152	212	45
15 Mar.	3.18.0	35.9	183	..	..	..	no transfer	213	49
1 Apr.	3.18.0	36.1	302	..	..	..	148	230	60
14 Apr.	3.18.0	36.1	315	..	..	..	140	221	66
2 May	3.18.0	36.1	335	..	..	..	154	234	60
13 May	3.18.0	35.4	352	..	..	..	167	237	68
1 June	3.18.0	35.8	610	525	500	..	210	290	140
17 June	3.18.0	34.11	745	480	490	..	208	335	105
1 July	3.18.0	34.5	950†	545	525	190	238	420†	145
15 July	3.19.6	34.10	890	620	580	230	240	390	150
2 Aug.	4. 1.6	33.11	840	595	530	250	230	365	138
16 Aug.	4. 0.6	34.1	790	570	505	230	227	360	127
1 Sept.	4. 0.6	33.11	775	490	430	150	227	345	130
16 Sept.	4. 0.6	34.1	520	320	240	30	210	270	65
1 Oct.	4. 0.6	35.1	290	80	10	..	190	195	50
14 Oct.	3.18.0	35.3	170	30	10	..	135	145	40
1 Nov.	4. 1.0	33	212	..	10	..	142	165	47
15 Nov.	4. 2.0	34	195	25d	15d	..	143	170	45
1 Dec.	4. 0.0	34	192	20d	10d	..	145	165	46
15 Dec.	4. 0.0	33.10	155	50d	20d	..	140	155	40

Source: J. Castaing, *The Course of the Exchange, and other things* for 1720. (For Castaing's price-list see below, p. 488.) Cf. the careful and elaborate chart of the prices of Bank, East India and South Sea stock in the end-cover of Scott, op. cit., vol. iii.

* All prices are the lowest for the day.

† Noted as 'for the opening'.

The chief increases in the price of South Sea stock came in the second half of March, the second half of May, and during June. The first of these was probably due to diversion of foreign speculation from Paris to London. The outlook in Paris at the beginning of March 1720 was not reassuring. Fears of a crash were being expressed, and it was said that foreigners were only deterred from selling out by the artificial value put on the coinage, which prevented remittances except at 40% to 50% loss.[1] A few days later it was reported that Parisians were making wagers that Law would be hanged before the New Year.[2] Dutch speculation prudently changed course. The *London Journal* reported in its issue of 19–26 March 1720 that 'orders are come from Holland to buy Stock at any Price', and on 12 April that £250,000 in specie had been sent in a sloop from the Netherlands to London.[3] A week later speculators were arriving in person from Holland.[4] Law's agents in London, according to the newspapers, were at work too; they were credited with having bought £400,000 South Sea stock, though whether only for profit, or to unload it later so as to spoil the rival market, is not clear.[5] Meanwhile a smaller flow of money was coming in from Ireland. The pound sterling appreciated sharply in terms of the pound Irish in the second half of March and throughout April. As late as October Bishop Nicolson of Londonderry was able to write to Archbishop Wake about Irish speculation

I cannot help assuring Your Grace, that the effects of it are as sensibly felt here in Ulster, as in any other Province of the King's Dominions. Most of the little Money that we had, is already drawn into Exchange–Ally, and the small Remainder is following very fast.[6]

There is also evidence that the Huguenot community in Dublin was busily investing in South Sea stock.[7]

The second major rise in the price of South Sea stock, in the second half of May 1720, was partly due to the continuance, and perhaps acceleration, of foreign buying. By this date Dutch speculators had perfected their arrangements. It was reported from Harwich on 26 May that 'several Dutch scouts lie here, to carry over South-Sea Messengers.'[8] A few days later the arrival

[1] *St. James's Weekly Journal*, 12 March 1720. On 30 March 1720 (N.S.) John Law had the South Sea director John Lambert expelled from France on the grounds that he had remitted 20m. livres to England in order to break the French exchange-rate. (Lüthy, *Banque Protestante*, i. 291.)

[2] *The London Journal*, 12–19 March 1720.

[3] Ibid., 9–16 April 1720. The gold arrived 'on Tuesday', i.e. 12 April.

[4] *Whitehall Evening Post*, 19–21 April 1720.   [5] *The London Journal*, 16–23 April 1720.

[6] Add. MS. 6116, ff. 113–14, Nicolson to Wake 21 October 1720.   [7] See below, p. 316.

[8] *The Weekly Journal*, 4 June 1720, report from Harwich dated 26 May.

of seven hogsheads of Dutch money was noted. It was said that they had been taken to the Bank of England and from there been swept into Exchange Alley.[1] Meanwhile, a heavy discount on Bank bills was reported from Paris and, in July, mob riots against Law.[2] Although as early as 21 May the Dutch States General were said to be considering 'a Company in Imitation of the French Mississippi' to 'reduce the Publick Debts',[3] the wave of company floatation which engulfed the Netherlands in August and September, diverting speculators from other ventures, had not yet begun.

But the increase in the price of South Sea stock was also due to other factors. On 14 April the South Sea Company announced that the midsummer dividend would be 10% and would be paid in stock.[4] Given the rise in stock-prices, this was a far more interesting offer than cash. Second, the relatively equitable terms offered on 19 May to the annuitants who had subscribed into the company reassured the market.[5] More important, the South Sea Company began to pump funds into Exchange Alley. On 21 April 1720 the General Court had given the directors a general power to lend money on security of South Sea stock.[6] The avowed object was to 'keep up' market prices. As the Sub-Governor informed the General Court, 'the profit of the Company . . . do's chiefly depend on the price of the Stock at the times of the execution of the Act'.[7] The directors decided to lend up to £500,000 for four months at 5%. On 20 May 1720 they further decided, with the Treasury's agreement, to lend to South Sea proprietors at 4% the £1m. in Exchequer bills which the company was empowered (by 6 Geo. I, c. 10) to borrow from the Government. These bills were not available until 4 June, but the expectation of their arrival in the market must have greatly influenced prices.[8] Further, there is little doubt, though it cannot be proved,

---

[1] *The London Journal*, 11–18 June 1720. This report presumably means that specie was remitted to agents' accounts at the Bank and used by them to speculate for their principals.

[2] *The St. James's Post*, 8–10 June 1720; *The Flying Post or Post-Master*, 12–14 July 1720.

[3] *The Weekly Journal*, 21 May 1720. For Dutch projects in August–September 1720 see below, p. 152.

[4] Add. MS. 25499, f. 9, South Sea D. Ct. Bk., 14 April 1720.

[5] For these terms see above, p. 135.

[6] The decisions of the company to make loans on its stock and scrip are summarized by the Committee of Secrecy (*HCJ* xix. 441).

[7] Add. MS. 25499, f. 10, D. Ct. Bk., 21 April 1720, agenda for the General Court.

[8] The Commons had resolved to make this loan on 16 February 1720, see above, p. 100. The Treasury Warrant, dated 4 June 1720, authorizing the Exchequer to pay the bills to the company is printed in *HCJ* xix. 470. According to Robert Knight in his examination by the Committee of Secrecy on 17 January 1721 'the first talk of the Exchequer Bills was by the Chancellor of the Exchequer [Aislabie] who said about a week before the first

that the company was buying its own stock in Exchange Alley. On 17 February 1720 the directors had resolved that their Committee of the Treasury should be entrusted 'to Employ the Company's Money in the Cashier's hands, in such manner as they see most for the Interest of the Company'.[1] On 20 May it was ordered that

> it be refer'd to the Sub and Deputy Governors and Committee of the Treasury and They are hereby empower'd to take care to maintain the Credit and Currency of the Company's Bonds, and to do all such things as they shall think necessary in order thereto and also to adjust and settle such other matters and things as have been transacted for the Company's Interest, and for Carrying on their undertaking of Encreasing the Company's Capital.[2]

This carefully ambiguous language gave the 'Junto of Managers' full powers over the company's cash. It was hardly necessary in July to make them more explicit by ordering the Treasury Committee 'to Lend or Imploy the Company's Money that is or shall be in cash between this & Michaelmas next in such manner as they shall judge for the company's Interest'.[3]

The third and most spectacular rise in the price of South Sea stock came in June 1720. At the beginning of the month it stood at just over 600, by the end of it at just under 1,000. Two months later it was still at 800. On 17 June £5m. new stock was marketed at 1,000, with over four years allowed for payment.[4] On the 22nd the company's transfer books were shut for two months to allow the 10% midsummer dividend to be made out.[5] While they were shut large numbers of purchases were concluded at 1,000 'for the opening'.[6] The causes of this very large (and as it proved, fatal)

proposal was offered to the House of Commons That the Company must undertake it . . . that the Company might afford to Circulate them for Nothing for the Government, those Bills being to be Lent to the Company to Enable them to Execute their Scheme'. Sir John Blunt in his evidence on 14 January 1721 had conceded that the initiative about the Bills came from the company, but said that Aislabie liked the argument that if lent out they would increase the price of stock. London Univ. MS. 89, f. 68 subff. 5–7. The printed version of Blunt's evidence however (HCJ xix. 434) makes him say that Aislabie was the initiator after all.

[1] Add. MS. 25498, f. 171, South Sea D. Ct. Bk., 17 February 1720.

[2] Add. MS. 25499, f. 19, South Sea D. Ct. Bk., 20 May 1720.

[3] Ibid., f. 33, South Sea D. Ct. Bk., 27 July 1720.   [4] See above, p. 125.

[5] Add. MS. 25499, f. 22, South Sea D. Ct. Bk., 2 June 1720, order for closing of transfer books on 22 June.

[6] Anderson, *Origin of Commerce* (1787 ed.), iii. 113; Grellier, 124; H.L.R.O., Parchment Coll., South Sea Company papers, Box 167, brokers' accounts showing contracts 'for the opening' at 1,000.

increase were basically the same as those of the previous ones, but this time the South Sea Company's own share of responsibility was far greater. On 9 June the directors made more generous the terms on which the £1m. Exchequer bills just borrowed from the Government could be lent to proprietors.[1] On 27 July, anxious to sustain the rise in prices this initiated, they decided to lend the third payment (due 15 August) on the first Money Subscription and the second payment (due 14 September) on the second Money Subscription.[2] This news was released to the papers on 12 August.[3] In executing this policy the company largely disregarded the limits it set itself. By the early autumn it had lent over £9m. on security of South Sea stock and over £2m. on subscription receipts.[4] Loans were concentrated in June and August; none were made in July, when it was perhaps hoped that the market could, at least for a time, sustain itself.[5] Loans on stock were made by an ordinary transfer of stock to the South Sea cashier Robert Knight, who gave an assignable receipt. This constituted the only title to the 'pawned' stock.[6] Loans were also made on stock which was not even transferred to the company.[7] Loans on subscription receipts were authorized verbally by directors without being entered in any books.[8] The company evidently retained the receipts, though the directors had originally ordered that they should be endorsed with the amount of the loan and returned to the borrower.[9]

[1] It was intended in May to lend £300 on £100 stock, with no more than £3,000 to one person. In June this was altered to £400 and £4,000.

[2] *HCJ* xix. 441.

[3] Add. MS. 25499, f. 36, South Sea D. Ct. Bk., 12 August 1720. The statement for the Press said that scrip was to be endorsed with the amount of the loan and returned to the owner.

[4] The Committee of Secrecy in its First Report (*HCJ* xix. 434) stated that £9,039,937 had been lent on £2,563,118 stock. The amount of 'pawned stock' in the company's hands at the end of 1720 was, however, only £2,141,868. The committee thought the balance had been sold with the intention of rebuying it at lower prices (ibid. 435). They stated the amount lent on subscription receipts as £2,219,089 on £773,600 receipts (ibid. 434). Slightly different amounts are stated in the 'Abstract of the Ledgers of the Loan' (H.L.R.O. Parchment Coll., South Sea Co. papers, Box 167) where the amounts borrowed are said to be £9,330,687 on £2,663,687 stock, and £2,228,089 on £776,600 scrip.

[5] 'Abstract of the Ledgers of the Loan' (H.L.R.O. Parchment Coll., loc. cit.). In its Seventh Report (*HCJ* xix. 593-4) the Committee of Secrecy showed that the company had made alterations and erasures in the original ledger of which this is a copy. It can therefore only be used with caution. Loans would have stopped in July because the funds authorized in May–June had been exhausted and the new powers given on 27 July were not yet operative. Scott, iii. 321, says the whole £11m. had been lent by the end of June.

[6] *HCJ* xix. 435, and *The Case of the Borrowers on the South-Sea Loans* (1721).

[7] *HCJ* xix. 555.   [8] Ibid. 436.   [9] See above, n. 3.

The copy ledgers of the loan, for what their evidence is worth, show that about 2,300 people borrowed from the company in 1720. This indicates an average loan of about £4,900, but some borrowers took up much larger sums. The biggest loan of all, for £97,576, was made to William Pulteney's father-in-law John Gumley, a rich Isleworth glass manufacturer. Walpole later sarcastically observed that when he saw this 'Gentleman's Name in that Book of Loans, no ways considerable but for his Relation of Marriage as a Borrower of £97,576' he asked himself 'what Consideration could give so private a person such an immense Credit.'[1] The money lent on stock must have come partly from the Money Subscriptions, on which over £6m. had been paid in by the end of June; partly from the £1m. Exchequer bills lent by the government; partly by issuing new South Sea bonds.[2] Loans on scrip were not in cash, but by enabling a subscriber to pay his calls on credit they released his cash for further speculation in the market.

The South Sea directors' handling of their scheme, which was the deciding, though not the sole, factor in bringing stock to 1000 and keeping it near there for two months, was irresponsible and dangerous, but brilliantly conceived and executed in the short run. The exchanges of Government debts for new South Sea stock — the original object of the whole proposal — were carefully divided so that the first set of terms, which were reasonably equitable, could reassure the market and help stock to rise to a point at which the second, inequitable, exchange could take place. The Money Subscriptions were made for large round sums to impress the imagination, but calls were deliberately (and increasingly) widely spaced. When calls did become due, the company at once allowed generous credit to holders of scrip. While pumping funds into the market by loans on stock, by the issue of cash and bonds to the Government creditors, and by using its own funds for under-hand buying, the company made every effort to restrict the market supply of stock and scrip by postponing the transfer of stock to the Government creditors, by taking 'pawned' stock and scrip into its hands, and by omitting to issue receipts for the third and fourth Money Subscriptions. The knowledge that stock and scrip actually available for transfer were in short supply was bound to push up their price, despite the fact that only a minority of bargains envisaged actual delivery.[3] Further, systematic use of forward

[1] [Sir Robert Walpole], *Some Considerations concerning the Publick Funds* (1735), p. 84. Walpole hints that Pulteney himself must have had part of the loan.

[2] Add. MS. 25499, f. 24, South Sea D. Ct. Bk., 9 June 1720, all bonds issued 'by way of Loan on the Companys Stock' to bear date 16 June and be repayable 16 January 1721.

[3] See below, pp. 497 ff., for market technique.

purchases at high prices by directors and agents encouraged market optimism, and at the same time yielded a handsome immediate return in hard cash. 'I have been credibly informed', wrote James Milner as late as the end of September, 'that some of the Directors have taken great sums at Forty and Fifty per cent., to deliver Stock at six Months for Fifteen Hundred Pounds.'[1]

Unfortunately for the directors their policy was viable only in the short run. In the first place, they had not the advantage of anonymity. Many speculators in the bull market must have reaped handsome profits and retired to spend them. The directors could not do this. If the market collapsed, as it was bound to do sooner or later, they would take a large share of the blame. Second, they were unable to control the multiplier effects of their own actions. Thus, their policy of loans on stock was at once imitated on a smaller scale by the Bank of England, which had lent over £1m. to its proprietors by September 1720, and the Royal African Company, which lent £102,000.[2] Although an article written in the South Sea interest early in June declared that Bank stock was held back from rising because the Governor and Deputy Governor were 'a Couple of Old Women', in fact its price had risen from 210 to 238 by the end of the month while that of the African and East India companies had doubled.[3]

Further, competition was not limited to existing companies. As the boom developed, expectations of profit on the part of projectors, investors, borrowers, lenders, became extremely optimistic. A flood of proposals for new companies appeared, whose scrip was hawked up and down Exchange Alley. These projects have usually been ridiculed. Their financial structure encouraged speculation, for like the South Sea subscriptions they relied on marketing stock on very deferred terms. Many of them were quite blatantly swindles. It is, however, worth noting that many others had respectable objectives. They aimed at increasing investment in industry and trade, and, in particular, like the Dutch companies in the autumn, at creating insurance facilities to reduce the prevailing risks of daily life and the conduct of business. This was the background for the successful floatation of the two chartered marine insurance companies in 1720, and the parallel take-over of the Sun

---

[1] James Milner, *Three Letters Relating to the South Sea Company and the Bank* (1720), p. 34, letter dated 28 September 1720.

[2] The Bank of England's loans and their repayment are described in the next chapter. For the Royal African Company's loans see A. B. Du Bois, *The English Business Company after the Bubble Act 1720–1800* (New York, 1938), p. 398 n. 87.

[3] *The London Journal*, 28 May–4 June 1720. The Governor of the Bank was John Hanger and his deputy Sir Thomas Scawen. For stock prices see Table 17 on p. 139 above.

Fire Office by a speculative syndicate.[1] The real danger of the bubble companies was not so much their objectives as their lax financial methods and the sudden increase in their number. The careful list of projects compiled by Scott shows that 5 were advertised in January 1720, 24 in February, 28 in April, 29 in May, 88 in June, and only 11 in the rest of the year.[2] Their heavy concentration in the short period coinciding with the peak of security prices obviously aroused the alarm and hostility of the South Sea directors. What they overlooked was that attempts to prick these bubbles might, and probably would, also prick their own.

For a time the price of land, the most sober of securities, rose as well, and diverted funds from Exchange Alley. 'Land itself', wrote one pamphleteer,

which one would have thought most solid, had taken its Frisk with the rest, and was got up to about Fifty or Sixty Years' Purchase; but this indeed was a Commodity fit for very few but Directors.[3]

Adam Anderson observes more soberly

It was indeed true that for a few months such as had sold out at high prices, eagerly coveting to purchase land with the money, occasioned lands to be sold at thirty five to forty years purchase; and some for somewhat more.[4]

The inventories of the South Sea directors' estates published in 1721 show that they had contributed to this land boom. Of the 31 directors and governors 16, besides the cashier Knight and his deputy Surman, had bought land in 24 counties, often at extravagant prices.[5] Surman alone had paid £76,000 for

---

[1] Dickson, *Sun Insurance Office*, ch. 3. The Welsh Copper Company was evidently also taken over in the summer of 1720 by another syndicate, headed by Cave Wiseman, see below, p. 502.

[2] List in Scott, iii. 445 ff.

[3] *A True State of the Contracts Relating to the Third Money-Subscription* (1721), pp. 12–13.

[4] Anderson, *Origin of Commerce* (1787 ed.), iii. 114.

[5] The directors who bought land were Astell, Blackwell, Blunt, Chaplin, Chester, Child, Delaporte, Eyles, Gibbon, Gore, Hamond, Hawes, Houlditch, Janssen, Page and Raymond. The trustees for selling the directors' estates refer in their first report in 1722 to many claims against the estates for land contracted for 'at Exorbitant Prices' (report in Bodleian Library copy of R. Chandler, *Votes of the House of Commons* for 1726). See also below, p. 188. Surman completed purchases of land in the counties of Dorset, Essex, Gloucester, Lincoln, Middlesex, Suffolk and Warwick for £75,930. He estimated their annual value as £2,630. This would be nearly twenty-nine years' purchase. He contracted for further lands in Dorset, Essex, Lincs. and Yorks., of an annual value of £2,800 for £102,812. This would be over thirty-seven years' purchase. Blunt contracted in July 1720 with Edward Paston to pay £12,000 for 992 acres in Norfolk of a computed annual value of £378. This would be just over thirty-one years' purchase. The normal top price of land at this date was twenty years' purchase, but leaseholds, life-tenancies, etc., sold for less.

land and contracted for £100,000 more. Knight had paid £67,000 for land. The only directors to come anywhere near these figures were Blunt, who paid £64,000, and Francis Hawes, who paid £73,000. Richard Houlditch paid £26,000; the rest were comfortably under £20,000. Payment, more-over, was sometimes partly made in over-valued South Sea stock and in South Sea bonds. In these instances the high price asked for land was merely a hedge against a fall in stock prices. The impact on the land market of the boom in securities was therefore probably less dramatic than was thought. At the time, however, these qualifications were ignored. Land seemed to be going the way of Exchange Alley. In June Lord Bristol wrote to his son that 'ye value of money is so sinking & consequently that of land so rising, that ye most foresighted men in these matters cannot at present guess where ye proportion between one & t'other is likely to fix.'[1] In August he com-plained to the South Sea director William Astell, who was negotiating to buy land from him, that 'land has almost doubly increased in value since ye time I first fix'd for your final answer'.[2]

Existing companies, new companies, and to some extent land itself, all diverted funds from South Sea speculation. But the biggest hazard proved to be state intervention, which, although the South Sea directors thought they could use it for their own ends, broke in their hands. A committee of the House of Commons had been appointed as early as 22 February 1720 to consider 'the several publick and private Subscriptions in and about the Cities of London and Westminster'.[3] In March, Parliament's hostility to the rising tide of speculation was noted in the Press.[4] At the end of April the *London Journal* welcomed the possibility of a Bill to make all subscriptions void, though sarcastically fearing that it might drive all the stock-jobbers into highway robbery.[5] The Bill in question was not in fact drafted until the following month. Besides the committee on 'unwarrantable practices', another had been appointed to prepare a Bill for incorporation of the London Assurance and Royal Exchange Assurance. On 12 May 1720 the Commons ordered the two committees to work together on a joint Bill, which was swiftly drafted, passed through both houses, and received the king's assent on 11 June.[6] This haste was no doubt partly due to George

---

[1] *Letter Books of John Hervey, first Earl of Bristol* (Wells, 1894), ii. 123, Bristol to Lord Hervey 25 June 1720.

[2] Ibid. 126, Bristol to Astell 4 August 1720.   [3] *HCJ* xix. 274–5.

[4] *The Weekly Journal*, 5 March 1720.

[5] *The London Journal*, 23–30 April 1720.

[6] *HCJ* xix. 361; *HLJ* xxi. 358.

D.F.R.

I's wish to leave for Hanover on 14 June. He did not return until 10 November.[1]

The statute, to be known to posterity as the Bubble Act, was an uneasy knitting together of two quite different measures, as its clumsy title indicated.[2] Its criminal sections made it an offence after midsummer 1720 to 'presume to act' as a corporate body, or to divert an existing charter to unauthorized ends. The legal consequences of the Act were far from straightforward, and were to be debated for most of the rest of the century.[3] At the time it was regarded, rightly or not, simply as a stroke at annoying rivals by the all-powerful South Sea Company, which feared

> that if there was not a stop put to this Affair, it might take off abundance of their Bubbles, and by lessening the number of their Buyers, lessen, if not spoil, their Market.[4]

It was at first noted that the new Act had emptied Exchange Alley.[5] But this check, administered when the market was at its strongest, was no more than temporary. New projects continued to be advertised, and it was not until 24 June that the lately reconstituted Treasury Board ordered the Attorney-General and Solicitor-General to consider how to stop the unlawful subscriptions 'daily increasing in the City of London'.[6] Throughout July, with the king in Hanover, 'the Town a desert and the world crammed into Change Alley',[7] no serious action was taken. On 12 July the Lords Justices, deputed to act during the king's absence abroad, dismissed eighteen petitions for incorporation from groups of projectors, but this was no more than a palliative.[8] Whatever the Attorney-General and Solicitor-General may have been doing as a result of the Treasury's first instructions, they

---

[1] According to other sources he left on 15 June and returned on 9 November.

[2] 6 Geo. I, c. 18, 'An Act for better securing certain Powers and Privileges, intended to be granted by His Majesty by Two Charters, for Assurance of Ships and Merchandizes at Sea, and for lending Money upon Bottomry; and for restraining several extravagant and unwarrantable Practices therein mentioned.'

[3] A. B. Du Bois, *The English Business Company after the Bubble Act 1720–1800* (New York, 1938).

[4] *The Original Weekly Journal*, 25 June 1720.

[5] *The London Journal*, 11–18 June 1720.

[6] P.R.O. T 29/24 (i), f. 275, Treasury Board Minutes, 24 June 1720. On 11 June 1720 a new Treasury commission had been issued under which William Clayton and John Wallop were replaced by Richard Edgecumbe and Sir Charles Turner. The other three members (Lord Sunderland, John Aislabie and George Baillie) remained unchanged.

[7] H.M.C. *Bath*, iii. 483, Matthew Prior to Lord Harley, 2 July 1720.

[8] The Lords Justices' decision is printed in Boyer, *Political State* xx. 51 ff.

gave no advice until the Treasury again approached the former, and the Treasury Solicitor, on 17 August about 'the Trade now carryd on in Defiance of the Laws with relation to the buying and selling unwarrantable Stocks.'[1] The advice returned, given with all speed, was evidently that writs of *scire facias* should be issued against three companies, the English Copper Company, the Royal Lutestring Company and the York Buildings Company, which were contravening the Bubble Act by misapplying their charters.[2] The Lords Justices were advised accordingly, and they authorized writs against these three companies and the Welsh Copper Company the following day, 18 August 1720.[3]

From this date the price of South Sea stock began to fall. The break was not at first disastrous. On 22 August the company's transfer books reopened, and on the 24th the fourth Money Subscription at 1000 was filled 'in less than Three Hours.'[4] On the 25th the directors decided to close the transfer books again on the 31st in order to make a new issue of stock, amounting to 20% of the existing capital and confined to those who were already proprietors.[5] By this stage, however, the ground was crumbling beneath their feet. On 30 August they made a desperate attempt to keep up prices by resolving to declare a 30% Christmas dividend and offering to guarantee a 50% dividend for the next twelve years.[6] The General Court on 8 September 1720 actually agreed to this piece of moonshine, but as a defensive move it was swept on one side by an avalanche of selling, which by mid-September had brought South Sea stock down 250 points to 520, and by 1 October another 230 points to 290. The Bubble had exploded.

Anderson attributes the catastrophe to the 'fatal *scire facias*', which according to him, the directors themselves had procured from the government, and which had acted on the market like the 'touch of Ithuriel's spear.'[7] A similar charge had been made against the directors when the Bubble Act was passed in June.[8] The evidence about the directors' responsibility for the *scire facias* is in fact evenly balanced, though it is clear that their general

[1] P.R.O. T 29/24 (1), f. 291, Treasury Board Minutes, 17 August 1720.

[2] Ibid.

[3] The Lords Justices' proclamation is printed in Boyer, op. cit. xx. 138 ff.

[4] Boyer, op. cit., p. 143.

[5] Add. MS. 25499, f. 44, South Sea D. Ct. Bk., 25 August 1720. Cf. too above, p. 128. The General Court on 8 September 1720 resolved that this subscription should not be held.

[6] Add. MS. 25499, f. 45.

[7] Anderson, *Origin of Commerce* (1787 ed.), iii. 98, 103.

[8] See above, p. 148.

attitude to the bubble companies was one of hostility.[1] What both the government and the South Sea directors failed to realise was that the smaller bubbles were unlikely to be suppressed without destroying the largest one as well.

Important external influences were in any case already affecting the market. Wharton had argued in the Lords in April that the South Sea project

gave foreigners an opportunity to double and treble the vast sums they had in our public funds, which could not but tempt them to withdraw their capital stock ... which might drain Great Britain of a considerable part of its gold and silver.[2]

Wharton was not the coolest of heads, but his prediction seems to have been borne out. As early as July 1720 there were sinister rumours that the Swiss Cantons had given their agents orders to sell out of South Sea stock.[3] The largest holder, the Canton of Berne, in fact retained its stock, but the mere possibility that it would sell was alarming.[4] By September, reports of sales by foreigners had become more definite, and were probably true. *Applebee's Journal* told its anxious readers on 10 September that

We hear the Agents for the French sold off last Tuesday, Wednesday, and Thursday, 300,000*l*. Capital in the South Sea Stock; As did the Dutch, Swiss, and many other Foreigners, which being much contrary to what was expected, the Stock fell to 645 and is expected to fall much lower very soon.[5]

A few months later a pamphleteer ascribed the prevalent 'want of money' to

the unhappy Management of South-Sea Stock, bringing that and other Stocks to such extravagant Advance that induc'd Foreigners to sell out and draw much more from us than otherwise they wou'd or cou'd have done; this the Exchanges demonstrate.[6]

---

[1] Professor L. C. B. Gower in 'A South Sea Heresy?', *LQR* lxviii (1952), 214, argues that there is no supporting evidence in contemporary sources for Anderson's assertion. Professor Gower's argument is strong but not conclusive. An application of this sort would probably have been made verbally, and Anderson as a South Sea clerk might have known of it. Cf. the letter from Lord Townshend to Robert Walpole on 23 August 1720 in which the South Sea Company is said to have complained to the Lords Justices about the bubble companies (J. H. Plumb, *Sir Robert Walpole*, i, 314).

[2] *Parl. Hist.* vii. 646, 4 April 1720.

[3] *Applebee's Original Weekly Journal*, 16 July 1720.

[4] For the Canton of Berne's holding of over £250,000, see below, p. 314.

[5] *Applebee's Original Weekly Journal*, 10 September 1720.

[6] *A State of South-Sea Stock* (n.d., but from internal evidence written in the winter of 1720–1).

The rate of exchange on Amsterdam, Europe's leading commercial centre, had indeed moved sharply against London from July 1720. 'The exchange is low owing to the continual remittance [to Holland] of large sums realised by the sale of stock', commented a London house to a Dutch client on 15 August 1720.[1] A temporary revival in mid-October was almost immediately reversed, and the exchange did not reach its former parity until the first half of 1721.[2] With the exchange against London, gold started to be remitted instead. The price of bar gold, normally just below £3 18s. 0d. an ounce, moved above par in July and stayed above it until well into the winter.[3] Early in August it was noted that bullion was being shipped to Holland,[4] and a month later that

The Quantities of Gold and Silver exported from this Kingdom to Holland have of late been very large and remarkable.[5]

As late as November it was stated that it was the great exports of gold that had raised its price to £4 2s. 0d. an ounce.[6] Alarmed by the situation, the Lords Justices approached the Bank of England. The Governor reported on 15 September that they had asked that

this Court would contribute their Endeavours for maintaining the Course of the Foreign Exchanges, and assured them, That the Loss that might be sustained thereby should be made good to the Bank.[7]

The Bank agreed to draw on debtors in Amsterdam to help ease the strain.[8] Early in October *Applebee's Journal* reported that the government had ordered the Mint to coin £1m. in gold and silver, and added that the king had contracted abroad for a further £2m. silver, to be imported via Holland.[9] The government also put out feelers to the East India and South Sea companies, and committees of directors of all three met to discuss the question of the exchanges on 15 and 16 September 1720.[10] But the tide of home events was now running so strongly against the South Sea Company that it was in urgent need of help itself, and in no position to give it to others. It

---

[1] 'De wissel is laagh door d'groote somma's continueel overgemaakt voor vercogte acties' (Schoppens & Edwards in London to Simon Bevel in Haarlem, 15 August 1720, quoted in F. Ph. Groeneveld, *De Economische Crisis van het Jaar 1720* (p. 142). See also Table 17 on p. 139, above.

[2] See Table 17.   [3] Ibid.   [4] *The Daily Post*, 5 August 1720.

[5] *The Whitehall Evening Post*, 13–15 September 1720.

[6] *The London Journal*, 5–12 November 1720.

[7] Bank of England D. Ct. Bk. H, ff. 169–70, 15 September 1720.

[8] Ibid., ff. 177–8, 27 September 1720.

[9] *Applebee's Original Weekly Journal*, 8 October 1720.   [10] See below, p. 163.

was at the committee meeting on 16 September that it used one of the East India directors as intermediary to make its first appeal for help to its hated rival, the Bank of England.[1]

The foreign-exchange crisis in the late summer and early autumn of 1720 was not entirely due, however, as contemporaries thought, to heavy sales of stock by foreigners. It was partly due also to two other factors. First, and less important, was a supposed improvement in the affairs of the Mississippi Company.[2] As late as September the *Weekly Journal* felt able to observe that John Law had entirely succeeded in his plans and renewed the strength of France.[3] More significant than this temporary rally in Paris was the floatation of numerous companies in the Netherlands from June 1720 onwards. Between mid-June and mid-October over forty projects were advertised there.[4] They resembled their English counterparts in having large nominal capitals the first payments on which were quite small; and also in having as their objectives the relief of points of tension or difficulty in the economy: insurance, loans and discounts, wool and linen production, tobacco-planting, sugar-refining and so on. Few of them survived the year of their floatation, but their initial success was enough to divert Dutch speculation from Paris and London, and to encourage English speculators to realize their gains at home and remit them to Holland. As early as mid-June 1720 the *London Journal* reported that

They tell us from Holland, that the Dutch are going to establish a great Fund, which shall be like a South Sea or Mississipi, and we find our Merchants here have already begun to remit Money thither, that they may come into the first of it.[5]

In August and September the Press reported the movement of individual speculators from England to Holland.[6] Englishmen and Scots appeared in the subscription lists of new Dutch companies.[7] Nor were they the only foreign subscribers. In Utrecht, where a company was floated in September, old men said they had never seen so many foreigners.[8] In the international financial débâcle of the next two months nearly all these fine projects toppled in ruins. But while they lasted they had financial allure.

English money began to flow on a smaller scale into Portuguese specu-

---

[1] Ibid.   [2] *The Weekly Journal*, 6 August 1720.   [3] Ibid., 3 September 1720.
[4] F. Ph. Groeneveld, *De Economische crisis van het Jaar 1720.*
[5] *The London Journal*, 11–18 June 1720.
[6] *The Evening Post*, 25–27 August 1720; *The Whitehall Evening Post* 13–15 September 1720.
[7] Groeneveld, op. cit., ch. v and app. i.
[8] Ibid., p. 160, quoting Jan van Breda to Simon Bevel, 16 September 1720 (N.S.).

lation as well. The puritan court of Madrid had rejected various 'projects' at the end of August,[1] but the financial climate across the frontier was evidently more temperate. On 3 September 1720 the *Weekly Journal* noted that 'Great Remittances are daily making from hence to Portugal to buy into the Brasil Bubble, newly set up at Lisbon'.[2] A lawsuit brought in London in 1722 contains among interrogatories the question 'Do you know of any Order that was sent by the Defts. the Arthurs to any person at Lisbon to buy on Account of the Defendt. Shadforth any stock or Subscription there?'[3] By November, however, the Portuguese prospect had clouded, as it had elsewhere. The *London Journal* reported

Our last Letters from Lisbon say, that of the many fine Projects that have been proposed there, none are like to succeed; the Fate of their Neighbour having quite spoil'd their Gust for such Chimeras.[4]

VII

The implications of the South Sea Bubble's collapse, and its interaction with the parallel and equally sudden collapse of the markets in France and the Netherlands, were spelled out with bitter clarity to an increasingly desperate English public as October succeeded September. First the South Sea Company itself and the government which had almost become its accomplice, then the king, then Parliament when it reassembled early in December 1720, were forced to recognize the harsh fact that the financial crisis threatened the nation with social and political ruin. This situation, and the measures taken to deal with it, are described in the next chapter. This one ends with some remarks and questions about the ground gone over so far.

It seems clear that the South Sea Bubble was not an isolated English event, but formed part of an international movement of speculation in 1719–20, touched off by John Law's grandiose schemes for French trade and finance. In Paris, London, and perhaps at first in the United Provinces,[5] this movement had at its core the wish to liquidate, or at least alter the structure of, the

---

[1] *The Flying Post or Post-Master*, 30 August–1 September 1720.

[2] *The Weekly Journal*, 3 September 1720.

[3] P.R.O. E 134, 8 and 9 Geo. I, Trinity Term no. 9, *Crossley* v. *Shadforth*, a suit arising out of speculation in Holland and Portugal in 1720. The quotation in the text omits several words which are due to legal redundancy.

[4] *The London Journal*, 12–19 November 1720.   [5] See above, p. 141.

vast debts created by the wars of 1689–1714. Superimposed on this wish
were schemes for economic betterment, which had a more solid basis in
contemporary needs than has usually been acknowledged, but which were
nearly all loosely controlled and unrealistically financed. These factors
underlay the most obvious feature of speculation in all the countries affected
— dealings in securities which brought their prices to dizzy heights. These
were most marked in countries (England, France, the Netherlands), where
a market in securities was already reasonably well organized before the
boom began. The boom itself lasted longer in Paris than in London, longer
in London than in the Netherlands, and longer in the Netherlands than in
Hamburg or Lisbon. There was considerable movement of speculative funds
between the three leading financial centres of Paris, London, and Amsterdam, and these movements affected the timing and duration of speculation.
Thus it was argued earlier that large-scale selling by foreigners was one of
the causes of the weakening of the London market in August–September
1720, and that another was the simultaneous division of English funds into
the new projects in the Netherlands.

There are still many gaps in our knowledge both of these developments,
and of the South Sea Bubble's social and economic consequences. Thus,
reliable lists of those who made fortunes, like Thomas Guy, or broke on a
staggering scale, like Sir Justus Beck, would be extremely interesting,
though there seems little hope of obtaining them.[1] It would also be interesting to know if the boom led to increased investment in urban building.[2]
Again, its effects on the land market in the provinces have never been
properly explored. Lastly, there may have been an influence on prices other
than those of securities. In France, as Professor Hamilton's researches
showed some years ago, massive creation of paper money by Law's bank led
to an equally massive inflation of the prices of consumer goods.[3] So far as is
known, price inflation in England was limited to securities, but it would be
interesting to know whether Pope's casual remark about the increase in the
price of venison in 1720 could be extended to cover a whole range of luxuries.[4]

This chapter ends with a more general subject, the social background to the

---

[1] For Guy see *DNB*. For Beck see below, p. 158.

[2] Great James Street, London, W.C.1, off Theobald's Road, a rare example of a complete early Georgian street, was finished in 1721. No other instances have so far been
traced.

[3] E. J. Hamilton, 'Prices and Wages at Paris under John Law's System', *Quarterly
Journal of Economics*, li (1936), 42; 'Prices and Wages in Southern France under John
Law's System', *Econ. Hist.* iii (1934–7), 441.

[4] Alexander Pope, *Moral Essays, Epistle*, iii, ll. 117–18.

South Sea Bubble. This has usually been ignored. It is, however, obviously relevant to the apparently hysterical and ungoverned behaviour of contemporaries, both in the boom and after its collapse. The setting for the Bubble was a great town, where the death-rate was high, and disease, misery and crime flourished. For the poor, employment was uncertain and badly paid. Commercial life was overshadowed by the fear of bankruptcy, ordinary life was profoundly affected by the threat of the debtors' prison. The risk of fire, which could cripple the most prosperous in a few hours, as it crippled the South Sea director William Astell in 1720, was only just beginning to be limited by insurance.[1] All classes were exposed to horrifying dangers from bad building, bad drainage, bad food, dangerous patent-medicines, and imperfect surgery — performed without anaesthetics.

Uncertainty stimulated fraud and brutality. Thus, deceit in revenue dealings, documented by the committee on Customs frauds in 1733, was a constant preoccupation of the legislature.[2] A year before the report on Customs frauds, the Bank of England discovered that a deceased former director, Humphrey Morice, had discounted at the Bank fictitious bills of exchange supposed to be drawn in the West Indies.[3] The directors of the Charitable Corporation and the York Buildings Company were shown in 1732–3 to be guilty of equally polished deceit on a larger scale. The collapse of the Charitable Corporation, indeed, reproduced many of the features of the South Sea Bubble: incriminating acts by directors, the flight abroad of company servants who knew too much, a parliamentary committee of inquiry, ejection of director M.P.s from the House of Commons, an Act for relief of the sufferers.[4] For the lower orders crime was more direct. The roads in and around London abounded with highwaymen, whose execution when caught was a spectacle for the eager mob. A proclamation against them on 21 January 1720, offering £100 reward for the capture of individuals, seems to have had little effect; in August it was noted that despite the proclamation highwaymen were still very numerous in and near the capital.[5]

[1] For Astell's loss see above, p. 119.

[2] *Report of the Committee appointed to enquire into the Frauds and Abuses in the Customs, Reports from Committees of the House of Commons*, i (1803). Cf. the preambles to 8 Geo. I, cc. 4 and 18 (1722), 9 Geo. I, c. 21 (1723), 10 Geo. I, c. 10 (1724).

[3] W. Marston Acres, *The Bank of England from within* (1931), i. 154–5; Bank D. Ct. Bk. L, f. 268, 20 January 1732.

[4] *Reports* of the committees appointed to inquire into the affairs of the Charitable Corporation (April 1732) and the York Buildings Company (May 1733), *Reports from Committees of the House of Commons*, loc. cit.

[5] *The Evening Post* 25–27 August 1720.

Furthermore, brutality and a wanton disregard for life permeated London society. In February 1720 it was nonchalantly reported that a hackney coachman demanding more than his fare had been run through by his passenger, who had then escaped.[1] The weavers' campaign against imported calicoes was partly conducted by attacking women wearing them.[2] Military violence complemented civil violence. In March and again in September 1720 naked soldiers were publicly flogged in St. James's Park. In the second incident each of the soldiers concerned received 900 lashes; they were presumably flogged to death.[3]

The fever of speculation during the Bubble, which affected so unfavourably the judgement even of those experienced in business, and the harshness of the attitudes taken up after its collapse, must be seen against this background, which was probably similar to that of the other great cities of Europe. Great and obvious disparities of wealth, together with social insecurity and the prevalence of corruption, fraud and violence, bred an appetite for gain, and a lack of scruple in obtaining it, which, given exceptional circumstances, could and did become uncontrolled. The *London Journal* in October 1720 invited the public to consider whether its own avarice and love of luxury were not the true cause of the South Sea boom and its collapse.[4] In March 1721 the *Weekly Journal*, looking back over the astonishing events of the previous year, concluded that they were basically the result of debauched public morality; the Bubble was 'but the natural Effect of those Vices which have reign'd for so many Years'.[5] As Adam Anderson wrote later: 'Avarice had at that time deeply infected persons of all ranks, whereby they contributed not a little to favour the South Sea managers, and to forward their own subsequent losses.'[6]

[1] *The Original Weekly Journal*, 27 February 1720.
[2] See above, p. 137.
[3] *The Weekly Journal*, 5 March and 3 September 1720.
[4] *The London Journal*, 8–15 October 1720.
[5] *The Weekly Journal, or British Gazeteer*, 4 March 1721.
[6] *Origin of Commerce* (1787 ed.), iii. 123.

7

Financial Relief and Reconstruction 1720–30 (I)

I

B y late September 1720 the prevailing mood in London, Paris, Amsterdam and most of the other great commercial centres of Europe was one of alarm shading into panic and despair. John Law's Mississippi Company had collapsed during the month as suddenly and desperately as the South Sea Company. In early September Law's prospects had been favourably assessed in England.[1] By October the bottom had dropped out of the Paris market. On 29 September the French government announced that after three weeks the notes of the Royal Bank would not be accepted in payments.[2] Late in December Law fled to Brussels to save his skin. In Amsterdam a similar climate prevailed. Extreme optimism changed abruptly to extreme pessimism. In November 1720 it was reported that 'The Fall of their [Dutch] Stocks has ruin'd many of their Famous Merchants; and Stopping of Payment there hath been almost as much in Fashion as with us.'[3] In February 1721 the news from Holland was that

the States of Holland are now deliberating, how to abolish all the Companies of Commerce and Insurance, which have been Established in the Southern and Northern Quarters of that Province: They now appear beyond Contradiction, extremely pernicious to Trade, Navigation, Manufactures, and the Circulation of Money in all Parts of this Republick.[4]

In London, where the market had crashed first, perhaps triggering-off the collapse in France and Holland, panic as extreme as the summer's euphoria tightened its grip on social and economic life. Foreign bills drawn on London from Holland, Portugal and Spain were returned protested.[5] On 29

---

[1] See above, p. 152.

[2] The announcement was made on 10 October 1720 (N.S.), i.e. 29 September (O.S.).

[3] *The London Journal*, 5–12 November 1720.

[4] *The Post-Man*, 11–14 February 1721.

[5] *The London Journal*, 8–15 October 1720, 5–12 November 1720.

September the Bank of England ceased for a month to discount bills at all.[1] The ties of trade between London and Amsterdam, in particular, were so close that the crisis in each was bound to affect the other. Thus on 11 October 1720 Robert Walpole's banker Jacombe wrote to him that

One house in Holland is broke, with whom sir J. Beck had great transactions, what effect it will have upon him, is not yet knowne.[2]

By 22 October Beck was bankrupt, for *Applebee's Journal* described how

you may meet with the melancholy Trophies of one eminent Merchant's Fall, a Pair of his remarkable Coach-Horses driven about the Streets in a Hackney-Coach.

A contemporary hand notes in the margin 'Sr. Justus Beck'.[3] Dutch sources show that Beck's liabilities amounted to £347,000. The most his creditors could obtain was 5s. in the £ by 1732.[4] Failures in London in turn affected houses in the provinces. In early October it was reported from Bristol that 'five of the most eminent Merchants have fail'd, which has caused a great Consternation'.[5] Liquidity preference in London moved sharply upwards and there were many runs on bankers.[6] On 24 September the Sword Blade Bank, whose directors were closely connected with the 'Junto' of South Sea directors, suspended payment. Many of those who had engaged in contracts for South Sea stock fled into the liberties of the City to avoid their creditors.[7] In Northern Ireland (and presumably also in Dublin) trade was at a stand-still. Bishop Nicolson of Londonderry wrote to Archbishop Wake on 21 October 1720: 'Yarn and Linnen-Cloath, our only Support, are already unsaleable; and we are indeed within an Ace of bartering one Commodity for another.'[8] A sidelight on the perturbation of the times is that, as in the summer, the volume of letters carried by the English Post Office was abnormally large, higher in 1720 and 1721 than in any other years between 1716 and 1733.[9]

---

[1] Bank D. Ct. Bk. H, f. 179, 29 September 1720, discounting of Bills of Exchange suspended until further order; f. 188, 20 October 1720, discounting resumed under limitations.

[2] Coxe, *Walpole*, ii. 193, Under-Secretary Jacombe to Walpole 11 October 1720.

[3] *Applebee's Original Weekly Journal*, 22 October 1720, copy in Nichols Newspaper Collection, Bodleian Library.

[4] Amsterdam, Archief Brants, 1649, Schoppens & Edwards in London to Simon Bevel in Haarlem, 1 November 1720, 9 June 1732 (in Dutch). The first letter describes Beck as 'a man of considerable capital and of the first credit on the Exchange'. He died in 1722.

[5] *Applebee's Original Weekly Journal*, 8 October 1720.

[6] Boyer, op. cit. xx. 198, 23 September 1720; Coxe, *Walpole*, ii. 191, Brodrick to Midleton, 27 September 1720; *The Weekly Journal*, 8 October 1720.

[7] *Applebee's Original Weekly Journal*, 29 April 1721.   [8] Add. MS. 6116, f. 114.

[9] Post Office revenue figures in *HCJ* xxii. 464, 16 April 1735.

On the Continent an even more sinister enemy than financial crisis made its appearance. This was the plague, travelling along the commercial routes from the Near East. 'Distempers reigning in several Parts of the Turkish Dominions' had been reported as early as December 1719, but the infection did not reach Marseilles until August 1720.[1] In that month and in September it spread to Mannheim and Paris, despite the construction of an elaborate *cordon sanitaire*.[2] Precautions were taken in Rome, Berne, Geneva and Savoy.[3] In England, the Lords Justices issued a proclamation on 25 August 1720 enforcing quarantine for ships coming from the Mediterranean.[4] Further and more stringent measures were taken in 1721 and 1722.[5] By April 1721 plague was reported to have ceased at Marseilles, but there were cases of it in Provence as late as June.[6] This scourge, coinciding with the great European financial collapse of 1720–1, must have exerted a most unfavourable influence on the revival of confidence.

As the English autumn shaded into winter, the crisis deepened. By the time Parliament reassembled in early December 1720 South Sea stock stood at 191, having lost nearly 600 points since 1 September. The company's bonds, which had increased in volume during the year by over £3m., were quoted at 15% discount by mid-December, despite the fact that their nominal interest had been increased from 4% to 5% at Michaelmas. Every class which had lost by the disaster was clamouring for relief: the Annuitants, the Money Subscribers, those who had borrowed from the company, the buyers and sellers of stock for time. Their interests were mutually conflicting, and it was obviously impossible to relieve some except at the expense of others. Moreover, as 'the famous Mr. W[alpo]le' pointed out in November 1720, 'he knew of no Scheme that would be able to Restore the Ruin'd Credit of those Affairs, to bear any Proportion to the Flourishing Circumstances they were lately in.'[7] Popular despair and frustration found a partial vent from October 1720 onwards in a tide of abuse against the South Sea directors.[8]

---

[1] *St. James's Weekly Journal*, 2 January 1720, report from Vienna dated 13 December 1719 (N.S.); *The Daily Post*, 6 August 1720.

[2] *The Post-Boy*, 18–20 August 1720; *The Evening Post*, 25–27 August 1720; *The Whitehall Evening Post*, 6–8 September 1720.

[3] *The Whitehall Evening Post*, 23–25 August 1720.

[4] Printed in Boyer, *Pol. State*, xx. 157.   [5] 7 Geo. I, c. 3; 8 Geo. I, cc. 8 and 18.

[6] *The London Journal*, 1 April 1721; *The Whitehall Evening Post*, 1–3 June 1721.

[7] *The London Journal*, 12–19 Nov. 1720, report that 'the famous Mr. W-le' had received and perused various plans for the restoration of public credit.

[8] *The London Journal*, 8–15 October 1720, 19–26 November 1720; H.M.C., *Bath MSS.*, iii. 493, Matthew Prior to Lord Harley, 3 Jan. 1721.

In January 1720 the London mob was crying 'break Janson and Lambert on the wheel — as in their countries they would have been served'.[1] The very severity of the crisis, which turned each man's hand to the retrieval of his own fortunes to the exclusion of those of others may, indeed, have prevented popular wrath from taking a more dangerous form. As Arthur Onslow, then a young M.P., later recorded:

I have often wondered that this [i.e. the crash] did not produce some convulsion in the State. That it did not was certainly owing to people of all denominations thinking of nothing but their own losses and flattering themselves with the hopes of some quick turn in the public credit as they called it, to recover their late fortunes. If otherwise, or some bold men had taken advantage of the general disorder men's minds were in, to provoke them to insurrection, the rage against the Government was such for having as they thought drawn them into this ruin, that I am almost persuaded, the King being at that time abroad, that could the Pretender then have landed at the Tower, he might have rode to St. James's with very few hands held up against him. I was at London in the midst of this confusion and well remember that I then made this reflection.[2]

At the heart of the prevailing stringency of credit was the complex network of sums due from and to the South Sea Company. The latter's obligations, as they were worked out later by the new directors elected in February 1721, are shown in Table 18.

This account overstated the bond debt, but as against this other debts amounting to £460,000 were omitted.[3]

The company's assets consisted in over £11m. due from those who had borrowed from it on stock and scrip in 1720; in the nominal £60m. to £70m. due from the Money Subscribers; and in the £15,743,500 South Sea stock it held itself at the end of 1720.[4] These items were worth little for four reasons. In the first place, punctual compliance with calls on the part of the Money Subscribers was wildly improbable; indeed the company was already considering remission of further calls. The same argument applied to the sums due on stock and scrip: it was unlikely that more than a fraction could realistically be claimed. Third, the stock the company held itself was

---

[1] Prior to Harley, loc. cit.

[2] H.M.C., *14th Report*, app. ix, *Onslow MSS.* 504. The king returned to England on 10 November 1720.

[3] £300,000 was due to the Bank of England (see below, p. 166), and about £160,000 more for unclaimed dividends, bills of exchange and sundry bills, 'An Account of what Sums of Money have been taken up . . . on Accot. of the SS Co.', dated 9 January 1721 (H.L.R.O., Parchment Coll., South Sea Company Papers, Box 167).

[4] For these amounts see above, pp. 125, 136.

TABLE 18

Liabilities of the South Sea Company at the end of 1720

	£
1. *Due to the state*	
(a) Premium for being allowed to make an offer to the state's creditors	4,156,306
(b) 4½ years' purchase of Irredeemable debts (annuities) exchanged for South Sea stock	2,847,321
(c) One year's purchase of Irredeemable debts *not* exchanged . .	161,364
	7,164,991
(d) Exchequer bills borrowed from the state 4 June 1720 and repayable 7 June 1721	1,000,000
(e) One year's interest on these bills at 4%	40,000
Total due to state	£8,204,991
2. *Due to others*	
(f) Due on bonds 'upwards of'	5,000,000
(g) 5% Christmas dividend on £26m. South Sea stock . . .	1,300,000
(h) Interest on bonds to Christmas 1720	125,000
TOTAL LIABILITIES	£14,629,991

Source : Statement presented by the new South Sea directors to Parliament 13 February 1721, *HCJ* xix. 421–2, partly rearranged. This statement would have been true for the end of 1720 as well.

virtually an unreliable asset, in view of the bitter memories of the issues of stock earlier in 1720. Lastly, the desperate condition of the subscribers of debts and money in any case provided the strongest justification for distributing this 'surplus' stock to them.

This apparently insoluble tangle of debts and counter-claims, of demands which could not be mitigated without grave loss nor met without intolerable hardship, was the core of the problem with which first the South Sea Company itself, and then Parliament, had to grapple in the winter and spring of 1720–1. Around it was an indefinite penumbra of preparations for legal action, and the threat of further preparations. Complex social groups and economic interests were involved. The public creditors affected alone amounted to some 30,000 individuals, groups and corporations, many of them rich London financiers and merchants, finance houses, banks and insurance companies.[1] Trustees for minors and for married and unmarried

[1] See below, p. 271.

women had compromised their beneficiaries' incomes by eagerly exchanging their securities for South Sea stock. The Money Subscribers numbered several thousand, including a majority of Members of Parliament and a minority of the House of Lords.[1] The mutual obligations for private loans and contracts entered into in 1720 may have been the largest group of debts of all. They were computed by a contemporary at £90m.; on more sober evidence it is known that the contracts for sale of stock and scrip registered at South Sea House alone in 1721 amounted to nearly £10m.[2] Together with a mass of small and middling interests, the financial crisis thus involved some of the greatest and most influential in the kingdom. The threat of ruin for the state — and the concurrent ruin of property — which the generation of 1688 had thought discarded with Shaftesbury and James II, had once more made its hideous appearance; more frighteningly, perhaps, because of the new and sophisticated form which it had assumed. The remainder of this chapter describes how a way out was eventually found, though not easily, nor without bitterness.

II

The initial moves were made by the South Sea Company in September 1720, when the house of cards was only just beginning to collapse. The company's General Court met three times in this month, its first sessions since April. On 8 September it agreed that dividends due on stock subscribed for should be allowed in payment of calls due on it; it was also suggested that the calls on the fourth Money Subscription should be more widely spaced.[3] Prices, however, were sinking daily, and these measures quickly proved insufficient. At the next court, on 20 September, the Sub-Governor, Sir John Fellowes, took powers to draft relief measures for the second group of public creditors (those whose terms had been announced in August) and for those concerned in the last two Money Subscriptions.[4] A committee of the whole directors'

---

[1] See above, p. 108.

[2] *Reasons for making void and annulling those Fraudulent and Usurious Contracts* (n.d., clearly 1721), p. 2; Anderson, *Origin of Commerce* (1787 ed.), iii. 123.

[3] Add. MS. 25499, ff. 47–48, South Sea D. Ct. Bk., 8 September 1720, report of decisions of the General Court.

[4] Add. MS., loc. cit., f. 53.

court appointed to study the problem presented its recommendations on 20 September 1720 to the third General Court to meet in the month.[1] The measures proposed were that the price at which South Sea stock should be valued for the second group of public creditors should be halved to a figure of 400 — this would effectively double their allocation of stock; that redeemable stock should be exchanged for South Sea stock at par, and not at £105 Redeemables for £100 South Sea stock as previously offered; that the 10% midsummer dividend in stock, declared on 14 April 1720, should be added to the stock already held by the public creditors; that the issue price of the last two Money Subscriptions should be reduced from 1,000 to 400; and that the calls on them should be more widely spaced. The company evidently still hoped that it could conciliate the public creditors by bettering their terms, and persuade the Money Subscribers to complete their subscriptions, though at a lower rate and over a longer period. Both hopes were to prove mistaken.

Meanwhile, the company's directors had concluded that something drastic must be done to improve public confidence in its own stock and bonds, and that this involved swallowing the bitter pill of soliciting the help of the Bank of England, whose power and prestige they had dreamed for a brief moment of eclipsing. The meetings about the foreign exchanges of committees of directors of the East India and South Sea companies and the Bank of England on 15 and 16 September 1720 provided an opportunity.[2] At the conclusion of the second meeting the South Sea directors asked William Dawsonne, one of the East India directors present, to hand on a paper to the directors of the Bank. This oblique approach indicated their understandable nervousness. The paper read

The Court of Directors of the South Sea Compa: Do think it of Importance to the Publick Credit that their Bonds to a Certain Sum be circulated for a time to be agreed on And are of Opinion that the same may best be done for the publick Service by the Bank of England; and if they are willing to Undertake the same; the Court of Directors of the South Sea Compa. have Empowered the Sub & Deputy Govr. to treat with them about it.[3]

The directors of the Bank, who were hard-headed men, were easily capable of penetrating the hypocritical language about the public service and

[1] Ibid., f. 58.   [2] For these meetings see above, p. 151.

[3] H.L.R.O., Parchment Coll., South Sea Company Papers Box 167, 'Copy of Minutes of the Committee [of South Sea directors] appointed to treat with the Bank', 15 September 1720–10 November 1720.

construing the paper as what it was, a cry for help. They promptly got in touch with members of the government, and on 19 September 1720 a conference was held at Postmaster Craggs's house 'at the General Post Office'. The Ministers who attended were evidently Aislabie, Postmaster Craggs, his son Secretary Craggs, Lord Townshend, and Robert Walpole, who had recently returned from Norfolk to attend to his affairs in London. There were also committees of directors of the Bank of England and the South Sea Company. At the end of a prolonged discussion Walpole, by far the most eminent financier present, was asked to draft a note recording with suitable blanks the basis for further negotiations. The basis was that the Bank would circulate £3m. South Sea bonds for one year, would hold a subscription to enable itself to do so, and would 'subscribe into' the South Sea Company the annuity of £188,751 which the government paid it as interest on funded Exchequer bills.[1]

The meaning of this 'first rough Draught, or Sketch of a future Agreement . . . void of all Form, or any manner of Obligation', as Walpole later described it, but which was almost at once labelled by public opinion 'the Bank Contract', became clearer during the next three days.[2] On 20 and 22 September the General Courts of the South Sea Company and the Bank of England empowered their directors to conclude an agreement.[3] On 21 September committees of the two companies had already met to discuss the terms of the first part of the scheme, support of the price of South Sea bonds. The arrangements for this, when completed in detail, were as follows. The Bank would open a subscription 'for the support of Publick Credit' on 23 September 1720. The contract with the subscribers was to run to Michaelmas 1721. They were to pay in 15% in Bank of England notes or in goldsmith-bankers' notes they had themselves endorsed, and were to be liable for further calls in tenths at ten days' notice. They were to be allowed 3% premium on the amount they *subscribed* and 5% interest on the amount they

---

[1] The sources for the meeting are the minutes of the South Sea Committee appointed to treat with the Bank (H.L.R.O., Parchment Coll., loc. cit.); A. Boyer, op. cit., xx. 187; *Applebee's Original Weekly Journal*, 24 September 1720; and Walpole's later pamphlet *Some Considerations concerning the Publick Funds* (1735), p. 87. The minutes of the South Sea Directors' Court for 20 September 1720 record a meeting on the previous day with several Bank directors 'in the presence of Several Persons of the first Rank' but do not give their names.

[2] Walpole, *Some Considerations*, loc. cit. See the photograph of the 'Bank Contract' on Plate 4.

[3] Add. MS. 25499, f. 53, South Sea D. Ct. Bk., 20 September 1720, report of proceedings of General Court held same day; Bank D. Ct. Bk. H, f. 173, 22 September 1720.

paid in. This amounted to a return of 25%. The total to be subscribed was settled at £3m.[1] This contract was an almost exact copy of those which the Bank had held since 1711 for the 'circulation' of Exchequer bills, and presumably had the same intention, namely that holders of in this instance South Sea bonds could be sure that the South Sea Company would be prepared to buy them at par, using the subscribed money to do so.[2]

While the subscription which it was hoped would save the South Sea bonds was being opened on 23 September 1720, committees of the Bank and South Sea Company were meeting to discuss the second part of the 'Bank Contract', aimed at salvaging the price of South Sea stock. What was envisaged was basically a straight sale of a large amount of South Sea stock to the Bank. It was obviously hoped that the news of this would support the market price and the market in general. The form of the transaction was somewhat complicated. The bank already received £188,751 p.a. from the Exchequer, as 5% interest on £3,775,000 Exchequer bills originally funded in 1709 and 1717.[3] What was proposed was that this annuity should be transferred to the South Sea Company with effect from Michaelmas 1720. In return, the Bank was to receive £943,750 South Sea stock valued at 400, which would make a nominal £3,775,000. Besides this, it would receive £94,375 additional stock for the 10% South Sea midsummer dividend, making a total of £1,038,125.[4] Since the government could only have redeemed the Bank's original annuity of £188,751 by paying £3,775,000 in hard cash, this was not the most prudent of bargains.

On 28 September 1720 the South Sea Company declared its not unnatural willingness to transfer the stock concerned.[5] The next day the Bank of England 'ordered, that the Secretary do attend Mr. Townsend with the Agreement made with the South Sea Company, for him to consider of a Form for putting the same in practice'.[6] Townsend, who was standing counsel to the Bank, took this knotty problem away to study. He was still

---

[1] Bank D. Ct. Bk. H, ff. 173–4; ibid. I, f. 120, 8 August 1722 for the preliminary meeting with the South Sea directors on 21 September 1720. The amount for which the subscription was to be held is given in Boyer, op. cit. xx. 198. The South Sea Company had issued over £3m. new bonds in 1720 (see above, p. 136). It were these which the subscription was primarily to underwrite.

[2] For the Exchequer bill contracts see below, p. 375.   [3] For details see above, p. 87.

[4] Bank D. Ct. Bk. H, f. 176, 24 September 1720, report of meeting with South Sea committee the previous day.

[5] Add. MS. 25499, f. 56, South Sea D. Ct. Bk., 29 September 1720, Robert Chester's report of a meeting with the Bank's committee on the previous evening.

[6] Bank D. Ct. Bk. H, f. 180, 29 September 1720.

pondering over it two weeks later on 15 October, when the Bank closed the books opened on 23 September for the support of public credit. The amount subscribed turned out to be only £2,281,200, substantially less than the £3m. intended.[1] This failure, contrasting so markedly with the ease with which all the South Sea subscriptions in the summer had been filled, indicated how deeply the market was depressed. It occurred despite the generous yield of 25% offered, the ostentatious subscriptions of £100,000 by the king and £50,000 by the Prince of Wales, and pressure by the Treasury on revenue officers and their friends to come in.[2] The amount actually paid in was 15% of the subscription, and amounted to £342,180. On 26 October 1720 the Bank of England paid over £100,000 of this to the South Sea Company, and on 16 November a further £200,000, taking as security £360,000 South Sea bonds.[3] The South Sea Company evidently thought that the subscription was fully paid up, or that the Bank would treat it as such, for on 28 October 1720 it presented to the Bank a statement of the money it would require over the next six months, amounting to £2,291,200 'which they took to be the Total Amount of the Subscription.'[4] Measured against this need, the sum which the Bank was able to transfer was no more than a drop in the ocean.

The subscription thus proved a disappointment. But a much worse shock awaited the South Sea directors. Townsend evidently advised the Bank that its agreement with the South Sea Company should not be completed without statutory authority. On 9 November 1720 the Governor of the Bank therefore informed the company that as regards the circulation of bonds and the purchase of stock his committee 'did not think fit for the present to proceed further in that matter'.[5] Despite the Treasury's impatient questioning and angry calumny on the part of the South Sea Company the Bank maintained its refusal to complete the contract.[6] In February 1722, in the course of different negotiations with the South Sea Company, the Bank suggested that

---

[1] The amount subscribed is stated in Bank D. Ct. Bk. I, f. 121, 8 August 1722.

[2] For the Prince of Wales's subscription on 1 October 1720, see Boyer, op. cit. xx. 380; the Treasury on 5 October ordered the king's intention to subscribe £100,000 to be published in the *Courant*, P.R.O. T 29/24 (i), f. 305, Treas. Bd. Mins. 1718–20. On 28 September Aislabie had urged the various revenue officers and their friends to subscribe (ibid., f. 300).

[3] Bank D. Ct. Bk. I, f. 123, 8 August 1722.

[4] Ibid., f. 122. Even this was £10,000 out.

[5] Bank D. Ct. Bk. H, ff. 194 and 195–6, 10 and 17 November 1720.

[6] For the Treasury's pressure P.R.O. T 29/24 (ii), f. 1, Treas. Bd. Mins. 16 November 1720, and Bank D. Ct. Bk. H, ff. 195–201, 17, 18, and 24 November 1720. For the South Sea General Court's instruction to its directors to prosecute the Bank see below, p. 178.

the contract, together with the 'Ingraftment' subsequently proposed, 'be no longer insisted upon by either Corporation'.[1] The South Sea directors tartly replied that they conceived 'the Contract for taking South Sea Stock and the Proposal of Ingrafting to Stand of very different Considerations'.[2] In June, however, they finally abandoned their untenable position. The cost of the subscription for support of public credit, amounting to £85,545 (15% interest on the sums paid in) was referred to arbitrators.[3] Their award in September 1720 predictably divided the cost equally between the two companies.[4] It seems likely, though not certain, from the surviving evidence that the contract was not binding at law, however much the Bank of England might be considered to have obeyed itself morally. 'It was afterwards denied', says Adam Anderson,

to have ever been executed as a legal contract; but had only been discoursed of between some ministers of state and the two companies: but although it never took place, it certainly drew in many new purchasers of stock to their great loss, and, for that reason, occasioned much noise and scribbling, though long since buried in oblivion.[5]

III

The South Sea Company's modification of the terms allowed to the public creditors and Money Subscribers, and the Bank Contract, were attempts to stem the tide of disaster by private action. Their failure made parliamentary action inevitable. Parliament had been in recess since June 1720. It re-

---

[1] Bank D. Ct. Bk. I, f. 52, 3 February 1722. The ingraftment is discussed below, p. 170.

[2] Add. MS. 25500, f. 155, South Sea D. Ct. Bk., 7 February 1722.

[3] Add. MS. 25544, f. 24, South Sea G. Ct. Bk., 22 June 1722. The arbitrators were Macclesfield, L.C.; Lord Carleton, Lord President of the Council; and Robert Walpole, First Lord of the Treasury.

[4] Arbitration award reported in Bank D. Ct. Bk. I, ff. 129–30, 6 September 1722.

[5] Anderson, *Origin of Commerce* (1787 ed.), iii. 114. On 13 January 1722 Sir John Chesshyre, standing counsel to the South Sea Company, gave his opinion that the contract was binding, though he stated no reasons. London Univ. MS. 89, ff. 66–67. If the contract had been one of those provided for by the Statute of Frauds of 1677, the fact that it was not signed would have rendered it unenforceable. But it is not clear that it was within the statute, which dealt with executors' interests, guarantee, sale of land, and agreements not to be performed within a year. Still, it seems likely that in court the informal nature of the agreement would have told in the Bank's favour.

assembled on 8 December in an atmosphere of crisis. Opinion in it can be divided for convenience into two main categories, though the neutral groups in both houses probably supported parts of different policies at different times. Those in the first category wished to resist investigation into the dubious origins of the South Sea scheme and to 'skreen' members of the Court and Administration who might suffer from such an inquiry. Its leaders were Aislabie, Secretary Craggs and Walpole in the Commons, and Stanhope and Sunderland in the Lords.[1] They considered that the ugly temper of public opinion provided no justification for 'unravelling' the scheme, which, as Walpole pointed out on 20 December 1720, had served its main purpose of converting most of the annuities for terms of years into South Sea stock 'without a breach of parliamentary faith'.[2] They were prepared to temper their firmness on this point by proposing drastic modification of the obligations of the South Sea Company's debtors and of the company itself.

The second group stood for a policy of investigation and revenge. They wished to exact every penny of the sums which the company owed the state. Their leaders were Thomas Brodrick, Archibald Hutcheson, Sir Joseph Jekyll, Lord Molesworth, William Shippen and Sir William Wyndham in the Commons, and Lord Cowper, Lord North and Grey and the Duke of Wharton in the Lords. (Jekyll, Molesworth and, in particular, Wyndham, had all been involved in the South Sea subscriptions of the summer of 1720.)[3] It gradually became apparent that neither this group nor the first could have its way completely. The vehemence of public feeling compelled the Court party to acquiesce in measures of revenge against Ministers and directors. The extreme stringency of credit, and the impossibility of making the South Sea Company pay what it had not got, compelled the popular party to agree to the remission of the greater part of the company's debts to the state.

The first task of the government's supporters was to defeat the possibility that the public creditors' exchanges of their debts for South Sea stock, the core of the whole scheme, might be rescinded. This objective was reached on 20 December 1720, when a vote of 232 to 88 confirmed the resolution of the Committee of the Whole House that

---

[1] The attitudes of the principal speakers on both sides appear from *Parl. Hist.* vii. 678–911, December 1720–July 1721.

[2] See above, p. 97.

[3] In the Money Subscriptions Jekyll subscribed £3,000 in the third; Molesworth £3,000 in the third, £500 in the fourth; Wyndham £3,000 in the first, £500 in the second, £2,000 in the third. Wyndham had also borrowed £4,000 from the company.

all Subscriptions of publick Debts and Incumbrances, Money Subscriptions, and other Contracts made with the South Sea Company, by virtue of an Act of the last Session of Parliament, remain in the present State, unless altered ... by a General Court of the South Sea Company, or set aside by due Course of Law.[1]

This firm stand, together with the subsequent measures of relief, put an effective quietus to the attempts of the public creditors who had agreed to take South Sea stock to get out of their bargains. But they were slow to believe it. As early as 10 September 1720 *Applebee's Journal* had reported a meeting of several of them at the Crown Tavern near the Royal Exchange 'to concert Measures for their Advantage'.[2] A note of protest against the subscription of debts, to be lodged at the Bank of England, was set out in *The London Journal* of 29 October–5 November 1720. In November and December 1720 groups of public creditors tried petitioning the Treasury Board.[3] In January 1721 the Board replied to one of these groups that it had done its part under the South Sea Act, but that the petitioners 'have the privilege of all Englishmen to take their Remedy in a due Course of Law'.[4] In the following month the *London Journal* reported that several former owners of redeemable stock had

resolved to withdraw their Subscriptions if possible, and stand Trial with the South Sea Company at Common Law and a Number of them have formed themselves into a Society to go on together, and support the Expence together; having already fee'd Council, and consulted upon the Measures they are to take, and it seems Council give it as their Opinion that they have Right on their Side.[5]

In view of the clear, if disastrously unfavourable, contract which the public creditors had signed in 1720 it is by no means obvious how counsel can have held such a view. Nothing evidently came of the projected lawsuit. At the end of June 1721 it was reported that 'the unfortunate Proprietors of the Redeemables have waited on the Rt. Hon. Mr. Walpole in a Body, to represent their Grievances'. His answer was not known, but it was added that 'they have resolved to deliver a Petition in French to the King in a Body'.[6] The last appearance of the government's luckless former creditors on the public scene was on 3 August 1721 when

---

[1] *HCJ* xix. 392.

[2] *Applebee's Original Weekly Journal,* 10 September 1720.

[3] P.R.O. Index 4635, ff. 187, 188, 192, 196, 200, Treasury Board Memorials 1719–21, November and December 1720.

[4] P.R.O. T 29/24 (ii), f. 28, Treas. Bd. Mins. 1720–22, 25 January 1721.

[5] *The London Journal,* 4 February 1721.

[6] *The Whitehall Evening Post,* 29 June–1 July 1721.

the Annuitants call'd Redeemables, went up to the Parliament House with their Petition, which being order'd to lie upon the Table, they seem'd displeas'd thereat, and so great a Crowd of People assembled in the Lobby of the House of Commons, and Places adjacent, that the Houses sent for the Justices of the Peace and Constables of Westminster to disperse them; who came and read the Proclamation; upon which all was quiet immediately.[1]

While the public creditors were vainly beating at the cage they had stepped into, Parliament was trying to devise more effective and far-reaching measures of relief. The first comprehensive plan to restore public credit was drawn up by Robert Walpole, with the counsel of his friend and banker Robert Jacombe, in October or November 1720, before Parliament met.[2] Walpole's plan, which was probably one of several he considered, had three main points.[3] The first Money Subscription would be completed, but no further calls would be made on the others. Subscribers should instead be credited with stock valued at 400 for as much cash as they had paid in. Second, the surplus stock in the company's hands should be distributed among the proprietors by way of bonus. Third, £18m. of the South Sea Company's swollen capital of over £37m. was to be cancelled, by exchanging it for £9m. Bank stock and £9m. East India stock. The capitals of these two companies were each to increase by £9m., on which the state would pay interest. The South Sea proprietor would cease to hold part of his South Sea stock, but would acquire an equivalent amount of Bank and East India stock, and, it was hoped, a more than equivalent share of these companies' profits. At the same time, the reduction in the South Sea Company's capital would better its market price. Unlike Walpole's two first points, which closely anticipated the settlement of 1721, this 'Ingraftment', which was less than realistic, proved a dead letter. It was formerly considered by the Bank of England on 28 November 1720, and discussed several times in the following month in acrimonious General Courts of all three companies.[4]

[1] *St. James's Evening Post*, 3–5 August 1721. Cf. *Parl. Hist.* vii. 902–10. The proclamation was that enjoined by the Riot Act of 1715.

[2] Undated paper in Coxe, *Walpole*, ii. 197–201. The paper was presumably drawn up between 11 October 1720, when Jacombe wrote to Walpole suggesting 'ingraftment' of part of the South Sea Company's capital into the capital of the Bank of England and East India Company, and before 28 November 1720, when the plan for an ingraftment was presented to the Bank of England.

[3] For a report that he studied several proposals see above, p. 159 n. 7.

[4] Bank of England D. Ct. Bk. H, f. 203, 28 November 1720, for the committee of six to negotiate the terms of the Ingraftment. The Bank of England held General Courts on 23 and 29 December 1720, the East India Company on 21, 22 and 28 December 1720 and 3 January 1721, and the South Sea Company on 23 December 1720 and 3 January 1721.

In these meetings, between the groans and hisses, doubts were expressed by South Sea proprietors of the credit-worthiness of the East India Company, and by Bank and East India proprietors about accepting South Sea stock at a time when the public creditors might still upset their bargains at law.[1] Despite the difficulty of their task, however, the directors of all three companies managed to secure assent to the plan and early in the new year made their formal offers to Parliament.[2] These were drafted into a Bill which received the royal assent on 23 March 1721.[3] But the statute was permissive only, and since neither the Bank nor the East India Company cared to go further, the Ingraftment died a natural death. In 1722 the Bank suggested that it be forgotten about, and the South Sea Company reluctantly acquiesced.[4]

The first measures designed to resolve the crisis — the South Sea Company's relaxation of the terms of its subscriptions, the Bank Contract, and the Ingraftment — had thus all proved ineffective. The next measures were ones not of relief, but of retribution. In December 1720 both Houses of Parliament called for a series of accounts from the unhappy South Sea Company, designed to elucidate its overt and covert actions in executing its scheme.[5] The evidence discovered was equivocal, and on 4 January 1721 the Commons ordered the appointment of a committee to investigate further.[6] On 9 January the committee was elected by ballot. Most of its thirteen members seem to have been in varying degrees hostile to the Administration.[7] From 16 January 1721 it sat in secret. In its seven reports between February and June 1721 it exposed at least part of the murky background to the

---

[1] The debates are reported in *The Proceedings of the Directors of the South Sea Company* (1721) and in several newspapers.

[2] The companies' offers are set out in *HCJ* xix. 398, 10 January 1721. The East India Company's is undated. The Bank's is dated 3 January, and the South Sea Company's 4 January 1721.

[3] 7 Geo. I, c. 5.

[4] See above, p. 167. Scott's statement (*Joint Stock Companies*, iii. 347), that the Bank purchased £4m. South Sea stock under the Ingraftment Act is incorrect; this sale was made under a different Act in 1722, see below p. 179.

[5] Indexes to *HCJ* and *HLJ* under 'South Sea Company'. The accounts submitted to the House of Lords largely survive in H.L.R.O., Parchment Coll., South Sea Company Papers Box 167 (see Bibliography).

[6] *HCJ* xix. 395.

[7] Ibid. 397, 399. The members were Thomas Brodrick, chairman, William Clayton, Archibald Hutcheson, Edward Jeffreyes, Sir Joseph Jekyll M.R., Nicholas Lechmere, Chancellor of the Duchy of Lancaster, Lord Molesworth, Sir Thomas Pengelly, General Charles Ross, William Sloper, Thomas Strangways, Dixie Windsor and Edward Wortley.

events of the previous year.[1] Its almost immediate discovery that £574,500 fictitious South Sea stock had been 'sold' while the South Sea Company's Bill was going through Parliament aroused the blackest suspicions. These were merely baffled, not allayed, by the flight abroad of Robert Knight the company's cashier on 22 January 1721, and by a train of alterations and erasures in the relevant South Sea records.[2] The early reports also showed unequivocally that Aislabie and Postmaster Craggs had used their official knowledge to increase their private fortunes, and had acted more like accomplices of the South Sea Company (as indeed they were) than as ministers of state. Considerable suspicion was also thrown on the roles of Lord Sunderland and the junior Treasury Secretary Charles Stanhope.

While these discoveries were being made behind closed doors, Parliament delivered its first blast of wrath against the South Sea directors. On 14 January six directors who held Crown offices were summarily removed from them.[3] On 23 and 28 January the four directors who were M.P.s were expelled from the House.[4] On 25 January two Bills about the directors received the royal assent. The first restrained them from leaving the realm for one year, and required them to draw up inventories of their estates and present them to Parliament.[5] The second disabled them for life from being directors or voters of the Bank of England and the East India and South Sea companies.[6] While they were busy compiling their inventories, the Committee of Secrecy made its first two reports on 16 and 25 February 1721. As a result, the parliamentary attack turned against the Administration. By this date death had already eaten into the ministry. On 5 February 1721 the fiery Lord Stan-

---

[1] The committee's reports are dated 16 and 25 February, 21 April, 22 and 26 May, 5 and 16 June 1721. They are printed in *HCJ* starting at pp. 425, 459, 519, 555, 561, 568 and 593. Cf. Scott's discussion of these reports, iii. 331 ff. The House of Lords also examined the directors who were not M.P.s early in February 1721. The depositions, including one by Robert Surman, are printed in *HLJ* xxi. 430–36, 15 February 1721.

[2] For the £574,500 stock and Knight's escape see above, pp. 110–12.

[3] *The St. James's Post*, 13–16 January 1721. James Edmundson held the sinecure office of Purser on H.M.S. *Royal Anne*. Reynolds was a Victualling Commissioner. Hawes, Houlditch, Ingram and Master held various revenue posts, see above, p. 117.

[4] *HCJ* xix. 406, 412–13, 23 and 28 January 1721. Janssen and Sawbridge were expelled at the first date, Chaplin and Eyles at the second. There were two further expulsions. On 10 March 1721 Sir George Caswall, the senior partner of the Sword Blade Bank, with which the South Sea Company had had extensive dealings; on 8 May 1721 Thomas Vernon, who had made the curious mistake of sounding General Ross about the terms on which Aislabie, Vernon's father-in-law, could go free.

[5] 7 Geo. I, c. 1. The inventories were to be sworn in the Court of Exchequer.

[6] 7 Geo. I, c. 2.

hope died of heart-failure after defending his government in the House of Lords. On 16 March Secretary Craggs died of smallpox. On the same day his father, who had been ill for three days, died at the General Post Office in Lombard Street, not without suspicion of suicide.[1] Parliament's attack was thus against failing ranks. On 28 February 1721 Charles Stanhope, the junior Treasury Secretary, was cleared of charges of corruption of which he was almost certainly guilty by three votes (180–177).[2] On 15 March Sunderland was saved by 233 to 172 in a Commons debate which lasted until 8 p.m. The exceptional attendance showed that members appreciated its significance.[3] Aislabie, on the other hand, was too deeply implicated, and too unpopular, to be spared. On 8 March 1721 the House passed eleven resolutions accusing him of corruption. He was expelled and committed to the Tower.[4] Onslow later said that he

was so little respected that he fell almost unpitied by anybody. It was thought he was given up at Court by way of composition, to save my Lord Sunderland, and he, chiefly against Sir Robert Walpole, resented it accordingly, as long as he lived.[5]

He retired to his Yorkshire estates, where he died aged 72 in 1742 — the year of Walpole's own fall from power.[6] It had also become apparent by this date that one of the junior Ministers, Richard Hampden, who had succeeded Aislabie as Treasurer of the Navy in 1718, had used his official balances to speculate in South Sea stock, and could not pay his debts. He was replaced as Treasurer by Sir George Byng. The extent of his liabilities took some time for the Exchequer's cumbrous machinery to disclose, and it was not until 1726 that a final reckoning became due. To avoid a Crown extent, under which 'the said Richard Hampden's Family (which is very Antient) would be entirely ruined' a private Act was then obtained to vest his estates (except the lands for his wife's jointure) in trustees, to be sold to pay what was due. Thus in the age of Liberty and Property John Hampden's great-grandson lost by speculation what his ancestors had so resolutely defended against

---

[1] *Applebee's Original Weekly Journal* for Saturday 18 March 1721 reports that 'We hear that Yesterday Morning James Craggs Esq; Post Master General of Great Britain, departed this Life, at his House in the Post Office in Lombard Street, after an Indisposition of three Days.' Onslow (H.M.C., *Onslow MSS.*, p. 511) says there was a strong suspicion that Craggs killed himself. *The Whitehall Evening Post*, 16–18 March, gives the date of Craggs's death as 16th March, at 10 p.m. This is confirmed by other newspapers.

[2] *HCJ* xix. 462, Cf. Scott, op. cit. iii. 337–41.

[3] *HCJ* xix. 482.   [4] Ibid. 472–3.   [5] *Onslow MSS.* p. 511.

[6] Cf. K. Darwin, 'John Aislabie 1670–1742', *Yorks. Arch. J.* xxxvii (1950), 262.

illicit taxes.[1] The fact that some Chancery Masters had also speculated with trust funds in 1720 had fortunately not yet come to light.[2]

IV

This train of disasters made the government's reconstruction inevitable. At the beginning of April 1721 Sunderland made way at the Treasury for his junior colleague Walpole, and retired from politics.[3] Walpole was to retain his office for twenty-one years. He succeeded to a most difficult inheritance, for effective measures to restore public credit, as distinct from placating public anger, had not yet even been drafted. Parliament was still intent on the past rather than the future. On 21 February 1721 it had returned to its attack on the South Sea directors by ordering a Bill to confiscate their estates, together with those of the cashier Knight, his deputy, Robert Surman, and the accountant, Grigsby.[4] Though called a measure for 'Relief of the unhappy Sufferers in the South Sea Company', among whom the property would be distributed, it was really a straight piece of revenge. The Bill was introduced on 3 April 1720.[5] On 1 May the estate acquired by the elder Craggs after 1 December 1719 was included in it.[6] At this stage it was evidently intended to put Aislabie's estate into the melting-pot as well as those of the directors.[7] Evidently owing to Walpole's own intervention, this was modified to confiscation of the estate acquired after 1 October 1718.[8] Despite Aislabie's eloquent speeches in his own defence in the House of Lords on 19 and 20 July 1721 the Bill received the royal assent on 29 July.[9] Besides the confiscations, it debarred the directors and Aislabie from sitting in Parliament, or voting for it, during their lifetimes.[10]

---

[1] The Bill for sale of Hampden's estates is 12 Geo. I, c. xxviii.   [2] See below, p. 292.

[3] The new Treasury Commission was dated 3 April 1721, with Walpole as First Lord. Dr. Plumb, however, *Walpole*, vol. i, ch. 10, stresses Sunderland's influence with the king until his death in 1722.

[4] *HCJ* xix. 455.   [5] Ibid. 502.   [6] Ibid. 533.

[7] Ibid. 522, 21 April 1721. The directors' estates were to be confiscated entirely and an allowance given them.

[8] *Parl. Hist.* vii. 833, 10 June 1720. Walpole proposed 25 December 1718 but was overruled.

[9] 7 Geo. I, c. 28. Aislabie's Speeches are in *Parl. Hist.* vii. 863–92. For the amounts realized for the South Sea Company from the estates of Craggs and Aislabie see below, p. 188.

[10] John Gore somehow got round this. He was M.P. for Great Grimsby 1747–61.

The assessment and sale of these estates, by trustees who were members of the new South Sea court of directors elected on 2 February 1721, proved to be a long and complex task, which is separately considered below.[1] Serious consideration of the measures needed to restore public credit was far more urgent. The new South Sea directors' statement of the company's liabilities to parliament on 13 February 1721 clearly implied remission of some at least of the debts due from and to it.[2] For the company these debts were principally £7m. due from it to the state for being allowed to make an offer to the government creditors in 1720; a further £1m. which it had borrowed from the government in Exchequer bills; and £6m. of miscellaneous debts, making a total of over £14m. Against this, it had claims against borrowers and Money Subscribers of up to £80m. or more. Parliament was at first reluctant to agree that this was an impossible situation. On 18 February, five days after receiving the company's claim for relief, the most the House felt able to agree to was a clause to postpone the payments of £7m. and £1m. for a year.[3] A series of petitions from cities and counties, between the end of March and the beginning of June 1721, deploring the alleged ruin of trade due to the wickedness of the South Sea directors, cannot have helped the moderates.[4] The more sensible view however, eventually prevailed. Between 3 May and 5 July 1721 a Committee of the Whole House carefully considered the very difficult problems involved, and drafted a series of important resolutions, which on 25 July were incorporated in an address to the king, drawn up by a committee presided over by Walpole himself.[5] As the rules of Parliament made a Bill impracticable in that session, Parliament was prorogued from 29 to 31 July 1721.[6] On 1 August a Bill to embody the resolutions was ordered, and was brought in by the senior Treasury Secretary, William Lowndes, the next day, clearly having been prepared in advance. On the 10th it received the royal assent, and Parliament could at last be prorogued.[7]

---

[1] See pp. 187 ff.   [2] See above, p. 161, Table 18.

[3] *HCJ* xix. 452. The clause was to be inserted in the Ingraftment Bill.

[4] See, for example, the petitions printed in *HCJ* xix between pp. 493 and 567, 24 March–3 June 1721.

[5] *HCJ* xix. 638. The chairman of the Committee of the Whole House was William Farrer, who had been chairman of the Committee of the Whole House which drafted the Reduction proposals of 1717, see above, p. 84. He was a Bencher of the Inner Temple and Master of St. Katherine's Hospital. He had been M.P. for Bedford since 1695. In 1700 he was made a Commissioner for Army debts, see below, p. 394.

[6] The address states that the 'ancient Usage and established Rules of Parliament' made a Bill impossible within the session, but does not say why.

[7] *HCJ* xix. 642–5.

The new Act 'to restore the publick Credit' incorporated the Commons' resolutions without substantial alteration.[1] The South Sea Company was to be excused payment of the sums of £4·1m., one year's purchase and four and a half years' purchase, but not of the £1m. due in Exchequer bills. In return, £2m. of its capital, and a proportionate part of the interest which the government paid the company, were to be cancelled at midsummer 1722. Further calls on the Money Subscriptions were to be remitted. Subscribers were to be credited with stock valued at 300 (first subscription) and 400 (others) for the cash they had already paid down. Additions were to be made from the company's surplus stock to the accounts of those in the last three subscriptions and to the public creditors whose terms were announced in August 1720. The additions for the latter aimed at giving them as much stock as those whose terms were announced in May 1720.[2] Any stock remaining in the company's hands after this was to be distributed rateably among all the proprietors. Sums owing to the company on stock or scrip could be compounded for 10%. Brokers were at first excepted from this, but were allowed to come in for 20% in 1723.[3] All contracts for the sale of company stock or scrip were to be invalid unless registered with the companies concerned by 1 November 1721. All contracts for the sale of securities which the seller did not possess within six days of the bargain were to be void unless performed by Michaelmas 1721.

There can be little doubt that Walpole was the main architect of these proposals, which applied the harsh cautery of common sense to the soaring dreams and megalomaniac expectations of the South Sea year. The company was forced to disgorge the surplus stock which it had accumulated at the public creditors' expense, and to give up its claims to be paid in full for the amount it had sold. The public creditors were forced to reconcile themselves to drastic losses of income and capital.[4] The airy fabric of speculative purchases and sales was cut down to a realistic size.

At the same time in France over £500m. of debts were written off, while the Dutch authorities applied themselves to liquidate the mushroom companies of the previous year. The financial storm dispersed almost as quickly as it had come, leaving statesmen to ponder its lessons, and private individuals all over Europe to piece together their shattered fortunes.

[1] 7 Geo. I, stat. 2.   [2] This is discussed below, pp. 183 ff.
[3] 9 Geo. I, c. 23.   [4] See below, pp. 183 ff.

8

Financial Relief and Reconstruction
1720–30 (II)

I

The new directors of the South Sea Company, elected in February 1721, had now reached the first and most important of their objectives, the remission of most of the vast sums which their predecessors had so light-heartedly engaged to pay the Exchequer.[1] They had also received statutory guidance about the contracts entered into by the public creditors, the Money Subscribers and speculators in stock and scrip. Sir John Eyles, who held the thankless position of Sub-Governor continuously from 1721 to 1733, thought that as a result of Parliament's work the outlook for the company was hopeful. The measures enjoined would

> put an end to all those Disputes and Perplexities which without the Authority of Parliament would have involved You and all that are concerned with You in Difficulties insuperable and Confusion without End ... Your Court of Directors have great Satisfaction in acquainting You, That as by the Wisdom and Authority of Parliament Your Affairs are pretty well disintangled from The Embarrassments in which they before labour'd, They have now a good prospect before them of your being very soon in a settled and flourishing Condition.[2]

It soon became apparent that this estimate was far too optimistic. Despite the remission of the greater part of its debts to the Exchequer, the company remained liable to private creditors, including the Bank of England, for over

---

[1] The king remained the company's governor. Sir John Eyles was elected Sub-Governor on 31 January 1721 and John Rudge Deputy-Governor. Eyles (1683–1745) was the eldest son of Sir Francis Eyles, Governor of the Bank of England in 1709. He was an East India director, 1700–13; a Bank of England director, 1715–17; M.P. for Chippenham, 1713–27, and for London, 1727–34; P.M.G., 1739. He married Mary, daughter of Joseph Haskin-stiles. Thirty new directors were elected on 2 February 1721.

[2] Ibid., ff. 9–10, 1 September 1721.

£7m. In addition, it had to pay back the £1m. Exchequer bills borrowed in 1720.[1] Its General Courts were in a truculent mood, and little disposed to pay attention to economic realities. The court on 7 December 1721 'order'd & directed' the directors to 'prosecute' the Bank of England about the Bank Contract, voted the Ingraftment proposal 'very Detrimental to the Interest of this Corporation', and demanded redress for the 'frauds' committed by the directors of 1720.[2] On 19 January 1722 Eyles confronted the proprietors attending the next General Court with some home truths about their situation. He said that the company could only pay its debts in three ways. First, it could do so from the half-yearly interest payments made by the government (the 'Exchequer annuity'). Trading profits were so slim that this step would compel the payment of dividends from capital. Second, stock could be issued for sale. Third, part of the 'Exchequer annuity' could be sold for a capital sum. Like many lists of possibilities, this was designed to exclude all save the last. The General Court reluctantly agreed to the sale, but with the impossible rider 'Provided such Purchasers remain Proprietors of the South Sea Company'.[3] Two days later Eyles got rid of this clause by securing from the adjourned General Court a general power to negotiate with the Bank of England.[4]

Negotiations between committees of directors of the two companies were opened at the beginning of February 1722.[5] The South Sea Company wanted to sell £200,000 p.a. of its 5% Exchequer annuity. It asked for a price of £4·4m., perhaps thinking of the amount of its bond debt. The Bank was unwilling to pay more than par, £4m., and recorded that

it will be impossible to raise the sum of Four Millions upon other Terms than what they have already proposed, and very Far from doing any Service to Publick Credit, to undertake what they apprehend they cannot execute with Success.[6]

On 8 February 1722, therefore, the meetings were broken off. Perhaps owing to stockholders' pressure for alternative means of settlement, one of the South Sea directors, Sir Thomas Crosse, M.P., made a motion in the Commons on the same day for a Bill to enable the company to sell part of its

---

[1] For the company's liabilities see Table 18 on p. 161, above. The £1m. Exchequer bill loan was not included in the debts remitted by Parliament.

[2] Add. MS. 25544, f. 14, South Sea G. Ct. Bk., 7 December 1721.

[3] Ibid., ff. 17–18, 19 January 1722.   [4] Ibid., f. 19, 24 January 1722.

[5] The committees, appointed on 31 January 1722, each had seven members. Their negotiations are recorded in the directors' court minutes (Bank D. Ct. Bk. I, ff. 49 ff., Add. MS. 25500, ff. 153 ff.).

[6] Bank D. Ct. Bk. I, 9 February 1722.

stock by lottery.[1] On amendment, the company was also given power to sell 'Part of their Fund, or Annuity, payable at the Exchequer'.[2] The Bill received the royal assent on 7 March 1722.[3]

No further action was then taken until June. Eyles, who had enough other work on his hands, perhaps hoped that the mutinous South Sea proprietors would come round to a more reasonable frame of mind if left to cool their heels. When he did raise the matter, on 7 June 1722, he complained bitterly about the stockholders' lack of trust in their directors.

It is not therefore to be Imputed to Us that your Affairs have not long Since been Settled and Flourishing, but to your want of a Just and Reasonable Confidence in Us whose willingness to Serve You in such a Juncture, under Troubles and Difficulties unexpected, greater than can be Imagined by any without Doors, and whose Steady Sincere Endeavours to promote your Interest, gave Reason to Expect more Agreeable Returns.[4]

Perhaps impressed by this straight talk, the proprietors gave their directors fresh powers to negotiate with the Bank for sale of part of the 'South Sea Fund'.[5] Meetings of the two companies' committees resumed, and within a fortnight terms of agreement had been settled. On 22 June 1722 the South Sea General Court ratified them by 2,742 votes to 275, the large number of voters, whether attending or proxy, showing the intense interest the 'Bank Treaty' had aroused.[6] The Bank's General Court approved the agreement on 26 June without division.[7] The draft was then ingrossed, the two companies exchanging sealed copies on 23 October 1722.[8]

The terms of the 'Bank Treaty', one of the most important of the measures which restored the badly-shaken South Sea Company to equilibrium, were as follows. The Bank was to pay £4·2m. for £200,000 p.a. from the South Sea Company's 'Exchequer annuity'. (This amount would be reduced, like the rest of the South Sea Company's interest, to 4% or £160,000 p.a. at midsummer 1727.)[9] The price payable was a straight compromise between the two companies' demands. The annuity was to be paid to the Bank from midsummer 1722. To finance the purchase, the Bank would issue new stock for sale at a price of 118. It could pay the £4·2m. to the South Sea Company in bonds, dividend warrants or cash. One-fifth was to be paid as soon as possible after the subscription for Bank stock was held, the rest in five instal-

---

[1] *HCJ* xix. 740.   [2] Ibid. 748, 751.   [3] 8 Geo. I, c. 21.
[4] Add. MS. 25544, f. 21, South Sea G. Ct. Bk., 7 June 1722.
[5] Ibid., f. 22.   [6] Ibid., f. 24.   [7] Bank G. Ct. Bk. ii, f. 202, 26 June 1722.
[8] Bank D. Ct. Bk. I, f. 142, 23 October 1722.
[9] Under the terms of the South Sea Act of 1720.

ments, the last falling on 24 February 1724. Lastly, the cautious rider was added that the Exchequer annuity purchased was to bear 'its proportion of any Deficiencies that may happen, until provided for by Parliament'.[1]

The Bank held its subscription on 4 July 1722.[2] One-fifth was payable on application, the rest in ten calls at two-monthly intervals, timed to coincide with the payments to the South Sea Company. Each Bank director was allotted £80,000, the East India Company £50,000, the South Sea Company £800,000. With the help of these lists there was no difficulty in filling the subscription. The amount of stock issued was £3,400,000 at 118, which realized £4,072,000. The Bank of England's capital accordingly increased from £5,550,995 to £8,959,995 from midsummer 1722.[3] The South Sea Company's capital decreased by £4m. to just under £32m. (2m. having already been cancelled at midsummer).[4]

With the £4m. paid over by the Bank, the South Sea Company was at last able to get out of the red. Its overdraft with the Bank of England alone was £490,000 in March 1723. By December it had reduced this to £3,217.[5] It paid back the £1m. it owed the Exchequer.[6] It paid the Bank the £300,000 lent in 1720.[7] And it made substantial inroads into its bond debt. In February 1721 the volume of its bonds outstanding was £4,415,950. By May 1732 this had been reduced to £1,967,850.[8] The company's sounder financial condition was reflected in the price of its stock, which in January 1723 reached par for the first time since October 1721. Its bonds, which had been at a heavy discount since September 1720, were also once again at a premium from August 1722. The last step taken to reconstruct

---

[1] Bank G. Ct. Bk. ii, ff. 199–201, 20 June 1722; D. Ct. Bk. I, ff. 93–94, 26 June 1722, explanation of various points in the agreement.

[2] For the terms see Bank D. Ct. Bk. I, ff. 96–106, 27–29 June and 3 July 1722. The subscription date was fixed on 29 June, ibid., f. 104.

[3] BPP (1898), lii. 341.

[4] Under 7 Geo. I, stat. 2.

[5] Bank of England Record Office, Drawing Office ledgers, South Sea Company account. The company's debtor balance on 30 March 1723 was £492,703. Until August 1722 the company had been in credit.

[6] Government revenue accounts in BPP (1868–9), xxxv. 70.

[7] As a result of the subscription for public credit, see above, p. 166.

[8] H.L.R.O., Parchment Coll., South Sea Company Papers Box 167, 'The Report of the Committee appointed to Inspect and Examine the Several Accounts of the South Sea Company'. This report was printed in 1733, see Bibliography. The dates of bond repayment are not given in this account. On 30 May 1723 the South Sea directors ordered that all bonds issued up to 25 June 1720 should be discharged, Add. MS. 25501, f. 66.

the company was to divide its capital at midsummer 1723 into halves.[1] Half was renamed 'South Sea Annuities', and was in effect a fixed-interest stock managed by the company. The other half was the 'trading capital'. At the same time the £2m. stock cancelled in 1722 was revived. The total of stock and annuities was thus £33,802,203.[2] Each proprietor's account was divided into two, the half which became South Sea Annuities being transferred to a new set of ledgers. This measure accurately reflected the wish of the majority of new South Sea proprietors to have a gilt-edged security rather than dividends liable to fluctuate with the profits of trade.

II

The difficulties which Eyles and his colleagues had overcome had indeed been formidable. In resolving them they had presided over the transformation of the South Sea Company from a corporation with serious trading pretensions to one whose members really wanted nothing more than steady payment of interest. As Pulteney said in 1729:

the greatest part of these Proprietors came in as Creditors to the Publick only, and are upon a very different Foot from Those, Who first, knowingly, became Members of Companies upon a Trading Bottom.[3]

The implications of this change for the company's trade to the New World were not at first apparent. But there is no doubt that they underlay the apathy of the mass of proprietors both to the directors' attempts to make it pay and towards Spanish intransigence, and their willingness in 1750 to give up the trade altogether. The proprietors' attitude was partly due to their social structure, which favoured conservatism and the avoidance of financial risks. But it was also due to the shock which the new proprietors experienced as a result of transferring out of Government securities into South Sea stock in 1720. Their losses of both capital and income made them avid for revenge against the old directors, and sullen and resentful against the new ones. The Money Subscribers, who had also suffered, shared these feelings.

---

[1] 9 Geo. I, c. 6. The opening ledgers for South Sea Old Annuities are in the Bank of England Record Office.
[2] Cf. also Appendix B.
[3] *Some Considerations on the National Debts* (1729), p. 73.

In order to trace these losses it is necessary to return to the winter of 1720. A South Sea General Court had been held on 23 December 1720 at which Sir John Fellowes had put forward Robert Walpole's plan for remitting further calls on the Money Subscriptions, and distributing the company's surplus stock by way of bonus.[1] But the proprietors were in no mood to give calm thought to constructive proposals. They were preoccupied with the more burning issues of the Ingraftment and the delivery of receipts for the third and fourth Money Subscriptions, and Fellowes could get no answer. The question was then pushed on one side by the dramatic events of January 1721 — the appointment of the parliamentary Committee of Secrecy, the flight of Robert Knight, the disablement of the South Sea directors, the preliminary moves to confiscate their estates. At the same time many of the public creditors were actively exploring the possibility of undoing at law their agreements with the South Sea Company.[2] The new South Sea directors elected in February 1721 took a little time to play themselves in, and had no proposals ready about the Money Subscriptions until 9 March 1721.[3] They then proposed to the General Court remission of calls on these subscriptions on the following basis. Stock was to be credited to each account for as much cash as had been paid in. It was to be valued at 300 for the first Money Subscription and at 400 for the other three. In the last two the mid-summer dividend of 10% in stock was to be credited 'to such of the proprietors as desire the same'.[4] Despite Eyles's exhortation to calm discussion, this apparently innocent clause aroused furious debate, perhaps because it implied a wish to take even more stock away from those who had already lost heavily. John Hopkins headed the list of those who demanded a ballot.[5] On 18 March 1721 the adjourned General Court learned that the clause had been defeated by 1202 to 384.[6] The rest of the proposals evidently stood firm.

They were underwritten by the Act 'to restore the publick Credit' in early August. The Act also extended relief to the unfortunate public creditors, who by this stage had effectively shot the bolt of their attempts to undo their bargains. The details of the arrangements were as follows. Further calls on the Money Subscriptions were remitted. Stock at the prices agreed to by the General Court on 9 March was to be credited to each

---

[1] For Walpole's proposals see above, p. 170.   [2] Ibid., p. 169.
[3] Add. MS. 25544, f. 6, 9 March 1721.   [4] Ibid.
[5] John Hopkins of Broad Street. He died in April 1732 worth £300,000 (*Gent. Mag.* for that month under 'Deaths'). Cf. his attitude about subscription receipts, above p. 128.
[6] Add. MS. 25544, f. 9.

account. The 10% midsummer 1720 dividend in stock was to be added to this. Further stock equal to one third of that already held was to be added to the accounts of those concerned in the last three subscriptions, but not the first. Those who had exchanged redeemable stock for South Sea stock were to have a similar stock bonus. The public creditors whose terms had been announced in August 1720 were to have stock priced at 150 added to their accounts so as to make their terms the same as those announced in May 1720. Unlike the first group of creditors, who had had to accept part of their exchange in South Sea bonds, the second group in the end only received stock.[1]

The effect of these provisions can be judged from the following examples. A subscriber of £1,000 in the third Money Subscription would be credited with £36 13s. 4d. for £100 paid in.[2] A creditor who had exchanged £100 redeemable stock for South Sea stock would be in the same position.[3] A former holder of a £100 p.a. long annuity who had exchanged in August 1720 now had £1,083 6s. 8d. South Sea stock, and so on. South Sea stock had fallen below par by the end of 1721 and did not recover until 1723, so the outlook for the new proprietors was still distinctly bleak. Some mitigation, however, was now given by the company itself. The relief Act had ordered all stock left in its hands after the statutory additions to be rateably distributed. The company accordingly ordered a further addition of $33\frac{1}{3}$% to each proprietor's account on 1 September 1721.[4] The revival in 1723 of the £2m. stock cancelled in 1721 provided a further bonus fund.[5] On 28 March 1723 the company's Committee of Treasury, which had been asked to study what distribution was appropriate, recommended a figure of $6\frac{1}{4}$%. It was ordered

[1] 7 Geo. I, stat. 2. For the terms allowed to the public creditors in May and August 1720 see above, p. 135.

[2] One-tenth was payable on application in this subscription, which was at 1000, the subscriber thus paid in £100. He now received £25 stock (at 400) plus the 10% dividend, plus one-third bonus. The financial effects of the various distributions are carefully worked out by Anderson, *Origin of Commerce* (1787 ed.), iii. 120 ff. As a South Sea clerk at the time he must have been familiar with the problems involved. Anderson, however, says that *all* the Money Subscribers received the $33\frac{1}{3}$% bonus. It was in fact limited to the last three subscriptions.

[3] Scott, op. cit. iii. 349, greatly overestimated the amount of stock a former holder of Redeemables acquired. This was because he took the one-third bonus to be one-third of the amount *subscribed* instead of one-third of stock *held*. As a compensating error he ignored the additions later made by the company, which are discussed below.

[4] Add. MS. 25544, f. 12, South Sea G. Ct. Bk., 1 September 1721.

[5] The £2m. stock cancelled by 7 Geo. I, stat. 2 (1721) was revived by 9 Geo. I, c. 6 (1723).

that the transfer books should be closed on 11 April 1723 to allow each owner's account to be credited accordingly.[1]

The additions made in stock to the new proprietors' accounts in the period 1721–3 can therefore be summarized as follows:

TABLE 19

Additions in stock to South Sea proprietors' accounts 1720–3

1. Midsummer 1720, 10% stock dividend.
2. 31 July 1721, '*Act to restore the publick Credit*'

    (i) orders distribution of $33\frac{1}{3}$% of stock already held to

      (*a*) those who had exchanged redeemable stock for South Sea stock;

      (*b*) those concerned in all the Money Subscriptions except the first.

    (ii) also orders additions of stock to the accounts of Annuitants whose terms were announced in August 1720 to make them equal to those whose terms were announced in May 1720.

3. 1 September 1721   South Sea Company distributes $33\frac{1}{3}$% stock to all proprietors' accounts.

4. 12 April 1723   Company distributes a further $6\frac{1}{4}$%.

Source: See pp. 182, 183.

An account made up in 1732 shows that these distributions amounted to £12,289,043 stock. This was about four-fifths of the £15,743,500 'surplus stock', representing its profit on the public creditors' exchanges, which the company had held at Christmas 1720.[2] The balance of over £3m. was increased in the period 1723–8 by £0·8m. stock realized from the sales of the 1720 directors' estates and some other sources, and diminished by the £4m. sold to the Bank of England in 1722.[3] The net balance of stock in May 1732 was £46,306.[4] Thus, while the South Sea Company's gains in

[1] Add. MS. 25501, ff. 41 (reference to Committee of Treasury 21 March 1723) and 47–49 (recommendation and order for closing transfer books 28 March 1723).

[2] H.L.R.O., Parchment Coll., South Sea Company Papers Box 167, 'The Report of the Committee appointed to Inspect and Examine the Several Accounts of the South Sea Company . . . 16th of June 1732', ff. 12–14.

[3] The sales of the 1720 directors' estates are described below, pp. 187 ff.

[4] 'Report of the Committee', f. 15.

1720 were clearly exorbitant, equally clearly they were liquidated during the following decade.

The final effect of all this on the old and new proprietors of South Sea stock can be judged from a series of examples.[1] Taking first the capital position, an old proprietor who had retained £100 stock through the South Sea year would by midsummer 1723, before his account was divided equally into stock and annuities, have £155 16s. 8d. stock. The position of those concerned in the last three Money Subscriptions and those who had exchanged £100 Redeemable stock for South Sea stock were identical. At midsummer 1723 for each £100 paid in they held £51 18s. 10d. stock. A former holder of a £100 p.a. long annuity who had exchanged it for South Sea stock in August 1720 was rather better off. A straight market sale of his annuity early in 1720 would have realized £2,000. At midsummer 1723 he held £1,543, 14s. 4d. South Sea stock. On the other hand, a former holder of £100 p.a. prize tickets in the 1710 lottery who had exchanged them for South Sea stock in August 1720 would at midsummer 1723 only have had £755 11s. 0d. South Sea stock. He could have sold his tickets early in 1720 for fourteen years' purchase or £1,400. The pattern of these examples is that the old proprietors had by 1723 received a 50% stock bonus, while the Money Subscribers and exchangers of Redeemable stock had suffered a 50% capital loss. This partly explains the persistence of their attempts to undo their bargains.[2] The short annuitants had lost almost equally heavily. The long annuitants, on the other hand, had not lost on a capital basis much more than 25%. This provides partial justification for Anderson's comment that 'all the irredeemable debts subscribed were put upon a much better footing than the redeemable ones, and the money subscribers; who certainly were very hardly used.'[3]

The income position for the annuitants was much more unfavourable. To take an example, suppose that *AB* in 1720 held a long annuity of £100 p.a. and a short annuity of the same amount, and that he exchanged both for South Sea stock in August 1720. By midsummer 1723 he would have received £1,544 South Sea stock for his long annuity, and £778 stock for his short annuity, a total of £2,322 stock, which at that date would be divided half-and-half into South Sea stock and South Sea annuities. The annuities

---

[1] Cf. the careful list in Anderson, *Origin of Commerce* (1787 ed.), iii. 120 ff.

[2] See above, p. 169.

[3] Anderson, op. cit. iii. 122. Anderson underestimates the capital loss suffered by the former holders of short annuities. As against this, however, their former annuities would have run out in 1742.

were at 5% until midsummer 1727, then at 4%. The stock paid a 6% dividend until the same date, then 5%.[1] The income over the period 1723–1730 would therefore have been as follows:

TABLE 20

Income loss of a new South Sea proprietor 1723–7

1	2	3	4	5
Year ending 31 Dec.	*Income from £1,544 South Sea stock, resulting from exchange of £100 p.a. long annuity*	*Income from £788 South Sea stock, resulting from exchange of £100 p.a. short annuity*	*Total (2+3)*	*Income if annuities had been retained*
	£	£	£	£
1723	79·1	39·9	119·0	200
1724	84·9	42·8	127·7	200
1725	84·9	42·8	127·7	200
1726	84·9	42·8	127·7	200
1727	73·3	36·9	110·2	200
1728	69·5	35·0	104·5	200
1729	69·5	35·0	104·5	200
1730	69·5	35·0	104·5	200

Taking the same figures for dividends and interest, a former holder of £100 5% Redeemable stock would have received £2·7 in 1723, £2·9 1724–6, £2·5 in 1727 and £2·3 1728–30. The income from long annuities therefore diminished by about a third, the income from short annuities by about two-thirds, and the income of those who had exchanged redeemable stock by about half. The latter, on the other hand, could not have expected the government to pay 5% indefinitely. These severe losses, which must have caused great hardship in many families, were the price paid for the relative success of the reconstruction of the National Debt in 1720. This was perhaps as near as the English government came in the eighteenth century to repudiating its obligations. Successive ministries remembered the lesson. The flourishing state of public credit after the Seven Years War was attributed as of course to 'the scrupulous exactitude with which

[1] Dividends and interest 1721–32 are shown in Add. MS. 25544, South Sea G. Ct. Bk., *passim*. Add. MS. 25561, f. 12, South Sea Memorials, also lists dividends and interest 1721–7. Scott, iii. 348–9, wrongly assumes a 5% dividend 1721–7.

interest has always been paid, and the confidence felt in parliamentary security'.[1]

III

As the new South Sea proprietors gradually and bitterly adjusted themselves to the losses to which their imprudence had exposed them, they had the doubtful consolation that the directors of 1720 were being sold up for nearly everything they possessed. The directors' estates, those of three of the company's servants and part of those of Aislabie and the elder Craggs, were vested in trustees in 1721 and sold in the course of the next decade.[2] Parliament allowed the directors and servants £354,600, which was evidently taken in cash or a number of other forms at the trustees' discretion.[3] Exclusive of this sum and of claims for debts, jointures and settlements amounting to £774,000, the forfeitures realized about £2·3m. for the South Sea Company by the early 1730s.[4] This included no less than £261,077

[1] I. de Pinto, *Traité de la Circulation et du Crédit* p. 41.

[2] The nine trustees appointed under 7 Geo. I, c. 28 (see above, p. 174), were members of the new South Sea Court of Directors. They were discharged in 1729, handing over the small balance of work remaining to the company itself. Their reports for 1722, 1726 and 1728 are printed in the Bodleian Library volume of *Votes of the House of Commons* for 1726. Their regular reports to the South Sea directors' court, which show their methods, are in Add. MSS. 25500–3, South Sea D. Ct. Bks., 1721–30. The company servants included in the confiscation Act were the cashier Robert Knight, who had fled abroad, Robert Surman the deputy cashier, and John Grigsby the accountant.

[3] The allowances Parliament originally made are summarized in R. Chandler, *Hist. and Proc. of the House of Commons* (1742), vi. 251–2. Four allowances were increased in June 1721 (*HCJ* xix, 620 ff.). These were William Astell (£5,000 raised to £10,000); Sir Lambert Blackwell (£10,000 raised to £15,000); Sir John Blunt (£1,000 raised to £5,000) and Francis Hawes (£31 raised to £5,000). Scott (iii. 346) says in error that Hawes's £40,031 estate was £400,031; this is repeated by Clapham, i. 91 and elsewhere. Surman was allowed £5,000. Grigsby £2,000. Knight's estate was all confiscated.

[4] Trustees' report for 1728 in Bodleian Library copy of *Votes of the House of Commons* for 1726; Add. MS 25561, ff. 4–6, accounts which the company presented to the House of Lords in May 1733, and H.L.R.O., Parchment Coll., South Sea Company Papers Box 167, 'The Report of the Committee Appointed to Inspect and Examine the Several Accounts of the South Sea Company, laid before the General Court of the said Company the 16th of June 1732'. The net amount realized is there stated as £2,312,518 (f. 17). By collating the accounts, it looks as though the gross sale value of all the assets was just over £3·5m., of which the directors' estates formed nearly £3m.

from the estate of Robert Knight, which was the only one entirely confiscated. Surman's estate realized £133,264 and Grigsby's £82,795.[1] The
partial confiscation of Aislabie's and Craggs's estates produced a further
£45,126 and £68,921.[2] A large part of the assets consisted of £816,000
South Sea stock, which the company took over at par in 1728–30.[3] Roughly
the same amount was in the form of land scattered over a number of counties.
Among the prominent buyers of these estates were Sarah, Duchesss of
Marlborough, whose agents laid out over £150,000 on her behalf; Denis
Bond, a director of the Charitable Corporation; John Hopkins of Old
Broad Street; Philip Hollingworth of Covent Garden, a prominent gold-
smith and East India jobber, later of Lombard Street; and Edward Turner
of Gray's Inn, who at his death in 1737 was still reputed 'very rich', despite
losing £70,000 when the Charitable Corporation collapsed in 1732.[4] Besides
South Sea stock, the 1720 directors held policies of the Amicable Assurance
Office, shares in the London Assurance, Royal Exchange Assurance and
Thames Water Company, and Bank, East India and Million Bank stock.
These securities were sold in 1728 and 1729. The main purchasers
were Abraham Atkins, Henry Carington, William Cole, Salomon
da Costa, Abraham Crop, John Edwards, Mussaphia Fidalgo, Moses
Helbut, Philip Hollingworth, Gabriel Lopes, Moses Machado, John
Montier and Joseph Pangbourne. All of these were prominent City
stock-jobbers.[5]

---

[1] Trustees' report for 1728. Knight none the less died 'immensely rich', see below, p.
190.

[2] Craggs's estate after 1 December 1719 and Aislabie's after 1 October 1718 were
included in the confiscation Act. The valuations of the two estates in the Court of Exchequer took time and were only ready by 7 March 1723. The South Sea Company then
learned that Craggs's estate was £144,061 at 1 December 1719 and £212,982 at his death
in March 1721. Aislabie's estate was £118,986 at 1 October 1718 and £164,112 in March
1721. The surplus in each case was transferred to the company in the form of South Sea
stock. This accounted for £114,000 of the £816,000 referred to in the text.

[3] Add. MSS. 25561, ff. 5–6.

[4] Gent. Mag., March 1737, under 'Deaths'. The names of purchasers of South Sea
property are from two volumes of Estates of the South Sea Directors as Sold (Bodleian
Library). These were annotated by John Read, the forfeiture trustees' chief accountant,
with reserve and sale prices and the names of purchasers. The Duchess of Marlborough's
agents were Thomas Broderick and William Wilson. The lands they bought were in Essex,
Huntingdonshire, Lincolnshire, Oxfordshire, Surrey, Wiltshire. Among them was the
Manor of Wimbledon, purchased from Sir Theodore Janssen, who, however, re-purchased
the dwelling-house.

[5] Manuscript lists of securities sold in Estates of the South Sea Directors, vol. ii, pt. ii,
pp. 39, 53, 92, 101–2.

This transfer of most of their property to others as rich as they had so recently been dealt the South Sea directors of 1720 a severe but not fatal blow. In the cases which can be traced they seem to have retained enough to support themselves and help endow their descendants. William Astell was succeeded in his Huntingdon estates by his son Richard, on whose death without heirs in 1777 they passed by marriage to the famous banking family of Thornton.[1] Sir John Blunt's descendants were prominent administrators in Bengal.[2] In his obituary in 1737 Sir William Chapman was celebrated as an eminent City merchant, who had evidently long outlived old scandals.[3] Edward Gibbon, according to his grandson, had acquired a second fortune by the time of his death in 1737.[4] Sir Theodore Janssen never recovered his colossal wealth, but he was able to lend substantially on the land tax as late as the 1740s.[5] His son Stephen Theodore Janssen was Chamberlain of the City and Lord Mayor of London. Charles Joye, the former South Sea Deputy Governor, was Treasurer of St. Thomas's Hospital in the late 1720s. He must have been able to exchange interesting reminiscences with his President, the veteran Bank director Sir Gilbert Heathcote.[6] Sir John Lambert's baronetcy descended in the male line into the present century. Colonel Hugh Raymond was a prominent East India proprietor in the early 1730s.[7] Robert Surman, the South Sea deputy cashier was a prosperous goldsmith-banker in the 1730s 1740s and 1750s, though his career ended, as it had begun, in bankruptcy.[8] Perhaps the most spectacular case of all was that of Robert Knight, whose part in the whole scandal seems to have been second to none. In August 1742, a few months after the fall of his old enemy Walpole, Knight, who had been living in Paris, received a pardon under the Great Seal for all his offences. In January 1743 he offered to pay the South Sea Company £10,000 in satisfaction of all its demands on him.

---

[1] *V.C.H. Hunts.* ii. 371–2.

[2] G.E.C., *Baronetage*.

[3] *Gent. Mag.* May 1737 under 'Deaths'. Chapman's son and heir John had married Rachel, daughter of the 1720 South Sea director James Edmundson.

[4] Edward Gibbon, 'Memories of my life and writings', *Misc. Works*, i. (1796), 13.

[5] See below, p. 436.

[6] St. Thomas's Hospital account in Old South Sea Annuities, Bank of England Record Office, joint account for Heathcote and Joye.

[7] East India G. Ct. Bk. i, f. 318, 20 September 1730, Raymond subscribed £5,000 to a loan to enable the company to pay dissentient bond-holders.

[8] Surman was a partner in Martin's Bank 1730–48 (G. Chandler, *Four Centuries of Banking*, i (1964), 106, 117, 131). He then founded his own firm, Surman Dinely & Cliffe, which went bankrupt in 1757.

In February the General Court reluctantly (410–257) agreed.[1] The way was clear for him to return to the country which he had left in such urgent haste twenty-two years earlier. But his exile was not long over before he had to leave on a new and more permanent journey. The *Universal Spectator* noted in its issue of 17 November 1744 that 'Last Week died, at his House in Great Russell-Street, Bloomsbury, the memorable Robert Knight, Esq.; Cashier of the South-Sea Company in the Year 1720, who has died immensely rich.'[2] No one seems to have taken the trouble to find out from him what he knew; or perhaps he was too discreet to indulge in reminiscences. The fortune he had accumulated, which the statutory confiscation was evidently far from exhausting, was in any case used to some purpose, for his son Robert Knight, after an assiduous political career, was made an Irish Earl by George III.[3]

IV

The long-drawn-out sales of the directors' estates, with their attendant complex legal and administrative problems, were not the only legacy of the Bubble which worried the new South Sea directors of 1721. They had also to try to get in the statutory 10% of the amounts borrowed from the company in 1720, at the same time that the Bank of England, which had itself lent over £1m. during the Bubble, was putting pressure on its own debtors.[4] At the same time private individuals were claiming and counter-claiming at law, to an extent which has not yet been properly explored or assessed. The echoes of the great boom and its collapse therefore reverberated through the following decade.

[1] *Gent. Mag.*, August 1742 (pardon reported), and 1743 at pp. 50, 101, for the South Sea Company's decisions. Knight's letter asking the Treasury Secretary James West to influence the South Sea Company to allow him to return, dated Paris 10 December 1742 (N.S.), is in Add. MS. 34728, f. 7. It is reasonable to suppose that Walpole, who resigned in February 1742, had opposed Knight's return as long as he was in office.

[2] *The Universal Spectator or Weekly Journal*, 17 November 1744.

[3] Robert Knight, M.P. 1734–72, created Baron Luxborough of Shannon in 1745, and Viscount Barrells and Earl of Catherlough in 1763.

[4] Under the 'Act to restore the publick Credit' (1721) the South Sea Company was entitled to recover 10% of the sums borrowed on its stock and scrip in 1720, see above, p. 176.

The effect of the Act of 1721 to restore public credit on an individual (and perhaps not unrepresentative) speculator's fortunes can be judged from a report later drawn up for counsel about the affairs of Colin Campbell in 1720.[1] Campbell, who was probably one of a speculative syndicate which bought up the majority of Sun Fire Office shares in the summer of 1720,[2] and had fled abroad after the crash, had incurred debts of three kinds. He had entered into seven contracts for the future purchase of a nominal £12,000 South Sea and other stock at high prices. He had borrowed £37,725 from five lenders for short terms, at rates of interest which on an annual basis were between 30% and 60%. The security for these loans was stock and scrip nominally worth £16,830, about half the debt. Third, he had entered into five penal bonds and nine notes of hand for sums lent to him without the deposit of security.

Each type of debt raised nice questions. Three in the first category were void because the contracts had not been registered by 1 November 1721, as was obligatory under the Act.[3] Two of these three, in counsel's opinion, were also void because they could not be performed: they were for receipts in the last two Money Subscriptions, and these receipts had never been delivered.[4] The remaining contracts had been registered, but were no longer enforceable, for Campbell had been in England when the cause of action accrued even though he subsequently left the country; he therefore received the benefit of the Statute of Limitations, by which personal actions had to be brought within six years. Debts in the second category, where stock had been deposited for security, were not enforceable, in council's opinion, since the plaintiffs were accountable for the security conceded. If, as was probable, they had sold it, they could be enjoined in equity from proceeding further. Anderson, who drafted the report, considered that the bonds were in any case void for usury, but counsel pointed out that this was not true. Unless the usury appeared on the face of the bond the lender could not be compelled to confess it. Brokers' accounts were no proof of usury, for they were not

---

[1] Add. MS. 17477, ff. 31 ff., notes drawn up in 1748–9 by Adam Anderson for submission to Charles Erskine.

[2] Dickson, *Sun Insurance Office*, ch. 3. As Colin Campbells have always abounded, identification is uncertain. A Colin Campbell, 'a Scots Gentleman of a good Estate and bright Parts, one of the Directors of the York-Buildings Company', who married a daughter of Sir William Clarges in July 1720 (*Flying Post*, 12–14 July 1720) is perhaps the same man.

[3] All contracts made in 1720 for sale of stock or scrip were to be registered with the company concerned by 1 November 1721.

[4] See above, p. 128.

signed at the order of the lender. If, therefore, as normally happened, the borrower's interest was incorporated with the principal, no remedy was available. Campbell's third group of debts was composed of penal bonds and notes of hand. Action on the latter was now barred by the Statute of Limitations, but he remained liable on the former. As counsel said, the 'general Rule of Law relating to Prescriptions upon account of Length of time does not take place here, as there is a probable Reason to be assigned why Payment was not demanded or made, as Mr. C—was the greatest part of the time beyond the Seas. And there is no Limitation by Statute for Bonds; only a general Rule of Law arising from a probable Presumption of Payment.'

Campbell's case shows the great difficulties which private creditors experienced in enforcing contracts entered into during the Bubble. Equal difficulties faced the monied companies, and the contrasting fortunes of the Bank and the South Sea Company in collecting their debts during the decade after 1720 can partly be ascribed to the fact that the South Sea Company was obliged to resort to litigation which, as Campbell's case shows, was hazardous and inefficient, while the Bank of England was able to avoid doing so.

The Bank of England's loans on its own stock in 1720 were an important subsidiary cause of credit inflation during the South Sea Bubble. They were also a remarkable episode in the history of a normally conservative and sober institution.[1] On 22 April 1720 the Bank's court of directors resolved 'that it be offered to the General Court on Thursday next as the Opinion of this Court, that it may be for the Service of the Bank, to lend Money to the Proprietors upon their Bank Stock'.[2] It cannot be coincidence that a proposal to empower loans on stock had been approved by the South Sea Company's General Court on the preceding day. The Bank's directors ordered their Committee of Treasury to prepare conditions and a form of receipt. Fifty pounds was to be lent for each £100 Bank Stock, at 5%. On 28 April the General Court gave the directors the required power in general terms. On 3 May the Committee's draft of the note to be signed by borrowers on stock and of the deed between the Bank and the trustees to be appointed to accept transfers, were read and approved. At the same court the two Governors, and three directors, were nominated trustees.[3] It was ordered that the pro-

---

[1] The loans are referred to by Clapham (i. 84), but not described.

[2] Bank D. Ct. Bk. H, f. 139, 22 April 1720. 'Thursday' was 28 April. The following section is almost entirely based on the court minutes and references are therefore omitted except for quotations.

[3] The Governor was John Hanger, the Deputy Governor was Sir Thomas Scawen, and the three directors were Sir Peter Delmé, Gerard Conyers and John Rudge.

missory notes should be printed and the deed between the Bank and the trustees engrossed, and that a 'new particular Transfer Book be prepared with the Trustees Names Printed in it, and that the said transfers be stamped'.[1] The Bank's Secretary was to be the trustees' attorney to accept transfers of stock. On 5 May the Court of Directors proposed that £100 should be lent on every £100 Stock, instead of £50 on each £100 as previously agreed.[2] At the same court the method of making the loans was settled. On 12 May it was ordered that the Bank's Accountant-General and Secretary should be the trustees' attorneys for retransferring 'mortgaged' stock when it was redeemed. The efficiency of these arrangements contrasted markedly with those adopted for similar purposes by the South Sea Company.[3] Only one addition was made to them, when the interest on loans was lowered to 4% on 14 July 1720. The South Sea Company had made a similar reduction on 20 May. There is no further mention of the loans in the directors' minutes until Michaelmas Day when, in the worsening financial situation of the early autumn, it was decided to call in 25% of the amount lent. From the ledgers for Bank stock, in which an account for the five trustees was opened on 10 May it appears that over £1 million had been borrowed by proprietors by the end of September 1720. The balance of 'mortgaged stock' held by the trustees at different dates is shown in Table 21.

After Michaelmas 1720 the Bank, like other lenders, was understandably concerned not to make further advances but to recover what it had already lent. The ledgers show that loans ceased at Michaelmas, although a formal resolution of the Court of Directors to suspend them until further order was not made until 6 October. The call of 25% ordered on 29 September was payable on or before 12 October on pain of forfeiture of the stock pledged. On 13 October the interest charged on the loans was raised to 5%. On the 25th it was ordered that a proportionate part of the stock should be sold to answer the 25% call, and on the 27th that the trustees should meet the defaulters 'to consider of the most easy Method for the Sale of so much of their said Stock as will Answer and Pay the said Call'.[4] On 3 November 1720 the court of directors heard an account of this meeting, at which the Bank's debtors had asked for further time in which to pay.

[1] Bank D. Ct. Bk. H, ff. 141–2, 3 May 1720.
[2] Ibid., f. 143, 5 May 1720. The alteration was to be offered to the General Court on Thursday next'; in fact no General Court was summoned until 28 July. The authority given to the directors on 28 April, however, included power to alter the terms of loans.
[3] See above, p. 143.   [4] Bank D. Ct. Bk. I, ff. 189, 191, 25 and 27 October 1720.

TABLE 21

Balance of Bank stock in the hands of trustees

for loans, 1720–3

1720					£000	*1721*					£000
17 May	.	.	.	.	.	191	14 August	.	.	.	.	514
31 May	.	.	.	.	.	345					
3 June	.	.	.	.	.	433	*1722*				
14 June	.	.	.	.	.	508	31 August	.	.	.	.	225
6 July	.	.	.	.	.	841					
21 July	.	.	.	.	.	861	*1723*				
5 August	.	.	.	.	905	18 December	.	.	.	.	56
26 August	.	.	.	.	965					
8 September	.	.	.	.	946					
29 September	.	.	.	.	1,021					
12 October	.	.	.	.	1,012					
31 December	.	.	.	.	738					

Source : Trustees' ledger, Bank of England Record Office.

The Bank was now in a difficult legal position. By the terms of the promissory note signed by its debtors it could enforce the whole of its obligations against them by selling their stock, but it was uncertain whether it could similarly enforce part of its obligations by sale of part of the stock. The problem was submitted to Townsend, the Bank's counsel. On 22 November he recorded his opinion that part of the stock could not be sold; it was a question of all or nothing.[1] Despite this advice, on 6 April 1721 the directors resolved to threaten to sell 25% of the stock pledged unless the 25% call was met by 20 April. On 13 April, mingling persuasion with force, the directors promised the Michaelmas 1720 dividend to those who paid the 25% call on their pledged stock. On 26 October 1721 the court ordered the Accountant to find what sums were due on the loan, and from whom. On 15 February 1722 the Secretary was ordered to write to all debtors to discharge their loans in full — it was not now merely a question of 25%. On 6 September it was decided to threaten to sell the stock unless loans were repaid by the 19th, but no action can have been taken, for on 27 June 1723 a call was ordered on all monies outstanding, payable on or before 31 August. On 15 August this resolution was suspended till further order. It seems clear

[1] Bank of England, 'Copies of Bonds and Opinions 1701–43', ff. 172–4.

that rather than enforce its rights by selling collateral security, with the attendant bitterness, disruption of credit, and risk of lawsuits which this would have caused, the Bank preferred to give its debtors further time, in the belief that they would all pay in the end. Its belief proved justified. The stock held by the trustees was steadily reduced, and only £56,000 was outstanding by the end of 1723.[1] The last transfer was made on 30 April 1729, when £2,250 stock was transferred to Dame Mary Skipwith, executrix of Sir Fulwar Skipwith, Bart. Over a period of nine years, therefore, the Bank had succeeded without litigation in getting all its money back.

The South Sea Company was not equally fortunate. During the Bubble it had lent over £9 million on the security of its stock, and a further £2m. on subscription receipts.[2] Under the Act of 1721 it was entitled to recover 10% of these sums, and to confiscate the stock pledged as security by borrowers. At first an optimistic view was taken of the probable proceeds. On 1 September 1721 the Sub-Governor, Sir John Eyles, told the South Sea General Court that he expected to realize over £1,100,000 in cash and £2,500,000 in forfeited stock and scrip.[3] But it soon became apparent that the recovery of the sums due would not be easy. On 6 July 1721 a Committee of Lawsuits was added to the five existing committees of the Court of Directors.[4] It had two major tasks. The first, and more complex, was to resolve the tangled claims and counter-claims arising from the Money Subscriptions and public creditors' exchanges of 1720. A large number of cases was examined. There were seemingly endless permutations of the possible difficulties. Subscriptions had been made but not credited, attorneys had exceeded their powers, trusts had been disregarded, transfers had not been registered. The stream of applications was not reduced to a trickle until the mid 1720s, and some claims were still being considered in the 1730s.[5] The Committee's second task was to coerce the 'borrowers on the loan'. It started by drawing up a list of thirteen persons claiming stock subscribed for in the names of third parties, where the latter were indebted to the company. Among these debtors was John Gay, under whose name 'Alexander Pope of Twittenham' claimed £1,000 in the third money subscription. No further action appears to have been taken until 23 October

---

[1] See above, Table. 21.   [2] See above, p. 143.

[3] Add. MS. 25544, f. 11; South Sea G. Ct. Bk., 1 September 1721.

[4] Its minutes for 1721–33 are in Add. MS. 25568. The committee had ten members. The remainder of this section is based on this source, and references are therefore omitted except for quotations.

[5] Ibid., *passim.*

1722, when Mr. Bootle, the company's counsel, was consulted about the 'borrowers on the loan'.[1] On 13 November the committee studied his opinion, which advised a suit at Common Law, aided by a Bill of Discovery in equity.

At the same time the company obtained statutory extension of the period within which the composition was to be paid. The date for the third payment of 5% was finally altered to Christmas 1723.[2] But this did not produce the required eagerness to pay, and on 11 February 1723 the directors ordered their solicitor to 'prosecute' four debtors: Lord Hilsborough, John Crookshanks, Robert Clarke and William Carter. The attempt, however, evidently came to nothing, for on 23 October 1724 the Solicitor and Cashier were told to select ten cases in which there was material proof, and sue the debtors concerned. By this date the period of statutory grace had expired. It is clear that the question of evidence was crucial. The loans which the company had made in 1720 were so large and, in contrast to those made by the Bank of England, had been so carelessly administered, that subsequent enforcement of its rights was gravely impeded. The poor state of its own records was shown when it wrote to the ten debtors selected on 23 October 1724. The first three addressed denied that they owed anything, and were able to prove it. Baffled, the company beat a temporary retreat, and engaged in a complicated suit with Richard Rigby, its agent in Jamaica. But matters could not be allowed to drift. In December 1725 the Solicitor reminded the directors that nearly six years had elapsed since the loan, and that it was advisable to bring a suit in order to prevent the debtors pleading the Statute of Limitations. Accordingly, in October of the following year the Lawsuits Committee decided to select as defendants those who had paid only half their composition. They hoped that proof in these cases would be easier to obtain. Nothing further seems to have been done, however; in February 1727 the committee changed its membership once again, and a year later was still industriously compiling lists of 'borrowers on the loan'. The causes of these repeated failures and delays were first, the unsatisfactory state of the records, in which those entered as debtors were often able to prove they owed nothing, and second, the company's willingness to accept compositions even at this date, rather than incur the expense of litigation.[3]

No definite legal action was taken until 24 January 1729, when the Solicitor was ordered to 'prosecute' eight debtors, who had paid only their first 5%, and five others, who had paid nothing. Perhaps for the reasons

[1] Add. MS. 25568, f. 12.   [2] 9 Geo. I, c. 23.
[3] As appears from numerous entries in the committee's minutes.

suggested earlier, this brief list eventually dwindled to two names, those of Jonah Crynes and Colonel John Duncomb. Each had borrowed £8,000 in 1720 on security of £2,000 South Sea stock. It was hoped to prove this by the evidence of two South Sea clerks, Bignol and Hayne, who claimed to know the defendants and their handwritings. The claim was mistaken. When Cryne's case came on at *nisi prius* at the Old Bailey on 24 May 1731, eleven years after the Bubble, Hayne admitted in cross-examination that he did not know the defendant after all, while Bignol confidently identified the wrong man.[1] In November of the same year the action against Duncomb was heard in the King's Bench before Chief Justice Raymond and a special jury, which, after a hearing lasting seven hours, reached a verdict against the company after withdrawing for only fifteen minutes.[2] After this double fiasco the 'borrowers on the loan' were left in peace. 'As for Mr. Campbell's Loan from the S.S. Co.,' wrote Adam Anderson later, 'that Matter will never affect him, the Company having been Cast some years ago in a Lawsuit for Recovery of a Loan, and therefore they are determined never more to make any Demand hereafter.'[3] From accounts made up in 1732 it appears that the net amount recovered 'on the Loan' was £717,860 in cash and £2,441,719 in forfeited stock and scrip, an indifferent return for the £11 million originally lent to the Company's proprietors.[4]

V

The South Sea crisis and its aftermath were the most dramatic financial storm in eighteenth-century England. Its results, still in many ways imperfectly worked out, were complex. First, it changed the structure of the National Debt. It enabled the government, at the expense of the public creditors, to turn the greater part of the annuities for terms of years into South Sea stock, and thus paved the way for reduction of both the capital and interest of the debt under Walpole and Pelham. The South Sea Company,

[1] Report of Lawsuits Committee to directors' court, 4 June 1731, Add. MS. 25568, ff. 95 ff.

[2] Ibid., ff. 106–7, 3 December 1731.   [3] Add. MS. 17477, f. 37.

[4] H.L.R.O., Parchment Coll., South Sea Company Papers, Box 167, 'The Report of the Committee appointed to Inspect and Examine the Several Accounts of the South Sea Company', ff. 8, 11.

used as the government's agent, completely changed its nature by the acquisition of so many new (and disgruntled) proprietors. This change underlay the conversion of first half its capital then, in 1733, of most of the remainder, into fixed-interest annuities, and the final abandonment of its trade in 1750.[1] The company had been forced to double its staff as a result of the Bubble, and began in 1725 to build a new and larger house in Broad Street, nostalgically described later by Charles Lamb, but for all intents and purposes, despite its size, the company was in future more and more an extension of the Exchequer.[2] At a political level the Bubble, combined with a remarkable series of deaths among his rivals, led to the emergence of Robert Walpole as First Minister, a position he was to retain for over twenty years. It has been argued in this chapter that the magnitude of the difficulties which he overcame in resolving the crisis can hardly be overestimated. There is no doubt that the hard, tough men who ran the City and its institutions recognized in his handling of this and subsequent financial issues a competence equal to their own, and not found at the Treasury for any length of time since the fall of Godolphin. Lastly, in a longer view the lesson of the crisis was that public faith should never again be subjected to the intrigues of politicians and company promoters. Despite all defects in the handling of English public finance, for the rest of the century it remained more honest, as well as more efficient, than that of any other country in Europe.

[1] See below, p. 240.

[2] On 24 March 1720 the South Sea Company reported the purchase of houses lying between Broad Street and Threadneedle and Bishopsgate Streets (Add. MS. 25499, f. 2). The house there is described as 'building' on 24 December 1725, ibid. 25502, f. 176. The company had thirty officers and clerks in 1719, just over eighty in 1721.

9

The National Debt under Walpole

I

WHEN Robert Walpole took up the reins of political leadership in April 1721 he was only forty-four, yet he had behind him more than a decade of experience of Parliament and responsible office, and was widely acknowledged as the country's foremost expert in public finance. His potential rivals had been removed by death or the disgrace of involvement in the South Sea Bubble. He was to hold the first position in the kingdom for twenty-one years. What were his political and economic aims during this long command of power?[1]

Walpole belonged to a generation which in boyhood had learned from its fathers of the horror and bitterness of the Civil War, and had seen the threat of civil war recur in the violent decade 1679–89. He came to manhood, and began his experience of politics, during the long wars that racked Europe between 1689 and 1714. These were dangerous years, with the shadow of treason and the block looming over domestic politics, and the ever-present threat that the new English state would be overwhelmed by France, the greatest and richest military power that Europe had yet seen. These wars disrupted commerce, burdened propertied Englishmen with heavier taxes than Charles I would have dared contemplate, and served up butchers' bills for recurrent battles of pitiless ferocity.[2] The peace of 1713–14, concluded in an atmosphere of mutual exhaustion, and on the English side in a pall of

[1] The latest general survey of the period is J. H. Plumb, *Sir Robert Walpole. The King's Minister* (1960). There is no recent monograph on Walpole's economic policies. N. Brisco, *The Economic Policy of Robert Walpole* (New York, 1907), is jejune and inaccurate. The following section is largely based on inference from the pamphlets and statutes of the period, and its conclusions are partly speculative.

[2] At Malplaquet, for instance, the combined numbers of the forces involved were nearly 200,000. The battle took only one day, but casualties were more than 30,000, Coxe's *Marlborough* (1914 ed.), ii. 435–6, 458–9. The heaviest were suffered by the Dutch. This frightful slaughter must have profoundly influenced the Republic's attitudes to foreign policy for the rest of the eighteenth century.

double-dealing and treason, was followed by harsh and laborious financial reckoning. It was in this immediate post-war period that Walpole won his political reputation, which his handling of the South Sea catastrophe confirmed and enhanced.

Walpole seems to have drawn a number of lessons from these dramatic experiences of his formative years. First, like many of the politicians of the 1930s, he had an active hatred of war, based on personal experience of its cost in blood and money. There is no reason to doubt his sincerity when he told the House of Commons, towards the close of his political career,

I have lived, Sir, long enough in the world to see the effects of war on this nation; I have seen how destructive the effects, even of a successful war, have been; and shall I, who have seen this, when I am admitted to the honour to bear a share in his majesty's councils, advise him to enter upon a war while peace may be had? No, Sir, I am proud to own it, that I always have been, and always shall be, an advocate for peace.[1]

Generalizing from his own experience, he argued, first, that the nation required a long period of peace to recover and develop its strength. Second, that such a period would have the additional advantage of taking the sting and rancour from domestic politics, and uniting the landed and trading classes behind the new dynasty. Third, that this unity could only be won and held in Parliament, which the war had shown to be an institution capable of considerable growth and development, despite its claims to have existed unchanged since the days of Alfred the Great. Lastly, that within Parliament the power of the purse, involving financial decisions of unprecedented magnitude, had effectively made the Commons the decisive centre before which national policy must be cleared.

These conclusions would have been inadequate if Walpole had not at the same time acquired an intuitive understanding of the balance of forces within English society. He knew that England had emerged victorious from the wars of 1689–1713 for two main reasons. The first was the consent of the political nation in Parliament to taxes and loans of unprecedented size. The second was the growing financial expertise of the City of London, without which the formidable problems of loan management, exchange remittance and economic warfare could not have been solved. Two major sectors of society had therefore been involved. On the one hand were the aristocracy gentry and farming classes: rooted in the land, suspicious of political innovation, social change, religious nonconformity and foreign entanglements, yet willing, from a mixture of patriotism and self-interest, first to pay heavy taxes and then to support an alien king. On the other was the socially and

[1] *Parl. Hist.* xi. 232, 21 November 1739.

religiously mixed community of the City of London, with its international outlook and contacts, only just beginning to feel its real strength and power, but already aware that without its services the Government would become ineffective. Its outlook and social structure were mirrored in the growing centres of regional trade like Bristol, Liverpool and Glasgow. Walpole realized that the support of both social groups must be won and held if policy was to command the assent of the political nation as a whole. He was further aware that both were growing in complexity, and that as they did so the links between them would strengthen, so that policies which affronted the interests of either must so far as possible be avoided. Some analysis of this kind, whether or not explicitly formulated, explains his deliberate shelving of Stanhope's projects for emancipating Protestant Nonconformists, his attempts to keep taxes on the landed classes low, and his cultivation of at least the politically more tractable members of the Revolution Families; while at the same time he conciliated Protestant dissent by Indemnity Acts and not merely maintained close contact with the powerful mercantile and financial houses of the City of London, but actively strengthened the government's relations with them, particularly the links between the Treasury and the Bank of England.[1]

This balancing of conservative and dynamic interests in society needed to be complemented by a policy of economic and administrative reform sufficiently neutral politically to command the assent of a broad spectrum of social groups. So far as England's trade was concerned, this policy as it was worked out was openly protectionist and restrictionist, like the policies of most contemporary European Powers. For example, the Habsburg government's council in Breslau in 1740, anxiously surveying the state of the Silesian economy only a few weeks before Frederick the Great summarily marched in and took over, noted how English tariffs were so high that they virtually excluded certain kinds of Silesian cloths, while the Spanish tariff discriminated in favour of French ones. The council was hardly entitled to grumble, since it had just stated as a 'chief principle' that taxation should discriminate against foreign products in favour of native ones, whose growth increased population and hence consumption.[2] In Whitehall similar reasoning prevailed, as the titles and preambles of several Acts of Parliament in the

---

[1] A. J. Henderson, *London and the National Government 1721–42* (Durham, North Carolina, 1945), shows that Walpole's relations with the City's government were poor, but ignores his more important relations with the financial community.

[2] Vienna, Österreichisches Staatsarchiv, Hofkammer Archiv, Hof-Finanz Akten 20 December 1740 (N.S.), Schlesische Cammer, Commerzien Protocoll, minutes dated 20 September and 24 October 1740 (N.S.).

1720s and 1730s show. Thus the Act of 1721 prohibiting the use of imported painted calico after Christmas 1722 was called one 'to preserve the woollen and silk manufactures and for more effective employing the poor'.[1] The preamble to the important statute of the following year which removed export duties on a large number of English goods states that the wealth and prosperity of the realm depend on fostering employment by the improvement and export of manufactures.[2] The sailcloth Act of 1731 repeated that the 'wealth and prosperity of this kingdom does very much depend upon the preservation and improvement of its manufactures'.[3] A further Act to encourage home sailcloth was passed in 1736.[4] The London correspondent of an Amsterdam mercantile house reported to his principals that its effect was virtually to exclude Dutch sailcloth from the English market.[5] Increased turn-over in foreign trade might also be fostered by making London a free port, or at least by putting under improved control the very important section of trade consisting of colonial re-exports.[6] This was the main intention of the so-called Excise Scheme of 1733, which would have enabled re-exporters of wine and tobacco to place them in Excise-controlled ware-houses pending re-shipment, and thus have avoided the delays and frauds involved in the standard customs procedures.[7] Chatham later pentitently acknowledged this, saying

he owned he was for an Inland Duty and a Free port, that every body must know by Inland Duties he meant Excise ... That Sir Rob. Walpole meant honestly in the Excise Scheme.[8]

At the same time, every effort was made to lessen manufacturers' costs, and to discipline labour, by keeping wages low, breaking up workers' combinations, and making the conditions on which poor-relief could be obtained harsher.[9]

These policies aimed, by cutting costs and protecting markets, at increasing

[1] 7 Geo. I, stat. 1, c. 7 (1721).   [2] 8 Geo. I, c. 15 (1722).
[3] 4 Geo. II, c. 27 (1731).   [4] 9 Geo. II, c. 37 (1736).
[5] Amsterdam, Archief Brants, 1344, Joseph Grove in London to de Neufville & Co. in Amsterdam, 10 June 1736.
[6] For Sir John Blunt's proposal in 1720 that London should be made a free port, see *Applebee's Original Weekly Journal*, 6 August 1720.
[7] Cf. the report in 1733 of the committee appointed to inquire into frauds in the customs, referred to above, p. 155.
[8] Add. MS. 32888, f. 428, West to Newcastle, endorsed 'March 9th 1759 Mr. West'. West was reporting the Commons' debate on the West Indian Sugar Bill.
[9] See, for example, 7 Geo. I, stat. 1, c. 13 (1721), regulation of London journeyman tailors; 9 Geo. I, c. 27 (1723), regulation of journeyman shoemakers; ibid., c. 7, amendment of conditions for poor-relief. *An Account of Several Work-Houses for employing and maintaining the Poor* (2nd ed., 1732) claims that the last statute checked a sharply mounting poor-rate.

England's share of world trade, and thus increasing her stature as a great power. Internally, it was hoped that they would draw on the large pool of endemically under-employed, and thus reduce the heavy burden of local poor-rates, while at the same time, by increasing excise and customs revenue, they would enable direct taxation to be kept at a reasonable level. They would also enable part of the National Debt to be repaid, especially now that its structure had been favourably changed by the South Sea Bubble. It could further be argued that such reductions would raise the market price of fixed-interest securities, and thus lower both public and private interest rates. This in turn would stimulate private investment.[1]

The argument put forward here is that Walpole was not simply concerned with letting sleeping dogs lie. He was instead concerned with creating a helpful political and social climate for individual economic initiatives, at strengthening the relations of the government with the financial community in the City of London, and at repaying as much as possible of the nation's debts, while at the same time taking care to conciliate the traditional landed and farming interests of the country, and to make it clear that the supremacy of the Established Church was not in danger. He aimed, in fact, at political unity partly achieved through social and economic progress. In several respects these policies had achieved their aims by the date of his fall from power in February 1742. He had firmly established the main political pattern of the next hundred years: the supremacy of Parliament in the formulation and expression of national opinion; the need for the leading Minister to sit in the Commons; the careful management of both court and Parliament; the leading role of the Treasury in executive government. Every time this pattern was departed from over the following century, circumstances pulled the country back to it. Second, the nation was socially and politically stronger and more united in 1742, on the eve of a renewed period of Jacobite threats and invasions, than had seemed possible twenty years earlier. This was not an automatic result of a long period of external peace and internal tranquillity. It was due as much to the increased complexity of business life and social organization which this period fostered. These changes occurred most noticeably in the fast-growing services of the City of London, where banking, fire-insurance, marine underwriting and shipping all made considerable strides. But they are also traceable in agriculture, for which London mortgage finance was of growing importance, in industry, and in the organization of internal and foreign trade.

In a number of respects, however, Walpole's policies enjoyed only quali-

---

[1] As Sir John Barnard in particular argued in 1737, see below p. 478.

fied success. He was not able to pursue all his aims in detail. On important issues like the repeal of the Salt duties (1730–2), the restrictions imposed on foreign lending in 1723 and 1730, and the Molasses Act of 1733, revenue needs were clearly influenced by the intrigues of sectional interests or the needs of diplomacy.[1] Public reactions to changes in revenue collection which would probably have benefited both government income and the economy as a whole could be seriously misjudged, as they were in the excise crisis of 1733. At a more general level, it can be argued that, despite important developments in the structure of the economy, it was not moving ahead fast enough. The growth of trade to America did not compensate for the relative stagnation of exports to a protectionist Europe. There also seems to have been depression in sectors of agriculture. The evidence, admittedly equivocal, suggests that Walpole's policies, however much they commanded general assent, were in the longer run inadequate to remove the obstacles to expansion of English overseas commerce. First among these obstacles was growing French competition in the Mediterranean, India, Africa, the West Indies and the mainland of North America. It is at least arguable that by the 1740s the aggressive mercantilism of Chatham had become a more appropriate cure for these problems than Walpole's pacific mercantilism, which was really a new version of Yarranton's outdoing the Dutch without fighting.[2] On the other hand, Walpole, by strengthening both the machinery of government finance and its social and political foundations, put into his successors' hands the means to change from the one policy to the other in the costly decades of war that followed his resignation.

II

We must now return from these general considerations to the specific question of Walpole's financial policy. This, like those of Austria, France and the United Provinces in the same period, aimed in the first place at reducing

---

[1] For the repeal of the salt duties see E. Hughes, *Studies in Administration and Finance* (Manchester, 1934), pp. 291 ff. The Acts restricting overseas lending were 9 Geo. I, c. 26 (H.M. subjects not to subscribe to the Austrian East Indian Company), and 3 Geo. II, c. 5 (H.M. subjects not to lend money to any foreign power without licence). The Molasses Act (6 Geo. II, c. 13) is discussed by C. M. Andrews, 'Anglo-French Commercial Rivalry 1700–1750', *Am. H.R.* xx (1914–15), 539.

[2] For Yarranton see above, p. 4.

the debts contracted during the wars of 1689–1714. The government's tax revenue, derived mainly from customs, excise and a two-shilling land tax[1] was by now sufficiently high — about £6m. p.a. — to cover ordinary expenditure, which had fallen by a third from its wartime peak. New long-term borrowing could therefore be kept at a low level, and at favourable rates of interest, as is shown in Table 22.

Loans were floated partly to redeem previous short-term debts (in 1721, 1726 and 1728), partly to help discharge part of the new debts owed to the South Sea Company as a result of the Bubble, and partly for current supply. Three of them were administered by the Exchequer, the rest by the Bank of England, and they were charged on the usual miscellany of indirect taxes. In addition to the sums raised in this way, the East India Company in 1730 gave the state £200,000 to secure continuance of its charter to 1769. It also agreed that the interest on the state's debt to it of £3,200,000 should be reduced from 5%, at which it had stood since 1708, to 4%.[2] This brought it into line with the other two monied companies.

The relatively small sums borrowed for long terms were more than offset by repayment of parts of the National Debt. By the late 1720s the Sinking Fund of 1717 had increased to over £1m. a year, so the government had plenty of money in hand.[3] Walpole began to look at the ways in which it could be used. The South Sea Bubble had led to conversion of most of the former redeemable debts into South Sea stock, but a residue of £2,561,000 of these debts remained. The government discharged this between 1721 and 1730.[4] Since it could not touch the Irredeemable annuities left over from the Bubble, it then turned its attention to the swollen capital of the South Sea Company itself. This had increased in 1720 from £11,746,844 to £37,802,203 and was not repayable before midsummer 1727. In 1722, however, the company had sold part of its Exchequer interest-entitlement to the Bank of England, and had cancelled £4m. of its stock. The remaining £33m. capital was divided in 1723 into £16,901,103 'South Sea Annuities' and £16,901,100 'Trading Stock'. This aimed at conciliating the new proprietors, who did not want to see their securities exposed to the hazards of trade. The dissatisfaction of the rank and file of the company with the

---

[1] In 1732 and 1733 the rate was reduced to 1s. in the £. Land-tax rates are listed below, p. 358 n.

[2] 3 Geo. II, c. 20 (1730).

[3] BPP (1686–9), xxxv. 682 ff. annual statements of Sinking Fund revenue and expenditure 1718–86.

[4] See Appendix B.

TABLE 22

Government long-term borrowing 1721–42

1 No. Date of royal assent to Loan Act	2 Sum raised £	3 Interest %	4 Fund on which interest charged	5 Purpose of loan	6 Administration of loan
1 29 July 1721	500,000	5	Hereditary revenue of Crown. Crown to reimburse itself by charging 6d. in £ on pensions and annuities.	To discharge debts of royal Civil List.	By Bank of England. Creditors to notify Bank which would then credit them with 5% stock.
2 24 February 1726	1,000,000	3	6d. pensions duty as above	Under 11 Geo. I, c. 17 (1725), £990,000 Exchequer bills were created to repay loan (1), above. This loan was to discharge these bills.	A lottery managed by Bank of England. Prize-winners were credited with 3% stock.
3 28 May 1728	1,750,000	4	Coal duties, extended in 1719 to 1751 and perpetuated by the South Sea Act in 1720.	The loan had five aims: (a) repayment of £500,000 South Sea stock; (b) discharge of £338,000 Supply Exchequer bills; (c) discharge of £90,000 loans raised by Commissioners for new churches; (d) £103,140 more for these Commissioners; (e) £718,060 for Supply of 1728.	The loan was made by the Bank of England.

4	24 March 1729	1,250,000	4	Part of 1714 lottery fund (duties on soap, paper, calico, vellum). The rest of this fund was payable to the South Sea Company.	The loan was to pay off a further £1,403,970 South Sea stock. In fact only £1m. was discharged (3 Geo. II, c. 16).	The loan was made by the Bank of England.
5	7 May 1731	400,000	3½	Duties on salt, stamped vellum, parchment and paper freed by reduction of East India Company's interest to 4% in 1730 (see text).	Supply of 1731.	Exchequer.
6	Same Act	800,000	3	Same fund.	Supply of 1731.	A lottery managed by the Bank of England. Prize-winners were credited with 3% stock.
7	20 May 1736	600,000	3	Sinking Fund.	Supply of 1736.	Exchequer.
8	14 June 1739	300,000	3	Sinking Fund	Supply of 1739	Exchequer.
		£6,600,000				

Source: Acts of Parliament authorizing these loans. Besides these sums, £141,094 St. Kitts–Nevis Debentures, originally made out to sufferers in those islands, were funded in 3% stock in 1721. Of this stock, £103,273 was exchanged 1727–30 for 3% (1726) stock, the 1726 lottery having been undersubscribed by that amount. The rest was absorbed into 3% Consols in 1752 (see below, p. 242).

directors' policies led within a decade to an extension of this principle. In January 1732 Sir John Eyles, then nearing the end of his long and relatively stormy term as the company's Sub-Governor, had bitterly complained, not for the first time, of the General Court's hostility to the directors.[1] This did not deter a group of nine proprietors in April sponsoring 'Heads proposed for a Bill in Parliament', whose object was to reduce the trading capital by three-quarters, the remainder becoming fixed interest stock like that of 1723. A ballot showed a large majority (619–180) in favour of the proposal.[2] The appointment two months later of a committee of fifteen to examine the company's accounts, on which no director or ex-director was to be allowed to serve, was a further example of the General Court's rancour.[3] No steps, however, were evidently taken to carry through the proposed Bill for capital reconstruction until May 1733, when its progress in Parliament was reported. In the following month it became law.[4]

As a result of it, the South Sea Company's trading capital was reduced by two-thirds (not three-quarters as originally proposed) to £3,662,784, a figure at which it remained until paid off in 1854.[5] The remainder of the trading capital of 1733, amounting to £10,988,319, became a fixed interest 4% stock, called South Sea New Annuities to distinguish it from the similar stock created in 1723, now known as South Sea Old Annuities. Both were administered at South Sea House, but for all practical purposes they were government stocks like those administered by the Bank of England.[6] The government had meanwhile (1728) begun to reduce the company's trading capital as soon as it was legally able to. It soon extended its repayments to the annuities, and between 1728 and 1738 paid off and cancelled £6·5m. in all.

The government was also able to repay part of the debts owed to the Bank of England for Exchequer bills which it had funded in 1709 (£1,775,028) and 1717 (£2m.). The Exchequer had paid 5% interest on this debt be-

---

[1] Add. MS. 25544, f. 89, South Sea G. Ct. Bk., 14 January 1732. Eyles was elected in 1721.

[2] Ibid., f. 101, result of ballot announced 25 April 1732.

[3] Ibid., f. 110, 16 June 1732. This seems to have been a counterblast to the report of the directors' own committee on the company's accounts, presented on the same day and now in the House of Lords MSS. (see Bibliography, below).

[4] Add. MS. 25545, ff. 13, 17, 25 May and 20 June 1733. The Act was 6 Geo. II, c. 28.

[5] Under 16 Vict. c. 23 (1853) the South Sea Company was to be wound up after Christmas 1853.

[6] The ledgers for South Sea stock were destroyed in the mid-nineteenth century when the company was wound up, see Bibliography below. The ledgers for the South Sea Old and New Annuities are now in the Bank of England Record Office.

TABLE 23

South Sea stock and annuities paid off 1728–37

Date	South Sea Stock	South Sea Old Annuities	South Sea New Annuities	Total paid off
£	£	£	£	£
1728	250,000	250,000	..	500,000
1729	1,000,000	..	..	1,000,000
1731	..	1,000,000	..	1,000,000
1732	1,000,000	..	..	1,000,000
1733	..	1,000,000	..	1,000,000
1736	..	..	1,000,000	1,000,000
1737	..	1,000,000	..	1,000,000
TOTALS	2,250,000	3,250,000	1,000,000	6,500,000

Source: BPP (1898), lii, 332–5, and the Acts of Parliament authorizing the repayments.

tween midsummer 1718 and midsummer 1727, when the rate was lowered by agreement to 4%.[1] In 1728 Walpole repaid £775,028 of the 1709 debt. In 1729 he repaid the remainder, £1m., and also paid off half a million of the £2m. debt of 1717. The funds thus obtained enabled the Bank to make a loan of £1·25m. for the service of 1729.[2] In 1739 the government paid off a further £1m., but the balance of £500,000 still forms part of its debt to the Bank. During the period in which Walpole held office he thus paid £3,275,028 debts due to the Bank but borrowed a further £3m. from it. To sum up, between 1721 and 1742 Walpole paid off the residue of the old Redeemable debts, and parts of those owed to the South Sea Company and Bank of England. Besides this, he liquidated nearly £1m. Civil List debts, including the £500,000 Civil List 5% stock of 1721, by a lottery loan in 1726.[3] These repayments amply outbalanced the new long-term borrowing previously discussed.

An important further point is that the reduction in 1727–30 of the interest which the state owed to the three monied companies lowered the annual charge of the debt more than in proportion to the reduction of its principal.

[1] 11 Geo. I, c. 9.　　　　　[2] See above, Table 22.　　　　　[3] Ibid.

TABLE 24
Decrease in the National Debt under Walpole

No.	Type of debt	£	£
1	Residue of former Redeemable debts paid off 1721–8	2,560,792	
2	South Sea stock and annuities discharged 1728–37	6,500,000	
3	Debts due to Bank of England discharged 1728–39	3,275,028	
4	Discharge of Civil List 5%s (1721) in 1726 . .	500,000	
			12,835,820
5	*Less* additions to National Debt by new borrowing (see above, Table 22)	..	6,600,000
	NET DECREASE		£6,235,820

Source: See previous text.

In 1721 the charge was £2,567,000, in 1741 only £1,890,000, a fall of 20%, or nearly one-third.[1]

At the same time that he was carrying through these operations, which resembled on a larger scale a clever landlord's reduction of his mortgage charges, Walpole was making important improvements in the machinery of short-term borrowing, which brought the Treasury into increasingly close contact with the Bank of England.[2] His policy created a general atmosphere of financial confidence, which encouraged substantial market investment by institutions, government departments and rich individuals. Combined with the reduction of the National Debt, this brought the market price of fixed interest stock higher and higher, and the rate of interest nearer and nearer 3%. In 1732 government 3% stock reached par for the first time, and in the first half of 1733 was at a small premium. Walpole described the new situation in the following terms.

The Sinking Fund was now grown to a great maturity, and produced annually about 1,200,000*l.* and was become almost a Terror to all the individual Proprietors of the Publick Debts; the high state of Credit, the low rate of Interest of money, and the advanced price of all publick Stocks and Funds above Par, made the great monied Companies, and all their Proprietors, apprehend nothing more than the being oblig'd

---

[1] *BPP* (1857–8), xxxiii. 171, 179, annual charge of the debt.
[2] See below, especially p. 383.

to receive their Principal too fast; and it became almost the universal consent of Mankind, that a Million a year was as much as the Creditors of the Publick could bear to receive, in discharge of part of their Principal.[1]

This was what Sir John Eyles had in mind when he told the South Sea General Court in March 1732 that the £1m. receivable from the government should probably be used to pay off part of the company's bonds,

Because this debt carrying 4 p. Cent. will be paid off at Par by Money, that if divided among the Proprietors, cannot be laid out in the Purchase of anything that bears the same Interest under 10 p. Ct. advance.[2]

In other words, now that 4% securities were at a premium, holders of 4% South Sea stock should stick to it — for if paid in cash they could not obtain the same income by new investment. A pamphleteer asserted, falsely or not, that the public creditors, presumably for this reason, did not want to be repaid.[3]

Walpole's opponents were at first unwilling to concede the success of his financial policy. Pulteney claimed in 1729 that, although the minister was careful not to produce satisfactory accounts of the National Debt, it had increased by over £400,000 between 1716 and 1729 — despite the government's claim that it had decreased by as many millions during the same period.[4] Pulteney also depreciated the originality of the Sinking Fund, which he said was clearly copied from the Aggregate Fund of 1715.[5] At the same time, he argued that the Sinking Fund could only legally be applied to national debts contracted before 1717, whereas Walpole had repeatedly used its balances for other purposes, with Parliament's consent.[6] Walpole agreed that the Sinking Fund had precedents, and that it should normally be applied to discharge the National Debt, but convincingly repudiated the claim that

[1] [Sir Robert Walpole], *Some Considerations concerning the Publick Funds* (1735), p. 56.

[2] Add. MS. 25544, f. 95, South Sea G. Ct. Bk., 24 March 1732.

[3] *A letter from a Member of Parliament to his friends in the Country* (1733), p. 11.

[4] [William Pulteney], *Some Considerations on the National Debts* . . . (1729).

[5] Ibid., p. 64. A further regular opposition complaint during the 1730s was the use of Votes of Credit. These were no longer loans on the strength of votes of the House of Commons repaid from the first supplies, as they had been in the 1690s. They were instead a power given by Parliament to use part of the annual supplies granted for unspecified purposes, see the concluding section of Walpole's *Some Considerations concerning the Publick Funds*. The money, according to him, was mostly used for diplomatic purposes. The opposition, of course, hinted that it was used to bribe supporters of the Administration.

[6] Pulteney, op. cit., and idem., *An Enquiry into the Conduct of our Domestick Affairs* (1734).

the Act of 1717 included a concession to the public creditors of an inalienable right to its produce.[1] He repeated his arguments in the Commons two years later, and extended his basic contention that Parliament had absolute control over the Sinking Fund by proposing that its balances should be used to anticipate annual taxes, rather than lying idly in the Exchequer until applied to discharge part of the National Debt.[2]

By this date it was no longer possible for his opponents to claim, as Pulteney seems to have been doing earlier, that his financial policy was compounded of lies and myths. They conceded that the Sinking Fund was 'one of the most useful funds that was ever established in this kingdom', and the only one that promised relief from the nation's heavy debts, though disagreeing with Walpole's proposal to pay off from it more of the South Sea debt; they argued that the discharge of those due to the Bank of England and East India Company was politically more urgent.[3] This Walpole rejected.[4] Later in the same month the opposition launched a more subtle attack. Government 3% stock, which had fallen away from par owing to the war rumours and difficulties of 1733–5, had again reached par in 1736, with the clearing of international horizons, and by March 1737 it was at 107. On 21 March Sir John Barnard, Member for the City of London, and an ardent exponent of cheap government, tabled a motion, of which he had given preliminary notice on 14th, to reduce the interest on the South Sea annuities from 4% to 3%.[5] This put Walpole in a cleft stick, for he either consented, and conceded the political initiative, or opposed, and in doing so appeared careless of an economy which the very success of his own policy had made possible. This was just the kind of subtle issue that might, and did, loosen the political ties that more dramatic ones held firm.

On 28 March 1737 Barnard supported his proposal in the Committee of the Whole House for which he had moved. The substance of his speech was

[1] [Sir Robert Walpole], *Some Considerations concerning the Publick Funds* (1735), esp. pp. 13 and 31.

[2] *Parl. Hist.* x. 34, debate of 9 March 1737. It became regular form between this date and 1742 to use Sinking Fund balances in this way.

[3] *Parl. Hist.* x. 39, 11 March 1737.

[4] For some of the arguments used see above, p. 1.

[5] *Parl. Hist.* 62–72, 14 and 21 March 1737. For Barnard see the *D.N.B.* and the jejune *Memoirs of the late Sir John Barnard, Knt.* (1820, repr. 1885). Barnard (1685–1764), a marine underwriter, was the son of a Quaker wine merchant in Reading. In 1703 he became an Anglican and from 1728 to 1758, when he resigned, was an alderman of London. From Michaelmas 1737 to Michaelmas 1738 he was Lord Mayor. He was knighted in 1732 and was M.P. for the City 1722–61. His statue was put up on the Royal Exchange in 1747. Barnard lived in Clapham, but was buried in Mortlake Parish Church.

that owing to her higher taxes and interest rates England was being ousted from her trade by her old rivals, the Dutch, and her new ones, the French. Reduction of interest on the National Debt, which would lead to lower private rates of interest, was part, though only part, of the cure for this dangerous situation.[1] He proposed that the holders of South Sea annuities should be given three choices: to be paid in cash; to be reduced to 3% and then have no further reduction for fourteen years; or to exchange their stock for life annuities or terminable annuities. The government speakers argued that Barnard's facts about taxes were mistaken, and his arguments about rates of interest muddled. They also expatiated on the hardship a reduction would cause the widows and orphans who held stock.[2] But the most telling intervention was made by Sir William Yonge at the close of the debate. He argued that Barnard's scheme was both too complex in its proposed methods and too narrow in its application. Instead of only the South Sea annuities, all 4% debts should be paid off at par or reduced to 3%. If so reduced, they should be irredeemable for fourteen years. The government should be empowered to borrow at 3% to pay dissentients.[3] This apparently realistic amendment impressed the committee, which moved two resolutions to embody it.[4] When they were reported to the House on 30 March 1737 the government tried to adjourn their consideration until 14 April. This motion, however, was defeated by 220 to 157, Henry Pelham and Horatio Walpole voting with the majority against Sir Robert Walpole and Sir William Yonge, 'and so it happened in many other instances among persons related to one another in the House, who never separated before'[5]. The House ordered a Bill to give effect to the resolution, with Barnard as one of the committee of three appointed to draft it.[6]

So far Barnard and those who supported him — for whatever motives — had gone a long way to break the normally solid ministerial front. But Barnard now, characteristically, overplayed his hand by moving, in conjunction with Sandys, Pulteney, George Speke and Micajah Perry, that taxes should be cut in proportion as soon as interest was reduced to three per cent.[7] This enabled the Government speakers, led by Lord Baltimore, Plumer, Sir Robert Walpole and Winnington, to attack his alarmist picture of the relative incidence of taxation in Holland, France and England, and to accuse him of trying to bind the hands of future parliaments. They were also

---

[1] *Parl. Hist.* x. 74 ff., 28 March 1737.
[2] Ibid. 94 ff.   [3] Ibid. 145–6, 28 March 1737.
[4] Ibid. 154.   [5] Ibid. 147 n. Horatio Walpole to Trevor 1 April 1737.
[6] Ibid. 155.   [7] Ibid. 155–6, 30 March 1737.

able to insist that taxes should not be cut back until the Sinking Fund had paid off the nation's debts.[1] This was just the kind of realistic husbandry that appealed to the House, and Barnard lost his motion by 200 to 142. Meanwhile, a vigorous pamphlet debate about the merits and demerits of the proposed reduction of interest was being waged outside Parliament. The numbers and social background of the public creditors, the effects of a reduction on overall demand and consumption, the links, if any, between the yield on the public funds and private investment, were all examined at some length.[2] The general climate of opinion seems to have been unfavourable to a reduction. This was as much as anything due to the long peace and the government's policy of redeeming the National Debt. Things seemed to be moving steadily in the right direction, so that there was no urgent need to alienate the public creditors by a further reduction of interest, coming less than ten years after that of 1727–30. Walpole, perhaps recalling the fiasco of his Excise proposals four years earlier, decided to back down. When Barnard's Reduction Bill came up for its second reading on 29 April 1737 he argued strongly against it. Though conceding that he had at first found the proposal plausible, he argued that in fact it discriminated against a group within society, and that a distinction should be drawn between public profit and public utility. He added that the Bill locked up the Sinking Fund for years ahead, and thus prevented any further reduction of interest, or any real flexibility in financial policy. It should therefore be rejected.[3] When the debate closed, the motion to commit the Bill was defeated by 249 to 134.[4]

The difficulty that Henry Pelham experienced in his reduction of interest in 1749, even after massive war borrowing had greatly increased the measure's urgency, argues in favour of Walpole's judgement in rejecting Barnard's scheme. 'You may remember, sir', a pamphleteer wrote about Pelham's plan, 'that a scheme of this nature was offer'd about ten years since and the great outcry it immediately raised. The administration at that time were too wise to try the experiment.'[5] Popular views in 1737 were probably well expressed in the doggerel, 'John the Quaker, did invent a wicked Calculation, To sink the Funds to Three *per Cent* and beggar all the Nation'.[6] Barnard had undoubtedly been used as a stalking-horse by members of the opposition who

---

[1] Ibid. 156–81.   [2] See above, p. 31, and below, pp. 478 and 480.

[3] *Parl. Hist.* x. 181–6, 29 April 1737.

[4] *Parl. Hist.* x. 187. No division lists for these debates have survived.

[5] 'A letter from a Gentleman in Town to his Friend in the Country', *Gent. Mag.*, November 1749.

[6] 'The Widows and Orphans Triumph', Milton Percival (ed.), *Political Ballads Illustrating the Administration of Sir Robert Walpole* (Oxford, 1916), p. 106.

wanted a stick with which to beat the Minister. And he was not the man to form and hold together a majority in the House. As he naively complained in March 1737,

As for my own part, if my reasons have any weight with those that hear me, I am sure I have but seldom been heard by the majority of this House, ever since I had the honour to sit in Parliament, and yet I have always raised my voice as much as I could.[1]

He had some compensation, though, twelve years later in the part he played in sponsoring Pelham's much more complex and important reduction of the interest on the National Debt.

[1] *Parl. Hist.* x. 65.

10

War and Peace 1739–55

WHEN Walpole fell from power in February 1742 the dark clouds of war were again gathering over Europe. England had declared war on Spain in October 1739, but this was at first little more than a colonial interlude. With the sudden Prussian invasion of Silesia in December 1740, which obliged England to come to the aid of Austria, and the official outbreak of war between England and France in March 1744, the issues became much more complex and dramatic, recalling the terrible years of the 1690s. Advocates of the Old System of foreign policy were happy to see England once more in league with the United Provinces and Austria to curb French power, and only gradually realized that the war aims of the allies were quite different from those of the early 1700s, that the spirit of the Dutch, who remained neutral until 1744, was broken, while Austria's real enemy was now not France, but Prussia. One thing remained constant and obvious, however: war was cripplingly expensive. Until 1744 new English government long-term loans were relatively small, and 3% stock remained at par or just below it. When France officially entered the conflict against her in March 1744, and the real struggle began, the 3%s at once sank to 92–3, and the scale of long-term borrowing sharply increased. Larger and larger loans became needed each year. By the end of 1747 Henry Pelham, who was First Lord of the Treasury from 1743, was seriously questioning, like his brother in 1761, whether England could fight for another year.[1]

The greater part of new government borrowing was by publicly-subscribed loans, which are listed in Table 25.

The two loans of 1747–8, which were in effect issued at a discount, increased the total government liability from £20·7m. to £21,730,000. Besides this, the government borrowed smaller sums from the monied companies. In 1742 the Bank of England agreed to lend £1·6m. without interest to secure extension of its charter from 1743 to 1764.[2] It financed

[1] Pelham to Cumberland, 8 September 1747, quoted in Mahon, *Hist. of England 1713–83*, iii (1838), 530; Newcastle to Hardwicke, 17 August 1761, *Rockingham Memoirs* (ed. Albemarle), i (1852), 31.
[2] 15 Geo. II, c. 13.

this loan by issuing £800,004 new stock, making its capital a round £9m.[1] The East India Company lent £1m. at 3% in 1744 to secure a similar extension of its own charter from 1769 to 1783.[2] In addition, the Bank agreed in 1746 to fund £986,000 Exchequer bills at 4%.[3] Since £3,072,472 departmental debts were funded in 1749,[4] the war added over £28m. to the National Debt, besides £67,500 p.a. life annuities created in 1745 and 1746, which at twenty years' purchase would have added another £1·3m. This was about a third of the total war costs of over £95m. Effectively the war was therefore as expensive in real terms as the War of the Spanish Succession — prices having remained fairly constant — though fought within a much shorter period. This pointed the way to the staggering costs of the next conflict.[5]

With the exception of the small amount of life annuities, handled at the Exchequer, the public loans of the 1740s were entirely administered by the Bank of England. This was a logical continuation of Walpole's policy of enlisting its support to by-pass the Exchequer's cumbrous procedures. The loans were entered at the Bank in special subscription ledgers. Starting with the loan of 1743, the lender was given an assignable subscription receipt, on which payment of subsequent calls was noted when made. The holder of the receipt at the date of the last payment was credited in the ledgers 'by subscription receipt' with the appropriate amount of stock.[6] The introduction, also in 1743, of loans divided into an ordinary subscription and a lottery, enabled the government to tap the popular enthusiasm for gambling without obliging itself to pay out large sums in prizes. The holder of prize or blank tickets simply exchanged them after the draw for a certificate from the Managers of the lottery stating their amount. He presented this at the Bank

---

[1] Bank G. Ct. Bk. iii, ff. 120–1, 8 July 1742. The issue was at 140, and was payable in six instalments by 20 December 1742.

[2] 17 Geo. II, c. 17.   [3] 19 Geo. II, c. 6. See below, p. 224.

[4] See below, p. 230.

[5] The new taxes imposed to service the war loans also led to an increase in the number of revenue officers. The total number in 1755 can be calculated from Chamberlayne's *Magnae Britanniae Notitia* as about 5,200. Dr. J. E. D. Binney, 'The Public Revenue and Expenditure . . . 1774–92' (Oxford University D.Phil. thesis, 1952), ii. 325, calculates the number as 14,203 in 1782. E. Halévy, *England in 1815* (English trans., 1949), p. 36, estimates the number of revenue officers in 1825 as 25,000.

[6] The subscription ledger for the loan of 1742 at the Bank of England Record Office is ruled with four columns, one for each instalment. The introduction of assignable scrip by 16 Geo. II, c. 13, did away with this; instead, payment of each instalment was noted in the subscription ledger *seriatim*. The only such ledger in the Bank Record Office for this period is for the 4% loan of 1748.

TABLE 25

Government long-term loans publicly subscribed 1742–8

No.	Date of royal assent to Loan Act	Sum raised £	Interest %	Fund on which interest charged	Administration of loan
1	16 June 1742	800,000	3	Sinking Fund.	Ordinary stock transferred at Bank of England. Subscriptions at Bank, payable in four instalments.
2	22 March 1743	1,800,000	3	Excise duties on spirits imposed same year.	£1m. was to be raised by subscription as in (1) and £800,000 by a lottery. Stock subscribed for was to be payable in four instalments, lottery tickets (£10 each) at once. Holders of both blank and prize tickets after the draw were to have stock credited to them in the same ledgers, whose total would therefore be £1,800,000. This was called 'funding tickets in stock'.
3	22 March 1744	1,800,000	3	Same as (2).	£1,200,000 was to be raised by subscription £600,000 by a lottery. Administration as in no. 2. However, lottery tickets, too, could be paid for in four instalments.

4	19 March 1745	2,000,000	3	Additional duty of £8 a tun on French wine imported and £4 a tun on other wines imported.	£1,500,000 was to be raised by subscription and £500,000 by a lottery, administration as in (2) and (3). In addition, each purchaser of ten £10 lottery tickets was allowed a 4½% Exchequer Annuity for his own life or a nominee's.
5	19 March 1746	3,000,000	4	Additional customs and excise duties on glass, low wines and spirits.	£2,500,000 was to be raised by subscription and £500,000 by a lottery, administration as in (2), (3) and (4). However, stock was now payable in seven instalments instead of four, The life-annuity offer (see (4)) was repeated but the rate was doubled to 9%.
6	5 February 1747	4,000,000	4	New Window duties.	Raised by subscription, managed by Bank of England. For each £100 paid in subscribers were allotted £10 extra stock. The government's total liability was therefore £4·4m. Subscriptions were payable in six instalments.
7	24 March 1747	1,000,000	4	Excise duty of £4 p.a. on coaches.	A lottery. The tickets were subsequently funded in 4% stock managed by the Bank of England.
8	18 February 1748	6,300,000	4	Additional shilling in pound	Raised by subscription, managed by Bank of England. Each subscriber of £100 received a free £10 lottery ticket; these were subsequently funded as usual in the same ledgers as the subscribed part of the loan. The government's total liability was £6,930,000.
		£20,700,070			

Source: Acts of Parliament authorizing these loans, and stock ledgers for them (Bank of England Record Office).

of England, which credited him 'by certificate' with that amount of stock.[1]
The other technical innovations in these loans were the *douceurs* of 1745–6
(life annuities) and 1747–8 (extra stock or lottery tickets). These expedients
were attempts to increase the yield of loans without increasing their nominal
interest — which, it was held, would depress the price of existing stock.
Their efficacy was probably only marginal.[2] A further point is that calls on
the loans were increasingly widely spaced. In 1748 there were ten spread
over nine months. Together with the other innovations, this stimulated the
growth of speculative practices like 'nursing' scrip and 'insuring' lottery
tickets. These increased the demand for loans, but also the risk of default.[3]

The administration of the war loans had certain common features, others
which varied and were subject to acrimonious debate. The Treasury drew up
proposals for the year's loan, generally towards the end of the previous year, after
consultation with the monied interests in the City. The draft was introduced
into the Commons' Committee of Ways and Means early in the year. After consideration there, it was worked up into a Bill by a subcommittee under the
expert guidance of the aged joint Secretary to the Treasury, John Scrope, who
on Lowndes's death in 1724 had succeeded to his office and his reputation
for financial omniscience.[4] Each Bill, as was inevitable where technical
matters of great complexity had to be precisely defined, was recognizably based
on the others, and something like a standard form of wording had appeared.
The Bill was normally read for the first time in the Commons in February
or March, and generally had an untroubled passage through the House.[5]

The main difference between loans was in the means used to ensure that
they were fully subscribed. The best method of underwriting was to negotiate
the terms in advance with a group of important monied men in the City,
each of whom undertook to take up a portion of the loan when it was opened.
He would do so not from his own resources, but by canvassing friends and
relations whose financial probity he could vouch for. Their subscriptions,

---

[1] Loan Acts, and stock ledgers in the Bank of England Record Office.

[2] Cf. also below, pp. 222 ff.

[3] See also below, p. 506. The structure of loan subscriptions is examined on pp. 287–9.

[4] Scrope, a former Baron of the Scottish Exchequer, was over sixty when he took office
in 1724; by the mid-1740s he was well into his eighties. Cf. *Bedford Correspondence* (ed.
Lord John Russell), i (1842), 7, 5 July 1742, Pulteney to the Duke of Bedford (who had
contemplated having Scrope replaced): 'What your Grace mentions is absolutely impracticable. Mr. Scrope is the only man I know that thoroughly understands the business
of the Treasury, and is versed in drawing money bills. On this foundation he stands secure,
and is as immovable as a rock.'

[5] See the Loan Acts and the *House of Commons Journals*.

added to his own, constituted his 'list'.[1] To this was added the 'Treasury list' composed of peers, M.P.s, and government and departmental officials.[2] The monied companies usually did not subscribe for themselves.[3] The total of these lists guaranteed the first payment on the loan, though apparently not more than the first payment.[4] By these means the loan was filled in advance, sometimes before the money Bill was drafted.[5] The subscribers appeared to have been bound in honour rather than in law to fulfil their promises. A pamphleteer said of the loan of 1746,

I dare say, Sir, you will agree, that every Person, who had suffered his Name to be put into any List delivered to the Treasury, was as much engaged in Honour to pay his Subscription, as if he had given his Bond for the Performance of it.[6]

The writer, although he admitted that Parliament could not be bound in advance by such an agreement, added,

Sir, I will venture to tell you . . . that if it was not taken for granted, that the House of Commons would always confirm those Agreements, no Set of Men whatever would treat with the Treasury at all upon this Subject.[7]

There are some earlier indications of consultation between the Treasury and the monied interest before loans were floated.[8] The systematic use of

[1] *Gent. Mag.*, April 1744, Hist. Chronicle under 9 April, shows the lists for the first payments on the loans for that year.

[2] Ibid. The composition of the Treasury's lists in the 1740s can be inferred from the practice of the 1750s, for which some lists survive.

[3] The London Assurance (£20,000) and the South Sea Company (£30,000) both appear in the opening ledger for the 3% loan of 1744, Bank of England Record Office. The South Sea Company, however, had not subscribed, but had bought scrip on which the first payment was already made.

[4] For example, Samson Gideon in his memorial submitted to the Treasury in 1758 claimed that in 1742 he had made himself answerable for the first payment on upwards of £600,000, Add. MS. 33055, f. 221, transcribed by Dr. L. S. Sutherland, 'Samson Gideon and the Reduction of Interest, 1749–50', *Econ. H.R.* xvi (1946), 15.

[5] This seems to have occurred in 1746. In 1744 the loan was reported to be filled 'in one Day' on the same day that the Bill for it received the royal assent, *Gent. Mag.*, March 1744, Hist. Chronicle under '22 March'.

[6] *A Letter to Sir John Barnard upon his Proposals for raising three Millions of Money for the Service of the Year 1746. From a Member of the House of Commons* (1746), p. 8.

[7] Ibid., p. 9.

[8] For example the partial failure of the Lottery loan of 1726 'was occasioned by some certain Favourites refusing to take out their Tickets, when they were at a Discount, which they had subscribed for, as usual, hoping to make an Advantage of them'. [William Pulteney], *Some Considerations on the National Debts* (1729), p. 28. (Of 100,000 tickets, 11,093 were at first unsold. They were subsequently given to holders of St. Kitts-Nevis debentures, see above, p. 207, Table 22.)

lists, however, apparently dates from the 1740s, judging by the intense controversy it then aroused.[1] It almost certainly derived, like the use of scrip, from the practice of the monied companies. The Bank's subscriptions of 1722 and 1742, for example, were divided amongst the directors, each of whom brought in his list of contributors, and in 1720 the South Sea Company had used similar methods, though in disreputable circumstances.[2] The Bank's annual subscriptions for circulating Exchequer bills were filled in the same way.[3] From the Treasury's standpoint the system had great merits. It used the mercantile community's knowledge of its own members' probity and business capacity, and by doing so enlisted in advance the support of interests in the City whose hostility would have impaired the success of any financial measure. This made it possible to raise the supplies in years of great credit stringency like 1746, when an 'open' loan would probably have failed. Unsubscribed loans were not, after all, unknown; their memory must have given the Treasury official nightmares. The Tontine of 1693, the first issue of Exchequer bills in 1696, the Malt Lottery of 1697, the Bank Circulation subscription of 1711, the 5%s of 1715, the Subscription for the Support of Public Credit in October 1720, the Malt Lottery of 1721, the 3%s of 1726, had all been left partly unfilled. Measures to prevent this recurring were correspondingly attractive. The Treasury therefore filled its loans between 1742 and 1747 by prior consultation with the monied men in the City. Its most prominent contractor was the great Jewish jobber Samson Gideon, whom the monied companies were also using in this period to buy and sell securities.[4] At the same time Gideon was actively dealing in

---

[1] Cf. Liverpool Papers 1715–45, vol. cxli, Add. MS. 38330, ff. 330–2, 'Plan to raise 3 Millions for the Year 1746': 'the Method practised of late Years to raise the money at once by Subscriptions of large Sums in few hands at a price much less than the old Funds.'

[2] In 1722 each director of the Bank of England was allowed £80,000, half of which was to be reserved for proprietors of Bank stock, Bank D. Ct. Bk. I, f. 96, 27 June 1722. In 1742 each director was allowed £18,000, and the Governors had the rest, D. Ct. Bk. O, f. 49, 8 July 1742. For the South Sea subscriptions see above, p. 125.

[3] The subscriptions were 'filled, for the most part by People in the Management and their Favourites', see below, p. 386.

[4] For an account of Gideon's career see Dr. L. S. Sutherland, 'Samson Gideon: Eighteenth Century Jewish Financier', *Trans. Jewish Hist. Soc. of England*, xvii (1951–2), 79. Gideon's role in the loans of the 1740s is described in his memorandum to the Treasury in 1758, *Econ. H.R.*, loc. cit. He was used by the South Sea Company to buy securities in 1744, 1745 and 1750 (South Sea D. Ct. Bk., 31 May 1744, 21 March 1746, 20 September 1750), by the Bank of England to buy the stock of defaulters on the call of 1746 (below, p. 224), and by the East India Company to buy silver in 1749, East India General Cash Journal 1742–50, f. 328, October 1749. For his activities as a jobber see below, p. 514.

East India stock for clients and on his own account. Good Protestants regarded him as a symbol of the corruption of English society by wealth and power.[1]

Gideon's activities, and those of his colleagues, aroused increasing dissatisfaction in orthodox City circles. This came to a head over the loan negotiations of 1746. In 1745, when even before the Jacobite invasion credit had become more stringent, it was apparently Gideon who suggested that by offering a life annuity to each subscriber of £100 in the lottery it might be possible to disguise the rise in the rate of interest allowed.[2] In 1746, when thanks to Charles Edward Stuart's invasion and march towards London, reversed only on 6 December 1745, no administration 'ever began a Session of Parliament . . . under greater Disadvantages as to raising the publick Money',[3] this device was again used, but the life annuity was doubled to 9% and the interest on the loan raised to 4%. These terms had been agreed upon by the Treasury and the loan contractors headed by Gideon early in 1746, apparently on the basis of a proposal submitted by John Bristow and Gerard Van Neck at the end of 1745.[4] They were generous,[5] but the situation was critical. A cash loan on the Land Tax at 4% had been only partially subscribed.[6] A call of 20% on the subscribers to the circulation of Exchequer bills in December 1745 had proved a failure.[7] By the end of January 1746 the price of 3% stock had sunk to 74.[8] In these circumstances the Treasury had its back to the wall, and, after delaying for over a month, accepted the terms in January as the best that could be obtained. It remedied

---

[1] See above, p. 34.　　　　[2] Gideon's memorandum, *Econ. H.R.*, loc. cit.

[3] *A Letter to Sir John Barnard* (1746), p. 3.

[4] *A Letter to Sir John Barnard* (1746), Barnard's reply, *A Defence of several Proposals for Raising of Three Millions for the Service of the year 1746* (1746), and Gideon's memorandum, *Econ. H.R.*, loc. cit.

[5] For the terms see Table 25 on p. 219 above. The author (possibly Barnard) of 'The merchants proposal in 1746' endorsed 'Remarks on the City Proposal for 3 Millions in 1746', Liverpool Papers, Add. MS. 38330, f. 332, argues that the loan was in effect being marketed at 76, and that it would have been better to offer a straight 5% stock reducible to 4% after the war.

[6] *A Letter to Sir John Barnard*, p. 4.　　　　[7] See below, p. 385.

[8] Bank stock was at 143½ on 7 September 1745, at 136¼ on 12 November, at 134 on 4 December, at 125 on 19 December and still at 125 on 22 January 1746. East India bonds were at 10s. discount in early September 1745, falling to £4 5s. 0d. discount by mid-December. By the end of February 1746 the discount was only £1 17s. 0d., and in April the bonds were again at par. Contemporaries differed about the seriousness of the crisis. The prevailing newspaper opinion seems to have been one of optimism throughout, though in mercantile correspondence it is usually asserted that trade is at a standstill.

the deficit of short-term supply in the same month by an agreement with the
Bank of England. The Bank undertook to fund £986,000 Exchequer bills at
4%, and to lend the government £1m. on security of the Land and Malt
taxes.[1] In order to finance this it made a call of 10% on its proprietors in
February and March, when credit was still extremely low. A small part
(£11,525) was unsubscribed.[2] In August 1746, however the defaulters'
stock was sold to complete the £986,000 due, Samson Gideon taking up
most of it himself.[3] Since the market price of all securities rallied after the
defeat of the Jacobites at Culloden on 16 April 1746, the government could
congratulate itself on having come unscathed through the worst financial
crisis since 1720, thanks to the capacity of the monied men.

The enemies of the 'Gideonites' drew a different lesson from the episode.[4]
Their leader, as might have been expected, was the veteran but muddle-
headed exponent of financial purity, Sir John Barnard. He claimed that the
loan contractors had taken advantage of very difficult circumstances to
wring extortionate terms from the Treasury.[5] In this they had been aided
by the selfishness of the Bank of England, which should have realized that
its 10% call would depress stock-prices and 'forestall the Government,
when it should have Occasion to raise Money by new-created Funds'.[6]
Barnard was aggrieved that his own proposal, which he had put forward in
the Committee of Ways and Means on 21 February 1746, had not been
accepted.[7] He had suggested raising £3m. by three lotteries of equal amount.
The first would be at 5% for ten years, and then be redeemable at par. The

---

[1] 9 Geo. II, c. 6. On 15 January 1746 the Bank's General Court had been summoned 'to
consider by what Ways or Methods the Bank which has hitherto been always ready to
shew its Zeal for the good of the Publick may advance Money towards furnishing the
supplies for the Year 1746' (Bank G. Ct. Bk. iii, f. 141). The proposal drafted by the
directors was submitted the same day, ibid. and its further progress reported to the Court
on 20 and 29 January, ibid., ff. 142–4.

[2] Bank stock, Journal of call of 10%, 1746, f. 59, Bank of England Record Office.

[3] The stock was sold at 137 under an order of the Bank's General Court of 21 August
1746 (ibid.). The total sold was £11,525, of which Gideon bought £10,685 on 29–30
August, Bank stock transfer books.

[4] The term 'Gideonites' was used in the 1740s to designate loan-contractors and stock-
jobbers as a class. Cf. *The Art of Stock-jobbing, a Poem. By a Gideonite* (1746). The author of
*Annotations on a late pamphlet intituled Considerations on the Proposal for reducing the
Interest on the National Debt* (1750) says (p. 9) that Barnard claims that great estates have
been gained by supplying the public with money, but 'Here the Author must mean the
Gideonites, for the old Proprietors of the Funds, have made a losing Account of it, ever
since the Year 1716'.

[5] Sir John Barnard, *A Defence of several Proposals*.   [6] Ibid., p. 2.   [7] Ibid., p. 9.

second would be at 3% but be issued at a discount of 30%. The third would be at 4%. The loans would be filled by a subscription open to all, and any unsubscribed tickets would be sold by auction.[1]

Barnard's opponents accused him, with some plausibility, of thinking he had only to stamp his foot upon the ground to raise millions.[2] They pointed out also, perhaps untruthfully, that 'we have had Lotteries for so many Years successively, that People begin to grow tired of them'.[3] There was a danger too, it was alleged, that the lotteries currently being raised in Holland would affect the success of English loans.[4] It was not difficult to represent Barnard's arguments as inspired merely by pique. He had made himself the spokesman of those who were excluded by the Treasury's lists and were aggrieved because they were excluded. There is a nice touch of hurt pride in his reference to the monied men by whose advice the loan of 1746 was supposed to have been composed:

It is very well known, that the Men who have Money in the City are very numerous . . . but it is possible . . . that a very few Persons [this was aimed at Gideon] may pass, with some, for the Monied Men of the City; and . . . may take on them to represent the Sense of the City, although perhaps quite contrary to the real Sense of the Citizens . . . I shall choose for the future to call them Undertakers; not liking that they should enjoy the Title of The Monied Men, as if they were the only Monied Men in the City.[5]

It is clear, however, that Barnard and his supporters had more than merely personal points to make. They claimed that 'the Methods of late used, for contracting with a few Persons, for raising the Supplies in a Lump' caused sudden fluctuations in stock-prices, since the subscribers sold out of the old stocks, whose price therefore sank, in order to come into the new ones.[6] Further, they subscribed only in order to sell again; most of them had not the capital to complete their payments.[7] In a crisis, therefore, as in 1745, the market became unnecessarily depressed, since those with money but no scrip held off in the hope of reducing the jobbers, who had scrip but no money, to

[1] Ibid., pp. 9 ff.   [2] *A Letter to Sir John Barnard*, p. 14.
[3] Ibid., p. 16.   [4] Ibid., and the postscript to the pamphlet.
[5] *A Defence of several Proposals*, pp. 38–39. One of Barnard's supporters in his *Remarks on a Letter to Sir John Barnard* (1746), p. 12, said that the latter had, in trying to obtain better terms for the public, shown himself a real friend to the nation, 'though not a Friend to that Mixture of all Nations, as well as Faiths, that are to receive the greatest Part' of the premium for the loan, i.e. the Gideonites.
[6] *A Defence of several Proposals*, postscript p. 72.
[7] *A Defence* and cf. Add. MS. 38330, ff. 330–2, 'Plan to raise 3 Millions for the Year 1746', cited above, p. 222 n.

the lowest possible point.[1] This was not really contradicted by the partisans of lists, who admitted that 'many of them [subscribers] . . . cannot keep their Subscriptions, and many more . . . never intended to keep them', but claimed that as they intended to sell out anyway it was to their interest that the price of the old stock should stay up.[2] If it fell, this was merely the natural effect of a new loan being raised at a higher nominal rate of interest.[3]

Barnard's sovereign remedy for what he saw as a corrupt and inefficient system was to eliminate the profits of middle-men by raising subscriptions directly from the public.

When Funds are sold by the Government, to Traffickers in Stocks, who design to sell them again, the Market continues in Agitation, until the Funds, by degrees, become settled in the Hands of Buyers, who keep them. Those Traffickers, who buy to sell again, will have more Encouragement than is necessary to be given to those who buy with a Design to keep; or else there would be no Profit arising to them. If, therefore, the Government should deal directly with Persons who buy to keep the Funds, a good Part at least of that immense Profit, which is now made by the Traffickers, would remain to the Government.[4]

An 'open' subscription would also make it easier for foreigners to subscribe.[5] Barnard's statement accurately described how the market worked when a loan was floated.[6] The belief that open subscriptions would eliminate the jobbers, however, was naive. If anything, the new method, which was in fact a return to an older method, loans being originally open, encouraged them. When credit was high, a loan would be oversubscribed by 'stags' who hoped to resell quickly at a profit. When it was low, those who held scrip would find it difficult to pay the calls due on it, and these might have to be deferred, like the South Sea subscriptions of 1720. Both risks were exposed in the loans of 1747 and 1748, which were raised by open subscriptions on the basis of schemes which Barnard had submitted.[7] The two loans in 1747 were heavily oversubscribed.[8] In the great loan of £6,300,000 in 1748 this at first happened again. The first subscriptions had been taken, following a resolution of the House of Commons, in November 1747, although the

[1] *A Defence of several Proposals*, p. 3. [2] *A Letter to Sir John Barnard*, p. 10.
[3] Ibid. [4] *A Defence of several Proposals*, p. 69.
[5] Ibid., p. 71. [6] See below, p. 289.
[7] Gideon says in his Memorial that the loans of 1747 and 1748 were based on Barnard's proposals, *Econ. H.R.* xvi (1946), pp. 16–17.
[8] *Gent. Mag.*, December 1746, Hist. Chronicle under 19 December, £6,000,000 subscribed in less than four hours to the £4,000,000 loan; ibid. March and April 1747, Hist. Chronicle under '30 March' and '1 April', £2,971,000 subscribed to the £1,000,000 loan.

Bill for the loan was only introduced in January 1748.[1] Only one-tenth had to be paid on subscription, and, as the London firm of John and Francis van Hemert wrote to Jan Isaak de Neufville in Amsterdam on 17 November 1747,

we are meanwhile informed that nine millions have already been subscribed, and the subscribers will again have to be considerably cut down so that the favourites [de lievelingen] can keep their subscriptions, as we have seen in previous loans.[2]

A danger of another kind, however, soon appeared. The calls on the loan were in tenths, and were widely spaced, the last falling on 20 September 1748. As the new year opened it became clear that they might not be punctually met. The war news was unfavourable, and in January and February credit became increasingly tight.[3] War loans in the Netherlands, as in earlier years, were thought to have harmed the price of English funds.[4] The exchange on Amsterdam moved against London.[5] The Bank of England restricted its discounts, and in February the new subscription, which, it was alleged, the monied men disliked, was 3% below par.[6] On 22 March Chesterfield wrote to Dayrolles that 12% was being asked for money in the City.[7] In the same month the government was obliged to postpone to October and November the calls due on the loan in April and

[1] *HCJ* xxv. 485, 25 January 1748, resolution of Committee of Whole House of 5 and 19 December 1747 read. A Bill was ordered the same day and introduced on 28 January (ibid. 494).

[2] Amsterdam, Archief Brants, 1344, 17 November 1747 (in Dutch). For subscriptions to this loan see also below, p. 289.

[3] Ibid., van Hemerts to de Neufville 8 January 1748: 'the rumour has spread here that the French have made some progress in Zeeland, but we hope this is ungrounded. The funds here are so fallen because of it that the new loan can be bought at 90¼'; same to same 19 January 1748: 'For anyone who has money idle now is a very good time to invest it.'

[4] Ibid., van Hemerts to de Neufville 16 February 1748: 'Loans on your side of the sea and the scarcity of money here have dealt the funds a severe blow. The new subscription is sold at 3% discount today, so that anyone who has money idle can invest it with a good prospect of high interest.'

[5] On 30 April 1747 Messrs. Gore & Gulston, exchange remitters for the Treasury, asked for an alteration of their terms on the ground that the Amsterdam exchange had moved against London. On 10 August 1748 they agreed that the rate had bettered, and changed their terms again in the Treasury's favour, P.R.O. T 29/31, Treas. Bd. Mins. 1747–51, ff. 9, 143.

[6] *An Essay upon Publick Credit in a Letter to a Friend* (1748), p. 15, the Bank has restricted discounts and has declined altogether to discount bills for Jews on the ground that they are exporting the cash of the realm. The *General Advertiser* of 20 February 1748 shows the subscription at 3½% discount.

[7] Quoted in Mahon, *Hist. of England 1713–83*, iii (1838), 544.

May.[1] At the beginning of April 3% stock, at 77, had reached its lowest price since early in 1746. At this point, however, the tide turned. On the 26th van Hemert & Co. wrote to de Neufville that

Yesterday the news was received here that the Peace Preliminaries have been signed. This caused a great movement of the Funds, principally in the new Subscription, which yesterday morning was at $3\frac{7}{8}$ p. Ct. discount and now is at $3\frac{1}{4}$ p. Ct. Premium, so it was a lucky day for some.[2]

It was also a lucky day for the Treasury, which had nearly suffered a damaging rebuff. Though credit remained tight until the formal conclusion of peace in October 1748, the loan was fully subscribed by November. Its near-failure, however, must have impressed the official mind. In the Seven Years War it was the methods Gideon had advocated, not those of Sir John Barnard, which were used to raise the supply loans whose size and success, as de Pinto observed, 'surprised and astonished Europe'.[3]

IV

At the close of the war, while the great Powers settled down to an uneasy peace, and the court at Vienna pondered new moves for the recovery of Silesia from its arch-enemy Frederick, the administration in England turned its attention, as its predecessor had in 1714, to the debts with which the conflict had saddled the revenue. The principal of additional long-term debts amounted to over £25m., and the whole of the National Debt, excluding annuities for life and terms of years, to over £68m., of which £54m. was at 4% and the rest at 3%.[4] Its annual charge had risen from £1,736,000 in 1739 to £2,623,000, wiping out at a stroke the diminution under Walpole, and restoring the level of charges of 1721 — though admittedly with a much larger nominal principal.[5] Besides these long-term debts, there was a floating debt of over £3m., largely in the form of Navy and Victualling bills,

---

[1] *Gent. Mag.*, April 1748, Hist. Chronicle, under '1 April'.

[2] Archief Brants, 1344, van Hemerts to de Neufville, 26 April 1748.

[3] I. de Pinto, *Traité*, p. 42, quoted above, p. 11.

[4] The figures for 1749, when £3m. had been added to the 4% debt, are shown on p. 232 below.

[5] *BPP* (1857-8) xxxiii. 178-81 (charge of redeemable debt and management 1739, 1748).

which burdened a money-market already strained by outstanding bonds of the East India Company amounting to over £4m.[1]

The market price of securities rose slowly in the second half of 1748, as the City gradually recovered from the crisis earlier in the year which had imperilled the success of government borrowing. But improvement in prices was not enough. Government action to clear the floating debt, and if possible reduce the charge on the remainder, was now — in contrast to the conditions of 1737 — urgently called for, with France making firm moves to reduce her debts and the prospect of renewed war on a vast scale clearly on the horizon.[2] This was the task that faced Henry Pelham, the First Lord of the Treasury, now, at fifty-four, at the height of his powers.[3] He had been in politics for a quarter of a century. For most of this time, like Attlee or Truman at a later period, he had never been expected to take the first place in government, and had been content to learn the ropes. Like them, once in control he astonished previous detractors by his grasp of public business. Contemporaries asserted that relations between the administration and Parliament had never been so harmonious. Above all Pelham, like Godolphin and Walpole, had the financial skill that earned the respect and co-operation of the great houses of the City of London. As he brooded over the difficulties of the financial situation in the Treasury Chambers at Whitehall, or in his pleasant old villa near the Thames at Esher, he must have been acutely aware of the ghosts looking over his shoulder and of the shadows of past events: Montague, backing the infant Bank of England and desperately anxious about the early issues of Exchequer bills; Godolphin, haggling with Furnese and Janssen about the remittances for Flanders; Walpole, negotiating with the monied companies the great reduction of interest in 1717; the panic and turmoil of the South Sea year, when the government's attempts to get rid of the National Debt had imperilled the dynasty; the abortive moves to reduce interest in 1737, when Pelham himself had been in the minority.[4] He knew that the difficulties of financial reconstruction were now greater

[1] For the floating debt see below, p. 405; for the bonds of the East India Company see p. 413.

[2] Cf. above, p. 23.

[3] Henry Pelham (?1695–1754), son of first Baron Pelham, brother-in-law to John Holles, Duke of Newcastle, whose title passed to Henry Pelham's brother Thomas Pelham-Holles. Treasury Commissioner 1721–24, Secretary at War 1724–30, Paymaster of the Forces 1730–43, First Lord of the Treasury 1743–54.

[4] Apart from Coxe's *Pelham Administration* (2 vols., 1829) and the excellent study by J. B. Owen, *The Rise of the Pelhams* (1957), there is little on Henry Pelham; his papers, unlike those of his irritating brother the Duke of Newcastle, were destroyed.

than they had ever been, owing to the increased size and complexity of the National Debt, the increased strength of the monied companies, the increased stake which foreign, particularly Dutch, investors had in English government securities.[1] He knew, too, that apart from the ageing Scrope at the Treasury he could rely on little assistance, since his colleagues were inexpert in financial matters. But he rightly judged that inaction was more dangerous than action, and that both honour and expediency urged him forward.

Pelham evidently argued that the first steps must be to reduce the charge and volume of short-dated securities. In April 1749 he made arrangements to fund £3,072,472 Navy, Victualling and other bills in 4% stock managed by the Bank of England.[2] This had an immediate effect on 3% government stock, which by the beginning of June 1749 had risen from 95 to just over par. At this stage Pelham allowed the Dutch government to float a small loan in London, but fended off the Poles, who also wanted to.[3] He then turned his attention to the East India Company, the largest short-term borrower in the market apart from the government itself. His agent was Samson Gideon, whose services as a contractor for war loans had evidently impressed Pelham as much as those of Herne, Lambert, Janssen and Furnese had impressed Pelham's predecessors Montague and Godolphin.[4] Gideon approached the East India directors on 18 August 1749 with a proposal to reduce the company's bonds to 3% from 31 March 1750. He brought with him a list of guarantors, who undertook to raise £1·5m. to repay dissentient bondholders. The directors agreed to his proposal, and arranged to raise a further half million themselves if necessary.[5] The majority of bondholders acquiesced, so

[1] Cf. below, pp. 321 and 324.

[2] 22 Geo. II, c. 23, based on a Commons resolution of 21 March 1749. Holders of bills were to take them to the appropriate departmental office by 20 April 1749. They were there to be cancelled and exchanged for a certificate assignable till Michaelmas. On or before Michaelmas the certificate was to be surrendered to the Bank of England, which would credit the holder with 4% stock. Most of the bills were those of the Navy and Victualling Boards, a minority those of the Ordnance Board and Transport Commissioners, see below, pp. 406 and 450.

[3] For the Dutch loan see Add. MS. 33038, ff. 243–4, John Gore's memorandum of his remittances. Gore says he was a trustee of the loan and remitted £48,273 of it, but it is not clear whether this was the whole amount. For the Polish government's attempt see Coxe, *Pelham*, ii. 75–76.

[4] Gideon claims in his memorandum (*Econ. H.R.* xvi (1946), 17) that Pelham employed him in the reduction of interest, though he gives no details.

[5] See below, p. 413, for this episode. The list of Gideon's guarantors is missing from the East India court minutes.

neither call was needed. A hostile pamphleteer observed in November 1749 that the reduction of interest on the National Debt

is now pretended to be more practicable, as means have been contrived to raise the three per Cents. above par, and to reduce India bonds from 4 to 3 per Cent.

He went on, however, to observe that, 'tho' these two little jobs have succeeded', the reduction of interest would probably fail.[1]

Thanks to the peace, and Pelham's preliminary spadework, the financial outlook was thus a good deal clearer when Parliament reassembled on 16 November 1749. The price of 3% stock had been above par for some months, the market had been cleared of government floating debts, and the interest on East India bonds was shortly due to fall to 3%. The National Debt at this stage, excluding from it the small amount of Exchequer life and terminable annuities and the £1m. Civil List 3% of 1726, amounted to over £70m., as is shown in Table 26.[2] The annual charge was now £2,692,273, of which £370,134 was at 3%, £14,000 at 3½% and £2,308,139 at 4%. It was the last and largest item that the government wished to cut down.[3]

The king's speech at the opening of Parliament urged the Commons to 'be watchful to improve any opportunity of putting the national debt in a method of being reduced, with a strict regard to public faith and private property'.[4] The House replied that they would 'apply ourselves, with all possible diligence to find out the properest means to accomplish so great and necessary a work'.[5] In the debate which followed, Henry Pelham asserted that it was

the indispensable duty of the servants of the crown and the public, to endeavour, as

---

[1] 'A Letter from a Gentleman in Town to his Friend in the Country' (*Gent. Mag.*, November 1749).

[2] The 3%s of 1726 were charged on the 6*d*. Civil List duty, see above, Table 22. They are treated in all contemporary accounts as being on a different footing from other government stocks. They were not affected by the consolidation of 3% stocks in 1752, and remained separately accounted for until the nineteenth century. By 1749 Exchequer life annuities, increased by £67,500 p.a. in 1745-6, amounted to about £95,000 p.a., and Exchequer terminable annuities to about £116,000 p.a., a total of £211,000 p.a.

[3] Contemporary accounts of the National Debt at this date do not agree on what should be included in it. They therefore differ, though within reasonable limits, about its total size. Thus a paper headed 'National Debt and Charge at Christmas 1749' (P.R.O. Treasury Papers T 1/335) adds in Exchequer annuities and Exchequer bills to make the total £74,221,687. Other accounts include the Navy and Ordnance debts and the Civil List 3%s of 1726.

[4] *Parl. Hist.* xiv. 573, 16 November 1749.   [5] Ibid. 578.

TABLE 26

The redeemable National Debt, 29 September 1749

No.	Category	At 3% £	At 4% £	Sub-totals £	Totals £
1	*Due to companies corporately*				
	(a) Bank of England . .	3,200,000	8,486,800	11,686,800	
	(b) East India Company .	1,000,000	3,200,000	4,200,000	
	(c) South Sea Company .	..	3,662,784	3,662,784	
					19,549,584
2	*Stock managed by companies*				
	(a) Government stock managed by Bank of England . . .	7,200,000	18,402,472	25,602,472	
	(b) South Sea Old Annuities . . .	..	13,651,100	13,651,100	
	(c) South Sea New Annuities . . .	..	9,988,319	9,988,319	
					49,241,891
3	*Managed at the Exchequer*				
	(a) 3½%s (1731) . .				400,000
	(b) Loans of 1736 and 1739	900,000	..	900,000	
	(c) St. Kitts–Nevis debentures	37,821	..	37,821	
	(d) Loan of 1720 charged on duties on Wrought Plate . . .	..	312,000	312,000	1,249,821
	TOTALS . . .	12,337,821	57,703,475	70,041,296	70,441,296

Source: Tables 22 and 25 (above, pp. 206–18) and *BPP* (1898), lii, esp. ff. 326 ff. on the debts owed to the monied companies.

soon as ever it should be found practicable, to ease the nation of its great debts, by consulting with persons of skill, and those of great property in the funds, and publishing the method, for general approbation . . . That, as within three years the 3 per cents had risen gradually from 75, and now were at 101, he thought it a demonstration of the rise of public credit; and as an instance of the flourishing condition of commerce, the duties on imports had added to the sinking fund one million in about nine months; and at the same time, for the great quantity of grain exported, there had been paid for bounties 221,000*l.*[1]

[1] Ibid. 575, from *Gent. Mag.*, November 1749, p. 1.

He convincingly repudiated Lord Egmont's fatuous argument that unless a reduction of interest were kept secret until the last minute the monied interests would sabotage it.[1] He then outlined his proposals. The interest on the debt which carried 4% was to be reduced after a year to $3\frac{1}{2}$%. It was to remain at this rate for seven years, and then to fall to 3%.[2] Pelham had, probably correctly, rejected the sudden reduction to 3% contemplated in 1737, but had at the same time avoided committing the government to a payment of $3\frac{1}{2}$% for more than seven years.[3]

On 29 November 1749 Francis Fane, the chairman of the Committee of the Whole House, reported that it had considered and accepted Pelham's plan.[4] The 4% debt was to be reduced to $3\frac{1}{2}$% from Christmas 1750. At the end of seven years it was to fall to 3%, but during this period was to be irredeemable. On amendment, the capital of the East India Company was exempted from this last provision; this later proved a very useful stick with which to beat the company.[5] The public creditors were given until 28 February 1750 to agree to the government's proposals, but no provision was made at this stage to pay them off if they dissented. The Commons ordered a Bill to embody their resolutions. It was introduced on 4 December 1749, and received the royal assent on 20th. It was, commented a writer, 'hurried through both Houses with the greatest Expedition possible even after two great Companies had shewed a dislike to it'.[6]

Parliament's complaisance was perhaps rather due to its social structure, for landed men had a keen interest in reducing the burden of taxes.[7] The public creditors, especially the stockholders of the monied companies, were less docile. It soon became apparent that the conversion would be won or lost in the companies' General Courts, to which the mass of holders of government stock, and the numerous foreign owners, looked for a lead. The

---

[1] Ibid.

[2] Ibid.

[3] The proposals of 1737 envisaged a fixed period at 3% of fourteen years, see above, p. 213.

[4] *HCJ* xxv. 903–4.

[5] Ibid. For the coercion of the East India Company see below, p. 238.

[6] *Annotations on a late pamphlet intituled Considerations on the Proposal for reducing the Interest on the National Debt* (1750), p. 15. The Reduction Act was 23 Geo. II, c. 1.

[7] This was argued by the author of *A Dispassionate Remonstrance of the Nature and Tendency of the Laws now in Force for the Reduction of Interest* (1751), pp. 8–9. Cf. also above, p. 29.

omens were unfavourable from the start.[1] On 7 December 1749 the directors of the South Sea Company put the government's plan before their General Court.[2] The Sub-Governor explained that the company's assent or dissent must be a corporate decision, unlike that of the holders of ordinary government stock or South Sea annuities, who could decide individually. The South Sea proprietors, angered by the long-drawn-out dispute with the government in Madrid about compensation for war damage, and acutely aware of the unpromising future of the South Sea trade, were in a hostile mood.[3] They asked whether the company could be heard by counsel against the Bill, and in the end the meeting adjourned without reaching a decision, the directors noting that

the General Court, as it appeared from their debates, were of opinion, it was at present too early to come to any Determination with Regard to the Resolution of the Honble. House of Commons.[4]

They instructed Mr. North, their solicitor, to find out whether legal representation could be made against the proposals. North's inquiry, however, ran into sand.[5]

On 13 December 1749 the General Court of the East India Company gave the government's plan an equally cold reception.[6] The directors recommended its acceptance, provided the government allowed the company to raise a loan to discharge part of its bond debt. The court, however, merely resolved that the directors' recommendation should be printed, and adjourned until 19 December. When it reassembled there was 'a very large Appearance of the Generality', whose dislike of the government's plan must have deepened when one of the directors, Sir James Creed, openly proclaimed

---

[1] Cf. van Hemert & Co. in London to J. I. de Neufville in Amsterdam, 15 December 1749 (in Dutch): 'The reduction of the 4% Annuities will certainly take place.' The Bank has not yet held a meeting, but will certainly assent, 'as all these things have had its approval'. On 22 December 1749, however, they write that the Reduction Act has passed Parliament this week, that large sums are still unsubscribed, and that some ask 'what one can lose by not subscribing on these terms' (Amsterdam, Archief Brants, 1344.)

[2] Add MS. 25545, f. 129, South Sea G. Ct. Bk., 7 December 1749.

[3] The company claimed £1,367,387 from Spain; it eventually received only £100,000 and had to give up its trade, see below p. 240.

[4] Add. MS. 25512, f. 71, South Sea D. Ct. Bk., 7 December 1749.

[5] Ibid., f. 73, 14 December 1749, North's report. He had asked Speaker Onslow about the point. Onslow said that the matter was difficult, and that he would search for precedents and consult with the South Sea directors who were M.P.s. He subsequently said he could not answer the question at all.

[6] East India G. Ct. Bk. ii, ff. 129–33, 13 December 1749.

dissent from his colleagues' views.[1] A motion to accept the directors' proposal was then read and carried, a counter-motion to adjourn being rejected. A group of nine influential proprietors at once asked that the issue be decided by ballot.[2] This was held on 3 January 1750, and was carried against the directors by 296 votes to 209.[3] When the reduction proposals were laid before the General Court of the Bank of England on 31 January 1750, therefore, the two other monied companies had already rejected them. It was hardly to be expected that the Bank's proprietors would refrain from following suit. Their restless mood is indicated by the Governor's plea that

their Debates on the Proposals be carried on with Calmness of Temper and Respect to One another as becomes Gentlemen who have but one View as design which is the Prosperity and Safety of this Corporation.[4]

The gentlemen evidently considered that their own prosperity counted for something too. They summarily rejected the government's plan.[5]

At this stage the success of Pelham's conversion seemed doubtful. If the rank and file of stockholders followed the companies' lead, and the evidence is that they were doing so, the government would either have to withdraw its proposal altogether or borrow over £60m. at $3\frac{1}{2}\%$ to pay off the dissentients.[6] The first course would be politically disastrous, and might well imperil government credit for years ahead. The second was economically impossible. It is difficult not to criticize Pelham's handling of this part of the operation. He had started well, and at the right point, the market in short-term securities. But he had made no provision for the repayment of dissentients in his parliamentary Bill, and had allowed his plan to come up first for discussion in the South Sea Company, whose proprietors were already in a bitter mood. If the Bank, with which the Treasury had such close contacts, could have been persuaded to give a favourable lead instead of being

[1] Ibid., ff. 133–4, 19 December 1749.
[2] Ibid., f. 135. The nine were Abraham Atkins, Joseph Gulston, Sir Thomas Hankey, Richard Holland, John Legg, Moses Mendes jun., Charles Savage, William Sloane and Pinckney Wilkinson. Atkins was a prominent East India jobber, Gulston a former contractor for remittances with the Treasury, Hankey the head of a banking house with a European reputation, Savage a director of the Bank of England who had been Governor in 1745–47, Wilkinson a rich merchant and loan jobber.
[3] Ibid., ff. 139, ballot held 3 January 1750, f. 142, 4 January, its result reported. Sir James Creed committed his dissenting views to paper in a pamphlet, *Three Letters to the Proprietors of Stock in the East-India Company, Relative to the Question to be Ballotted for on Wednesday, January 3d., 1749* [i.e. 1750]. *By a Director*.
[4] Bank G. Ct. Bk. iii, f. 164, 31 January 1750.   [5] Ibid.
[6] For the reluctance of the South Sea annuitants to move at this stage see below, p. 237.

left until last, the attitude of the other companies might have been different, while the rank and file of holders of ordinary government stock, both in England and abroad, would have been favourably impressed. Lastly, Pelham seems completely to have neglected the arts of behind-the-scenes influence, coupled with propaganda, for which the situation obviously called.

With disaster staring him in the face he set about repairing his mistakes. His first move seems to have been the difficult but shrewd one of persuading Sir John Barnard to co-operate with the Treasury at the same time that it was using the services of Barnard's *bête noire*, Samson Gideon. Pelham's diagnosis evidently was that Barnard's reputation as the Cato or Brutus of public finance made him the right man to appeal to the public creditors at large, while Gideon, with his vast wealth and many financial contacts, was the right man through whom to work on opinion in the Bank of England. This proved to be correct. On 6 February 1750 Barnard published his *Considerations on the Proposal for Reducing the Interest on the National Debt*. It at once made a great impression.[1] He defended Pelham's aims and tactics, and urged the holders of government stock to subscribe immediately without waiting to see what the three monied companies would do. He argued that the trend of interest rates was downward, and that those who chose to be paid off in cash would have difficulty in reinvesting at even 3%. He added, incorrectly, that the government was unlikely to extend the time for subscribing (the deadline at this stage was still 28 February 1750). Meanwhile, Gideon had been working on important stockholders of the Bank of England with a view to persuading the Old Lady to change her corporate mind.[2] On 22 February 1750 he and twenty-four other proprietors exercised their right to summon a special General Court.[3] When this met on 27 February it asked the directors their views of the government's plan. They recommended its acceptance. The court acquiesced, and asked the directors to notify their assent to Parliament.[4] It would be nice to know what arts Gideon used to turn the lion of January into the lamb of February.

Foreign observers, in close touch with their London correspondents, noted

[1] Barnard's preface is dated 6 February 1750. The effectiveness of his pamphlet is noted in *A Dispassionate Remonstrance of the Nature and Tendency of the Laws now in Force for the Reduction of Interest*, p. 11.

[2] Gideon's memorandum to the Treasury in 1758, printed in *Econ. H.R.* xvi (1946), 17.

[3] Bank D. Ct. Bk. O, f. 531, letter from Samson Gideon, James Colebrooke and twenty-one other proprietors 'having each of us Five Hundred Pounds or more' stock. With the exception of Gideon, Colebrooke and one or two others, the signatories were not well-known names. Some of them were probably Gideon's agents.

[4] Bank G. Ct. Bk. iii, ff. 165–6.

that the financial atmosphere had quite suddenly changed. On 24 February 1750 Gerrit Blauw in Amsterdam wrote to his uncle, David Leeuw, at his country house in Warmond that

Advice has been received that there has been a considerable change in the subscription. In one or two days 1½ million has been subscribed. . . . The last day of this month is the last day one can subscribe. People are now beginning to be frightened about the possibility of being left out.[1]

TABLE 27

Subscription of South Sea annuities to Pelham's reduction of interest December 1749 — February 1750

Subscribed by	South Sea Old Annuities £	South Sea New Annuities £	Total £
26 December 1749	68,043	62,311	130,354
31 January 1750	182,133	112,177	294,310
28 February 1750	8,772,711	6,102,769	14,875,480
TOTALS £	9,022,887	6,277,257	15,300,144

Source: Notes on fly-leaves of Old Annuity ledger T–Z, 1744–51, f. 906, New Annuity ledger T–Z, 1747–51, f. 872, Bank of England Record Office; sums rounded and partly re-arranged. The final figures were slightly different, see below, p. 239.

The figures for subscription of South Sea annuities, the largest single government stock, show that February was indeed a decisive month. By the end of February 1750 £38,806,976 of a possible 4% debt of £57,703,475 had been subscribed for conversion.[2] This enabled Pelham to bring the second part of his plan into force, by extending the date for subscription to 30 May 1750, but at the same time stiffening the terms allowed to these

[1] Amsterdam, Archief Brants, 395 (in Dutch). The letter is dated 7 March 1750 (N.S.), i.e. 24 February (O.S.). Similar views are expressed by van Hemert & Co. in a letter to J. I. Neufville & Co. dated 23 March 1750 (Archief Brants, 1344). Professor C. H. Wilson, *Anglo-Dutch Commerce and Finance in the Eighteenth Century* (1941), p. 150, dates this letter in error 23 March 1749.

[2] See Table 29 on p. 239.

subscribers. They were only to have 3½% for five years, after which they were to be reduced to 3%. At the same time the government took powers to repay dissentients at stated times in 1751.[1] The same Act provided that the whole of the £4,200,000 due from the state to the East India Company should be repaid to it in 1751 unless it agreed to the reduction by 30 May 1749. If it did agree, it would be allowed to borrow up to £4·2m. to discharge its bond debt.

Pelham had recovered his touch. These were measures which nicely blended the stick and the carrot, and recovered the government's authority, which had wavered for a long and unpleasant moment. Their effect on foreign opinion can be judged by isolating from the overall figures for subscription of South Sea annuities those for subscription by Dutch proprietors, who were easily the most important foreign holders.

TABLE 28

Dutch subscriptions of South Sea annuities to Pelham's reduction of interest 1750

	Subscribed by 28 February 1750 £	Subscribed by 30 May 1750 £	Total £
South Sea Old Annuities . .	214,175	547,028	761,203
South Sea New Annuities . .	206,365	478,881	685,246
TOTALS	£420,540	£1,025,909	£1,446,449

Source: South Sea annuity ledgers, Bank of England Record Office. Only a minority of foreign holders elected to be paid off, see below Ch. 12.

On 25 April 1750 the East India proprietors, aware that the tide of events was running against them, capitulated — after acrimonious debate — and agreed to the government's terms.[2] By the end of May 1750, therefore, the financial situation had greatly improved, only £7m. of the 4%s remaining unconverted, of which half was due to the unhappy and bitter South Sea Company, still on its lonely pinnacle of resistance.

[1] 23 Geo. II, c. 22. This received the royal assent on 12 April 1750 but its provisions were known earlier. Money to repay dissentients was to be raised at 3½% or less in cash or by creating new Exchequer bills.
[2] East India G. Ct. Bk. ii, ff. 163–71, 25 April 1750.

TABLE 29

Four per cent debts subscribed by 30 May 1750

Type of debt	Amount £	Subscribed by 28 February 1750 £	Subscribed by 31 May 1750 £	Total subscribed £	Remaining unsubscribed £
1. Due to Bank of England	8,486,800	8,486,800	..	8,486,800	..
2. Due to East India Company	3,200,000	..	3,200,000	3,200,000	..
3. Due to South Sea Company	3,662,784	..	..	..	3,662,784
4. South Sea Old Annuities	13,651,100	9,050,911	3,353,359	12,404,270	1,246,830
5. South Sea New Annuities	9,988,319	6,284,809	2,673,446	8,958,255	1,030,064
6. Govt. 4% stock managed by B. of E.	18,402,472	14,857,956	2,713,618	17,571,574	830,898
7. 4% stock managed by Exchequer	312,000	126,500	3,250	129,750	182,250
TOTALS	£ 57,703,475	38,806,976	11,943,673	50,750,649	6,952,826

Source: BPP (1890–1), xlviii. 665, rearranged, except the sums for Old and New South Sea Annuities, not given there, which are taken from the ledgers, Bank of England Record Office.

Effectively, therefore, 88% of the 4% debt had been reduced to $3\frac{1}{2}$% (with effect from Christmas 1750) and would fall to 3% from Christmas 1757. This reduced the cost of servicing the funded debt as a whole by about 12% initially and nearly 25% from 1757, though by that date the fall had been offset by new borrowing on a large scale.[1] Particularly in contrast to its doubtful prospects earlier, the conversion had been virtually as successful as Walpole's in 1717, a fine achievement considering the increased complexity of the problems involved.

[1] The charge of servicing the former 4% debt fell by £286,654 p.a. 1750–5, £346,372 p.a. 1755–6 and £577,036 p.a. 1757 ff. BPP (1890–1), xlviii. 665 makes the first two of these figures £272,067 and £350,101 by taking the South Sea Company's capital as being at $3\frac{1}{2}$% 1750–7 when it was in fact at 4%, see the text.

The next task for the government was to clear off the 4% debts left unsubscribed. In October 1750 it issued sufficient new Exchequer bills to cancel the unsubscribed stock transferred at the Bank of England and Exchequer, amounting to £1,013,148. The bills were subsequently paid off from the Sinking Fund.[1] This left the much thornier question of the South Sea Company. The government had to sell the company three main propositions. The first was that its trade with the New World, which had been the proximate cause of war in 1739, was no longer a viable proposition, and must be abandoned. The second was that its claims against Spain for war damages, amounting to £1,367,387, were hopelessly unrealistic politically, however just they were as a matter of accountancy, and must be drastically cut down. The third was that it was no longer possible for the company to stand out against the reduction of interest, now that the other monied companies, and nearly everyone else, had agreed to it. The process of bringing the company to see reason was not easy, and argumentative South Sea General Courts debated the issues involved in December 1749, February 1750, January 1751 (twice) and February 1751.[2] But the company had few bargaining-counters, and the proprietors were forced to realize it. In January 1751 they agreed to accept £100,000 in settlement of their claims against Spain, and to give up their trade to the New World.[3] In the next month they reached agreement with the Treasury. The company's capital was to stay at 4% until Christmas 1757, and then to fall to 3% like the state's other debts. It was also to be allowed to borrow £2·1m. at 3% to discharge most of the unsubscribed South Sea annuities, which amounted to £2,276,894. This loan was successfully floated in the same year, £1·4m. by subscription and £700,000 by a lottery whose tickets were funded in the same stock, the South Sea 3%s of 1751.[4] Interest was charged on the Sinking Fund. Effectively, this was the end of the South Sea Company as anything more than a department of the Treasury. It had on at least two occasions (1719–21 and 1737–40) exerted as dramatic an influence on the state as the East India Company was ever to do in the second half of the eighteenth century, but it never had the overseas interests which were to make John

[1] Bank G. Ct. Bk. iii, f. 171, 25 October 1750 and Add. MS. 33038, f. 388.

[2] Add. MS. 25545, ff. 129–47, 7 December 1749, 26 February 1750, 10 and 16 January 1751, 28 February 1751. Other General Courts in this period were held only to declare dividends.

[3] The acceptance of £100,000 was cleared at the General Court on 10 January 1751; the sum was paid over by General Wall on 26 February 1751, Add. MS. 25513, f. 9.

[4] 23 Geo. II, c. 22. The ledgers for this stock in the Bank of England Record Office show that the lottery tickets were not funded until 1752.

Company's politics of such moment for powerful social groups at home. In May 1752 the South Sea directors disconsolately informed the commissioners of the Land Tax that they would no longer pay tax on their personal stock and effects, 'they being no longer a Trading Company'.[1]

V

Pelham's conversion had sailed through rough waters into safe harbour. Pelham, like any administrator of comparable ability, was more concerned with what was wrong than with what was right. The operation had indeed greatly cheapened the servicing of the National Debt, and had in doing so asserted the government's authority against its creditors. But it had left some important problems behind it. Each of the five former 4% stocks administered by the Bank of England was serviced by a separate 'fund' of customs and excise duties. And each set of ledgers for these stocks had had to be broken into two in 1750 in order to record the first (February) and second (May) subscriptions separately.[2] Besides these former 4% (now $3\frac{1}{2}$%) stocks the Bank managed six separate 3% stocks and the Exchequer three others. These were also serviced by different funds, and the transfer books for them opened on different days. Once the reduction of interest was completed, there was therefore a strong case for consolidating all the reduced 4%s into two sets of ledgers, and all the 3%s into another set.[3] Interest could then be met from the Sinking Fund, to which the duties formerly settled to pay interest on the separate stocks could be carried. The Treasury's point of view is set out in a memorandum of 1754 which, though concerned with the 3%s, applies equally cogently to the 'reduced Threes'.

The Annuities at 3 li p. Ct. were transferrable at the Bank, and because the Funds of most of them were deficient and the several Transfer Books open upon different days which was extremely troublesome to the Proprietors, It was therefore thought

[1] Add. MS. 25513, f. 13, South Sea D. Ct. Bk., 14 May 1752. In the following year the number of directors was reduced from thirty to twenty-one.

[2] Ledgers for these stocks, Bank of England Record Office. The stocks were for one loan of 1746, two of 1747, one of 1748 and one of 1749.

[3] $3\frac{1}{2}$%s had to be consolidated in two sets of ledgers, not one, because the subscriptions in February and May 1750 ran for different periods (seven years and five years) before reducing to 3%.

proper to Consolidate and make them into one Transferrable Stock, and by that means to save the Proprietors a great deal of trouble, and at the same time to get rid of making good the Deficiencies every Year out of the Supplies. The Annuities were charged on the Sinking Fund and all the Duties carried there.[1]

This further major operation was carried through in 1752, with the cooperation of the Bank of England.[2] The stocks affected are shown in Table 30.

TABLE 30

Consolidation of the National Debt 1752

Managed by Bank of England	Managed by Exchequer	at 3% £	at 3½%, formely 4% £	Fund from which interest paid
..	1720	..	129,750	Wrought Plate Duties
..	1721	37,821†	..	General Fund
1731	..	800,000	..	Additional Paper Duties
..	1736	600,000	..	Sinking Fund
..	1738	300,000	..	Sinking Fund
1742	..	800,000	..	Sinking Fund
1743	..	1,800,000	..	Duties on Spirits
1744	..	1,800,000	..	Duties on Spirits
1745	..	2,000,000	..	Additional Wine Duties
1746	..	..	2,824,429	Glass and Spirits Duties
1747	..	..	4,189,365	Window Duties
1747	..	..	929,277	Coach Duty
1748	..	..	6,660,007	New Customs
1749	..	..	2,968,496	Sinking Fund
1750*	..	1,000,000	..	
TOTALS		£ 9,137,821	17,701,324	

Source: Add. MS. 33038, f. 388, figures rearranged, and *BPP* (1890–1), xlviii. 629–36.

* Supply loan for 1750.

† St. Kitts–Nevis Debentures, see above, p. 207, Table 22.

[1] Add. MS. 33038, papers and memoranda of the Duke of Newcastle on taxation and finance 1688–1756, f. 388.

[2] 25 Geo. II, c. 27.

The £400,000 3½% Exchequer stock of 1731 was not included in the scheme but was largely paid off in 1753, the remainder being cancelled in 1754 and 1758. The holders of Exchequer 3%s of 1736 and 1738 surrendered their tallies at the Bank of England and were credited with 3% stock instead. The reduced 4% stock soon became known by the somewhat misleading name of 'Reduced Threes', and the consolidated 3%s simply as 'Consols'. The duties from the various tax funds were carried to the Sinking Fund, from which the new stocks were serviced from October 1753.[1] This was a logical continuation of Walpole's policy of making the Sinking Fund a general and flexible reserve, as against Pulteney's rigid insistence on its application to discharge the early part of the National Debt.[2] It was noted in 1754 that 'altho' the Funds used to be deficient yet since this Alteration the produce has been so great that the Sinking Fund has been a Gainer'.[3] Pelham died in 1754 just after these changes had been carried through. Completing Walpole's earlier work, he had greatly strengthened and simplified the machinery of public borrowing. In 1752 the market price of 3%s was higher than it was to be for nearly a hundred years. These changes can perhaps be seen as part of a modest programme of administrative and social reform, of which the Naval Discipline Act of 1749, the Calendar Act of 1751 and the Marriage Act and abortive Jewish Naturalization Act of 1753 were other parts. It is uncertain what Pelham's influence would have been had he lived, and how, in conditions of renewed war, he would have agreed with his turbulent colleague Pitt. As he retired to render a different and more subtle account, he perhaps reflected with Charles II that he was leaving control of the kingdom 'à la sottise de mon frère'.

V

This chapter may perhaps usefully conclude by recapitulating the main conclusions reached in this part of the book. Government long-term borrowing had gone through five main phases between 1693 and the outbreak of the Seven Years War. The first, from 1693 to 1697, was marked by experiment

---

[1] The consolidation statute said that interest was to be paid from the Sinking Fund from midsummer 1752, but this was subsequently altered to 10 October 1753, Add. MS. 33038, f. 388.

[2] For this argument see above, p. 211.　　　　[3] Add. MS. 33038, f. 388.

and confusion, but during it at least three important lessons were learned. The first, that the capital for long-term loans was available and that its owners were willing to lend it. The second, that there was a real, if not strictly defined, line between long- and short-term borrowing, and that it was dangerous to blur it. The third, that the Caroline pamphleteers had in no way exaggerated the need for and uses of a central bank in London, even though they had not foreseen that it would originate as part of government war finance rather than as part of a planned expansion of the economy. The second phase of long-term borrowing coincided with the War of the Spanish Succession. During it Godolphin imposed a much stricter control of government credit operations, and confirmed the Bank of England's importance in them. Long-term loans, though used to meet a third of war costs, were floated at much more favourable rates than in the 1690s. They were still, however, regarded as repayable or self-liquidating.

In the third phase, from the peace of 1713 to the outbreak of war in 1739, this concept was modified. Definite plans to discharge the National Debt were shelved; in 1720 the greater part of the annuities for terms of years, which were self-liquidating, were turned into lower-interest ordinary stock, which was not. In compensation, a sinking fund was created in 1717 which could be used to pay these and other debts. Its operation, however, was capricious. It might be used to pay off the capital of old debts, but it might also be used to service new ones, thus removing the need for new taxes. And since no time limit was set to the redemption of the debt, it was fairly clear from the start that renewed war borrowing might overtake the sinking fund's operations. Walpole did in fact reduce the capital of the National Debt by over £6m. His argument, however, seems to have been that what mattered from the government's point of view was the annual charge of the debt rather than its nominal capital, provided that the government's creditors had no legal claim against the state for the principal which they had lent it. Given this reasoning, the larger the proportion of the long-term debt in the form of ordinary stock, which could be paid off but need not be, the better. In the war of 1739–48, which marks the fourth phase of long-term borrowing, Walpole's successors followed this policy out: nearly all their long-term loans took the form of ordinary stock whose holder could not ask the government to repay it. Although this sent the nominal principal of the National Debt soaring to over £70m. by 1749, it was more realistic, given the relative inelasticity of the revenue, than attempting to set a definite term for repayment of loans, or than floating them in self-liquidating form — life annuities, terminable annuities — at higher rates of interest. In the final phase of long-term borrowing in this period, from 1749 to 1752, Henry Pelham took advantage of the peace and the buoyant demand for government stock to underline the advantages of this policy by forcing through a reduction of the charge on the long-term debt to a level not much above that of 1714. This was about a third of ordinary revenue.[1] Pelham also consolidated most of the existing government stocks, thus paving the way for the massive loans of the Seven Years War, which took a similar form to those of the previous conflict.

Some of the conditions for the success of government financial policy over this period are apparent from the previous chapters: effective parliamentary government, executive skill and flexibility, the co-operation of the monied interest in the City of London, the fact that there was a good deal of slack in the economy, so that Government borrowing did not have disrupting consequences on prices and private investment. Other conditions, which have still to be examined, were clearly of equal importance. For example, if an efficient market in securities had not developed in London, where lenders could sell their claim to annual interest in return for a capital sum, the state would hardly have been able to float long-term loans without promising to repay them. Thus, the absence of such a market in Vienna compelled the Habsburg government in this period to borrow on the basis that it would repay over a fixed number of years: in consequence it had to tie up an unrealistic proportion of its scanty revenues for decades ahead. Again, the development of English government long-term borrowing was matched, and partly made possible, by important changes in short-term borrowing. These changes, and the rise of a market in securities, are discussed later. The next two chapters are concerned with a different but even more important problem, the sources of the capital invested in government long-term loans. It seems clear that the government itself worked almost entirely in the dark as far as the supply side of loans was concerned. It took care to ensure through underwriters that loans were filled, and they always, or nearly always, were. But Ministers can have had little more than a general idea of where the money for their very extensive credit operations came from. The following pages, based largely on the records of the Exchequer and Bank of England, try to work out a clearer picture.

[1] The service of the debt continued to absorb between a third and a half of ordinary revenue for the remainder of the eighteenth century. The charge of the debt is abstracted from *BPP* (1868–9), xxxv, in B.R. Mitchell and P. Deane, *Abstract of British Historical Statistics* (1962), pp. 389–91.

PART THREE

The Public Creditors

II

Public Creditors in England

CONTEMPORARIES were uneasily aware that the government creditors who were helping to finance Britannia's wars formed a powerful and perhaps sinister new interest in society. 'The Publick Funds', wrote a pamphleteer in 1737,

divide the Nation into two Ranks of Men, of which one are Creditors and the other Debtors; the Creditors are the Three Great Corporations and others, made up of Natives and Foreigners; the Debtors are the Land-holders, the Merchants, the Shop-keepers, and all Ranks and Degrees of Men throughout the Kingdom.[1]

Another writer nearly twenty years later gave this theme a different twist.

The public debt has produced a difference of interests in this country, that we have lately suffered by, and if not remedied, can have no end. It is the interest of the stockholders, to involve the nation in war, because they get by it. It is the interest of landed men and merchants, to submit to any insult rather than engage in war, since they must bear the whole burden of it.[2]

According to him the public creditors, threatened by Barnard's proposal of 1737 for reducing their interest, were responsible for the clamour for war with Spain in 1739.[3]

Discussion of who the government's creditors were was not always at this level of generality, but it did not attain great precision. Convincing demonstration of the supposed separation of the public creditors from other sectors of society, or serious analysis of where the capital to finance government borrowing came from, especially if land and trade were supposed not to be contributors, were not forthcoming. There was instead a vague running commentary, with its emphasis on social categories rather than economic analysis. Briscoe in 1694 told his readers that large traders who had lent up to £10,000 apiece were prominent in the subscriptions to the Million Act of

---

[1] *Reasons for the more speedy Lessening the National Debt* (1737), p. 22.

[2] [Patrick Murray, Lord Elibank], *An Inquiry into the Original and Consequences of the Publick Debt* (Edinburgh, 1753), p. 16.

[3] Ibid.

1693, and the Bank of England in 1694.[1] Elibank (himself a not unsuccessful speculator in Government stock) described these early proprietors half a century later as follows.

The first proprietors . . . of that share of the profits of the industrious called public debt, were such vermin as from nothing took advantage of the public folly; and, by furnishing them their own money at an extravagant premium, got annuities assigned them at 7 per cent. interest.[2]

More coolly and in a more limited context, a director of the Bank of England in 1707 asserted (falsely) that the proprietors of Bank stock were '2,000 . . . Men of various Professions, and Manner of Living, and dispersed all over the kingdom.'[3]

In the discussions of 1737 and 1749 about the reduction of interest on the public debt these descriptions became somewhat more specific. The national creditors were treated as a group of ascertainable size and domicile, whose members' economic habits and reactions could be predicted. Their number was estimated in 1737 as about 25,000 in a total population of 10 million.[4] It was agreed that the majority were English, and that the greater part of this majority lived in and around London.[5] The majority of the domestic holders of the South Sea annuities (which at that date formed about half the National Debt) were described as 'Widows, Orphans under Trust, single Women, and those never educated in any Trade or Business, or who are past it'.[6] This tallies with Lechmere's contention in 1717 that the greater part of government annuities were settled for jointures and portions, though of course both statements were primarily intended to wring a tear from the public eye.[7]

---

[1] John Briscoe, *A Discourse on the Late Funds of the Million Act* . . . (1694), p. 23. See below, p. 304, for Briscoe's estimate of foreign investment in the Funds.

[2] Elibank, op. cit., p. 6. Elibank bought £3,200 4% (1748) stock September 1748–September 1749 and sold it in December 1749. (Ledgers, Bank of England Record Office.) The price went up 10% before he sold.

[3] [Nathaniel Tench], *A Defence of the Bank of England* (1707), p. 22. For the concentration of ownership of Bank and other stocks on London, see below, p. 256.

[4] *Queries relating to the Reduction of the National Redeemable Debts from Four to Three per Cent. per Ann.* (1737), p. 6, 'the Mass of the People of this Kingdom who may be supposing 10,000,000'. It is not clear whether this refers to England or the British Isles.

[5] *Considerations upon a Proposal for Lowering the Interest upon all the Redeemable National Debts to Three per Cent. per Ann.* (1737), p. 19, 'the Cities of London and Westminster, where, 'tis supposed, most Part of the Proprietors constantly reside'.

[6] *Considerations Occasioned by a Proposal for Reducing Interest to Three per Cent.* (1737), p. 24, 'most of the present Proprietors'.

[7] For Lechmere's assertion see *Parl. Hist.* vii. 427, 8 March 1717.

The spending habits of the government's creditors were the subject of disagreement. Opponents of a reduction of interest argued that these creditors usually spent their dividends, so that a reduction would lead to diminished consumption and falling prices.[1] Advocates of Barnard's measure insisted that they spent no more than a quarter to a third of their dividends, and reinvested the remainder.[2]

During the discussions about Pelham's reduction of interest in 1749 the estimates of 1737 were suitably revised, the total number of public creditors being put at 'above thirty thousand Persons' or 'thirty or forty thousand People'.[3] The general structure of the discussion of 1737 was, however, left unaltered.

II

Before moving from the opinions and conjectures of contemporaries to the evidence of the records for government loans, it is necessary to consider a serious possible objection to doing so, which may be stated as follows. The structure of ownership of securities as formally recorded in the stock ledgers of the monied companies and the receipt books and annuity rolls of the Exchequer might be held to be largely a fiction. For it is possible that by ingenious use of nominee holdings, secret trusts, and other devices, the real owners of securities concealed their identities, for reasons of business secrecy and perhaps of tax evasion. Foreign holders might be thought to be particularly adept at these practices, since, it could be alleged, they wished to conceal from the English government the true scale of their investment in English funds. If this were so, the central records, far from being an accurate check on the assertions of the pamphleteers, would be doubly dangerous, both because they would in fact be equally uncertain, and because they seem to be extremely precise.

This hypothetical case has some evidence to support it, and, since the objection applies to ownership of all securities indifferently, it does not matter

[1] *A Speech Without-Doors*, pp. 18–19.

[2] *Considerations upon a Proposal*, p. 19; *Reasons for the more speedy Lessening the National Debt*, p. 15.

[3] For these two estimates, see *A Copy of a Letter wrote to a Member of Parliament* (1750), p. 10, and *Annotations on a Late Pamphlet* (1750), p. 3. See below, p. 286, for a possible explanation of Hume's estimate in 1752 that the public creditors totalled only 17,000.

that some of this relates to short-term loans. Thus in the Land Tax loan of 1693 Obadiah Burnett of Fenchurch Street subscribed £200 'on account of Thomas Clarke of Enfield'. In the same loan Thomas Symonds and John Hunt subscribed £200 'in trust for Elizabeth Symonds', and James Wallis senior £395 'in trust for James Wallis junior'.[1] In a private declaration of 1697 Lord Coningsby acknowledged that £1,000 he had subscribed towards the circulation of Exchequer bills was in trust for the banker Sir Stephen Evance.[2] Again, in 1692 Sir Joseph Herne and Sir Stephen Evance lent £9,000 each at the Exchequer 'for the Duke of Savoy'.[3] In all these instances the tally and Order of Payment, or the Circulation Receipt, if made out in the name of the subscriber, would conceal the true beneficiary. A further example of this is the subscriptions that partners, agents or officials made to Land Tax loans for banks, companies and noble clients, which were acknowledged in the agent's name, not the beneficiary's.[4] Similarly, tallies of fictitious loan made out in the name of individual paymasters were an administrative device used to market tallies, and are not a record of true loans to the government.[5] In long-term securities individual holdings might also conceal trusts for others. Thus Christian Georg Dosten of Heidelberg in 1723 held £120 South Sea stock 'in trust for his children'.[6] In 1727 Simon Bevel held £6,500 Bank stock, of which, as his private papers show, £1,500 belonged to his sister Christine and £500 to his brother Dirk.[7] There are also grounds for believing that the use of nominees to buy and hold stock became more common in the second half of the century; it was, for example, a method used extensively by Henry Fox.

Trusts and agencies, whether overt or covert, thus modify the pattern of ownership. But in nearly all the instances cited the beneficiary is either a member of the same family or is disclosed on the face of the records. If not, it is not too difficult, as with Peter Walter's loan, to deduce his existence. Similarly, the numerous multiple accounts in South Sea annuities (and to a

[1] All these examples are taken from the list of subscribers reconstructed from P.R.O. E 401/1991–92 and Guildhall MS 40/57: see below, p. 422.

[2] P.R.O. C 111/50, Evance Papers, declaration by Lord Coningsby dated 30 April 1697.

[3] P.R.O. T 29/627, extracts from Treasury Board Minutes, 17 August 1692.

[4] See below, pp. 429–30 (loans by Peter Walter), pp. 438, 450 n. 1 (loans by Child's Bank) and p. 435 (loan by the South Sea Company in the name of its cashier).

[5] This system is explained on p. 351 below.

[6] South Sea Old Annuity ledgers for 1723, Bank of England Record Office.

[7] Amsterdam, Archief Brants, 927 (de Flines) under date 7 February 1727 (N.S.).

less extent in other stocks) by the mid-eighteenth century are clearly those of executors and trustees, and can be classified accordingly.[1] They were not part of a conspiracy to obscure true ownership. As regards foreign proprietors, the advantages of registration of their stock in their own names must have outweighed any loss of secrecy this involved. (In any case, the companies seem to have kept their secrets well, otherwise pamphleteers' estimates of who held stock might have been more reliable.) If an English agent had held a foreign investor's stock for him under the terms of a private agreement the investor would have been at hazard. For at any time the agent could have sold or pledged the stock, and since the beneficiary was outside the jurisdiction of the English courts he would have had to bring a suit for redress through another agent against the first one — who would almost certainly have prudently vanished. An age as acutely aware as the eighteenth century of the risks and uncertainties of life would not have been inclined to tempt providence in this way. And, since dividends were untaxed until the Napoleonic Wars, there was no particular incentive to do so. It is therefore not surprising that the fairly large mass of correspondence and accounts in the Archief Brants at Amsterdam shows no trace of secret arrangments more complicated than the kind of family trust Simon Bevel was involved in.[2] Finally, in view of the large numbers of foreign owners of English government securities who appear on the face of the records, it is inherently implausible to assume that there was a secret technique of foreign ownership as well, because if there had been these owners would presumably have taken advantage of it. The general conclusion is that the records of both long- and short-term loans, if handled with appropriate caution, are an adequate source of information about the savings flowing into government borrowing over the whole of this period.

III

What were the number and social background of the 'publick creditors' in the 1690s? Some conclusions about this can be reached by examining the subscriptions to the Tontine of 1693 and the Bank of England in the following year, and comparing them with the ownership of Bank stock in 1697 (see Table 31, below). The Tontine was the first English long-term loan to

---

[1] For these accounts see below, p. 299.   [2] See above, p. 252.

be floated. Between 3 February and 1 May 1693 £377,600 was subscribed to it in minimum units of £100, but owing to a gap in the Exchequer records the names of only 1,257 subscribers of £297,500 (79% of the whole) are available.[1] The Bank of England's subscription for £1,200,000, one-quarter payable on application, was opened on 21 June 1694 and, in marked contrast, was filled in ten days.[2] There were 1,268 subscribers,[3] 192 of whom are in the partial list for the Tontine in the previous year; the overlap in ownership between the two loans was thus of the order of 8%.[4] Making the assumption that if 1,257 persons contributed £297,500 to the Million Loan the total number of contributors needed to complete it would have been about 4,200, adding to this the 1,268 Bank subscribers, and deducting 8% for overlap between the two sectors, it may be surmised that the total number of 'vermin [who] took advantage of the public folly' at this early stage was of the order of 5,000.[5]

Table 31 analyses the two subscriptions of 1693–4 and the ownership of Bank stock at Christmas 1697.[6]

The Tontine subscribers evidently committed themselves to the novel experiment of government long-term borrowing with a good deal of caution. Their average contribution was only £236, and 88% of them subscribed less than £500. This was an exceptionally high proportion of small subscribers, due to exceptional circumstances, but a proportion of about 50% remained characteristic of government long-annuity ownership, and later of ownership of South Sea annuities, into which the bulk of long annuities were converted in 1720.[7] The largest subscription to the Tontine, Sir

---

[1] The names of the Tontine lenders were extracted from the entries in the Pells' Receipt Books and re-sorted in alphabetical order (P.R.O. E 401/1991, 1992). The first of these receipt books ends on 24 March 1693, the second begins on 20 April; Easter Day was 16 April. There is no sign of leaves having been extracted. Unfortunately, there is no Receipt Roll for this year to act as a check.

[2] Bank of England Subscription Cash Book, f. 45. Subscribers had to pay a further 35% by the end of the year.

[3] Alphabetical list of subscribers compiled by the Bank of England from the subscription ledgers. I am indebted to the Bank for giving me a copy of this list.

[4] The joint numbers were 2,525, of which 192 is 7·6%.

[5] The quotation is from Elibank, op. cit., p. 6.

[6] The categories adopted in this and subsequent analyses are a modified version of those introduced by Mrs. A. C. Carter in her article, 'Analyses of Public Indebtedness in Eighteenth-Century England', BIHR xxiv (1951), 173.

[7] The proportion of owners of less than £500 was 55·7% in the 14% long annuities in 1719, and 52·8% in South Sea Old Annuities in 1744, see below, Tables 37 and 40.

TABLE 31

Subscribers and owners, Tontine loan and Bank of England, 1693–97

Unit £	1693 Tontine (part)				1694 Bank of England Subscription				Dec. 1697 Ownership of Bank stock			
	Nos.	%	£	%	Nos.	%	£	%	Nos.	%	£	%
Under 500	1,107	88·1	180,100	60·5	442	34·9	77,700	6·5	919	42·3	195,616	8·9
500–999	118	9·4	70,700	23·8	435	34·3	227,150	18·9	614	28·2	357,980	16·3
1000–4999	32	2·5	46,700	15·7	347	27·4	571,250	47·6	569	26·2	1,067,777	48·5
5000–9999	..	..	..	..	32	2·5	203,900	17·0	53	2·4	331,478	15·0
10,000 and over	..	..	..	..	12	0·9	120,000	10·0	19	0·9	248,320	11·3
Average holding or subscription	..	..	[236]	..	..	..	[946]	..	..	..	[1,013]	..
TOTALS .	1,257	100·0	297,500	100·0	1,268	100·0	1,200,000	100·0	2,174	100·0	2,201,171	100·0

Source: for the Tontine and Bank of England subscription see above, p. 254 n. 1, 3. For the ownership of Bank stock at December 1697, Bank of England dividend list for that date (Bank of England Record Office).

Robert Howard's, was only £4,200.[1] On the other hand, in the Bank of England subscription, which must have been regarded as a test of the new regime's ability to survive, 31% of the contributors, putting up 75% of the capital, subscribed £1,000 or more, and forty-four lenders of £5,000 or more took up between them £323,900, 27% of the whole. Nor were these big lenders just stagging (buying to resell). For example, of the twelve subscribers of £10,000 or more, eight appear as holders of Bank stock at Christmas 1697. One of these had reduced his holding to £9,000, one had kept it intact, the other six had increased theirs.[2] Indeed, the structure of ownership of the enlarged capital of the Bank after the 'Ingraftment' of 1697 is remarkably similar to that of the subscription of 1694.

Table 32 shows the geographical spread of the Tontine and Bank subscriptions, and the proportion of subscriptions by women, whose role in the ownership of government stock was to become increasingly important as the century went on.

The major part of the capital was subscribed by those resident in London and the Home Counties,[3] though this was less evident in the Tontine than in the

TABLE 32

*Geographical spread of subscriptions to the Tontine 1693
and the Bank of England 1694*

Category	1693 Tontine (part)				1694 Bank of England Subscription			
	Nos.	%	Sum subscribed £	%	Nos.	%	Sum subscribed £	%
London, Middlesex, Surrey, Herts.	875	69·6	230,600	77·5	1,111	87·6	1,077,775	89·8
England outside these counties	336	26·7	56,700	19·1	130	10·2	99,225	8·3
From abroad	46	3·7	10,200	3·4	27	2·2	25,000	2·1
Women	234	18·6	35,300	11·9	151	11·9	70,675	5·9

Source: Same as Table 31.

[1] Howard, who was Auditor of the Exchequer of Receipt, subscribed £8,000 to the Bank of England in 1694.

[2] The names are shown on p. 257, below.

[3] As defined in the Table. This definition applies to all references to Home Counties in the text until the analyses for the mid-century when Essex is added; see below p. 297 n.

Bank subscription. There were three Irish subscribers but no Scottish ones, (Scottish ownership of English government securities was negligible even at the middle of the eighteenth century). The average provincial contribution, as well as the total of such contributions, was smaller than the London average: in the Tontine £169, compared with £263; in the Bank £763 compared with £970. Only comparatively small sums were lent from abroad, mostly from the United Provinces. The proportion of women subscribers was a good deal higher in the Tontine than in the subscription to the Bank of England.

Who were the plutocrats whose lead must have been a decisive factor in the success of the Bank of England subscription? The twelve subscribers of exactly £10,000 were as follows:

TABLE 33

Subscribers of £10,000 to the Bank of England, 1694

Name and description	Stock held, December 1697
	£
1. King William and Queen Mary jointly	none
2. James de la Bretonnière, Esq.	none
3. William Brownlowe, Esq., Woodcott, Surrey . . .	10,000
4. Abraham Houblon, merchant, London	11,900
5. Sir John Houblon, Knight and Alderman	13,225
6. Thomas Howard, Esq., Westminster	9,000
7. Matthew Humberstone, Esq., London	10,000
8. Theodore Janssen, London	10,000
9. Thomas Mulson, Esq., Middle Temple	none
10. Anthony Parsons, Esq., London	none
11. William, Earl of Portland	19,750
12. Sir William Scawen, Knight	16,075

Source: Bank stock subscription list, see above, p. 254 n. 3.

This was a cross-section of London political, official and mercantile society. The king and queen can only have been showing the flag, for they quickly disposed of their subscription. The two Houblons were members of the dynasty, of sixteenth-century Huguenot extraction, which had played a major part in the scheme for the Bank, of which Sir John Houblon was the first Governor. Thomas Howard was one of the four Tellers of the Exchequer. Matthew Humberston was a prominent lender on short-term funds throughout the 1690s, and held the (presumably sinecure) office of Usher of the London Customs. Theodore Janssen, another Huguenot, had emigrated to England in 1683, was created a baronet in 1715, was an M.P. from 1717 to 1721, and was the richest of the South Sea directors of 1720. The Earl of Portland was the King's favourite and political adviser. Sir William Scawen was a prominent City merchant and clothing contractor.

Loan subscriptions in 1693–4 from the peerage and Members of Parliament were relatively unimportant. One spiritual and one temporal peer and forty-two M.P.s, several of whom were baronets, subscribed to the Tontine, and nine peers and thirty M.P.s to the Bank of England.[1] The peers in the Bank subscription included the newly created Duke of Devonshire, the Duke of Leeds (Lord Danby of Charles II's reign) and, once more, William of Orange's favourite, the Earl of Portland. Several of the M.P.s, like the three Cumberland baronets, Sir George Fletcher, Sir Wilfred Lawson and Sir John Lowther, who, no doubt after consulting together, contributed £500 each to the Tontine, Sir Robert Cotton 'of Hattley St. George, Cambridge', or Sir William Cowper 'of Hertford Castle, baronet', who contributed £500 and £2,000 respectively to the Bank of England, were country gentlemen asserting their faith in the Revolution Settlement. Other M.P.s, like John Blencowe, Sir Robert Clayton, Charles Godfrey, Sir Joseph Herne and Sir George Treby in the Tontine, and Gilbert Dolben, Sir Stephen Fox, Sir Robert Howard, Charles Montague and Sir William Scawen in the subscription to the Bank, were drawn from political, legal and mercantile circles in London.

At the other end of the social scale to these top subscribers was a number of tradesmen and artisans: apothecaries, carriers, clothworkers, embroiderers, farmers, mariners, wharfingers. (These descriptions are all from the Bank list, for the Tontine records do not show occupations.) The majority of

---

[1] For convenience 'peer' here and later in this chapter is confined to those entitled to sit in the English House of Lords. Gilbert Burnet, Bishop of Salisbury (£200), and Francis, Lord Howard of Effingham (£800), were the peers in the Tontine loan. Some identifications of M.P.s are uncertain. Their subscriptions totalled £23,700. In the Bank list the peers were John, Lord Berkeley (£1,000); the Earl of Bradford (£1,000); William, Duke of Devonshire (£6,000); Sidney, Lord Godolphin (£6,000); Thomas, Duke of Leeds, (£4,000); William, Lord Leominster (£1,000); John, Lord Ossulston (£3,000); Thomas, Earl of Pembroke (£2,000) and William, Earl of Portland (£10,000). The M.P.s subscribed £78,500. Five were also in the Tontine subscription.

subscribers to both loans, however, belonged to the mercantile middle classes of London, though there were also important ancillary contributions from lawyers, office-holders, and clergy of the Church of England. The absence of precise information about membership of Protestant Nonconformist churches makes it impossible to say how important Nonconformist owner-ship of government stock was, either at this date or later, though specific owners can be identified.[1] The likelihood is that at this early period most domestic Nonconformists were artisans or tradesmen, and their ownership of securities was therefore probably insignificant. Two other religious minorities whose members can be identified fairly accurately are Huguenots of recent domicile and Jews. Allowing for some uncertainty of classification, there were fifty-three Huguenots subscribing £16,200 in the Tontine and 123 lending £104,000 in the subscription to the Bank, fourteen being common to both groups. The number of Jewish contributions — all from members of the Sephardi (Iberian) community in London — was very much smaller: six subscribed £1,800 to the Tontine and four £3,700 to the Bank, Peter or Pedro Henriquez jun. being common to both groups.[2] Lastly, virtually all subscriptions were from individuals. Ownership by corporations

---

[1] For identification of some Nonconformist stock-jobbers see below, p. 515. The best lists of Nonconformists seem to be the indexes to the Minutes of the Dissenting Deputies (Guildhall MS. 3083/1), the certificates requesting construction of Nonconformist churches under the Toleration Act (Guildhall MS. 9579) and the index to Walter Wilson, *The History and Antiquities of Dissenting Churches* (4 vols., 1808–14), but all these are of course very incomplete. Dr. Williams's Library at 14 Gordon Square, W.C.1, has copies of the eighteenth-century lists of congregations compiled by John Evans and Walter Wilson, but these are of little help. Despite the pioneer work of Dr. E. D. Bebb, *Noncon-formity and Social and Economic Life 1660–1800* (1935), and Dr. Arnold Lloyd, *Quaker Social History 1669–1738* (1950), the social history of Nonconformity in this period, so often boldly generalized about by historians, seems to be largely a blank.

[2] Identification of Huguenot names from the careful lists in W. A. Shaw, *Letters of Denization and Acts of Naturalization . . . 1603–1700* and *1701–1800* (Publ. Huguenot Soc. London, xviii [1911], xxvii (1923); also the suppl. vol. by William and Susan Minet (ibid. xxxv (1932)); of Jewish names from J. A. Giuseppi, 'Sephardic Jews and the early years of the Bank of England', *Trans. Jewish Hist. Soc. of Eng.* xix (1953), 53. (The lists of names referred to in this article are published in ibid., *Miscellanies*, 1962.) Ownership of govern-ment securities by the much poorer Ashkenazik (East European) Jewish community in London was rare throughout this period. On Huguenot ownership cf. also Mrs. A. C. Carter, 'The Huguenot contribution to the early years of the Funded Debt, 1694–1714', *Proc. Huguenot Soc. of London*, xix (3), (1955), 21. 'Recent domicile' for Huguenots is taken for convenience as meaning post-1650, to distinguish recent arrivals from the Elizabethan immigrant families, many of which, like the Desbouveries, Houblons, Lethieulliers, Lordells and Papillons, were established City dynasties by the later seventeenth century.

and groups of trustees, so characteristic later, had barely begun. Only one of the Tontine subscriptions, for example, was from a group of subscribers.[1] In general, this evidence suggests that in its initial phase English government long-term borrowing leaned heavily on the financial expertise and accumulated capital of the London *bourgeoisie* and office-holders, and only marginally on other sources, and on other classes of the community.

IV

The next analyses, in Table 34, are of part (71%) of the subscription to the Government long annuity loan of 1707; and of the whole of the subscription to double the capital of the Bank of England in 1709. These are compared with the structure of ownership of Bank and East India stock in 1709.

Total government long annuities created by the end of 1707 amounted to £546,567.[2] By the same rough proportionate rule as before, if 719 subscribers put up 71% (£51,253 p.a.) of the £72,188 p.a. created by the 1707 loan, the total number of long annuitants, controlling £546,567 p.a., would have been roughly 7,700. This ignores the difference between subscribers and holders, but it squares fairly well with later evidence.[3] Adding to this figure 3,439 proprietors of Bank and East India stock in March 1709, a gross figure of about 11,000 national creditors at the middle of Anne's reign is arrived at. Comparison of a sample of 608 of the Bank stock subscribers of 1709 with the list of 719 annuity subscribers of 1707 shows seventy-six names common to both lists, an overlap of the order of 6%.[4] The overlap between the 'old' and 'new' proprietors of the Bank of England was understandably rather higher. An estimate of September 1709 suggests a figure of 15%.[5] Overlap at somewhere around or between these two figures seems to

[1] William Allen, and John and James Sawyer, £100.   [2] For details see above, Ch. 3.

[3] Below, p. 274. The figure in the text is arrived at by dividing 719 by 51,253 and multiplying by 546,567 = 7,660.

[4] Defining overlap (as above, p. 254 n.) as the number of accounts common to two stocks, expressed as a percentage of the total of accounts in both.

[5] The Bank of England raised a further £400,000 by a call of 15% in September 1709. A note on the flyleaf of the 'List of the Proprietors in the Additional Stock of the Bank Sept. 24th 1709' (Bank of England Record Office) says there were 1,437 'proprietors in the New Subscriptions', i.e. presumably the two subscriptions of 1709 as owned in September 1709. The note continues that there were 1,924 'in the Original Stock' and 499 common to both. This would be a 15% overlap.

TABLE 34

Subscribers and owners 1707–09

Category	1 Part of subscription for 99 yrs. Annuities (6 Anne, c. 2), 1707				2 Subscription to double capital of Bank of England, 22–25 February 1709			
£	Nos.	%	£	%	Nos.	%	£	%
Under 500 .	354	49·2	78,528	9·6	175	16·3	39,272	1·8
500–999 .	148	20·6	92,285	11·2	281	26·1	149,200	6·8
1000–4999 .	191	26·6	355,685	43·4	515	47·9	941,200	42·8
5000–9999 .	17	2·4	101,650	12·4	57	5·2	329,300	14·9
10,000 and over	9	1·2	191,700	23·4	48	4·5	742,200	33·7
Average subscription .	..		[1,140]	..	..	..	[2,045]	
TOTALS .	719	100·0	819,848	100·0	1,076	100·0	2,201,172	100·0

Category	3 Ownership of Bank stock 25 March 1709, before capital doubled				4 Ownership of stock of United East India Company 31 March 1709			
£	Nos.	%	£	%	Nos.	%	£	%
Under 500 .	822	42·9	177,783	8·2	384	25·3	62,794	2·0
500–900 .	481	25·1	289,087	13·1	479	31·6	304,526	9·6
1000–4999 .	539	28·1	1,019,860	46·3	514	33·9	1,107,848	35·0
5000–9999 .	50	2·6	319,716	14·5	91	6·0	643,364	20·4
10,000 and over .	24	1·3	394,726	17·9	49	3·2	1,044,668	33·0
Average holding .	..	..	[1,148]	..	..	..	[2,984]	
TOTALS .	1,916	100·0	2,201,172	100·0	1,517	100·0	3,163,200	100·0

Source: For 1: P.R.O. E 401/2018, Receipt Book (Pells') Michaelmas 1706–Easter 1707. This records £819,848 of the total £1,155,000 subscribed. All except eleven entries are recorded under 8 April 1707. In the next receipt book no subscriptions were recorded: they were entered instead in a 'Liber Annuitatum', which has not survived. Its totals were regularly added to the 'Summa diei' in the receipt book. For 2, 3, and 4: Bank stock subscription books 1709, Bank stock dividend list 25 March 1709, and list of United East India Company proprietors at 31 March 1709, all in the Bank of England Record Office. There is a copy of the Bank stock subscription book in P.R.O. E 401/2594.

have been constant to the middle of the century, though only a complete comparison of the holders of all securities at a given date could test its accuracy.[1] In this instance it suggests that the net number of public creditors in 1707–9 was of the order of 10,000.

The difference in structure between the subscriptions to the government annuity loan and the Bank of England is striking. In the former, nearly 70% of the subscribers lent less than £1,000. In the Bank subscription the proportion was only 42%. At the other end of the scale big subscribers (£5,000 and more), who were respectively 3·6% and 9·7% of total numbers, contributed only 35% of the annuity loan, but nearly 49% of the subscription to the Bank. The middle group of subscribers (£1,000 to £4,999) lent roughly the same proportion of the whole on both occasions, but formed a much larger proportion of total numbers in the Bank subscription. The ownership of Bank and East India stock also shows some interesting contrasts. The distribution of holdings in Bank stock resembled that of the subscription to annuities, and had changed little since 1697.[2] There was a high (43%) proportion of units of ownership of less than £500, and a less proportion (3·9%) than later of ones of £5,000 or more. In East India stock, on the other hand, the pattern of ownership in March 1709 was as monopolistic as that of the subscription to the Bank in the previous month. Of the total stock, 53% was held in units of £5,000 or more and only 2% in units of less than £500 — though these small holdings accounted for a quarter of all proprietors.

It might at first be thought that the structure of the Bank stock subscription and the ownership of East India stock were due to special circumstances: in the first to 'stagging' by speculators, in the second to the financial jobbery which preceded the formation of the United Company. This is partly true. Examination of the accounts of several of the big subscribers to the Bank of England shows that some of them like Alvaro da Fonseca (£32,200), Thomas Guy (£10,200), Raymond de Smeth (£9,000), the Duke of Somerset (£5,000) and the Earl of Sunderland (£10,000) sold part of their subscription stock fairly quickly.[3] In East India stock the enormous holding of Samuel Waters and Thomas Granger (£126,264) was probably part of the capital reconstruction of the two companies; by 1724 the Waters

---

[1] For overlap at the middle of the eighteenth century, see below, p. 284.

[2] For the structure of Bank stock holdings at December 1697 see Table 31 on p. 255 above.

[3] Bank stock ledger accounts for these subscribers, Bank of England Record Office.

and Granger account was reduced to £239 10s. 2d.[1] But the structure of ownership of both Bank and East India stock by the early 1720s shows that these instances are not of great importance. By 1724 the pattern of *ownership* of Bank stock had come to resemble that of the *subscription* of 1709.[2] This was presumably partly due to large blocks of the subscriptions of 1709 and 1722 being taken up — and retained — by existing proprietors. For example, many of the big subscribers to the Bank in 1709 did not sell out or reduce their holdings like those previously referred to, but retained or increased them. This was true, for instance of Sir James Bateman (who subscribed £10,000), Sir Richard Child (£12,000), Alvaro da Costa (£15,000) Sir Francis Dashwood (£12,100), Sir John Houblon (£10,000), the Duke of Marlborough (£20,000) or Dr. John Radcliffe (£20,000).[3] Similarly, the structure of ownership of East India stock in 1724 was not unlike that of 1709, though there had been some increase in the share of the middle group of proprietors (£1,000–£4,999).[4]

The group of nearly 5,000 subscribers and proprietors of 1707–9 was headed by the cosmopolitan mercantile plutocracy of the City of London. This can be seen from the group of seventy-four holders of £5,000 or more Bank stock in 1709, who were also extensively involved in the other three loans. Only three lived outside London and the Home Counties: George Dodington, the rich Somersetshire squire (£5,000); Sir John Elwill, Bart., 'of Langley, Kent'; and Benjamin England of Yarmouth. None were peers. Ten were Jews: Alvaro da Costa (£16,350), Anthony da Costa (£7,700), Peter Henriquez jun. (£25,200), Francisco de Lis jun. (£17,150), Sir Somomon de Medina (£16,600), Francis Pereira (£13,200), Alphonso Rodriguez (£11,700), Jacob Teixeira de Mattos (£5,375), Jacob da Veiga (£6,050), and Rodrigo Ximenes (£6,600). De Medina, Pereira, Rodriguez and Ximenes were all holders of £5,000 or more East India stock as well. Pereira and Teixeira de Mattos subscribed £5,000 or over to the Annuity loan of 1707. Peter Henriquez jun. had subscribed £20,500 to the Annuity loan, held £46,591 East India stock in 1709, and subscribed £31,200, for himself only, to the doubling of the Bank's capital in the same year.[5]

There seem to have been only two capitalists of recent Huguenot ex-

---

[1] East India stock ledgers, account for Samuel Waters (deceased) and Thomas Granger at 25 March 1724 (Bank of England Record Office).

[2] For the ownership of Bank stock in 1724 see below, p. 275 Table 37.

[3] Bank stock ledger accounts for these subscribers, Bank of England Record Office.

[4] See below, p. 275.

[5] The ledgers show whether subscribers contributed for others or for themselves only.

traction among these seventy-four big owners: Peter Fabrot (£5,885) and Sir Theodore Janssen (£24,900).[1] It is worth noting, however, that the big (£5,000 and over) subscribers to the doubling of the Bank's capital in 1709 included Moses Beranger (£16,000), John Martin Couvreu (£5,000), John Francis Fauquier (£26,400), Sir Theodore Janssen (£25,000), Anthony Laroque (£6,000) and Stephen Seignoret (£6,800), while the big holders of East India stock at the same date included René Baudouin (£7,417), Francis Beuzelin (£6,008), Peter Fabrot (£8,266) and Stephen Seignoret again (£14,187). Another sub-group among the seventy-four big holders of Bank stock in 1709 comprised those of recent foreign (non-Huguenot and non-Jewish) origin. They were Sir Justus Beck (£8,450), noted in the alphabet book as 'Joost, alias Sir Justus Beck, knight', William Henry Cornelisen (£11,200), Dennis Dutry (£7,238), Jacob Jacobsen (£40,289), Philip Martins (£8,000), Peter Vansittart (£8,700) and Pieter Vandermersch (£6,000). Jacobsen was the son of Heinrich Jacobsen of Hamburg and was a South Sea Director in 1720. The others were probably all of Dutch extraction.[2] The majority of the seventy-four big holders were, however, native-born, even if like Sir James Bateman (£10,300) and Sir Peter Delmé (£14,300) their father or grandfathers were naturalized foreigners.[3] Gerard Conyers (£6,200), Sir Henry Furnese (£10,000), Sir Stephen Fox (£5,000), Sir John Houblon (£10,900), Sir John Lethieullier (£6,500), Alexander Merreall (£5,300), Captain Thomas South (£5,000) and Nathaniel Tench (£5,000), to take names at random, were among other big holders of stock.

Precise information about many of these stockholders is not available, but enough is known about some of them to throw light on the group as a whole. Francis Beuzelin, of French extraction, was later (1716–18) a director of the Royal African Company. Peter Henriquez jun. was one of the most prominent members of the Sephardi Jewish community in London, a big lender on short-term tax funds, and an agent for Dutch Jewish investors in English securities. Sir Theodore Janssen was one of the two most important

[1] John Emilie, a Bank Director 1708–10, who died in 1711, held £5,000 stock in 1709. He may have been of Huguenot extraction.

[2] Philip Martins may have been of Jewish origin. For Jacobsen see above, p. 114.

[3] Sir Peter Delmé (1667–1728), a director and later Governor of the Bank of England, was the grandson of the pastor of the Walloon Church at Canterbury. Sir James Bateman (c. 1660–1718) was the son of Joos Bateman of Flanders, who was naturalized in 1660. Sir James was Governor of the Bank of England 1705–7. In 1710 his interest and credit abroad were said to be second only to that of Sir Henry Furnese (H.M.C. Portland, iv. 559).

agents remitting government money for payment of the troops overseas; Sir Henry Furnese was the other. Sir Justus Beck had close ties with his native community in Amsterdam. During the South Sea Bubble he went bankrupt for nearly £350,000.[1] Sir James Bateman was one of the merchant princes of London, and was the first Sub-Governor of the South Sea Company in 1711. Sir Stephen Fox, who was sixty in 1707, was a veteran politician and civil servant. Alexander Merreall was a rich stationer. Thomas South, described in the alphabet book simply as 'mariner, London', may have been an East India ship's husband. Nathaniel Tench was a director and former Governor of the Bank of England. Some members of the group were also members of the Court of Alderman of the City of London: Sir James Bateman, Sir Robert Beachcroft, Sir John Houblon and Sir Joseph Woolfe. Others would clearly not have been admitted to that highly conservative and exclusive body. This evidence as a whole suggests that war and war finance had brought into a position of very considerable power a group of capitalists of international outlook and connections, and of mixed origins. A substantial minority were Huguenots and Jews, who were excluded from formal participation in local or central government. Nearly all were self-made men, whose vast wealth had been built up during the long wars since 1689. Even if it was not due to these wars, it must have been tempting for hostile critics to say that it was. This helps to explain the increasingly bitter hostility of the squirearchy to the 'Plumb Men of the City of London', and the ignorant ferocity of the attacks on monied wealth, foreign refugees and overseas commitments in the Parliaments of 1710–14.[2]

In each of the four loans previously analysed there was a minority of subscriptions or holdings by peers and M.P.s.[3] The figures, allowing for some uncertain identifications, were as shown in Table 35.

In the annuity loan the Duke of Newcastle subscribed £15,000 and Lord Townshend £5,000. The other peers came in for smaller sums: Lord Ashburnham (£4,000), Fulke, Lord Brooke (£2,500), William, Lord Leominster (£2,000), Charles, Earl of Sunderland (£3,900) and Thomas, Earl of Westmorland (£2,000); since the surviving list is defective, other peers may also have subscribed. Only a handful of peers owned Bank and East India stock in March 1709. In Bank stock they were Charles, Earl of Berkeley (£2,500), Francis, Earl of Bradford deceased (£1,000), Lord Chancellor Cowper (£2,400), David Boyle, Earl of Glasgow, who was a

---

[1] See above, p. 158. [2] For Tory views on the monied interest see above, p. 26.

[3] Defining 'peers' (above, p. 258 n. 1) as those entitled to sit in the English House of Lords. From the Union of 1707 this included Scottish Representative Peers.

TABLE 35

Peers and Members of Parliament subscribing to loans or owning stock 1707–9

Subscription or stock		Peers				M.P.s			
	Nos.	% of total numbers	£	% of total stock	Nos.	% of total numbers	£	% of total stock
Annuities	1707	7	0·1	34,400	4·2	25	3·5	107,600	13·1
Bank subscription	1709	14	1·3	93,700	4·3	52	4·8	205·700	9·3
Bank stock	1709	6	0·3	9,900	0·4	28	1·5	137,997	6·3
East India stock	1709	4	0·3	15,624	0·5	29	1·9	136,632	4·3

Source: as in Table 34 (above, p. 261).

Scottish Representative Peer (£1,000), William, Lord Leominster (£1,000) and the Duke of Marlborough (£2,000). In East India stock there were only four peers: Robert, Lord Ferrers (£8,000); Charles, Lord Halifax (£4,800); David, Lord Lawarr (£904), and Henry, Earl of Romney (£1,920). In the subscription to the Bank of England in February 1709, on the other hand, noble subscriptions were more numerous. The names, among others, of the Duke of Bedford (£4,000), Lord Cowper (£5,000), Lord Godolphin (£6,000), Lord Halifax (£10,000), the Duke of Marlborough (£20,000), the Duke of Newcastle (£5,000), Lord Somers (£3,000), the Duke of Somerset (£5,000), the Earl of Sunderland (£10,000), and Lord Townshend (£3,200) give the subscription lists the appearance of a gesture of support for the Bank of England from the Revolution Families at a critical moment in the war.

M.P.s' subscriptions and holding of stock were, like those of the peerage, a good deal less important than they were later to become. The most prominent M.P. in the annuity loan of 1707 was Lord Treasurer Godolphin's son Lord Ryalton, who subscribed £55,000, part of which must have been on behalf of others. Among other M.P.s in this list were Marlborough's brother, General Charles Churchill (£5,000), the elder James Craggs, who was to achieve notoriety in the South Sea Bubble, the London bookseller Thomas Guy (£2,050), the City magnates Sir Gilbert Heathcote (£3,500) and John Ward (£6,750), the Secretary to the Treasury, William Lowndes

5. Early subscriptions to the Tontine loan of 1693

(£700), and an eminent lawyer, Sir Thomas Powys (£500).[1] The prominent High Tory, William Bromley, M.P. for Worcestershire, subscribed £1,700. Craggs, Heathcote and Ward all reappear as owners of both Bank and East India stock in 1709. Among other M.P.s who were holders of both stocks at this date were Sir Francis Dashwood (£2,000 Bank stock, £11,556 East India stock), Sir Henry Furnese (£10,000 and £6,400), Admiral Sir John Norris (£2,114 and £480) and Sir William Scawen (£29,466 and £19,200). The lawyers John Dolben and Sir Joseph Jekyll were other M.P.s who were proprietors. In general, the M.P.s interested in securities were office-holders, merchants, lawyers, and naval and military men, rather than landed men, a pattern still observable at the mid-century.[2]

The solid core of medium subscribers and owners (£500–£4,999), which provided 50% of both numbers and capital in both subscriptions and both monied companies, also consisted largely of merchants, financiers, office-holders and professional men. Most of them lived in and around the capital. The addresses for Bank and East India proprietors, for example, are nearly all in London and the Home Counties.[3] There is only a handful of foreign names.[4] Among the subscribers of 1707 were Dr. John Arbuthnot, F.R.S., later physician to the Queen, and a friend of Swift and Pope (£500); Marlborough's secretary, Adam Cardonell (£2,000); Admiral Richard Haddock, who was Comptroller of the Navy (£500); and the rich physician Dr. John Radcliffe (£15,000). Among subscribers to the Bank of England in 1709 were Generals Cadogan (£4,000) and Earle (£3,000), Robert Eyre, who was Solicitor-General (£2,000); Brigadier Wade (£2,000); the physician Nehemiah Grew (£5,000);[5] Dr. White Kennett, Dean and later Bishop of Peterborough (£400); and the physician and collector, Dr. Hans 'Slone' (£1,000). Less prominent clergy, soldiers, sailors, lawyers appear in all the lists, though the majority of the identifiable names are those of members of the London mercantile and financial community.

As in the 1690s, an important minority of holdings and subscriptions belonged to married, widowed and spinster women. There were also important contributions from the London Huguenot and Sephardi Jewish communities.[6]

---

[1] Powys became a judge of the Queen's Bench in 1713. Sir Littleton Powys, judge of the King's Bench from 1700, and a lender on short-term tax funds (below, p. 428), was his brother.

[2] Below, p. 296.

[3] The domicile of Exchequer subscribers is less certain, except where the same names occur in other records, for those of the Exchequer give no addresses. The Tontine records, which show subscribers' counties, seem to be unique in this respect.

[4] For these see below, p. 309.   [5] For Grew cf. also below, p. 426.

[6] For the definition of 'Huguenot' see above, p. 259 n. 2.

Table 36

Women, Huguenot and Jewish subscribers and owners 1707–9

Subscription or stock	Women				Huguenots				Jews			
	Nos.	% of total nos.	£	% of total stock	Nos.	% of total nos.	£	% of total stock	Nos.	% of total nos.	£	% of total stock
Annuities 1707 .	146	20·3	76,595	9·3	71	10·0	43,960	5·4	17	2·4	54,000	6·9
Bank subscription 1709 .	92	8·5	69,300	3·1	72	6·7	150,500	6·8	13	1·2	108,100	4·9
Bank stock 1709 .	318	16·6	181,738	8·3	92	4·8	133,291	6·1	49	2·6	206,322	9·4
East India stock 1709 .	161	10·6	124,156	3·9	110	7·3	277,368	8·8	65	4·3	386,131	12·2

Source: as in Table 34 (above, p. 261).

Women were less important as subscribers to the Bank and as East India stockholders than as subscribers to government annuities and as stockholders of the Bank of England. Huguenot investors were more numerous than Jewish ones, but both their average and aggregate contributions were smaller. The evidence does not seem to justify Wortley Montagu's assertion in February 1709 that Huguenot refugees had contributed £500,000 to the Bank subscription, and 'were reckoned to have above two millions sterling in the government'.[1] It is, however, worth remembering that there were several Huguenots and Jews among the biggest owners of stock.[2]

Nearly all subscriptions in 1707–9 were still for individuals, and not for corporations or groups. An exception to this was the Bank of England's purchase in 1706 of £12,000 p.a. of the government loan for that year; at 15½ years' purchase, the issue price, this would have cost £186,000. The Bank sold the whole of this investment in the difficult autumn of 1709.[3] In Bank and East India stock, on the other hand, two trends were already discernible, which developed considerably by the middle of the century. The first was the tendency for stock to be held in the name of dead owners. Thus, in Bank stock in March 1709 196 accounts were for deceased proprietors. This was 10·2% of the total number of accounts, and controlled £182,289 (8·3%) of the total stock. In East India stock at the same date the corresponding figures were 109 accounts (7·2%) controlling £187,620 (5·9%) stock. In addition, there were accounts, normally but not invariably for two or more proprietors, stated to be held in trust. Thus in the Bank stock dividend list of Michaelmas 1712 there are 104 such accounts controlling £118,699.[4] In the same list there are thirty-four joint accounts, controlling £42,424, not specifically stated to be in trust. The high mortality of the period could and did quickly create a cat's cradle of relationships in such multiple holdings, with executors taking over from partners and trustees, and trustees from executors, or even executors of executors. Presumably owing to this, the Bank and the other monied companies soon gave up the attempt to classify multiple holdings, and merely stated the names of the holders without 'in trust' or other labels.[5] 'Deceased' was, however, normally added against individual names in printed voting lists, and each company

---

[1] *Parl. Hist.* vi. 782–3.   [2] Above, p. 263.

[3] Bank D. Ct. Bk. E, f. 94, 1 and 13 March 1706, £12,000 p.a. of the annuities of the year to be purchased; ibid., F, f. 27, 20 October 1709, the committee for discounting tallies to sell all annuities purchased from the government.

[4] Bank stock dividend list 29 September 1712, Bank of England Record Office.

[5] For example, the Bank gave up separate listing of trust accounts in Bank stock after 1720.

kept a careful register of deaths, in which the details of wills, administrations and so on were noted.[1]

The second trend away from individual ownership was corporate investment in securities. By far the most important corporate owner at this early stage was the Million Bank, founded in 1695. Within a year of its establishment it had given up banking and had concentrated instead on the purchase of government life annuities and their reversions.[2] The total of Exchequer, single-life annuities under the three loan Acts of 1693 and 1694 was just under £140,000 p.a. When the Government decided in 1695 to convert them into long annuities in return for additional payments, it gave third parties permission to buy the reversion of the term of years on each annuity if the life-tenant did not wish to do so himself.[3] The Million Bank took advantage of this so energetically that by November 1702 it had acquired £59,566 p.a. in reversionary annuities, about 43% of the total available.[4] It was of course not entitled to draw the annuities until the life-tenants died. But even before this happened the reversion was a valuable investment, and the Bank did a brisk trade, both in buying out life interests where it held the reversion, and in selling reversions to the tenants for life.[5] By 1720 these transactions, and the falling in of lives, had reduced its holding of reversionary annuities to £36,000 p.a., and increased its holding of ordinary long annuities to nearly £15,000 p.a.[6] In consequence it was one of the government's most influential creditors on the eve of the South Sea Bubble.

V

The number and type of the public creditors affected by the South Sea Company's proposals in 1720 for the reconstruction of the National Debt, and the effect of the Bubble itself on the structure of ownership, might well

[1] Cf. below, p. 299.

[2] 'Account of the Transactions of the Million Bank Society . . .', B.M. Collection of Palty Papers 1731–1800, vol. 96.

[3] See above, p. 56.

[4] P.R.O. Chancery Masters' Exhibits C 46/1, list of reversionary annuities dated 24 November 1702. The sub- and main totals are entered on the dorso of each skin. The British Museum printed list of the Million Bank's annuities (B.M. 8223.e.7) appears to be an alphabetical version of this one.

[5] 'Account of the Transactions', passim.

[6] P.R.O. C 114/9, Million Bank ledger 1717–21; see also below, p. 276.

have been thought sufficiently interesting, indeed urgent, for the government to investigate the subject and publish the results. For reasons of haste and carelessness beforehand, and (no doubt) prudent caution afterwards, nothing of the kind was in fact attempted. What might such an inquiry have shown?

The public debts affected by the 'South Sea Scheme' were the long annuities amounting to £666,566 p.a., the short annuities and lottery annuities of £121,669 p.a., and £16·5m. of 'Redeemables' (ordinary stock).[1] The only long-term securities not affected by the scheme were the small amount of government life annuities and the capital of the Bank of England and the East India Company. How many public creditors did this involve? The Issue Roll for 14% long annuities at Michaelmas 1719 contains about 3,600 names.[2] Allowing for duplication — many names being entered twice or oftener for different amounts — the probable number of proprietors on it is about 1,800. The 14%s amounted to about £124,000 p.a., and the total long and short annuities to about £788,000 p.a. If 1,800 proprietors owned £124,000 p.a., the number of proprietors of £788,000 p.a. would have been about 11,000 without allowing for overlap of ownership, or about 10,000 after deducting 10% for overlap.[3] According to Adam Anderson the number of proprietors of the £14·3m. 'Redeemables' (Government ordinary stock) offered for exchange for South Sea stock in 1720 was 'about sixteen thousand'.[4] On this basis the total number of proprietors of Redeemables would have been about 18,500.[5] The number of accounts in the largest part of this debt, the 5%s of 1717, whose capital amounted to £9·5m., was 12,887 at Michaelmas 1719.[6] On the same basis as before, if about 13,000 owned £9·5m. stock, £16·5m. stock would have been owned by about 23,000 proprietors. Here again 10% must be deducted for overlap to give just over 20,000 proprietors, a figure rather higher than Anderson's. Added to the figure of 10,000 owners of annuities it suggests that about 30,000 public creditors were affected by the South Sea Company's proposals.

---

[1] See below, Appendix B. [2] P.R.O. E 403/1400.

[3] See above, p. 260, for derivation of the figure of 10%. The Million Bank's holding of £14,766 long annuities in 1719 (below, p. 277) is not a sufficient fraction of the total to distort the calculation.

[4] Adam Anderson, *An Historical and Chronological Deduction of the Origin of Commerce* (2 vols., 1764), ii. 288. Anderson was a South Sea Company clerk at the time of the Bubble.

[5] The Redeemables totalled £16·5m.

[6] Bank of England Record Office, ledgers for this stock. The six original ledgers were closed at Michaelmas 1719 and the accounts posted to six new ledgers, the number of whose opening entries thus equals the number of proprietors. When the ledgers were opened in 1717 there had been 12,228 proprietors (ibid.).

The other way in which this calculation can be made is by working back from the number of South Sea Company proprietors' accounts at midsummer 1723. At this date the company's capital was broken into halves. Half of each proprietor's holding of South Sea stock was made into fixed-interest stock at 5%, the so-called South Sea annuities, later known as South Sea Old Annuities. As the ledgers for South Sea stock no longer survive, the opening ledgers for these annuities are the only existing cross-section of ownership of the whole of the South Sea Company's capital shortly after the Bubble. This amounted to roughly £34m., of which about £22m. had been created by the exchange of government annuities and ordinary stock for new South Sea stock in 1720. (The actual sum added to the company's capital in 1720 was larger, about £26m., but £4m. of this was sold to the Bank of England in 1722).[1] The number of opening entries in the South Sea annuity ledgers is about 27,000.[2] If 27,000 proprietors owned nearly £34m. stock, the number of proprietors of nearly £38m., the company's capital at the beginning of 1721, would have been about 30,000, of whom 5,000 would have been 'old' owners and 25,000 those who had come in by exchange of their government bonds for South Sea stock during 1720. Since these 'new' proprietors owned about five-sixths of the government bonds qualifying for exchange, the total number of these owners again comes to about 30,000. The figure of 5,000 for 'old' South Sea owners in 1720 is an estimate from the size of the capital at that date (£11·7m.), the number of owners (4,662) of nearly £9m. Bank stock in 1724 (Table 37), and the probability that because of large subscriptions in 1711 (p. 449 below) the number of 'old' owners in 1720 was still relatively restricted.

The *total* number of long-term government creditors in 1720 included these 'old' owners and holders of life annuities and of Bank and East India stock, not included in the scheme. The life annuitants cannot have been numerous by 1720, since the greater part of their holdings had been converted into long annuities in the 1690s. In 1719, 637 of the 1,013 nominees under the Tontine loan of 1693 were still living, so 637 persons must still have been drawing annuities.[3] There would also have been holders of a

---

[1] For details see above, p. 179, and below, Appendix B.

[2] South Sea Old Annuities, opening ledgers, Bank of England Record Office. The ledgers mingle opening accounts and working accounts.

[3] Add. MS. 38330, Liverpool Papers 1715–45, f. 327, 'An Account Shewing the Total Number of Nominees for Life-Rents' lists the number of nominees dying annually since 1693. The number of nominees, by definition, was equal to the number of annuitants.

small number of annuities for two and three lives created in 1694 and 1704.[1] The number of accounts for proprietors of Bank stock in 1712, when its capital was the same as in 1719, was 3,894.[2] The number of East India proprietors in 1724, when its capital was the same as in 1720, was 1,892.[3] Probably therefore the overall number of public creditors not affected by the South Sea Company's proposals was of the order of 10,000,[4] and the total number of public creditors of all kinds on the eve of the South Sea Bubble about 40,000 when allowance is made for the minority of accounts in joint or multiple ownership.

Some conclusions about the structure of ownership of long-term securities just before and just after the South Sea Bubble can be drawn from Table 37, which compares the distribution of holdings in long annuities and 5% stock at Michaelmas 1719 with that of Bank, East India and South Sea stock in 1723–4.

The table shows the persistence of the differences in structure already observable in the middle of Anne's reign. In the long annuities and the 5%s of 1717, and also in South Sea stock in 1723, which was heavily weighted by government stock and annuities exchanged for it during the Bubble, the number of small proprietors (under £500) was between 55% and 63% of total numbers. The proportion of stock they owned, however, was a mere 8% in South Sea stock, only 14% in the 5%s, and less than a quarter in the long annuities. Since the minimum South Sea voting qualification was £1,000 stock, this meant that control of the company was in the hands of the 28% who held this amount or more, the other 72% being excluded from voting at General Courts. This helps to explain both the turbulence of these courts in the period 1721–3 and the relative conservatism of the settlement voted for by the propertied minority.[5]

In the Bank of England and the East India Company small investors were also numerous, but owned an even smaller fraction, under 3%, of the total stock. The proportion of owners of £1,000–£4,999 stock in these two companies was a good deal higher (40%–42%) than in the South Sea Company (22%), the 5%s (18·5%) and the long annuities (16%); the

---

[1] £22,633 p.a. created by 5 & 6 Wm. and M. c. 20 and £14,508 p.a. created by 2 & 3 Anne, c. 3.

[2] Bank of England Record Office. Bank stock dividend book for 29 September 1712.

[3] See Table 37 on p. 275.

[4] Taking 11,000 Bank, East India and South Sea accounts, adding 1,000 for life-annuitants and reducing by 10% for overlap.

[5] For this settlement see above, p. 179.

TABLE 37

Ownership of certain stocks 1719–24

Category £	1 Sample of 14% long annuities at Mich. 1719, capitalizing each annuity at 20 y.p.				2 Sample of 5% (1717) at Mich. 1719				3 Sample of South Sea stock midsummer 1723			
	Nos.	%	£	%	Nos.	%	£	%	Nos.	%	£	%
Under 500	131	55·7	37,090	23·5	1073	62·9	193,415	14·3	466	55·2	94,528	8·8
500–999	64	27·2	40,320	25·5	280	16·4	182,842	13·6	141	16·7	93,650	8·7
1000–4999	38	16·2	66,960	42·4	315	18·5	585,557	43·3	184	21·8	387,392	36·2
5000–9999	2	0·9	13,600	8·6	25	1·5	155,617	11·5	41	4·9	272,956	25·5
10,00c and over	..	..	..	..	11	0·7	234,324	17·3	12	1·4	222,696	20·8
Average holding	..	..	[672]	..	..	..	[793]	..	..	..	[1,269]	..
TOTALS	235	100·0	157,970	100·0	1704	100·0	1,351,755	100·0	844	100·0	1,071,222	100·0

Category £	4 Bank of England stock 25 March 1724				5 East India stock 25 March 1724			
	Nos.	%	£	%	Nos.	%	£	%
Under 500	1,116	24·0	242,629	2·7	479	25·3	92,480	2·9
500–999	1,204	25·8	684,323	7·6	518	27·4	292,330	9·2
1000–4999	1,941	41·6	3,638,158	40·6	765	40·4	1,427,708	44·7
5000–9999	262	5·6	1,692,021	18·9	82	4·3	541,396	16·9
10,000 and over	139	3·0	2,702,865	30·2	48	2·6	840,166	26·3
Average holding	..	..	[1,921]	..	..	..	[1,688]	..
TOTALS	4,662	100·0	8,959,996	100·0	1892	100·0	3,194,080	100·0

Source: For 1 the Issue Roll for 14% long annuities at Michaelmas 1719, P.R.O. E 403/1400; for 2 all names starting A and B in the ledgers for the 5%s of 1717; for 3 all names in Ledger R, opening ledgers for South Sea Old Annuities; for 4 Bank stock dividend list for 25 March 1724; for 5 East India stock ledgers for the same date. The ledgers for 2, 3, 4 and 5 are all in the Bank of England Record Office.

proportion of the total owned by this group was, however, roughly the same in all five (36%–45%). At the top big owners (£5,000 and over) were unimportant in the long annuities. In the 5%s of 1717 they were only 2% of total numbers, but controlled 29% of the total stock. In South Sea, Bank and East India stock they were between 6·3% and 8·6% of total numbers, and controlled between 43·2% (East India stock) and 49·1% (Bank stock) of the whole capital. The trend towards plutocracy, observable earlier, had become fully confirmed, and was only partly offset by the continued importance of the medium (£1,000–£4,999) holders.

The greater part of the government's creditors on the eve of the South Sea Bubble still lived in London and the Home Counties. Samples of addresses from the biggest stock, the 5%s of 1717, show that only about 6% of English proprietors lived outside this area. Addresses north of the Trent were rare. Foreign owners were small in number before the Bubble, but increased markedly as a result of it.[1] The majority of accounts were still individual ones. In the annuities, however, the Million Bank retained the important position it had begun to build up during King William's reign. At Michaelmas 1719 it held £14,766 p.a. in direct long annuities, and £36,019 p.a. in reversionary long annuities, a total of £50,785 p.a. It valued its holding at the massive figure of £495,708.[2] On the eve of the South Sea Bubble it was thus by far the largest single government creditor. It is interesting that one of its directors, Jacob Sawbridge, was an active South Sea Company director as well, while another director, Thomas Hawes, was closely related to the South Sea director Francis Hawes.[3] Whether or not because of these ties, the Million Bank's directors decided early in 1720 that they would exchange their annuities for new South Sea stock. In some ways this decision was the most critical one taken in 1720, for unless this very large creditor had agreed to the South Sea scheme it is unlikely that the smaller holders of annuities would have followed suit.

If the Million Bank was to participate in the scheme as fully as possible,

---

[1] See below, p. 311.

[2] P.R.O. Chancery Masters' Exhibits, C 114/9, ledger of the Million Bank 1717–21, ff. 48, 72.

[3] The names of Million Bank directors present at court meetings are shown in its minutes, P.R.O. Chancery Masters' Exhibits C 114/17, Million Bank Directors' Ct. Bk. 1714–24. The directors in 1720 included Urban Hall, Sir Dennis Dutry, Laurence Hatsell Thomas Hawes, Sir Bibye Lake and Jacob Sawbridge. Hall and Lake were both connected with the Royal African Company. In 1710 Hall was an African director, as well as being an East India director. In 1723 Bibye Lake was Deputy Governor of the African Company.

however, it would have to accelerate the process, which had been going on since the 1690s, of acquiring direct long annuities, since these alone could be exchanged for South Sea stock. As it could hardly kill off the life-tenants, it had no alternative to bribing them by high prices into selling their reversions. On 25 February 1720, before the South Sea proposals had even passed the House of Commons, the Million Bank directors accordingly resolved

that this Bank will from this Day give One hundred and thirty Pounds for the Estate for life of each fourteen Pounds p. ann. of which they [i.e. the Bank] have the Revertion.[1]

This was about $9\frac{1}{2}$ years' purchase. In June they raised their offer to 12 years' purchase, and in July, at the height of the Bubble, to 14 years' purchase.[2] In the course of the spring and summer they paid 'about 40,000 li' for life interests, bringing the bank's holdings of direct annuities up from £14,766 p.a. to £19,264 p.a., all of which was exchanged for South Sea stock and bonds, the greater part in May, the rest in August.[3] The bank received £154,308 South Sea stock and £84,172 South Sea bonds.[4] The transaction may have been coloured by the fact that to finance its purchases of life interests and to pay a 20% midsummer dividend it had had to borrow £60,000 from the South Sea Company itself.[5] The Bank of England followed a similar policy to that of the Million Bank. By August 1720 it had bought up a quarter of a million ordinary stock. It exchanged the whole of it for South Sea stock in August.[6] When institutional investors as important as these were so eager to climb on the South Sea bandwagon, it is hardly surprising that the rank and file of government creditors acted as precipitately as they did.

In ordinary ('redeemable') government stock there were no very large holdings on the eve of the South Sea Bubble equivalent to the Million Bank's portfolio of annuities, but there was an important minority of holders of £10,000 and upwards. Thus in the big (£9·5m.) 5% (1717) stock there were 75 such accounts at Michaelmas 1719, controlling £1,368,000 stock, an average holding of £18,240.[7] Just as the attitude of the Million Bank to the South Sea scheme was likely to decide the fate of the annuity subscrip-

---

[1] Ibid., f. 254. [2] Ibid., ff. 275 (2 June 1720) and 292 (21 July 1720).
[3] For these figures ibid., ff. 331–2, 6 April 1721, report for the General Court.
[4] Ibid. [5] Ibid.
[6] Bank of England General Ledger 7, f. 162. At 31 August 1720 the Bank held £289,680 'redeemable' stock, all save £32,500 of which it had bought in the course of the year. It exchanged it all for South Sea stock.
[7] List compiled from the ledgers for 5% (1717) stock, Bank of England Record Office.

tions, the attitude of these and a handful of other big holders was likely to decide the success of the subscriptions of 'Redeemables'. The list opens with the Amicable Society for a Perpetual Assurance Office, which owned £10,000 stock. There was one other corporate holder, the Bank of England, which owned £32,500, but the remaining accounts were for individuals. Six of these were women, including the rich widow Elizabeth Howland of Streatham (£10,820). There were thirty-three merchants, four goldsmith bankers, and eleven lawyers, five of whom were Chancery Masters. All had London addresses. Among the nineteen others were James Lowther, Esq., 'of Whitehaven in Cumberland' (£11,541), Sir John Sherrard, Bart., 'of Lepthorp in Lincolnshire' (£13,000),[1] and Frederick Tylney 'of Rotherwick, Hampshire' (£10,000).

Broadly the same pattern of top ownership is characteristic of Bank, East India and South Sea stock in 1723–4,[2] but by this date foreign plutocrats had joined the English ones. Of 48 proprietors of £10,000 or more East India stock at this date, for example, fourteen were foreigners (three of whom were women).[3] The big English East India proprietors all had London addresses. Six were Jewish, including the merchant Anthony da Costa, who held £31,331 stock, the merchant Francis Pereira (£85,075), and the physician Fernando Mendes (£27,010). Merchants were also prominent among the remainder: for instance Abraham Craiesteyn (£36,800), Sir Peter Delmé (£47,700), Sir Dennis Dutry (£14,271), Sir Gregory Page (£10,000) and Charles Savage sen. (£10,000). John Morse (£12,000) was a goldsmith banker, and William Fellowes (£20,000) a Chancery Master. The only two domestic women proprietors of £10,000 or more East India stock were the widows Leonora Frederick (£10,533) and Lady Elizabeth Germain (£25,000).[4] Other large proprietors were Spencer Compton, M.P., Speaker

---

[1] The estate was Lopthorpe, North Witham, Lincs. Sherrard had contributed £400 to the Tontine loan in 1693.

[2] For sources see those listed under Table 37, above, p. 275.

[3] For big foreign stockholdings at this date see below, p. 315.

[4] Lady 'Betty' Germain (1680–1769), second daughter of Charles, Earl of Berkeley. Married (1706) as his second wife Sir John Germain, a soldier of fortune who was reputed a bastard son of William II of Holland. Germain inherited great wealth from his first wife (d. 1705), the heiress of Henry, Earl of Peterborough. Germain died in 1718, leaving Lady Betty all his property. He asked her to leave it, if she did not remarry, to one of the children of Lionel Sackville, Duke of Dorset, the son-in-law of his comrade in arms, General Walter Colyear. When Lady Betty died in 1769, allegedly with £120,000 in the funds, she left her fortune to Dorset's second son, Lord George Sackville, on condition that he

of the House of Commons (£12,000), Lucy Knightley, Esq., of Fawsley (£26,000) and the physician Caleb Cotesworth (£25,010).

Nineteen of these forty-eight big East India proprietors, including five of the foreigners, were among the 139 holders of £10,000 or more Bank stock at the same date, an overlap of top ownership between the two stocks of about 10%. For example Anthony da Costa held £42,929 Bank stock, Caleb Cotesworth £14,000, Abraham Craiesteyn £70,550, Sir Dennis Dutry £34,738, William Fellowes £18,500, Lucy Knightley £32,500 and Francis Pereira £109,162. These big Bank stock proprietors included twenty-three foreigners.[1] Of the domestic owners, eleven lived in England outside London and the Home Counties, the remainder lived in London itself. The provincial stockholders included Abraham Crompton sen., 'Derby gent.'; (£25,600), Sir William Daines, Knt., Bristol (£11,000); Caleb Dickinson, Esq., 'of Monk's House. Wilts.' (£10,600); and Sir John Sherrard (£10,000) and Frederick Tylney (£13,000), who had been big proprietors of 5% (1717) stock a few years earlier.[2] Nine of the London proprietors were lawyers, including Sir Littleton Powys, a judge of the King's Bench (£15,000). Among other big holders were the Exchequer officials John Grainger (£10,000) and John Taylour (£20,000), Richard Crawley, 'deceased, of Doctors' Commons', Sir Isaac Newton 'of St. Martin's street near Leicester Fields, Knt.' (£11,000) and Sir Thomas Colby, Bart., 'of Kensington'. Four big holders were peers — William, Earl of (sic) Cadogan (£18,753), William, Earl Cowper deceased (£14,300), John, Duke of Marlborough deceased (£83,355) and Thomas, Earl of Pembroke (£77,500). The only English women proprietors in this group were all members of the aristocracy: Lady Elizabeth Germain (£11,700) and the Duchesses of Devonshire (£11,600), Marlborough (£25,280), and Kendall (£10,000).

The majority of the big London owners of Bank stock were members of the mercantile bourgeoisie. An alphabetical list would start with Abraham Craiesteyn 'London, merchant' (£70,550) and run through Sir Gerard Conyers, 'Knight and Alderman' (£12,660), Sir Peter Delmé, similarly described (£118,358), and Sir Dennis Dutry 'London, Bart.' (£34,738) to John Thompson 'Crooked Lane, London, merchant' (£10,700) and Sir

change his name to Germain. It was by this roundabout route that in 1770 Lord George Sackville became Lord George Germain, and inherited a vast fortune, without any tie of blood and purely on the strength of a military friendship dating from the 1690s. Thus the fortunes of war did not always deal him reverses.

[1] See p. 315 below.   [2] See above, p. 278.

John Ward 'Knight and Alderman' (£20,000). There were also the London brewers Thomas Beacon (£35,400) and Josias Nicolson (£13,500), the distiller Philip Hall, of Aldgate (£12,050), the London bankers (described as 'goldsmith'), Francis Child (£12,900), Henry Hoare (£13,375) and James Martin (£28,700), the bookseller Thomas Guy (£16,335) and the broker Thomas Shuttleworth 'of Bartholomew Lane' (£10,000). Only one large proprietor, Anthony da Costa (£42,929), was Jewish. Lastly, only two of the big holdings were in more than one name; one of these was a trust account for the Bank of England itself.[1]

Many of these big Bank and East India proprietors were also holders of £10,000 or more South Sea stock at midsummer 1723.[2] Sir Peter Delmé, for instance had £122,103 stock of his own and held a further £150,468 with his fellow director John Hanger in trust for the Bank of England. (This was presumably largely acquired when the Bank exchanged its redeemable stock in 1720.)[3] Delmé's personal account was only exceeded by that of Sir Dennis Dutry (£141,660). Among other large South Sea proprietors were George Dodington, deceased, (£28,540), Sir Robert Furnese (£36,000), King George I (£15,383), Lady Elizabeth Germain again (£50,520), the Duchess of Kendall (£47,000), James Lowther, Esq., of Whitehaven (£29,400), Dudley North, Esq. (£31,108), and the Earl of Pembroke (£69,052). As a corporate owner of stock, the Bank of England was only rivalled by the Million Bank (£136,147) and the Canton of Berne. whose vast holding of £253,000 was easily the largest at this date. It originated in a loan which the Canton had made to the English government in 1710, the securities for it being exchanged for South Sea stock in 1711. Subsequently the Canton increased its holding, retained it during the Bubble, despite rumours that it had sold out, and later bought Bank stock as well.[4]

Holdings by peers in three important stocks — Bank and East India stock and the 5%s of 1717 — were not significant on the eve of the South Sea

---

[1] John Hanger and four other directors held £41,350 stock which had been pledged for loans made in 1720, see above, p. 192. The other multiple account was for Robert Heysham, deceased, Peter Godfrey, Esq., and Micajah Perry jun. (£10,000).

[2] Opening ledgers for South Sea Old Annuities, Bank of England Record Office. These ledgers were opened when the company's share capital was divided in two, see above p. 272.

[3] See above, p. 277.

[4] For the Canton's original loan of £150,000 see above, p. 62; for rumours of it selling out in 1720 see above, p. 150; for its holding in 1750, see below, p. 329. The growth of the original holding was presumably due to reinvestment of dividends.

Bubble.[1] There were forty-five accounts in the names of six spiritual and thirty-nine temporal peers. Several peers were acting as trustees and some acted more than once. The total they owned was £154,881, less than 1% of the nearly £18m. stock involved. Only a few of these noble accounts were of any size. Lord Cadogan owned £5,132 Bank stock. Lord Cowper had £24,757, in two stocks. Lord Halifax held £10,000 Bank stock, and the Duke of Marlborough £27,830, by far the biggest peer's holding. George, Earl of Orkney, a Scottish Representative Peer from 1708 to 1737, held £7,000 Bank stock. All the other accounts were for amounts well under £5,000.

Holdings of stock by M.P.s were beginning to be more numerous. In these three stocks, and in the 14% long annuities, there were 158 accounts for M.P.s in January 1720. Of these M.P.s, sixty-eight held in one stock only, twenty-eight in two, ten in three and one, Sir Gilbert Heathcote, in all four, reducing the net number of holders to 107, nearly a fifth of the House.[2] The total stock controlled, £573,056, was however less than 3% of the total of about £21m.[3] The greater number of these M.P.s belonged to the official, legal, financial and mercantile groups in Parliament. To take some examples from Bank stock, John Aislabie, the Chancellor of the Exchequer, held £4,000, Sir George Caswall, a leading director of the Sword Blade Bank, £42,668, Sir John Cope, a director of the Bank of England, £4,000, the East India merchant Sir Matthew Decker £14,025, Alexander Denton of the Middle Temple £1,000, Fleetwood Dormer of Lincoln's Inn £2,000, and so on. There were some holders who were country gentlemen, like Sir Dewey Bulkeley of Burgate, Hants (£300 Bank stock), or Sir Richard How, Bart., of Whishford, Wilts. (£244 5% (1717) stock), but the amount they owned was generally small. This rough-and-ready division between 'funded' and 'landed' M.P.s was still true at the mid-century, though by then the former and their investments had both increased.[4]

Women stockholders were an important minority of all owners. The figures for five stocks before and after the South Sea Bubble are shown in Table 38.

[1] Ledgers for these stocks, Bank of England Record Office. The date taken was 1 January 1720.

[2] The number of accounts, followed by their amount was: Bank stock 53 (£239,716); East India stock 39 (£129,344); 5% (1717) stock 47 (£152,396); 14%s 20 (at 20 years' purchase £51,600).

[3] Capitalizing the £124,000 p.a. 14% at fourteen years' purchase and adding this to the capital of the other three stocks.

[4] See below, p. 296.

TABLE 38

Women as owners of stock 1719–24

Sample of 14% annuities Mich. 1719			Sample of 5%s (1717) at Mich. 1719			Sample of South Sea stock midsummer 1723		
Nos.	% total in sample	£	% total in sample	Nos.	% total in sample	£	% total in sample	
Nos.	% total in sample	£	% total in sample	Nos.	% total in sample	£	% total in sample	
50	21·3	29,140	18·4	592	34·7	271,400	20·1	176	20·9	127,390	11·9

Bank stock 25 March 1724				Sample (A–C) East India stock midsummer 1724			
Nos.	% total in sample	£	% total in sample	Nos.	% total in sample	£	% total in sample
964	20·7	1,124,984	12·6	83	19·0	83,709	11·0

Source: See Table 37 (above, p. 275). The Table includes a minority of women stock-holders domiciled abroad. For foreign-domiciled women stockholders see below, p. 325.

The very high proportion of women holders in the 5%s was probably due to the fact that this stock originated in the state lotteries of 1711–12, in which many small investors would have had a flutter. The proportion of women proprietors to the total number of proprietors was much the same — about one-fifth — in each of the other four stocks, but the amount they owned was higher (18%) in the long annuities than in the three companies (11%–12%).

By this date the Huguenot community in London had become fairly well absorbed into English society, and its ownership of securities is therefore no longer of particular significance. In Bank stock in March 1724 there seem to have been about 250 accounts for English Huguenots out of the total of 4,662 accounts, a proportion of about 6%, as in 1709.[1] In a sample of 400 accounts in East India stock at the same date only fourteen (just over 3%) were for English Huguenots. The Jewish contribution, too, was small. In

[1] See above, Table 36.

the same East India sample there were only half a dozen English Jewish accounts. In Bank stock there were about 130 English Jewish accounts at the same date. It must of course be remembered that some of the biggest holders of stock were Jews or — less significantly — of Huguenot extraction. In general, however, these domestic minorities were of less significance by this date than the growing body of foreign, particularly Dutch, investors; with whom English Jews and Huguenots sometimes had close ties of trade and family.[1]

Although most owners were individuals, trustee and other joint holdings continued to be an important minority of all accounts. For example, in Bank stock in March 1724 there were 202 trust, joint or multiple accounts (just over 4% of total accounts) controlling £287,021 stock (just over 3% of total stock).[2] In addition, about 290 individual Bank stock accounts are noted as 'deceased', a further 6·2% of the total number. It is a reasonable assumption that the greater part of the joint or multiple accounts were for trustees or executors and that the deceased proprietors' accounts would in due course be transferred to executors. Any increase in the time needed to clear an estate legally for distribution to beneficiaries would have had the automatic effect of increasing the amount of stock thus held. This is perhaps the explanation, or part of it, for the increase in multiple holdings of stock by the mid-century.[3]

Another aspect of the importance of trust accounts was the proliferation of small corporate or quasi-corporate holdings. In Bank and East India stock such accounts, like Clare Hall's £3,600 Bank stock, or the £70 East India stock held by the 'Clergy Mens Sons Charity', were infrequent. In South Sea stock they were numerous. Among them at this date were the Clothworkers', Clockmakers', Fishmongers', Stationers' and Scriveners' Companies; Magdalen and Merton Colleges, Oxford (£409 and £500), and King's College, Cambridge (£233); various charity schools in London; the Workhouse for the Poor at Hackney (£100); the Hospital for Poor French Protestants in Great Britain (£2,140); the Corporation, President and Fellows of Sion College (£145); the Dean and Chapter of Rochester Cathedral (£780); the corporation of Yarmouth £2,798); the Master and Governors of 'the Scotts Corporation' (£860); the Mayor, Constables and

---

[1] See below, p. 314.

[2] These totals exclude the £41,350 Bank stock held in trust by five Bank directors; this was the balance of stock pledged to the Bank as security for loans in 1720, see above, p. 194.

[3] See below, p. 299.

Society of Merchants of the Staple of England (£262).[1] These examples could be multiplied. In view of the relative infrequency of such accounts in Bank and East India stock, and of the proportionately large number of very small South Sea proprietors, they suggest that as a result of the Bubble numerous quasi-charitable holdings of government securities were transferred into the South Sea Company, and that its stock quickly came to be regarded as a trustee investment, which ought not to be subjected to the fluctuations of trade. This helps to explain the conversion of the greater part of the company's capital in 1723 and 1733 into fixed-interest annuities, in which very large trustee holdings had been built up by the 1740s.[2] Bank and East India stock, where the average unit of ownership was a good deal larger than in South Sea stock, can have had far less attraction for poor trustees.

VI

Examination of some of the subscriptions to war loans in the 1740s, and of the ownership of certain government stocks in the same period, shows that several of the trends previously noticed had remained constant, while others had become more pronounced. By the middle of the eighteenth century the total of government stock had increased to about £77m.[3] In 1719, when it was about £52m., the number of public creditors was about 40,000.[4] Assuming a constant proportion between numbers and stock, one would expect the number of public creditors in 1752 to have been about 59,000. Examination of the ledgers at this date shows that the total number of *accounts* was in fact about 59,000, distributed as in Table 39.

Sample comparison of various stocks suggests that the allowance of 10% made for overlap of ownership in previous analyses is still reasonably accurate.[5]

---

[1] South Sea Old Annuities, opening ledgers (Bank of England Record Office).

[2] See below, p. 299.

[3] i.e. £70·4m. at Michaelmas 1749 (above, Table 26, p. 232) with the 3%s of 1726 (£1m.) the East India 3½% (1750) (£2·9m.) the South Sea 3%s (1751) (£2·1m.) and the Exchequer annuities (£0·2m.) added.

[4] See above, p. 273.

[5] For instance a sample of one hundred names chosen at random from the alphabet books for 3% Consols contained fourteen names which also occur in South Sea Old Annuities (1st subscription ledgers). Of one hundred names in South Sea Old Annuities, twenty-five occur in South Sea New Annuities. Of a given number of names chosen at random from

TABLE 39

*Estimated number of accounts in Government
and allied stock 1752*

Bank stock	4,750
East India Stock	2,140
South Sea stock	4,000
South Sea annuities	19,539
South Sea 3%s (1751)	1,322
East India 3½%s	1,150
Reduced 3%s	12,645
Consols 3%	7,373
3% (1726)	900
Exchequer annuities	5,000
	58,819

Source : Ledgers for these stocks at the Bank of England Record Office,
except South Sea stock and Exchequer annuities. The estimate
for South Sea stock is based on the printed list of voting proprietors at 25 December 1747 (Goldsmiths' Library Extra Size
Fol. xviii (49)), which contains 1,740 names. It has been
assumed that these were about 40% of the total number of
owners (only those with £1,000 or more stock could vote). The
figure for Exchequer annuities is based on their amount, which
was £0·211m. p.a., assuming (on the basis of an average £33
p.a. in 1719, see p. 274) an average holding of £40 p.a.

This would give a net total of about 53,000 owners. Since about 10% of all
accounts were in joint or multiple ownership, however, the actual number of
public creditors on the eve of the Seven Years War was probably around
60,000.[1] As several of these were corporate or quasi-corporate bodies, the
number of those (shareholders, litigants, beneficiaries under trusts) involved
in government bonds at one remove must have been at least as large again.

the Consols alphabets, twelve to fifteen usually occur, too, in the alphabets for 'Reduced
Threes'. These and some other figures suggest an overlap of about 7% between some
stocks and about 12% between others (overlap being defined as above, p. 260 n. 4). 10%
overlap seems a reasonable compromise allowance. Overlap between big holdings at this
date was as high as 18% (below, p. 292).

[1] Adopting from this the very rough formula that the net number of accounts was
three-quarters of the public debt divided by 1,000, the number of accounts in 1815, when

Hume's estimate in 1752 that the public creditors numbered only 17,000 is thus clearly much too small, but may derive from confusion of the number of owners of 3% Consols and Reduced Threes, who totalled about 18,000, with the whole body of stockholders.[1]

During the War of the Spanish Succession there had been marked differences between the structure of subscriptions to government annuities and subscriptions for company capital, and between the ownership of Bank and East India stock.[2] Table 40, which compares the subscription to the government loan of 1742 with the ownership of four important stocks, shows that these contrasts had persisted, and, if anything, become more noticeable.

The greater part (69%) of the 1742 loan was taken up by big subscribers, many of whom must have been stags, i.e. have come in in order to resell at a profit. When the stock ledgers for this loan were opened, six of the twenty subscribers of £10,000 or more had sold all their stock, and four more had reduced their subscriptions by 50% or more. Of the thirty-nine subscribers of £5,000 — £9,999, ten sold out, and a further eight reduced their subscriptions by 50% or more. The twenty largest subscribers, with the stags starred, were as shown in Table 41. What were their backgrounds?

Backer, Colebrooke, Dobree, Gideon, both Isaacs, Lascelles (a partner in Lascelles & Maxwell), Muilman, Newnham and Salvador were all prominent merchants.[3] Gibson, Martin, Mee and Snow were financiers. Wilkinson, who in the early 1720s was 'of Copthall Court bookkeeper', was rising into prominence as a government loan and remittance contractor; in 1748 he subscribed £10,000 to the huge loan which made the conclusion

the debt reached a peak of £670m., would have been of the order of 510,000. In June 1815 the Bank of England stated that it had deducted income-tax from 565,600 accounts for the year ended 5 April, 1815 ('Resolutions Proposed concerning [the] Bank of England', dated 26 June 1815, in the author's possession). Presumably tax was deducted from all domestic accounts. There were in addition around 20,000 exempt foreign accounts and around 25,000 accounts at East India House and South Sea House, making the total number 605,000 or 545,000 if 10% overlapped. A figure of about 530,000 may thus be taken as the approximate size of the 'funded interest' that Cobbett and the squirearchy detested.

[1] Hume's estimate is in his essay 'Of Public Credit' (*Philosophical Works*, ed. Green and Grove, iii (1875), 373 n.). The number of accounts in Consols and Reduced Threes, if reduced by 10% for overlap, would give about 18,000 proprietors.

[2] See above, p. 261.

[3] Muilman was in partnership in London with his brother Pieter from about 1740. They were sons of Pieter Schout Muilman, a banker of Amsterdam. (J. Elias, *Vroedschap van Amsterdam*, ii (Haarlem, 1905), 866, 869.)

TABLE 40

Ownership of loan subscription and various stocks
1742–53

Category	1 Subscription to 3% loan 1742				2 South Sea Old Annuities, balances in first ledger, 25 March 1744			
£	Nos.	%	£	%	Nos.	%	£	%
Under 500 .	24	9·5	5,200	0·7	805	52·8	156,962	8·7
500–999 . .	52	20·6	27,650	3·5	274	17·9	184,136	10·2
1000–4999 .	117	46·4	215,650	26·9	393	25·8	754,768	41·8
5000–9999 .	39	15·5	230,500	28·8	36	2·4	251,740	14·0
10,000 and over .	20	8·0	321,000	40·1	17	1·1	456,591	25·3
Average holding	..	..	[3,175]	..	..	..	[1,183]	..
TOTALS .	252	100·0	800,000	100·0	1525	100·0	1,804,197	100·0

Category	3 East India stock, 25 March 1748				4 4% stock (1748) sample February–May 1750			
£	Nos.	%	£	%	Nos.	%	£	%
Under 500 .	460	21·3	100,714	3·2	843	38·2	142,320	4·2
500–999 . .	678	31·4	367,197	11·5	422	19·1	258,241	7·7
1000–4999 .	908	42·0	1,607,482	50·3	782	35·4	1,454,258	43·3
5000–9999 .	77	3·6	479,363	15·0	113	5·1	692,566	20·6
10,000 and over .	37	1·7	639,324	20·0	49	2·2	815,207	24·2
Average holding	..	..	[1,478]	..	..	..	[1,522]	..
TOTALS .	2160	100·0	3,194,080	100·0	2209	100·0	3,362,592	100·0

Category	5 Bank stock, balances in first ledger, 10 October 1753			
£	Nos.	%	£	%
Under 500 .	264	21·5	64,329	2·4
500–999 .	282	22·9	172,237	6·3
1000–4999 .	583	47·5	1,168,688	42·8
5000–9999 .	62	5·1	400,531	14·7
10,000 and over .	37	3·0	923,867	33·8
Average holding	..	..	[2,223]	..
TOTALS .	1228	100.0	2,729,652	100·0

Source : Ledgers for these stocks, Bank of England Record Office.

TABLE 41

Subscribers of £10,000 or more in the 3% loan 1742

	£
*John Backer	
Mark Lane, merchant	10,000
†James Colebrooke	
New Broad Street	20,000
William Dobree	
Monument Yard, merchant	10,000
Thomas Gibson	
Lothbury	10,000
Samson Gideon	
Ludgate Street, merchant	35,000
*Benjamin Isaac	
Magpie Alley, Fenchurch Street, gent. . . .	15,000
†Henry Isaac	
Fenchurch Buildings, gent.	15,000
Henry Lascelles	
Mincing Lane, merchant	20,000
†Lord William Manners	
Burlington Street	15,000
*James Martin	
Lombard Street	10,000
†Benjamin Mee	
Gracechurch Street, later Clapham, merchant . .	15,000
*Henry Muilman	
Devonshire Square, merchant	25,000
Nathaniel Newnham	
Watling Street	10,000
Martha Parker	
Leicester Fields, spinster	10,500
Duke of Rutland	20,000
*Francis Salvador	
Lime Street, merchant	10,000
Judith Sambrooke	
Basinghall Street, later Berkeley Square, spinster .	15,500
Thomas Snow	
Temple Bar, goldsmith	10,000
Duke of Somerset	20,000
*Pinckney Wilkinson	
New Bond Street	25,000
	321,000

* Sold out before stock ledgers opened.
† Reduced by 50% or more.

Source: Subscription ledger for 1742 3% loan, Bank of England
Record Office. Descriptions from the alphabet to this stock.

of peace feasible.[1] The introduction of assignable subscription receipts in 1743 must have facilitated this kind of stagging.[2] In 1744 the government loan of £1·8m. was largely taken up by the lists of nine contractors:[3]

	£			£
Samson Gideon	. 300,000	Richard Jackson	.	90,000
John Gore	. 150,000	John Edwards	.	90,000
John Bristow	. 150,000	Peter Burrell	.	90,000
Gerard van Neck	. 150,000	Henry Lassels [sic]		90,000
Roger Drake	. 90,000			

Each of these would have subscribed heavily on his own account. Yet when dealings in scrip ended, and the stock ledgers were opened, four had already sold out, and none of the other five had more than a few pounds of stock.[4]

The government loans of 1747 and 1748 were floated on Sir John Barnard's principle of bypassing the contractors by throwing subscriptions open to the public.[5] Ironically, this method accentuated instead of diminishing the trend to monopoly. Thus, in the great loan of £6·3m. in 1748, £2,851,500 — 45% of the total — was taken up by 139 subscribers, an average of £20,514 each.[6] When dealings in scrip closed, and the stock ledgers were opened, 21 of these big subscribers had retained or increased their original contributions, and 15 others had not reduced theirs by more than half. The other 103 had either drastically reduced their balances or sold out completely.[7] These stags included Samson Gideon, the chief government loan agent, whose enormous subscription of £590,000 was reduced to nothing by the time the ledgers opened, and Jeremiah Joye 'of Winchester Street, merchant', whose subscription of £155,000 was reduced by the time the ledgers opened to £1,000. None of the stags was a foreigner, but at least

[1] Wilkinson is described as a bookkeeper in East India stock ledger 1718–23, f. 735 (Bank of England Record Office). He proposed to remit to Flanders with Henry Muilman in January 1743 (Cal. T. Papers 1742–5, 226).

[2] 16 Geo. II, c. 13. Previously transfers of scrip were registered at the Bank and entered in the subscription ledger, see above, p. 217.

[3] Names of the loan contractors from Gent. Mag. (1744), 'Hist. Chronicle' under '9 April'; in addition to the contractors the Treasury put in a list for £600,000. For the system of subscription lists see above, p. 220.

[4] Ledgers for 3% (1744) stock, Bank of England Record Office.   [5] See above, p. 226.

[6] Subscription ledger for this stock, Bank of England Record Office. Apart from the ledger for 1742 this is the only subscription ledger to survive for the 1740s. Initial entries were for first payments, the loan being in ten instalments. Subsequent payments were entered seriatim.

[7] Stock ledgers for 4% (1748) stock. Bank of England Record Office.

two, John Edwards and Henry Muilman, were clearly subscribing on behalf of foreign, mainly Dutch, correspondents.

Among the big subscribers to this loan who retained or increased their contribution were several of the politically-favoured investors who were presumably able to come in on the ground floor when a loan was floated. They included the peers Lord Anson (£20,000) and Lord Ilchester (£15,000), and the M.P.s Henry Fox (£15,000), George Grenville (£10,000), Sir Dudley Ryder (£10,000), Admiral Sir Challoner Ogle (£14,000) and Admiral Isaac Townshend (£12,000).[1] But most of the M.P.s among big subscribers sold out; of twenty-six who subscribed £10,000 or more, twelve had sold out by the time the stock ledgers opened, and seven others had reduced their subscription by well over 50%.[2]

This evidence suggests that the services of a relatively small circle of London financiers were essential to the success of government loans. The political hangers-on, whom ministers were able to gratify by letting them into subscriptions early, were dependent on the skill of these professionals. Their boycott would put any subscription in peril, as the Pitt–Devonshire ministry discovered in the early stages of the Seven Years War.[3] There was therefore some justification for Sir John Barnard's contention that the 'Undertakers' had acquired an entrenched — and lucrative — monopoly position in government finance.[4] Disappointingly for him, however, the flank of their position was not turned by making subscriptions open to the public. The process of initial partly speculative subscriptions, followed by brisk dealing in scrip until the latter reached its final owners' hands, was characteristic of both closed and open loans. And if anything it was more characteristic of the second than the first.

The structure of ownership of stock at the mid-eighteenth century (Table 40 on p. 287 above) differed in important respects from the structure of subscriptions. There were many more small investors. In both Bank and East India stock at the mid-century they formed 21% of the total number of accounts. In the 4%s at the same period they formed 38%, and in South Sea annuities a few years earlier as much as 53%, of all accounts. The proportion of stock this group controlled was, however, very small: as low

---

[1] Townshend, who was M.P. for Portsmouth, subscribed £6,000 and later increased this to £14,000. The other four listed retained the amount they subscribed.

[2] Ledgers for 4% (1748) stock. Bank of England Record Office.

[3] Dr. L. S. Sutherland, 'The City of London and the Devonshire–Pitt Administration, 1756–7', Raleigh Lecture on History, British Academy, 1960.

[4] For Barnard's complaints see above, p. 224.

as 2·4% in Bank stock, and even in South Sea annuities only reaching 8·7%. Investors holding between £500 and £1,000 were far more important in East India stock (31·4% of all accounts) than in Bank stock (22·9%) or in South Sea annuities and the 4%s (18% to 19%); this must have been connected with the £500 East India voting qualification. The proportion of stock which this group controlled ranged from 6·3% in Bank stock to 11·5% in East India stock, with the 4%s (7·7%) and South Sea annuities (10·2%) in between. The holders of £1,000 to £5,000 stock were very important. In the Bank of England they controlled 47·5% of all accounts, and owned 42·8% of the stock, and in the East India Company 42% of all accounts, owning no less than 50% of the stock. In the 4%s the proportions (35·4% and 43·3%) were a little lower. In South Sea annuities this group was less as a proportion of total numbers (25·8%) but, surprisingly, owned a nearly equal proportion (41·8%) of total stock.

At the top of the scale (£5,000 and over) big investors were only 3·5% (South Sea annuities) to 8·1% (Bank stock) of total numbers, but owned a large proportion of total stock. This varied from 35% in East India stock to as high as 48·5% in Bank stock, with South Sea annuities (39·3%) and the 4%s (44·8%) in between. South Sea annuities were clearly still the characteristic stock for small investors, though the 4%s (and presumably government stock in general) were also popular. This left a proportionally smaller group of medium owners (£1,000–£5,000) in South Sea annuities than in Bank or East India stock, but their average holding must have been larger than in the companies for their proportion of the total stock to be similar. Concentration at the top was less marked in the East India Company than in either of the other three stocks. John Company's medium stockholders (£1,000–£5,000) had clearly been gaining ground at the expense of the biggest proprietors since 1709. They had then controlled 46·3% of total stock and the big stockholders (£5,000 and over) 53·4%.[1] In 1724 these proportions were 44·7% and 43·2%.[2] By 1748 they were 50·3% and 35%. In contrast to this spreading of East India ownership, big holders of Bank stock controlled 48·5% of the stock in 1753 compared with only 30·7% in 1709. The proportion of 48·5% was virtually unchanged since 1724 (49·1%) but the holders of £10,000 and more had increased their holdings from 30·2% in 1724 to 33·8%.

There was thus some substance behind the complaints in Parliament in 1737 about 'our over-grown rich stockholders',[3] or Bolingbroke's reference

[1] See above, p. 261. Table 34. [2] See above, p. 275. Table 37.
[3] *Parl. Hist.* x. 90, 28 March 1737.

in 1749 to the 'principal men in our great companies, who, born to serve and obey, have been bred to command even government itself'.[1] What was the structure of this plutocracy, whose decisions must have been so important to the success of Henry Pelham's reduction of the interest on the public debt? Some light can be thrown on this by examining the accounts containing £10,000 and over in five important stocks at 1 March 1750. The total number of accounts was 447 in the names of 365 proprietors, an overlap between stocks of 18%. The group held £8,985,201, 21% of the total. The most important subgroup within it was ten corporate or quasi-corporate bodies controlling between them £1,946,975.

TABLE 42

Large corporate owners of stock 1 March 1750

	£
The Accountant-General of Chancery	1,138,188
The Amicable Society for a Perpetual Assurance Office .	12,400
Queen Anne's Bounty	224,800
The Bank of England	52,467
The Canton of Berne	357,311
Nathaniel Blackerby, dec., Treasurer to the Commissioners for building 50 new churches	20,859
The Drapers' Company	20,950
The Goldsmiths' Company	15,000
The London Assurance (Fire)	76,500
The Parnassims of the Portuguese Jewish Nation at Amsterdam	28,500
	£1,946,975

Source: Ledgers for Bank, East India and 4% (1748) stock and for South Sea Old and New Annuities, all at the Bank of England Record Office.

The office of the Accountant-General of Chancery was created in 1726 to unify the administration of suitors' funds previously under the control of the Chancery Masters. This step was taken after speculation by individual Masters during the South Sea Bubble, and the sale of Masterships by Lord

[1] Henry St. John, Viscount Bolingbroke, *Works* (1754), iii. 169.

Chancellor Macclesfield, for which he was impeached in 1725, had cast doubts on the previous system.[1] A major part of government and company stock affected by Chancery suits was evidently transferred to the Accountant-General's name. He also invested suitors' cash in government stock, and was a considerable purchaser of short-term securities.[2] The growing volume and dilatoriness of Chancery business put more and more funds under his control; by the middle of the eighteenth century he held nearly £1·4m. in various government stocks.[3] So far as the market was concerned this sum was virtually immobilized. The holdings of the Commissioners of Queen Anne's Bounty, who had started buying in 1725, of the Canton of Berne, whose ownership dated back to Anne's reign, and of the Parnassims of the Portuguese Jewish Nation, were similar in their effect. This withdrawal of large blocks of securities into trust accounts must have helped support the price of the remainder. A second sub-group of large holdings consisted of accounts held jointly or by three or more persons. There were twenty-three of the first, and thirty-four of the second kind, and these fifty-seven accounts controlled £779,327 stock, 8·6% of the total. Several of the accounts are stated as subject to the orders of the Court of Chancery. It seems plausible to assume that the majority were trustee and executors' accounts of one sort or another.

A third sub-group, whose holdings were almost as important as those of the first, consisted of ninety-four foreign accounts, which controlled £1,633,715 stock. If the Canton of Berne's £357,311 is added, this becomes £1,991,026. Most of these proprietors were Dutch. Only a handful were

---

[1] See 12 Geo. I, c. 32, 'An Act for better securing the Monies and Effects of the Suitors of the Court of Chancery.' Cf. also 11 Geo. I, c. 2, which indemnified Masters for disclosing what price they had paid for their offices, and 12 Geo. I, c. 23, 'An Act for the Relief of the Suitors of the High Court of Chancery.' *The Accompts of the Several Masters of the High Court of Chancery* were published by J. Buckley in 1725. The Accountants-General in this period were Henry Edwards, July–December 1726; Francis Cudworth Masham, December 1726–May 1731; Mark Thurston, May 1731–August 1749; John Waple, August 1749–October 1759. The next Accountant-General was Peter Davall. All were Chancery Masters as well.

[2] See below, pp. 434–5. In addition to the stock controlled by the Accountant-General, officers of the Court of Exchequer and other law courts sometimes held stock in trust. For an example see p. 295 below.

[3] Taking the balances transferred to John Waple in August 1749, which were £116,060 Bank stock, £1,057,659 South Sea annuities, £164,510 4% stock, £11,631 3% stock and £26,262 East India stock, a total of £1,376,122 (ledgers for these stocks, Bank of England Record Office).

Jewish.[1] Fourth, there were twenty-eight accounts for members of the English, Irish and Scots peerage, often acting as trustees under wills and settlements. Headed by the Marlborough family, with £276,154, they controlled £787,947 stock.[2] Several of these aristocratic proprietors were women, including Frances, Lady Dillon (£18,000), the inevitable Lady Elizabeth Germain (£83,400), the Duchess of Montague (£20,000), and the deceased Duchesses of Kendall (£10,000) and Marlborough (£88,000). There were seventeen other women among the big stockholders, nearly all widows or unmarried daughters of London merchants: for example, Dame Mary Abney, widow (£11,000), Ann Crayle of Arlington Street, spinster (£40,000), Dame Henrietta Decker 'of St. James's Square, widow' (£11,000), Ann Halsey, deceased, 'per Ralph Thrale, surviving executor' (£11,000) and Ann Jennens, 'widow, Grosvenor Square' (£40,000).

Nineteen (7%) of the 270 English proprietors lived outside London and the home counties.[3] Among them were John Burton of Leeds (£44,000); Samuel Crompton jun., 'gent. Derby' (£21,000); Sir Nathaniel Curzon of Kedleston (£13,250); Thomas Gisborne, Esq., of Derby (£15,000); Sir James Lowther, Bart., of Whitehaven (£108,400); Henry Peirse, Esq., 'of Bedel, Yorks' (£20,000); Beilby Thompson, Esq., 'of Escrick, Yorks' (18,633); Thomas Thornhill, Esq., 'of Fixby, Yorks' (£96,350)) and Richard Weddell, Esq., 'of Eastwick, Yorks' (£27,500). William Jennens 'Esq., Acton Place, Suffolk', held £52,000; Mrs. Millicent Neate of Swindon, one of the two women in this list, £11,555; and Alicia Harris 'Kent, spinster', the other, £14,000. Sir Danvers Osborn, Bart., of Chick-sands Priory held £11,700 with two co-trustees.

The big London proprietors were nearly all merchants, officials, lawyers and naval and military men. Only five were Jewish.[4] Among the merchants were William Baker, 'Esq and Alderman' (£12,230); Abraham Craiesteyn (£53,200) and Francis Craiesteyn (£131,053), both described at first as 'London, merchant' later as 'Esquire'; Marshe Dickinson, 'Esquire and Alderman' (£22,975); Jonathan Forward, 'Esq. London' (£10,000); Samson Gideon 'London merchant [erased], Lincoln's Inn Fields Esq.' (£76,450); and Galfridus Mann 'the Strand, woollendraper' (£49,200).

---

[1] For these foreign holdings see below, p. 327.

[2] Holdings by English peers, including those of less than £10,000, are given below, p. 295.

[3] Essex, Herts., Middlesex and Surrey, see below, p. 297 n. 2.

[4] Samson Gideon (£76,450), Isaac Lamego (£10,750), Moses Lamego (£30,150), David Salomons (£10,000), Francis Salvador (£13,840).

Thomas Bridges of the Six Clerks Office (£10,000); John Dive, 'Esq., the Exchequer' (£14,000); and Charles Taylor, Esq., 'Deputy Remembrancer of the Exchequer, in trust to attend the orders of the said Court' (£14,861) were officials. Christopher Arnold (£82,766), Samuel Child (£49,500), James Colebrooke sen. and jun. (£10,000), George Lee (£11,000) and Joseph Martin (£12,000) were goldsmith bankers.[1] 'The Rt. Hon. Henry Fox, Secretary at War' held £11,000 stock, 'the Hon. George Grenville, St. George's Hanover Square' £15,358, Sir Paul Methuen, K.B., £11,000 and Sir Dudley Ryder, the Attorney-General, £24,800. The list also includes Admirals Lord Anson (£30,000), Sir Challoner Ogle (£14,000), William Rowley (£11,000) and Isaac Townshend (£19,000) and Generals James Cholmondeley (£12,000) and Sir John Cope (£12,900).

This evidence suggests that big ownership of stock at the mid-eighteenth century was more complicated than Bolingbroke and others assumed. Three of the largest single holdings were for the suitors of Chancery, the poor clergy of the Church of England and the Commissioners for New Churches. By the severest Tory standards these accounts were for admirable causes, and could not plausibly be fitted into the picture of a sinister plutocracy. Similarly, the important minority of trustees could not very well be accused of financial legerdemain; many of them were flies caught in the intricate web of Chancery proceedings. It is also clear that the circles of ownership just described overlapped, for instance several holdings by peers or merchants were trustee accounts. Contemporaries who disliked the 'overgrown rich stockholders' would have been forced, if they were consistent, into maintaining that merchants or bankers were wicked when owning for themselves but without blemish when acting as trustees. But despite these qualifications, the structure of top ownership, concentrated on a minority of the peerage, rich officeholders, the mercantile oligarchy of the City of London, and successful naval and military men, and supported by a minority of foreign owners from similar backgrounds, shows that Tory fears of the great world of wealth and influence, which they hated with the intensity of the excluded, were based on something more solid than ignorance and prejudice.

Members of the peerage, whom the Squire Westerns of the day so heartily detested,[2] were less prominent as owners of stock than the minority of very big holders described above suggests. In the same five stocks there were 140 accounts in which peers were concerned on the eve of Pelham's conversion

---

[1] Described as both goldsmith and banker in different alphabets. Cf. below, p. 450, for the Bank of England's usage.

[2] Fielding's *Tom Jones* was first published in 1749.

scheme.[1] The number of account-holders was only 116, owing to owner-ship of more than one stock by several of them. The actual number of peers involved was lower still, only ninety-four, owing to the fact that several acted more than once. Further, in a handful of cases the account is in the name of a deceased peer, with his successor and others joined as executors. Only forty-nine account-holders were individuals, the remaining sixty-seven were groups of two or (generally) more, the co-trustees mostly being untitled. The amount of stock controlled was £689,199, the greater part of which was Bank stock and South Sea annuities, which seem to have become the favourite aristocratic investment by this date. Noble holdings were thus less than 2% of the total of £47·5m. stock. This was only a fractionally larger proportion than in 1719.[2] In the meantime, however, the actual number of peers with a stake in the funds had doubled, even though many were only drawn in by lawsuits or by acting as trustees. Fundholding peers therefore increased as a proportion of the peerage as a whole, which remained constant in size. Of the 116 account-holders in the five stocks examined, eleven held less than £500, thirteen £500–£999, fifty-five £1,000 to £4,999, eighteen £5,000–£9,999 and nineteen £10,000 or over. The last group included the two largest accounts, for John, Duke of Marlborough, deceased, (£84,790) and for Sarah, Duchess of Marlborough, deceased, and Francis, Earl of Godolphin (£71,763). Only three of the other large accounts exceeded £20,000.[3] As stockholders the peerage concentrated in the medium bracket.

Members of Parliament concerned in four of the same five stocks at this date numbered 157 and controlled 225 accounts.[4] In a number of cases they, like the peers who held stock, were involved as co-owners, but the number of individual accounts was proportionately larger than it was with members of the Upper House. This was largely due to the difference in social struc-ture, for owners in the House of Commons were mostly drawn, as they were

[1] The stocks were Bank and East India stock, South Sea Old and New Annuities and 4% (1748) stock, above, p. 292. 'Peers' as before are those entitled to sit in the English House of Lords. The date taken was 1 December 1749.

[2] See above, p. 281.

[3] The Duke of Leeds and Henry Furnese (£22,627); Francis, Lord North and Guild-ford, the Hon. Robert and William Herbert and the Hon. Richard Arundell (£20,500); Thomas, Lord Onslow, deceased (£23,925). The Pembroke holding of £69,052 South Sea stock (above, p. 280) had greatly lessened by this date. Henry, Earl of Pembroke held £5,000 South Sea annuities and £3,000 4% stock. He was also a co-trustee in four other accounts for £2,857, £5,550, £18,700 and £2,230.

[4] Bank and East India stock, New South Sea Annuities and 4% stock (1748), Bank of England Record Office.

at an earlier period, from a mercantile, legal or office-holding background. To take some examples from the beginning of the alphabet, Alderman William Baker held £15,860; Alderman Sir John Barnard £10,321 in five accounts, four of which were with co-owners; Stamp Brooksbank, a director of the Bank of England, £8,700; Merrick Burrell, another Bank director, £15,000; Samuel Child of Osterley Park, the great banker, £20,000, and so on. A list of office-holders who were proprietors of stock would begin with William Aislabie, Auditor of the Imprests (£2,150), Richard Arundell, Clerk of the Pipe (£8,000) and Walter Cary, a Clerk Comptroller of the Household (£2,000). A similar list of lawyers would begin with Isaac Hawkins Browne (£1,700), Thomas Clarke, 'K.C., Hampstead' (£4,310) and John Garth, Recorder of Devizes (£3,271). Among naval and military men were Lord Vere Beauclerk, Admiral of the Blue (£3,200), Lt.-General Henry Cornewall (£6,000), Capt. Richard Evans, Lt.-Governor of Sheerness (£500) and so on. Some country gentlemen M.P.s were holders of stock. Thus Sir John Hinde Cotton held £1,845 with two co-owners; William Drake of Shardeloes held £6,625; Sir Robert Grosvenor held £1,500 for himself and £650 as a co-trustee; and the rich Sir James Lowther of Whitehaven held £73,640.

The greater part of the English government's creditors at the mid-eighteenth century still lived in and around London, as they had done thirty years earlier, though by this date the number and importance of foreign owners had greatly increased.[1] In the large Reduced $3\frac{1}{2}\%$ stock in the first two years of its existence (1752–4), samples from the alphabets give a proportion of about 7% of domestic proprietors living outside London and the Home Counties.[2] In a large sample of South Sea annuity accounts at 25 March 1744 7·2% of the proprietors lived in the provinces; they controlled 5·5% of the stock sampled.[3] In East India stock at 25 March 1748 only 0·01% of accounts were outside London, though they were big enough to control 8% of the stock. It is worth noting in this context that as late as 1790 less than 18% of the proprietors of shares of an important London insurance company, the Sun Fire Office, lived in the provinces.[4] The majority of ordinary owners of government stock at the middle of the eighteenth century

[1] For foreign owners see the next chapter. For the position in 1719–24 see above, p. 276.

[2] Ledgers and alphabets for Reduced $3\frac{1}{2}\%$s, Bank of England Record Office. In a random sample of 781 domestic proprietors 51 (6·5%) were resident in the provinces and the rest in London and the Home Counties. In these analyses Essex has been added to the home counties, previously (above, p. 256) defined as Herts. Middlesex and Surrey.

[3] Ledger A–B for South Sea Old Annuities 25 March 1744.

[4] Dickson, Sun Insurance Office, p. 290.

were members of the London *bourgeoisie* and *petite bourgeoisie*. They were
merchants, bankers, brokers, jobbers, clergymen, doctors, lawyers, shop-
keepers, artisans. Domestic servants were also often small owners of stock,
like John Turner, 'servant to Lady Cater', who bought £10 South Sea
annuities in December 1752.

Women continued to be an important minority of all owners. The figures
for Bank stock, South Sea Old Annuities and 4% (1748) stock were as follows:

TABLE 43

Women as owners of stock 1744–53

South Sea Old Annuities, balances 25 March 1744 in ledger A–B				East India stock 25 March 1748			
Nos.	%	£	%	*Nos.*	%	£	%
485	31·8	352,565	19·5	485	22·5	527,734	16·5

4% stock (1748) sample February–May 1750				Bank stock, balances 10 Oct. 1753 in ledger A–C			
Nos.	%	£	%	*Nos.*	%	£	%
379	17·2	270,070	8·0	312	25·4	513,211	18·8

Source: Ledgers for these stocks, Bank of England Record Office. Cf. also the note
to Table 38 on p. 282, above.

In Bank and East India stock women owned proportionately more than they
had thirty years earlier, and had also somewhat increased as a proportion of
the total number of owners.[1] Their average holding was much larger than
in the other two stocks. In South Sea annuities they were more numerous
than in the other stocks, presumably because it was thought more suitable
for trustee investment. Besides accounts for women, this stock contained a
much larger proportion than others of joint and multiple accounts, the greater
part of which must have been for administrators, executors and trustees.

[1] The figures for 1724 (above, p. 282) were 20·7% and 19·0% for Bank and East India
women proprietors, owning respectively 12·6% and 11·0% of the total stock.

6. Letter of attorney by a Dutch investor in the English Million Loan of
1693

7. Dutch acknowledgement of sale of Bank of England stock, to be delivered in London, 1730; (above) an Amsterdam broker's note of the sale of £1000 East India stock, 1736

TABLE 44

Joint and multiple holdings of stock 1744–53

South Sea Old Annuities, balances 25 March 1744 in ledger A–B				East India Stock 24 March 1748			
Nos.	%	£	%	Nos.	%	£	%
282	18·5	648,633	35·9	161	7·5	229,482	7·2

4% stock (1748) sample February–May 1750				Bank stock, balances 10 October 1753 in ledger A–C			
Nos.	%	£	%	Nos.	%	£	%
98	4·4	140,338	4·2	141	11·5	242,866	8·9

Source: Ledgers for these stocks, Bank of England Record Office.

In a sample of 450 proprietors' accounts taken at random from the alphabets to Reduced $3\frac{1}{2}\%$ stock for 1752–4 seventy-nine (17·6%) were joint or multiple ones.[1] Trustee accounts were a function of the age and social structure of the stock concerned. Thus the 4%s of 1748 had not existed long enough by 1750 to build up a trustee sector, while East India stock was clearly not regarded as very suitable for such investments. In Bank stock, joint and multiple holdings were more common than in the early 1720s, perhaps because of delays in clearing estates for probate, which would have kept stock in executors' hands longer.[2] South Sea annuities were clearly the most important trustee stock, over a third of the total being in accounts of this sort. The figure in Table 44 confirms a return which the South Sea Company made to Parliament in 1737, which showed that £8,397,254 South

[1] Alphabets to Reduced $3\frac{1}{2}\%$ stock 1752–4, Bank of England Record Office.

[2] As was suggested above, p. 283. The Bank and East India and South Sea companies kept registers of proprietors' deaths. To take an example, the number of deaths of Bank stock proprietors each year between 1731 and 1752 fluctuated between 148 (1734) and 228 (1746). The number of proprietors was roughly 5,000 throughout the period. Thus 3% to 4% died annually. This by itself would have kept a steady proportion of stock in the hands of executors and trustees, even assuming that the time taken to clear an estate for distribution did not lengthen.

L   D.F.R.

Sea annuities were 'holden by Executors, Administrators, and Trustees'; this would have been 34% of the £24,639,419 stock.[1]

Besides these holdings in the names of two or more proprietors, the South Sea annuities contained numerous accounts, as at an earlier period, for corporate bodies of a charitable kind. Such holdings also occur in other stocks, like the £2,800 4% (1748) stock owed in 1750 by 'the President and Governors of the Corporation for Relief of Seamen in the Merchants' service' but they are rarer. Taking South Sea Old Annuities alone, in the same year there were accounts for the 'Charity for Relief of Poor Widows of Clergymen' (£2,491), the Charity School of St. Martin-in-the-Fields (£100), the Treasurer of Christ's Hospital (£2,407), the 'President and Governors of the Hospital or Infirmary at Bath' (£5,000), the 'Dean and Canons of the Free Chapel of St. George, Windsor' (£200), the Minister and Churchwardens of Hampstead (£50) New Windsor (£100) St. James's, Westminster (£100) St. Bartholomew (£100), and Whittington, Gloucs. (£225), the 'President and Governors of Queen Elizabeth's College at East Greenwich' (£1,500), the 'Governors of Peirpoint's Free School in Lucton' (£700), the Guardians of the Poor at Plymouth (£2,100), the Mayor and Aldermen of Gloucester (£100), the Society for the Propagation of the Gospel (£6,200), the Treasurer and Masters of the Bench of the Middle Temple (£6,000), eleven London livery companies, All Souls (£100), St. John's (£1,100), Magdalen (£3,100), Pembroke (£200) and Wadham (£3,520) Colleges, Oxford, and Christ's College (£600) and Pembroke Hall (£365), Cambridge. These smaller holdings, like the larger ones of Queen Anne's Bounty or the Accountant-General of Chancery, widened the circle of those who — at first or second hand — had a stake in the National Debt.

VII

To sum up. The domestic capital invested in English long-term government loans in this period came mostly from London and its environs. The substantial provincial stake in the earliest loan of all, the tontine of 1693, was not maintained, and at the mid-eighteenth century the circle of home

---

[1] HCJ xxii. 827, 25 March 1737. The accounts were ordered on 22 March (ibid. 819) to test assertions made during the debate on Sir John Barnard's proposal to reduce interest rates that a large part of the annuities were trustee holdings.

investors was more solidly based on London than it had been six decades earlier. This is in contrast to the United Provinces, where, as the next chapter shows, the trend of investment in English government securities was away from Amsterdam towards the provincial towns. In qualification of the English pattern it must be noticed, first, that there was a growing, though still small, number of really rich provincial investors by the 1750s; second, that funds invested in government and allied securities by institutions in London — banks, insurance offices, trading companies, charities — partly derived from provincial deposits, insurance premiums and assets contested at law.

It seems clear that in London and its environs at least there was from the 1690s onwards plenty of capital available for long-term investment yielding a 'safe' return. This was presumably due to several factors. First, the national income was growing, and perhaps growing faster in London, which was the mercantile hub of the kingdom and contained a tenth of the total population, than anywhere else. Second, the national income was distributed in favour of the middle classes and the rich, and was not significantly redistributed towards the poor by government taxation. Even in war-time, taxes tended to hit landed rather than personal property. A high rate of saving among the traditionally thrifty mercantile and professional classes, particularly since the price level was fairly stable, was the natural result. The outlets for safely investing part of these savings (ignoring as irrelevant to the argument the part reinvested in trade and industry) were presumably limited. The market in private fixed-interest securities was in no way comparable with the market in railway debentures and municipal bonds of the nineteenth century. And all loans on personal bonds were subject to grave risks. This would have left the government, once it had established its competence and good faith, in a virtually monopoly position as a long-term borrower until well into the second half of the eighteenth century.

Most investors in the earliest period of government long-term borrowing were individuals: joint, multiple and corporate holdings of securities were rare. This picture quickly changed, however, the change beginning with the Million Bank's massive purchases of government annuities and the reversions to them from the late 1690s. By the mid-eighteenth century there were substantial institutional investments, and holdings by trustees particularly by executors, were also of growing importance over the period. These institutional and trustee funds provided part of the new capital for government war loans in the 1740s. After the peace of 1748 they helped drive up market prices by steady demand for stock and — since trustees and charities in particular tended to hold it for longish periods — by restricting its supply. (It is interesting to speculate whether investment of such funds in government stock slowed down the rate of charitable and educational building, to which the capital might otherwise have partly been devoted.)

In London, the *bourgeoisie* were the most important individual investors in government loans. They included members of the Church, Civil Service and professions, but the majority were merchants and financiers, or, as smaller owners, tradesmen, craftsmen and artisans. Religious minorities — Huguenots, Jews — were less significant as investors than contemporaries thought, but they included some very important capitalists, whose activities helped to magnify the importance of these groups as a whole. Insufficient evidence is available about Protestant Nonconformists to make similar generalization possible, though it seems plausible that their pattern of investment was broadly the same as that of these other religions. Only a minority of the peerage had investments in the funds, though it was a growing minority; here, too, there were some very large individual holdings. The proportion of Members of Parliament owning stock also increased over the period, but they were drawn from the monied and professional rather than the landed interests in the House. It seems fair to generalize that the landed classes as a whole were not significant contributors of new capital for public loans. Lastly, at all social levels women were an important minority of investors.

The structure of ownership of government and allied securities (and presumably therefore of the pattern of savings) shows a mass of small investors, an important 'middle class', and a small number of really large owners. There seems always to have been a much higher demand from small (£500 and under) investors for government stock and South Sea annuities than for the stock of the Bank of England and the two trading companies. Small holders, however, even when comprising up to 50% of total investors, generally controlled only a quarter or less of total stock. At the other end of the scale the big investors (£5,000 and over) were only a fractional proportion of total investors, but at the mid-eighteenth century normally controlled a quarter to a third of most stocks. Medium holders (£1,000– £4,999) maintained a constant proportion of between 40% and 50% of total holdings throughout the period. In the East India Company they increased at the expense of the big owners. The services of loan brokers were important from the 1740s in passing stock created by new loans and issues into the hands of these 'final' holders. As is to be expected, the structure of subscriptions by 1750 was much more monopolistic than that of final ownership, since the large subscribers took up blocks of scrip and marketed them to others.

The government's success in financing war by public borrowing in this period, however, was only partly due to the ready availability of domestic funds and the growing sophistication of the methods used to mobilize them. It was also and increasingly due to ability to tap an international market as well. This is discussed in the next chapter.

12

Public Creditors Abroad

I

THE type and volume of foreign investment in England have been a subject of interest and concern to English governments at least since the days when the Bardi and Peruzzi underwrote the wars of Edward III. By the mid-seventeenth century the acute anxiety about payment of interest on loans from abroad, characteristic of an earlier period, had faded with the development of a rudimentary domestic capital market. It had been replaced by fear of the economic power of international rivals whose trade balances with England were consistently favourable. The most important of these rivals were the Dutch. Sir Josiah Child in his *Brief Observations concerning Trade* stated as a possible major objection to his case for reducing domestic interest-rates the likelihood that such a reduction would lead to the withdrawal of foreign, especially Dutch, funds 'put out at interest in England, by their Friends and Factors'.[1] His dismissal of the argument on the grounds that it was not true, and even if true would not matter, cannot have seemed entirely plausible to his contemporaries. The political revolution of 1688 gave new point to English fears. First, the fuller and more accurate statistics collected by the new Board of Trade from 1697 confirmed the view that English visible trade with the Dutch annually showed a large balance in the latters' favour. Second, the great increase in government borrowing under William and Anne drew in foreign capital whose amount was not centrally recorded, and was thus open to the alarmed estimates of pamphleteers. Briscoe in 1694 told his readers that among the subscriptions to the Million Act in the previous year there were 'very considerable Sums . . . remitted from Foreign Parts, and paid in by Foreigners'.[2] A writer of 1726 computed that foreigners had lent one-sixth of the sums borrowed for long terms between 1690 and

[1] [Sir Josiah Child], *Brief Observations concerning Trade and Interest of Money*. By J. C. (1668), p. 10.

[2] John Briscoe, *A Discourse on the Late Funds of the Million Act*, p. 23. For the Million Act see above, p. 53.

1702, or about £1m., and a similar proportion, amounting to about £6½m., between 1702 and 1714.[1] With the inconsistency typical of most discussions of the subject he estimated current (1726) foreign holdings not at over £7m., but only at £6m., 'about the ninth part of our Debt'.[2] Meanwhile in 1711 Defoe had found it plausible to assert that 'Foreigners withdrawing their Money' was one of the causes of embarrassment of Harley's Ministry, though he did not say whether he meant by this that they were liquidating English investments or merely drawing more heavily than usual on their English correspondents.[3]

Controversy about the type and number of foreign owners of English government stock revived during the discussions of 1737 about reducing the interest on the National Debt to 3%. Estimates of foreign ownership then varied from as low as £4m., one-twelfth of the public debt, to as high as £12m., about a quarter of it.[4] 'The chief of these Foreigners for Number and Value', it was stated, 'are the Dutch'.[5] These calculations were scaled upwards, but not radically revised, at the end of the 1740s, when foreigners were still thought to hold a quarter (£17m.–£18m.) of the by then considerably enlarged National Debt, and to have contributed about £5m. to the loans made during the war.[6] Lower estimates seem by this stage to have faded away.

II

The records give a more complicated and less tidy picture of foreign investment than the bold but haphazard statements of the pamphleteers. In the subscriptions to the earliest English government long-term loan, the Tontine of 1693, and to the Bank of England in 1694, foreign names are

[1] Erasmus Philips, *The State of the Nation, in Respect to her Commerce, Debts and Money* (1726), pp. 22, 36. The author computes the increase in the debt since 1701 as 'about forty Millions . . . of which it is suppos'd they [foreigners] generally had a sixth part'.

[2] Ibid., p. 49.

[3] [Daniel Defoe], *Eleven Opinions about Mr. H—y; with Observations* (1711), p. 40. For an example of increased Dutch drawing of bills in 1710 see below, p. 451.

[4] *Considerations upon a Proposal for Lowering the Interest upon all the Redeemable National Debts to Three per Cent. per Ann.*, p. 28, 'four or five millions'; *Reasons for the more speedy Lessening the National Debt* (1737), p. 9, £12m.

[5] *A Speech Without-Doors Addressed to the National Creditors at 4l. per Cent*, p. 15.

[6] *An Essay upon Publick Credit* (1748), pp. 7, 11. £5m. would have been about a quarter of the sums subscribed 1740–8.

few.[1] In the first, there were thirty-four Dutch subscribers, with total subscriptions of £8,200, and twelve other foreign subscribers, with total subscriptions of £2,000. In the Bank subscription, which included only one foreign Tontine lender, there were nineteen Dutch subscribers with £15,300, and eight others with £9,700. A majority of Dutch-domiciled subscribers to both loans were Huguenots, Jews and English resident abroad.[2] It is argued below that foreign investment in Bank stock and East India stock only became significant after the peace of 1713.[3] But it would be incorrect to deduce that foreigners were uninterested in English government securities at this early stage. When the Million Bank was buying reversions of single-life government annuities in the 1690s, it found that foreign annuitants were willing to sell to it on an extensive scale.[4] The Bank's total purchases by 1703 amounted to £59,566 p.a. (43% of all such annuities); of this, £10,080 p.a. (16·9%) was in the names of foreign nominees.[5] The Bank was entitled to draw each of these annuities once the original nominee died. Meanwhile, it had to wait. The willingness of these foreign annuitants to sell their reversions suggests that they had come into the original sub-scription to the Million Act less as long-term investors than from motives of speculation, or at the most of buying additional life assurance for themselves or their dependants. The average sum they contributed was only about £140, and they were evidently unwilling to pay the further substantial amounts needed to take advantage of the English government's offer to turn single life annuities into annuities for terms of years.[6] In the absence of any com-plete record of the nominees under the Million Act, it is no more than a

---

[1] For the sources see above, p. 254 n.

[2] Of the 19 Dutch subscribers to Bank Stock (only four of whom were Amsterdamers), fourteen have Huguenot names. In the Tontine, where twenty-one Dutch subscribers were Amsterdamers, and the other thirteen lived in The Hague, Haarlem, Rotterdam and Utrecht, nine were Jewish (all in Amsterdam) eight were Huguenot (mostly outside Amsterdam), and six had English names: George Barrons, Reginald Calthorpe, Thomas Kirby, Robert Pease, Benjamin Furly, John Gay. Subscribers outside the United Pro-vinces came from Flanders (4), Fort St. George, India (1), Germany (4), Ireland (3), Switzerland (4), and one each from Italy, Jersey, Portugal and Spain. (Both lists.)

[3] See pp. 311 ff.

[4] For the Million Bank and its purchases see above, p. 270.

[5] The manuscript list of the Million Bank's total purchases is in P.R.O. C 46/1 (with totals endorsed). The names of foreign nominees have been extracted from B.M. 8223.e.7, 'A List of the Several Reversionary Annuities to which the Million Bank are Intituled' n.d.). The latter is a printed version of the former, which is dated 24 November 1702.

[6] For this offer see above, p. 56. The additional sum to be paid was between four and a half and five years' purchase of the annuity.

presumption that the foreign names in the Million Bank List are all, or the bulk, of original foreign investors in Million Loan life annuities. A contributory piece of evidence that the presumption is correct is the card-index to the Amsterdam Notarial Archives, which, when examined (1961), covered 75% of the material for 1700–10. The number of entries relating to English securities was 63. Owing to various ambiguities, only forty-nine of these entries are clearly identifiable. Of these, twenty-eight are about Exchequer life annuities and government lottery tickets, ten about Bank stock, a further ten about East India stock and one about African Company stock: none are about Exchequer long annuities.[1]

The foreign nominees in the Million Bank list were overwhelmingly concentrated in the United Netherlands: 378 names are Dutch out of the total of 430. (There is no indication in the list whether the beneficiaries were normally the nominees themselves or someone else.) Many of the families concerned — Clifford, Crommelin, Dussen, Dutry, Eelbo, Heemskerk, Muyssart, de Neufville, van Roye, Scheepers, Schuylenburch and others — were to reappear later as investors in other stocks. Members of all the families just mentioned, for instance, were holders of East India stock in 1750. Within the United Provinces, the nominees were widely distributed: only 139 (36%) came from Amsterdam. Exactly half (189) of the Dutch nominees were women. Of nominees from other countries, sixteen came from Switzerland, thirteen from the Spanish Netherlands,[2] ten from Germany, five from France, three from Dublin, two from Sweden (one of whom was the painter Michael Dahl 'of Stockholm', who was nominee for £56 p.a.)[3] two from Jersey and one from Vienna, Philip Plantamore, who was perhaps an English merchant residing there.

The Million Bank list does not indicate who the London agents for these foreign investors were. In the subscription to Bank stock in 1694, London agents of Huguenot extraction acted as agents for Dutch Huguenot subscribers. These agents included David Debarry, Theodore Janssen, Theodore Le Coq de St. Leger and Alexander Mariette.[4] Dutch Jewish investors' London agents included Pedro Henriquez jun., Isaac Lopez Milhado, Isaac Senior Henriquez, Isaac Pereira Cortiso and Gomer Rodriguez, all members of the London Jewish community, and also the London goldsmiths

---

[1] Amsterdam, Gemeente Archief, card-index to the Notarial Archives.

[2] Which became the Austrian Netherlands in 1714.

[3] Dahl is so described in the list of nominees, though he was normally resident in London. The other Swedish nominee was Charles, Hereditary Prince of Sweden.

[4] Bank stock subscription ledger, 1694, see above, p. 254 n.

William Sheppard and Charles Shales.[1] Some further information is available from the card-index to the Amsterdam Notarial Archives for the years 1700–10, though it often leaves agents unspecified. The names mentioned are as follows:

TABLE 45

Some London agents for Dutch investors 1700–10

Simson de Costa Athias & Co. . . .	Peter Henriquez jun.
Sarah Boone	Theodore and Jacob Jacobsen
Jacob George Beck & Sons	Elias Lindo
Petre Delmé	Moses de Medina
Dennis Dutry	David and Raphael Penso
Isaac Senior Henriquez	Peter Renew
Pieter and Pierre Henriquez . . .	Melchior de Ruuscher
	Nicholas Tourton and Tobias Guiguer

Source: Amsterdam, Gemeente Archief, card-index to the Notarial Archives 1700–10.

Most are described as 'of London, merchant'. Most acted only for one investor. The trend towards specialization in agencies, which developed as foreign investment in the Funds increased, is not yet noticeable.[2]

III

The English government's lottery loans of 1710–14 attracted a certain number of foreign speculators, like Simon Bevel of Haarlem, who in February 1710 noted in his ledger that Schoppens & Edwards in London had laid out £104 in buying him eleven tickets in the 'Lotery van 't Parlament te London'.[3] In March he bought twenty-two more tickets for £209 11s. 0d.,

[1] Tontine subscription list (Shales and Sheppard); Amsterdam, Gemeente Archief, Notarial Archives, 3317/69, 3320/89, 310. 311; 3151/1171 (others). I am indebted to Dr. S. Hart for these references to the Notarial Archives. For the Tontine list see above, p. 254.

[2] For this trend see the list of agencies on p. 318, below.

[3] Archief Brants, 1736, ledger of Simon Bevel 1710–14, 20 February 1710 (N.S.).

selling them in July for £235 19s. 0d. In September 1712 he bought fifty blank tickets 'op't Parlament to London' for £382 10s. 9d., selling them the same day for £398 19s. 5d. In February 1713 he sold the eleven tickets of 1710 for £80 17s. 2d.[1] At the same time (February 1712–August 1713) he was buying and selling a small number of tickets in two of his own country's national lotteries.[2] Again, a list of 857 prizewinners in the second English Government Classis Lottery of 1711 contains the names of twenty-two foreigners, twelve of whom were from the United Provinces, five from Ireland, three from Germany and one each from Denmark and Jersey.[3] The prizes in this, and the three other lotteries of 1711–12, were funded in 5% stock in 1717, and the opening ledgers at that date contain about three hundred foreign names, the majority of which are Dutch, followed by a Swiss group and a handful of accounts for the Channel Islands, Denmark, Germany and Ireland.[4]

The evidence so far reviewed suggests that in the early years of English long-term government borrowing foreigners were unwilling to invest on a large or permanent scale, though they were happy to spend limited sums on life annuities, and to speculate in lottery tickets. This conclusion is confirmed by a study of the ledgers for East India and Bank stock. There is only a handful of identifiable foreign names in the first list of proprietors of the United East India Company, dated 31 March 1709.[5] Ten years later, at Lady Day 1719, sixty-two East India accounts, half of which were Dutch, can be identified as those of foreigners. These accounts controlled £134,118 (just over 4%) of the total East India stock of £3·2m.[6] In Bank stock, the precision of the ledger alphabet books (indexes) makes it possible to reconstruct the number of accounts opened for foreign proprietors each year between 1694 and 1720.

[1] Ibid. at New Style dates 11 March and 14 July 1710, 19 October 1711, 27 September 1712 and 16 February 1713. Bevel also paid £200 on 18 April 1710 (N.S.) for a 32-year £9 p.a. annuity, which he sold on 19 October 1717 (N.S.) for £247.3.9. In the interim Schoppens & Edwards had annually remitted the £9.

[2] Ibid., accounts for 'Hollandse Lotery' and 'Hollandse Lotery van Zes Millioenen'.

[3] P.R.O. E 401/2600, list of prize-winners in the second (Classis) lottery of 1711 (9 Anne, c. 16).

[4] Opening ledgers for 5% (1717) stock, Bank of England Record Office. There were nearly 13,000 proprietors of this stock, see above p. 271.

[5] List of proprietors of the United East India Company 31 March 1709, Bank of England Record Office. The list does not give addresses of proprietors, so some identifications are uncertain.

[6] Names extracted from the East India stock ledgers, Bank of England Record Office.

TABLE 46

Accounts opened for foreigners in Bank stock
1694–Michaelmas 1720

| Year | DUTCH | | | | Swiss | German | Spanish, later (1714) Austrian, Netherlands | Other | Total |
	Amsterdam	The Hague	Other	Total					
1694	6	8	8	22	..	2	1	..	25
1695	..	..	..	..	..	..	..	..	..
1696	..	1	..	1	..	..	..	1	2
1697	2	..	1	3	..	..	1	..	4
1698	1	..	2	3	..	..	..	1	4
1699	1	1	2	4	..	1	..	..	5
1700	..	..	..	..	..	..	..	..	..
1701	3	..	..	3	..	..	..	..	3
1702	2	..	1	3	..	1	..	..	4
1703	2	..	..	2	..	..	..	..	2
1704	7	..	1	8	..	..	..	..	8
1705	1	1	..	2	..	..	..	..	2
1706	..	..	1	1	..	..	..	..	1
1707	1	1	..	2	..	..	..	..	2
1708	..	..	..	..	..	..	..	..	..
1709	4	1	1	6	13	1	..	1	21
1710	3	1	1	5	17	8	1	3	34
1711	4	3	..	7	15	3	..	..	25
1712	4	..	..	4	8	2	4	2	20
1713	1	4	..	5	6	1	1	1	14
1714	4	..	..	4	5	..	1	..	10
1715	7	..	3	10	1	7	..	..	18
1716	9	..	4	13	5	1	..	1	20
1717	15	2	3	20	1	4	1	..	26
1718	24	3	6	33	2	1	3	3	42
1719	22	5	2	29	6	..	1	1	37
1720	34	7	13	54	4	1	1	1	61
TOTALS	157	38	49	244	83	33	15	15	390

Source: Bank stock ledgers and alphabets 1694–1720, Bank of England Record Office.

From the table it seems that after an initial spurt foreign investment in Bank stock fell away for some years. Swiss investment increased substantially in the years 1709–11, which saw the opening of 50% of all Swiss accounts during the period.[1] Dutch investment showed a rising trend after 1713. Lastly, a larger number of foreign accounts opened in the first nine months of 1720 than in any previous year since the Bank of England was established. Analysed by countries, Dutch investment (244 accounts) was the most important, followed by Switzerland (83 accounts), Germany (33) and the Austrian Netherlands (15). Other countries were Denmark (1) France (4) and Italy (5). English merchants resident abroad held the remaining 5 accounts.[2] Principal sellers to Dutch buyers were Cornelius Backer, Sir Justus Beck, Gerard Bolwerk, Sir Mathew Decker, John Leonard d'Orville, James Martin and John Olmius, all prominent London merchants and financiers, and all, except Martin, of Dutch origin.[3]

IV

On the eve of the South Sea Bubble of 1720, foreign investment in English government stock was therefore limited in amount, although it was already showing a rising trend. At the same time, the earlier pattern of temporary or speculative commitment (life annuities, lottery tickets) was changing towards a more permanent interest, in the forms of annuities for terms of years and holdings of government and company stock.[4] As a result of the South Sea Bubble this trend was markedly accentuated. By 1723–4 foreign holdings of English government securities had reached — for the first time — a really

---

[1] It was in 1710 also that the Canton of Berne lent England £150,000, see above, p. 62.

[2] They were resident in Constantinople, Jamaica, Jersey, Lisbon and Oporto.

[3] Names of sellers extracted from the ledgers for Bank stock. For Sir Justus Beck's bankruptcy in 1720 see p. 158; for the d'Orville family see below, p. 314.

[4] A by-product of foreign investment was an increase in notarial work. Thus the annual number of procurations about English securities drawn up by the prominent Amsterdam notary Philip de Marolles was 19 in 1715, 43 in 1716, 36 in 1717, 78 in 1718, an estimated 180 in 1719, and 284 from 1 January to 9 August 1720. (Figures for 1715–March 1719 from a manuscript list compiled by Dr. S. Hart of the Amsterdam Gemeente Archief; this shows 31 procurations for 1 January–3 March 1719, hence the estimate of 180 for the year. Figures for 1720 from C. H. Wilson, *Anglo-Dutch Commerce and Finance in the Eighteenth Century*, app. B. Of the 207 procurations listed by Dr. Hart, 35 concern Exchequer annuities and the rest Bank, East India and South Sea stock.)

substantial size. They were to go on increasing in amount until the massive
foreign disinvestment of the last twenty years of the eighteenth century.

Table 47 shows the number of foreign accounts in South Sea stock at
midsummer 1723, and in Bank and East India stock at 25 March 1724.

TABLE 47

Foreign accounts in Bank, East India and South Sea stock 1723–4

Stock	Nominal capital £	No. of foreign accounts	As % of total no. of accounts	Stock held £
Bank stock	9,800,000	567	12·2	1,260,790
East India stock	3,194,080	277	14·6	505,106
South Sea stock	33,802,202	1,077	4·5*	2,569,762
TOTALS	46,796,282	1,921	6·3*	4,335,658

Stock	As % of total stock	Average foreign holding £	Average holding all proprietors £
Bank stock	14·2	2,223	1,921
East India stock	15·9	1,859	1,688
South Sea stock	7·6	2,386	1,269
AVERAGE	9·3	2,156	1,626

Source: Ledgers for these stocks, Bank of England Record Office.
To obtain the figures for South Sea stock, foreign accounts
in South Sea annuities were listed and doubled (the stock
of the company having been divided into two equal parts
at midsummer 1723).
* Estimate.

The slight difference in dating, and uncertainty about the nationality of a
small number of accounts, do not seriously qualify the pattern of ownership
that the table indicates. Foreign holdings totalled about 9% of this large
section of the National Debt. In Bank and East India stock they had become
a significant fraction of the total equity, though nowhere near the size they

were to reach by the mid-century. In South Sea stock they were greater in aggregate amount, but proportionally smaller. The average foreign holding was larger than the overall average in Bank and East India stock, and significantly larger in South Sea stock, where there were much fewer very small foreign than very small native holders.

The geographical distribution of accounts (Table 48) shows the Dutch with a clear preponderance, followed at increasing distances by the Swiss, the Irish and the Germans.

TABLE 48

Geographical distribution of foreign holdings of stock 1723–4

Country	Accounts in					
	South Sea stock		Bank stock		East India stock	
	Nos.	£	Nos.	£	Nos.	£
United Netherlands .	587	1,562,197	430	1,024,589	219	426,644
Switzerland . .	216	564,178	62	71,541	25	19,415
Austrian Netherlands	30	70,189	25	42,045	14	11,600
Germany . .	79	121,847	22	69,694	12	36,932
Ireland . . .	100	81,988	9	6,807	..	..
Other . . .	65	169,362	19	46,115	7	10,515
TOTALS . .	1,077	2,569,761	567	1,260,791	277	505,106

Country	Totals		% total foreign accounts	% total foreign holdings
	Nos.	£		
United Netherlands .	1,236	3,013,430	64·3	69·5
Switzerland . .	303	655,134	15·8	15·1
Austrian Netherlands	69	123,834	3·6	2·9
Germany . .	113	228,473	5·9	5·3
Ireland . . .	109	88,795	5·7	2·0
Other . . .	91	225,992	4·7	5·2
TOTALS . .	1,921	4,335,658	100·0	100·0

Source : See preceding table.

The number of account-holders was smaller (1,654) than the number of accounts owing to a 19% overlap between holdings: 1,268 held in one stock only, 172 in two, 103 in three. The majority of account-holders in all countries were individuals, though there was a small number of joint or treble holdings, and at least two corporate ones, the huge account of the Canton of Berne, which held £253,000 South Sea stock,[1] and another for 'Frederick Middendorf, Andrias Dortman, William Falck and others, Directors of the Provincial Company of Utrecht', who held £5,667 South Sea stock. About one-fifth of all accounts, controlling just under a sixth of the total stock, were in the names of women.[2]

A majority of account-holders in Ireland and Germany, and a minority of the larger number of Dutch investors, had Huguenot names. They formed part of a small international community which had not yet put down deep enough roots in its countries of adoption to outweigh memories of its common origins. The d'Orville family was not untypical. John Leonard d'Orville was a London merchant, and acted as agent for Dutch investors. Lewis Frederick d'Orville lived at Exeter; Susanna d'Orville, spinster, lived at Salisbury. Gédéon Duchat d'Orville lived at Berlin, and Frederick Philip d'Orville at Amsterdam. All held South Sea stock in 1723 and their accounts cluster together in the ledger.[3] The Sephardi Jews, too, formed a small but significant international community. Thus, the index to the Bank stock ledgers for 1720–5 contains twenty-two da Costas, of whom thirteen lived in London, eight in Amsterdam, one in Lisbon; twenty-one Henriquez, of whom five lived in London and the rest in Holland; fifteen Mendes of whom four were Londoners and the rest Dutch. Between 1694 and 1726, 371 Jews opened accounts in Bank stock. Of these, 108 were domiciled abroad, 102 of these in turn being Dutch. The great majority (88) of the 108 accounts were opened in the years 1716–25.[4]

---

[1] See above, p. 280.

[2] The proportion varied between stocks. In Bank stock women had 19·6% of the total number of foreign accounts and controlled 16·6% of the stock. In East India stock the figures are 19·5% and 20·1%, in South Sea stock 24·7% and 16·8%.

[3] South Sea Old Annuities, opening ledgers, Bank of England Record Office.

[4] Based on an analysis of the very careful list of early Jewish holders of Bank stock compiled by Mr. J. A. Giuseppi for his article 'Sephardi Jews and the early years of the Bank of England', *Trans. Jewish Hist. Soc. of Eng.* xix (1953), 53. The lists of names are published in ibid., *Miscellanies* (1962). I am grateful to Mr. Giuseppi for giving me a typescript and copy of the list before his article was published. The remaining six foreign Jewish holders referred to in the text lived in Antwerp (1), Portugal (2), Switzerland (2), and Jamaica (1). As with English Jewish investors, members of the Ashkenazik (mid-European) Jewish community were conspicuous by absence.

But most of the Dutch and Swiss accounts in 1723-4 were in the names of native inhabitants. Dutch proprietorship centred on the mercantile aristocracy which in the previous century had made the United Provinces the richest and most powerful society that Europe had seen since the fall of the Roman Empire. Of the 456 male Dutch owners of Bank stock, the indexing of which is the most precise, 189 are described as merchants. Other stockholders were clergymen, doctors, office-holders. Thus Pieter van Eys, 'Minister of Zutphen', held £500 Bank stock. Hieronimus von Alphen, D.D. of Utrecht, held £500 Bank stock and £1,063 South Sea stock. Renate Vincent, 'Comte de Hompesch, Lt. Gen. of ye Dutch Army', held £2,480 South Sea stock. Jacob Hop, 'Treasurer General of Holland', had £2,400 in the same company. Adrian Mollerus, 'Agent and Solicitor General, of the Hague', held £500 Bank stock, and Bonifacius Pous 'of Zerikzee, Zeeland, Rentmaster General', a further £1,000. Jan Abraham Thilenus, 'Secretary to the States of Holland' held £4,250 South Sea stock. Noble owners like Wigbolt van der Does, 'Lord of Noordwyck, one of the College of Nobles of Holland', who held £3,000 Bank stock, were infrequent. Ownership concentrated on Amsterdam: 52% of South Sea accounts, 59% of East India accounts, and no less than 67% of Bank stock accounts were for proprietors living there. This contrasts with the earlier figure of only 36% Amsterdam nominees in life annuities.[1]

Dutch ownership, like English ownership, concentrated at the top. Of a total of £3,013,430 Bank, East India and South Sea stock in Dutch names, £1,117,122 (37%) was owned in units of £10,000 or more by 52 proprietors. Thirty of these proprietors held units of all three stocks, ten held in two and twelve in one stock only. Between them, therefore, they controlled 122 (10%) of the 1,236 Dutch accounts, though they were less than 3% of the total number of proprietors. Two of these large proprietors were partnerships, the rest were individuals. Eleven were Jewish, six Huguenot, the rest native Dutch.[2] The two largest holdings were for Jeronimo de

---

[1] See above, p. 307.

[2] Jewish holders were: Moses Abrabanel (£13,642), Francis Duarte (£16,410), Francis de Lis sen. (£53,600), Francis de Lis jun. (£17,800), Isaac Franco Mendes (£17,250), Anthony de Pinto (£13,000), Jacob de Pinto (£10,316), Joseph de Jacob de Pinto (£10,450), Moses, Joseph and David de Aaron de Pinto (£10,625), Joseph Teixeira de Mattos (£10,000), Manuel Teixeira jun. (£21,000). Holders with Huguenot names were Daniel Bernard (£13,938), Henry de Cheusses (£11,220), Nicholas Clignet (£14,000), Michael de la Court (£19,000), John Antoine de Normandie (£14,125) and Peter Testas (£10,625).

Haze de Giorgio, Burgomaster and Senator of Amsterdam (£82,292, in Bank and South Sea stock), and Magdalena Clara de Haze, his wife (£65,500, in all three stocks). The holdings of one stock only were all in South Sea stock, presumably as a result of the Bubble. Seven of the fifty-two large proprietors were women, who controlled between them £225,030 stock, just over 20% of the total.

Most of the Swiss owners of English government stock in the early 1720s belonged to the families of the interlocking financial patriciate which dominated the country's economic and political life: the families of Calandrini, Cambiague, Couvreu, Favre, Gallatin, Huguetan, Lullin, Pellisari and others, whose ramifications M. Lüthy has so skilfully traced.[1] There were also clergy like Jacob Bordier, 'one of the ministers of the Church of Geneva', who held £700 Bank stock, or John Alphonse Turrettin, 'Geneva, Professor of Divinity' (£2,000 Bank stock), and nobles like Nicholas Fischer, 'Berne, one of the Lords there' (£1,200 Bank stock) or Stephen Potier, 'Lord of Vernand, Lausanne' (£574 Bank stock). Really large individual holdings were, however, very much less common than in the United Provinces: there seem to have been only two for individuals.[2] There was, however, the Canton of Berne's massive holding of £253,000 South Sea stock.

German stockholders at this date centred on Berlin (in South Sea stock forty-four out of seventy-nine had a Berlin address); others came from Danzig and Hamburg, and there was also a number of interior addresses: Dresden, Heidelberg, Hanover, Magdeburg. A substantial number of the German-domiciled proprietors had French names, and were presumably Huguenot refugees. Other German holders were office-holders, nobles, merchants. Jerome de Grapendorff, 'Chamberlain to the King of Prussia, Berlin', held £3,000 Bank stock and £3,000 East India stock. Members of noble families included Frederick William, Baron de Gromkow, Berlin (£800 South Sea stock), Christian Ulrich, Baron Hardenberg, of Berlin (£3,000 East India stock), John Sigismond, Baron de Heiden, Berlin (£633 Bank stock) and Maria Margaretha, Baroness von Offenbergen, 'widow, Danzig', (£26,578 East India and Bank stock), who was one of three German-domiciled stockholders with over £10,000 stock.[3] Irish ownership resembled German ownership in its core of Huguenot names. Of the 100

[1] Herbert Lüthy, *La Banque Protestante en France de la Révocation de l'Edit de Nantes à la Révolution* (2 vols. Paris, 1959–61).

[2] Andrew Gallatin £16,107; James Andrew Saladin £22,500.

[3] The other two were Reynhold Colmer of Danzig (£25,148) and Francis Mathieu, Baron de Vernezobre de Laurieux, of Berlin (£26,563).

Irish-domiciled owners of South Sea stock (eighty-three of whom lived in Dublin), no less than eighty-five had Huguenot names. The contrast comes in the average unit of ownership, which was only £815 compared with the German average of £2,033 (and an overall foreign average of £2,156). The flow of Irish funds into South Sea speculation, on which contemporaries in 1720 remarked, must have owed a great deal to this recent sector of Irish society.[1]

Among holders of English government securities in relatively peripheral areas of ownership were Donat Chabbert 'of Paris banker' (£2,240 South Sea stock), and Lewis Guiguer 'of Paris' (£52,000 South Sea and Bank stock),[2] Gottlieb de Schmettau, 'Lt. Genl. of the King of Poland' (£2,600 South Sea stock), and the mysterious trio 'Josephus, Count Teleki, Stephen Guila Szigeti and Stephen Komaromy of Enyed in Transilvania', who jointly held £6,000 South Sea stock. There were three stockholders who lived in the British North American colonies, and seven who lived in Central America and the West Indies.[3] This trend towards geographical spread of ownership was to develop markedly during the following three decades.

The Bank stock dividend list for 1724 shows the names of all the English agents used at the this date by foreign holders of Bank stock, many of whom were also owners of East India and South Sea stock. It seems clear that the increase in business had led to distinct specialisation. A sample of 200 Dutch stockholders were catered for by fifty-six agents acting under power of attorney. But four of these fifty-six attorneys acted for sixty-four owners, and a further eight for fifty-three more. These specialist agents' names are given in Table 49.

The description common to all these is 'London, merchant'. Jacobsen's is the only name from the partial list of Anne's reign.[4] Of the new men, Craiesteyn, who was in business as a merchant with his brother Abraham,

---

[1] For Irish remittances to England in 1720 see above, p. 140.

[2] Both were Paris bankers, see the index to Lüthy, op. cit.

[3] The North American owners were: Andrew Faneuil of New England, merchant (£3,800 Bank stock), Captain Thomas Miller of New England (£25 South Sea stock) and Thomas Morrey of 'Pensilvania', merchant (£108 East India stock). The Caribbean owners were Thomas Blechynden, factor at Panama (£52), Capt. Edward James, Jamaica (£2,480), Jonas Langford, Antigua (£780), Henry Nelson, planter in Jamaica (£150), Azariah Pinney, Nevis (£1,560), James Pym, 'Carthagena' (£632) and Robert Robertson, Nevis (£106). Apart from Nelson, who held Bank stock, all these holdings were in South Sea stock.

[4] See above, p. 308.

TABLE 49

Some prominent London agents for Dutch stockholders, 1724

Cornelis Backer . . . (11)*		John Leonard d'Orville . . (10)		
Nicholas van Beeck . . . (7)		Francis Pereira . . . (8)		
Gerard Bolwerk . . . (6)		Jacob Abenatar Pimental . . (5)		
Francis Craiesteyn . . . (9)		Raymond de Smeth . . (6)		
John Edwards . . . (22)		H. Martins jun. . . . (7)		
Henry Muilman . . . (21)		Theodore Jacobsen . . . (5)		
				(117)

Source : Bank stock dividend list 25 March 1724, Bank of England Record Office.
* Figure in brackets is the number of clients out of the sample of 200 for whom the agent acted.

and Henry Muilman were to be prominent members of the London financial community for the next thirty years.[1] Specialization by religion seems to have been common but not invariable. Thus Cornelis Backer and John Leonard d'Orville both acted indifferently for native Dutch and Huguenot Dutch owners, while Francis Pereira (who at this date owned over £106,000 Bank stock) acted for Dutch gentiles as well as Dutch Jews. Some of these agents for Dutch stockholders also acted for investors in other countries. John Edwards acted for some holders in the Austrian Netherlands. He and Theodore Jacobsen, who was of German descent, also acted for Germans. The three main agents for Swiss stockholders were Robert Caillé (5), Peter Fabrot (9), Isaac Levinet (9) and Stephen Riou (11), but between them they handled only 10% of Swiss accounts. It was evidently in the Dutch sector of ownership that specialization of agency work had gone farthest.

Some of these correspondents can have done no more than collect and remit dividends and arrange sales and purchases of stock for their foreign clients, in the same way that a banker or other agent would for a client domiciled in England. Thus in the 1740s Edward Brown of London acted out of old friendship as securities agent ('Zyn afaires in de fondsen') for John Alexander van Susteren, Lord of Gravenwesel.[2] Many of them, however,

---

[1] Cf. above, p. 286. Abraham Craiesteyn was later (1750) 'of Witcomb, near Bath'.

[2] Amsterdam, Archief Brants 1344, van Hemert & Co. in London to J. I. de Neufville in Amsterdam, 13 May 1748.

were mercantile correspondents as well, and handled security business merely as part of a spectrum of financial and commercial activities. For more than a century the mercantile communities of England and the United Provinces had had close links not only of trade, but of mutual residence and apprenticeship, and exchange of visits. By the early eighteenth century it seems to have been an established custom for English youths to serve an apprenticeship in Holland, and Dutch ones in England. For example on 6 April 1701 (N.S.) Cornelis van Leeuwen of Amsterdam gives a letter of attorney to Pieter Mortier of London to look after the former's son Pieter, 'apprenticed in a shop in England'. On 25 June (N.S.) in the same year George and Isaac Clifford of Amsterdam accept Thomas Roycraft as apprentice for six years, the cost of £200 to be borne by Roycraft's father Samuel, a London merchant.[1] Foreign residence was not confined to apprenticeship. English merchants in the United Provinces and elsewhere were among the earliest contributors to English long-term government loans.[2] Scottish merchants also had a long and successful tradition of residence abroad. Andrew Russell, for example, to whom Dr. Smout has recently drawn attention, was Scottish factor in Rotterdam from 1688 to 1697, and had commissions from many of the leading merchants of his homeland.[3] Similarly, Dutch merchants resident in London like John Crellius, Henry Muilman or John and Wolfgang van Hemert were obvious choices as mercantile agents for houses in Holland.[4] Superimposed on this pattern were the international ties of the Huguenot and Jewish communities, which spanned all the important commercial centres of Western Europe. Permanent residence, and absorption into the society of the country of adoption, which during the seventeenth and eighteenth centuries occurred mutually between most of the states bordering the North Sea, establishing the Vansittarts in England, the Dicksons in Sweden, the Hopes and Cliffords in Amsterdam, was thus merely the final stage of a process of exchange in men, ideas, friendship and family ties, as well as trade, which made the old North Sea community in some ways as important as the rising Atlantic community in the West.

[1] Both examples from Amsterdam Gemeente Archief, Notarial Archives, 5880/85 and 3351/1297.

[2] For examples see above, pp. 306–7.

[3] T. C. Smout, *Scottish Trade on the Eve of Union 1660–1707* (Edinburgh and London, 1963).

[4] For the correspondence between London agents and their Dutch principals see the extensive treatment in C. H. Wilson, *Anglo-Dutch Commerce and Finance in the Eighteenth Century.*

V

At the middle of the eighteenth century the pattern of foreign investment in English government securities was broadly the same as it had been thirty years before. But its size had greatly increased, and there were some interesting variations in its details. Table 50 shows the number of foreign accounts in 1750 in the same three stocks that were examined for 1723–4. The amount of stock concerned (£35·3m.) was about half the total National Debt. Compared with the position in 1723–4, the capital of the Bank of England had increased by just under £1m., the East India Company's was the same, and the capital of the South Sea Company had been rearranged and reduced.[1] Foreign ownership in this sector of the National Debt had increased from just under 10% in 1723–4 to just under 20%. But this average conceals the disproportionately large increase in certain stocks. In Bank stock foreign ownership had moved up from 14% (1723–4) to over a third of the whole, in East India stock from 16% (1723–4) to nearly a quarter.[2] This very large overseas ownership of Bank and East India stock at the mid-eighteenth century partly explains contemporary estimates that foreigners held a quarter of the National Debt.[3] The average foreign holding at this date was still larger than the overall average in East India stock and South Sea annuities (though not in Bank stock), but the foreign, like the overall average, had fallen since the earlier period.

Apart from Bank and East India stock and South Sea annuities, the major stocks comprising the National Debt at this date were the new 3%s and 4%s created by the recent War of the Austrian Succession, the trading capital of the South Sea Company (£3,662,784) and the portion (£2,276,894) of South Sea annuities not subscribed to Pelham's reduction of interest. Examination of the ledgers for the great 4% loan of 1748, by far the largest of the war loans, shows that in 1750 nearly £750,000, just over 10% of the whole stock, was in the hands of foreign owners.[4] If foreign ownership of

---

[1] The company's trading capital, the ledgers for which do not survive, had been reduced by this date to £3,662,784.

[2] The Swedish ambassador's opinion in 1735 (cited A. B. Du Bois, *The English Business Company after the Bubble Act*, p. 308) that foreigners owned about a third of East India stock was true — of the wrong company.

[3] See above, p. 305.

[4] Ledgers for this stock, Bank of England Record Office. Cf. also below, p. 331, for a more detailed analysis.

Table 50

Foreign accounts in Bank and East India stock and South Sea annuities 1750

Stock	Nominal Capital £	No. of foreign accounts	As % of total no. of accounts	Stock held £	As % of total stock	Average foreign holding £	Average holding all proprietors £
Bank stock . . .	10,780,000	1,712	36·0	3,800,126	35·3	2,219	2,222
East India stock . .	3,194,080	490	22·9	760,626	23·8	1,552	1,478
South Sea Old Annuities	12,404,270	619	6·1	1,159,654	9·3	1,873	1,183
South Sea New Annuities	8,958,255	680	7·3	1,063,237	11·9	1,563	..
TOTALS/AVERAGES . .	35,336,605	3,501	13·2	6,783,643	19·2	..	..

Source: Ledgers for these stocks. Bank of England Record Office. Bank and East India holdings at 1 March 1750; South Sea annuity holdings subscribed to Pelham's reduction of interest March–May 1750.

the other war stocks was proportionate, its total would have been about £2·1m. No ledgers survive for South Sea stock, but there is a list of voting members of the company for 1747 which shows 323 foreign domiciled proprietors, 219 of whom held between £1,000 and £3,000 stock, twenty-two £10,000 stock or more, and the remaining eighty-two between £3,000 and £10,000. Making the assumptions that the members of the largest group had an average holding of £1,500 stock, the next largest of £5,000 and the smallest of £20,000, total foreign holdings of South Sea stock would have been £1,178,500, which small foreign accounts without voting rights would probably have brought up to £1,200,000, or about a third of the £3·6m. total.[1] Lastly, assuming that the proportion of foreign holdings of South Sea annuities not subscribed to the reduction of interest in 1750 was two-fifths of the holdings subscribed (as it was in the 4% (1748) stock), a further £450,000 or so should be added.[2]

These estimates together come to £3·75m., which when added to the £6·78m. in Table 50 gives a total of foreign ownership of English government stock at the mid-eighteenth century of about £10·5m. The National Debt was then just over £70m., so this proportion would be just under 15%. An apparently authoritative account of 1762, reproduced by Sinclair, computes foreign holdings at that date at about £15m., which Sinclair expands to £17m., roughly 14% of the total debt of £123m.[3] Sinclair thought that the corresponding figure in the late 1780s was just under £24·5m. (this would have been about 10% of the whole debt), Dutch investment in Bank stock in particular having been drastically reduced at the close of the American War.[4] From accounts drawn up for the Commissioners for Taxes during the Napoleonic Wars it seems that in the period 1807–10 foreign

[1] London University, Goldsmiths' Library, Extra Size Folio xviii (49), 'A list of the names of the corporation of the [South Sea Company]'. This list stars proprietors for one, two, three or four votes. (The stock to be held for one vote was £1,000, two £3,000, three £5,000, four £10,000.) Cf. below p. 323n. for similar foreign holdings of South Sea stock in 1810.

[2] Foreign holdings in the 4% (1748) stock in 1750 totalled £748,269. Of this, £550,599 was subscribed to the reduction of interest and £197,670 was sold off or repaid in cash.

[3] Sir John Sinclair, *The History of the Public Revenue of the British Empire* (3rd ed., 1804), app. V, and Sinclair's comments. For the question of foreign ownership see also Mrs. A. C. Carter, 'The Dutch and the English Public Debt in 1777' and 'Dutch Foreign Investment 1738–1800'; both in *Economica*, New Series, xx (1953).

[4] Sinclair, op. cit., pp. 367–8. His figure is £24,435,478. He refers to 'the interest which foreigners possess in our funds' without giving a date. The first edition of volume iii of his book was published in 1790. The National Debt then totalled about £238m.

ownership of English government stock was about £20m.; the National Debt was then well over £500m.[1] By this period, therefore, foreign support had become of marginal importance in government borrowing. The government was able to draw instead on the rapidly increasing national income, which was already financing the growth of industry and would shortly provide massive investment overseas as well.

Table 51 shows the geographical distribution of the foreign accounts in Table 50.

Dutch accounts had increased from 64% of total foreign accounts (1723–4) to 78%. The number of Swiss accounts had diminished by a third, and as a proportion of the total had fallen from 15·8% (1723–4) to 5·8%; though still ranking second they now barely exceeded in number accounts in the Austrian Netherlands, which had increased to 5·5% from a 1723–4 proportion of 3·6%. Italian accounts, too, had greatly increased in number by the mid-century. Irish accounts, like Swiss ones, had diminished both in number and as a proportion of the whole. The peripheral areas of ownership, though insignificant in terms of the stock they controlled, had become more numerous; on the eve of the Seven Years War the English government's creditors were dispersed over the civilized world.

The number of foreign account-holders in 1750 was 2,592, 26% less than the total number of foreign accounts.[2] In 1723–4 the overlap was only 19%; this argues for extension of existing holdings. Although the majority of foreign account holders were still individuals, in Bank stock there was a minority of jointly or trebly-held foreign accounts,[3] and there were also more accounts than previously in all stocks in the names of corporate bodies, many of them charities. For instance, the Directors of the Reformed Bethlemian College of Alba, 'at Emyet in Holland', held £2,150 South Sea Old Annuities. 'The Pastors of the French Church at Basle' held £300 of the same stock, and 'the Rector and Deans of the University of Basle' a further £500. The 'House of Charity of Neufchatel in Switzerland' held

---

[1] B.M. *Collection of Parliamentary Papers* (1806), xii. 447 (1806–7), iv. 49, B.P.P. (1810–11), x. 483. These accounts, drawn up because foreign holdings were exempted from income-tax, show the principal held and the dividends payable in 1803, 1806, 1810 and 1811. The fullest account is for 1810–11. At that date foreign holdings of East India stock were £449,725 and of South Sea stock £1,121,000. No figures for Bank stock are given in any of the accounts.

[2] Taking 'account-holder' to include double or treble holders as well as individual ones. There were 1,744 single-stock owners, 787 in two stocks and 61 in three.

[3] Of the 1,429 Dutch accounts in Bank stock, controlling £3,263,044 stock, sixty were joint or treble accounts, controlling £151,348 stock.

TABLE 51

Geographical distribution of foreign holdings of stock in 1750

Country	Accounts in											% total foreign accts. Nos.	% total foreign £
	Bank stock		East India stock		South Sea Old Annuities		South Sea New Annuities		Totals				
	Nos.	£	Nos.	£	Nos.	£	Nos.	£	Nos.	£			
America	15	36,125	..	..	..	..	4	8,150	19	44,275		*	0·7
Austrian Netherlands	81	119,922	19	15,100	49	82,364	42	79,357	191	296,743		5·5	4·4
Channel Islands	6	2,487	..	..	44	24,083	34	17,544	84	44,114		2·4	0·7
France	5	11,070	..	..	7	22,165	6	7,823	18	41,058		..	..
Germany	48	99,417	23	30,924	12	11,866	22	35,669	105	177,876		2·9	2·6
Ireland	5	5,791	1	1,000	19	17,927	6	2,313	31	27,031		0·9	0·4
Italy	48	105,674	12	17,500	6	6,571	9	6,649	75	136,394		2·1	2·0
Madeira	..	..	1	800	..	..	..	..	1	800		..	..
Minorca	..	..	..	..	2	2,360	..	..	2	2,360		..	..
Portugal	2	1,685	..	..	3	3,329	3	4,900	8	9,914		..	..
Russia	3	7,200	1	1,200	..	..	..	..	4	8,400		..	..
Spain	1	1,025	..	..	..	..	..	..	1	1,025		..	..
Switzerland	64	140,431	18	10,950	55	214,719	66	193,599	203	559,699		5·8	8·3
United Netherlands	1,429	3,263,044	414	682,152	414	761,203	468	685,246	2,725	5,391,645		77·8	79·5
West Indies	5	6,255	1	1,000	3	5,300	..	..	9	12,555		0·2	0·2
Uncertain	..	..	..	..	5	7,767	20	21,987	25	29,754		0·7	0·4
TOTALS	1,712	3,800,126	490	760,626	619	1,159,654	680	1,063,237	3,501	6,783,643		98·8	99·2

Source : See Table 50.

* Very small numbers omitted.

£6,000 South Sea New Annuities, and the 'General Hospital of the City and Republick of Geneva' £180. The Orphans' Chambers of Middelburg (£750) and Utrecht (£250) held East India stock. The 'Directors of the Common Cash of the Collegers holding their Congregation on the Keysersgraft [*sic*] over against the Play House within the City of Amsterdam' held £2,800 Bank stock. As a counterpart to this increase in charitable holdings, there was a marked increase in the proportion of stock held by women, as Table 52 shows. This trend was presumably due partly to the greater

TABLE 52

Women's Share of Foreign Holdings 1723–50

	1723–4		1750	
Stock	Accounts for women %	Stock held %	Accounts for women %	Stock held %
Bank stock .	19·6	16·6	35·6	30·7
East India stock .	19·5	20·1	32·0	28·2
South Sea anns. .	24·7	16·8	38·0	28·0

Source: See notes to Tables 47 and 50 (pp. 312, 321 above).

longevity of women, and partly to the increasing practice of investing widows' dowers and spinsters' legacies in English government stock. It was a tribute to the trust which foreigners felt in the security of the English funds. It also throws some doubts on the hypothesis that the lure of the English National Debt was attracting risk capital away from foreign economies, especially the Dutch economy. For in this sector of investment, at least, it must have been above all security, stability and the absence of risk that were sought.

At the same time there was a widening of the sources of Dutch ownership. In 1723–4 Dutch holdings of East India and South Sea stock, and in particular of Bank stock, centred on Amsterdam, where half the owners of Bank stock were described as 'merchants'.[1] By the middle of the eighteenth century only 45% of Dutch Bank stock accounts were for holders living in Amsterdam, while in East India stock (39%) and South Sea annuities (32%)

[1] See above, p. 315.

the proportion was lower still.[1] Even when allowance is made for the less accurate indexing of the East India and South Sea ledgers, it seems fair to conclude that by the 1750s about two thirds of Dutch owners of English government stock lived outside Amsterdam, mostly in provincial towns like Bois-le-Duc, Dordrecht, Flushing, Haarlem, Leiden, Middelburg, and Utrecht. Further, the extension of provincial holdings seems to have implied as well a shift away from mercantile ownership towards offices and professions. Only 25% of Dutch Bank stock owners in 1750 are described as 'merchant' compared with 44% in 1724, while at the later date other occupations proliferate. To take some examples of Bank stock proprietors: Cornelis Beck 'Secretary of the Ryp in Holland', held £550 Bank stock; Jacob van Belle, 'Lord of Sleewyck, Secretary of Rotterdam', held £1,705; Daniel van Berkelom, 'Middleburg, Military Solicitor', held £500; Pieter Bertrand de Jonge, 'Middleburg, surgeon', held £1,000; Pieter Boddaert, 'Middleburg, Griffier of the Admiralty College of Zeeland', held £1,600; Nicholas de Bye, 'Sheriff and Councillor of Haarlem', held £300; Gysbert Craeyvanger, 'Advocate of the Court of Utrecht', held £1,100; Christoffel van Dam, 'Commissary of the Petty Court of Justice of the City of Haarlem', held £1,000. It would be easy to extend the list through the alphabet. The absence of occupational labels against many foreign names in the East India and South Sea ledgers prevents a similar analysis, but the shift towards provincial ownership in these stocks suggests that a similar change in background occurred there too.

It does not follow that the new sector of Dutch ownership excluded the old. Comparison of lists of owners for 1724 and 1750 shows there was considerable continuity between the two dates. And in nearly every case where an owner of stock in 1724 was still an owner in 1750 he had increased his holding. Thus, Daniel Bernard Guilliamszoon of Utrecht held £7,438 South Sea stock in 1723; in 1750 he held £14,000 South Sea annuities and (in 1747) over £10,000 South Sea stock. His holding of Bank stock was £4,000 in 1724 and £6,600 in 1750.[2] John Berndt Bicker of Amsterdam

---

[1] Based on examination of a sample of 500 Dutch Bank stock accounts; all the Dutch East India stock accounts; and all Dutch accounts in the second subscription of Old South Sea annuities.

[2] Bernard is referred to as 'Guiliamsz' or 'Guilliamsz' in all the ledgers and alphabets. Had he been of Dutch not Huguenot extraction this label would have been Willems[zoon]. His address is given as both Amsterdam and Utrecht in different lists. He has four stars against his name (denoting £10,000 stock or more) in the South Sea list of 1747 (for this see above, p. 285).

held £2,250 Bank stock in 1724, £12,250 in 1750. Allard de la Court held £4,000 Bank stock in 1724, £11,500 in 1750. Maria Duist van Voorhout held £2,125 South Sea stock in 1723 and £9,300 South Sea annuities in 1750. Very substantial increases between the two dates were not uncommon. Thus by 1750 Renate Vincent, Comte d'Hompesch, 'Lt Gen. of ye Dutch Army', had raised his £2,480 South Sea stock of 1723 to £23,331.[1] William Munter, who figures laconically in 1724 as 'Amsterdam, gent.', at that date held £1,000 Bank stock and £1,200 South Sea stock. In 1750, transformed into 'the Rt. Hon. Willem Munter, Burgomaster and Councillor of Amsterdam',[2] he owned £6,600 Bank stock, £9,000 South Sea annuities and between £3,000 and £5,000 South Sea stock.[3] Dirk Roest, still modestly styled 'Amsterdam, gent.' in 1750, held at that date £10,000 or more South Sea stock, £10,000 South Sea annuities, and £15,000 Bank stock; in 1723–4 he had only £638 South Sea stock and £500 Bank stock.[4] William Henry van Schuylenburch held £3,400 South Sea stock in 1723; in 1750 he held in addition £14,000 South Sea annuities.[5] In many other instances the owners of 1723–4 had died, but members of the same family had maintained or increased their holdings.[6] In general, where the same owner, or family, were still concerned in 1750, their stake in the English funds had doubled or trebled. The pattern of Dutch investment in English government stock in the period 1720–50 is thus one of new capital coming partly from new owners and partly from an increase in existing owners' commitments.

Of the 365 English and foreign owners of £10,000 or over in five major stocks in 1750, who between them controlled £8,985,201 stock, eighty-nine were Dutch, controlling £1,550,845.[7] Only £56,308 in the names of

[1] Hompesch is mentioned above, p. 315. He does not appear in the list of voting proprietors of South Sea stock in 1747, so his holding in 1750 was presumably in South Sea annuities only. In the Bank stock alphabet 'deceased, per exor. Gerard van Assendelft' is written against his name, but the alphabet extends several years beyond 1750.

[2] He is so described in the alphabets to the Bank stock ledgers.

[3] He has two stars against his name in the 1747 South Sea voting list. This denotes between £3,000 and £5,000 stock.

[4] Roest has four stars in the 1747 South Sea list.

[5] Schuylenburch has two stars against his name (£3,000–£5,000 stock) in the 1747 voting list, so it is likely that his holding of South Sea stock remained unchanged.

[6] A minor holding which increased in this way belonged to the Brants family, whose archive is now such a valuable source of information for the mercantile history of eighteenth-century Holland. Christoffel Brants held £1,000 Bank stock in 1724. In 1750 Jan Brants held £1,200 Bank stock.

[7] For this list of 1 March 1750, see above, p. 292. The stocks were Bank stock, East India stock, South Sea Old and New Annuities and 4% (1748) stock.

five of these proprietors, was in the 4%s of 1748: the remainder, in the names of eighty-five proprietors, with 108 accounts between them, was in the other four stocks, Dutch holdings in which totalled £5,391,645, in 2,725 accounts.[1] Between them these eighty-five therefore controlled just under 4% of all Dutch accounts and 27.7% of the stock. This agrees well enough with the conclusion reached in the previous chapter that at the mid-eighteenth century 2 to 3% of owners with £10,000 or more each controlled about a quarter of most English government stocks.[2] It was shown earlier that in 1723–4 3% of Dutch proprietors owned 37% of total Dutch-held stock. The proportion in 1750 would probably be similar, since the list of large stockholders in 1750 includes only units of £10,000 or more in each stock, whereas the earlier list was cumulative. Of these 'fine stately capitalists' of 1750 twenty-two (26%) were women, owning between them £423,975, 21% of the total.[3] Only one of these, and four of the male owners, were Jews.[4] A further handful of owners, like Allard de la Court (£11,500), Daniel Bernard Guilliamsz (£20,600) or Peter Huguetan (£10,000) were — for what the distinction was still worth — of Huguenot extraction. The majority, however, were native-born Dutch. Nearly all accounts are in the names of individuals. With the exception of the holding of the Parnassims of the Portuguese Jews, there are no big corporate holdings corresponding to those of the English Accountant-General of Chancery or the London trading companies and insurance offices. In this sector, Dutch investment at the mid-eighteenth century was still personal, not institutional. Finally, it is worth noticing that fifty-one (60%) of these big stockholders lived in Amsterdam. At the top, the geographical concentration of ownership characteristic of the 1720s was thus still observable.

Ownership of English government stock in the Austrian Netherlands centred on Antwerp, where, for instance, sixty-two of the eighty-one holders of Bank stock in 1750 lived. They included Jean Baptiste van Delft,

---

[1] For these figures see Table 51 on p. 324 above. Of the five holders of 4% stock, only one, Anne de Haze, held £10,000 or over in other stocks.

[2] See Table 40, above.

[3] The phrase quoted was actually used by van Hemert & Co. apropos of John de Neufville's London correspondents, van Hemert & Co. in London to J. I. de Neufville in Amsterdam, 2 November 1744, Archief Brants, 1344.

[4] Rachel Mendes de Costa (£13,052); and Abraham Nunes Henriquez (£15,009); Abraham Teixeira de Mattos (£16,000); the Parnassims of the Portuguese Jewish Nation at Amsterdam (£28,500) and Antonio de Pinto (£11,250), a total of £83,811.

'Banker', who held £1,464 stock.[1] In Germany, holders of stock were, as in the 1720s, merchants, officials and professional men. Justus Anton Conradi of Hanover 'Secretary of the Private Cabinet', who held £200 Bank stock and £100 East India stock, and Carl Dietrich Ebell of Hanover, 'Assessor of the Court of Judicature', with £540 Bank stock, and £275 East India stock were in the orbit of the Hanoverian court. Major Jean Penvaise, 'Major of the King of Prussia's Horse Grenadiers', (£1,100 Bank stock) must have been of Huguenot extraction. Other holders lived in Danzig and Berlin. In Switzerland, where there had been considerable disinvestment from English securities since the early 1720s, the most important holding of stock was still that of the Canton of Berne, which owned £69,850 Bank stock and £287,461 South Sea annuities (which it prudently refrained from subscribing until the second stage of Pelham's reduction of interest). James de Hervart (£10,350 South Sea annuities) was the only other Swiss owner of more than £10,000 in any one stock. Swiss owners were nearly all domiciled in Geneva (thirty-five of the sixty-four Swiss Bank stock accounts, for example, were for owners in Geneva), Berne and Lausanne. Most holdings were for individuals, but there were three for hospitals at Berne and Geneva, one for 'the Abbey of Tanners at Berne,' one for 'the Pastors of the French Church at Basle', and one for the 'President and Assessors of the House of Charity of Neufchatel'.[2] The families of de Graffenried and de Watteville, both of Berne, invested their 'common cash' in English stock.[3] Some of these Swiss noble accounts lasted for many years. When the South Sea 3%s of 1751 were paid off in 1854, a small number of accounts was converted into 2½% stock, among them £3,300 held by 'the

---

[1] Aimé Grenier of Vevey in Switzerland, who held £1,200 Bank stock is similarly described as 'citizen and Banker'. Cf. the description of Donat Chabbert as 'banker' in the South Sea ledgers in 1723, above, p. 317. By 1750 the Bank of England largely also used 'banker' for Londoners too, but sometimes still called them by the older name of 'goldsmith', see below, p. 450.

[2] The President and Directors of the Great Hospital of Berne held £220 Bank stock and £1,091 South Sea annuities. The President and Directors 'of the Hospital of the Sick call'd Lisle of Berne' held £770 Bank stock and £812 South Sea annuities. 'The Syndic, Procurators and Directors of the Hospital General of Geneva' held £1,650 Bank stock and £180 South Sea annuities. The Abbey of Tanners held £956 South Sea annuities, the Pastors of the French Church at Basle £300 more and the Neufchâtel House of Charity a further £6,000.

[3] 'The President and Directors of the Common Cash of the Noble Family of de Graffenried of Berne' held £200 East India stock. The de Wattevilles, similarly described, held £200 East India stock and £545 South Sea annuities.

Directors of the Purse of the Poor of the Noble Family of Gallatin of Geneva'.[1]

Italian ownership of English government stock had markedly increased since the early 1720s. There had then been only seven Italian accounts in the ledgers. By 1750 there were seventy-five. Virtually all these owners lived in Genoa or Leghorn. The description in the Bank stock alphabets against Leghorn names is usually simply 'merchant', and against those from Genoa, ' a noble Genoese', or 'a nobleman of Genoa', appropriately Shakespearian usage for Garrick's contemporaries. Among these families were those of Carrega, Cattaneo, Centurioni, Doria, Fiesco, Lomellino, della Rovere and Spinola. Here, as elsewhere, nearly all accounts were for individuals. There were sixteen French stockholders, owning between them £43,659. Four were women, of whom one, Marguérite Girardot de Préfond of Paris, had the largest single French holding (£8,300). Only six of the sixteen lived in Paris.[2] The four Russian-domiciled owners of English stock were Wilhelm Grote, merchant of Riga (£1,000), Lt.-Gen. Georg Wilhelm de Hennin of 'Petersburgh in Russia' (£2,200) and John Tamesz, 'Esq. of Moscow' (£4,000), all in Bank stock.[3] In East India stock there was one Russian proprietor, Earl Moise Vladislavich of 'Petersburg' (£1,200), who sold his stock in October 1750. On the other side of the world, there were 15 American-domiciled owners of Bank stock in 1750. Among them were Charles Apthorp (£4,500), James Boutineau (£4,400) and Benjamin Faneuil (£3,030), all merchants of Boston; the 'hero of Louisburg', Sir William Pepperell, Bart. (£1,200); the South Carolina merchants Alexander and Henry Peronneau (£2,045 and £1,295); Edward Bradley, a merchant in Philadelphia (£105); Addington Davenport of Boston, clerk (£4,290), and Nicholas Salisbury, (£1,600), a barber in the same town. The

---

[1] Ledgers for South Sea 3% (1751) stock, Bank of England Record Office.

[2] The French stockholders were Felles Baudry, Dieppe, £1,400; Jean Masson de Bessé, Esq., Paris, £2,200; John Boucoiron, Languedoc, £400; Anne Calandrini, wife of Jean Huber of Lyons, £220; Isaac DuPont, Paris, £1790; Paul Girardot, Paris, £4,600; Marguérite Girardot de Préfond, Paris, £8,300; John Augustus Hauteclaire, Caen, £634; Anna Gomez Henriquez, Bordeaux, £3,375; Marie Locher, spinster, Paris, £7,150; John de Moraes, Bordeaux, £7,010; Francis de Nogaret, St. André, £1,000; Antonio Rodriguez Nunes, Bordeaux, £2,180; Stephen de Peyre, 'Milhau in Languedoc' £400, Peter Simard, Loriel, £2,800; Isaac Thelluson, Paris, £200.

[3] John Tamesz also held £1,018 4% (1748) stock at this date. Two members of the Tamesz family (Jean and Paulus) were Moscow correspondents of David Leeuw of Amsterdam in the period 1712–25 (Catal. Archief Brants (see Bibliography under 'Archief Brants'), no. 985), but it is not clear whether the John Tamesz mentioned in the text is the same as Jean Tamesz.

Rev. Colin Campbell of 'Pensilvania' (£550), John Catherwood of New York (£600), the Hon. George Clinton, Governor of New York (£3,000) and Edward Fenwick, Esq., of South Carolina (£4,000) held South Sea annuities. There were accounts in Bank and East India stock and in South Sea annuities for five proprietors living in Antigua, one in Barbados, two in Curacao and one in Montserrat.[1]

In concluding this section, it is worth noticing that the structure of foreign ownership in 4% (1748) stock in 1750 was broadly similar to that in Bank and East India stock and South Sea annuities. Examination of the foreign holdings suggests that the same sources provided capital both for war loans and investment in the stock of the monied companies. The total of 4% (1748) stock in 414 foreign accounts in 1750 was £748,269.[2] Of this, £278,322 in 144 accounts was subscribed at the first stage of Pelham's reduction of interest, £272,277 in 154 accounts at the second stage and £197,670 in 116 accounts was sold off, or repaid by the government. Of the £748,269, £510,723 (68%) was held in 309 accounts (74% of total foreign accounts) by investors in the United Provinces. Of these 309 accounts, only 127 were in Amsterdam. Eighty-five (27%) of the Dutch proprietors were women, a somewhat lower figure than in the stocks previously examined. The largest sector of ownership after the United Provinces was Ireland, with fifteen accounts controlling £72,400, but this was largely due to the £51,000 held by Nathaniel Clements of Dublin. Next to Ireland came the Austrian Netherlands (thirty-nine accounts controlling £53,900 stock) and Italy (thirteen accounts, £45,900 stock). There was one account in America, for Charles Apthorp, merchant of Boston (£5,328). There were two in the Channel Islands, one in Russia, for John Tamesz, merchant of St. Petersburg (£1,018), one in Scotland for Alexander le Grand of Edinburgh (£500) and three in France (John Black, merchant in Bordeaux, £1,000; John Masson de Bessé of Paris, gent., £11,200; Madalène Susane Marie de St. George, Paris, spinster, £450). There were only nineteen Swiss accounts, totalling £20,600. Lastly, Hendrik Swellengrebel, governor of the Cape of Good Hope, held £6,700. Most foreign holders, whether in the United Provinces

[1] Archibald Cochran, merchant, Antigua (£2,750 Bank stock); James Doig, 'Planter', Antigua, a further £2,255; Samuel Martin of Green Castle, Antigua (£1,800 South Sea annuities); Dorothy Thibou, widow, Antigua (£440 Bank stock); Harry Webb of Antigua (£2,500 South Sea annuities); Arthur Upton, Esq., Barbados (£150 Bank stock); William Meyer, Curaçao, merchant (£660 Bank Stock); Moses Penso of Curaçao (£1,000 East India stock); Dominick Trant of Montserrat (£1,000 South Sea annuities).
[2] Ledgers for this stock, Bank of England Record Office.

M   D.F.R.

or outside, came, as these examples show, from families already familiar as investors in Bank and East India stock or South Sea annuities.

VI

To recapitulate the argument to this stage. Foreign investment in English long-term securities went through three main phases between 1688 and 1756. In the first, from roughly 1688 to 1713, there was a fairly large flow of overseas funds into government single-life annuities, and a smaller speculative flow into purchases of lottery tickets, but foreign purchases of government long annuities and of the stock of the Bank and East India Company were infrequent. The next phase, from 1713 to 1724, shows, first, a gradual increase in foreign investment in all securities, then a very rapid acceleration of this trend during the period of the South Sea crisis (1719–22), which brought overseas holdings to a significant level for the first time. In the third phase, lasting until the eve of the Seven Years War, the foreign sector of ownership expanded more than the increase in the public debt, and by the early 1750s was proportionately, though not absolutely, as large as it was ever to be in the eighteenth century. Within this overall pattern the main subordinate trends, mostly developing during the period 1720–50, were the increase of Dutch ownership at the expense of other countries, particularly Switzerland, a higher proportion of foreign owners in Bank stock and East India stock than in South Sea and other government annuities, a shift in the proportions of Dutch ownership away from Amsterdam towards the provinces, and a significant increase in the proportion of women owners of stock.

Why had this movement of long-term capital occurred, and what were its significance and consequences? Contemporaries stressed the importance of the lower Dutch rate of interest, which forced her capitalists to look for higher yields abroad. The difference between English and Dutch rates probably was important, though it was not as great as was often supposed.[1] It must also be noted that the gap was largest in the early part of the period (1690–1715) rather than in the decades 1720–50 when Dutch investment in English securities increased most. A second general factor must have been the comfortable current account surplus of the Dutch balance of pay-

<hr>

[1] See below, p. 474.

ments with England, which enabled the Dutch patriciate to export their funds on a sizeable scale. Other factors which must have affected the decisions of all foreign investors were, first, successful English management of the public debt in the period immediately after the peace of 1713, and the maintenance of public faith during the storms of the South Sea Bubble; second, the fact that English securities, unlike those of several foreign countries, including the United Provinces, were free of tax, and transfer charges were low. In trade, 3% to 4% was a quite insufficient yield, as the London merchant Claude Bosanquet pointed out to Jan Isaak de Neufville in July 1749.[1] But on government securities it must have seemed an acceptable, because net, return.

The dividends payable on foreign holdings would, assuming a 4% rate and taking the estimates of aggregate foreign ownership arrived at earlier in this chapter, have been of the order of £175,000 p.a. at the beginning of the period 1720–50 and £420,000 p.a. at the end of it. It is unlikely that there was much offset to this in the form of English investment in European government securities, though the whole subject has been little studied.

Loans for foreign governments were raised in London at intervals during the eighteenth century. The Emperor, for example, borrowed £250,000 in 1706, £89,950 in 1710, a further £250,000 in 1735 and £320,000 more in 1737. The Dutch government evidently borrowed £50,000 in 1749.[2] The only subscription lists to survive, for the loan of 1706, show that the lenders were primarily London merchants and financiers, though understandably, as the loan was intended for an ally in grave difficulties, the queen and leading Ministers were the first to put their names down.[3] The total of these foreign loans raised in London during the whole of the eighteenth century was probably small, but English investors must also have contributed to foreign loans raised abroad, such as the Emperor's million reichsthaler loan of 1730 secured, like the one raised in London in 1735, on the Silesian revenues. It is known that 400,000 thalers of this came from Holland; English contributions may have helped to complete it.[4] So far as

[1] Archief Brants, 1344. Bosanquet to de Neufville 4 July 1749.

[2] The Austrian borrowing is listed by F. von Mensi, *Die Finanzen Österreichs von 1701 bis 1740* (Vienna, 1890). For the Dutch loan see p. 230, above.

[3] The subscription books for this loan are in the Bank of England Record Office. The episode is described by H. L. Mikoletzky, 'Die Grosse Anleihe von 1706', *Mitt. des Österreichischen Staatsarchivs*, vii (1954), 268–93.

[4] Österreichisches Staatsarchiv, Hofkammerarchiv, Hof Finanz Akten 21 February 1730, order for receipt of 400,000 thalers lent by 'einige holländische particulares' towards the one million Silesian loan. One million *reichsthaler* would have been about £180,000.

Dutch securities were concerned, the motives of English buyers whose correspondence is in the Archief Brants in Amsterdam are entirely speculative. Thus Thomas Church of London writes to Jan Isaak de Neufville in Amsterdam in September 1732

You was so kind to Promise me yt that you would Examine some Tickits for me in ye Hague Lottery; & when you have any Other Business to Write to Mee I should be glad if you'l Insert ye Sucksess of each Tickit; & you'l much oblige your very humble servt.[1]

Similar London requests came to de Neufville from Kelsey Bull & Co. in 1742, John Dupré in 1748 and Nathaniel Torriano in 1750.[2] Torriano sent him three tickets 'as they were bought in London', so there must have been fairly regular English interest in these Dutch loans.[3] There is, however, no trace in the correspondence of serious English buying of Dutch securities, or of regular agency arrangements for this purpose.

It is not certain whether foreigners' dividends were always remitted from England when received. Jan Isaak de Neufville's London agents regularly credited his account with dividends due on his English securities, and on at least one occasion, in 1745, used a dividend to help finance the purchase of new stock.[4] Dividends credited in this way became part of the miscellany of debts and credits between mercantile firms, who settled balances due to each other by periodic drawing of bills of exchange, though admittedly this complicated the bookkeeping, rather than altering the economic significance, of foreigners' earnings. Other Dutch investors simply drew their dividends when due. Thus Simon Bevel's London agents regularly remitted him his £9 p.a. Exchequer annuity in the years 1710–17. In the years 1721–5 his new agents Abraham and Francis Craiesteyn equally remitted twice a year

[1] Archief Brants, 1344, Church to de Neufville 6 September 1732. He gives the numbers of his four tickets at the foot of the page.

[2] Ibid., Kelsey Bull & Co. to de Neufville, 2 November 1742; Dupré to de Neufville, 12 February 1748; Torriano to de Neufville, 8 March 1750.

[3] P.R.O. C 107/47 contains an entire book of tickets of the first class of the Groningen lottery of 1721, presumably sent over for sale in London. Cf. E. Victor Morgan and W. A. Thomas, The Stock Exchange (1962), p. 43, for an advertisement of Groningen lottery tickets by Matthew West in 1722.

[4] Archief Brants, 1344, van Hemert & Co. in London to de Neufville 15 February, 9 April, 9 August and 11 October 1745, 29 July 1746 (in Dutch). In their letter of 11 October 1745 van Hemerts said they would use £264 16s. 0d. dividends due on de Neufville's Bank stock and South Sea annuities to help finance the purchase he had requested of £500 Bank stock, and would draw the balance at sight.

the dividends due on his Bank stock.[1] It may be surmised that the increase in ownership of English securities by the *rentiers* of the Dutch provincial towns in the period 1720–50 increased direct dividend remittance as distinct from the treatment of dividends as one of a number of items in a trading account.

Following logically from the rising curve of foreign, especially Dutch, investment in English securities, a close link grew up in the period 1720–50 between the Amsterdam Bourse and the London market in securities. Dealings in English securities in Amsterdam were (like those in London) partly real and partly speculative. One aspect of 'real' Dutch ownership was that English securities were increasingly used by Amsterdamers as collateral for short-term loans. The index of loans recorded in the Amsterdam Notarial Archives compiled by Professor Hamilton shows that up to about 1719 the collateral used was mostly Dutch government securities, but that after this English government securities were increasingly used, and by the mid-1720s predominated.[2] These loans were nearly all for periods from three months to a year, and the lenders were members of solid patriciate families.

English securities were bought and sold on the Amsterdam Bourse for delivery in London. Thus in January 1750 van Hemert & Co. in London thank Jan Isaak de Neufville in Amsterdam for buying them £4,000 South Sea stock at 111, for which they had asked in December 1749.[3] In February 1750 they write, 'We shall receive the £4,000 S.S. Shares into our name tomorrow and have remitted you f. 169·9 for costs and commission.'[4] The form of contract note for such purchases was a straight obligation to deliver (or accept) £*x* stock in London. Thus a contract dated 4 April 1730 between Jacob Reynst and David Leeuw, both of Amsterdam, translates as follows:

I the undersigned acknowledge to have Bought from *Heer David Leeuw One Thousand* Pounds Sterling Capital Shares of the *Bank of England* at London, at a price of a *Hundred and Forty Five and a Quarter per Cent* remaining after the Dividend paid last *October*, for settlement on next 15 *May*, the which £1000 I oblige myself to receive in London at the stated Price. And in case in the interim any

---

[1] Archief Brants, 1736, Bevel's ledger 1710–14 (agents Schoppens & Edwards); ibid. 1739, Bevel's ledger 1721–25 (agents Abraham and Francis Craiesteyn). See also above, p. 308, for Bevel's purchases.

[2] Amsterdam, Gemeente Archief, index of *obligaties* and *leningen* in the Notarial Archives drawn up by Professor Earl J. Hamilton for his forthcoming work on John Law. I am indebted to Professor Hamilton for allowing me to see this data. Cf. also p. 473 below.

[3] Archief Brants, 1344, van Hemert & Co. to de Neufville, 5 January 1750 (in Dutch).

[4] Ibid., same to same 13 February 1750 (in Dutch).

Dividend is paid, it shall be to my profit and to reduction of the above Price. Contrarywise all Supplementations and Calls shall be at my expense, in the usual way. All done in good faith at Amsterdam the *Fourth April* Seventeen hundred *and thirty*.[1]

A written footnote adds that this bargain is to be outside the Rescounters, the quarterly settlement day (in this case 15 May) at which contracts could be carried forward on payment of a fee.[2] It looks, therefore, as though this stock was actually transferred. The form of the contract note, however, did not make this really necessary. It was equally well adapted to a merely speculative bargain, in which at settlement day only the rise or fall in the price of stock since the contract day would be adjusted, and it is clear from de Pinto's description that a very large number of the bargains in English (and Dutch) securities on the Bourse were 'on margin' in this way.[3]

At a political level, foreign, especially Dutch, investment in English government securities was an important ancillary cause of English success in the wars of 1739–63. The Dutch, perhaps, supplied the extra margin of funds without which, on de Pinto's argument, the rest would have been committed in vain.[4] And they did this whether combatant, as in the later stages of the War of the Austrian Succession, or neutral, as in the Seven Years War. This foreign support enabled England to extend aid by way of subsidies to powers like Austria, and later Prussia, whose export of capital was negligible.[5]

At a technical economic level, the rise of the Dutch sector of ownership in the English funds affected the Amsterdam market by expanding the collateral available for short-term loans, and the range and amount of securities dealt in on the Bourse, while accelerating the emergence of quarterly settlement days in London, and leading to close liaison between the

---

[1] See Plate 7. A printed footnote adds that the contract must be fulfilled within two months of settlement day or be void. The phrase 'remaining after the Dividend' was common form in Dutch contracts and probably originated in the days of terminable joint-stock companies.

[2] For the introduction of English Rescounters see below, p. 509. The English days were also on 15 February, 15 May, 15 August and 15 November, but owing to the difference between the Dutch and English calendars were actually eleven days later, hence could take account of bargains done in Amsterdam (ibid.).

[3] [Isaac de Pinto], *Traité de la Circulation et du Crédit* (partly written in the early 1760s). The most recent treatment of the whole subject of Dutch share-dealings is in C. H. Wilson, *Anglo-Dutch Commerce and Finance in the Eighteenth Century*.

[4] For de Pinto's argument see above, p. 9.

[5] Though, as this chapter has shown, this was diminishingly true of the Austrian Netherlands.

London and Amsterdam markets. Its significance for the Dutch and English economies as a whole is still subject to debate. It can be argued that it deprived the Dutch economy of the funds needed for growth, and thus accelerated Dutch economic decline in the eighteenth century.[1] It can also be argued that the import of foreign capital released English funds, which would otherwise have been tied up in government loans, for industrial development. But there are other factors to be considered. It is not clear from the evidence reviewed in the last two chapters that the savers who were investing in English government securities in either Holland or England would willingly have switched their money into risky industrial ventures. Again, it might be argued that Dutch purchases of English securities, however they affected the long-term position, actually improved the Dutch *short-term* capital market, by giving it better collateral for loans, and providing a regular flow of income for such loans in the form of dividends and interest on English securities. Further, the 'decline' of the United Provinces in the eighteenth century is recognizably a relative one, due to the faster growth of the two much bigger neighbouring powers, France and England, with their larger markets and larger populations.[2] Perhaps the real financial weakness of the United Provinces in this period was its failure to develop an institutional structure able to provide long- as well as short-term capital, on the lines which the London banks and insurance companies had evolved by the eve of the Seven Years War.

[1] C. H. Wilson, op. cit.

[2] J. de Vries, *De economische Achteruitgang der Republick in de Achtiende Eeuw* (Amsterdam, 1959).

PART FOUR

Government
Short-term Borrowing

13

Borrowing by Exchequer Tallies

I

THE provision of long-term capital to finance the state's war expenses was the most novel feature of the Financial Revolution, and the one that attracted most contemporary notice. But the arrangements made for government short-term finance were of equal, though less conspicuous, importance. These included anticipation of annual tax revenue; payment on credit for goods and services supplied to the Army and Navy; and co-ordination of the government's short-term financial needs with those of the monied companies, particularly the East India Company and the Bank of England, the former, in particular, being a prominent short-term borrower. Care had also to be taken that short-term needs did not conflict with those for longer-dated finance, since the two were closely connected. This was a problem of which the monied companies were well aware. As Sir John Eyles, the Sub-Governor of the South Sea Company, told his shareholders in September 1721, 'the Maintaining the Credit of your Bonds is the only way to support the true Value of the Stock, the one alwayes suffering proportionally to the Discredit of the Other'.[1] From a government point of view, issue of short-dated paper beyond the capacity to redeem it regularly (and thus maintain public confidence in it while outstanding) was a perennial fiscal temptation. The French government, for example, after 1704, fell prey to this temptation to such an extent that its whole machinery of credit was soon virtually ruined. The English seemed likely in the 1690s to tread a similar path, but recovered in time.

II

The hard core of anticipation of government revenue under the early Stuarts was the advances made by the Customs farmers in anticipation of

---

[1] Add. MS. 25544, f. 11, South Sea G. Ct. Bk., 1 September 1721.

their stipulated payments.[1] Owing to the price changes, administrative mis-management and political tensions of the period, the system did not work well, the Crown always borrowing more than it could repay from current income. The system itself, however, was not in principle wrong, and was continued in an altered form after the Restoration, particularly from 1671, when Customs revenue was placed in the hands of commissioners. The Customs cashier became a principal source of annual advances, and from 1683, when the Excise revenue was also put into commission, the two Cashiers Richard Kent (Customs) and Charles Duncombe (Excise) supplied the greater part of the £150,000–£250,000 annually anticipated in cash.[2] As Dr. Chandaman says,

the revenue which passed through their hands as Cashiers offered unrivalled security for loans, and as government creditors the partners played a part during the decade before the Revolution not unlike that of the goldsmith bankers in the period before the Stop of the Exchequer.[3]

There are obvious resemblances to the advances made by the General Farmers to the French Crown in the eighteenth century and, more speci-fically, the advances made to the Exchequer by the Bank of England from the 1690s onwards. The system's main defect was that the cashiers had no parliamentary guarantee for repayment of their loans, and were thus de-pendent on the competence and goodwill of the government, without any guarantee of redress if things went wrong.

A second important source of government short-term finance in the later Stuart period was the City of London, whose Chamberlain normally acted as agent for the citizens' loans. Surviving records show twelve loans of this kind from the citizens between 1660 and 1680, largely concentrated in the 1660s and in the period 1677–9. The total lent was just over £1m., £406,000 of which was lent in 1678 and 1679.[4] According to Dr. Chanda-man's figures the government borrowed and repaid just under £6m. between 1660 and 1688, so the City contributions on the eve of the Exclusion Crisis were second in importance only to the advances of the revenue cashiers.[5]

[1] R. Ashton, *The Crown and the Money Market, 1603–1640* (Oxford: Clarendon Press, 1960).

[2] C. D. Chandaman, unpub. London University doctoral thesis 1954, 'The English Public Revenue (1660–1688)'.

[3] Ibid. i. 198 n. 'Offered unrivalled security for loans' should perhaps be spelled out as 'gave them unrivalled security for the loans which they made to the government'.

[4] Corporation of London Records Office, index under 'loans'.

[5] Chandaman, op. cit. i. 512, untotalled table of sums annually borrowed in cash and repaid 1660–88. I have totalled the figures, repeating the previous ones where there are gaps, as £5,879,904 lent and £6,064,945 repaid.

The attractiveness of the loans from the lenders' standpoint was, first, that they were authorized by Parliament and charged on specific direct taxes, and were therefore a reliable investment. Second, procedure was simple. For example, the ledger for a loan of £100,000 made in anticipation of the Poll Tax of 1678 shows the Chamberlain receiving 653 separate contributions on behalf of the Exchequer between 11 and 26 April 1678 and repaying them with interest (having first collected the money from the Exchequer) between 3 July 1678 and 29 March 1679.[1] Interest rates went as high as 10% on at least one loan (on the Six Months Assessment of 1661, 12 Ch. II, cc. 27–28) but on others were 6% and, in 1678–9, 7%. Part (one-third) of a loan on Fee Farm rents in the 1670s was raised at 5%.[2] These were lower rates than the government was to pay in the 1690s. The development of the struggle between Crown and Parliament from 1679, however, into which the City of London was increasingly drawn, impaired the development of this sector of public borrowing. After 1680 no new direct taxes were imposed until after the political revolution of 1688, and City loans in anticipation came to an end for a decade.

III

In contrast to the relatively modest sums which the government borrowed in cash during the 1680s, the total of short-term loans recorded at the Exchequer between 1688 and 1697 was very large. The total was over £32m.[3]

It was not long before the strains imposed by these heavy demands began to show. In negotiations for individual advances from the Excise and Customs Cashiers and other lenders in the period 1691–3, the Treasury seems invariably to have allowed 2% 'gratuity' as well as 6% interest; yet it was on such privately-negotiated loans that it might have expected more favourable rates than on public ones.[4] In April 1693 Sir Joseph Herne and Sir Stephen

---

[1] Corporation of London Records Office, MS. 40/43. Only £90,000 is listed as repaid; the rest of the volume is blank. The Act was 29 & 30 Ch. II, c. 1.

[2] Corporation of London Record Office, index under 'loans'.

[3] See Table 53 on p. 344.

[4] Details of loan terms in P.R.O. T 29/627, extracts from Treasury Board Minutes 1691–1702. Cf. Davenant's character Double in *The True Picture of a Modern Whig* (1701), p. 11: 'for some time I drove a Trade of getting people to lend Money to the Government; Per Manus Double was very well known in the Treasury, the Prem[i]ums I shared with the Lender, many more did the same, and by this we fleec'd the Publick bravely'.

TABLE 53

Government short-term borrowing 1688–97

Years	£	No. of tax funds on which loans charged	Interest %
1688–91	7,880,080	19	7–8
1691–92	3,058,292	9	7–8
1692–93	4,300,428	10	7–8
1693–94	3,188,802	13	7–8
1694–95	5,521,827	12	7–8
1695–96	4,971,104	15	5–8
1696–97	3,156,729	6	6–8
	£32,177,262		

Source : Cal. T. Bks. IX (i) and XI (i), statements of income and expenditure printed from P.R.O. T 30/1, Treasury Account Books. Interest on loans on direct taxes was at a fixed rate: 7% to 1694, 5% in 1695, 6% in 1696, 8% in 1697 and 1698, 7% in 1699, 5% in 1700, 6% in 1701 and 1702. Loans on the Customs in 1695 were scaled from 5% to 8% according to the priority of repayment of a given tally. This was also done in 1696 and (in a reduced range, 7 and 8% and 6 and 7%) in 1698 and 1701.

Evance, in a proposal for remittances to Leghorn and Genoa, suggested they should receive 2% gratuity 'for Hazard of bills and grave loss by selling Tallies'.[1] (Tallies were the Exchequer's formal wooden receipts, which could in certain circumstances be used also to make payments.[2]) In May the gunmakers of the City of London complained to the Treasury that the Board of Ordnance, instead of paying them for their work in cash, had offered them tallies, on which they could raise no money. Like most petitioners of the period they were 'ready to perish' unless quickly helped.[3] In June, the Navy Board Commissioners were told they would receive part

[1] P.R.O. T 29/627, 19 April 1693. [2] Cf. also below, p. 350.

[3] *Cal. T. Papers 1557–1696*, p. 294. For the Ordnance Board's system of debentures see below, p. 397. The gunmakers were presumably offered tallies instead of cash for their debentures when they became due for payment.

of their supply in tallies, and 'must endeavour to raise the money at as reasonable rates as may be'.[1] In September 1693 the Commissioners for Sick and Wounded Seamen reported that government credit was very bad at Rochester and Chatham.[2] A year later, in September 1694, the Board of Ordnance claimed that £20,000 Land Tax tallies imprested to them for payment of contractors were 'nothing worth'.[3] In the following month a memorial from the officers of Lord Oxford's Royal Regiment of Horse stated that £5,000 in tallies had been paid them as part of their arrears, and that they could only dispose of them at 25–30% loss.[4] In January 1695 the artificers of the Ordnance were threatening to take their case to the House of Commons.[5] The House might perhaps have given them relief, but the Treasury could not; in the same month it plaintively minuted an offer to contract for mourning facilities for the late Duchess of Modena: 'we have not creditt enough to furnish His Majesty with a mourning coach or mourning for a footman to waite on him'.[6]

Worse was to come, as the control which the Treasury exerted over the situation weakened, and the terms offered by the monied men and contractors increasingly determined government credit bargains. A note of desperation begins to appear in the Treasury Board's proceedings. In May 1696 the East India Company, which had been paid £10,000 in Land Tax tallies for saltpetre supplied to the Ordnance, was authorized 'to obtain the mony to be advanced on those Tallys as Cheap as is possible and be allowed the Discount at the King's Charge'.[7] In March 1697 the Board agreed to the Ordnance accepting 26% discount when making payment in tallies.[8] In the same month the Ordnance Commissioners told the Treasury that the contractors in Flanders refused to bring one horse into the field until their last year's arrears were paid. Moreover, said the Commissioners, 'persons are now very shy in treating about the discompt of any talleys'.[9]

Weakened credit also affected the remittances for payment of the troops overseas. As early as January 1695 it was said of the great London merchant Sir Joseph Herne that without his credit and assistance the artillery train in Flanders would have starved during the winter.[10] The massive remittances, and the weakening of government credit, were already affecting the rate of exchange on Amsterdam, which sank 15% between January 1694 and

---

[1] P.R.O. T 29/627, 21 June 1693.   [2] *Cal. T. Papers 1557–1696*, p. 319.

[3] Ibid., p. 391, 4 October 1694.   [4] Ibid., p. 397.   [5] Ibid., p. 424.

[6] Ibid., p. 425.   [7] P.R.O. T 29/627, 12 May 1696.   [8] Ibid., 3 March 1697.

[9] *Cal. T. Papers 1697–1702*, p. 17, 15 March 1697.

[10] *Cal. T. Papers 1557–1696*, p. 424.

August 1695. In the early part of 1695 the Bank of England took over the main remittance contract for Flanders for one year, and set up an office staffed by three directors in Brussels to carry it out. Over the next two years this imprudent heroism, without which the campaign in the Netherlands would have collapsed, involved the Bank in a loss of £128,000.[1] Yet even this did not remove the Treasury's need to allow generous discounts in other exchange contracts. In June 1696 the Ordnance Board declared itself unable to discount tallies for a remittance to Flanders under 18%, and was directed to raise £5,000 at such discount 'as the same will be done for'.[2] In the same month the Treasury ordered that care should be taken that bills drawn by Richard Hill, Paymaster of the Forces in Flanders, should not be protested, 'and rather than to suffer that to raise the money on any discount'.[3] In July Lord Ranelagh was authorized to meet the bills payable to Francis Eyles that Hill had drawn by selling tallies 'at any discount'.[4] In May 1697 Ranelagh was ordered to transfer £4,500 Land Tax tallies to Francis Eyles. Eyles had been paid £30,000 in tallies for 330,000 guilders that he had supplied for subsistence in Flanders. The extra sum was to make up the 15% discount on these.[5] A few days earlier it was minuted that the 'gentlemen concerned in the Savoy remittances' were to have £8,000 in tallies at 35% discount.[6]

Financial stringency, resort to desperate, even heroic, expedients, virtual abandonment of Treasury control over government credit: the evidence suggests all these. But it is not self-explanatory evidence. The discount on tallies means little (save as a general indicator of financial distress) unless the nominal rate of interest on a given tally and its priority for repayment are known. As these varied, so the tally's market price varied. This was what Lancelot Burton had in mind when he told the Treasury Board in October 1695 that the tallies for the fictitious loan of £31,163 lately made in his name on the Hereditary and Temporary Excise were not repayable until after £500,000, so that 'it will be very difficult to raise money thereupon'. He suggested the Board should give an extra 2% to purchasers, over and above the 6% already allowed on the tallies, and this was agreed to.[7] The

---

[1] A careful account of this episode, based on the Remittance Ledgers, has been drawn up recently by the Bank of England staff for internal purposes. The Bank estimated its total loss on the Exchange contracts as £128,333. Cf. also the discussion in R. D. Richards, *The Early History of Banking in England* (1924), ch. vii.

[2] P.R.O. T 29/627, 30 June 1696.   [3] Ibid.

[4] Ibid., 28 July 1696. Francis Eyles (c. 1650–1716) was Governor of the Bank of England 1707–9 and was created a baronet in 1714.

[5] Ibid., 11 May 1697.   [6] Ibid., 7 May 1697.

[7] P.R.O. T 29/627, 23 October 1695. For tallies of fictitious loan see below, p. 351.

Bank of England was accused by its opponents of never lending to the Exchequer except on tallies ranking first for repayment, though it denied the charge.[1] Unfortunately, the order of priority for repayment of tallies and the interest on them are generally not stated. Table 54 brings together a number of instances in which they can be traced.

TABLE 54

Discounts on government tallies 1695–7

No.	Month and year		Discount	Yield of tally %		Tax fund from which tally to be repaid	Whether fund deficient in 1697
				nominal	actual		
1	March	1695	20–22	6	7·5–7·7	¾ Customs	Yes
2	September	1696	25–30	5	6·6–7·1	3rd 4s. Aid	Yes
3	October	1696	28	5	6·9	Annuity Act 1695	No
4	March	1697	26	6	8·1	4th 4s. Aid	Yes
5	April	1697	36	6	9·4	4th 4s. Aid	Yes
6	May	1697	25	7	9·3	Salt Duties	Yes
7	May	1697	15	8	9·4	3s. Aid	No
8	June	1697	10	8	8·8	Malt Tax	No
9	August	1697	33¼	8	10·0	3s. Aid	No

Source: Nos. (1), (2) and (3), *Cal. T.P.* i. 433, 547, 552; (4), (5) and (6), ibid. ii. 13–14, 35–36, 39; (7), P.R.O. T 29/627; (8) and (9), *Cal. T. Bks.* xii. 211, 296. For the funds deficient in 1697 see below, p. 354.

The discounts before 1697 are all for tallies carrying only 5% or 6% interest. The discount raised this to 7% or 8%, which had generally been allowed on similar loans between 1688 and 1695.[2] Presumably in view of this, 8% was allowed on loans on both direct and indirect taxes in 1697, but by this time public confidence had waned so far that a still higher rate was needed. It must also be noted that the yields in the table are based on the assumption that the tallies would not be repaid when due, but would continue to circulate for some years until the government was able to fund them, or promise graduated repayment, as in fact happened.[3] If the yields are calculated on the basis of repayment of the tally a year or so after its issue

[1] *A Short View of the Apparent Dangers and Mischiefs from the Bank of England* (1707); [Nathaniel Tench], *A Defence of the Bank of England.*

[2] See Table 53, above, p. 344. [3] See below, p. 353.

they become very much higher. In the last instance in the table *AB* can buy now for £66 a claim to £100 with £8 interest payable in, say, one year's time. This was why Burnaby said that in 1696 the short-term rate of interest had, so far as the government was concerned, risen to over 40%.[1]

The financial crisis that developed from 1693, reflected in the sharp rise in interest rates, threatened by 1696–7 to bring the whole English war machine grinding to a halt. The collapse of the Bank of England, political as well as economic bankruptcy, and resumption of Stuart rule under French auspices, were far from distant threats. 'The Malcontents,' remarked a contemporary

were certain that this Evil was never to be cur'd; and therefore look'd upon the Government as near its End; gave it up as desperate; and triumph'd in the Expectation of a sudden Revolution.[2]

What was it that had gone wrong? As with most crises the causes were complex. First, the amount which the Government tried to borrow for short periods in the 1690s was too large in relation to long-term borrowing and total expenditure. More should have been raised for long terms, thus taking some of the pressure off the short-term capital market. The reluctance to do so was partly due (as in France) to over-optimistic assumptions about the length of the war.[3] A connected point is Parliament's unwillingness to impose new taxes for more than limited periods, on the ground that consumers should not be unnecessarily burdened by continuing war taxes after war conditions had ceased. This was admirable, but futile, for the taxes were at once saddled with short-term loans, even though the taxes themselves were likely to expire before the loans were repaid. Thus, among ten loan funds derived from indirect taxes listed as deficient in 1697, two were due to expire in that year, two in the following year, one in 1700 and one in 1701.[4] Such uncertainties were bound to affect both public willingness to lend, and market confidence in existing tallies.

Third, the number of taxes on which loans were charged was so large as almost to get out of hand; bigger individual loans charged on fewer taxes would have been more effective. Fourth, and more important, there seems little doubt that insufficiently close attention was paid to the prospective yield of new taxes, and that the latter were therefore generally saddled with

---

[1] A. Burnaby, *An Essay upon the excising of Malt* . . . (1696).
[2] Alexander Justice, *A General Treatise of Monies and Exchanges* (1707), p. 85.
[3] For English expectations see Burnaby, op. cit.
[4] See below, p. 354, Table 56.

larger loans than they could repay. Owing to the pressure of war and lack of adequate statistics, the Commons' Committees of Supply showed themselves willing again and again to accept estimates of tax yields which were only optimistic guesses. Davenant writes in 1698 that 'the Projectors of most new Funds, have hitherto been generally mistaken two parts in three', an opinion later confirmed by Defoe.[1] Burnaby, Davenant, King and others correctly insisted that systematic study of patterns of consumption was needed before the yield of new indirect taxes could be estimated accurately; but neither the time nor the facilities for this were available.

Reinforcing these general difficulties was the recoinage of 1696–7.[2] This was decided upon in view of the deterioration of the silver coinage in circulation, the export of silver, and the appreciation of the price of gold guineas caused by the undervaluation of the English guinea in terms of silver. The chief decisions taken in Parliament were to recoin the existing silver in stages at the old standard, and to call down the price of guineas. Coin amounting to a nominal £5,729,183 was called into the Tower of London mint alone; when recoined it amounted to only £3,307,284. A further £1·8m. was called in to county mints. In effect, the coinage in circulation had been written down by 50%. This measure

restor'd the Honour of the English, confirm'd the Shaking Government, and laid the Foundation of that Honourable Peace, which after ensued.[3]

However, together with the shock given to the Bank of England by the royal approval of the National Land Bank in 1696, and the failure of the first issue of Exchequer bills, it created an extremely deflationary fiscal situation, in which only the most attractive terms on government loans were likely to bring funds into the Exchequer.[4] Yet it was just at this point that the rate of interest on several short-term loans was lowered to 5%.[5]

These factors were important separately, and more important cumulatively. They do not, however, entirely explain the government's financial

---

[1] [Charles Davenant], *Discourses on the Publick Revenues* (1698), p. 27; [Daniel Defoe], *An Essay upon Publick Credit* (1710), p. 17.

[2] The most recent account of the controversy which accompanied this step is in J. K. Horsefield, *British Monetary Experiments 1650–1710* (1960), pp. 37–90.

[3] Alexander Justice, op. cit., p. 83. For sums coined at the Tower Mint: Shaw, *Cal. T. Bks.* (1695–1702), p. cxii. For the county mints: Mitchell and Deane, *Abstract of British Historical Statistics* (1962), p. 440. Cf. *Gazette d'Amsterdam*, 27 February 1696 (N.S.), for favourable Dutch opinion of the recoinage.

[4] For the Land Bank and Exchequer Bills see below, p. 366.

[5] See above, p. 344, Table 53.

embarrassment. How was it, for instance, that loans of over £30m. are recorded in the Exchequer receipt books between 1688 and 1697 if credit was so low? How was it that paymasters had large sums of tallies in their hands which they were using for payments? In order to answer these questions it is necessary to look more closely at the technicalities of Exchequer practices.

The Exchequer's time-honoured form of receipt for money was a wooden tally, notched according to a code for amounts, and with the sum received generally added to it in writing. The tally was split down the middle, the Exchequer retaining the foil or minor portion, and the payor the stock or major portion. This venerable ritual had roots going back deep into a primitive and largely illiterate past. To some, like Edward Chamberlayne, it still seemed admirable in the stirring world of later Stuart London. Tallies, he claimed, were businesslike because they could not be forged, and, partly owing to them, 'the Exchequer of the King of England, is become the best ordered publick Revenue in the World'.[1] The forms of the Exchequer had, however, always been less unchanging than the encomiums of its admirers suggested, and it seems clear that the use of tallies in the 1690s differed in important respects from that of earlier periods.

The two main kinds of tally used to record loans to the government in the 1690s were the tally of Pro and the tally of Sol.[2] The former was charged on a specified revenue, normally the Customs or Excise, and was encashable, together with interest, either with a revenue collector or at the Customs House, Excise Office, Post Office, etc., in London.[3] By the later seventeenth century such tallies evidently conveyed to their holder the legal title to a portion of the public revenue. Thus Lowndes records

These words on the Pro Side [of the tally] by the Course of the Exchequer which is common Law do assigne and transferre the Right of the Money (though otherwise a Chose in Accon) from the King to the Subject in Such Manner that the Subject may in his owne Name Sue the Receivor when he has so much in his hands to pay him.[4]

---

[1] Edward Chamberlayne, *Angliae Notitia* (1682 ed.), pt. ii, p. 106.

[2] This section is based on William Lowndes's paper 'The Course of the Exchequer on the Receipt Side', Add. MS. 15898, ff. 101 ff., evidently written in James II's reign, see f. 108. 'Sol' is short for *solutum*'. An early-eighteenth-century account of Exchequer of Receipt procedures in Add. MS. 24689 is clearly based on Lowndes.

[3] Cf. 8 & 9 Wm. III, c. 20, s. lviii, for encashment at government offices. The Bank of England's General Ledger 1, covering the period 1694-7, regularly shows an interest column in Pro tally accounts.

[4] Add. MS. 15898, f. 109.

It seems likely that the loans made by revenue cashiers were acknowledged by tallies of Pro. They were also used in the 1690s to pay judges and other officials; when used in this way the tally became a kind of post-dated cheque.

The second type of tally, of Sol, increasingly ousted the first, which after the 1690s seems to have disappeared from use. Tallies of Sol were, like tallies of Pro, used for payments, when they were described as tallies of anticipation.[1] The practice may have originated in the reign of James I,[2] and analogous juggling with Exchequer forms can be traced back to the Middle Ages.[3] When used to acknowledge loans at the Exchequer, tallies of Sol were accompanied by a written Order of Payment. These had first been made out in 1665, following an idea of Sir George Downing.[4] From 1688, with the increase in their volume, they were printed, only the lender's name, and other details, being written. They were serially numbered, and ranked for payment in priority.[5] Unlike the tally of Pro they could only be encashed at the Exchequer, but the holder of a tally could assign it by endorsement and delivery. Assignees were noted in the margin.[6] Assignment was supposed to be registered at the Exchequer, but this procedure seems largely to have been a dead letter.[7]

An important modification of this type of tally and Order was the Tally of fictitious loan. The idea behind this was simple. When Parliament authorized a loan of £x in anticipation of a specific tax, the Exchequer would make out tallies of receipt for, say, one third of this sum, together with the corresponding Orders of Payment. The Orders would be in the name of a departmental paymaster, such as the Treasurer of the Navy. Though the latter had not himself lent a penny, the tallies and Orders he held were valuable claims on future revenue, and could be used for payment, or as security for private advances. The introduction of this device can probably be dated to May 1690.[8] It is clear from the long lists of paymasters' 'loans'

---

[1] Ibid. [2] Chandaman, 'Public Revenue', i. 29 n.

[3] G. L. Harriss, 'Fictitious Loans', *Econ. H. R.*, 2nd ser., viii (Dec. 1955), 187.

[4] They were written on paper (not parchment) and were first made out under authority of 17 Ch. II, c. 1 (1665). For Downing's Order experiment see above, p. 43.

[5] See Plate 8. There are several specimens of Orders in Add. MS. 34195, collection of original letters, warrants and papers 1576–1763, and also in P.R.O. E 404/520.

[6] Ibid. and see the procedure for assignment in the various tax Acts.

[7] For disregard of registration see below, p. 356.

[8] P.R.O. E 401/1985, Pells' Receipt Book Easter–Michaelmas 1690. Long lists of 'loans' by Edward Russell the Navy Treasurer begin in May, in a form characteristic of all subsequent entries for fictitious loans. There are no such entries in the previous half-year (Michaelmas 1689–midsummer 1690. E 401/1984). In the Treasury Minutes the authorization of this expenditure takes the form 'out of loans to be made by' Russell and others.

which occur in all the Exchequer receipt books from this date that the new device was being extensively used. How extensively is only known in specific instances, for the overall distinction between loans in cash and tallies of fictitious loan is, significantly, only observed in the Treasury accounts from 1703.

TABLE 55

Sources of short-term loans 1689–93

Tax on which loan charged	Date	Lent through City Chamber		Lent by others in cash		Tallies of fictitious loan	
		£	%	£	%	£	%
Two Shilling Aid (1 Wm. and M. sess. 2, c. 1)	1689–90	182,533	30·1	423,524	69·9	..	..
Poll Act (3 Wm. and M. c. 6)	1692	165,680	29·5	254,214	45·3	141,257	25·2
First Four Shilling Aid (4 Wm. and M. c. 1)	1693	244,340	22	605,385	54·4	262,945	23·6

Source: For the Two Shilling Aid, *Cal. T. Bks.* ix (v), 1991 ff.; for the Poll Act, *HCJ.* x. 723; for the Four Shilling Aid, Exchequer Receipt Books listed in notes to Table 69, p. 421, below.

The figures for 1703 were £1,906,690 (60·1%) borrowed in cash and £1,200,000 (39·9%) by means of tallies of fictitious loan. The inference from these figures, and from the evidence previously examined, is that the proportion of tallies of fictitious loan followed a steadily rising curve during the war years, thus placing large sums of tallies (instead of cash) in the hands of departmental paymasters. These tallies were used to pay government creditors, or as collateral for loans. The system was not in itself vicious, for if all the tallies had been adequately covered by the taxes they were charged on it would not have mattered how they were marketed. As — for reasons discussed earlier — they were not adequately covered, the system placed a strain on the machinery of government credit that it was unable to bear.

The crisis reached its peak in the spring of 1697; by this date deficiencies on short-term tax funds were over £5m., and in April a lottery loan for £1·4m. was almost entirely unsubscribed.[1] By this date busy consultations

[1] See above, p. 49. For the deficiencies see Table 56, p. 354.

about a remedy for public credit had been going on for some months between the government and the Bank of England. ('I am sorry 'twas not sooner perceived that their credit rightly supported would have carryed us thro this War', Montague wrote bitterly to Blathwait in June.)[1] The upshot was a long and complicated statute which received the royal assent on 1 April 1697.[2]

The first part of the Act was concerned with fifteen tax funds which were deficient, in the sense that they would not yield enough to repay the short-term loans charged on them. Two of the loans dated from as far back as 1691, two others from 1693, and a fifth from 1694. The total deficiencies were stated to be £5,160,460; subtotals were given for only twelve of the fifteen funds, as shown in Table 56.

The remedy put forward was to extend three of these funds (nos. 8, 9, and 11), together with five others, which in turn were due to expire between March 1697 and March 1703, to 1 August 1706, and to settle them, together with a temporary addition to the salt duties, as 'the General Fund for making good the particular Funds before expressed . . . [not to] be divertible to any other Use Intent or Purpose whatsoever until all the said Principal and Interest shall be fully . . . paid off' (s. xxxviii). In a landowning Parliament it is not surprising that this measure at once became known as 'the First General Mortgage'. The duties included in it were, with some exceptions and additions, continued in 1702 until 1710 to discharge further deficiencies amounting to £2,498,678.[3] By statues of 1707, 1708, 1709 and 1710 further extensions of the term were authorised to create a basis for new loans. These third, fourth, fifth and sixth 'General Mortgages' continued the duties concerned to August 1720, and in 1711 they were made perpetual as part of the South Sea Company's fund.[4] The whole episode showed how easily debts at first meant only to be temporary could become a permanent charge on the state's revenues. In later wars the attempt to find a short-term solution to the problem of floating debts was frankly abandoned, and the holders were required to convert them into ordinary stock.

The second stage of operations was for the Bank of England to hold an unlimited subscription for new Bank stock, payable four-fifths in government tallies and one-fifth in its own notes. The aim was to clear the market of part of the floating debt at once, and thus increase confidence in the re-

[1] Add. MS. 34355, Charles Montague to William Blathwait, 25 June 1697.
[2] 8 & 9 Wm. III, c. 20.   [3] 1 Anne, sess. 1, c. 13.
[4] Third General Mortgage, 5 Anne, c. 27 (8 April 1707); fourth, 6 Anne, c. 19 (20 March 1708); fifth, 7 Anne, c. 8 (21 April 1709); sixth, 8 Anne, c. 13 (5 April 1710).

TABLE 56

Tax funds listed as deficient in 1697

Tax fund	Created by	Rate of interest on loans	Date of expiry of fund	De-ficiency £
1 First Four-Shilling Aid . . .	4 Wm. & M. c. 1	7	..	55,622
2 Third Four-Shilling Aid . . .	6 & 7 Wm. III, c. 3	5	..	470,372
3 Fourth Four-Shilling Aid . . .	7 & 8 Wm. III, c. 5	6	..	917,102
4 Quarterly Poll . .	5 & 6 Wm. and M. c. 14	6	..	9,276
5 Three-quarters Customs . . .	2 Wm. and M. c. 4	6	..	213,448
6 Duties on salt, glass, stoneware, earthenware, and tobacco pipes . . .	7 & 8 Wm. II, c. 1	7	..	1,711,500
7 Two-thirds excise of 18*d.* barrel and excise on beer and ale .	2 Wm. and M. sess. 2, c. 10	7	17 May 1697 (then other uses)	160,000
8 Additional imposition on goods . .	4 Wm. and M. c. 5	8	1 March 1697	445,177
9 Vellum, parchment, paper . . .	6 and 6 Wm. and M. c. 21	8	28 June 1698	224,114
10 £300,000 p.a. from Customs . . .	6 & 7 Wm. and M. c. 1	5 to 8	25 Dec. 1698	142,666
11 Marriages, births, burials, bachelors, widows . . .	6 & 7 Wm. III, c. 6	8	1 May 1700	648,000
12 Wines, vinegar, tobacco, E.I. goods . .	7 & 8 Wm. III, c. 10	5 to 8	29 Sep 1701	146,182

£5,143,459

Source: 8 & 9 Wm. III, c. 20.

mainder. The subscription realized £1,001,172, four-fifths, or about £801,000, of which must have been in tallies, that is, about one-seventh of the total tallies outstanding. Until the 'ingrafted stock' (another agrarian metaphor) added to the Bank of England's capital by this subscription was repaid, the Treasury was to pay it 8% interest on the tallies (the title to which had passed to the Bank under s. xxiii. of the Act) and 8% on tallies already held by the Bank itself, up to a sum equal to the cash portion of the subscription. This arrangement was intended to safeguard the Bank's own very large holdings of tallies, which at 25 June 1697 amounted to £1,830,281, of which about £480,000 seems to have been secured on funds listed as deficient by the Act.[1] In effect, therefore, the Treasury paid 8% on the whole £1,001,171 10s. 0d. until all the tallies concerned had been repaid, and the Bank could therefore cancel the new (1697) stock, a process not completed until 1707. In that year a director, Nathaniel Tench, claimed that only the Bank could have carried out the 'ingraftment', without which government credit could not have been retrieved.[2] Tench was an interested party, for now that the debts of 1697 had been repaid the Bank's charter could be cancelled at a year's notice after 1 August 1710, under s. xxvii of the Act of 1697, and brisk controversy about its renewal was already under way. But the claim was substantially just.

The remainder of the 1697 Act, aiming at strengthening government credit by punishing those who dealt in it on adverse terms, was less realistic Certain sections tried to restrict the activities of stock-jobbers.[3] Others were concerned with the price of tallies. The statute noted, in words which might have been written by the great Lord Burleigh, that

it is found by Experience that many avaricious or ill disposed Persons taking an Advantage of the Necessities of those who have occasion to sell or dispose of such Tallies and Orders ... do in the buying or purchasing of such Orders or Tallies extorte and gaine to themselves an exorbitant and unreasonable Allowance Premium or Consideration out of the principal Moneys besides the Interest accruing for the same to the unspeakable Damage and Prejudice of his Majesty and many of his good subjects in Trade and otherwise and in a great measure to the ruine of the publick Credit which cannot be repaired as long as such Practises are continued or suffered.[4]

---

[1] Bank of England General Ledger 1, Balance Sheet at 25 June 1697. There is some uncertainty about which of the tallies listed there were deficient, as their names were abbreviated. The ones in question seem to be 'Paper' £7,659, 'Marriages' £469, 3rd 4s., Aid £129,363, 'Salt' £333,208, 2/3 excise £9,441, and '4th year's Land Tax' £95, a total of £480,235.

[2] [Nathaniel Tench], A Defence of the Bank of England.

[3] For these clauses see below, p. 516. [4] 8 & 9 Wm. III, c. 20 (1697), s. lvii.

It went on to say that for a period of six years from 10 June 1697 no one was to buy a tally at more than 6% discount. To make sure that buyers complied with this rule, they were obliged to swear an affidavit at the Exchequer that they had done so, within ten days of registering the assignment of the Order of Payment there. No sales were to be valid without such registration — an indication that the rules for assignment previously made had largely been ignored. For tallies of Pro, payable at the Excise Office, General Post Office or 'any other publick Office', the procedure was to be the same, and the necessary registers were to be kept in each office. If anyone infringed the Act by charging more than 6% discount he could be sued for three times the tally's value, one-third of the proceeds to go to the Crown and the rest to the informer.

These clauses resembled much of the later legislation about stock-jobbing, and were equally futile. Like most previous attempts to regulate the economy, they were the product of a specific crisis, and embodied no long-term ideas — except the time-honoured belief that all economic hardship was due to the villainy of middlemen. In fact, of course, it was the government, including Parliament, which had created the situation that it now tried to regulate. Fortunately for the commercial public, the funding clauses of the Act, the success of the Bank's 'ingraftment' subscription held in the summer of 1697, and the completion of the government's peace negotiations (forced on it by financial exhaustion) with the signature of the Treaty of Ryswick in September, proved more effective remedies for the crisis than the coercion of the dealers in money. In December 1696 Bank stock, at 77, had fallen 26 points since the start of the year, and its notes were at 16% discount, a reflection of the difficulties that the stringency of credit and adverse foreign exchange had created.[1] 'Money continues so scarce as ever,' wrote the London merchant Henry Phill to correspondents abroad on 8 December 1696,

which is ye bane of all trade, discounts on Bank notes is at present 16 p.Ct: has been at 17 or 18 & yt. within ye hund[red].[2]

He added gloomily that one of his ships had been unable to sail up the Thames, which was 'at present full of ice, haveing frozen many days very hard'.[3] In the spring and summer of 1697 government tallies were still at high discounts, and Bank stock, with the effects of the ingraftment still uncertain, continued to fluctuate around seventy. At the end of May 1697 Phill still

[1] Prices from J. E. Thorold Rogers, *The First Nine Years of the Bank of England* (1887), table I.

[2] P.R.O. C 111/127, Chancery Masters' Exhibits, *Crow* v. *Phill*, letter book, f. 220, Phill to Knipe and Hoyle 8 December 1696.

[3] Ibid.

found credit very bad, and confidently predicted that Bank notes, then at 21% discount, would 'come much lower'.[1] 'Tallies here go for nothing', wrote Montague to Blathwait on 11 June.[2] But in the autumn the situation dramatically improved. By mid-September Bank notes were at par, and Bank stock, quoted at 60½ on 3 September, suddenly rose to 82 on 10 September and 97½ on 1 October; in 1698 it fluctuated between 86 and 97, and in the following year was consistently at a premium.[3] The conclusion of peace had its effect on Exchequer tallies as well. In January 1698 Sir William Scawen and other clothiers were still asking for a generous discount, 15%, if they were to be paid in Salt tallies for clothing they had supplied in 1697.[4] But in November 1698, when a Mr. Levy proposed discounting £220,000 Salt tallies at 6%, the Treasury Board told his agent 'My Lords expect a better Market'.[5] They were justified in their attitude, for later in the month the Victualling Commissioners were able to discount £120,000 Salt tallies at an average of £4 9s. 9⅕d.%.[6] By 1700 6% tallies were regularly at par, and discounts vanish from the Treasury Board Minutes.[7] Meanwhile, the pound sterling's exchange rate in Flemish shillings in Amsterdam, 36·6 in February 1687, 34·5 in February 1692, 33·6 in February 1693 and 27·11 in August 1695, had climbed back to 35 by May 1700.[8] The crisis was over.

IV

There can be little doubt, however, that it had left its mark on contemporary minds. In particular, Lord Godolphin, the official head of the Treasury Board between 1690 and 1696, seems to have been determined while Lord Treasurer between 1703 and 1710, when he clearly had far greater control, that the near-disasters of the 1690s should not recur if good management

---

[1] Ibid., f. 229. Phill to Knipe and Hoyle 21 May 1697.

[2] Add. MS. 34355, Montague to Blathwait 11 June 1697.

[3] Prices from J. E. Thorold Rogers, op. cit. Cf. Phill to Knipe and Hoyle, 2 September 1697, Bank Bills have fallen to 2½% discount and will 'shortly be as good as mo[ney]'. The sudden rise of Bank stock may have been partly due to advance rumours of the 20% increase in the paid-up capital, though the decision to call this amount in was only reached by the directors on 29 September.

[4] P.R.O. T 29/627, 16 January 1698. [5] Ibid. 18 November 1698.

[6] Ibid. 30 November 1698. [7] Ibid. 1700-2.

[8] The rate was 34 to 35 for most of the eighteenth century. Figures from N. W. Posthumus, *Nederlandsche Prijsgeschiedenis* (Leiden, 1943).

could prevent them. Godolphin understood the realities of the money market, in particular the way in which the various sectors of government and private credit interlocked. His methods between 1702 and 1710 are visibly a re-action to the qualified chaos of the previous decade. First, he increased the proportion of public expenditure covered by long-term loans, and was there-fore able to reduce the amount annually needed in anticipation of taxes to around £3m.[1] Second, he cut down the number of tax funds on which short-term tallies of loan were charged to five or six each year, the most important being the annual Land Tax of four shillings in the pound, the Malt Duties and the miscellaneous taxes grouped in the 'General Mortgages' of 1707–1710.[2] Third, he took care that deficiencies on tax funds never reached alarm-ing proportions. This point requires examining more closely.

Parliament's practice was to fix an estimated value and a loan value on the main direct taxes. By the 1700s the estimated yield of the four-shilling Land Tax, the chief pillar of direct taxation, had become stereotyped at a figure just below or just above £2m., and the loan value at between £1,800,000 and £1,880,000.[3] This was not unrealistic, but as the period of collection was lengthening the fairly high loan value could lead to temporary difficulties. For example, the Land Tax granted for 1707 was estimated to yield £1,997,763, a loan value of £1,850,000 was set on it, and in the winter of 1706–7 cash loans on it at 5%, totalling £1,375,000, were received at the Exchequer. (The rest of the loan value was taken up by creating tallies of fictitious loan.) The yield of the tax was as shown in Table 57.

Although 95% of the estimated tax yield was received by the end of 1712, only 89% of the estimated loan value had come in by Michaelmas 1708; interest at 5% had to be paid on top of this. Hence only £1,676,446 of the loans were repaid by Michaelmas 1708. The sum of £263,758 was carried forward, and at Michaelmas 1710 £59,084 was still due. This was again carried forward, and eventually discharged from the Land Tax of 1711.[4] It

---

[1] For long-term loans see above, p. 60. For the amounts raised by short-term loans see Appendix C.

[2] This process can be followed in *Cal. T. Bks.* for 1702–10, particularly the volumes abstracting the P.R.O. T 30 (Annual Accounts) series; also in James Postlethwayt, *History of the Public Revenue* (1759). The Land Tax was at 4s. in the £ 1693–7, 1701–12, 1716, 1727 and 1740–9; at 3s. 1698–9, 1717–21, 1728–9 and 1750–1; at 2s. 1700, 1713–15, 1722–6, 1730–1, 1734–9, 1753–5; at 1s. 1732–3 (all years inclusive).

[3] Annual estimated yields and loan values in the Land Tax Acts (*Statutes of the Realm*). The practice seems to date from 1698. The Land Tax loan value was £1,800,000 1702–3, £1,850,000 1704–7 and £1,880,000 1708–12 (years inclusive).

[4] Postlethwayt, op. cit., p. 76.

TABLE 57
Collection of the 1707 land tax

Exchequer year ending at Michaelmas	£
1707	172,642 ⎱ £1,705,304 = 88·7%
1708	1,532,662 ⎰ of loan value
1709	179,191
1710	12,490
1711	2,223
1712	4,026
TOTAL . .	1,903,234 = 95·3% of estimated value

Source: Annual Revenue accounts 1707–12 printed in *Cal. T. Bks.* xxi–xxv.

seems probable that the cash loans from the general public (as distinct from the tallies held by paymasters) were repaid from the first receipts of the tax, so that these delays would not seriously affect government credit. This general picture explains the confident assertion of the Agents for Taxes in February 1708 that 'there is not unpaid to her Majesty upon all the Land Taxes . . . above Ninety thousand Pounds; which is constantly bringing in and in no danger of being lost'.[1] At Michaelmas 1710 the deficiencies on short-term loans amounted to only £358,021, the deficiencies on the Land Taxes of 1706, 1707 and 1708 totalling £116,707. Dr. Sperling calculates that over a sufficient period 98% of the estimated yield of the Land Tax in this period was collected, a very close approximation for a country with relatively undeveloped fiscal machinery.[2] Similar methods were used for loans on the Malt Duties. When the latter brought in insufficient revenue to repay the loans punctually, the tallies on the end of the course were carried forward as a prior charge on the next year's tax, the cash loans on which were proportionally reduced.[3]

[1] *HCJ* xv. 562.
[2] J. G. Sperling, 'Godolphin and the Organisation of Public Credit, 1702 to 1710', Cambridge University Ph.D. thesis, 1955, pp. 9 ff. Dr. Shaw's confusion of arrears with deficiencies enables him to arrive at a total of £2,070,347 'deficiencies' on the Land Taxes of 1702–7. This is clearly quite mistaken. (*Cal. T. Bks.* xxi (i), pp. xxiv, xxvii.) Shaw cites the same figures differently in different places. Cf. also Sperling's excellent exposé of Shaw's mistakes, loc. cit.
[3] This can be followed in Postlethwayt, op. cit.

From his experience of the 1690s, Godolphin might have drawn the lesson that the tally of fictitious loan was a dubious instrument, and should be suppressed. Correctly, he drew the different lesson that it was potentially extremely useful, but had been misused. Under his intelligent direction it became an important part of a successful short-term borrowing policy. The change was primarily due to two factors. First, Treasury management was remarkably prudent. The annual total of such tallies was kept within a limit of £1·5m. except in the difficult years 1709–11, and their volume was accurately recorded in the Treasury account books for the first time.[1] Godolphin also developed the practice of impresting to paymasters tallies which carried no interest until indorsed by the Treasury for assignment, thus avoiding the practice of William's reign by which the interest on tallies was credited to the paymaster and entered by him as a charge item in the accounts.[2] Lastly, the Treasury carefully regulated the terms of bargains made by paymasters to raise cash on tallies in their hands. A further factor, without which this careful stewardship would have been of little use, was the co-operation of the Bank of England. With the exception of the tallies pledged to the foreign-exchange contractors, it made the major part of the loans to departments between 1702 and 1710, and indeed until the end of the war. This was an immense help to the Treasury, which was no longer obliged in this sector of borrowing to expose itself to the hazards of the money-market, and was another step towards the quasi-monopoly of short-term lending which the Bank had established by the mid-century.[3] Finally, though the details are not within the scope of this discussion, Godolphin established careful control over the rates at which the very large sums needed for Marlborough's armies and those in Spain were remitted overseas.[4]

The combined effect of these changes, and of Marlborough's chain of victories, was a startling improvement in public credit. In the years 1703–9 inclusive the Land Tax was anticipated without difficulty at 5%, and eight long-term loans to finance budget deficits were floated between 1703 and 1708 at 6·6% to 6·25%.[5] As a contemporary wrote in 1707, apropos of the dangerous years 1696–7,

---

[1] For figures see Appendix C.

[2] As for instance in the Declared Accounts by Lord Ranelagh and Lord Orford in *Cal. T. Bks.* ix (i), pp. cclxxviii, cclxxxvii.

[3] Cf. below, p. 417.

[4] See Sperling, op. cit. ch. iv.

[5] Short-term rates from Postlethwayt, op. cit. For long-term loans see above, p. 60.

We are, God be thanked, greatly recover'd from that dangerous Crisis which we then were in, our Credit retriev'd, our Money recoin'd, great part of our Debts paid, and almost all provided for. And though we have since been for some Years in an expensive War, by the prudent Management of the Treasury, our Interest [is] at a moderate rate; and we croud more to get our Money into the Funds, than heretofore to get out of them.[1]

Walpole wrote later that 'Large Sums were constantly advanc'd, and almost forc'd upon the Government at Five or Six per Cent.'[2] Defoe's view was that 'we have not . . . found any Fund the Parliament has rais'd, unsupply'd with Loans and Advances upon it, even faster than could be desired'.[3] Though writing for Harley's new ministry, Defoe says of the fallen Treasurer

The late Lord Treasurer . . . has done Honourably, has manag'd the Finances with great and unusual dexterity, and has acquir'd thereby the Fame of the Best Officer, that has for many Years acted in that Post.[4]

A contemporary character sketch of Godolphin says

This Queen has deservedly made him Lord High Treasurer, in which Station he hath so improved the Revenue, and put it into so good a Method, notwithstanding the Debts of the Nation, that Money is lent to the Publick at Five per Cent.[5]

In 1729 it was asserted, not entirely accurately, that

the late Earl of Godolphin, by good Management only, and without the great Advantage of Exchequer Bills, seldom paid at a medium above 4 per Cent upon the whole Land Tax, during the War.[6]

Godolphin was playing a very difficult game with coolness and skill, making up the rules as he went along. For the first time the emergent class of merchants and financiers, whose services were indispensable to the conduct of a war waged on an unprecedented scale, came up against financial management as prudent, realistic, and successful in assessing risks as their own. But there was a joker in the pack. Just as in the 1690s the volume of tallies of fictitious loan had increased out of proportion to the money-market's capacity to absorb them, so the floating departmental debt, accumulating with every year of war, came after 1708 to imperil the structure of credit

---

[1] *A Short View of the Apparent Dangers from the Bank of England* (1707), p. 6.
[2] [Robert Walpole], *The Debts of the Nation Stated and Considered in four Papers* (1712), p. 7.
[3] [Daniel Defoe], *An Essay upon Publick Credit*, p. 28.   [4] Ibid., p. 14.
[5] *Memoirs of the Secret Services of John Macky Esq.* (Roxburghe Club, 1895), p. 42.
[6] [William Pulteney], *Some Considerations on the National Debts*, p. 78.

which Godolphin had so carefully built up. The reasons for the growth of this debt, and the Treasury's inability to check it, are discussed in a later chapter.[1] By Michaelmas 1710 the debt amounted to well over £6m., about a year's revenue.[2] Simultaneously, the triumphant military and economic progress of the Allies began to falter. The failure of the negotiations for peace at The Hague in August 1709 was followed in September by the bloody and equivocal battle of Malplaquet. Further, the iron winter of 1708–9, which froze the rivers all over Europe, and paralysed commerce, was followed by a disastrous corn and wine harvest in France, and by equally bad harvests in parts of Germany and southern Europe. Bid up by French demands, grain reached prices not equalled until the 1770s.[3] In April 1709 the chief French financial agent, Samuel Bernard, was unable to meet his payments at Lyons, thus triggering off a chain of bankruptcies among his French and Swiss correspondents.[4] In 1709–10 the bankruptcy rate rose sharply in London and Amsterdam. From Venice it was reported that everyone had gone bankrupt one after the other.[5]

These shocks to the delicate spider's web of European commerce were bound to affect the credit of the English government, particularly as rumours grew in the early months of 1710 that Godolphin was about to be dismissed. Six per cent Navy bills, a principal item in the floating debt, were already at 12% discount at the end of 1708. This discount increased to between 13% and 20% in 1709, to 26%–30% in 1710, and to 33% in the following year. Victualling bills, also at 6%, had gone to 45% discount by March 1711.[6] Other securities were affected, though not so greatly. At the end of 1710 discounts of up to 2½% had appeared on Exchequer bills.[7] In April 1711 tallies of loan on the annual Malt Tax were at nearly 5% discount, and even those on the Land Tax, the safest fund, were at over 2% discount in the following month, despite the fact that the rate of interest on both was raised from 5% to 6% in the years 1710–12.[8] Effectively, the short-term rate of

---

[1] See below, p. 403.   [2] See above, p. 68.

[3] I am indebted to Dr. Sperling for allowing me to see his unpublished paper on the harvest, based on contemporary newspaper reports.

[4] H. Lüthy, *La Banque Protestante en France*, i, ch. ii (6).

[5] See G. Chalmers, *An Estimate of the Comparative Strength of Great Britain* (1804), p. 291; N. W. Posthumus, *Geschiedenis van de Leidsche Lakenindustrie*, iii (The Hague, 1939), 1159, for the English and Dutch bankruptcy figures; *Wienerisches Diarium*, February 1710 for the report from Venice.

[6] Figures from the careful list of discounts compiled by Dr. Sperling, op. cit. p. 110.

[7] See below, p. 375 n.

[8] *Cal. T. Bks.* xxv (ii) (1711), 42, 58. Loan rates from Postlethwayt, op. cit.

interest had therefore risen to between 10% and 11%.[1] Godolphin's dismissal in August 1710, and the return in the autumn of a Tory Parliament eager to attack the financial oligarchy of the City of London, made the Navy creditors, in particular, relentless in their pressure on the Treasury.[2] But despite appearances the crisis was much less severe than that of 1696–7. The Bank had no difficulty in acquiring an extra Exchequer bill allowance from the Treasury, the floatation of the South Sea Company in June 1711 absorbed the floating debt, and by the autumn tax tallies were at par.[3] Generous discounts on the lottery loans of 1710–12, which made their nominal return nearly 8%, brought capital flooding in to fill them, as Harley's supporters gleefully pointed out. With the approach of peace in 1713 it was possible to reduce the interest on Land Tax loans to five per cent.

V

The combination of good Treasury management and the co-operation of the Bank of England had by 1710 put government anticipation of annual revenue on a sound basis. This explains the relative ease with which the potentially very dangerous crisis of 1710–11 had been overcome. In the long years of peace after the Treaty of Utrecht these trends developed further, and the terms on which the government was able to borrow for short terms became cheaper and cheaper.

Between 1713 and 1726 methods of anticipation of tax revenue remained broadly the same as those used by Godolphin. As overall expenditure was smaller, the amounts borrowed annually were limited to between £1·5m. and £2·5m.[4] The taxes on which loans were secured were generally the Land and Malt taxes only, a far cry from the multiple funds of the 1690s. Tallies continued to be divided into those given as receipts for cash loans and

---

[1] Calculating the yield on Navy and Victualling bills as though they were ordinary stock, and the yield on tallies on the assumption that they would be repaid after one year with interest.

[2] See above, p. 64.

[3] The Treasury noted on 11 September 1711 that Land Tax tallies were now in such good repute that money could be raised on them at par, *Cal. T. Bks.* xxv (ii), 453. For the Bank of England's Exchequer bill allowances see below, p. 374, and for the South Sea Company above, p. 64, and below, p. 404.

[4] See Appendix C.

TABLE 58

*Rates of interest on loans in anticipation of Land, Malt
and Salt duties 1714–56*

Year	%	Year	%	Year	%
1714	5	1723–6	3	1740	3½
1715	4	1727	4	1741	4
1716	6	1728–33	3	1742	3½
1717–20	5	1734	3½	1743–4	3
1721	6	1735	3½	1745	3½
1722	5	1736–9	3	1746–9	4
				1750–6	3

Source: James Postlethwayt, op. cit., for 1714–53, then Public General
Acts (Land Tax Acts), for 1754, 1755, 1756.

those of fictitious loan imprested to departments, the proportion between the
two kinds evidently varying with departmental needs. After the Exchequer
year 1725–6, however, these methods were changed. Increasing reliance
was placed on Exchequer bills circulated by the Bank of England and annually
paid off from incoming taxes.[1] Tallies of fictitious loan were struck for the
last time in the Exchequer year 1728–9, and subsequent loans in cash were
nearly always exceeded in amount by the creation of Exchequer bills. The
two kinds of anticipation continued to run in double harness until 1763–4,
but more as a political device to conciliate the lenders on the tax funds than
as an economic necessity. From the end of the Seven Years War cash loans,
and the tallies that went with them, disappeared, and the Exchequer bill
managed by the Bank reigned alone until the 1870s. Characteristically,
governments continued to take powers to anticipate the annual taxes in cash
until 1808, but did not use them.[2] The accumulated tallies in the Exchequer
were finally got rid of by fire in 1834, with appropriate symbolism burning
down the old Palace of Westminster in the process.

[1] See p. 382, below.   [2] *BPP* (1868–9), xxxv. 152.

14

Borrowing by Exchequer Bills

I

F R O M the 1720s Exchequer bills, mainly charged on the annual Land and Malt taxes and paid off when these were collected, became the most important form of annual anticipation of government revenue. From 1763, with the cessation of cash loans at the Exchequer, Exchequer bills reigned supreme until their supersession by Northcote's Treasury Bill of 1877.[1] Yet when first introduced in 1696 no one could have predicted a long and successful history for them. They were a product of the crisis of state credit in the 'Year very likely to have proved many ways Fatal to England',[2] and even their sponsor, the Chancellor of the Exchequer Charles Montague, was doubtful of their success.

The idea of 'turning the Exchequer into a Bank', by issuing notes charged on the revenue, originated with Sir George Downing's 'Order experiment', which led to the Stop of the Exchequer in 1672.[3] The shock this gave to royal credit, the relative easiness of the government's financial situation in the 1670s and 1680s and the stability of the arrangements for short-term finance in this period, deferred fresh consideration of the idea for twenty years. The mounting curve of government expenditure after 1689 caused its reappearance. On 17 June 1694 Godolphin, the First Lord of the Treasury, wrote to William III that soon the only remedy for the government's difficulties would be 'to give out bills from the Exchequer'.[4] The successful foundation of the Bank of England, chartered in the following month, put off the hour of decision, though the Bank's issues of notes

---

[1] Exchequer bills were formally abolished in 1897, almost exactly 200 years after their first creation.

[2] *Some Remarks on the Bill for Taking . . . The Publick Accounts* (1702), p. 7.

[3] See above, p. 43. On Exchequer bills cf. also R. D. Richards, 'The Exchequer Bill in English Government Finance', *Economic History*, iii (1934–7), p. 193, though this article contained a number of inaccuracies.

[4] *Cal. State Papers Domestic*, 1694–5, 189.

probably increased the plausibility of similar action by the Exchequer. The creation of bonds by the Royal African and East India Companies, and the proposals of the Land Bank promoters of 1695–6 to issue notes, also cannot have escaped Treasury notice.[1]

Exchequer bills were thus the product both of a general climate of economic thought and of specific precedents. The immediate cause of their creation was the financial crisis of 1696. According to a contemporary, a plan for them was first put up to the Chancellor of the Exchequer, Charles Montague, by Mordecai Abbot, who had been concerned in founding the Million Bank in the previous year.[2] Montague worked out the details, probably in conjunction with Godolphin, the head of the Treasury Board, and John Smith, one of the Commissioners.[3] Montague conceded that the project was doubtful. On 5 June 1696 he wrote to William Blathwait, Secretary at War, who was attending the king in Flanders as his secretary:

As to the Credit in the Exchequer how that will succeed no man can answer, only I assure you no pains shall be wanting to establish it.[4]

He was particularly worried about the activities of the Commissioners of the National Land Bank of England, whose success in persuading Parliament in March to incorporate the bank if it could raise and lend to the government £2,564,000 (and thus render any creation of Exchequer bills unnecessary) had given them official standing.[5] It became gradually clear that they were not able to fulfil their grandiose promises, and that the Exchequer bills would thus be needed after all, but until this was finally proved by the complete failure of their subscription in August 1696 they were a thorn in Montague's side. His advisers were sure the Land Bank's supporters 'depend much upon baffling the Currency of the Exchequer bills, and to bring them

---

[1] The East India bond debt increased from £318,000 in 1694 to £809,000 in 1696.

[2] [Charles Davenant], *The True Picture of a Modern Whig* (1701), p. 25. For other suggestions about the authorship of Exchequer bills see J. K. Horsefield, *British Monetary Experiments 1650–1710*, pp. 122–4. Abbot subscribed £1,000 to the Million Bank in 1695, P.R.O. C 46/1. He was appointed Customs Cashier in 1698 but died soon after; his widow acted as his administratrix in the office April–December 1699. Abbot is also listed in Chamberlayne's *Angliae Notitia* for 1700 as Deputy to the Paymaster of the Forces, Lord Ranelagh. Chamberlayne's lists tended to go unrevised into new editions.

[3] Add. MS. 34355, letters from Charles Montague to William Blathwait May 1696–October 1697. Most of the following section is based on this correspondence, part of which is published by W. A. Shaw, Introduction to *Cal. T. Bks. XI–XVII*, pp. lix–lxxiii.

[4] Montague to Blathwait 5 June 1696.

[5] For the Bank see J. K. Horsefield, *British Monetary Experiments*, pp. 156–217.

to be sold upon the Exchange for 20 p. Ct. loss'.[1] The Land Bank Commissioners also tried to take advantage of the current recoinage. One of their reiterated claims was for permission to lend the government clipped coin taken as par, which the Crown's advisers rejected as illegal.[2]

This general background explains the tentative form of the first creation of Exchequer bills, and Montague's pessimism about them. Authority to make out the bills was given in the Land Bank Act passed in April 1696. This envisaged the possibility that the £2,564,000 loan promised by the bank's promoters might not appear, and authorized short-term loans for the same amount. Up to £1,500,000 might take the form of bills carrying 3d.% a day interest (4·6% p.a.). The rest was to be by 7% tallies.[3] The Land Bank had until 1 August to fill half its subscription, the first condition for its incorporation. Montague, though bitterly opposed to the bank as such and hoping for its failure, awaited the date with frayed nerves, for if the Land Bank loan did not come in the Exchequer bills would have to go out. 'Wee are now come to the experiment of our Exchequer Bills', he wrote to Blathwait on 23 June 1696,

for when ye 24th of June is over the fear of having clipt money poured in upon us is over, and wee must set our shoulders to it, to make them pass, 'tis a terrible prospect, and I have yet no comfort, nor hopes of being successfull, for all credit is so entirely destroyed by the fatal project of a new Bank coming at the same time with the deficiency of species that wee know not how to turn our selves.[4]

He enclosed for Blathwait's comments his 'scheme how to set up the credit of the Exchequer' and added

The design has been approved by the Treasury, and Wee are endeavouring to engage the most considerable men in all parts to assist us in it. Wee have brought it to great perfection at Exeter by the help of Sir Joseph Tiley, and I have letters from Sir Wm. Blacket of Newcastle, Mr. Yates of Bristoll and Mr. Blofield of Norwich that give us encouragement and if wee do carry it on, 'tis the most difficult thing yt was ever brought about.[5]

The enlistment of these local capitalists was presumably to make sure that Bills would be accepted in the provinces. In July Montague hoped that 'in a

---

[1] Montague to Blathwait 3 July 1696, enclosed paper initialled 'J. B.'.

[2] Montague to Blathwait, 29 May 1696. For the recoinage see above, p. 349.

[3] 7 & 8 Wm. III, c. 31.

[4] Montague to Blathwait, 23 June 1696. Clipped coin ceased to be legal tender on 1 February 1696, but could be taken in payment by revenue collectors until 4 May, and paid by them into the Exchequer up to midsummer.

[5] Ibid.

little time you will hear Wee have established a litle Bank' at Exeter for this purpose.[1] Meanwhile, he asked Blathwait to see if the States General would agree not to protest any bill of Exchange that had been paid in Exchequer bills. Treading the governmental maze between the Treasury Board, the Lords Justices (who 'are not very conversant in these matters')[2] and the Council he succeeded in getting this proposal accepted at home, and left Blathwait to promote it abroad, commenting: 'for the Exchequer bills wch have the Government of England for their security it should not be refused'.[3]

Despite Montague's care, however, the first set of Bills was not very skilfully devised. The rate of interest allowed, under 5%, was an unhappy compromise between allowing nothing (like many banknotes) and allowing 6% to 8%, like the Exchequer's short-term tallies. Blathwait feared the hostility to the project of all dealers in money 'except the Old Bank' and wondered whether a higher interest should not be conceded.[4] The Treasury was perhaps calculating that (as Bagehot later pointed out) the success of a bank largely depends simply on the willingness of its clients not to present its bills for payment. But it showed its uneasiness about this by admitting the possibility of a 'failure of Cash coming into the Exchequer to answer' the Bills, and providing for it by allowing holders to choose a 'perpetual annuity' of 7% instead.[5] This was a farcical proviso, particularly in a year of financial crisis and high liquidity-preference. Further, it was not said that the bills could be used to pay taxes. It is thus not surprising that only £158,589 were issued, about a tenth of the sum authorized. Of these, £99,910 were cancelled between Christmas 1696 and midsummer 1697. In September 1697, £41,975 of the remainder were in the hands of the Paymaster of the Forces Abroad, Lord Ranelagh, £16,019 in those of Charles Fox, Paymaster of the Forces in Ireland, and the balance of £685 in those of 'Private Persons'.[6]

Meanwhile, the Treasury tried again. In January 1697 a new statute authorized the creation of a further £1,500,000 Exchequer bills. They

[1] Montague to Blathwait, 3 July 1696.
[2] Montague to Blathwait, 23 June 1696. The Lords Justices were deputed to act for the king during his absence abroad.
[3] Ibid.
[4] Blathwait to Montague 2 July 1696, one of three Blathwait letters in the correspondence.
[5] Section lxxii of the Act.
[6] P.R.O. E 406/89, Exchequer Bill Certificate Book, at end. This states that £99,910 bills were made out, £158,589 issued. The figures agree substantially with those in Add. MS. 20721, revenue accounts 1685-99, f. 41.

could be used to pay current (1697) taxes, except the Land Tax, and might be redeemed either at the Exchequer or by presenting them to a Crown revenue collector (like tallies of Pro). Deficiencies were to be provided for in the following year.[1] Nothing was said about interest. These clauses were not conspicuously better than those of 1696. The London merchant Henry Phill, writing to his correspondents Knipe and Hoyle on 21 May 1697, described Exchequer bills as 'a paper credit newly come out, ye discount of wch. is run up already to 7 p. Ct. & upwards'.[2] Montague commented gloomily to Blathwait on 25 May

The Exchequer Bills do as well as could be expected from so new a thing, under a great opposition, but Wee are almost at the end of our Tedder in them, and how Wee shall find Remittances on any other fund is yet to be tryed.[3]

Already, however, the Treasury had taken an important step towards improving the bills. In April 1697 a statute empowered the Board to make arrangements with private financiers for the advance of sums to encash them after they were paid out from the Exchequer. Interest was to be payable at the rate of $5d.\%$ a day (7·6% p.a.). Care was taken that it did not accrue while bills were in the hands of revenue collectors or the Exchequer, by providing that the date at which either of these acquired or paid bills was to be endorsed on them.[4] These regulations were evaded with considerable profit in the same year by the revenue officials Bartholomew Burton, Charles Duncombe and John Knight, but, despite this scandal, proved workable and were included in subsequent Acts.[5]

This statute, which was part of the general settlement in spring 1697 of the government's desperate financial situation, was followed by a third, also in April, authorizing the creation of a further £1·2m. bills, but stipulating that not more than £2m. were to be outstanding at a time.[6] By dint of yearly cancellations this limit was observed. Of the £2,700,000 bills authorized in 1697 £2,699,990 were issued, but repayments reduced the principal by Michaelmas 1702 to £553,417 and by midsummer 1710 to £1,925. With the contrariety of Exchequer practice a final balance of £1,495 was solemnly

---

[1] 8 & 9 Wm. III, c. 6.

[2] P.R.O. Chancery Master's Exhibits, C 111/127, *Crow* v. *Phill*, f. 229*v*.

[3] Add. MS. 34355, Montague to Blathwait, 25 May 1697.   [4] 8 & 9 Wm. III, c. 20.

[5] Burton had just succeeded Duncombe as Excise Cashier. Knight was Cashier of the Customs. Their fraud, which turned on evading the regulations about indorsements so as to increase the interest due, is described in *BPP* (1857–8), xxxiii. 261 ff. from the Treasury Board Minutes.

[6] 8 Wm. III, c. 24.

carried forward for half a century, but for all practical purposes the 'Old Bills', which had been 'an effectual, tho' a Paper, Prop to support the State, when its Silver Pillars were for a time remov'd', had been liquidated.[1]

At this point it is worth looking at the 'circulation' contracts which had gone a good deal to uphold their credit while they were outstanding. At first there were twelve 'Trustees for the Circulation', six nominated by the subscribers and six by the Treasury. By 1702 their number had fallen to three, Sir James Bateman, John Heathcote and Henry Fermor, who continued to act until the last contract was signed in 1710.[2] The details of the contracts, which were entered into under the statutory powers given to the Treasury in 1697, are shown in Table 59.

The terms of the contracts moved very quickly in the Treasury's favour, Godolphin, as usual striking a good bargain for 'the publique service'. The trustees at first took subscriptions covering a quarter to a third of the bills, put this up to between 55% and 95% 1698–1703, then became more confident about what they were doing and reduced cover to 20% to 30% of bills outstanding. The subscriptions, though in instalments, were evidently fully paid, in contrast to the Bank of England's later subscriptions for the same purpose, which were only a tenth paid with a liability for the remainder. Thus, a surviving, undated, printed receipt for the third subscription of 1697 acknowledges £375 paid by John Lade as the third instalment of the £1,500 he had subscribed, 'which Sum . . . was repaid to *him* at the same time in Exchequer-Bills'.[3]

The last sentence raises the question of how the bills were circulated. Dr. Shaw argues that the trustees undertook to cash them at sight, but this cannot be right.[4] The statutory powers given to the Treasury in 1697 were to

covenant and agree with any Persons for the immediate advancing of Money from Time to Time for exchanging such Bills as shall be refused or not accepted in repayment of Tallies and Orders . . . such Persons shall upon their advancing any Moneys pursuant to their Contracts have for their Security & Satisfaction the said Bills.[5]

---

[1] For totals see Appendix C. The quotation is from Alexander Justice, *A General Treatise of Monies and Exchanges* (1707), p. 90.

[2] The contracts are printed in the *Cal. T. Bks.* xii–xxiii, see Introduction to *Cal. T. Bks. XI–XVII* for references. The Secretary to the Trustees was Lionel Herne, First Clerk to the second Exchequer Teller, and the Cashier was Samuel Edwards, First Clerk to the Fourth Teller.

[3] Corporation of London Records Office, Assessments Box 1.2. Word italicized in ink, remainder printed.

[4] W. A. Shaw, Introduction to *Cal. T. Bks. XI–XVII* (1695–1702), p. cxlviii.

[5] 8 & 9 Wm. III, c. 20 (1697), s. lxvi (omitting some words).

TABLE 59

Treasury contracts for circulation of Exchequer bills 1697–1710

1	2	3	4	5	
No.	Date	Amounts to be subscribed £	Interest allowed to Trustees %	Volume of Exchequer bills outstanding £	Ratio of 3 to 5 %
1	27 April 1697	431,450	10 ⎫		22·9
2	9 July 1697	695,170	10 ⎬	1,881,475	36·9
3	26 October 1697	517,345	10 ⎭		27·5
4	3 March 1698	300,000	8 ⎫		20·0
5	28 April 1698	1,000,000	4 ⎬	1,498,713	66·7
6	1 February 1699	1,000,000	3	1,051,707	95·1
7	15 April 1700	500,000	3	876,062	57·1
8	16 June 1701	500,000	3	651,092	76·8
9	1 June 1702	500,000	3	553,417	90·3
10	24 May 1703	300,000	1½	539,497	55·6
11	22 May 1704	150,000	1	538,412	27·9
12	21 May 1705	150,000	1	535,312	28·0
13	10 May 1706	150,000	1	529,377	28·3
14	12 May 1707	50,000	1	409,184	12·2
15	5 May 1708	50,000	1	258,049	19·4
16	9 May 1709	50,000	1	107,910	46·3

Source: Cal. T. Bks. xii–xxiii, and Appendix C.

The situation this envisaged was that John Doe, on presenting an Exchequer tally at the Exchequer for payment, might refuse to be paid in Exchequer bills, and demand specie instead. The trustees were a safety-net for such demands rather than being prepared — as the Bank of England later was — to cash all Exchequer bills at sight. The first Treasury contract faithfully reproduced the limited statutory arrangement.[1] Endorsements on surviving bills of this period show the dates at which they were received by revenue officials and the dates at which they left the Exchequer again. This second entry — 'from the Exchequer' — is sometimes but by no means always followed by 'Exchanged per ye Trustees.' This is followed in turn by the

[1] Contract printed in *Cal. T. Bks.* xii (April–September 1697), pp. 141–3.

next revenue collector's endorsement.[1] What became of bills which the trustees cashed? Shaw thought that after they had given cash for a bill they 'handed the bill to the Exchequer which reissued it'.[2] But had this been done there would in all likelihood have been a second 'exchange per ye trustees' (which does not appear on any of the bills examined), and thus an endless shuttling of bills between the trustees' office and the Exchequer. They would never have got into circulation at all. By the terms of their contract the trustees were assured that

as any . . . part of the money subscribed . . . shall be required and paid for exchanging the said Bills, the Bills that shall be exchanged therewith shall and may immediately be delivered out to the use of the contractors and be current from them as from any other person or persons whatsoever.[3]

This gave the trustees *carte blanche* to dispose of bills in their hands, and it looks from the circulation receipt previously described as though subscribers were given an equivalent sum in Exchequer bills for the money which they paid in calls.

The nature of the bills made this viable. Shaw argues that they passed by endorsement and delivery, like bills of exchange, and deduces from the limited number of endorsements on surviving bills that their velocity of circulation was low.[4] But as the necessity for endorsement was limited to the Exchequer, revenue officials, and the trustees, this cannot be correct. There is every reason to suppose that bills changed hands as freely as bank-notes. One bill of 1697 got as far as Bridgenorth in between being encashed by the trustees and paid in again to a revenue collector; unfortunately most endorsements merely give a name.[5] The low denomination of many of the bills of 1696–7 must have helped this process. Those of April 1697 had a blank for the sum; those of September included ones of (printed) five pound denomination.[6] Curiously, the shuttling process which, if Shaw's interpretation were right, would have replaced the free circulation of bills, and would

[1] Based on surviving Exchequer bills of 1697, 1701, 1709 and 1720 in P.R.O. E 407/134 (ii) and Add. MS. 31025. The latter is a particularly good collection, donated by the Comptroller and Auditor-General in 1879. Cf. also Plate 9.

[2] Introduction to *Cal. T. Bks. XI–XVII*, p. clii.   [3] *Cal. T. Bks.* xii, loc. cit.

[4] Introduction to *Cal. T. Bks. XI–XVII*, pp. cli–iii.

[5] Add. MS. 31025, bill of 26 April 1697; see Plate 9.

[6] See the collection of bills referred to in the previous note. The bill of 26 April 1697 was for (written) £5. Cf. Alexander Justice, *A General Treatise of Monies and Exchanges*, p. 89: 'A great number of these Notes were only for five or ten Pounds, which answer'd the Necessities of Commerce among the meaner People, for the common Conveniencies of Life.'

at this period have proved fatal to their credit, was later to characterize the arrangements between the Bank of England and the Exchequer which ensured their survival and development.

II

Long before the first issues of Exchequer bills were paid off, the War of the Spanish Succession made it necessary to create new and much larger amounts. The principal of bills issued for supply in 1707, 1709 and 1713 was £5·6m., besides further bills used to pay interest on those already made out.[1] Godolphin considered that the syndicate which had underwritten the Old Bills was not powerful enough financially to secure the credit of these much larger sums, and instead turned for support to the Bank of England. The first batch of bills underwritten by the Bank, under a statute passed in March 1707, amounted to £1·5m.[2] The Bank undertook to cash bills, when presented, at sight or within twenty-four hours. The interest allowed on bills was left to its discretion.[3] The Treasury was to pay the Bank an allowance of $4\frac{1}{2}\%$ on the principal of bills outstanding, a sharp rise above the rate of 1% currently allowed to the syndicate financing the small balance of Old Bills. The House Duties were perpetuated from 1 August 1710 to provide a fund for discharging the New bills. In the meantime, the Exchequer might create further bills to pay the Bank its quarterly circulation allowance. This was credit supporting credit with a vengeance. With the curve of war expenses mounting, the Treasury, like the French *Trésor Royal*, became increasingly concerned about the threat to public credit from an uncontrolled increase in the volume of short-dated paper.[4] But unlike Desmaretz, basing his financial operations on Samuel Bernard's increasingly precarious juggling in the Lyons money-market, Godolphin was able to rely on the Bank of England's good faith and financial power. Early in 1709 he approached the directors with a four-point proposal. The existing bills and the interest due on them should be funded at 6%, thus converting the

[1] The Acts concerned are 6 Anne, c. 21, 7 Anne, cc. 30, 31, 9 Anne, c. 7, 12 Anne c. 11.

[2] 6 Anne, c. 21.

[3] It recouped itself when it returned the Bills to the Exchequer, see below, p. 378.

[4] For its amount see Appendix C.

government's short-term debt into a long-term one: the Bank should undertake to circulate a fresh issue of £2·5m. bills; it should undertake to advance the government £400,000 in cash; its charter would be extended from 1710 to 1732. The directors agreed, and put the recommendation to their General Court on 2 February 1709. On 4 February the adjourned Court met to consider the details of the scheme. The Governor, Francis Eyles, said that

it was evident to them all That the want of Species in the Kingdome required some Remedy for the Circulation of the Great yearly paymts. to her Majty. for carrying on the War, and that perhaps no other Remedy was to be found at this time, but by Excheqr. Bills.[1]

The Court agreed that the directors should put forward a proposal to the Commons' Committee of the Whole House, and on 10 February was told it had been accepted. On 22–25 February a subscription to give the Bank the extra resources it would need, by doubling its existing capital of £2,201,172, was heavily oversubscribed. On 21 April the Act incorporating the agreement with the Bank received the royal assent.[2]

The bills funded amounted to £1,500,000 principal and £123,338 interest, and it was agreed that 6% on the whole sum should accrue until Michaelmas 1710. From this date, when the principal would be £1,775,028, 6% interest was to be paid each year from the House Duties. By the same Act, a further £2·5m. bills were to be issued, which the Bank agreed to cash after they had been paid into the Exchequer and reissued from it. As against this stiffening of its 1707 attitude (when it had agreed to encash bills at sight) it accepted an allowance of only 3% (as against 4½%) on the total of bills outstanding. Holders of bills were to be allowed interest of twopence a day (3·04% p.a.). An elaborate 'General Fund and Security' derived from Customs dues was settled for payment of interest and allowances and the discharge of a yearly £200,000 of the principal, but, as the great part of this fund would not be available until 1714, it was once more agreed that these obligations should meanwhile be met by further bills, made out quarterly and paid to the Bank. In September 1709 an additional £400,000 bills were issued on the same terms and charged on the same funds.[3] In February 1711, as a result of the severe pressure on the money-market in 1710, which had driven Exchequer bills to a small discount, the government agreed to pay the Bank an additional 'circulation allowance' of £45,000 p.a. from the fund

---

[1] Bank of England G. Ct. Bk. ii. 46.   [2] 7 Anne, c. 30.   [3] 7 Anne, c. 31.

settled in 1709.[1] In return, the Bank undertook to cash all bills at sight. In July 1713, by the last Act authorizing the creation of Exchequer bills until 1720, a further £1,200,000 bills were made out, which the Bank agreed to cash when presented, on condition that its £45,000 p.a. allowance be increased by £8,000 p.a. to £53,000 p.a., charged on the same fund. These allowances were to last until the total of bills was reduced to £1·9m.[2]

As all the allowances payable under the four Acts of 1709, 1711 and 1713 ranked in priority to the proposed redemption of £200,000 p.a. principal, and as the total of bills outstanding in June 1713, before the new issue of £1·2m., was already £3,395,312, the day when this reduction would occur must have seemed distant. But, unlike the French government, the English administration had preserved the good name of Exchequer bills, which reached the end of the war at par. This had been primarily due to the Bank's willingness to help, which in turn depended on the fact that Parliament and the whole realm stood behind its promises, as one of Controller-General Desmaretz's correspondents pointed out to him in November 1709.[3]

The Bank of England provided itself with the funds which it needed to finance its new Exchequer bill commitments by increasing its capital by 50% in 1707–8, doubling it in February 1709, and making further calls of 15% in December 1709 and 10% in 1710. But there were obvious objections to increasing paid-up capital simply to finance short-term bills, particularly after the Treasury increased its Exchequer bill allowances to the Bank in 1711 and 1713. From 1711 the Bank relied instead on its 'subscriptions for circulating Exchequer bills as specie', under which the underwriters (subscribers) paid a tenth down, and remained liable for one year for the remainder. The system was introduced in March 1711, when the Bank borrowed £1m. at 6%, £100,000 of which was subscribed in cash, and remained intact until 1759.[4]

How did the Bank handle the bills of 1707–13? To record transactions in them it opened a new account headed 'Act. for Exchequer Bills' on 26

---

[1] 9 Anne, c. 7. The Bank opened an account to record discounts on Exchequer bills coming into its hands in May 1710 (General Ledger 4, f. 366). It closed it in August 1711, debiting profit and loss with £4,384. The rate of discount was between 1½% and 2½%.

[2] 12 Anne, c. 11.

[3] A.N. G 7, 1119, du Casaux du Hallay to Desmaretz 17 November 1709 (N.S.), enclosing an extract from a letter from London dated 4 November 1709, presumably N.S. The writer was a friend of the deceased Patrick Sarsfield, but his name is not stated. The phrase referred to in the text is 'vous avez le parlement, et ainsy tout le Royaume pour caution'.

[4] For this system see below, p. 384.

April 1707. This listed bills paid on the debtor side and Bills issuing from the Bank on the creditor side. There was a flow of bills in and out as they were presented and reissued. They were separated by columns into different denominations. Thus from 15 November 1707 to 17 January 1708 the Bank paid £788,325 Bills and reissued £729,850. The bills were made out in denominations of £100, £50 and £25. There were 6962 of the first, 728 of the second, 2,229 of the third.[1] The Bills of 1709 included in addition some for £12 10s. 0d. each.[2] But the Bank clearly disliked this attempt to create small bills again, like those of the 1690s, and asked in July 1713 that the new bills to be made out should be for £100 each.[3] This was the standard denomination until 1742.[4]

TABLE 60

Principal of Exchequer bills outstanding 1715–20

						nearest £
December 1715 .	.	.	.	.	.	4,561,025
December 1716 .	.	.	.	.	.	4,561,025
July 1717	.	.	.	.	.	4,561,025
December 1717 .	.	.	.	.	.	2,561,025
December 1718 .	.	.	.	.	.	2,561,025
December 1719 .	.	.	.	.	.	1,279,738
June 1720	.	.	.	.	.	1,056,263
December 1720 .	.	.	.	.	.	1,919,613

Source: Exchequer bill Certificate Books, see notes to Appendix C.

In 1709 the Bank had asked that 'sufficient Funds be appropriated for the Cancelling or Paying off the Whole Sum [of Bills issued that year] in some certain time'.[5] But despite the provision of an hypothetical sinking fund of £200,000 p.a. in 1709, nothing serious was done to discharge the principal of the post-1707 Bills until 1715, when the Act establishing the Aggregate Fund appropriated £271,000 p.a. to regular cancellation of outstanding Bills.[6] These then amounted to £4,561,025. This plan, too, had little effect,

[1] Bank of England General Ledger 3, f. 608.
[2] The 1709 bills in the collections referred to above p. 372 n. are all for this amount. The Bank's ledgers show that others were for £25, £50 and £100.
[3] P.R.O. E 406/208, f. 2, 22 July 1713.
[4] When bills for £1,000 were introduced, below p. 384.
[5] Bank of England G. Ct. Bk. ii, f. 47 (4 February 1709).   [6] See above, p. 83.

and it was not until drastic funding (as in 1709) was again resorted to in 1717, when £2m. Bills were cancelled,[1] that the principal began to sink rapidly. (See Table 60.)

One effect of the post-1707 Exchequer bill system was that at a given date the Bank, in virtue of its importance in circulating the bills, was always a large holder of them. Thus at selected dates its holdings were as follows:

TABLE 61

Bank of England's holdings of Exchequer bills 1707–20

| Bank's holding | | Total Bills outstanding | |
Date	£	Date	£
August 1707	861,950	September 1707	1,879,409
August 1708	1,194,925	September 1708	1,827,899
August 1709	606,725	September 1709	2,631,785
August 1711	1,406,013	September 1711	3,193,433
February 1712	1,065,925	December 1712	3,343,713
September 1715	1,004,025	December 1715	4,561,025
November 1716	2,330,650	December 1716	4,561,025
December 1717	2,438,000	December 1717	2,561,025
September 1718	471,938	December 1718	2,561,025
October 1719	154,225	December 1719	1,279,738
February 1720	166,675	June 1720	1,056,263
August 1720	4,675	August 1720	2,056,263

Source: Bank's holdings: Bank of England General Ledgers 2–5. Volume of bills outstanding: Appendix C.

These figures provide partial confirmation of Walpole's later statement that the Bank had 'generally been the Bearers, or Holders of all, or the greatest Part of the Exchequer bills standing out'.[2] From the beginning of 1720, however, the Bank was rapidly liquidating its holding, and finally closed this account in August 1725.

With the exception of the period April 1709–February 1711 the Bank agreed — unlike the trustees who had underwritten the Old bills of 1696–7 — to encash bills at sight or within twenty-four hours, with accrued

[1] Ibid., p. 87.
[2] [Sir Robert Walpole], *Some Considerations concerning the Publick Funds*, p. 24, referring to 1717.

interest. In return, it received an allowance of 3% (4½% 1707–9) on the bills outstanding in the current year, computed and paid quarterly in more Exchequer bills. It got back the interest it had paid on bills encashed when it returned these to the Exchequer. (In this respect it was in no different position from any other holder of bills.) The Exchequer Bill Act of 1709 (7 Anne c. 30) authorized the Treasury to reimburse the Exchequer Tellers what they allowed for interest to those who presented bills to them, and on 22 June 1709 Lord Treasurer Godolphin's warrant created the offices of Paymasters of Interest on Exchequer bills, which were filled at first by the Treasury clerks Samuel Edwards and Lionel Herne, and later by Edwards, George Jerman and John Stockwell, who declared their last account in July 1720.[1] They were handling sums of £50,000 p.a. and more, but their function was nevertheless relatively subordinate, and not to be confused with the encashment of bills, for which the Bank, not the Exchequer, was responsible, nor with their cancellation, which was not undertaken until after the peace of 1713. By this date the rate of interest which the Treasury allowed on bills had fallen from the 4·6% (1696) and 7·6% (1697) of the previous war to just over 3% (2d. a day). This rate seems to have been constant from 1709 to 1717, when it was halved to a penny a day. From the 1720s the Bank of England became the government's agent for underwriting bills on the annual taxes, and paid the interest itself, without right to reimbursement from the Exchequer. It had power to vary the rate, which did in fact rise to 2½% in 1745 and 4% 1746–9.[2] As the Bank itself was the main holder, however, these changes must have been intended primarily to keep the bills good currency in case it had to use them in payments.

The argument to this stage may now be briefly recapitulated. The Exchequer bills of 1707–13 were far greater in volume than the experimental bills of 1696–7, and of larger denomination. They were all, however, supply bills, and not bills in anticipation of given taxes paid off when these came in. In this they resembled the later stages of Downing's 'Order experiment' of 1665–72, or the issues of *Billets de Monnaie* by the French

[1] P.R.O. Audit Office 1/876/16, Declared Accounts of Paymasters of Interest on Exchequer Bills 1709–20. The first account recites Godolphin's warrant of 22 June 1709. The two first Paymasters were to receive £500 p.a. for themselves and their clerks. They were already acting as Secretary and Cashier to the Trustees for circulating the Old (pre-1707) bills, see above, p. 370 n.

[2] Add. MS. 33038, f. 241. The earlier (1696–1717) rates stated in the text are those organized by the statutes creating the bills, but the Treasury clearly had power to vary the rate, for several bills of the period are indorsed 1d. or ½d. a day only. Other bills carried no interest.

treasury after 1704 rather than the Exchequer bills of the Walpole period. Unlike either, however, their credit was sustained by regular and businesslike encashment by the Bank of England. When the system wobbled in 1709, the Bank's help was enlisted to fund nearly £2m. bills, and thus clear the way for the issue of new ones. The system resembled a well-managed bank-note issue. Despite its success, strikingly contrasting with the French government's failure in the same field, it was regarded at its inception and for some years after the war as a temporary device, which by implication was to be got rid of as soon as the recovery of the national finances permitted. Exchequer bills were debts, and debts must be repaid. The steady reduction of the principal of Exchequer bills between 1717 and 1720 reflects this attitude and the policy derived from it. The actual course of events, however, was to be quite different.

III

An important if indefinable aspect of the great South Sea scheme of 1719–20 was the desire of the company's inner ring of directors, headed by Sir John Blunt, to dish the Bank of England by sapping its privileged financial position. This motive, which had also been a factor in the company's flotation in 1711, lay behind the grandiose first South Sea proposal of late 1719 to take over the Government debts owed to the Bank and the East India Company, as well as those owed to the general public. Though this plan came to nothing, at a more modest level the company did succeed in robbing the Bank of its circulation of Exchequer bills from midsummer 1720. Under the South Sea Act of April 1720 the company, whose commercial record so far revealed only modest financial expertise, agreed to circulate £1m. Exchequer bills (which were in fact to be lent to it) until midsummer 1727.[1]

The motive — support of the company in executing its scheme — which prompted the Treasury to agree to this, is clear, even if the judgement involved was, to say the least, erratic. The results were unhappy. On 24 May 1720 the company named three of its directors, John Blunt, Sir Robert Chaplin and Sir William Chapman, to act as Trustees for the Circulation, and the Treasury named three others (this was reminiscent of the first

[1] 6 Geo. I, c. 4. The bills were made out in June and lent to the Company, see above, p. 141.

contract of 1697).[1] During the hectic summer of 1720 the South Sea trustees had more pressing matters to occupy them, and consistently neglected their official duties. In the autumn, when the bottom dropped out of the security market, the Treasury belatedly acted. On 1 October 1720, inappropriately presided over by the Chancellor of the Exchequer John Aislabie, whose dark ambition and lack of scruple were important factors in the South Sea scheme's original acceptance, the Board summoned the three delinquent trustees before it, and Aislabie severely reprimanded them. They had conducted their office carelessly and contrary to their solemn contract. The Treasury on its part had 'taken the proper caution . . . to support the Credit of the Excheqr. by their having a much greater Cash than is necessary to support their proportion of the Circulation'. The reproof was given verbally, and not by a public letter, 'lest the world's being acquainted with their Carelessness and mismanagement might heighten the diffidence & Distrust mankind hath of them'. Aislabie, who was soon to be made painfully aware of the diffidence and distrust mankind had of him, ended by telling the three directors to hold a Court to discuss raising 'their proportion in Specie but to take especial care that the Methods they shall think the most proper to use do not in any wise affect the credit of the Bank.'[2]

It was in fact already obvious that the South Sea Company's attempt to exclude the Bank of England from exercising its increasing role as the government's financial supporter had broken down in this as in the more important sector of management of the public debt. In July 1722 a new circulation contract for Exchequer bills was signed between the Treasury and the Bank.[3] At this date the volume of bills outstanding was £1,919,913, £1m. new bills having been created in 1722 to pay off part of the Navy Debt.[4] (The special £1m. bills made out in 1720 and lent to the South Sea Company were recorded in separate books at the Exchequer and by the end of 1722 were reduced by repayment to £30,000; in July 1723 only £400 was outstanding.)[5] In 1723 £100,000 more bills were charged on a new tax on Roman Catholics, and in 1725 the issue of a further million was authorized, partly to pay off stock issued in 1721 and partly to make further

---

[1] Add. MS 25499, f. 19, South Sea D. Ct. Bk., 24 May 1720. In 1697 the Treasury had named six trustees and the subscribers six more, see above, p. 370.

[2] P.R.O. T 29/24 (i), Treasury Board Minutes 1718–20, ff. 302–3.

[3] P.R.O. E 406/209, f. 24, circulation contract between the Treasury and the Bank dated 24 July 1722. In 1721 the Bank has no account for Exchequer bills in its General Ledger.

[4] By 8 Geo. I, c. 20.   [5] P.R.O. E 406/94–95.

provision for the Civil List.[1] Most of these bills were cancelled at the end of their year of issue, and the new office of Paymasters of Exchequer bills was created in April 1723 to manage the business involved.

The duties of these officials were defined as cancelling bills when ordered to do so by the Treasury, and paying the Bank its quarterly circulation allowance. The first paymasters, Edmund Britiffe, Thomas Genault and Thomas Newman, were allowed £700 p.a. for themselves and their clerks.[2] In October 1725 the further office of Comptroller of Exchequer bills was instituted.[3] The Comptroller's duties were defined in 1755 as the cancellation of bills each week (presumably after the paymasters had paid them), the inspection of the paymasters' books, and the quarterly audit of the Bank of England's circulation accounts to determine its allowance. The original Comptroller, Thomas Le Heup, was still in office at this date, at a salary of £350. He only needed to attend once a month.[4] A further step was to charge a senior clerk and two junior clerks in the Exchequer of Receipt with the preparation of Exchequer bills. This had been done by 1727; by the end of the century the title of the small department had become 'the Office for the Issue of Exchequer Bills'. Its staff establishment was still three in the 1840s. Over the years a regular system evolved for engraving or altering plates for new issues of bills, manufacture of special paper at mills near Exeter, and the printing and signature of the bills themselves.[5]

The government's next innovation after introducing Exchequer offices for handling the creation and discharge of bills was to issue bills in 1725–6 charged on the annual Land and Malt taxes and redeemed when these came in, besides small additional amounts for supply. This experiment was repeated in each of the four following years, and after the Exchequer year 1728–9 the use of tallies of fictitious loan, whose history dated back to the 1690s, ceased altogether. From this date, the government relied increasingly on the Exchequer bill for anticipation of its annual revenue. 'What has rendered the invention of exchequer bills of the utmost use and service to the public', wrote Walpole,

[1] 9 Geo. I, c. 18, 11 Geo. I, c. 17.

[2] P.R.O. E 406/209, Warrants relating to Exchequer bills, ff. 36–37, 24 April 1723.

[3] Ibid., f. 58, 12 October 1725.

[4] Add. MS. 33038, f. 470, 'The Business of Comptroller of Excheqr. Bills'. This account says that when bills were for £100 regular attendance was needed. The introduction of £1,000 bills [in 1742] made this unnecessary.

[5] John Chamberlayne, *Mag. Brit. Notitia* for 1727 records the officials for the first time. For later developments see *BPP* (1842), xviii, report on making out and issue of Exchequer bills.

is the late great improvement thereon, by registering them, and paying them off in course, as the monies come in, on the land-tax and malt.[1]

The new system was recognizably an adaptation of the loans by Exchequer tallies and Orders, for in these, too, Orders had been serially numbered, registered on a given tax, and paid in course when it came in. But Exchequer bills eliminated the need for tallies of receipt, and were altogether more easily handled and dealt in. Further, while tallies were not always certain, Exchequer Bills were as good as gold. The reason for this, in turn, was the part played in the new system by the Bank of England, without whose help it would not have worked.

The Treasury's arrangements with the Bank were in the form of regular annual contracts signed each July, by which the Bank normally undertook to circulate (cash on sight or within twenty-four hours) £2·5m. bills. Its allowance was 3% on the bills outstanding, unless their principal was less than £1m. when it fell to 1%. These terms were constant from the 1720s up to the Seven Years War.[2] In addition, supplementary contracts were drawn up, at first endorsed on the main one but after 1743 written separately, stipulating the additional bills charged on the annual Land, Malt and sometimes other taxes, which the Bank agreed to circulate.[3] Examination of the Bank's ledgers shows how the new system operated. The Bank took up bills in batches as they issued from the Exchequer, and then 'set them off'; that is received the cash for them (and handed them over for cancellation) as the tax monies came in. It seems clear from the dating and the completeness of the serial numbers that the Bank held the bills till they were due for payment.[4] This was in effect a shuttle-service between Bank and Exchequer, which must virtually have excluded other lenders, as is seen by continuing the table of the Bank's holdings of bills.

Allowing for the difference between the months at which the two balances were struck — the Exchequer account usually shows a higher balance of bills in June than in December — the figures correlate sufficiently to prove that the fears expressed in 1705 that the Bank would monopolize govern-

---

[1] Coxe, *Walpole*, iii. 621–2, dated by Coxe 1724 but probably a year or two later. For tallies of fictitious loan see above, p. 350.

[2] Add. MS. 33038, f. 362. It is there alleged that before 1726 there were intermediate rates of 2½% and 2% for volumes over £1m. but under £1·5m., which were subsequently omitted.

[3] Based on examination of surviving Exchequer Bill contracts for the period 1735–56 in the Bank of England records.

[4] Bank of England General Ledgers, Exchequer Bill accounts for this period.

TABLE 62

Bank of England's holdings of Exchequer bills 1723–56

Date	Bank's holding (1 September)	Total Bills outstanding (Michaelmas 1723–5, then Christmas)
	£	£
1723 . . .	1,072,900	1,819,913
1724 . . .	1,424,700	1,756,113
1725 . . .	1,470,612	1,470,013
1726 . . .	1,649,213	1,680,709
1727 . . .	2,165,900	1,027,720
1728 . . .	2,152,600	2,453,065
1729 . . .	1,779,800	1,892,124
1730 . . .	2,172,400	2,142,031
1731 . . .	2,035,200	1,615,202
1732 . . .	1,832,100	788,912
1733 . . .	1,606,100	1,545,278
1734 . . .	2,089,300	2,066,785
1735 . . .	2,516,800	2,140,346
1736 . . .	1,967,100	1,760,391
1737 . . .	1,896,700	2,369,175
1738 . . .	2,163,500	2,643,700
1739 . . .	2,084,000	2,168,555
1740 . . .	1,890,500	2,241,400
1741 . . .	2,095,900	2,263,347
1742 . . .	3,000,300	2,506,858
1743 . . .	3,002,700	3,057,510
1744 . . .	4,245,400	3,687,361
1745 . . .	3,577,400	3,179,805
1746 . . .	2,582,200	2,740,272
1747 . . .	2,478,250	2,649,163
1748 . . .	2,098,400	2,475,422
1749 . . .	3,207,562	3,160,316
1750 . . .	3,313,600	2,439,709
1751 . . .	3,454,031	2,864,121
1752 . . .	3,536,103	3,483,476
1753 . . .	2,901,600	2,093,062
1754 . . .	1,927,600	1,533,475
1755 . . .	1,548,000	1,608,533
1756 . . .	2,307,000	2,033,183

Source: for Bank's holdings, Bank of England General Ledgers; for total bills see Appendix C.

ment lending were, in this sector, already justified.[1] But the position evidently changed considerably during the next fifty years, for during the Napoleonic Wars London banks were extensive holders of Exchequer bills.[2] This is not surprising in view of the numerous changes which had occurred during the earlier part of their history, and the great increase in their volume in the later eighteenth century.

The denomination of bills was scaled upwards to meet the changed arrangements of the 1720s and 1730s. As was seen earlier, the first bills went as low as £5, and those of 1709 were for £12 10s. 0d., £25, £50 and £100. Subsequent issues of bills were in units of £100 only, though occasional use was made as early as 1715 of a Bill for £5,000 in internal Bank–Exchequer transfers. By 1750, however, the only denomination was for £1,000, first introduced in anticipation of the Land and Malt Taxes of 1742.[3]

In view of the Bank's monopoly position in the new Exchequer bill system, its arrangements for providing contingent finance — the 'Subscriptions for the Circulation' — were increasingly anomalous, a relic of a more unsure and less well-organized period. They were, however, a handsome source of profit for those able to take advantage of them, and it was perhaps argued that they gave the Bank (and thus the bills it circulated) a useful line of reserve in emergency. It was not until October 1759, therefore, that the subscriptions were discontinued. By this date forty-six had been held since the first in March 1711.[4] The amount subscribed varied between £1m. and £2m., only reaching the upper limit in 1727 and 1728, and was one-tenth paid, the subscriber remaining liable for the other nine-tenths if called upon. The Bank allowed its 'premium' on each £1,000 *subscribed*, which was of course only £100 *paid*, and added to this the 'interest' on the amount actually paid in by the subscribers. The yield on the investment was therefore at first very high: between 1711 and 1727 it was below 11% in only two years. From 1727 to 1735 it fell to between 8% and 9%. From 1736 to 1738 it was only 4%, but rose to 6½% in the early years of the war (1739–44), and then to 9% (1745–7). After the end of the war it was gradually reduced to

[1] *Remarks upon the Bank of England by a Merchant of London* (1705), p. 28, 'the Bank will be, in a short time, not only the great, but the only Lender to the government'.

[2] W. T. C. King, *History of the London Discount Market* (1936), p. 13, citing evidence given before the Lords Committee on the Bank in 1848. Cf. also *BPP* (1842), xviii, chart showing the purchasers of Exchequer Bills.

[3] Based on examination of the Bank of England General Ledgers.

[4] This section is based on an 'Abstract of the several Subscriptions for Circulating Exchequer Bills as Specie' in the Bank of England Record Office.

4½% (1753–4) but increased again to 6½% in the first three years of the next war (1756–9).[1]

These yields were considerably higher than those on other short-dated securities. The difference was undoubtedly intended as compensation for the subscribers' liability to pay calls, but according to Nicholas Magens in 1753 the risk was not taken seriously.

> The Subscriptions are 1000 Pounds each, and for 10 per Cent paid in, or 100 Pounds is given 6 per Cent. and for all future Calls 4 per Cent. only, the Advance 20 on the first 100, makes the Subscription courted; and those who have Interest to procure it, commonly dispose of it again in Change-Alley at a handsome Advance, before even they have paid in their Subscription-money; and as this can be so done, it is of great Advantage to the Directors and their Friends; and as much of this is so disposed, it rests in the Hands of the Purchasers, who, generally speaking, have neither Interest in, nor Account with the Bank, nor often any other Money, it being thought no Risque, as the Calls have never been made, but on very extraordinary Emergencies.[2]

This account needs qualifying. The rate of interest allowed on calls was 5% not 4%, and the bigger 'subscribers to the circulation' such as the London Assurance, or Martin's bank, seem to have held not sold, whatever the smaller ones did.[3] Calls were also not infrequent to begin with. Two were made in 1713, a further two in 1715, and another one in 1718. After this, however, there was only one more, in December 1745.[4]

Magens was right in thinking that calls if made would come when money was tight, and would fluster the subscribers. This was particularly true of those which coincided with the two Jacobite invasions of 1715 and 1745. In November 1715 the northerner Henry Liddell wrote from London to William Cotesworth in Gateshead that

> There had been a run since 24th July daily and especially ye last three weeks so that the Directors were oblig'd to call in 20% from those that subscribed to ye Circulation and a second call which puts a greater stop to Trade of all sorts.[5]

The call of December 1745 created worse confusion still. In Magens's words:

---

[1] The yield is calculated by multiplying the premium by ten (because it was per £1,000 *subscribed*) and adding the interest, which was per £100 *paid*.

[2] [Nicholas Magens], *The Universal Merchant* (1753), p. 30 n.   [3] See below, p. 446.

[4] The calls are noted in the 'Abstract of the several Subscriptions'.

[5] Liddell to Cotesworth, 5 November 1715, quoted in E. Hughes, *North Country Life in the Eighteenth Century*, i (Oxford, 1952), 413.

although upon all other Occasions, the Subscription has been filled, for the most part, by people in the Management [of the Bank] and their Favourites, it was whispered, at this Time, not to be full, and only upon a further Call for 10 per Cent. more, the Subscribers were out of their Wits, and sold at [blank] per Cent. Loss to saddle it on other People.[1]

The Bank of England's ledgers show that in 1715 the two calls of 20% were met, but that the invitation to pay in the other half of the subscription, amounting to £750,000, had produced only £254,100 by March 1716. Similarly, in 1745 the Bank called for 20%, and added the option of paying the whole. If all the subscribers had responded, the full subscription of £1·8m. would have come in. As it was, only £478,350 was paid in between 19 December 1745 and 10 February 1746.[2] These episodes help to explain why the system was discarded. The final blow seems to have been the panic of 1759, when only a strong letter from the veteran Samson Gideon, urging the Bank not to make a call on the Circulation, restored confidence and enabled the government loan to be completed.[3]

From the Bank of England's point of view the subscriptions were not only unreliable, they cut into the profits of circulation. For the premium and interest paid to the subscribers were the largest charge against the premium which the Exchequer paid to the Bank for its services.[4] This premium was in turn calculated, or supposed to be calculated, on the total of bills outstanding. There is an unresolved puzzle here, for as this total was nearly always well over £2m., the annual premium should have been well over £60,000. Yet, as Table 63 shows, it was usually a good deal less. The explanation may be that Exchequer bills deposited by the Bank with the Exchequer as security for government balances at the Bank were not treated as 'outstanding' bills for the purpose of calculating the Bank's allowance.[5] In any case, even on the reduced basis the system showed a handsome profit for the Bank, a profit which must have been larger still once the subscriptions for the circulation were discontinued.

---

[1] Magens, op. cit., p. 30.

[2] For 1715 Bank of England ledger 6, ff. 132, 189; for 1745 General Ledger 10, f. 246, 11, f. 267.

[3] Dr. L. S. Sutherland, 'Samson Gideon: Eighteenth Century Jewish Financier', *Trans. Jewish Hist. Soc. of England*, xvii (1951–2), 79.

[4] The Bank had to pay interest on bills but as it was itself virtually the only holder of them this cannot have been a significant item.

[5] These deposits are described below, pp. 388 ff. Newcastle's informant in 1754 thought the deposit bills were treated as outstanding (ibid.), but this is not conclusive.

TABLE 63

Bank of England profit on the circulation of
Exchequer bills 1738–1756

1	2	3		4	5
		Total bills outstanding		Paid to	
	Premium			subscribers	Bank's gross
Date	on bills	a	b	(premium	profit
	outstanding	given (2)=3%	actually	plus interest)	(2 less 4)
	£	£	£	£	£
1738 . .	35,360	1,178,700	2,643,700	6,400	28,960
1739 . .	65,390	2,179,700	2,168,555	4,000	61,390
1740 . .	41,785	1,392,800	2,241,400	7,800	33,985
1741 . .	37,297	1,243,200	2,263,347	9,750	27,547
1742 . .	40,133	1,337,700	2,506,858	9,750	30,383
1743 . .	43,351	1,445,300	3,057,510	9,750	33,601
1744 . .	25,140	838,000	3,687,361	11,700	13,440
1745 . .	40,604	1,353,500	3,179,805	11,700	28,904
1746 . .	56,636	1,887,800	2,740,272	14,140	42,496
1747 . .	14,988	499,600	2,649,163	13,500	1,488
1748 . .	40,811	1,360,300	2,475,422	16,200	24,611
1749 . .	48,477	1,615,900	3,160,316	9,750	38,727
1750 . .	66,589	2,219,600	2,439,709	9,000	57,589
1751 . .	40,229	1,340,900	2,864,121	9,075	31,154
1752 . .	39,026	1,300,800	3,483,476	8,250	30,776
1753 . .	72,308	2,410,300	2,093,062	7,110	65,198
1754 . .	64,354	2,145,100	1,533,475	7,200	57,154
1755 . .	47,210	1,573,700	1,608,533	7,200	40,010
1756 . .	59,835	1,994,500	2,033,183	6,187	53,648

Source : Bank of England General Ledgers; Appendix C.

IV

The advantages of the new system of Exchequer bill finance built up by
Walpole and the Bank of England after 1722 are fairly obvious: the ready
availability of large sums at 3% in anticipation of government revenue, and
the limitation of negotiations about this to a restricted circle. Critics of the
system, however, retorted that it was monopolistic and, further, that the

Bank, in virtue of its position as account-keeper for revenue and other officials, was lending government money to the government itself. 'The Exchequer Bill contract', wrote an informant of the Duke of Newcastle when the latter was playing himself in at the Treasury after his brother's death in 1754,

> is signed annually in July and is advantagious to the Bank; because as they are Cashires to the Exchequer, and have seldom less in their hands than a Million of Exchequer Cash, they lend the Government their own Money. For this they lodge in the Tellers hands, by way of Security, Exchequer Bills for the Value.[1]

The point was reiterated,

> N.B. The Bank being made the constant Channel to conduct to the Exchequer all the Publick Monies, as Land Tax, Excise, Customs & ca. and having the Exchequer Cash, they must have in their Hands at most times 12 or 15 hundred thousand Pounds of Publick Money.[2]

The amount of 'Exchequer Cash' in the Bank's hands at 5 September 1754 was said to be £1,035,000, for which it deposited with the Exchequer an equivalent sum in Exchequer bills.[3] These sums, claimed Newcastle's informant, ought to be set off against the total Exchequer bills outstanding before the Bank's circulation allowance was calculated.[4]

The sums concerned presumably consisted partly of funds passing through the Bank in the form of subscriptions to state loans, or money imprested to it to pay the interest on them; partly of balances held by departmental paymasters and the receivers of the Customs, Excise, Land and other taxes. Only the second category of funds remained in the Bank's hands long enough to be relevant to the discussion. How far were these deposits available to the Bank? Second, what other large balances, besides these, could it draw on for the purposes of Exchequer bill finance?

In the earlier part of the period the Bank claimed that it received insufficient help from either government departments or revenue collectors. In October 1711 the directors complained to the Treasury Board that not more than five or six Receivers of the Land Tax kept their cash with the Bank, and that the departmental paymasters mostly lodged their balances 'in goldsmiths' hands', that is with private bankers.[5] An example of this is

---

[1] Papers and memoranda of the Duke of Newcastle on taxation and finance 1688–1756, Add. MS. 33038, f. 362, one of a series of anonymous papers on public finance evidently written late in 1754, see f. 358 *dorso*.

[2] Add. MS. 33038, loc. cit. [3] Ibid., Exchequer balances, 5 September 1754.
[4] Ibid., f. 366. [5] *Cal. T. Bks.* xxv (ii), p. 104, 10 October 1711.

Thomas Austin, Receiver-General of the counties of Montgomery, Merioneth, Caernarvon, Anglesey, Denbighshire, Flint and Cheshire, who in September 1699 instructed the London goldsmith bankers Fowle and Wotton to pay into the Exchequer any money credited to him as receiver.[1] The Bank of England was, however, incorrect in saying that few paymasters banked with it. Its Drawing Office ledgers show accounts for 1695–7 for Lord Ranelagh, Paymaster of the Forces Abroad, and for 1711–13 for James Brydges, who held the same office. John Lansdell, a senior clerk in the Ordnance Office, opened an account in January 1705, which must have been for the Treasurer of the Ordnance, Charles Bertie. Lansdell ran it until 1720 when he acted briefly as caretaker Treasurer. The new Treasurer, John Plumptree, who took office in June 1720 and served until 1751, took over the account in his own name.[2] In the General Ledgers there are also accounts in 1710–11 for John Howe (Paymaster of Guards and Garrisons), for Robert Walpole (Treasurer of the Navy, 1710–11) and for his successor, Charles Caesar. These accounts, however, did not have large cash balances. They existed to record Bank of England loans to the paymasters on security of Exchequer tallies, and were of little technical assistance to the Bank itself.[3] Soon after the peace of 1713 this picture began to change. Edward Pauncefort, cashier of the excise, kept his very large cash account with the Bank from April 1714. The new customs cashier (and South Sea director) Francis Hawes kept his account there from July 1716, a month after his appointment.[4] For most of the Walpole period the funds of the Paymaster General of the Forces, and the Navy Treasurer, were kept elsewhere. Then, in March 1739, Daniel Finch opened an account at the Bank for Arthur Onslow, the Treasurer of the Navy; in January 1744, Thomas Winnington, the new Paymaster of the Forces, followed suit. How far by this date were the provincial receivers of taxes also using the Bank? Of 35 receivers of the Land Tax for 38 counties or districts listed in the receipt books of the Exchequer for 1742–3, 21 had accounts at the Bank of England.[5] The main features of these accounts, however, are their high turnover and low average balances. The total balances in 1742 were £46,599, an average of only £2,219: the money was quickly paid away to the Exchequer.[6]

[1] P.R.O. Chancery Masters' Exhibits, C 103/123, Fowle and Wotton papers.

[2] Bank of England Record Office, Drawing Office ledgers.   [3] See below, p. 391.

[4] Hawes was appointed as cashier jointly with Horatio Walpole senior on 20 June 1716, *Cal. T. Papers 1714–19*, p. 261. The Drawing Office account is in the name of Hawes only, and has a very large turnover.

[5] List of receivers compiled from P.R.O. E 401/2090, Receipt Book (Pells) 1742–3.

[6] Balances at dates varying from November 1741 to May 1742.

Other large cash balances held by the Bank of England at the mid-eighteenth century were those of the Accountant-General of Chancery, the East India Company and the South Sea Company. Thus, on 27 February 1742 the East India balance was £106,628 and on 27 April 1742 the South Sea Company's was £144,133. The Royal Bank of Scotland's modest balance of £3,920 on 18 March 1742 was greatly exceeded by that of the banking firm Freame & Barclay, struck on 6 October 1741 at £24,753.[1] In general, however, the balances of London private banking houses are conspicuous by their absence. Thus, of nine goldsmith bankers funding £10,000 or more Navy Bills in 1749, not one had an account at the Bank.[2] In contrast, at 1 January 1755 four major government accounts had the following balances.

TABLE 64

Departmental balances at the Bank of England
1 January 1755

	£
Cashier of the Customs (Roger Townshend)	
Bill account	1,374
Cash account	60,480
Cashier of the Excise (Sir William Milner) . .	42,818
Paymaster of the Forces (William Pitt) . . .	308,280
Treasurer of the Navy (George Grenville) . .	7,120
	£420,072

Source: Bank of England Drawing Office Ledgers.

The balance of the Accountant-General of Chancery at this date, £248,489, brings the total for five large official accounts to £668,561. If the figure for Land Tax balances was about the same as ten years previously, a total of about £700,000 is arrived at. This takes no account of the balances kept at the Bank by receivers of other taxes, especially the Malt Tax, which may have increased official holdings at the mid-century to the million mark. There can be little doubt that the strengthening of the Bank's short-term

---

[1] Bank of England Record Office, Drawing Office ledgers for these accounts.
[2] For these bankers see below, p. 450.

financial position as a result of these changes was the result of deliberate ministerial policy.[1]

The disappearance of the system of government short-term borrowing based on the tally of fictitious loan must have greatly assisted the Exchequer bill finance which superseded it.[2] For as long as departmental balances were largely held in tallies they were of no use to the banking system; they were frozen capital. For example, the accounts of Charles Fox, Paymaster to the Forces in the Low Countries in succession to Lord Ranelagh from Christmas 1702, show the following balances in 1703.

TABLE 65

Balances of the Paymaster of the Forces 1703

Period	Receipts during period	Tallies undisposed of at end of period	Cash balance at end of period
	£	£	£
25 December 1702– 8 February 1703 . .	350,995	200,000	5,321
27 February– 15 March 1703 . .	625,890	615,037	10,853
29 September– 12 October 1703 . .	109,444	44,000	39,244

Source : P.R.O. T 1/87, Treasury Papers 1703, ff. 276 ff.

Discount of tallies or loans on their security would be followed almost at once by disbursements, leaving only small balances in ready cash. Thus James Brydges's Bank of England account in June–July 1711 was credited with £232,527, which was paid away almost immediately.[3] The accounts of Caesar, Howe and Walpole in 1710–11 referred to earlier were all to record

[1] Cf. a statement in 1815 that 'at present, and during many years past, . . . considerable Sums of the Public Money have been deposited with, or otherwise placed in the custody of the Governor and Company of the Bank of England, who act in this respect as the Banker of the Public.' (*Resolutions Proposed concerning [the] Bank of England* (1815), in the author's possession.)

[2] For the end of tallies of fictitious loan see above, p. 364.

[3] Bank of England Drawing Office Ledger 27, f. 196.

loans from the Bank on security of deposits of Exchequer tallies. These loans could not be asked for, nor the tallies pledged, until the Treasury gave directions, and when it did the money was quickly paid out. The cash balances available for banking purposes, and the paymasters' own freedom, were thus extremely restricted.[1] This contrasts with the paymasters' huge cash balances at the mid-century. The intervening changes had strengthened the financial machine; but had also increased the opportunities for a Fox or a Rigby to make the public purse a source of private gain.[2]

[1] For the Caesar, Howe and Walpole accounts see Bank of England General Ledger 4, ff. 10, 15, General Ledger 5, f. 36.

[2] Cf. also Dr. L. S. Sutherland and J. E. D. Binney, 'Henry Fox as Paymaster of the Forces', *Eng. Hist. Rev.* (1955), 229.

15

Departmental Credit

I

THE fighting services in the eighteenth century had their own systems of credit, which had been largely built up since the Restoration. During the period under review these systems greatly expanded in size and importance, but were at the same time brought increasingly under Treasury control. By the middle years of the eighteenth century they formed an important sector of the London market in short-dated securities, and an integral part of government credit as a whole.

II

The Army depended on credit less than the Navy, but credit was important to it. In the desperate conditions of the 1690s this mostly took the form of running up unsecured debts. Officers found themselves paid in doubtful tallies, and, more often, not paid at all.[1] In the two years after the Peace of Ryswick, Parliament voted substantial sums for arrears of pay and disbandment of troops over and above the 19,000 authorized as the peace-time establishment, but this left substantial arrears of officers' pay still due.[2] In December 1699 Lord Ranelagh, as Paymaster of the Forces, presented to the Commons, according to order, an account of the arrears still due for pay, clothing, forage and foreign subsidies. It amounted to £1,746,519, of which £1,218,196 was due to regiments for pay and clothing allowances, £177,000

---

[1] For payment of officers by tallies see above, p. 345.

[2] For the Votes for arrears and disbandment see J. Postlethwayt, *History of the Public Revenue* (1759). According to him the sums due to the Army were £3,373,728 in December 1697 and had been reduced to £1,018,657 by December 1701 (p. 41).

for bread and forage, and £245,055 to six foreign governments for arrears of subsidy payments.[1]

It is not clear from Ranelagh's account whether it was exclusively (or largely) for arrears of officers' pay, but it seems probable that it was, both because of the sums voted for pay of the troops in the two previous years, and because the commissioners created shortly after his account was presented were asked to examine only what was due to officers. The question of putting the debts due to the Army in such a form that they could be paid off was raised on 6 February 1700.[2] A Bill to appoint commissioners to state and adjust the debts of both Army and Navy was ordered six days later.[3] As agreed to by the Lords on 10 April 1700 it was 'an Act for appointing Commissioners to take examine and determine the Debts due to the Army Navy and for Transport-Service and also an Account of the Prizes taken during the late Warr'.[4] But the text of the Act makes it clear that its scope was narrower than its title suggests. The five commissioners appointed to examine Army debts were required to determine the debts due to officers for arrears of pay and clothing allowances. Their inquiry was to include garrison gunners in England; otherwise troops are not mentioned.[5]

When the commissioners were satisfied that a sum was due to an officer, they were to certify it to the Paymaster of the Forces, who was to give him a debenture for the amount owing. How were these debentures to be paid? One solution would have been to incorporate their holders, on the lines of the ingraftment of 1697, and as was actually done in 1711 with the creation of the South Sea Company. An anonymous and undated memorandum in the Portland papers, probably of 1700, put such a solution forward:

That a Corporation be made for the whole Debt due to the Army and for Transport Service and every one that has any of the said Debentures be obliged by a certain time to bring them in to the Corporacon, and everyone as he brings them in to have Credit in the Books of the Corporation for the Amount of their Debentures.[6]

But the solution adopted was different. Another Bill, also ordered in February 1700, placed the Irish estates forfeited since 1688 in the hands of

---

[1] *HCJ* xiii. 79–82, 19 December 1699. Dr. Shaw makes the total of items, excluding forage and subsidies, £1,562,939 by mistakenly adding the sub-total columns to the totals, *Cal. T. Bks.* xi (1), p. ccx.

[2] *HCJ* xiii. 182.   [3] Ibid. 203, 12 February 1700.

[4] Lords' assent, ibid. 321; text of the Act in *Statutes of the Realm*, 11 Wm. III, c. 8.

[5] The five commissioners, three of whom were to be a quorum, were Samuel Atkins, William Farrer, George Langton, Thomas Liston and Thomas Morrice. Clothing debts were to be stated to 24 December 1699, pay to 13 February 1700.

[6] B.M. Portland Loan 29/291.

Ḡ. B. ẘ ḻ̇

Bank

1837

Hon: Henry Boyle *Esq:*

in Repayment of Loan on the Eleventh 4 s. Aid, Anno 1708.

ORder is taken this 20 Day of
Janry 1707 ——by Vertue and
in Purſuance of an Act lately paſſed in
Parliament, (Entituled, *An Act for Granting
an Aid to Her Majeſty, to be raiſed by a Land-
Tax in* Great Britain, *for the Service of the
Year* 1708.) That you deliver and pay of
ſuch Her Majeſty's Treaſure as remains in
your Charge, ariſing by Vertue of the ſaid
Act, unto *Honble — Henry Boyle Esq —*

or *his* Aſſigns, the Sum of *One
Thouſand Pounds* — — — —

in Repayment of the like Sum by *him*
lent upon Credit of the ſaid Act, and paid
into the Receipt of Her Majeſty's *Exchequer*
the ſaid 20th Day of *Janry* 1707—
as by a Talley bearing Date the ſame Day
appears ; together with Intereſt for the
ſame, after the Rate of *five* Pounds *per
Cent. per Annum*, at the end of every Three
Months, from the Date of the ſaid Talley, until Repayment of the Principal. And
theſe, together with *his* or *his* Aſſigns
Acquittance, ſhall be your Diſcharge herein-

8. Order of Payment for a loan on the Land Tax of 1708

9. Front and reverse of an Exchequer bill of 1697

trustees, to be sold to pay the Army's debts.[1] The Commons hoped to kill two birds with one stone. The Act, which revoked all grants of forfeited Irish estates made since February 1699, was part of the angry parliamentary attack on William III's gifts to his favourites, which recalled the bitterness of the Exclusion Parliaments.[2] It was also intended to liquidate the Army debts on lines similar to those of the late 1640s. The officers who had borne the first shock of defending the settlement of 1689, which guaranteed Liberty and Property for Englishmen, were to be paid by a massive expropriation of Irish property: this was neither the first nor the last time that Irish history resembled English history in reverse. The Forfeitures Act required the thirteen trustees which it appointed to sell the estates vested in them by 25 March 1702. Payment could be made in a miscellany of government paper, including Army and Transport debentures, Land Tax tallies and Exchequer bills, 'as fully and freely as if the same were Sterling Money'.[3]

Claims for jointures, dowries, debts, etc., charged on the estates were to be made by 10 August 1700 or to be void.[4] It looks as though these charges came to a sizeable amount, for in December 1702 the trustees stated the gross revenue of the estates as £133,414 and the net revenue as only £83,086.[5] In their first report, dated 30 November 1702, the commissioners for Army debts stated that they had certified £950,516 debts to 30 November 1702.[6] In a final report, dated 22 February 1705, they certified the total for which debentures had been made out as £1,257,669.[7] The net Irish rental, capitalized at ten years' purchase (a not ungenerous rate for Irish land) would thus have covered only part of this. In December 1710 a detailed account presented to Parliament shows that the total of Army debentures made out was £1,150,141, and of Transport debentures £449,087, a total of £1,599,228. Of this, £612,071 had been exchanged for Irish lands,

---

[1] HCJ xiii. 222, 17 February 1700. The Bill was agreed to by the Lords on 10 April. For the text of the Act see Statutes of the Realm, 11 Wm. III, c. 2.

[2] For the Commons' attack on William's land grants see the Commons Journal for the early months of 1700.

[3] 11 Wm. III, c. 2, s. xl. The trustees, seven of whom were to be a quorum, were Francis Annesley, John Baggs, John Cary, William Fellowes, James Hamilton, Thomas Harrison, James Hooper, John Isham, Henry Langford, Thomas Rawlins, Sir Henry Sheers, John Trenchard and Sir Cyril Wyche.

[4] 11 Wm. III, c. 2, s. xi.

[5] H.M.C., Hse of Lds MSS. v. 134–49, report of the trustees dated 1 December 1702. The account referred to is at p. 142.

[6] Ibid. 128–33. Of this, £31,507 was for Transport debts.

[7] Ibid. vi. 290–4. Transport debts were by then £150,743 and £22,425 was also due to Chelsea Hospital.

O

leaving £987,157 debentures still outstanding, which for some years before
1710 had been quoted in the London market at prices between 75 and 90.
In 1711 they were subscribed into the South Sea Company.[1] A substantial
part of the debentures 'sunk in Ireland' is accounted for by the land purchases of the Sword Blade Bank. Originally chartered in 1691 as a manufac-
turing firm, this company had fallen by the early 1700s under the unscrupulous control of George Caswall, Elias Turner and John Blunt, all later to be
prominent in the affairs of the South Sea Company. They were looking for a
new field of activity, and found it by increasing their capital — allowing
payment to be made in Army debentures — then using these debentures
to buy forfeited Irish estates. In effect the Bank acted as broker between the
forfeitures' trustees and the debenture-holders.[2] The gross value of the estates
it purchased was about £270,000. The subsequent history of the company's
Irish holdings, however, showed that the project was ill-judged, and that
those who had held on to their debentures were wiser. The long fingers of
claimants to the company's lands slowly pulled its imposing rent-roll to
pieces. The Irish courts were unsympathetic, and a statutory limitation by
the English Parliament of the period within which action could be brought
against the company was of little help.[3] At the same time the company's
claims to act as a corporate bank were defeated by the Bank of England in
1708. The firm was forced back on partnership banking; it was finally
ruined by its involvement in the great crash of 1720.[4]

Meanwhile, Godolphin had taken care to pay the Army's debts regularly

---

[1] For the principal outstanding see the *Cal. T. Bks.* xxv (i) (1711), p. xlvii; for the prices
of debentures see Scott, *Joint Stock Companies*, iii. 439; for their subscription into the South
Sea Company see above, p. 68.

[2] The Bank also lent the government £20,000 secured on Cornish tin, *Cal. T. Bks.* xix
(1704–5), 268.

[3] 6 Anne, c. 61. The period was two years, except for minors, for whom it was two years
from the end of their minority.

[4] The Bank stopped payment in September 1720, see above, p. 158. This section is
based on Scott (*Joint Stock Companies*, iii. 435 ff.), who was working from pamphlets
published by the Sword Blade Company. Mr. Carswell follows Scott's account closely
(*The South Sea Bubble* (1960), ch. 2). The net value of the Sword Blade's lands was
£208,867, and it claimed to have paid off over £70,000 incumbrances. Dr. Shaw (*Cal. T.
Bks.* xi, p. ccxii) says that the 'grants and conveyances' of the Sword Blade lands are set out
in the report of the Irish Record Commission dated March 1828. In fact this report (*BPP*
(1830), xvi) says nothing about the subject. In an earlier report, of 1819, the Record
Commissioners list the records handed over by the forfeitures trustees to the Irish Revenue
Commissioners in August 1703 (*The Sixth, Seventh, Eighth, Ninth and Tenth Reports from
the Commissioners . . . respecting the Public Records of Ireland* (1820), p. 613).

during Marlborough's campaigns; his skill led those like Prince Eugène to the mistaken belief that in England finance was no problem.[1] At the conclusion of peace in 1713 the sums due to the Army were therefore relatively small. The commissioners appointed in 1715 to 'take examine and state the debts due to the Army' (on the lines of the commission of 1700) reported in March 1717 that the accumulated total was only £205,800.[2] Over a tenth of this (24,672) was due to the Anglo-Dutch contractor Sir Solomon de Medina for bread and bread waggons supplied to the English forces in the Low Countries in 1711; the rest (as in 1702) was for arrears of pay and clothing due to colonels and other officers. The commissioners, however, were continued in 1717 and 1718, and by the second statute were empowered to receive claims from foreign princes for arrears of subsidies.[3] This change inflated the debts payable to £1,603,987. Debentures had been made out for the sums certified, as in the earlier period, but, thanks to subsequent financial progress, the problem of paying them could now be solved not by 'sinking in Ireland', or other dubious devices, but by funding them at 4%, the stock created being managed by the Bank of England.[4] The ledger opening entries show that many holders had in any case already parted with their debentures to professional financiers like Sir Matthew Decker, John Marke, Thomas Snow and others.[5] Pulteney in 1729 observed that

These Debentures were from 30l. to 35l. per Cent Discount, before any Fund was settled for the Payment of the Interest; but a little before that was done, they were pick'd up, at that low Price, by some few Persons; which, it is said, have laid the Foundation of Estates, that may vie with the most antient Families of this Kingdom.[6]

As far as soldiers' and officers' pay and clothing allowances were concerned, the Army was planned to run on cash not credit, and the appearance of army debentures was thus an admission that something had gone wrong. For goods as distinct from services however, a well-managed system of credit was an advantage. The Board of Ordnance, which handled all Army contracts for guns, powder and auxiliary items, had an excellent credit system in operation

---

[1] For example Eugène's remarks on Marlborough's cavalry at their first meeting in 1704, quoted in Coxe's *Life of Marlborough* (1914 ed.), i. 163.

[2] Commissioners appointed by 1 Geo. I, stat. 2, c. 24. The commissioners' report is printed in full in *Cal. T. Bks.* xxxi (iii) (1717), 735 ff.

[3] 3 Geo. I, c. 17; 4 Geo. I, c. 9.

[4] The Act authorizing this was 4 Geo. I, c. 10 (1718).

[5] Ledgers for 4% stock (1718), Bank of England Record Office.

[6] [William Pulteney], *Some Considerations on the National Debts, the Sinking Fund, and the State of Public Credit*, p. 27.

by the 1690s, which was unchanged in the 1750s. It paid in cash those directly in its employ. Numbers were small, but included technical officers, clerks, storekeepers, labourers, petardiers, bombardiers and gunners. The Board's very numerous and complicated contracts were recorded in debentures, which the contractors later presented for payment. No interest was allowed. A careful record of all receipts and issues, including a register of all debentures paid, was kept at the head office. Inspection of sample ledgers at the beginning and end of the period (1696–7, 1754) shows that at the earlier date 2,051 debentures were paid during the year, having been made out twelve to eighteen months previously; in 1754 1,071 debentures were paid, mostly after a delay of less than twelve months.[1] Debentures were printed, and were presumably assignable in equity, but in view of the relatively short delay in payment and the absence of interest they tended to be held by contractors until paid.[2] The Board of Ordnance was not, of course, exempted by its efficient book-keeping from the problems created by shortage of government funds. The City of London's gun-makers were complaining in 1693 that the Board paid them in tallies. In June 1696 Sir Henry Goodrick, a member of the Ordnance Board, complained to the Treasury that the Ordnance Commissioners were unable to discount at less than 18% the tallies imprested to them for making payments in Flanders.[3] In 1711 and again in 1749 the debts of the Board were cleared by funding them in long-dated stock.[4] In general, however, the control exercised by the Board, together with the absence of interest on its debentures, made the latter relatively unimportant in the market.

Transport Commissioners were appointed *ad hoc* in war-time to deal with the business of carrying troops by sea. This included incoming as well as outgoing troops, for instance the Dutch and Swiss troops sent from Holland to England in 1719, and the 6,000 Dutch troops sent to England in 1744.[5] It has already been seen that the Commissioners ran up substantial debts

---

[1] P.R.O. W.O. 48/35 and 95, ledgers of the Ordnance Treasurer for July 1696–June 1697 and for the calendar year 1754. Both books are beautifully written. The debentures are numbered serially, and include full details of the work done.

[2] For a form of debenture — a short document certifying the sum due and the fund it is payable from — see P.R.O. T 48/21, Lowndes Papers, bundle 6, debenture dated 25 March 1711 made out to John Jeffreys for £6,526. For assignments in equity see below, p. 401.

[3] Above, p. 345, and P.R.O. T 29/627, extracts from Treasury Board Minutes, 30 June 1696.

[4] Above, p. 230.

[5] P.R.O. Index to Declared Accounts, Commissioners of Transports.

during the 1690s, £150,000 of which were still outstanding in 1705.[1] In 1711 over £480,000 of new Transport debts were funded in South Sea Stock.[2] Transport debentures were also among the securities funded at 4% in 1749.

Clothing Assignments, which were a form of trading in Army clothing allowances, were an important development in military credit during this period. The system, as explained to a committee of the House of Commons in 1746, was that colonels of regiments received every three years a War Office allowance for the pay and clothing of their men, known as Off-Reckonings. A Clothing Assignment was an assignment by the colonel to the clothier, with whom he or his agent contracted to clothe his troops, of the Off-Reckonings for the ensuing three years. The clothier paid the other tradesmen concerned, and eventually collected payment on the assignment from the government when the contract was fulfilled.[3] The records of the Sun Fire Office show that in the 1740s it started to accept Clothing Assignments as security for short-term loans to colonels of regiments and regimental agents.[4] No doubt other financial institutions did the same. In this way the growth of the money-market enabled the formal process of assignment to be abridged by, in effect discounting the colonel's claim for ready cash. By adding a new dimension to military credit, this development helped to account for the disappearance of the Army debenture from the financial scene.

III

The Navy, the most powerful in the world, needed the services of the money-market on a far larger scale than the Army. Britannia ruled the waves — on credit. The Navy Debt was a tangle of items, several of which were merely estimates, but its most important components were always seamen's wage tickets and the bills of the Navy and Victualling Boards. Wage tickets dated from the great expansion of the Navy under the Commonwealth. They were paid out at sea and encashed, without interest, on the sailors' return to port. Though their amount in war-time during this period was over £2m., it is unlikely that they were of much importance in the money-market. Navy

---

[1] See above, p. 395.   [2] See above, p. 68.
[3] *Reports from Committees of the House of Commons*, ii. 73 ff.
[4] Dickson, *Sun Insurance Office*, pp. 242, 254.

and Victualling bills on the other hand, were a barometer for naval credit, and sometimes, particularly in 1710–11, for government credit as a whole.[1] Navy bills were made out to contractors for ships and ships' stores, Victualling bills to contractors for food and drink. From 1666 Navy bills had always been registered and paid in sequence — 'in course' — as they became due. They bore interest until paid: at 6% until 1713, then at 5% until 1748, when the rate fell to 4%. (These relatively high rates were justified by the Navy Board on the ground that they kept the discount on bills lower than it would otherwise have been.)[2] The Victualling Board, originally set up in 1683 to replace procurement by the Navy Surveyor's department, registered and paid its bills in the same way and at the same rate of interest as the Navy Board, though the course of payment of the two sets of bills often differed in length.

In form, both Navy and Victualling bills were orders to the Treasurer of the Navy from the Navy or Victualling Commissioners to pay a named person for goods or services supplied, details of which were set out on the face or back of the Bill, with a certificate of good workmanship from the dockyard commissioners in appropriate cases. The bills were usually printed after about 1700. They were only 'assigned for payment' in this way on Treasury authorization, a note of which, and of the tax fund from which payment was to made, was added to the bill.[3] Bills were nearly always for broken amounts, like any tradesman's account, and indeed the whole procedure by which they were created and changed hands resembles a set of tradesmen's bills acknowledged by the government and fed into monetary circulation.[4]

Six months after a bill was issued, its holder became entitled to quarterly interest at the prescribed rate. The commissioners authorized this by a warrant made out in similar form with the bill, short particulars of which were sometimes endorsed on it. For instance, a warrant of 23 January 1702 authorizes the Treasurer of the Navy to pay 7s. 11d. being 111 days' interest at 6% on £21 16s. 3d. due to Christopher Bostock for glaziers' ware, the bill for which was made out on 28 March 1701, and numbered in course 3 April 1701.[5] Interest warrants were written in William III's reign but in

---

[1] Annual statements of the Navy Debt in *House of Commons Journals* (for figures see Appendix C); Sperling, op. cit., ch. ii, a careful discussion based on original sources; Lord Beveridge (ed.), *Prices and Wages in England*, i (1939).

[2] *Cal. T. Bks. and Papers 1742–45*, p. 452, 16 February 1744.

[3] P.R.O. Adm. 49/11 (original Navy bills) and 49/13 (original Victualling bills).

[4] For assignment of bills see below.   [5] P.R.O. Admiralty 49/11.

Anne's were printed. In September 1706 Godolphin changed the system of separate warrants by ordering that interest should accrue on bills until they were discharged.[1] This removed the need for a separate register for interest, and probably followed from a similar order made for bills of the Transport Commissioners in November 1705.[2] The disappearance of interest warrants, however, increased the discount on bills, and in September 1709 Godolphin restored quarterly interest payments in a vain attempt to check the downward movement of the market price of Navy bills.[3] By the 1740s separate interest warrants had again been abandoned. The Navy and Victualling Commissioners, when the Treasury ordered them to pay interest on bills in course, simply advertised in the *London Gazette* that

all Persons possessed of such Bills may at any Time carry them to the Treasurer's Office in Broad Street and receive the Interest due thereon, and have the same wrote off upon the Bills.[4]

Both Navy and Victualling bills were assignable, though only in equity. This was presumably on the ground that the original bill was a contract of debt between the Navy or Victualling Board and the contractor, so that John Doe, the contractor's assignee, could not, in Common Law, derive rights from it. In all other cases — Exchequer annuities and tallies, government stock transferred at the Bank of England, and the stock and bonds of the monied companies — the state had given parliamentary sanction to the assignment of debts, a benefit which private individuals were unable to obtain until the era of Victorian law reform. It was perhaps appropriate that the Navy and Victualling Boards, with their cumbersome procedures, should have taken a more restrictive attitude, which enabled them, when they wished, to block payment of bills by relying on the intricacies of the law of notice of defects in a seller's title.[5] The elaborate wording of assignments (which, too, were printed from the early 1700s) is clearly an attempt to guard against such defects. For instance, an assignment of a £350 Navy bill by the great contractor Nathaniel Gould to another prominent Navy supplier, Francis Collins, dated 4 April 1707, includes the clause

---

[1] *Cal. T. Bks.* xx (iii), 761, 11 September 1706.

[2] Ibid. xx (ii), 37, 20 November 1705.   [3] Ibid. xxiii (ii), 375, 28 September 1709.

[4] *London Gazette*, No. 8605, 10–13 January 1747.

[5] P.R.O. T 54/19, f. 609, 16 December 1706, opinion of the Attorney General, Sir Edward Northey, about a stopped Victualling Bill: 'In Justice the Bill is to be paid to Mr. Jackson for altho in point of Law ye sd Bills made payable to Mr. Armiger and not to him or Order are not Assignable, Yet such Delivery and Assignmt. for Value is in Equity a good Assignmt.'

I the said *Nathaniel Gould* for my Self my Executrs. and Administrs. the said bargained premises unto ye said *Francis Collins his* Executrs. Admrs. and Assignes against all Persons shall and will warrant and for ever defend and make good the aforesaid *Navy Bill* against the Claim of any person or psons. Free and Cleer of and from all manner of former Gifts Grants Forfeiture Claim or Demands of or to the same by any way or means whatsoever.[1]

This is very reminiscent of similar clauses in the assignment of government annuities; both probably derived from the cumbrous forms of land transfer, and they contrasted sharply with the simple procedure for sales of company stock.[2] However, the difficulties cannot have been too severe, for Collins reassigned the bill to Francis Upton of London, gent., twelve days later.

It seems clear, in fact, that the system of naval contracting depended on such assignments. Sir George Caswall explained to Parliament in 1733 that many small suppliers financed their contracts with the Navy Board by borrowing, making a contract with the lender to assign to him the Navy bills which would later be made out.[3] The Gould–Collins transfer just described, and the extent to which Navy bills, often of large dimensions, found their way into the hands of London financiers, for instance in 1709–11 and in 1747–9, suggests that transfer facilities were also useful to the large contractors.[4] Steps were evidently taken around the mid-century to facilitate assignments. A form of transfer for bills dated May 1745 is virtually the same as in the early years of the century, but Mortimer, writing in 1761, refers to Navy bills as 'made out with blank assignments, so as to be sold without any difficulty'.[5] It is interesting to notice, though, that he thought that the large denomination of most bills made them specialized investments. They were not

a general commodity because they are mostly for large sums, they are confined to a few hands at J's; and to the public in general . . . they are upon the whole not the most elligible commodity: though to some particular people, who can afford to lie out of their money some time, and have large sums to spare for this purpose, they are very advantageous.[6]

---

[1] P.R.O. Admiralty 49/11. The clause should read as though there were a comma after 'warrant'.

[2] See below, p. 459.   [3] *Parl. Hist.* ix. 52, 30 April 1733.

[4] For ownership of Navy bills at these dates see below, p. 449.

[5] Thomas Mortimer, *Every Man his own Broker* (5th ed., 1762), p. 189. The 1745 transfer is in P.R.O. Adm. 49/11.

[6] Mortimer, loc. cit. 'J's' is Jonathan's, the leading centre of dealings in securities, see p. 490, below.

The volume of Navy and Victualling bills standing out at a given date affected the length of time within which they would be paid, i.e. the Course of the Navy and the Course of the Victualling, as can be seen from the following table.[1]

TABLE 66

Navy debts and the course of payment of bills 1701–56

Years	Approximate volume of Navy bills outstanding	Course of payment (months)	Approximate volume of victualling bills outstanding	Course of payment (months)
	£		£	
1701–3	393,029*	29	158,347*	23
1709–10	1,779,509†	40	1,709,252†	35
1715–19	353,189‡	19	182,749‡	9
1729–30	572,725†	52	457,498†	41
1735–42	127,541§	17	94,786§	7
1747–8	2,115,391†	23	950,765†	25
1753	475,296	17	157,728	27
1754–7	526,283¶	22	247,351¶	7

Source: For the volume of bills, Appendix C. For the Course of the Navy and Victualling, Lord Beveridge (ed.), *Prices and Wages in England*, i (1939). The table adopts the longer periods cited by Beveridge, i.e. for bills last in payment.

    * Figures for 1702.

    † Figures for *second* year cited, i.e. 1710, 1730, 1748.

    ‡ Figures for 1717   § Figures for 1738.

    ¶ Figures for 1756.

Correlation was not invariable; the last of a relatively small volume of bills might not be due for payment for over one and a half years, as in the later 1730s. The damaging combination was a high volume of bills and a long Course, as in 1708–10 and 1746–8. The increase in the Navy debt during King William's War and the War of the Spanish Succession was due to the coincidence of a number of causes. Parliament was not always willing to vote

[1] The volume of bills outstanding is taken from the figures for the Navy and Victualling debt in the *House of Commons Journals*. These figures include the accrued interest on bills and are therefore up to 10% larger than the true figure each year. For an example of net and gross figures see p. 404, below.

the full naval estimates. For the years 1691–7 inclusive the estimates came to £15,962,653 and the supply to £15,577,444, a difference of £385,209.[1] The Treasury was not always willing to release to the Navy the full amount voted for it by Parliament. Dr. Sperling shows that between 1702 and 1710 £18,898,064 was voted for naval supply, while the Treasury only assigned £17,323,460 to the naval departments.[2] And the latter could, by credit, spend above their appropriation anyway; in the same period they overspent £2,534,302 in this way.[3] The general causes of overspending were summarized by the Treasury in a report to Queen Anne dated 31 August 1710 as the general dearness of naval provisions (the estimates had obviously been overtaken by the war-time price rise), freights to the Mediterranean '& other remote Parts where the occasions of the Warr have called for the same', the furnishing of Gibraltar with stores, expenditure on victuals for marines and soldiers not allowed for in the naval supply, the payment of interest on Navy and Victualling bills (for which Parliament made no allowance) and, lastly, the high discount at which these bills then stood.[4] A year later the victualling contractors were asking a price of £10 if paid in cash and £17 if paid in bills.[5]

The situation was retrieved by the subscription of the greater part of the Navy Debt into the South Sea Company during the summer and autumn. A statement of the debt at Michaelmas 1711 in the *Commons Journals* shows that the total Navy Debt was then £7,231,788. Of this, £4,256,932 had been 'discharged by the South Sea Stock'. Included in this were £3·4m. Navy and Victualling bills.[6]

	Principal	Accrued Interest	Total
	£	£	£
Navy bills . . .	1,677,064	177,033	1,854,097
Victualling bills .	1,764,762	165,112	1,929,874
TOTALS . . .	£3,441,826	£342,145	£3,783,971

The main item in the £2,974,857 debts still unpaid was £2,126,979 for seamen's wage tickets. These tickets were not subscribed into the South Sea

[1] Based on the figures in the *House of Commons Journals* for these years (see *Cumulative Index* under 'Accounts, Navy' for references).
[2] Sperling, 'Godolphin and the organisation of public credit', table at p. 74.
[3] Ibid.
[4] B.M. Lansdowne MS. 829.
[5] *Cal. T. Bks.* xxv (ii) (1711), p. 85, 27 July 1711.
[6] *HCJ* xvii (1711–14), 20–21.

Company, and were gradually paid off as ships returned to port.[1] With the old bills cleared off, it was possible to begin a new Course of the Navy at Michaelmas 1711, and a new victualling Course in April 1712.

With the conclusion of peace, and the fading of the bitter memories of the four last years of the queen, the Navy Debt seems again to have become 'concealed'.[2] In 1729 it was alleged that Navy bills had gone to 'a very great Discount' in 1721 (presumably owing to the stringency of credit after the South Sea Bubble) and that their volume was currently greater than in any year since 1710.[3] From 1733, however, the volume of Navy and Victualling bills was steadily reduced as part of Walpole's policy of peace and retrenchment, and in 1737 their combined volume (£122,364) was lower, with the exception of 1712–14, than in any other year between 1688 and the Seven Years War. The outbreak of war with France in 1744 immediately changed this situation. By the end of 1746 the Navy Debt was once more — for the first time since 1709 — causing ministerial alarm. Not inappropriately, on 28 November 1746 Henry Bilson Legge, one of the Admiralty Commissioners, wrote to the First Lord, the Duke of Bedford, suggesting a repetition of the solution adopted in 1711.

I should hope the next consideration ... will be to find some expedient for easing that most intolerable burthen — *the debt of the navy*. Mr. Pelham, who sees and feels the weight of it, has had it much in his consideration, and, I believe, has thought of the only expedient which can have any considerable effect; which is, to get a part of it taken into the S.S. [South Sea] Company by way of increase to their capital, as has been practised heretofore. But this is a secret I should not dare to tell to any man living but yourself. For as it cannot be put in execution till after the supplies of the year are raised, or beyond all doubt, so neither should it be suspected, or get the least wind, for fear of any bad effect it may have upon the raising those supplies.[4]

But this was financial atavism, however agreeable it might have been to twist the arm of the company whose pretensions had been a major cause of the war. The Navy creditors, who included some of the most powerful financial houses of the City of London, would not have been flattered at the chance of acquiring South Sea stock, particularly in view of the Spanish

---

[1] A clause in the South Sea Act (9 Anne, c. 15, s. lxviii) said that tickets might be subscribed but, if not, were to be paid in cash. The sailors obviously preferred cash.

[2] The Navy Debt was described in 1711 as 'too long conceal'd, and no visible appearance of a Method to work it off', [Daniel Defoe], *Eleven Opinions about Mr. H—y: with Observations*, p. 37.

[3] [William Pulteney], *Some Considerations on the National Debts . . .*, p. 32.

[4] Lord John Russell (ed.), *Correspondence of John, Fourth Duke of Bedford*, i (1842), 197–8.

government's intransigence towards the company's claims.[1] Pelham must have known this, and he knew, too, that the Bank of England could be relied on to help. Although in December 1746, therefore, he was still trying to find 'a fund for part of the debt',[2] he contented himself with grants of £1m. in 1746 and again in 1747 to pay part of the bills, and in 1749 arranged with the Bank of England and Parliament for the remainder, together with various Ordnance and Transport debentures, to be funded in 4% stock transferred at the Bank of England.[3] This method was to be used in every future war up to 1815.

[1] For the City's discounting of Navy bills see below, p. 449.

[2] *Bedford Correspondence*, i. 200, George Grenville to the Duke of Bedford, December 1746.

[3] 22 Geo. II, c. 23. The total funded was £3,072,472. (See above, p. 230.) The statute says that Navy and Victualling bills and transport debentures made out in 1748 totalled 'at least' £3m. and Ordnance debentures made out up to Christmas 1748 a further £230,382. The ledgers, which are labelled 'Navy 4%s 1749' (Bank of England Record Office), make no distinction between the type of debts funded. But the fall in the combined volume of Navy and Victualling bills between the end of 1748 and the end of 1749 from £3,066,156 to £296,076 shows that they must have formed by far the greatest part of the total.

16

The Bonds of the Monied Companies

BETWEEN the political revolution of 1688 and the Seven Years War the largest short-term borrowers in the London money-market, apart from the government itself, were the East India and South Sea Companies. Their bond-debts amounted to considerable sums. Between 1688 and 1709 the volume of bonds of the Old or London East India Company varied between £270,000 and £1·1m.; the nominal capital of the company in this period was about £1·5m. From 1709, when the United East India Company was established, until 1744 the volume of its bonds was between £2½m. and £3½m.; in this period the company's capital was about £3·2m. In 1744 it created a further £1m. bonds with government consent, but in 1750 funded half the total, and in 1755 only £2·1m. bonds were outstanding.[1] The bonds of the South Sea Company were first issued in 1712 to finance its trade to America. More were subsequently created to pay dividends. In 1720 their volume increased by over £3m. as a result of the conversion of government long annuities into South Sea stock, and for a short period in the early 1720s was greater than the volume of East India bonds. By 1732, however, the total had been reduced to under £2m., and ten years later to under £5,000. The combined volume of the two companies' bonds at its peak in the early 1720s (over £7m.) was equal to the combined volume of government short-term tallies, Exchequer bills, Navy and Victualling bills and the Bank of England note-issue.[2]

Company bond-finance had developed in the course of the seventeenth century. Company share-issues and bond-debts corresponded to, and were perhaps modelled on, the mortgage loans and personal bonds of private individuals. Thus the Royal African Company made extensive (even imprudent) use of bonds from the 1670s to raise working capital, and the East India Company's own bond-debt goes back well before 1688.[3] These

[1] The yearly balances of East India and South Sea bonds are shown in Appendix C.

[2] Based on the figures in Appendix C. The sources are indicated in the notes to the appendix. For early issues of South Sea bonds see also above, pp. 70, 136.

[3] K. G. Davies, *The Royal African Company* (1957), ch. 2; East India General Ledgers, India Office Library.

bonds seem often to have been, at least nominally, for quite short periods. Some of the early Royal African Company bonds were for as little as three months, while the East India Company in the 1680s was borrowing from month to month.[1] The foundation of the Bank of England in 1694, and the subsequent growing sophistication of the money-market, changed the situation in two ways. In the first place, the Bank was not willing to tolerate rival corporate note-issuers, and in 1708 obtained statutory prohibition of the right of any company, or partnership of more than six persons, to take up money on bills or notes payable at less than six months.[2] It was aiming at the Sword Blade Bank, but equally hit the East India Company, which was now prevented from borrowing on bond for less than six months. When the South Sea Company was established in 1711, with a right to issue bonds written into its Act of foundation, it found itself in the same position.[3] Secondly, however, the Bank of England provided both companies with an alternative source of very short-dated finance in the form of overdraft facilities, of which they made extensive use. Between 1720 and 1727, for instance, the East India Company borrowed and repaid £1·4m. in this way. Combined with the apparent willingness of their bond creditors to go on renewing their bonds almost indefinitely, this put the two companies in a much more flexible financial position.[4]

The bonds of the United East India Company and of the South Sea Company were normally for £100 each, though some South Sea bonds were for £50 only and others for £200, £300 and £500; one issue in 1720 was in units of £600.[5] They were transferable by indorsement and delivery. No East India bonds have been traced, but they were presumably in the same form as South Sea bonds, whose wording was decided by the Court of Directors on 12 June 1713 as follows.

---

[1] Davies, loc. cit.; East India General Ledger 1682–94, interest ledger account.

[2] 6 Anne, c. 22 (1708). This Act effectively gave a monopoly of corporate banking to the Bank of England until it was repealed in 1826.

[3] 9 Anne, c. 15, ss. xlvi, lxi.

[4] The East India overdraft figures are from East India General Ledger 1720–8, which shows total borrowings from the Bank of England and subsequent repayments as totalling £1,414,183 between July 1720 and June 1727. The early years of the South Sea Company's account with the Bank of England are discussed by R. D. Richards, 'The Bank of England and the South Sea Company', *Econ. Hist.* ii (1930–3), 348. For the two companies' credit balances at the Bank in 1742 see above p. 390.

[5] East India bonds are discussed by Mortimer, *Every Man his own Broker*, pp. 180 ff. He says India bonds were normally for £100. The denomination of South Sea bonds appears from the company's 'Register of Bonds 1720–1734', Add. MS. 25580.

No........ For £........

The Governor and Company of Merchants of Great Britain Trading to the South Seas and other Parts of America and for encouraging the Fishery Do hereby oblige themselves and their Successors to pay unto *A.B.* or his Assigns (by indorsement hereon) ... pounds with Interest after the rate of Six p. cent p. ann. on the ... day of ... one thousand seven hundred and ... For the true payment whereof they bind themselves and their Successors in the penal Sum of ...

London, the ..... day of ..... One thousand Seven hundred and....[1]

The South Sea bonds created in 1715 were stated to be for six, twelve or twenty-four months at the choice of the lender.[2] Those created in the 1720s were for one year, from Michaelmas to Michaelmas.[3] An issue of East India bonds in 1732 was for eighteen months, and it seems to have been anticipated that at least six months' notice of repayment would be given.[4] When these bonds were reduced to 3% in 1737 they were put on the basis of six months' notice of repayment.[5]

Both East India and South Sea bonds were, in effect, secured on the debts due from the government to the two companies. Thus a statute of 1721 empowered the East India Company to take up money on its common seal up to the sum which the government owed the company.[6] (This was an analogous position to that of the Bank of England, whose notes in its early days were, at least in theory, largely backed by the long-term debts which the government owed it.) From one point of view this application of the 'fund of credit' meant that the companies were lending long and borrowing short. But in practice neither seems to have had any difficulty in renewing their bonds when due, and what was in form short-term borrowing thus became equivalent in practice to long-term debenture finance.

Special legal provision was made to protect holders of bonds. Counterfeiting the company seal (impressed on all bonds) was made a felony by the Act creating the South Sea Company.[7] A statute of 1726 guarded against forged indorsements on East India and South Sea bonds.[8] Another, of 1729, made stealing South Sea bonds a felony without benefit of clergy.[9] These precautions probably reflected the brisk demand for bonds, in particular East India bonds. The latter were said in 1737 to be of great utility to those

---

[1] Add. MS. 25495, f. 60, South Sea D. Ct. Bk., 12 June 1713.

[2] Ibid. 25496, ff. 5–6, 9 February 1715.   [3] South Sea Register of Bonds.

[4] East India G. Ct. Bk. i, f. 319, 20 September 1732.

[5] Ibid. ii, ff. 36–37, 24 September 1736, from 31 March 1737 bonds to bear 3% interest and be repayable at six months' notice.

[6] 7 Geo. I, stat. 1, c. 5, s. 32.   [7] 9 Anne, c. 15, s. lxi.

[8] 12 Geo. I, c. 32.   [9] 2 Geo. II, c. 25, s. 3.

who wished to 'have those securities which they can turn into money upon an hour's warning'.[1] It was noted in 1750 that their form

makes them of great convenience to the Bank, private Bankers, and such who have large sums lying by them, to be employed at a future time,

particularly as they were admitted at par in payments at the company's biennial sales.[2] Mortimer writes in 1761 that

India bonds are the most convenient and profitable security any person can be possessed of, who has a quantity of cash unemployed, but which he knows not how soon he may have occasion for.[3]

The evidence about their ownership discussed in Chapter 17 bears these statements out; so does their price, which was fairly consistently high even when they carried no more than 3% interest.[4]

The interest on both companies' bonds fluctuated downwards, largely in step, from 6% at the beginning of the period to 3% at the end of it. (Table 67.) The successive alterations corresponded to changes in the yield on other (mostly government) securities. Hence the rise in bond rates in 1708, 1719, 1726 and 1746, and the reduction to a 3% level in the 1730s. Bondholders faced with a reduction of interest had to bear this correlation in mind. As the Sub-Governor of the South Sea Company, Sir John Eyles, put it in 1732,

this Debt carrying 4 p. Cent will be paid off at Par by Money, that if divided among the Proprietors, cannot be laid out in the Purchase of any thing that bears the same Interest under 10 p. Ct. advance.[5]

Early reductions in interest rates seem to have been negotiated in a very gentlemanly style. On 3 April 1705 the East India directors, who had recently decided to reduce the rate from 6% to 5%, were informed that the bondholders still wanted 6%. It was agreed they might have it until Michaelmas 1705, when the lower rate would take effect.[6] In June the Committee of Treasury was ordered to pay the bonds due at Michaelmas or to continue

---

[1] *Parl. Hist.* x. 109, 28 March 1737.

[2] *Considerations on the Proposal for the Reduction of Interest so far as it relates to the East-India Company* (1750), p. 6.

[3] Mortimer, op. cit., p. 180.

[4] The yield on East India bonds is shown in the chart on p. 471.

[5] Add. MS. 25544, f. 95, South Sea G. Ct. Bk., 24 March 1732.

[6] East India D. Ct. Bk. 39, f. 336, 3 April 1705.

TABLE 67

Interest rates on East India and South Sea bonds 1688–1754

East India bonds	%	South Sea bonds	%
1688–September 1705	6	June 1712–December 1714	6
September 1705–September 1708	5	December 1714–May 1720	5
September 1708–September 1716	6	May 1720–September 1720	4
September 1716–June 1718	5	September 1720–June 1723	5
June 1718–April 1719	4	June 1723–March 1726	4
April 1719–December 1724	5	March 1726–March 1728	5
December 1724–March 1726	4	March 1728–September 1733	4
March 1726–March 1728	5	September 1733–March 1737	3½
March 1728–March 1733	4	March 1737–1742	3
March 1733–March 1737	3½		
March 1737–March 1746	3		
March 1746–March 1750	4		
March 1750–1754	3		

Source: Directors' and General Court Minutes of both companies, and the South Sea 'Register of Bonds 1720–34', Add. MS. 25580.

them to the following Michaelmas at 5%.[1] Similarly, the South Sea Company laconically noted in November 1714 that the 6% bonds due on 31 December would be continuable at 5%,[2] apparently without encountering opposition.

As security yields moved towards 3%, however, resistance to further reductions of bond interest understandably grew. In August 1732, with government 3% stock only fractionally below par, the East India directors, anticipating the maturity of the company's 4% bonds at the end of March 1733, invited schemes for lowering the interest on them.[3] On 20 September twenty capitalists, most of whom were proprietors, submitted a proposal to lend the company £250,000 at 3% by 30 September 1732 and double this by the end of the following March, when the bonds matured. A further £185,200 was offered by sixty-one others, making a total of £435,200. Subscribers were to be asked to deposit 10% by Michaelmas 1732, and make

[1] Ibid., vol. 42, f. 7, 6 June 1705.
[2] Add. MS. 25495, f. 224, South Sea D. Ct. Bk., 10 November 1714.
[3] East India G. Ct. Bk. i, f. 315, 9 August 1732.

full payment by Lady Day 1733.[1] With this offer behind them, the General Court resolved that bondholders should be paid off on 31 March 1733, with 10% premium in lieu of notice, but might instead exchange their 4% bonds for 3% ones from Michaelmas 1732. A group of proprietors immediately demanded a ballot.[2] When it was held, on 26 September 1732, it confirmed the General Court's decision by 185–147.[3] On 3 November 1732, perhaps because this mandate was relatively feeble, the General Court referred reduction of bond interest to the discretion of the Court of Directors.[4] The latter seem to have decided to convert £425,000 bonds to 3% and the rest to $3\frac{1}{2}$%. On 20 December 1732 they were able to tell the General Court that 'upwards of two million were marked to be continued at $3\frac{1}{2}$ p. cent' and promised to notify it if any difficulty was experienced with the remainder.[5]

The South Sea Company followed suit, reducing its bonds to $3\frac{1}{2}$% from 25 May 1733. Just over £1m. bonds were then outstanding; £792,425 were marked for continuance at $3\frac{1}{2}$%, 'since which' it was explained to the General Court on 20 June 1733

many Persons, and particularly the Accountant General of the high Court of Chancery, on behalf of the Suitors of that Court, have applied to your Court of Directors for Liberty to have their Bonds mark'd, alledging they were prevented bringing them in to be mark'd in due Time, by unavoidable Accidents.[6]

The General Court agreed to extend the time limit to 20 July 1733. Over the next five years the bonds were being steadily paid off. In December 1736, when it was resolved that they should carry only 3% interest from Lady Day 1737,[7] less than £250,000 were outstanding. In reducing to 3% the

---

[1] East India G. Ct. Bk. i, f. 317, 20 September 1732. The names given, in fact for a total of only £240,000, were: Abraham Atkins (£30,000); Miles Barne (£10,000); Joseph Barrett (£10,000); James Colebroke (£10,000); Charles Colli (£10,000); John Edwards (£10,000); N[athaniel] Elwick (£10,000); Christopher Emmott (£10,000); Edward Hulse (£10,000); Alexander Hume (£10,000); Gabriel Lopez (£15,000); John Marke (£10,000); Benjamin Mendes da Costa (£10,000); Thomas Motley (£10,000); Thomas Edlyne for William Phips (£10,000); John Scofield (£10,000); William Steel for Henry Selwyn (£10,000); Joseph Shaw (£15,000); Thomas Snow (£15,000); William Steele (£15,000).

[2] Ibid., f. 318. The ten proprietors were: Thomas Aynscombe, John Caswall, George Heathcote, Nathaniel Newnham, Charles Newton, James Peachey, Samuel Perry, John Roberts, Charles Savage, Henry Vanderstegen.

[3] Ibid., f. 321.   [4] Ibid., f. 323, 3 November 1732.

[5] Ibid., f. 326, and ii, f. 37, 20 December 1732 and 22 December 1736. At the second date the quantity of 3% bonds made out in 1732 is stated.

[6] Add. MS. 25545, ff. 6 (reduction of bond interest) and 18 (quotation). South Sea G. Ct. Bk., 22 March and 20 June 1733.

[7] Ibid., f. 63, 17 December 1736.

company was once more following the East India Company, which in September 1736 had resolved to reduce its own bonds to 3% from 31 March 1737.[1] Neither seems to have had any difficulty, not surprisingly in view of the current premium on 3% government stock, which was shortly to lead Sir John Barnard to propose the reduction of long-term government debts to 3%.

By this date South Sea bonds were already insignificant in amount. At Lady Day 1740 nearly the whole of the company's remaining interest-bearing bonds were redeemed.[2] East India bonds, on the other hand, were increased by £1m. in 1744 to finance the company's loan of this amount to the government.[3] In March 1746 the interest on all East India bonds was raised to 4%. At the end of the War of Austrian succession they formed a substantial part of aggregate short-dated securities, and their reduction in both cost and amount became part of government and company policy. In August 1749, with 3% government stock at a small premium, the East India chairman raised at a Court of Directors the question of reducing the company's bonds to 3%. The matter was referred to the Committee of Treasury.[4] Two days later Samson Gideon attended the Court with a proposal in writing. He had 'advised with Several Proprietors and others mentioned in the Annexed List'. (The minutes do not give the list itself.) Those on it were willing to deposit 4½% of the sums they subscribed by 13 November 1749. The company was to allow them ½% premium, making 5% in all. The subscribers would pay in full by 31 March 1750, and Gideon himself undertook to be answerable for them. The list evidently totalled £1·5m.[5] This proposal seems to have been modelled on that of 1732, and there is little doubt that it was introduced with the government's blessing.[6] It enabled the directors to subscribe a further £500,000 themselves, and to order the redemption of all bonds at 31 March 1750, with the option of reduction to 3%.[7] In November they learned that only £218,457 bonds had not been reduced, so a call on the guarantors was unnecessary.[8] In December they paid Gideon £4,000 gratuity for his services.[9]

---

[1] East India G. Ct. Bk. ii, ff. 36–37, 24 September 1736.

[2] Add. MS. 25545, ff. 86–87, 4 December 1739, resolution to cancel interest-bearing bonds (£95,900) at Lady Day 1740; f. 92 (20 March 1741), bonds still in existence totalled £6,550; f. 180 (September 1759) £4,600 still outstanding.

[3] 17 Geo. II, c. 17; East India G. Ct. Bk. ii, ff. 78–79, 2 February 1744.

[4] East India D. Ct. Bk. 63, f. 419, 16 August 1749.

[5] Ibid., ff. 427–9, 18 August 1749. [6] Above, p. 230.

[7] East India D. Ct. Bk. 63, loc. cit. [8] Ibid., f. 503, 8 November 1749.

[9] Ibid., f. 534, 1 December 1749.

This still left the principal of the bond debt intact. Its reduction became involved with the government's proposals to reduce the interest on the National Debt, including the debt owed to the East India Company. One of the moves in this struggle was a government offer to let the company fund part of its debt. On 25 April 1750, the East India chairman explained to the General Court, which was in a difficult mood, that

in regard to the largeness of the Company's present Bond Debt . . . it will be for the Benefit of the Company to take Advantage of the liberty given them by the late Act of Parliament by converting a considerable part of that Debt into Transferable Annuitys, and issuing new Bonds for the rest of it.[1]

After much debate this proposal was adopted. In effect, the government, having run the company into debt by borrowing from it under duress, now used its permission to reduce the debt as a carrot to persuade the East India proprietors to agree (25 April 1750) to a general reduction of interest.[2] The bond subscription was held between June and December 1750, £2,992,440 being paid in in bonds. Subscribers were given one-quarter of their subscription in 3% stock, one-half in stock carrying $3\frac{1}{2}$% to Christmas 1755 and then 3%; and one-quarter in 3% bonds.[3] The effect of this operation is partly obscured in the company's ledgers by the creation of new bonds, but it seems clear that by 1755 the total had been reduced from its 1749 level of £4$\frac{1}{2}$m. to just over £2m.[4] No further attempt at diminution was made at this stage, and the company's bonds continued to be a factor in the London money-market for another century, until superseded by the debentures of the early railway companies.

---

[1] East India G. Ct. Bk. ii, f. 168, 25 April 1750.   [2] See above, p. 238.
[3] Terms in G. Ct. Bk. loc. cit.; total subscribed in *BPP* (1898), lii. 326; dates of subscription from ledger opening entries, Bank of England Record Office.
[4] East India General Ledger 1750–6, f. 10, balance of £2,101,270.

17

The Ownership of Short-dated Securities

I

THE changes in the pattern of short-term borrowing described in the previous chapters were accompanied and to some extent made possible by important changes in the pattern of short-term investment, which are discussed in the present chapter.

In the 1690s the commissioners and cashiers of the Customs and Excise were prominent leaders to the government, as they had been for many years before 1688.[1] Thus, on 4 May 1692 John Knight, Cashier of the Customs, proposed to lend £6,000 on the Quarterly Poll; on 9 May the Excise Commissioners and their cashier Charles Duncombe proposed to lend £20,000 on the Hereditary and Temporary Excise at 6%, with an extra 2% 'for procuring ye Loan'.[2] Similar examples could be multiplied. The flow of revenue into the Exchequer was in this way drawn off into new loans — at the public expense. For the government, in effect, was paying the cashiers a premium for taking the risk of lending either from their revenue balances, for which they were strictly accountable at the Exchequer, or from their own resources, including those of their friends, or from both. The system amounted to a short-cut through the tedious process of Exchequer collection and accounting. And while it might work reasonably in peace-time (as in the 1680s), when repayment could be depended on, in war-time it became increasingly risky for the cashiers. In February 1697, when a brisk discussion of the whole problem was held at the Exchequer, Charles Duncombe, who had been Excise Cashier since 1680, was told that he had come into his office on the understanding that he would make advances formerly amounting to £100,000 p.a. Would he now lend £1,000 a week? He retired behind a smokescreen of protests of his sensibility of the king's necessities and his own willingness to give up his post to someone else — for in view of his refusal to use the 'running cash' for his own benefit it was, he said, worth only £800 p.a. Finally, he stated that the lack of parliamentary security in

---

[1] See above, p. 341.   [2] P.R.O. T 29/627 at dates cited.

these Excise loans made it impossible for him (rather late in the day) to agree to what the Treasury wanted.[1] In April 1697 he was turned out in favour of Bartholomew Burton, who appears to have been expected to lend the government £1,000 a week from his revenue balances.[2] Burton, however, almost at once became involved in Exchequer bill frauds, together with Duncombe and the Customs Cashier John Knight, and was himself deprived of office in December.[3] His successors as Excise Cashier, Thomas Hall (1697–1705) and Henry Meriton (1705–10), evidently paid their receipts into the Exchequer as they came in; advances on tax funds were discontinued.[4] This change was connected with the improved provision for the Civil List in 1698,[5] which enabled loans on the Hereditary and Temporary Excise to be stopped. It was also connected with the increasing charge on the Excise revenue for interest on long-term loans, which made less and less of it available for current advances. A further factor was the emergence of the Bank of England as a large short-term lender, which made the former sources of loans no longer so necessary.

One effect of the system of borrowing by tallies of fictitious loan in the 1690s was to freeze undisposed tallies in the hands of departmental paymasters, who thus became for practical purposes holders of large amounts of short-dated securities. The tally balances of the Paymaster of the Forces in 1703 were shown in an earlier chapter.[6] In 1710 the whole of £1,296,000 in loans on the Sixth General Mortgage was taken up in the form of tallies of fictitious loan given out to the departmental paymasters. They were still holding the greater part of these in 1711, and subscribed them to the South Sea Company.[7] Most of another loan of 1710, on candles, was in similar form. The paymasters concerned were still holding £360,000 of these tallies in 1717.[8] The development of close liaison between the Treasury and the Bank of England about short-term advances under Godolphin had, however, already altered the significance of departmental holdings of tallies. In the first decade after 1688 a tally balance in a paymaster's hands was often, perhaps usually, due to failure to persuade anyone to accept the tallies in payment or as security for advances. After this period, however, it was much

---

[1] *Cal. T. Bks.* xi. 353 ff.   [2] Ibid. xii. 5.

[3] Ibid. xiii. 35, 169, see above, p. 369.

[4] Based on the annual revenue accounts printed in *Cal. T. Bks.* xi–xxiv.

[5] 9 Wm. III, c. 25.   [6] See above, p. 391. For tallies of fictitious loan see p. 351.

[7] For tallies struck on the Sixth General Mortgage (8 Anne, c. 13) see *Cal. T. Bks.* xiv (ii), 244–5, and James Postlethwayt, *History of the Public Revenue*, p. 71.

[8] The Candle Act was 8 Anne, c. 6. Loans on it are shown in P.R.O. E 401/2595. For sums still in the hands of paymasters in 1717 see 3 Geo. I, c. 7 (1717).

more a useful device for freezing departmental balances in a non-negotiable form until the Treasury asked the Bank of England to lend money on their security.[1]

The Bank of England's short-term advances to the government were at first in the form of straight loans on tax funds. In 1695 it lent £344,000 on the Land Tax, £149,000 on the Coal Act, £51,000 on the Post Office, £370,000 on the Customs, and £100,000 in anticipation of contributions to Reversionary Annuities, some of these loans being financed by the repayment of others. In 1696 it lent £210,000 on the Land Tax and £132,000 on the Salt Duties.[2] In view of these generous (even imprudent) advances, it was little wonder that there was talk, then and later, of the mercantilist dream of 3% interest being realized, and the usurers being put out of business.[3] After 1696, owing to changes, discussed below, in its arrangements with the Treasury, the Bank's cash loans at the Exchequer were rarer, but it continued to make some up to the 1740s. On the Land Tax, for example, it lent £300,000 in 1715, £400,000 in 1718, £336,000 in 1725 and £220,000 in 1726. In 1727 it lent £450,000 on the Malt Tax, and in 1736 and 1741 sums of £500,000 and £600,000 on the newly imposed Salt Tax.

The main current of its business in this sector had meanwhile flowed, first, towards discounting tallies. Between 1695 and 1698 it discounted Exchequer tallies struck on thirty-one different funds.[4] Second, it began to make extensive advances to the government on security of deposits of tallies. The heyday of this system was between 1700 and the 1720s and centred on the tally of fictitious loan. A typical entry in the Bank of England's minutes in November 1702 shows the sort of Treasury request which it was now meeting.

Mr. Deputy [Governor] Reported, That he with the Committee had attended the Lord Trear. according to his notice, That his Lordp. desired the Bank to lend £100,000 upon a Deposit of Tallies on the 5th. 4s. Aid, and struck without Interest next in Course after £1,883,000.[5]

The committee referred to was a small subcommittee of the Board specially established to handle this business. In this instance, as was commonly the

---

[1] See above, p. 391.

[2] The history of the Bank's early advances is far from clear, because the powers to lend recorded in the Court's minutes were not always fully used, and the ledgers are often ambiguous. This section is largely based on an examination of the Bank's General Ledgers.

[3] See above, pp. 15–16.

[4] Bank of England, General Ledger 1, index under 'discounts'.

[5] Bank of England, D. Ct. Bk. D., f. 164, 18 November 1702.

case at this time, the tallies ranked last for payment, but the Bank agreed to make the loan at 5% and covered itself by taking £106,000 tallies 'to be done in ye same method that ye former Loans in like Cases have been made'.[1]

The system depended on negotiation, and the Bank was capable of refusing a loan 'for fear of a Deficiency'[2] but on the whole it worked very well. It was intact in the 1720s, and functioned as steadily in civil crises as it had in war-time. Thus, in August 1720, at the height of the South Sea Bubble, the directors resolved

That the Lords of the Treasury be accommodated with a Loan of One Hundred Thousand Pounds upon Tallies and Orders on Malt 1720. . . . Their Lordships having represented it to be at this time much for the Service of the Government.[3]

The tallies of fictitious loan in question had been imprested to the Paymaster of the Forces in 1719 when the usual annual loans were made on the Malt Tax, and, having been held by the Bank as security for its advance, were duly repaid before all other loans when the tax money reached the Exchequer in 1720–1.[4]

With the disappearance of the tally of fictitious loan from the financial scene after 1729, the system of borrowing from the Bank on which it depended disappeared too. Clapham implies that the Bank continued to make cash advances 'on the security of the revenue, to government as a whole or to particular departments' throughout the Walpole period, but in fact the Bank's last cash loan to an individual paymaster seems to have been in October 1726.[5] Its last short-term cash loans to 'government as a whole' were the two on the Salt Tax in the thirties and forties.[6] From the late twenties its regular advances took instead the form of agreements to circulate extra quantities of Exchequer bills.[7] The effect of this change was that the Bank's holdings of Exchequer tallies diminished and its holdings of Exchequer bills increased; from the mid-1720s it had virtually a monopoly of all Exchequer bills outstanding.[8]

The way in which the Bank's various tally accounts worked in the early part of the period is not wholly clear from the ledgers, for these do not always

---

[1] D. Ct. Bk., loc. cit.

[2] Ibid., f. 156, 23 September 1702. Cf. also the *Calendar of Treasury Books* for this period, *passim*.

[3] Bank D. Ct. Bk. H., f. 163, 4 August 1720.

[4] P.R.O. E 403/1889, 1890, Issue Books (Pells) 1720–1.

[5] Clapham, *Bank of England*, i. 92; Bank of England D. Ct. Bk. K., f. 228, 13 October 1726, a loan to the Paymaster of the Forces.

[6] See above, p. 417.   [7] See above, pp. 382 ff.   [8] Ibid., p. 383.

TABLE 68

*Bank of England's holdings of tallies and Exchequer bills
at selected dates 1696–1750*

Date	Exchequer tallies	Exchequer bills	Date (31 Aug.)	Exchequer tallies	Exchequer bills
	£	£		£	£
15 March 1696	1,561,861	..	1729	122,800	1,779,800
25 June 1697	1,830,281	..	1734	195,000	2,089,300
2 January 1699	819,709	..	1739	500,000	2,084,000
28 February 1703	1,366,939	..	1744	615,000	4,245,400
3 September 1706	1,151,232	..	1749	151,320	3,207,562
29 February 1712	871,862	1,065,925	1754	136,185	1,927,600
1 September 1718	477,934	471,938			

Source : For holdings of tallies up to 1718, Bank of England General Ledgers 1–6, balance-sheets. For 1729–54, Bank of England Yearly Accounts 1729–62. For holdings of Exchequer bills, General Ledgers 1–12.

distinguish between tallies discounted and those deposited by the Exchequer as security for loans. A typical situation, however, seems to be that the Bank was acquiring tallies at the same time that it was encashing at the Exchequer those higher on the same register. Thus between 14 and 18 March 1698 the Bank acquired fifty-seven tallies on the 3s. Aid and encashed thirty-nine. The serial numbers of the former run from 2,042 to 2,341 and those of the latter from 2,825 to 2,890, in both cases with some interruptions. The denominations of tallies acquired were £100 to £500 in round hundreds, of those encashed £50 or £100.[1] In view of the relative continuity of the serial numbers, it is unlikely that the entries on the debtor side of the account were for tallies discounted for individuals. They probably represent loans to the Exchequer for which the latter gave tallies in receipt, and the entries on the creditor side represent the Exchequer repaying loans with interest, which is carefully entered in a separate column. The whole system bears a strong resemblance to the later one for Exchequer bills, for which this must have prepared the way.[2] The number of tax funds on which the Bank made advances to government or to individuals was at first high: 17 in 1696, 15

[1] Bank of England, General Ledger 1, f. 459.
[2] For the Bank's Exchequer bill accounts see above, p. 375.

in 1697, 21 in 1703, 15 in 1706, 12 in 1712. By 1718, however, the number had sunk to six, and from 1730 was no more than two or three each year. At 31 August 1744, for instance, the Bank's holdings of tallies consisted of £600,000 Salt Tax tallies, the result of its loan to the Exchequer on this fund in 1741, and £15,000 tallies struck on the Land Taxes of 1743 and 1744, presumably discounted for individuals.[1] This accurately reflected the simplification of the pattern of government short-term borrowing described in previous chapters.

As the example just given shows, while most of the tallies which the Bank held at a given date were for loans to the government, it was also prepared, on a limited scale, to discount them for individuals. In the 1720s and 1730s it acted in this way on several occasions for the Marlborough estate and the Accountant-General of Chancery. In contrast to its holdings of tallies and Exchequer bills, its balances in other short-term securities — East India bonds, Navy and Victualling bills — were small. It did hold £360,000 South Sea bonds in the early 1720s, but this was security for a special loan and the balance was gradually run off between 1720 and 1723.[2] It is understandable that the Bank should have felt that it had enough in short-term government securities already and preferred to use the balance of its funds in advances and in discounting mercantile bills.

II

The gradual dominance of the Bank of England in the field of short-term government finance weakened, but did not remove, the importance of individuals' cash advances to the Exchequer in anticipation of annual taxes. Over the period under review, important changes occurred in the size and structure of the groups making these advances. This can be studied with reference to loans on the Land Tax, 'the Flower of the Supplies'.[3] Table 69 analyses these loans (using the same categories as those for holdings of government stock) for the years 1693, 1707, 1720, 1730, 1743 and 1750.

---

[1] Bank of England Yearly Accounts 1729–62.

[2] For this loan see above, p. 166. It was for £300,000 and was secured by a pledge of £360,000 South Sea bonds. An account was opened in the Bank's general ledger and gradually written off as the South Sea Company repaid the loan.

[3] *A Letter to Sir John Barnard*, p. 4.

TABLE 69

Structure of subscriptions to the Land Tax 1693–1750

Subscribed	1693				1707			
	Nos.	% of total Nos.	Sub-scription	% of total subscrip-tion	Nos.	% of total Nos.	Sub-scription tion	% of total subscrip-tion
£			£				£	
Under 500	871	67·3	163,162	19·2	759	57·0	135,006	9·7
500–999	201	15·6	121,586	14·3	238	17·9	146,074	10·5
1,000–4,999	200	15·5	334,827	39·4	284	21·4	528,277	38·0
5,000–9,999	10	0·8	62,600	7·4	29	2·2	187,685	13·5
10,000 and over	10	0·8	167,550	19·7	20	1·5	393,911	28·3
TOTALS	1,292	100·0	849,725	100·0	1,330	100·0	1,390,953	100·0

Subscribed	1720				1730			
	Nos.	% of total Nos.	Subscrip-tion	% of total subscrip-tion	Nos.	% of total Nos.	Subscrip-tion	% of total subscrip-tion
£			£				£	
Under 500	171	51·4	27,053	2·7	14	53·8	2,300	0·4
500–999	44	13·2	28,297	2·9	1	3·8	850	0·1
1,000–4,999	91	27·3	193,057	19·4	7	27·0	12,350	2·5
5,000–9,999	12	3·6	82,640	8·3	2	7·7	10,000	2·0
10,000 and over	15	4·5	662,259	66·7	2	7·7	474,500	95·0
TOTALS	333	100·0	993,306	100·0	26	100·0	500,000	100·0

Subscribed	1743				1750			
	Nos.	% of total Nos.	Subscription	% of total subscription	Nos.	% of total Nos.	Subscription	% of total subscription
£			£				£	
Under 500	82	36·6	15,045	1·5	58	54·7	6,770	1·4
500–999	29	12·9	17,272	1·7	11	10·4	7,050	1·4
1,000–4,999	76	33·9	160,360	16·0	26	24·5	50,690	10·1
5,000–9,999	16	7·2	103,000	10·3	6	5·7	33,700	6·7
10,000 and over	21	9·4	705,800	70·5	5	4·7	401,500	80·4
TOTALS	224	100·0	1,001,477	100·0	106	100·0	499,710	100·0

Source: The Land Tax subscriptions made through the City Chamber in 1693 are recorded in Corporation of London Records Office MS. 40/57, the rest of the 1693 names in P.R.O. Exchequer Receipt Books (Pells') (E 401/1991, 1992). Subscriptions in the other years shown in the table are all from the relevant Receipt Books (E 401/2018–20 (1707); 2044–5 (1720); 2064–5 (1730); 2090–1 (1743); and 2103–4 (1750). In each the lenders' names were extracted from the miscellany of other items, and re-sorted in alphabetical order. Tallies of fictitious loan were excluded. Owing either to errors in transcription or in the records the totals in the table do not agree precisely with those given in the Treasury Account Books. These are: £826,924 (1693); £1,375,223 (1707); £995,448 (1720); £500,000 (1730); £1,000,000 (1743); £500,000 (1750). The margin of error is, however, sufficiently small not to affect the conclusions drawn from the table.

The most immediately striking thing about these figures is the reduction in the number of lenders between the beginning and end of the period. In the early 1690s it took 1,200 subscribers to raise what 200 could provide sixty years later. To put it another way, the average sum subscribed rose from about £650 to not far short of £5,000. It is worth remembering that the average holding of government stock at the mid-century was not much more than £1,000. Even in Bank stock it was only £2,000.[1] Thus in the Land Tax loans the plutocrats had taken over. Loans of £10,000 or more formed 20% of the total in 1693, 28% in 1707, 67% in 1720 and 70–80% by the 1750s. Yet the number of these large lenders did not exceed twenty-five, and was often less. At the other end of the scale, small lenders of less than £500 comprised 67% of total subscribers at the beginning of the period, and

[1] See above, p. 287.

continued with some exceptions to form around 50%, though their actual numbers sharply declined. So did their share of the total subscribed, from 20% to 1 or 2%. The individual sums lent in this group were in some cases as little as £10. The middle group of subscribers of £1,000–£5,000, so important in the funded debt, was largely squeezed out over the period.

The Land and Malt taxes were the most important funds for short-term loans, and by the 1750s were the only ones of any significance. In the war years 1688–97, on the other hand, there were up to a dozen different taxes on which advances were made, and even in Godolphin's time there were four or five. How far should the conclusions drawn from loans on the Land Tax be modified by the evidence of loans on these other funds? Without complete lists of subscribers for every loan made in this period it is impossible to answer this exactly. Perusal of the Exchequer receipt books, however, suggests that the circle of subscribers of all kinds at this time was not very much larger than the circle of subscribers to Land Tax loans. Several of the newly created (and short-lived) tax funds of the period 1688–1713 were anticipated by impresting tallies of fictitious loan to the departmental pay-masters; these tallies remained in their hands.[1] The customs and excise loans tended to be monopolized by the commissioners and their cashiers. In the advances on the Malt and Poll taxes in the early 1690s, there were many subscribers who were also concerned in loans on the Land Tax. Although the government had not at this stage got the proportions right between long- and short-term borrowing, and greatly exaggerated the extent to which the war could be financed by short-term methods, it seems unlikely that it was borrowing much more than £2m. annually in cash between 1688 and 1697.[2] This demand could be met by a circle of 2,000 to 3,000 lenders, particularly after the creation of the Bank of England, which was able to make very large advances of its own. The factor by which the number of Land Tax lenders should be multiplied to reach the total number of lenders at any one time in the 1690s is, if these conclusions are correct, not much more than two; certainly not the eleven or twelve which the proliferation of short-term tax funds might suggest. The argument applies more closely as the number of funds lessens. By the 1750s short-term lenders to government of all kinds probably numbered less than 250.

How far were short-term lenders at the Exchequer also concerned in long-term loans? Here, too, the complexity of the records makes certainty impossible; moreover, from about 1713 the difference in size of the two

---

[1] See above, p. 416.
[2] See pp. 344, 352. The balance was in the form of tallies of fictitious loan.

groups of proprietors is so great that their overlap is clearly no longer of much significance. In the early part of the period the question is of some interest. In 1693, 129 of the 1,292 lenders on the Land Tax also subscribed to the Tontine loan of the same year. The lists for the latter are incomplete so the total proportion was probably nearer 15% than 10%. In the subscription for the Bank of England in 1694 there are 181 names of Land Tax lenders of 1693, an overlap of 14%. In 1707, 148 of the 1,330 subscribers to the Land Tax loan also figured in the long-term annuity loan of the same year. For this, too, the records are incomplete, and a proportion of 15% would probably not be far out. Taking the big lenders only, two of the twenty lenders of £5,000 or more on the Land Tax of 1693 were also among the thirty-two lenders of £1,000 or more to the Tontine in the same year; in 1707 five of the forty-nine lenders of £5,000 or more on the Land Tax were among the twenty-six subscribers of £5,000 or more to the annuity loan of the same year. With the important holdings of plutocratic owners like the Marlborough estate and the London insurance companies from the 1720s, this interlocking of the two sectors of the monied interest at the top must have become increasingly important.

What kind of people were involved in the Land Tax loans, and who were the great lenders who eventually swallowed up most of the others?[1] The number of women lenders was high, between a quarter and a third of total numbers, rather more than their holdings in the funds. Their share of the total lent, however, fell from 9% in 1693 to 4% in 1750. Most of their subscriptions were for £500 or less, but a few were for substantial amounts. The number of peers and peeresses and their near relations was small.[2] Apart from the important Marlborough loans — which would distort the figures and are discussed later — the totals were as shown in Table 70.

Most of these subscriptions were of medium size, but some were large. For example, the dowager Lady Rivers lent £10,000 in 1707, and the dowager Ladies Dillon and Castlehaven £6,000 and £7,000 respectively in 1743. John, Duke of Buckingham lent £10,000 and Charles, Lord Sunderland £6,600 in 1707, Christopher, Lord Barnard and Thomas, Lord Parker £10,000 each in 1720, Philip, Lord Hardwicke £21,000 and Spencer Compton, Lord Wilmington £8,000 in 1743. Sunderland's son-in-law Lord Ryalton, M.P. for Helston and Cofferer of the Household, was also a big subscriber (£16,300) in 1707. Quite a few of these lenders — Sunderland, Ryalton, Parker, Hardwicke, Wilmington — were well placed

---

[1] For source see Table on p. 422 above.
[2] Peers being defined as those entitled to sit in the English House of Lords.

TABLE 70

Subscriptions to Land Tax loans by English peers and their relations

Date	Peers	Peeresses (including dowagers)	Sons and daughters of peers	subscribed Amount	% of total lent
				£	
1693	4	2	4	15,420	1·8
1707	7	8	18	100,830	7·3
1720	6	2	7	57,800	5·8
1730	..	1	..	2,000	0·4
1743	5	2	4	76,000	7·6
1750	1	1	2	12,300	2·5

Source : See Table 69.

politically to secure subscriptions for themselves and their friends, and less likely than others to be squeezed out when the sums required by government diminished.

Members of Parliament are not much more prominent in the subscription lists than members of the peerage.[1] The figures (allowing for some uncertainty in identification) are as shown in Table 71.

The conclusion which this evidence suggests — that the loans on the Land Tax, unlike the subscriptions to long-term loans, were relatively unpolitical — is confirmed by the fact that the largest single subscriptions during the Walpole period came, as will be seen later, from the Marlborough estate, whose chief trustee, the Dowager Duchess Sarah, was the Prime Minister's bitter enemy. Lastly, Jewish and Huguenot contributions to the Land Tax loans were of little importance. There were only five Jewish subscribers in 1693 and one — Peter Henriquez, a man of substance — in 1707: in later years there were none. About seventy-five first-generation Huguenot lenders can be distinguished in 1693, about twenty in 1707. In later years there were hardly any.

The general run of smaller Land Tax lenders (lending less than £5,000) were members of the London mercantile community, with additions from

[1] There is some overlap between Tables 70 and 71, because some M.P.s were sons of peers. Lord Ryalton, for instance, is common to both tables.

TABLE 71

Subscriptions to Land Tax loans by Members of Parliament

Year	Numbers	Amount subscribed	% of total lent
		£	
1693 . .	18	54,187	6·4
1707 . .	23	64,081	5·0
1720 . .	8	36,102	3·6
1730 . .	1	5,000	1·0
1743 . .	14	60,800	6·1
1750 . .	5	42,500	8·5

Source : See Table 69.

the professions and government departments. Women lenders were mostly members of the same families. 'Merchant' is the most frequent description against the names of those who subscribed to the Land Tax of 1693, either through the City Chamber or directly at the Exchequer. Several of these 1693 lenders were aldermen of London. Among the others were Sir Salathiel Lovell, Recorder of the City (£1,000), Dr. Nehemiah Grew, physician and botanist, 'of Racquet Court, Fleet Street' (£1,600) and another physician, Dr. Robert Pitt of Princes Street (£2,000); all three, incidentally, subscribers to the Bank of England in the following year. Sir Robert Legard (£1,500) was a Chancery Master and was perhaps investing suitors' funds (the Chancery Masters Roger Meredith and Sir Adam Ottley had invested small sums in the Poll Tax loan of 1692).[1] The future Chancery Master John Orlebar subscribed £1,000. Sir Robert Atkins (£2,200) was the Chief Baron of the Exchequer in 1693 and Sir William Dolben (£1,000) a judge of the King's Bench. John Gibbon and Peter Le Neve, both well-known members of the College of Arms, contributed small sums. The Huguenot broker John Castaigne (as he is spelt in the list), 'of the Three Black Posts, Berwick Street, Soho', lent £100. The Clockmakers', Clothworkers', Silkthrowers', Skinners' and Weavers' companies lent amounts totalling £2,500, and the Society of Watermen £1,500 through trustees.[2]

---

[1] The names of lenders on this tax are in *HCJ* x. 723. Meredith lent £100 and Ottley £2,000.

[2] The trustees were John Knight, George Oldner, Thomas Daniell, William Hill, William Jones and Thomas Huntley. For Castaing's *Course of Exchange,* see below, p. 488.

The records for the part of the 1693 loan subscribed at the City Chamber give lenders' addresses, unlike the Exchequer records. There were few outside London, and nearly all of these were in the Home Counties. Among those further afield were William Bodley of Oxford (£200), Dr. Fairfax, Dean of Norwich (£100), William Francks of Leicester (£500), Henry Greenhill of Plymouth (£500), Thomas Hobby of Brickton, Hants (£900) and Henry Webster of Bungay in Suffolk (£300). The only address outside England is for Robert Gay of Dort in Holland, merchant, who lent £1,200. These 'out of town' lenders, and a few others, appointed agents to whom notice of repayment was to be delivered. Gay, for instance, asked for notice to be sent to William Willis of Hackney, and Thomas Hobby for notice to be sent to James Harrison of 'Red Lyon Street Holborn, next to a Bakehouse, a Messenger on purpose'. Some of these agents, like John Sweetaple, a prominent goldsmith who was later knighted, or the goldsmiths' firm of Smith & Spincke, which acted for several lenders, were professionals; others were obviously just friends of the lenders: for instance, Thomas Attwood asked for notice of repayment of his £100 to be sent 'to Mr. Leneave at the Herault's Office'.

A similar pattern is found in later years, though with the cessation of loans through the City Chamber addresses are unfortunately no longer available. In 1707 the bulk of subscribers of less than £5,000 are identifiable as London merchants, some of whom later achieved considerable eminence. For instance, John Baker, who lent £1,450, was later a director of the Royal African Company and the Royal Exchange Assurance; Edward Bellamy (£900) became a director of the Bank of England and an alderman of London; Abraham Craiesteyn (£250) was later to become a trading magnate and, like his brother Francis with whom he was in partnership, a lender of importance in the 1740s. Edward Haistwell, a Russia merchant (£1,500) had been a lender in the 1690s, and was a contractor with the Navy Board.[1] Francis Hawes (£1,000) was Cashier to the Treasurer of the Navy, became joint Customs Cashier in 1716, and was a South Sea director from 1714 to 1721. Herman Olmius (£200) was a prominent Bank stock proprietor, and one of the commissioners for the Bank subscription of 1709; his son John was later a Bank director and his grandson was made a peer in 1762.

---

[1] He is referred to as deceased in 1715 (Add. MS. 25496, f. 88). Edward Haistwell, South Sea director 1736–42, was probably his son. In 1724 Richard Baker and Thomas Edwards held £2,000 East India stock 'for the use of Rachel Haistwell', presumably Edward senior's widow, Bank of England Record Office. Richard Baker is perhaps the same Richard Baker who was a South Sea director 1748–63.

P   D.F.R.

Among the other lenders in 1707 were at least six clergymen, six doctors of medicine, including Hans Sloane (£100) and one of law; the insurance projector Charles Povey (£300); the diarist Narcissus Luttrell (£1,300,) 'Grimlin' Gibbons (£1,000); Adam Cardonell, the Duke of Marlborough's secretary (£2,000); and Admiral Sir Clowdisley Shovell, M.P. for Rochester, and a Bank stock proprietor, who was drowned off the Scillies in October 1707 just about the time that his Land Tax loan of £3,500 became due for repayment. Sir Littleton Powys (£750) was a judge of the King's Bench, Sir Thomas Trevor (£4,000) Chief Justice of the Common Pleas, Thomas Jett (£300) a senior Exchequer Clerk, and Charles Sergison (£1,000) Clerk of the Acts to the Navy Board. Charles Pinfold (£1,400) was related to Edward Pinfold, a goldsmith banker of Fleet Street, and to Dr. James Pinfold of Doctor's Commons, who were his two referees when he became a South Sea Company clerk in 1711.[1]

In 1720, the social structure of the much smaller group (201) of male lenders subscribing less than £5,000 on the Land Tax was much the same. A number are identifiable as London merchants. Clerks and departmental officials included Edmund Ball of the Exchequer (a modest £64); William Lowndes, the Secretary to the Treasury (£4,000), and the South Sea director Francis Hawes's relative Thomas, a senior official of the Navy Board (£1,000). The Bishop of Chichester lent £2,400, four clergymen (only one of whom was among the six of 1707) £7,600 in all. In 1743 there were still a handful of representatives of medicine and the Church, including Benjamin Hoadly, Bishop of Winchester, who subscribed £2,000, some merchants, some goldsmith bankers like Christopher Arnold (£3,000), John Bosanquet (£2,300), Nathaniel Newnham (£2,000) and Thomas Snow (£1,400), and at least one official, the Treasury Clerk Peter Leheup, who subscribed £4,500. In the loan of 1750 the category of male lenders of less than £5,000 had shrunk to fifty-eight, but characteristically included two members of the Lowndes dynasty, one of whom was a Chief Clerk in the Treasury.

To determine precisely what proportion of lenders on the Land Tax and other funds renewed their loans each year would require annual lists of subscriptions, but even in the fairly widely separated years examined here the tendency seems to have been towards some continuity, with the same names or the same families recurring, though deaths and the reduction in the total number of lenders over the period would have worked in the opposite

---

[1] Add. MS. 25494, f. 102. In 1750 Lt.-Colonel William Pinfold of Walton, Bucks., and Charles Pinfold jun., LL.D., of Doctors' Commons, had accounts in 4% (1748) stock (Bank of England Record Office).

direction. Continuity is also observable in the large loans of £5,000 or more which, after 1713, became of ever-increasing importance.

III

In the subscription to the Land Tax in 1693 the most prominent large lenders were London merchants and financiers. Thus Sir John Cutler (£11,000) was a noted miser, whose character Pope later sketched in acid. Charles Duncombe (£20,000) was a partner in Child's Bank and was currently the Excise Cashier; his subscription may have come from his revenue balance, but is more likely to have come from his banking funds. Though dismissed from his revenue post for fraud in 1697, and expelled from the House of Commons in the following year, he was knighted in 1699, sat as M.P. for Downton until his death (unmarried) in 1711, and was Father of the City from 1707. Sir Joseph Herne (£5,000) was a prominent East India merchant, one of the government contractors for remittances to Flanders, and governor in 1691 of the newly floated Company of Copper Miners in England. Sir John Pye, Bart. (£23,050), a rich Derbyshire land-owner, had been a prominent lender in James II's reign. His father had been Auditor of the Exchequer of Receipt, and this was probably where the family wealth came from. Robert Fowle, (£13,000), Richard Lassells (£10,000) and Thomas Wotton (£18,000 jointly with his partner Fowle) were goldsmith bankers, and acted as agents in the Tontine loan of this year. Peter Henriquez jun. (£13,300) was a London merchant of Dutch Jewish extraction, a big East India jobber in Anne's reign, and a London agent for Dutch investors. Other big subscribers were Joseph Haskinstiles, a promi-nent London merchant (£10,000), Admiral David Mitchell (£5,000), John Rawkins (£8,000) a Portsmouth brewer, contractor to the Navy Board and revenue collector, and the Whig politician John Smith (£7,500), who was one of the Treasury Lords, Chancellor of the Exchequer 1699–1701 and 1708–10, Speaker of Parliament 1705–8, and an Exchequer Teller from 1710 until his death in 1723.

Smith (£12,200) and Henriquez (£17,200) were two of the three big lenders of 1693 to reappear in the much longer list of 1707. Other big subscribers in this year were the great London merchant Sir James Bateman (£10,250), who was Governor of the Bank of England and an East India director, and became Lord Mayor of London in 1716 (his son William was created Viscount Bateman in 1725); John Sheffield, first Duke of Buckingham and Normanby (1647–1721), the grandson of Lionel Cranfield, Earl of Middlesex (£10,000); Gerard Conyers (£6,400) a Bank director, who became Lord Mayor of London in 1723; William, Lord Cowper, the Keeper of the Great Seal (£8,200); Sir John Lethieullier (£8,500), alderman of London from 1676 until his death in 1719, and formerly a director of the East India and Levant Companies; and Henry Morse (£40,000) a goldsmith banker. Thomas Pitt (£16,470), James Medlycott (£400) and William Rogers (£2,100) were Chancery Masters, and their total of £18,970 was presumably an investment of suitors' funds. The attorney Peter Walter, who lent £8,000, perhaps for one of his noble clients, was entering the most prosperous phase of his career as land agent, money lender and man of business to the aristocracy. He had recently (1701) opened an account with Child's Bank, which in 1707 had a turnover of £20,000–£25,000 a year. Described by Pope as 'a rogue of truly ministerial kind', and allegedly the original of Peter Pounce in Fielding's *Joseph Andrews*, Walter is a background figure—like Joseph Demar of Dublin, the creditor of 'Lords, Knights and Squires', who died in July 1720 worth over £300,000, or the sinister money-lender John Manners of the later eighteenth century — whose activities, if properly reconstructed, would throw a new light on the period.[1]

The list of big lenders on the Land Tax of 1720 is in some respects similar to that of 1707. Christopher, Lord Barnard, the younger Sir Harry Vane's son, who had married the sister of John Holles, the millionaire Duke of Newcastle, subscribed £10,000; Spencer Compton, who could trace his lineage back to the voracious Baptist Hicks of Jacobean days, £15,000; Sir Peter Delmé, director and formerly Governor of the Bank of England, £8,000; John Grainger, a First Clerk in the Exchequer, £5,000; and

---

[1] Peter Walter (1662–1745) is not in the *DNB*. There are notes about him in Pope's *Works* (ed. Elwin and Courthope (1878)), iii. 141, 361; vii. 101 and in the *Herald and Genealogist*, viii. 1–5. He was Clerk of the Peace for Middlesex, and bought Stalbridge Park near Sherborne from the Boyle family. His account at Child's Bank opens (ledger for 1698–1715) on 28 July 1701 with £934. The form of the entries is laconic and generally ambiguous. (The account shows no trace of the Land Tax loan mentioned in the text.) Among other clients Walter acted for the rich Duke of Newcastle, whose account in Child's ledgers for 1685–1713 shows that in December 1704 Walter had lent £10,000 for him on the 8th 4s. Land Tax. For Joseph Demar of Dublin see *The London Journal*, 16–23 July 1720; for John Manners, Miss S. Campbell, 'Usury and Annuities of the Eighteenth Century', *Law Quarterly Review*, xliv (1928), 473. Demar (or Damer)'s fortune was eventually inherited by his great-nephew Joseph, created Earl of Dorchester in 1792.

Thomas, Lord Parker, the Lord Chancellor, £10,000, perhaps part of the profits from his sale of Chancery Masterships, for which he was dismissed in 1725. Sir Littleton Powys, a justice of the King's Bench lent £6,950, John Taylour, formerly joint Secretary to the Treasury, £10,000, Sir George Thorold, Lord Mayor of London, £15,000, and Sir William Withers, formerly an African Company and East India Company director, M.P. for London 1701 and 1707–15, alderman of the City until his death in 1721, £15,000. The mixture of rich aristocrats, rich office-holders and rich merchants and financiers, and the concentration on London, are familiar. But the trend to monopoly in these loans, already recognizable by the close of Anne's reign, had now become sharply accentuated by a new factor, the massive investments of the Marlborough family.

On 8 December 1688 Child's Bank struck the balance of the account of 'Lord Churchill, later Earl of Marlborough', who had played a decisive if not wholly creditable part in the recent 'Grand Revolution' at a modest £1,201 15s. 10d.[1] The account unfortunately closed in 1693, and the steps by which the Duke built up his personal fortune during the subsequent wars have never been properly worked out. By 1711 he was reputed to draw £40,000 p.a. from open sources, and by the peace of 1713 he must have been one of the richest private citizens in Europe. Meanwhile his erstwhile rival, Patrick Sarsfield, who in 1687 had been struggling with debts, had been forced, after the brief glory of the Irish campaign of 1689–90, to retreat to exile and death.[2]

At the end of 1718 Marlborough began to invest some of his wealth in short-term loans to the government which had given him the opportunity to make it. The history of advances from his estate (he died in 1722) can be reconstructed, with some omissions, from his account with the Bank of England, supplemented by the Exchequer Receipt Books. (See Table 72.)

From 1751 no subscriptions to loans appear in the Bank's ledgers, but receipt of interest is recorded until 1754. From this date the figures for

[1] Child's Bank ledger 1688–1732. For Child's records see below, p. 437.

[2] For Marlborough's income in 1711 see the DNB. The phrase 'the Grand Revolution' occurs in a Chancery case, White v. Evance, P.R.O. Chancery Masters' Exhibits C 111/50, Evance Papers. Sarsfield, described as 'then of St. Martins in the Fields' also appears in the Evance Papers. On 9 May 1687 he had executed a bond for £830 to Gregory Wale, a London merchant. The letter assigned it to Evance and the latter's partner Percivall on 19 March 1688. Wale later failed, and Evance in 1693 was trying to get paid from Sarsfield's confiscated Irish estate. For information sent from a friend of Sarsfield to the French Controller-General of Finance in 1709 see above, p. 375. Sarsfield was killed at the Battle of Landen in 1693.

TABLE 72

Advances on annual tax funds from the Marlborough estate

Year			Amount	Fund		Year			Amount	Fund	
			£						£		
1719	.	.	155,600*	Land tax		1739	.	.	100,000	Malt duty	
1720	.	.	445,775	,, ,,					100,000	Land tax	
1720–6	.	.	? ‡			1740	.	.	306,500	,, ,,	
1727	.	.	?450,000†	,, ,,		1741	.	.	305,600§	,, ,,	
1728	.	.	440,000	,, ,,		1742	.	.	276,000	,, ,,	
1729	.	.	440,000	,, ,,		1743	.	.	276,000	,, ,,	
1730	.	.	440,000	,, ,,		1744	.	.	306,000	,, ,,	
1731	.	.	? ‡			1745	.	.	305,500	,, ,,	
1732	.	.	350,000			1746	.	.	260,000	,, ,,	
1733	.	.	{ 100,000	Malt duty		1747	.	.	280,000	,, ,,	
			{ 100,000	Land tax		1748	.	.	260,000	,, ,,	
1734	.	.	345,000	Salt duty		1749	.	.	184,000	,, ,,	
1735	.	.	? ‡			1750	.	.	269,000*	,, ,,	
1736	.	.	150,000	Malt duty		1751	.	.	266,200¶	,, ,,	
1737	.	.	{ 130,000	Malt duty		1752	.	.	203,300	,, ,,	
			{ 50,000	Land tax		1753	.	.	233,700	,, ,,	
1738	.	.	{ 116,700	Malt duty		1754	.	.	203,000	,, ,,	
			{ 83,300	Land tax							

Source: Exchequer Receipt Books: Bank of England Drawing Office ledgers. No loans are recorded in the Exchequer Receipt Books for 1715–18. The first loan begins to be paid in instalments in December 1718. The Drawing Office account for the Duke opens in Bank of England Drawing Office Ledger 61 on 25 February 1726 with £65,000 in cash received from Lancelot Burton. All figures are from this account unless otherwise stated.

* From Exchequer Receipt Books.

† Between 22 May and 19 June 1727 £456,275 was received in cash for sale of tallies on the 17th 4s. Aid of 1727. No subscription for these tallies is noted earlier, but it seems probable they were subscribed for rather than purchased subsequently.

‡ No loan recorded.   § The figure is so recorded despite the similar one for 1740.

¶ From the Drawing Office ledger. Thereafter only interest is recorded.

interest diminish, and it seems that only small sums were lent from the account until it was closed in June 1759.

The loans from the duke's estate were supplemented by others by the Dowager Duchess Sarah from 1739 until her death in 1744; the loans were then continued by her executors until 1750; after that they apparently stopped.[1] The sums recorded in her account at the Bank of England are as follows:

TABLE 73

Advances on annual tax funds by Sarah, Duchess of Marlborough

Year			Amount	Fund	Year			Amount	Fund
			£					£	
1740 .	.	.	30,000	Land tax	1746 .	.	.	40,000	Land tax
1741 .	.	.	40,000	„ „	1747 .	.	.	40,000	„ „
1742 .	.	.	?82,000*		1748 .	.	.	44,000	„ „
1743 .	.	.	36,000	„ „	1749 .	.	.	?	
1744 .	.	.	123,000	„ „	1750 .	.	.	40,500†	„ „
1745 .	.	.	70,000	„ „					

Source: Bank of England Drawing Office ledgers. Sarah's account opens in D.O. ledger 63 on 26 August 1725 but though on several occasions she discounted tallies for the duke's estate no subscriptions on tax funds are noted until 1740.

    * Perhaps a purchase of tallies, not a subscription.

    † From the Exchequer Receipt Books.

So far as can be ascertained, both these loans and those made by the duke's executors were primarily for investment and not for re-sale, though on several occasions the duke's trustees discounted batches of tallies at the Bank of England.[2] It may be noted that other large sums were taken up by Marlborough relatives; in 1750, for example, £52,000 was advanced on the Land Tax by William Pitt and James Stephens, the executors of Sarah's favourite grandson, the Hon. John Spencer. Taken together, therefore, the Marlborough loans between the 1720s and 1750s virtually cornered this

1 The last loan recorded in the executors' Bank of England account is for 1748, though the account itself was not wound up for several years after that.

2 Cf. above, p. 420.

particular market. Sarah's own opinion, recorded in 1737, was that she had helped a hostile Minister to financial success. As she put it:

From the beginning of the reduction of interest [this seems to refer to 1717] I lent such sums to the government as reduced the interest from six per cent to four per cent (*sic* for three per cent); thinking it would have had a good effect for the security of the nation; and at that time he [sc. Walpole] could not have compassed such sums without me. But he has returned this with letting me know that he will take no more of the trust-money upon the land tax or malt, though it is but at three per cent; and even that favour, though it is not a great one, he will do for everybody but our family. . . .[1]

The assertion must be taken cautiously. As the figures previously given show, the latter part of it is untrue; and the former oversimplifies a complex issue. Still, it is clear that the very large Marlborough advances were an important factor in government short-term borrowing during this period; perhaps sufficiently important to have been a cause of the increasing stability of the Hanoverian dynasty. The situation was stated clearly in a memorandum of 1755: 'It is proposed this year that the Bank shall lend On the Malt 750 000 li. On the Land Tax 500 000. The other 500 000 li. is generally taken in by Loans of wch. the Duke of Marlbro' & his people usually want near 400,000 li.'[2]

The funds of Chancery were another important source of capital for short-term government loans in the period 1720–50. The Chancery Master's published accounts for the early 1720s show that they were already putting a fair amount of money into purchases of East India and South Sea bonds, South Sea stock and annuities and loans at the Exchequer.[3] The Exchequer loans continued a tradition dating back at least to the 1690s.[4] In 1733 the Accountant-General of Chancery, whose office was created in 1726 to unify the administration of suitors' funds, was referred to as an important holder of South Sea bonds.[5] Meanwhile, he had become an important investor in Land Tax loans. The advances which he made between 1727 and 1745 are shown in Table 74.

After 1745 there are no further references to advances in the Bank's ledgers, and the Exchequer Receipt Books for 1750 do not record any Land

---

[1] William King (ed.), *Memoirs of Sarah, Duchess of Marlborough* (1930), p. 299.

[2] Add. MS. 33038, f. 466, papers and memoranda of the Duke of Newcastle on taxation and finance, 1688–1756.

[3] *The Accompts of the several Masters of the High Court of Chancery* (1725). These were published as a result of the Macclesfield scandal, see above, p. 292.

[4] See above, p. 426.

[5] See p. 412 above.

TABLE 74

*Advances on the Land Tax by the Accountant-General
of Chancery*

Year	Amount	Year	Amount
	£		£
1727	31,300	1736	40,000
1728	(bought £33,000 Land	1737	40,000
	Tax tallies from	1738	?
	Bank of England)	1739	(bought £36,850 Land
1729	?		Tax tallies)
1730	34,500	1740	42,300
1731	?	1741	43,200*
1732	36,000	1742	44,800
1733	?	1743	50,100
1734	20,000	1744	47,000
1735	19,300	1745	47,000

Source : Bank of England Drawing Office ledgers. The Accountant-
  General's account opens in ledger 66 in July 1726 in the name
  of Henry Edwards.
  * So recorded despite the similar figure for 1740.

Tax loans by the Accountant-General. The reasons for this change are not
clear.[1]

The expansion of government borrowing during the 1740s brought some
new big contributors into the field of short-term advances. Among them in
1743 was the South Sea Company, which had had a share in bringing the
war about. In December 1742 its directors had decided to subscribe £50,000
to the new Land Tax loan when the Act was passed, and the money was
duly paid in on 3 January 1743 in the name of the company's chief cashier
Rowland Rogers.[2] The loan was evidently not repeated in 1744, but in 1745
and again in 1746 the company lent £40,000 on the Land Tax.[3] In 1748

[1] For the Accountant-General's cash balance of £248,489 at the Bank in 1755 see above,
p. 390.
[2] Add. MS. 25511, f. 35, South Sea D. Ct. Bk., 23 December 1742; P.R.O. E 401/2090,
entry for Rowland Rogers, 2 January 1743.
[3] Add. MS. 25511, ff. 121, 169, 7 March and 5 December 1745. The company also
bought £40,000 Salt Tax tallies at 4% discount through Samson Gideon on 21 March
1745, ibid., f. 124. Early in 1751 it held £119,900 Salt Tax tallies, Add. MS. 22513, f. 13.

and 1749 it increased the sum lent to £100,000, cashing the tallies when they matured in 1750.[1]

Other large new lenders in 1743 were Sir Edward Dering, Bart., M.P. for Kent (£5,000), and Sir Robert Rich, Bart. (£19,500), a former M.P. and shortly (1745) to become a General of Dragoons. Henry Fane, who was one of the four Chief Clerks of the Treasury and Keeper of the Treasury Books and Papers lent £8,000, and Charles Eyre, one of the six Sworn Clerks of the Exchequer, £20,000. Sir James Colebrooke (£10,000) and James Martin (£15,700) were London bankers, while Charles Savage (£10,000) was Deputy Governor of the Bank of England from 1743 to 1745. Merchants included the Anglo-Dutch brothers Abraham and Francis Craiesteyn, who subscribed £25,000 (Abraham had lent £500 on the Land Tax as far back as 1693), John Hanbury, probably 'a rich Virginia merchant' of Great Tower Street (£20,000) and Sir Theodore Janssen, Bart., the former South Sea director (£7,000).[2] A handful of politicians included Francis, Earl of Godolphin (£15,000) and the Lord Chancellor, Hardwicke, who lent £21,000. The next year (1744) only £600,000 was borrowed instead of £1,000,000 and there was an increase in the Marlborough loans, which in all took up £429,000 of the amount subscribed. However, some of the big lenders of 1743 reappear, among them Henry Fane (£5,000). Godolphin (£7,000), Hardwicke (£11,000) and Savage, who maintained his figure of £10,000. In 1745, when he was elected Governor of the Bank of England, Savage raised his subscription to £16,000. Fane, Godolphin and Hardwicke also subscribed again, Hardwicke reducing his loan to £7,000, Godolphin increasing his to £15,000, Fane remaining unchanged at £5,000. By 1750 the monopoly pattern of the 1730s had been restored, with the Marlborough loans taking up £376,500 of the £500,000 subscribed.

The evidence examined so far suggests that the circle of subscribers to short-term government loans shrank over the period, and that a high proportion of advances under Walpole and the Pelhams was taken up by the Marlborough family and its connections, while much of the remainder was supplied by institutions like Chancery and the London companies, members of the aristocracy, office-holders and big financiers. Meanwhile, the im-

---

[1] Add. MS. 25512, f. 42, South Sea D. Ct. Bk., f. 42, £100,000 evidently subscribed in 1748 to be carried over to the Land Tax loan of 1749. For encashment, ibid., f. 95, 26 April 1750.

[2] For Hanbury, see Thomas Wright, *History and Topography of Essex*, i (1836), 365. According to Wright the Hanbury family lived at Holfield Grange, Essex, and in the 1740s were tobacco brokers in Great Tower Street.

portance of these loans in anticipation of revenue diminished with the growth of Exchequer bill finance centring on the Bank of England, so that in 1763 it was possible to do away with them.

IV

One of the most important developments of the first half of the eighteenth century was the rise of specialized financial institutions with a professional interest in, and attitude toward, government securities. Examination of the investments of some of these houses shows how the pattern of their short-dated holdings changed in response to the development of government finance over the period.

Child's Bank, founded in the 1670s, was solidly established by Queen Anne's reign, and continued to prosper under the first two Georges.[1] In 1704 the bank's assets (not including its buildings or goodwill) were £178,195. In 1755, on the same basis, they were £734,020. By the 1740s the bank, with three partners, was averaging profits of over £12,000 a year.[2] Its clientele was weighted with aristocratic names like Egerton, Holles, North, Russell and Seymour.[3] The pattern of its investments probably differed in important respects from that of one of the primarily mercantile banks, particularly in virtually ignoring dealings in bills of exchange, and continuing to make large mortgage advances. But its records, which are full, and excellently preserved, show that it was closely in touch with the City financial community, as well as with the landed aristocracy, and the conclusions to be drawn from its operations are therefore of more than limited application.

In the early part of the period Child's, like other London banks, was taking diamonds, jewels and plate as securities for loans. For instance on 9 March 1691 the bank lent William Emerton £500 on 'jewels and 10 shares

---

[1] The bank merged with Glyn, Mills & Co. in 1924. Its records are kept at Child's Branch, No. 1 Fleet Street. This house, which until the introduction of street numbers in the later eighteenth century was simply known, from its sign, as 'the Marygold', was the site of Child's business from its inception. There is an anecdotal history of the bank by F. G. Hilton Price, *Temple Bar, or some account of 'Ye Marygold', no. 1 Fleet Street* (1875).

[2] Child's Bank, Balancing Book 1746–1770, containing some earlier accounts.

[3] Child's Bank, P. ledger 1717–59.

in the Linen manufacture'.[1] But as early as 1689 they were also lending at the Exchequer, discounting short-term government tallies, and making loans on the latter's security. Some entries in 1689 and 1690 were as follows:

TABLE 75

Acquisition of Exchequer tallies by Child's Bank 1689–90

			£
1689	27 June	Lent at Exchequer in Cratford's name	2,000
	20 July	Exchequer	3,000
	26 July	Exchequer per Jackson	3,500
	12 August	Exchequer per Jackson	2,000
	13 September	Exchequer in name of John Rogers*	4,000
		In name of R. Grainge	3,000
	20 November	Exchequer in name of R. Grainge	6,000
1690	13 April	[Lent] Thomas Brouncker on 3 tallies £500 each	1,500

Source : Child's Bank Ledger 1688–1732.
* A partner.

The form of ledger entries is often ambiguous, but discounts (purchases) of tallies seem early in the 1690s to supersede direct loans at the Exchequer. Sometimes the seller of a tally is noted. For instance, an entry of 25 June 1691 'Excheqr. in Russels name of Eyles 510' presumably means a tally of fictitious loan issued to Russell, the Navy Treasurer, which came into Eyles's hands, and then into those of the bank.[2] Sometimes these tallies are noted as at par ('Exchr. 500 and 500 in Foxs name 1000') but an entry of 10 July 1691 'Exchr. in Dyve's na. 250 & 250 480' indicates a 4% discount. In July 1694 '46.17.0. less' is marked against an entry for a £2,000 tally on Parchment and Paper, and '38 less' against tallies for £1,900 on the Poll Tax. These are discounts of only about 2½%; in 1696–7 discounts of 3% to 4% are noted. Tallies acquired by discount were sometimes rediscounted: in the critical month of January 1696, for instance, the bank sold over £20,000 worth. On most other occasions tallies were evidently held to maturity, and then redeemed at the Exchequer.[3] Between 1689 and 1713

[1] Child's Bank, ledger 1688–1732. Cf. P.R.O. C. 103/123, papers of the goldsmith's firm of Fowle & Wotton, which show them making loans on security of silver, watches, jewels, diamonds and pictures.
[2] For tallies of fictitious loan see above, p. 351.
[3] The whole of this section is based on Child's Bank, ledger 1688–1732.

the number of tally items in the bank's payments column (representing direct loans at the Exchequer, discounts — the majority — or loans to clients on security of tallies) was as follows:

TABLE 76

Tally items in Child's Bank ledger 1689–1713

1689	8	1694	46	1699	44	1704	16	1709	4
1690	1	1695	27	1700	28	1705	12	1710	5
1691	31	1696	9	1701	11	1706	11	1711	11
1692	16	1697	46	1702	13	1707	8	1712	7
1693	43	1698	68	1703	23	1708	1	1713	3

Source: Child's Bank ledger 1688–1732.

After this date these entries cease for many years to be of significance. This pattern reflects the confused state of government short-term borrowing in the 1690s, and its retrieval and simplification, with the Bank of England's help, under Godolphin.

In the 1740s Child's once more became interested in short-term tallies, on a considerable scale. During this period it made cash loans at the Exchequer on security of the Land Tax as shown in Table 77.

In addition, the bank was buying tallies. In May 1742 it paid Giles Earle £5,187 18s. 0d. (principal and interest) for £5,000 Land Tax tallies of 1741, and Samuel Child £10,376 12s. 6d. for a further £10,000 worth. In July, it bought £5,000 more from Thomas Tower for £5,039 19s. 3d., and encashed them at the Exchequer in the following month. In February 1744 it bought £6,500 Land Tax tallies of 1743 from John Edwin (who had subscribed £20,000 to the loan) for £6,626 18s. 0d. Between March and May 1746 it bought £10,900 tallies at 1¾ to 3¾% discount; between May 1746 and December 1747 £10,500 more.[1] In February 1748 it still held £6,600 tallies; the rest had been paid off at the Exchequer at par. Finally, in December 1749 Francis Fane sold the bank £10,000 tallies.[2]

Loans to clients on security of Land Tax tallies seem to have been of less importance in the 1740s, though some were made. The most important

---

[1] Child's Bank, Posting Book 1717–57. Cf. Archief Brants, 1344, van Hemert & Co. in London to J. I. de Neufville in Amsterdam, 4 March 1746: they hold Land Tax tallies, but no one wants to buy; they can only dispose of them at 4% loss.

[2] Child's Bank, Posting Book 1717–56.

TABLE 77

Land Tax subscriptions by Child's Bank 1740–52

Date of subscription	£	Disposal of tallies
April 1740 . . .	10,000	Held to maturity
January 1745 . .	10,000	Held to maturity
April–June 1749 .	30,000	Held to maturity
February–May 1750 .	23,000	Held to maturity
May 1751 . . .	3,500	Held to maturity
March 1752 . . .	20,000	Held to maturity

Source: Child's Bank, Posting Book 1717–56 and Balancing Book 1746–70.

securities for the bank in this period were, in order of liquidity, mortgages, government and allied stock, and insurance shares, East India bonds and Navy bills, and bonds of other kinds, including notes of hand. The last category was miscellaneous. It included Bedford Corporation bonds, on £1,000 of which John Floyer was lent a cautious £600 in July 1741, and 'corn debentures' which Lejay & Co. pledged (in unspecified quantity) for a loan of £6,000 in May 1752.[1]

The bank bought and sold other short-dated securities on its own account over the whole period. There seems to be no trace of subscriptions to the circulation of Exchequer bills before 1761. Exchequer bills rarely occur (nor do they figure as security for clients' loans). In July 1697 there are entries 'Peters for Exchequer Bills 3720' and 'Exchr. Bills 2000', but nothing further. In 1717 the bank held £9,800 Exchequer bills; in the balance sheets of the 1740s they do not appear at all. There were occasional purchases of Navy and Victualling bills in the early part of the period, but nothing of real significance even in 1710–11. In May–December 1747 the bank bought fifteen such bills totalling £22,676 10s. 7d, for £21,396 15s. 10d., increased its holding to £29,258 9s. 8d. in 1749 and funded it the same year.[2] In 1753 the bank bought over £3,000 more bills and in 1754 a further £7,725, at $1\frac{3}{4}$ to $1\frac{5}{8}\%$ discount. The bills were held to maturity and encashed at the Navy Office.[3]

[1] Ibid. [2] For funding of Navy bills in 1749 see above, p. 406.
[3] All these examples are from Child's Bank, Posting Book 1717–56, and Balancing Book 1746–70.

The bank purchased East India bonds more regularly, particularly towards the end of the period. In the later months of 1699 it bought £21,300 bonds which were paid by the company at maturity in April 1700. Between 1708 and 1711 it bought and sold a further £14,000 worth. In the 1720s its holdings of bonds were accumulating: it bought £14,750 at a premium for £15,546 and sold only £3,500. By July 1739 its balance was over £50,000. It sold £10,000 of these, mostly at discounts of £1 3s. 0d. to £2 1·0d%, in the crisis month of October 1745, but further purchases in 1747 and 1749 brought the total it held to £60,000, £45,000 of which was funded in 1750 in 3% and 3½% stock as part of Pelham's conversion plan. In its balance-sheet of October 1755 the bank showed £30,000 East India bonds, valued at £34,057. In contrast to East India bonds, those of the South Sea Company were unimportant for it. The bank bought £15,000 between 1720 and 1726: these were paid off by the company. In 1728–30 the bank bought a further £17,100 bonds, all of which it had sold by the end of 1731.[1]

As the bank prospered, and its funds increased, it began to make extensive mortgage advances, and by the mid-century its assets-structure was more rigid than it had been in Anne's reign. (See Table 78.)

Government stock was the bank's second line of reserve; in the crisis of October–December 1745 it sold £32,000 Bank and South Sea stock, besides £10,000 East India bonds. Mortgage advances, however, were not necessarily so illiquid as they seemed. They were sometimes repaid fairly quickly; for instance a loan of £13,000 in 1741 to the merchant Thomas Hammond was repaid in 1743; a loan of £5,000 to 'Carnarvon and Cotton' in 1743 was repaid in 1745; William Pescod's £2,500 mortgage loan in January 1745 is noted '12mos.'. Some advances were by way of assignment of an existing mortgage: John Depestres borrowed £2,000 in this way in November 1744, and in August 1746 Lynch Salusbury Cotton borrowed £1,800 'on mortgage per assignment from Eliz. Lutwych.' Here, presumably, the deeds were deposited as collateral, the bank becoming an equitable mortgagee. Many, perhaps most, mortgagors, were incontestably aristocratic. Thus, Lord Dysart borrowed £26,000 in 1741, Sir Charles Wyndham £4,000 in 1745, Lord Byron £2,000 in 1745, a further £6,500 in 1750 and £2,500 more in 1752, making £11,000 in all; Lord Granville borrowed £4,000 in 1746, the Duke of Beaufort £4,056 in 1747, Lord Gower £12,000 in the same year, and so on.[2] It looks as though mortgagors were a mixed bag including merchants and financiers, as well as landowners tapping city funds, Perhaps for this reason, the bank's money continued to flow into these loans

[1] Balancing Book 1746–70.   [2] All the instances cited are from Posting Book 1717–56.

TABLE 78

Child's Bank balance sheet 2 October 1755

		£ (incl. valuations)	%
Total assets		734,020	100·0
'Sundry mortgages and other securities' . .		232,542	31·7
Long-dated stock:	£ nominal		
East India	5,000		
South Sea	10,000		
Million Bank	1,000		
South Sea 3%	50,000		
East India 3%	45,000		
Bank 3%	30,000		
	141,000	146,355	19·9
East India bonds	30,000	34,057	4·6
Sundry		990	0·1
Arrears of interest		16,079	2·2
Cash		303,997	41·5

Source: Balancing Book 1746–70. This is the only balance sheet to break down the Government securities item.

throughout the latter part of the period, though there seems to have been a trend towards a reduction in the number of advances, accompanied by an increase in their average amount. (See Table 79.)

Child's records also throw some light on the private financial dealings of two of the partners, Sir Francis Child for the period 1700 to his death in 1713, and his son Samuel Child for the period 1740 to his death in 1752. The entries in their ledgers are a characteristic eighteenth-century jumble. For instance, Samuel Child records a payment of £31 for the funeral of his daughter Jane, closely followed by a payment of £200 to St. Dunstan's Charity School, and of £30 to buy sheep. The general pattern of their investments is broadly similar to those of the bank over which they presided.[1]

Sir Francis Child bought and sold East India bonds. In 1710 he was also buying and selling Exchequer bills, which at the end of the year were at a

[1] The following section is based on Sir Francis Child's Posting Book 1700–13 and Samuel Child's Posting Book 1740–52.

TABLE 79

Mortgage loans by Child's Bank 1740–56

Year	No. of loans	Total lent	Average sum lent
		£	£
1740	10	14,100	1,410
1741	9	36,100	4,011
1742	7	24,300	3,471
1743	3	7,600	2,533
1744	4	10,000	2,500
1745	10	23,800	2,380
1746	2	5,800	2,900
1747	8	37,856	4,732
1748	1	782	782
1749	2	2,400	1,200
1750	1	3,500	3,500
1751	6	40,600	6,766
1752	3	3,800	1,266
1753	3	17,500	5,833
1754	6	14,179	2,363
1755	1	10,800	10,800
1756	4	24,750	6,187

Source : Child's Bank, Balancing Book 1746–70.

small discount; thus on 13 December 1710 he paid £1,963 for £2,000 bills. As security for loans he accepted government annuities, short-term tallies, Navy bills (once), bonds and notes and foreign money.[1] He discounted Land and Malt Tax tallies which he seems normally to have held to maturity.[2] He sometimes subscribed directly to these loans, for instance lending £4,000 on Malt in 1702 and £3,000 on Land in 1710. He also sub-

[1] For instance, two loans made to Daniel Arthur on 5 and 19 February 1705. The first was £1,200 secured on 4898 oz. 'foreign money' for two months at 6%; the second £800 on 3467 oz. dollars, the terms not specified.

[2] Hence such entries as the following:

   9 May 1702 Recd. 4 Malt Tallies (17–20) £2,019.
   21 April 1703 Recd. 4 Malt Tallies (829–32) £4,170.
   28 July 1708 Cashed at Exchequer a Malt Tally £529.

scribed to government long annuity loans (in 1704, 1706 and 1707) and later sold part of the annuities acquired, besides infrequently buying Bank, East India and (in 1711–12) South Sea stock. He also made mortgage loans. In 1702 he lent Charles, Earl of Dorset £6,000, in 1703 Gabriel and Matthew Hale £2,000 and Jonathan Prideaux £2,300, and in 1711 Isaac Hancock £1,100 and Richard Bundy £360. Like Child's Bank's mortgage advances in the 1740s and 1750s, these seem to have been of a mixed kind, some short-term and some long.

The structure of Samuel Child's investments is very similar, despite the interval of thirty years. He subscribed £10,000 to the Land Tax loans of 1741, 1742 and 1750 and £20,000 to those of 1749, 1751 and 1752. He sold the 1741 tallies to his own bank in May 1742, but held the remainder to maturity. On one occasion only, in March 1746, he bought £2,000 Land Tax tallies of the current year, for £1,922 2s. 10d., holding them till they matured in April 1747. He bought and sold East India bonds fairly regularly; they were probably the first line of his investment reserves, for in the second half of the difficult year 1745 he sold 63 of them for £6,334. In 1748 he laid out £6,350 in Navy and Victualling bills at an average $5\frac{1}{2}\%$ discount. He must subsequently have added to this holding, for in the ledger opened to fund Navy bills in 1749 he is credited with £9,858.[1] The security on which he lent money to individuals was nearly always a mortgage or a personal bond; his practice in this respect was less flexible than his father's, and his own bank's. An incomplete and untotalled list of his assets at his death on 14 October 1752 is shown in Table 80.

The largest mortgagors were the Earl of Abingdon (£30,000), Colonel Cholmondeley (£5,633 17s. 10d.) and Lord Granville (£11,000); against the last entry, however, is noted 'setled'. Other mortgagors were George Branston (£3,500 direct and £3,616 10s. 0d. 'on assignment from Sir John Abdy'), Sir Richard Chase (£3,000) Pitt and Rudyard £3,819 19s. 3d., Charles Waller (£3,000) and Lord Wenman (£3,000).

The evidence of Child's Bank's records suggests the following conclusions. In the early part of the period the bank made some cash advances directly to the Exchequer, but later in the 1690s preferred to discount short-term tallies and lend on their security. Sometimes it rediscounted tallies to increase liquidity. It limited its discounts to good tallies which ranked high for payment and therefore only went to a small discount in a crisis year like 1696–7. After the conclusion of peace in 1713, tally-discounting became relatively unimportant for it, though it continued to make occasional loans on security

[1] Bank of England Record Office, opening ledger for Navy 5% stock (1749).

TABLE 80

Samuel Child's assets at his death in 1752

	£	%
Total listed assets	207,743	100·0
Mortgages (16 advances) . .	75,493	36·4
Land Tax tallies	20,000	9·6
East India bonds	15,000	7·2
Long-term securities (nominal value)	85,750	41·3
Cash, about	11,500	5·5

Source : Samuel Child's Posting Book 1740–52.

of tallies. When government short-term borrowing in cash again increased in the 1740s, the bank made substantial cash subscriptions (£10,000–£20,000) to Exchequer loans, the tallies for which it normally held to maturity. Individual partners followed a similar policy with their own funds. Tallies could be purchased when they were wanted, though there was probably a ceiling on the amount available. In the 1740s, when the seller to Child's of short-term tallies is noted it is usually a subscriber to the original Exchequer loan. By this date such tallies as security for loans to clients were rarer, their place being taken by government stock and East India bonds. By the 1740s the latter were clearly the bank's favourite short-dated paper. In the early 1750s it was holding about £30,000 East India bonds and Samuel Child held a further £15,000 for his own account. Since the volume of bonds at this date was not more than £2m., it seems probable that the London banking community of about thirty houses could easily absorb a million in bonds at any given time, leaving only a million for other holders.

In contrast, Child's showed little interest in Exchequer bills, except on a moderate scale in the early part of the period, and they do not appear in the 1740s as security for clients' loans. There are no subscriptions to the circulation of Exchequer bills. The bank's interest in Navy and Victualling bills was spasmodic, but in years when the growing debt of the Navy forced bills to a discount (1710–11, 1747–8), the bank or its partners purchased some of the bills which appeared in the market. Lastly, by the 1740s the bank had developed its very modest mortgage business of the early 1700s to a point where it was putting £10,000 to £20,000 a year into the hands of mortgagors. Many of these were aristocrats, but there was a fringe of mercantile borrowers, whose loans were probably only for short or medium periods. This overall pattern is consistent with the general development of government short-term borrowing: a glut of tallies in the 1690s, a well-managed policy under Walpole and Pelham which made Land Tax tallies, in particular, a gilt-edged investment, and virtually withdrew Exchequer bills from the market, and a less successful management of the Navy Debt, which was mitigated by the facilities for discounting Navy and Victualling bills in the London money market.

The London insurance offices were also interested in short-dated securities, particularly Bank Circulation receipts and East India and South Sea bonds; they occasionally purchased Navy and Victualling bills at a discount as well.[1] The London Assurance, for instance, established in 1720 primarily for marine business, invested in circulation receipts nearly every year from 1720 to 1746, and was also a substantial holder of company bonds. (It began buying and selling South Sea bonds in the period 1720 to 1728, but was only a regular holder of them from 1730 onwards.) The table shows holdings of certain classes of securities in the first quarter-century of business. This is one of the few solid pieces of evidence about the ownership of circulation receipts. It is also known, however, that Martin's Bank was a regular subscriber in the 1740s, while the South Sea Company in the years 1722–7 subscribed £300,000 p.a.[2] In comparison with the substantial sums which it invested in other short-dated bills, the London Assurance's purchases of Navy and Victualling bills were insignificant. Between April and September 1746 it paid £3,201 for bills at 6% and 12% discount. In November 1747 and December 1748 it laid out a further £3,799 for two Navy bills, which were funded at par (£3,945) in Navy 5% Stock in May 1749. In March 1745 it also came forward, evidently for the first time, with a loan of £50,000 on the Land Tax, which was repaid at the Exchequer in the following year. In 1746 it repeated its subscription of £50,000, and made a series of purchases which ran its holding of tallies up to £68,600. This account was cleared in October 1748 with the Exchequer's repayment of the £50,000. The other tallies had already been sold.[3]

[1] Cf. also A. H. John, 'Insurance Investment and the London Money Market of the 18th Century', *Economica*, New Series, xx (1953), 137.

[2] J. B. Martin, *The Grasshopper in Lombard Street* (1892), p. 140; Add. MS. 25561, f. 14, South Sea Memorials, for South Sea Company subscriptions. The East India Company general ledgers do not show subscriptions to the circulation. Martin's Bank evidently disposed of part at least of its subscriptions, for in the periods 1750–1 and 1757–60 it let the London merchant William Braund have £3,000 worth of circulation receipts (one-tenth paid) each year. Dr. L. S. Sutherland, *A London Merchant 1695–1774* (Oxford, 1933), p. 135.

[3] London Assurance, ship charter ledger A 1720–63.

TABLE 81

London Assurance, holdings of certain short-term securities
1720–46

'Money at Interest'*	Year	Bank circulation*	South Sea bonds†	East India bonds‡
£		£	£	£
..	1720	50,000	..	..
..	1721	5,000	..	..
..	1722	10,000	..	..
..	1723	10,000	..	..
..	1724	10,000	..	..
..	1725	10,000	..	..
..	1726	10,000	..	..
..	1727	10,000	..	..
20,916	1728	10,000	4,923	..
7,813	1729	10,000	..	..
9,327	1730	5,000	10,569	..
3,684	1731	..	10,326	..
19,444	1732	9,000	18,871	..
50,379	1733	10,500	10,004	..
..	1734	..	3,250	3,683
..	1735	..	10,255	17,442
..	1736	..	12,465	27,567
..	1737	10,000	2,720	27,567
..	1738	12,000	..	32,942
..	1739	10,000	..	32,942
..	1740	5,000	..	32,942
..	1741	10,000	..	32,942
..	1742	10,000	..	11,491
..	1743	..	..	4,849
..	1744	42,000	..	16,849
..	1745	8,000	..	16,849
..	1746	20,000	..	16,849

Source : London Assurance, ship charter ledger A, 1720–
1763, and balance sheets 1728–38 (the next
balance sheet is for 1762).

* The ledger account shows numerous different
securities.

† 15% paid 1720, thereafter 10% paid.

‡ Evidently at market value.

The records of the Royal Exchange Assurance, which was also established in 1720, also primarily for marine business, were largely destroyed in the fire of 1838 which burned down the old Royal Exchange. A surviving balance-sheet for 1734 shows total assets of £594,238, including £17,900 'loans at interest' on security of bills of exchange, and a massive holding of £100,000 East India bonds, valued at £102,938.[1] The Sun Fire Office, established in 1710 and growing rapidly from 1720, was also a holder of East India and South Sea bonds on a more modest scale.

TABLE 82

Sun Fire Office purchases of East India and South Sea Bonds
1728–59

Year	East India bonds*	South Sea bonds*	Year	East India bonds*	South Sea bonds*
	£	£		£	£
1728	..	6,000	1736–7	3,000	..
1729	10,000	4,000	1740–1	13,000	..
1730	..	..	1744	4,400	..
1731	..	..	1747	10,000	..
1732	..	..	1752	7,000	..
1733	..	..	1753–4	11,600	..
1734	1,000	..	1758–9	22,000	..

Source: Sun Fire Office, ledgers 1728–62.
* Nominal.

In 1728–32 the Office held £24,737 Navy and Victualling bills as security for a loan of £22,700 at 4% to Edward Jasper, one of its Managers (directors). In 1734–6 and again in 1737 Jasper pledged further bills for smaller advances. By April 1749 the total of such bills pledged by him was reduced to £12,155 which were funded at 5% in 1749.[2] Apart from this, in September 1746 the Office bought a Navy bill of £1,803 for £1,708 and sold it at £72 profit in March 1747.

[1] Royal Exchange Assurance, Doomsday Book compiled in 1876 by the corporation's Accountant J. A. Iligham to record the surviving records, balance-sheet dated 31 October 1734.
[2] Sun Fire Office, ledgers 1728–1762; Dickson, *Sun Insurance Office*, p. 242.

The records for conversion of navy and other debts into South Sea stock in 1711, and of Navy and Victualling bills into 5% stock in 1749, throw some further light on the use of the money-market by holders of government paper. A list drawn up for Lord Treasurer Harley in 1711, of 232 subscribers of £3,000 or more to the new South Sea Company shows that they contributed altogether £2,532,980, about 30% of the subscribable debt of £8·6m. Of this sum, however, £990,678 was subscribed by government trustees or paymasters, so 226 private subscribers held £1,542,302 paper, about 17% of the total.[1] Forty subscribers of £10,000 or over held £653,517 or 25%. A few addresses are not given; the great majority of those that are, are London ones, though there was a handful of subscribers from outside — Hertfordshire, Kent, Bristol, Portsmouth. Dr. Sperling shows that the majority of the subscribers were not regular contractors for the Navy, Victualling or Ordnance Boards, and must therefore have purchased the bills in their possession.[2] An important sub-group consisted of a dozen goldsmith bankers, who subscribed between them £105,000.[3] One of the parents of the South Sea project, John Blunt, who subscribed £7,556, and Laurence Hatsell, who subscribed £4,339, were London scriveners. Lawyers included Richard Belasyse of Lincoln's Inn (£3,045), William East of the Middle Temple (£3,812), James Lowther of the Middle Temple (£3,562) and James Medlycott, one of the Chancery Masters (£3,209). The

---

[1] The list is B.M. Harleian MS. 7479. This is in rough alphabetical order and untotalled. The names have been re-sorted and added. The government sums were £223,900 subscribed by the trustees of the Genoa loan, £353,100 by Brydges, Paymaster of the Forces Abroad, £168,100 by Caesar, the Navy Treasurer, £138,265 by Howe, the Paymaster of Guards and Garrisons, £45,319 by Lansdell, the Deputy Ordnance Treasurer, and £61,993 by Mordaunt, the Ordnance Treasurer. The Genoa Loan, of 800,000 pieces of eight, was the cargo of two captured Genoese ships. The republic was virtually obliged to let the English government have the use of the money until the war was over. Security was in the form of tallies on the Sixth General Mortgage, which the trustees for the republic exchanged for South Sea stock. See Cal. T. Bks. xxv (ii), 356–7, 6 July 1711.

[2] Sperling, 'Godolphin and the organisation of public credit', p. 117, based on a comparison of a list of 117 contractors compiled from the Navy and Ordnance ledgers 1702–10 with the British Museum list.

[3] The twelve described as 'goldsmith' are John Branfill, £5,051; John Brassey, £16,589; William Brassey, £3,397; John Campbell, £3,880; George Caswall, £14,671; William Hales, £4,915; Thomas Martin, £13,491; John Mead, £7,128; James Metcalf, £4,260; Stephen Ram, £9,188; Benjamin Tudman, £10,530; Joseph Wilson, £12,091, a total of £105,191. To these should probably be added James Colebrooke, £16,344; Thomas Coutts, £5,205; Sir Richard Hoare, £3,256, and Thomas Le Heup, £5,957.

Chancellor of the Exchequer, Robert Benson, (£3,002) and Harley himself (£8,041) were included; so were officials in departments, like Thomas Colby sen. (£4,511) and Thomas Colby jun. (£3,233), both of the Navy Office. The commonest description, however, is simply 'merchant'.

By the mid-century these trends had developed. Of the £3,072,472 Navy and Victualling bills and ordnance and transport debentures funded in 1749 at the Bank of England, £844,987 or over 26% of the whole was held by a small group of subscribers of £10,000 or more. They included at least nine bankers, two of whom are still described as 'goldsmith', who subscribed between them £165,193.[1] All the large subscribers had London addresses, except Thomas Holmes, Esq., of Yarmouth (£15,430). Among the other big subscribers was Admiral Lord Anson (£19,480); William Corbett (£11,440) and Savage Mostyn (£11,806), both of the Navy Office; and Lady Susannah Warren (wife of Vice-Admiral Sir Peter Warren), who subscribed £12,364, probably on behalf of her husband. Thomas Bray of Spitalfields, weaver, subscribed £11,511, John Lefevre of West Ham, distiller, £15,469 and Peter Lefevre of Walthamstow, distiller, £26,332. Merchants included William Baker (£13,491), Samson Gideon (£10,000), Henry Lascelles (£50,077), John Major (£12,304) and Edmund Proudfoot (£19,376). The jobber Samuel Bull, of South Sea House, and the brokers Edward Lambert of Cornhill and John Shipston of Cornhill, subscribed respectively £26,021, £11,396 and £30,415. Some of these big holders, like Lefevre, Lefebure and Lascelles, were probably government contractors. But the majority must have acquired their bills by discount, and among this group the London banking community was especially prominent.

It was stated rather wildly in 1699 that half a million a year of interest on the nation's debts, which were computed at £16·6m., 'falls into Foreigners hands'.[2] This presumably referred to short as well as long-term investments,

---

[1] Bank of England Record Office, opening ledgers for Navy 5% stock (1749). (For this stock see above, p. 406.) The bankers were Christopher Arnold, £20,840; Barnaby Backwell, £29,258 (this was for Child's Bank, of which he was a partner); James Colebrooke, £20,190; William Denne, £12,773; Richard Fuller, £10,172; Philip Hollingworth, £12,257; Fraser Honywood, £11,204; Joseph Martin, £19,500; Robert Surman, £28,999. Arnold and Denne are described as 'goldsmith'. Cf. the Bank's usage about foreign bankers, above p. 317. In the alphabet to the 4%s of 1748 Fraser Honywood's description 'goldsmith' is struck through and 'Banker' substituted.

[2] Add MS. 20721, Revenue Accounts 1685-99, f. 61.

and was a product of the same vague apprehension about foreign, particularly Dutch, ownership of English assets that Sir Josiah Child had referred to a generation previously.[1] But it is difficult to trace any significant foreign ownership of short-dated English securities, though there are occasional instances of it. In April 1701 Lidia Lacam of Amsterdam, widow of Jean Passalaigne, now married to Isaac Chavat, declares formally that she is the owner of three tallies on Coals and fifteen on Malt, in the hands of Pierre Renew of London.[2] In the period 1711–17 Lewis Fernandes Parfamo of Brussels held £650 East India bonds, and in 1729 he held £8,000 South Sea bonds, though there is no trace in his accounts of short-term tallies.[3] Claude Bosanquet of London occasionally included the price of East India bonds in his letters to de Neufville & Co. in Amsterdam in the 1730s and 1740s.[4] In October 1732 William Isaac Kops of London was telling his principal, Simon Bevel of Haarlem, that East India bonds were currently thought good value, though Bevel ordered Bank and East India stock instead.[5] By and large, however, both the English records and the Dutch correspondence and ledgers are uninformative about foreign ownership of short-dated English securities. A foreign merchant's favourable balance with his English correspondent was, of course, a first line of reserve, to be drawn on when times were difficult. Thus Simon Bevel, who normally did not draw much on England, drew heavily in the crisis year of 1710: £796 in April, £2,400 August–September, £2,000 on 2 October, £1,420 in November and £200 in December, a total of £6,816. After this his drawings fell off again.[6] If this was in any way typical, there were at a given date substantial cash balances in England earmarked, as it were, for foreign creditors, even though they might temporarily be invested in the English debtor's name. Since the overall balance of trade between England and Holland was in Holland's favour, this amounted to a hot money situation, for in a crisis these balances were liable to be run down suddenly, creating tight conditions in the London market. It was probably of this that Child and Defoe were partly thinking.[7]

[1] See above, p. 304.

[2] Amsterdam, Gemeente Archief, Notarial Archive 5880/22, 1 April 1701.

[3] P.R.O. C 11/695/35, *Cortisois and Others* v. *Da Costa*. Among the documents in this case is a schedule of accounts kept for Lewis Fernandes Parfamo by Anthony da Costa, merchant of London, for the period 1711–30.

[4] Gemeente Archief, Archief Brants, 1344.

[5] Ibid. 1649, Kops to Bevel 24 October 1732, in Dutch.

[6] Archief Brants, 1736, ledger of Simon Bevel 1710–14.

[7] See above, pp. 304–5.

VI

The evidence reviewed in this chapter suggests the following conclusions. The number of those directly involved in short-term cash loans to the government greatly diminished between the political revolution of 1688 and the Seven Years War, and the average size of advances correspondingly increased. The circle of lenders was largely restricted to London and its environs; this helps to bear out Allen's statement in 1734 that 'perhaps above two Thirds of the Nation's Cash are the Property of those who reside in and about that City.'[1] Foreign subscriptions were probably not of importance. In the 1690s tallies subscribed for were discounted with London companies and banking houses, who sometimes rediscounted them, but after 1713 the fall in the supply of tallies and the rise in the demand for them tended to make subscribers retain them until maturity. The tallies that were available for purchase in the 1730s and 1740s tended to change hands between the big owners, for instance from the Marlborough account to the Bank of England, or from Samuel Child to his own bank.

Exchequer bills throughout the period, and particularly from the 1720s, were largely monopolized by the Bank of England, and they appeared infrequently in the money-market. Such evidence as is available about those who (at least in theory) backed the circulation of these bills suggests that they came from a relatively limited circle of London banks and trading and insurance companies, and from friends and relatives of the Bank of England's own directors. Navy and Victualling bills appeared more often in the market, especially in periods when they were purchasable for less than their face value. They were bought and sometimes sold by individual merchants and financiers, and by banks and insurance companies, and were accepted as security for advances. The most popular short-dated security for London financiers by the 1750s was the bonds of the East India Company, which were held in substantial quantities as a first line of reserve.

Something can be inferred from this evidence about the sources of government short-term finance. In the early part of the period the cash loans of the customs and excise cashiers, and at a later date their balances and those of other government officials at the Bank of England, which helped the latter finance the circulation of Exchequer bills, were extremely important.

---

[1] William Allen, *Ways and Means to Raise the Value of Land* (1736, written 1734), p. 9. For this pamphlet see below, p. 476.

Government taxes, from which the revenue balances derived were in turn drawn from all over England. Although throughout the period London probably provided the greater part of customs revenue, nearly half the excise revenue came from outside the capital.[1] The Bank of England's private depositors, numbering about 2,000 by the mid-eighteenth century, were largely drawn from the financial and mercantile community of the City of London.[2] It seems likely that marine-insurance premiums, which provided the greater part of the income of the London Assurance and Royal Exchange Assurance, also came largely from the London area. A sampling study of the insurance premiums of the Sun Fire Office, on the other hand, shows that in 1716 only 37% of its premiums came from London, and as late as 1790 only 58%.[3] Provincial savings and tax payments thus indirectly helped finance central government borrowing. The same is also true of the deposits of a bank like Child's, whose clientele was aristocratic and landowning. It would be interesting to know how widely scattered was the circle of Chancery suitors whose funds the Accountant-General was investing in short-term Exchequer loans and East India and South Sea bonds.[4]

The Marlborough wealth had largely been accumulated from the profits of office, and the same must have been true of the politicians John Smith or Lord Ryalton, of the lawyers like Macclesfield and Hardwicke, of the sailors like Shovell and Anson, of the Exchequer Clerks like Samuel Edwards and Charles Eyre. Finance and jobbing had made the fortunes of Samuel Bull, James Colebrooke, Samson Gideon, Peter Walter. The profits of trade were perhaps a less important direct source of short-term government finance by the mid-eighteenth century, though they underpinned the lending capacity of the great financial institutions like the Bank of England, the marine- and fire-insurance offices, and the private banks. This trend towards specialization, which is evident in other parts of the financial field, underlay the complaints of contemporaries that finance was ousting trade, though in retrospect it seems an understandable consequence of the country's social and economic development.

[1] Harrowby MSS., 'An Account of the Gross Produce of the several Duties in each [excise] Collection for the year ended Michaelmas 1741' shows total excise revenue as £1,764,522, of which London provided £903,117. I am indebted to Lord Harrowby for allowing me to see this MS.

[2] Based on inspection of the ledger indexes, Bank of England Record Office.

[3] Dickson, *Sun Insurance Office*, p. 77.

[4] The Accountant-General's ledgers are not in the Public Record Office. The Supreme Court Pay Office, which took over the Accountant-General's functions, informs me that they hold no ledgers, but only the individual suitors' records, for the period 1726–56.

PART FIVE

The Market
in Securities

18

The Turnover of Securities

I

THE development of a market in securities in London in the period 1688 to 1756 was one of the most important aspects of the Financial Revolution. For unless facilities had existed to enable lenders to sell to a third party their claim on the state to annual interest, the government's system of long-term borrowing would never have got off the ground. The state would have been obliged to promise repayment in a limited number of years — and to keep this promise. This would have effectually stopped it from borrowing on the scale it needed. The rise of the market solved the dilemma by — to adapt a Keynesian phrase — making debts that were permanent for the state liquid for the individual; subject only to the risk of capital loss if market prices fell. The last part of this book examines three aspects of this question: first, the turnover of securities; second, their yield, and the general question of interest rates; third, the techniques of the market itself, as it evolved into the formal Stock Exchange of the 1770s.

II

The procedures which the Exchequer worked out after 1688 for the assignment of the government debts which it administered were cumbersome and at certain points seriously defective. They contrasted with the easy and efficient methods of transfer used by the monied companies. The increase in the portion of the National Debt administered by these companies after 1717–20 was therefore of importance in speeding up the transfer of securities, and increasing their turnover in the market.

Little information is available about the turnover of short-dated Exchequer tallies. For although they were supposed to be registered at the Exchequer each time they were transferred, it seems that in practice this formality was omitted.[1] They thus became bearer bonds, like Exchequer bills or East India bonds. Procedure for transfer of long-term securities administered by the Exchequer, originally devised for the Tontine loan of 1693, was more strictly adhered to.[2] The Act allowed each lender to assign by deed or will the annuity due to him. (There was no procedure for assigning only a part of the annuity.) The assignment or devise was to be registered at the Exchequer within two months. No fee was payable for this. Since the lender was only entitled to draw his annuity during the lifetime of his nominees, he was required each time that he collected his half-yearly payment to produce a certificate that the nominee was still alive.[3] Presumably an assignee would have had to do the same. Similar methods of transfer were used in the annuity loans of 1695–1710, and the lottery loans of 1710–14. No stamp duties were imposed on transfers as they were on Bank, East India and South Sea stock.

This system had three consequences. First, the officials of the Exchequer of Receipt never knew at a given date who the proprietors of government annuities were. The equivalent of a dividend list in the Exchequer was a parchment roll recording all the annuity payments for a given half-year, against the names of those paid.[4] No addresses were included. The lists were obviously made up from the Standing Orders presented by each annuitant.[5] There can thus have been no guarantee that *AB* was entitled to the Order he presented; nor that, if he was a transferee, the requisite transfer procedure had been carried out. Further, the names were entered in a jumble anyway; one annuitant might appear two or three times under different Orders, so that even retrospective knowledge of who the annuitants were, and how much each owned, depended on an elaborate resorting into alphabetical order, which there is no evidence that the Exchequer undertook. From its point of view the records fulfilled the desired aim of recording every penny paid out.

---

[1] See above, pp. 76–8. Comparison of the lists for *repayment* of the 1743 Land Tax loan with the lists of original lenders shows the two were identical (P.R.O. E 401/2090–1, E 403/1935–7). Assignees must therefore have been treated as though they were the original lenders; the same would have applied to thieves unless the true owner notified the Exchequer.

[2] 4 Wm. and M. c. 3.

[3] S. xi. If the nominee lived in Scotland or abroad, proof of his life was to be sworn before a Baron of the Exchequer. Otherwise the certificate was to be from the minister and churchwarden of the nominee's parish. In 1694 (5 Wm. and M. c. 5) this was amended by allowing the annuitant to swear to the nominee's existence before a J.P., a clause repeated in subsequent Acts.

[4] P.R.O. E 403/1330–1692, Issue Rolls for Annuities 1696–1796.

[5] For Standing Orders see above, p. 76.

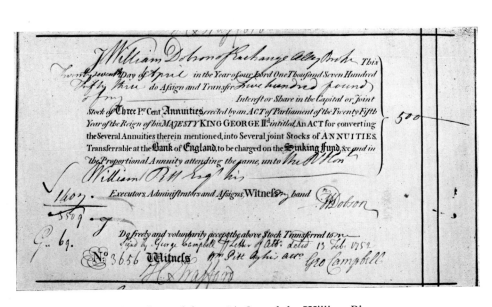

10a. Ledger account of Sir Peter Delmé in 5% stock, 1717–20

10b. Purchase of £500 3% Consols by William Pitt, 1752

11. Transfer of partly paid long annuity from Joseph Wilson to John Narbone, August 1706

The fact that the system was otherwise slow, obscure and inefficient was considered irrelevant.

Second, the cumbersome procedure for Exchequer assignments, the system of Standing Orders giving an effective title to payment, and the provisions about life-certificates, all opened the door to mistake and fraud, and therefore to dangerous uncertainties about the title to annuities. Standing Orders were constantly being lost, burned, and eaten by vermin, and Acts of Parliament were needed to give the holders redress.[1] Hence the title to an annuity had always to be examined as carefully as the title to land, as two eminent barristers explained to Parliament in 1733,[2] and transfers of annuities resembled in length and complexity a conveyance of land. Private errors were compounded by official carelessness. In 1697, for instance, Lord Ranelagh, Paymaster of the Forces in Flanders, was imprested large sums in reversionary annuity Orders for the current supply of the Army.[3] He assigned them by endorsing them to purchasers, without troubling to register the transfers at the Exchequer. Statutory relief was required in 1699 and again in 1719.[4] The records for 14% annuity payments at Michaelmas 1719 show that about £14,000 p.a., roughly 12% of the total, were still in Ranelagh's name.[5] He had then, of course, been dead for many years; his Orders had become bearer bonds of uncertain title. The third consequence followed from the first two. Exchequer annuities changed hands much less often than the stock of the monied companies, which was transferred by simpler and securer methods. It is necessary to describe these before discussing the evidence about turnover as a whole.

In contrast to the Exchequer's single-entry book-keeping, the companies used a double-entry system which must have derived from the practice of contemporary merchants.[6] Each proprietor of stock had a ledger account,

---

[1] For example, 7 Anne, c. 31, s. xxiii. Cf. Exchequer bills 'eaten by mice' and 'blown from aboard ship', and a bank-note 'torn to pieces by vermin', in Bank of England D. Ct. minutes at dates 14 and 21 January 1714 and 9 July 1719.

[2] See the opinions of Mr. Glanville and Mr. Bootle in *Parl. Hist.* ix. 65, 67, 30 April 1733, and the photograph of an annuity transfer on Plate 11.

[3] 9 Wm. III, c. 24.

[4] 11 Wm. III, c. 3, s. xii; 5 Geo. I, c. 2. The second Act gives the history of the episode.

[5] P.R.O. E 403/1400, Issue Roll for 14% long annuities 1 October 1719–25 March 1720.

[6] The similarity of the book-keeping methods used by both individuals and companies was presumably in turn due to the widespread adoption of the Italian double-entry system in the seventeenth century. There was probably also some borrowing of other countries' methods: for instance the Bank of England's transfer books are virtually identical to those of the Dutch East India Company, founded in 1602 (The Hague, Algemeen Rijksarchief, Oostindische Compagnie transfer books).

which was debited with sales and credited with purchases. The Bank of England kept separate indexes ('alphabets') the other two monied companies put the addresses in the ledgers. The title to stock was transferred by entry in a transfer book signed by buyer and seller: no further documentation was required. Each half year (or each year with government stock administered by the Bank) a dividend list was prepared from the ledger accounts, setting out the names of each owner of stock, the amount he held and the dividend due to him. When the proprietor or his representative came to collect his dividend he was given a payment warrant to present to the company cashier.[1] These methods ensured that the right people were paid (and not merely the owner of pieces of paper as at the Exchequer) and that the company knew at all times who the owners of its stock were, how much each of them held, and what transactions had occurred in it over a given period. It also kept the formalities involved in the transfer of title to a minimum.

Looking at the system in more detail, it seems clear that the main features of the form of stock transfer were already settled by the 1690s. Bank stock, for instance, was transferred as follows.[2]

I . . . this . . . Day of . . . in the Year of Our Lord One Thousand Six Hundred and . . . do Assign and Transfer . . . [pounds of] my Interest or Share in the Capital Stock and Fund of the Governor and Company of the Bank of England and all benefits arising thereby unto . . . his Executors and Assigns. Witness my hand

[*Signature*]

I . . . of . . . do freely & voluntarily accept the sum of . . . Transferr'd to me by . . . as abovesaid. Witness my Hand the day of the Date above written.
[*Witness*] [*Signature*]

This wording was retained up to the present century. From March 1696 transfers were printed, only the details being completed in ink. East India transfers in the early 1690s were similar in their wording to those of Bank stock. A written one dated 6 June 1694 runs as follows.[3]

---

[1] There is a bundle of printed warrants for unclaimed East India dividends in the Bank of England Record Office. The form of a warrant of 1730 was as follows (written words italicized): 'To the Committee of the Treasury. You may please to pay unto *Mr. Newdigate Owesley One shilling and five pence* being Four Pounds per cent. for one Half Years Dividend, due this day, on *£1. 16. 4* Capital Stock in the United Company of Merchants of England Trading to the East Indies, and take a Discharge for the same on the Back hereof.
LONDON, *25th December* 1730
Thomas Hort.'
[2] Bank of England Record Office, Bank stock transfer books.
[3] Bank of England Record Office, Old East India Company transfer books.

London the 6 June 1694

I John Smith of London Scrivr. Doe Sell Assigne & transferr unto Jacob Mazahod of Londo. Mercht. One thousand pounds of my Credit in the Generall Joint Stocke for East India with all present & future Proceeds except such Dividents [*sic*] as have been ordered to this day. Witness my hand

& ca. *Wm. Thorowgood*   Jon. Smith.

I Accept of the fforegoing Adventure on the Conditions Exprest in the Preamble dated 16 March 1664 Subject Nevertheless to the Alterations and Regulations of their Majesties Charter of the 11 Novr. 1693.

Jacob Mazahod

Signed in the presence of *Wm. Thorowgood.*

All stock transfers of the Old East India Company were written out in longhand, but from 1709 the United Company imitated the Bank's system of printed transfers. After several small changes the wording of the East India transfer became virtually identical with that of the Bank, and must have been based on it.[1]

I ... this ... day of ... in the Year of Our Lord One Thousand Seven Hundred and ... do assign and Transffer ... my Interest or Share in the Principal Stock and Fund, Additional Stock, Stock in Trade, Possessions, and Estates of the United Company of Merchants of England Trading to the East Indies and all the Benefits arising thereby unto ... Executors Administrators and Assigns

Witness my Hand

[*Signature*]

I Freely and Voluntarily accept the above Transffer.

[*Signature*]

Signed in the Presence of [*Signature*].

No transfer books survive for the South Sea Company for this period, but it appears from the company's minutes that it used a similar form.[2] Government stock administered by the Bank of England after 1715 was transferred by the same wording as Bank stock, with the addition of the title of the Act creating the stock and the words 'And in the Proportional Annuity attending the same', since the stock was fixed-interest and did not depend on a dividend

[1] Bank of England Record Office, United East India Company transfer books. The wording shown in the text was that adopted from 1 December 1730; previously the words 'Additional ... Estates of the' were omitted. From 2 October 1750 after 'East Indies' was added 'and a proportional part of the Fund due to the said Company'. The wording then remained the same until the nineteenth century.

[2] Add. MS. 25501, f. 70, South Sea Company D. Ct. Bk., 20 June 1723, a form of transfer for South Sea annuities virtually identical with that of Bank Stock. There are no surviving South Sea Stock transfer books. Those for South Sea annuities from 1791 are in the Bank of England Record Office.

being declared.[1] These government stock transfers were, like transfers of Exchequer annuities, unstamped. Company stock was stamped at a low fixed rate: 6*d.* from 1694 to 1698, 1*s.* from 1698 to 1712, 3*s.* 3*d.* from 1712 to 1714 and then 7*s.* 9*d.* until the end of the century. The terrors of *pro rata* transfer duties were reserved for a more prosperous age; brokerage (at $\frac{1}{8}$%) was a far more serious expense than stamp duty in the eighteenth century.[2]

The similarity of forms of transfer of government and allied stock between the 1690s and the middle of the eighteenth century suggests that Mortimer's description of transfer business, first written in 1761, is applicable to the whole period.[3] The method was simple. The seller of stock ascertained the buyer's name and address, filled out a slip in the form '*A.B.* of . . . [*address*] £1,000 Bank Stock to *C.D.* of . . .', and handed it to the transfer clerk standing under the relevant letter of the alphabet. The clerk verified from the ledger that the seller had the requisite amount of stock, and filled in the first part of the transfer. He then called out the seller's name. The seller and buyer attended, the latter having the purchase money ready. Each signed the transfer book. Their signatures were witnessed by the clerk. The buyer paid the seller his money, and obtained from him a printed receipt, witnessed by the clerk, in the following form:

London, the 20 Day of *Janry.* 1725
Received of *Henry Edwards Esq.* the Sum of *Two hundred & five pounds* being⎫
in full for *Two hundred pounds* in the Joint-Stock of South-Sea Annuities, this ⎬ £205
day transferr'd in the said Company's Books unto the said *Henry Edwards Esq*⎭
              By John Grove
683
Witness *A. Anderson*[4]

On the face of it, this procedure should have led to the company transfer offices being crowded with buyers and sellers all day and half the night. Three factors modified this in practice: restricted times for stock transfers, the prevalence of jobbing purchases, and the use of attorneys. Transfers were allowed only on a limited number of days, and within specified hours. No transfer business was allowed on Sundays or holy days (in 1754, for instance,

---

[1] Bank of England Record Office, transfer books for government stock, beginning with the 5%s of 1715.

[2] Stamp duty rates traced from the transfer books for Bank and East India stock in the Bank of England Record Office. For brokerage rates see below, p. 493.

[3] Thomas Mortimer, *Every Man his own Broker*, pp. 130 ff.

[4] Bank of England Museum, no. 166. There is also a specimen receipt in Mortimer, op. cit., p. 144.

there were forty-six holy days, only five of which coincided with Sundays). On the other days in the year the Bank of England allowed transfers on Tuesday to Friday inclusive, before noon; the East India and South Sea companies allowed transfers every weekday before one o'clock. This in turn was modified for particular sorts of stock: for instance the South Sea Company allowed transfers of South Sea stock on Monday, Wednesday and Friday and of South Sea annuities on Tuesday, Thursday and Saturday. Further, the ledgers were shut once or twice yearly, generally for a month, to prepare dividends.[1] All this tended to reduce available transfer days to not much more than two hundred a year, ending at latest at one o'clock.[2]

The second factor tending to reduce numbers at the transfer offices was the development of a system of stock-jobbing, in which the transfer-clerks themselves, acting as jobbers, played an important part. This is discussed in Chapter 20. The third factor was the use of powers of attorney. These were either particular — a power to buy only, sell only or draw dividends only — or general, a combination of all these. At least as early as the 1720s printed versions of these documents were available, and were extensively used.[3] At Lady Day 1724, for example, 4,662 proprietors of Bank Stock were due to receive dividends. About 2,000 of them used attorneys to do so. Approximately a quarter (567) of the 2,000 were foreigners; the remainder were English residents.[4] This use of attorneys was convenient, but risky. Mortimer warned his readers of the danger of empowering a man of doubtful substance.[5] From the standpoint of the companies, powers of attorney opened the way to fraud, and they therefore did their best to restrict their use. Thus, in October 1721 the South Sea Company restricted the right of residents within the London Bills of Mortality to use an attorney to those who satisfied the Accountant that they were ill.[6] In the following month, the Bank of England followed suit, by confining the right for London residents to those

---

[1] The shutting always cut across calendar months, so that some stock transfers were possible in each month.

[2] Based on Mortimer, op. cit. p. 168; *The Weekly News and Register* for the 1730s; and J. Castaing, *The Course of the Exchange*, which shows the dates at which transfer books were closed. The books for government stock were closed once a year, those for other stocks (Bank, East India, etc.) twice a year.

[3] For types of power see Mortimer, op. cit., pp. 159–60. There is a collection of powers of attorney relating to the South Sea Company in Add. MS. 27871, and another relating to government securities generally in Add. MS. 34195. The Bank of England Record Office has the originals of all powers relating to Bank stock.

[4] Bank stock dividend list for Lady Day 1724, Bank of England Record Office.

[5] Mortimer, loc. cit.

[6] Add. MS. 25500, f. 111, South Sea D. Ct. Bk., 5 October 1721.

known personally to the directors or chief officers of the Bank.[1] These decisions seem to have been taken as a result of successful frauds on the South Sea Company by Edmund Cheesborough and Benjamin Shambler; in March 1722 this type of offence became a felony without benefit of clergy.[2] How effective the attempt to cut down Londoners' use of attorneys was is uncertain. Those who were ill or had influence must have continued to use them, as the example of the 1724 Bank stock dividend shows. The companies were even prepared to accept casual notes in lieu of formal powers from proprietors they trusted.[3]

II

The remainder of this chapter discusses the turnover of stock transferred by the methods previously described. Table 83 shows the average size of certain transfers at different dates. Only (3) was transferred at the Exchequer.

It seems from this that the average unit of government stock transferred was fairly constant over the period, while the average transfer unit of Bank and East India stock markedly increased. This is not surprising in view of the more plutocratic structure of ownership in the companies, discussed in Chapter 11, and the need to transfer stock in amounts of £500 or more if voting rights were to go with it; hence a Dutch reference of 1733 to £500 East India stock as 'a Share' ('*een Actie*').[4]

Table 84 multiplies the stock transferred in the quarter or half-year by four or two in order to make an approximate assessment of total turnover, and its relation to nominal capital.

The ratio of turnover to nominal capital declined in all these stocks. Consols at the mid-century, for instance, had little more than a third of the

[1] Bank of England D. Ct. Bk. I, f. 32, 9 November 1721; the transferor had to be known to one or more directors, the Cashiers, Accountant-General, Chief Officer of the transfer books, or any two of them.

[2] 8 Geo. I, c. 22. Cheesborough impersonated a South Sea stockholder; Shambler drew South Sea dividends by a forged power of attorney, Add. MS. 25568, ff. 9–10, South Sea Company Committee of Lawsuits 30 June and 31 July 1722.

[3] Add. MS. 27871, f. 11, for examples of these unstamped and handwritten notes.

[4] Amsterdam, Gemeente Archief, Archief Brants, 1741, Simon Bevel's ledger, East India stock account at 1 December 1733 (N.S.).

TABLE 83

Average units of stock transferred 1704–55

Stock	1704 July–Dec. incl.	1716 whole year	1718 Oct.–Dec. incl.	1727 Oct.–Dec. incl.	1731 July–Dec. incl.	1755 Jan.–March incl.
	£	£	£	£	£	£
1. Bank stock . .	468	..	1,198	1,122	..	1,002
2. East India stock .	622	..	..	1,107	..	820
3. 'Bankers' annuities' .	..	320*	..	..	..	..
4. 5% (1717) stock .	..	..	362	..	..	..
5. 3% (1726) stock .	..	..	..	..	304	316
6. 3% Consols . .	..	..	..	..	..	381

Source: Except for the Bankers' annuities, the figures are from the transfer books at the Bank of England Record Office. The East India figures for 1704 are for the Old or London Company. The transfer book for Bankers' annuities is P.R.O. E 407/17. The figures for 1755 for Bank stock, Consols and the 3% stock of 1726 are from Mrs. A. C. Carter, 'Transfers of Certain Public Stocks . . . 1 Jan. to 31 March 1755', *BIHR* xxviii (1955), 202.

* The average price. The average annuity transferred was £18 18s. 0d. p.a.

turnover of the equivalently large 5% stock in 1718. There was the same trend in Bank and East India stock, though the latter still had twice the former's turnover at the end of the period. The earlier East India figures confirm, and indeed exaggerate, Sir Josiah Child's claims in 1692 that

without Restraint, Cramping, or taking care for Rotations or Changes in the East India Company, the whole Stock . . . is in a kindly, natural and continual changing Motion; insomuch that the Value of the whole Stock, once in Two Years, or thereabouts, changes Owners,

though Child underestimated the extent to which speculators continuously buying and selling to each other weighted East India turnover figures both then and later.[1]

Although the turnover of stock transferred by company methods declined over the period, it was higher even at the end of it than that of Exchequer

[1] Child's statement is in *HCJ* x. 705, 17 November 1692. For jobbing in East India stock see below, Ch. 20.

TABLE 84

Ratio of stock turnover to nominal capital 1704–55

1 Stock	2 Period of transfers	3 Approximate total transferred in year	4 Nominal capital	3 as % of 4
		£	£	
Bank stock . .	1704 July–December	531,042	2,201,172	24·1
	1718 October–December	2,463,812	5,559,996	44·3
	1727 October–December	2,181,824	8,959,996	24·4
	1755 January–March	1,519,664	11,686,800	13·0
East India stock .	1704 July–December	1,611,769	1,574,609	102·4
	1727 October–December	1,643,072	3,194,080	51·4
	1755 January–March	856,033	3,194,080	26·8
5% (1717) . .	1718 October–December	4,868,628	9,534,358	51·1
3% (1726) . .	1731 July–December	507,953	1,000,000	50·8
3% Consols .	1755 January–March	1,684,736	9,137,821	18·4

Source: As in Table 83.

annuities had been at the beginning of it, if the Bankers' annuities, the only stock managed at the Exchequer for which transfer records survive, were in any way typical.[1] In 1716, the last full year of its existence, there were 159 transfers of these annuities, of which 137 were for money. The total capital transferred was £43,960; if all the transfers had been for money nearly £51,000 would have changed hands, about 4% of the £1,328,526 capital of the stock.[2] Given the clumsy forms of Exchequer management described earlier, this relatively small turnover might be expected. It is therefore probable that one of the effects of the conversion of the greater part of

[1] For the origin of these annuities in the Bankers' Debt of 1672 see above, p. 44.
[2] Transfer book for Bankers' annuities 1716, P.R.O. E 407/17. The twenty-two remaining transfers were for nominal consideration, 'natural love and affection' or 'a competent sum of money'.

Exchequer annuities into stock managed at the Bank or South Sea House in 1717–20 was an increase in their velocity of circulation. As a pamphleteer wrote in 1729, the Act of 1717

at once removed the Payment of above Nine Millions and a Half from the ancient Course of the Exchequer to the Bank; and this change of our old Constitution, by turning the Bank into the Exchequer, was the first Step that led the Way to the fatal South-Sea Scheme, which is little more than the Copy of this Act. . . . This Incorporation of the National Debt hath certainly put the Publick Credit on the most precarious Bottom, by facilitating and increasing the ruinous Trade of Stock-Jobbing, which it would have been impossible to have carried on to such a Degree, as it hath been, if our Debts had continued in their old Shape, and been paid at the Exchequer. . . .[1]

This lament can be rewritten as the proposition that the change of form, by making the securities more attractive to both professional and amateur buyers, increased demand and turnover, and therefore helped to increase the market price. The conversions of 1717–20 may therefore have been one of a number of factors in the period 1720–40 tending to raise the price of fixed-interest securities, and correspondingly to lower the long-term rate of interest.

The evidence so far reviewed can be supplemented by the figures for aggregate annual transfers, shown in Appendix D. These are subject to certain reservations: in particular no records exist for turnover of stock managed at South Sea House. But they justify a number of conclusions.[2] First, projection of the pre-1720 figures forward confirms that, although aggregate turnover increased, the *rate* of turnover declined. Thus, a median of the figures for 1718 (17,172) and 1719 (13,740) may be taken as 15,000 transfers. The total stock available for transfer was about £22m., In 1754, when total stock was £43·8m., the number of transfers should therefore have been about 30,000. It was in fact 21,000. Similarly, if £43·8m. stock in 1754 gave rise to 21,000 transfers, £71·4m. — the total of the funded debt at that date — would have given rise only to about 35,000 transfers — not much more than twice the figure for 1718–19, when the amount of stock was three times as small.

Second, as a specific instance of a declining rate of turnover, the number of annual transfers in Bank and East India stock was fairly constant, despite the considerable increase in both companies' nominal capital over the period. Indeed, in the 1730s and 1740s East India turnover was tending to fall.

---

[1] [William Pulteney], *Some Considerations on the National Debts*, pp. 69, 71.
[2] The derivation of the figures is explained in the notes to Appendix D.

This is consistent both with the evidence previously discussed, and with the reduction in the number of market quotations for East India stock. Thorold Rogers, for instance, gives prices for it for 312 days in 1732, and 313 in 1733, but for only 218 days in 1753, and 181 in 1754.[1] The failure of Bank and East India turnover to expand was probably partly due to the tendency for new issues of stock to be taken up by existing proprietors, so that the amount available for purchasers was not correspondingly increased. Second, the market demand for these stocks was primarily from those interested in securing a vote (£500 stock) for the Court of Directors, and from big institutions like the London banks and insurance companies. This is reflected in the high average size of Bank and East India transfers compared with those of government stock. It is significant that 3% Consols, with a nominal capital rather less than that of Bank stock, had about three times its number of transfers. A third factor was presumably the tendency for market demand to be diverted to new government stocks in the 1740s. Fourthly, the development of a Stock Exchange, in which speculative purchases outweighed real ones, and for whose purposes only marginal transfers of stock were needed, must have tended to reduce turnover.[2]

Though the trend in Bank stock turnover (for which the most complete figures are available) was fairly uniform, there were important short-term fluctuations in it. Some of these must have been partly technical. For instance, when the nominal capital was increased by new subscriptions turnover would tend to increase correspondingly, until the pattern of ownership once more settled down. This would help to explain the larger turnover of 1697–1700, 1710–14 and 1722–6; in 1742 there is no marked increase. On the other hand, the political excitement of 1697–1700 and 1710–14 must also have affected the figures. This is clearly true of the threefold increase in the number of transfers in 1710 and 1711; while apprehension about the Hanoverian succession kept turnover at a high rate until 1715. The violent rise in 1720 is a by-product of the South Sea Bubble, the increase in 1746 a by-product of the Jacobite invasion. Lastly, there does not seem to be any marked correlation between the market price of stock and its annual turnover. The price of Bank stock in 1711–15, for instance, was rising, while turnover was falling. In 1717–19 it was rising while turnover was constant. In 1720 prices and turnover rose together. In the 1730s turnover and prices were both fairly constant. The same seems to be true of

[1] J. E. Thorold Rogers, *History of Agriculture and Prices*, vii (Oxford, 1902).
[2] This development, and the corresponding decline in the number of jobbers in Bank and East India stock over the period, are discussed in Ch. 20.

East India stock. In the early 1750s, for instance, its price was a good deal higher than it had been in the 1730s, but turnover was the same. In general the trend over the period for both companies was towards a higher market price and reduced dividends, while turnover was either constant or reduced.

19

The Rate of Interest in Theory and Practice

IT is clear from the discussion in previous chapters that the terms on which the English government was borrowing for both long- and short-term purposes moved steadily in its favour over the period. In the early 1690s it was paying up to 14% for long-term loans, and up to 8% for short-term ones. By the early 1750s it was able to borrow much larger sums for under 4%. The chart shows this diagrammatically. It gives the changes in short-term *rates*, and adds the *yields* on government long annuities and 3% stock, on East India stock — the leading equity of the period — and on East India bonds.[1]

Several conclusions can be drawn from these graphs. First, the long-term rate of interest, as measured by the yield on government stock, was between 7% and 14% in the 1690s, fell to 6–7% in the period 1702–14, and then fell to about 5% in the immediate post-war period. In the period 1720–40 it showed a fairly steady secular decline, and from the mid-1730s was at or below 3%. With the renewal of war on a serious scale in 1744 it moved above 4% again, only to fall with the peace which made Pelham's conversion of 1750 possible. Noticeable short-term fluctuations on this trend were the abnormal behaviour of interest rates during the South Sea Bubble, when owing to the frantic demand for money to buy securities short-term rates soared while the yield on long-term securities sank well below 3%;[2] and the rise in long-term interest rates during the last three years of wars: 1711–13 and 1746–8 (1695–7 was a partial exception owing to the very high rates

---

[1] Cf. also the careful yield charts in A. H. John, 'Insurance Investment and the London Money Market of the 18th Century', *Economica*, xx (1953), 137 and L. S. Pressnell, 'The Rate of Interest in the Eighteenth Century', in *Studies in the Industrial Revolution presented to T. S. Ashton* (ed. L. S. Pressnell, 1960), pp. 211–14. For a general discussion of interest rates in England and Europe in the eighteenth century see Sidney Homer, *A History of Interest Rates* (Rutgers University Press, 1963), chs. xi and xii, esp. the graph of yields on English government stock at p. 158. Cf. also J. M. Low, 'The Rate of Interest: British Opinion in the Eighteenth Century', *Manchester School*, xxii (1954), 115.

[2] For evidence that money was borrowed during the Bubble at up to 60% see above, p. 191.

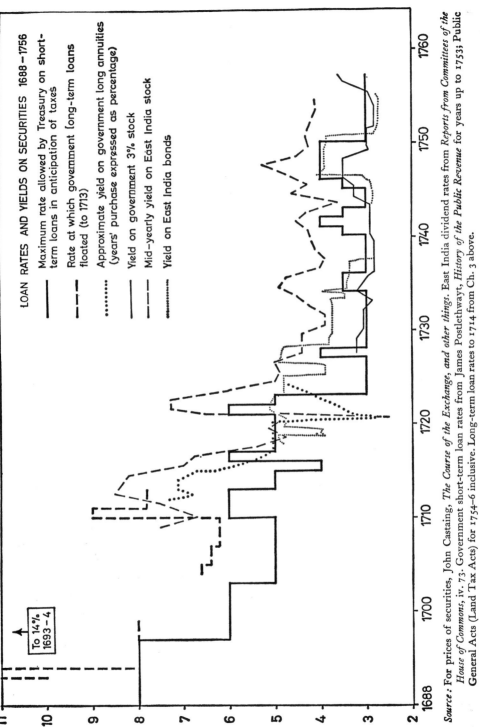

LOAN RATES AND YIELDS ON SECURITIES 1688–1756

Maximum rate allowed by Treasury on short-term loans in anticipation of taxes

Rate at which government long-term loans floated (to 1713)

Approximate yield on government long annuities (years' purchase expressed as percentage)

Yield on government 3% stock

Mid-yearly yield on East India stock

Yield on East India bonds

To 14% 1693–4

Source: For prices of securities, John Castaing, *The Course of the Exchange, and other things*. East India dividend rates from *Reports from Committees of the House of Commons*, iv. 73. Government short-term loan rates from James Postlethwayt, *History of the Public Revenue* for years up to 1753; Public General Acts (Land Tax Acts) for 1754–6 inclusive. Long-term loan rates to 1714 from Ch. 3 above.

which the government had to pay when the system of long-term borrowing began in 1693). The same basic pattern was repeated in the second half of the eighteenth century, with long-term interest rates moving up in war-time and sharply up at the end of wars (1780–3, 1797–1801, 1811–14), though in this period the *secular* trend of long-term interest rates, as measured by the yield on Consols, was gently upwards, rather than gently downwards as it had been to the middle of the eighteenth century. The primary reason for this change must have been the very much larger quantity of fixed-interest government stock marketed in the period (roughly £590m. 1756–1815 compared with roughly £75m. 1693–1755), which drove down its price.[1] Probably too there was greater competition for available funds from the private sector, making rates of interest higher all round.

The second conclusion from the chart is that rates of interest in the private sector tended to follow the same trend as yields on government stock. This was true for instance of East India stock and East India bonds. The Sun Fire Office was usually charging 5% on loans on its own shares and on pledges in the 1720s, but from the mid-1730s only 4%; and less on some mortgages.[2] From 1746 to 1752 it charged 5% for loans, then 4% from 1752 to 1756 4½% from 1756 to 1758, 4% again from 1758 to 1761, 4½% from 1761 to 1762 and 5% from 1762 to 1767.[3] The concurrence of these trends with the yield on government securities is, however, subject to two qualifications. First, contemporaries denied that rates in the London market were necessarily indicative of those elsewhere, as will be seen later. Second, the East India Company was owed such large sums by the government that its stock was not truly distinct from government stock itself. These qualifications make generalization about the rate of interest, and comparison of gilt-edged and equity yields, much more difficult than they are for the more developed capital market of the nineteenth century. It does not, however, make them impossible or meaningless.

Third, the yield on East India bonds was actually above the rate of long-term interest (as measured by the yield on government stock) during the 1720s and early 1730s, though below the yield on East India stock. From the mid-1730s the yield on bonds and on 3% stock tended to converge. The yield on East India bonds was highly dependent on their nominal rate: thus the yield fell abruptly in 1728, and again in 1737, when the nominal rate was reduced respectively to 4% and 3%.[4] This suggests that the demand for bonds was relatively constant, and that those who held government stock

[1] For these figures see Table 1 on p. 10, above.   [2] Sun Fire Office ledgers 1728–62.
[3] Dickson, *Sun Insurance Office*, p. 257.   [4] See Table 67 on p. 411, above.

were not prepared to switch into short-dated bonds instead — for otherwise their price would have risen, and that of government stock would have fallen, until the two yields converged. On the other hand, the yield on Consols or its earlier equivalents clearly helped to decide the timing of reductions of East India bond interest rates, and the willingness of proprietors of bonds to acquiesce in these reductions. Lastly, and connected with this point, the gap between government loan rates and private rates in London, and between long- and short-term rates, which were quite wide at the start of the period, gradually lessened towards the mid-eighteenth century. This suggests that a series of relatively separate and imperfect money-markets were becoming unified as technique improved and financial stability increased.

It is interesting to compare English rates of interest in this period with Dutch ones. Contemporaries always pointed to Holland as a land of cheap capital, and a writer of 1737 was merely restating an accepted point when he wrote that

in Holland they have such a plenty of Money already, that on Bullion, or coined Silver, on Jewels and Things not perishable, they lend at 1 or $1\frac{1}{2}$ per Cent. and on Goods and Merchandizes, Ships or Vessels, 2 or $2\frac{1}{2}$ per Cent. . . .[1]

How far does the available evidence bear out this theme, originally devised by Child, Barbon, Yarranton and other later Stuart economists? Table 85 brings together four series of interest rates from Dutch sources. The first and second are from the business ledgers of Quirijn Brants & Son, and of Simon Bevel. The third is from the registers of loans recorded before the Justices of Amsterdam (*Registers van Schepenkennissen*). The fourth is from an index of loans recorded in the Amsterdam Notarial Archives, which is being constructed by Professor Earl J. Hamilton in connection with his forthcoming work on John Law. When consulted (1961) this index covered the years 1711–25.[2] The periods of time for which the Brants and Bevel loans were made are not recorded in their ledgers, and probably varied from a few months to several years. The loans recorded before the Justices of Amsterdam were for from one to ten years, with a period of five, six, or seven commonest. The loans in Professor Hamilton's index were nearly all for three months to a year. Where more than one rate is indicated, the lenders were charging different rates to different borrowers at the same time. Thus, in the 1730s Quirijn Brants was asking some of his borrowers to pay only $3\frac{1}{2}\%$ at the same time that he was charging others 6%.

---

[1] *Considerations upon a Proposal for lowering the Interest* (1737), p. 26.
[2] I am indebted to Professor Hamilton for allowing me to see this data.

TABLE 85

Some Dutch rates of interest 1690–1752

Date	1	2	3	4
	%	%	%	%
1690–1730 . .	..	..	5, 4½, 4	..
1709–13 . .	..	4, 4¼, 4½	..	..
1712 . . .	6	..	..	..
1712–13 . .	..	..	..	5
1714 . . .	..	4½, 4	..	..
1715–16 . .	..	4	..	..
1716 . . .	4	..	..	..
1717–19 . .	..	..	..	3½, 4
1721–3 . . .	..	3	..	..
1724–5 . .	4	3	..	..
1725 . . .	..	..	..	3½
1725–9 . .	..	3½, 3	..	..
1729–35 . .	..	3½, 3	..	..
1730–37 . .	3½–6	..	..	..
1730–40 . .	..	..	4, 3¾, 3½	..
1740 . . .	3½–4	..	..	..
1741–44 . .	3, 3½	..	..	..
1741–45 . .	..	..	3, 3½	..
1747 . . .	3½	..	..	..
1748–49 . .	..	..	4	..
1750 . . .	..	..	4, 3½	..
1751 . . .	2½–4½	..	..	..
1752 . . .	4	..	..	..

Source: 1. Ledgers of Quirijn Brants en Zoon 1715–63, Amsterdam, Gemeente Archief, Archief Brants, 565–7.
2. Ledgers of Simon Bevel 1710–36, ibid. 1736–42.
3. Amsterdam, Gemeente Archief, Registers van Schepenkennissen.
4. Amsterdam, Gemeente Archief, Hamilton index of loans in Notarial Archives 1711–25.

These figures indicate that Dutch interest rates followed an approximately similar trend to English ones. But the high point of the curve at the beginning of the period was much lower ($4\frac{1}{2}$–5%), and a rate of 3% was reached earlier, in the 1720s rather than the 1730s. In the later 1730s 3% seems to be the common rate; one loan recorded before the Amsterdam Justices in December 1737 was at $2\frac{1}{2}$%. In the 1690s, therefore, the gap between Dutch and English rates was considerable. In the period 1700–30 it was of the order of 1%. After 1730, however, the divergence seems a good deal less than the sort of English comment quoted earlier would suggest.[1] In comparison with their thrifty neighbours, the English reached the mercantilist goal of 3% a good deal more quickly, and from a less favourable starting-point.

II

Contemporaries were well aware of the fall in the interest on public loans, but differed about its causes and significance. In the preamble to finance Acts of 1717 and 1742, the fall in 'the Common Rate of Interest for money' observable since 1714 was ascribed to 'Your Majesty's most auspicious government'.[2] The logic of this contention, which might be called the Confidence Argument, was presumably that the success of Hanoverian government had inspired ever-greater confidence in its trustworthiness as a borrower. A parallel case was that it had cheapened private borrowing (since private citizens felt more secure) and thus made cheaper government borrowing possible. The reduction of interest on the National Debt in 1717, for instance, was specifically designed to bring government interest rates down to those paid by private debtors.[3] Alternatively, and implausibly, the statute of 1714 reducing from 6% to 5% the maximum rate allowed by the Usury Laws on private loans was invoked as a sufficient cause. The reduction of 1717, declared Pulteney in 1729, was

so natural a Consequence of quiet and peaceful Times, that the Hopes and Appearance of it only in the year 1717 had done this to the Hands of our Ministers . . . they could not any longer have delayed lowering the Interest of the Redeemable National Debts from 6 to 5 per Cent. which was then the legal Interest of the Kingdom, and had been so for some Years before, by Virtue of an Act passed in the late Queen's Reign. This was owned by a very intelligent Person (a Member of the House of

[1] See above, p. 473.   [2] Geo. I, c. 8, 15 Geo. II, c. 13.   [3] See above, p. 83.

Commons, and a Director of the Bank, since deceased) who declared, upon the late Debates, that the Sinking Fund was not the Product of any one Man's Invention, but the natural Consequence of the Act of Parliament, in the Queen's Time, for reducing Interest.[1]

The argument, allowing for its muddled exposition, seems to be a restatement of the thesis debated between Child and Locke in the previous century that statutory reduction of the legal maximum rate would lead eventually to a general fall in interest rates.

As the yield on securities approached 3% towards the end of the 1720s, a new argument began to appear. This ascribed the rise of security prices in the London market, and the subsequent fall in yields, to artificial or special causes. Thus Sir Nathaniel Gould in 1726, alluding in passing to the importance of diminished capital risk in increasing the price of securities, contended that the real determinant was speculative buying in Exchange Alley. The general level of prices there was such that a conversion of the interest on the National Debt to 3% was possible in theory. It would, however, be inadvisable in practice, unless 'the real Proportion of our ordinary Necessities for Money to our Capacity and Disposition to supply them, have been so far altered as to admit of it'.[2] According to him, the yield on government stock was not an adequate measure of this proportion, for the price of securities was not determined by real purchases: 'By which Purchases of late Years the Prices of our Stocks have so seldom been determined, that perhaps it may be more reasonable in this Case to conclude from an Enquiry into the Rate of Interest ordinarily reserved on private loans'.[3] He was, however, prepared to argue that a reduction in the interest allowed on government loans would 'quickly reduce either the Price of our Publick Securities or the Rate of Interest in such Private Transactions as aforesaid'.[4]

The thesis that the price of government stock was determined by special causes was restated in 1734 in a tract written by William Allen, a Pembrokeshire landowner. Allen, who dedicated his work unhopefully to the Duke of Newcastle, thought that 'The Interest of our British Landholders has been declining several Years last past.'[5] He was particularly concerned with the plight of the remoter counties (like his own) which did not profit from

---

[1] [William Pulteney], *Some Considerations on the National Debts*, p. 68.

[2] Sir Nathaniel Gould, *An Essay on the Publick Debts of this Kingdom* (1726), pp. 76, 82–83.

[3] Ibid., p. 84.   [4] Ibid.

[5] William Allen, *Ways and Means to Raise the Value of Land* (1736), p. 1. It appears from a note on p. 14 that the pamphlet was written in 1734.

the contiguity of a large town, or the multiplier effects of government contracts in war-time. For want of better investments, landowners in these counties, Allen asserted, had to fall back on enclosures.[1] And when they wanted to borrow they found it costly.

Money, except in those Counties that are within Sixty or Seventy Miles of London, is not in general to be obtained at low Interest, nor under four per Cent. and a Mortgage for it; and then it must be in a Maritime County, or near a great Trading Town. Vast Sums of Money at London, got by South-Sea, Stock-Jobbing, &c. being in few Hands, lower the Interest of Money there; perhaps above two Thirds of the Nation's Cash are the Property of those who reside in and about that City.[2]

Allen concluded with a programme for relief of his class: it included the prosecution of sea-war rather than land-war; lowering of servants' wages; more export of ale; preventing colonial ships from taking wine instead of beer back to the colonies; hindering Irish distilling and the smuggling of meat from Ireland; and preventing the mainland American colonies from shipping food to the West Indies. To such 'mere gentry', Exchange Alley must have seemed far away. Its ill-understood activities merely confirmed their suspicions of the great London world of wealth, power and influence from which they felt themselves to be excluded.

Allen's contention that the capital market was imperfect was supported by several of the pamphleteers who debated Sir John Barnard's proposed reduction of interest in 1737. It was admitted by a supporter of the scheme that 'It is the Force of Money drawn from all Parts of the Country into one Place, that has operated so strongly to reduce the Rate of Interest of the Publick Securities'.[3] Another writer, opposing the reduction on just these grounds, stated that

Some Arguments might be brought to confirm what I advance concerning the Rate of Interest, from the Price of other Things regulated by that rate; as Money lent on Mortgages, Jewels, Plate, and other Pledges. . . . These, I should think, would be better Standards to judge of the natural Rate of Interest, than the Price of Stocks fluctuating much from other Causes. From this it would seem, as if the natural Use of Money in most parts of England were rather above than under 4 per Cent.[4]

[1] Ibid., p. 6. Allen says that for this reason more enclosures were to be seen on the Milford to Bristol road than on the Gloucester to London road.

[2] Allen, op. cit., pp. 8–9.

[3] *Reasons For the more speedy Lessening the National Debt and Taking off . . . Taxes* (1737), p. 11.

[4] *Reasons against Lowering the interest of the Redeemable National Debt* (1737), p. 21.

Another form of this argument was that in London itself private loans were made at rates well above the yield on government stock. There was no reason to fear that the government could borrow at 3% to pay off its 4% creditors, wrote one of Barnard's critics, 'When all the Traders in London, who have to borrow Money, willingly pay 5*l.* per Cent.'[1] Virtually the same contention was made from an opposite point of view in 1750 by a supporter of the recent reduction of the government's debts to 3½%. He argued that 'the industrious Labourer and Manufacturer' were forced to pay from 5% to 10% for money, in contravention of the usury laws. The reduction of interest would free them from this bondage by diverting capital from the funds into trade.[2]

The most eloquent and consistent exponent of the view that the return on government stock was the true determinant of private rates of interest was Sir John Barnard himself. He argued in Parliament during the debates of 1737 that the connection between the two rates was self-evident.

that the rate of interest upon public securities has always had, and always will have, a great influence upon the rate of interest between man and man, is what, I believe, Sir, no gentleman will question ... the natural rate of interest upon public securities will always be lower than the natural rate of interest upon private; therefore the only method of reducing the latter is, to reduce the former; and ... then, you may safely ... reduce the legal.[3]

He added that the price of government stock was high because the government had been so punctual in paying its creditors (the Confidence Argument again),

for by the long and regular payment of the interest upon such securities, and by the growing provision we have made for paying off the principal by degrees, they are got into such credit, that no man will lend upon a private security for the same interest he can have upon a public; except a very few persons who have large sums, which they are willing to lend at the same interest upon mortgages of land only.[4]

A reduction of interest on the Funded Debt was therefore (according to him) a necessary condition of cheaper capital in the economy as a whole.

The argument to this stage may be summarized as follows. Contemporaries were well aware of the decline over the period 1700–40 in the yield on government stock, and on allied securities such as those of the Bank of

---

[1] *A Speech Without-Doors Addressed to the National Creditors for the Redeemables at 4l. per Cent.*, p. 10.

[2] *A Copy of a Letter wrote to a Member of Parliament* (1750), pp. 18–20.

[3] *Parl. Hist.* x. 75, 28 March 1737.   [4] Ibid. 84.

England and East India Company. Explanations for the fall in the rate of interest (as so measured) divided into three main categories: the Confidence Argument (Barnard); the first type of Special Causes Argument, that the price-level in Exchange Alley was determined by speculative rather than real purchases (Gould); and the second type of this argument, that security prices in London were a function of high demand peculiar to that area, and did not necessarily affect provincial interest rates (Allen). By adjusting theory to take account of the more sophisticated financial world that had developed after 1688, this debate advanced a stage beyond the Locke–Child controversies of Charles II's reign. It assumed a causal relationship between the rate of interest and political stability; between the rate of interest and increased demand for securities (whether this demand was real or speculative); between the rate of interest and an increased supply of money or, alternatively, a concentration of money turnover in a limited area. It also conceded that the yield on government securities in London was not necessarily reflected in private loan-rates, either there or in the provinces, in other words that the capital market was an imperfect one.

The exposition of these relationships, was, however, neither rigorous nor free from confusion. As an example, Sir John Barnard's previously-quoted argument may be examined.[1] Barnard states that the 'natural rate of interest upon public securities', that is, the yield on government stock, tends to determine private rates of interest. He does not explain why. It may be assumed that he observed that private rates were falling, though tending to fall at a slower rate, and assumed that this relationship was a constant without bothering to examine it further. In any case, he then gets into a muddle between the market yield, the nominal rate of dividend paid on stock, and the legal maximum rate of interest. If his argument was correct that the first of these determined the price of capital in the economy as a whole it was, strictly speaking, unnecessary for him to advocate a lowering of either of the other two.

What sort of argument might Barnard have used to support his thesis? Perhaps it could have run something like this. Over a given period a given flow of savings becomes available for lending. Part of this will, assuming sufficient security, be invested in government stock, the rest will go to private borrowers. As the market yield on government stock falls, owing to this steady new demand for it, some investors will switch their funds into private loans in order to get a higher return. The more the yield on government stock falls, the more this process will occur. The rates paid by private

---

[1] For Barnard's argument see above, p. 478.

borrowers will therefore tend to decline in step with the yield on government stock, but at one stage behind it. An individual private lender cannot afford to ignore this state of affairs and charge a very high rate since there will always be other lenders who will charge a more reasonable one in order to obtain the business. It will be seen that this argument requires at least three assumptions. The first is a growth of the supply of loanable funds (portion of the National Income devoted to investment instead of consumption) rather greater than the growth in the opportunities for investing them. The second is a fairly perfect arbitrage between the two sectors of the capital market. This implies homogeneity among owners of capital, such that any capitalist is willing to switch his funds at any time to the point of highest return. The third, a variant of the second, is an absence of any substantial difference between the markets for long- and short-term capital, so that the shorthand term 'the rate of interest' can be used realistically to denote a complex of varying rates. The simultaneous existence of higher and, even usurious, interest rates can be explained by differences in degrees of security for loans.

The extent to which this interpretation of Barnard's argument can plausibly be taken as a description of early eighteenth-century conditions is discussed later. What must be noted first is that from the 1740s onwards the connection between public and private rates, on which Barnard insisted, was regarded with growing scepticism. Joseph Massie argued in 1750 that the yield on government stock and the price paid for capital by individuals were separately determined.[1] The former was influenced by public confidence in the government's good faith. 'Publick Faith is like a Merchant, whose Credit falls and rises as his Trade declines or prospers', so that in peacetime government yields are lower than private rates, while in years of crisis like 1745 they are higher. On the other hand, 'the natural Rate of Interest is governed by the Profits of Trade to Particulars', and is independent of the former.

It is owing to the before-mentioned Causes, that the Government has at one Time been able to borrow Money at 2 per Cent. below the legal Rate of Interest; and at another Time been obliged to pay as much above it, when neither the landed Gentleman, Merchant, or Tradesman (who are the People to determine natural Interest by) have at the same Time paid more, nor above 1 per Cent. less than the legal Rate; and many People have paid invariably one and the same Rate, and this either one of those last mentioned, or some intermediate one for the whole Time; so that no Inferences can justly be made from the Rate which the Government at any

---

[1] [Joseph Massie], *An Essay on the Governing Causes of the Natural Rate of Interest* (1750).

Time pays, as it oftener differs [from] than agrees with the natural Rate of Interest here.[1]

The contention that real ('natural') interest rates were governed by the 'profits of stock' was endorsed by Hume (1752) and Adam Smith (1776).[2] By the time that Ricardo published his *Principles* (1817) it had become orthodoxy. Ricardo restated the case against regarding market yields as a barometer for interest rates as follows.

The price of funded property is not a steady criterion by which to judge of the rate of interest. In time of war, the stock market is so loaded by the continual loans of Government, that the price of stock has not time to settle at its fair level, before a new operation of funding takes place, or it is affected by anticipation of political events. In time of peace, on the contrary, the operations of the sinking fund, the unwillingness which a particular class of persons feel to divert their funds to any other employment than that to which they have been accustomed, which they think secure, and in which their dividends are paid with the utmost regularity, elevates the price of stock, and consequently depresses the rate of interest on these securities below the general market rate.[3]

For Ricardo, the price of private capital was ideally, like all other prices, the point of intersection between the curves of demand and supply in a (theoretically perfect) national market.

III

Contemporary explanations for the rise in the market price of securities during the first half of the eighteenth century can be expanded along the following lines.[4] A first condition for a continuing flow of capital into state loans (and into the purchase of existing stock) was public confidence in the government's stability and its financial honesty and competence. This condition had largely been fulfilled by 1714; the Hanoverian succession,

---

[1] Ibid., p. 27.

[2] David Hume, 'Of Interest' (written in 1752), in *Writings on Economics*, ed. E. Rotwein (1955), p. 47; Adam Smith, *The Wealth of Nations* (1776), bk. I, ch. ix.

[3] David Ricardo, *Principles of Political Economy and Taxation* (1817) in *Works*, ed. P. Sraffa, i (1951), 298.

[4] The following section is based on the discussion in the previous chapters.

the defeats of the Jacobite attempts of 1715 and 1719, and the financial reforms of 1717, confirmed it. The Sinking Fund created expectations of the eventual redemption of the state's debts, and the General Fund expectation that the interest on them would meanwhile be regularly paid. Public confidence was thus strong enough by 1720 to withstand the shock of the South Sea Bubble, which ten years earlier might have destroyed it. Under Walpole, new government long-term borrowing was small in amount, and the operation of the Sinking Fund not only offset it but reduced the principal of the debt by over £6m. At the same time, owing to changes in the technique of government short-term borrowing, the use of tallies of fictitious loan ceased from the late 1720s, and Exchequer bills (which were largely a monopoly of the Bank of England) were largely relied on instead. The amount of cash borrowed from the public in anticipation of taxes correspondingly declined in the 1720s and 1730s to about half its previous level. In consequence, the quantity of short-dated tallies in the market was markedly reduced. Further, the bonds of the South Sea Company, which amounted to over £4m. in 1722, had been paid off by 1740. The volume of East India bonds was meanwhile constant from 1709 to 1744.

Given unchanged public confidence in the government's reliability, and a rate of demand for securities which remained constant through the period 1720–40, this reduction in the volume of securities would in itself have raised their price. And it is clear that in fact demand did not merely remain constant, it increased. It was in the 1720s that the Marlborough family began to invest up to half a million a year in short-dated securities. After 1726 the Accountant-General of Chancery invested lesser but considerable sums (£40,000–50,000 p.a.) in the same market, and institutional buyers like Child's Bank, the Sun Fire Office and the London and Royal Exchange Assurances were also regular purchasers, particularly of East India bonds. The Marlboroughs, the Accountant-General and the banks and insurance companies were also large buyers in the 1720s and 1730s of the declining quantity of government stock. This was just at the time when foreign, particularly Dutch, funds were flowing into it on an increasing scale. Other constant purchasers of stock, like the Commissioners of Queen Anne's Bounty, or the Society for the Propagation of the Gospel, helped to keep up its price-level, while their large holdings restricted its supply.

What significance has the rise in the price of fixed-interest securities in the London market for the capital market as a whole? Professor Ashton's theory is that the fall in the yield on government stock over the first half of the eighteenth century denoted capital accumulation on a scale sufficient to make subsequent industrialism financially viable.[1] The immediate inference from the evidence reviewed earlier is that this conclusion is implausible. It looks as though the fall in yields was, as contemporaries argued, due to special causes, specifically to an increase in the savings seeking gilt-edged investments just at the time when the bonds available for purchase were diminishing in amount.

But there is evidence the other way. (The subject demands a monograph of its own — as Gould asserted in 1726 — based on careful research into interest rates on private loans.)[2] It has already been shown that there is some correlation between the return on government stock, the bond rates of the East India Company, and the mortgage rates of the Sun Fire Office.[3] Dutch private interest rates (Table 85) followed a similar trend. Further, the behaviour of Exchange Alley in years of government financial crisis like 1711 and 1747–8 seems to have affected private borrowers in both London and the provinces. Thus Defoe writes in February 1711 that

A general want of Money among the Trading part of the Nation has rais'd the Rate of Personal Credit, and I am mistaken, and very much misinform'd, if very good Security has not been given lately to borrow Money, and 12 or 15*l.* per Cent. privately paid as a Premio.[4]

The Northumberland landowner Henry Liddell commented in the same year 'now on the best land security no money can be had; credit is so sunk'.[5] At this date government securities were yielding up to 10%.[6] In January 1747 Mathew Ridley, also a northerner, wrote that 'As this is a time when so much money is turning on Government Securities, it is not easie to raise any immediately on Land'.[7] A year later Chesterfield told Dayrolles that 12% was being offered for money in the City.[8] Both comments come from the closing stages of the Austrian Succession war, which were accompanied by considerable stringency of government credit. In the reverse direction, speculation in London in 1720 seems to have affected the land market in the provinces, and brought some estates there to up to forty years' purchase.[9]

[1] T. S. Ashton, *The Industrial Revolution, 1760–1830* (1948); *Economic Fluctuations in England 1700–1800* (Oxford, 1959); *An Economic History of England: the 18th Century* (repr. with corrections 1961).

[2] For Gould see above, p. 476.   [3] See above, pp. 472–3.

[4] Daniel Defoe, *Review of the State of the British Nation*, 10 February 1711.

[5] Quoted in E. Hughes, *North Country Life in the Eighteenth Century*, i. 158 n.

[6] See above, p. 363.   [7] Hughes, loc. cit.

[8] Quoted in Mahon, *History of England 1713–1783*, iii (1838), 544.

[9] See above, p.146.

Logically, of course, there is no reason to suppose a causal relationship between the London market in government and allied securities and the rest of the capital market. It could be assumed that each was distinct, and financed from a separate flow of savings. Periods of contraction like 1710–11, or 1747–8, or of euphoria like 1720, might then be treated as the product of a single general cause — a state of confidence or its absence — affecting all investors indifferently. If this were so, then the expansion of Barnard's case argued earlier, which postulated a high degree of interpenetration between the two sectors of the market, would be wrong.

In fact, both hypotheses are probably overstated. The two markets were not entirely separate; nor did they coincide. On the one hand they were not entirely separate, because the savings flowing into government securities partly derived from, or were administered by, sources like London banks and insurance companies which were concerned as well in mortgage loans to landowners (some at least of which must have been used for agricultural investment), in the general finance of trade, and in building up economic services like fire and marine insurance. This qualifies, though it does not invalidate the fact that the absence of a market in industrial bonds in any way equivalent to the market in government bonds necessarily impaired arbitrage between public and private capital requirements. On the other hand, they did not coincide, because there were clearly specialized sectors of finance like the underpinning of London retail trade, the finance of the growing outports like Glasgow and Liverpool, or the market in insecure loans at usurious interest rates, which did not compete for the funds of the London institutions, and of the London-based aristocracy and *bourgeoisie* who put their money into government securities.

In conclusion, some further hypotheses may be suggested. The generation of larger provincial incomes from the middle of the eighteenth century, in turn due to the expansion of foreign trade in the Atlantic sector and the growth of the Midland industries, may have accelerated the creation of a partly autonomous provincial capital market, centring on family resources and the activities of local consortia with expert knowledge of local business conditions, and underpinned by the rise of provincial banking houses closely involved in the fortunes of local trade. This in turn would help to account for the growing contemporary denial of a close link between yields on government stock in London and private interest rates. Another factor must have been specialization in particular types of finance. The savings flowing into purchases of government stock were seeking a gilt-edged long-term investment. The growing need of industry was for short-dated funds to provided working capital. By the 1750s the pattern of the capital market of the 1840s was already partly apparent. The early Victorian market depended on a flow of savings from the agricultural districts into London to help finance (by bill-discounting) the short-term needs of industry; while the industrial areas' insurance contributions to the London fire and life offices helped the latter accumulate very large funds, a substantial part of which were returned to the agricultural districts in the form of mortgage loans to landowners. This circular process of short- and long-term lending was still only embryonic by the mid-eighteenth century. It was, however, already creating a complexity in interest rates, and of the terms for which capital was lent, which made the yield on Consols an uncertain barometer of the needs and prices of the capital market as a whole.

20

The Origins of the Stock Exchange

I

By 1688 London was already an important centre of public and private credit, though hardly as yet challenging the international supremacy of Amsterdam. Dealings in mortgages and personal bonds had been common there since the Middle Ages. The growing volume of foreign trade since the mid-seventeenth century stimulated the creation of bills drawn on or discounted in the capital, and familiarized merchants with the details of their negotiation.[1] The stock and bonds of the East India Company changed hands regularly.[2] During Charles II's reign new securities appeared, in the form of Exchequer orders, Navy bills and the stock and bonds of the Royal African and Hudson's Bay Companies. Private bankers lent extensively on pictures, plate and jewels. Other financial services, particularly insurance of various kinds, were beginning on a small scale.

Thus the big increase in the market after 1688 was built on existing foundations. But contemporaries were so impressed by the swift-moving events in which they were caught up that they tended to ignore this, and to treat the market as a new phenomenon. They ascribed its rise, in the first place, to the diversion of investment to internal projects by the war, which had disrupted foreign trade. As John Houghton, F.R.S., who started a specialized list of prices for the shares of these projects in 1692, explained to his readers in his issue of 15 June 1694,

A great many Stocks have arisen since this War with France; for Trade being obstructed at Sea, few that had Money were willing it should be idle, and a great many that wanted Employments studied how to dispose of their Money, that they might be able to command it whensoever they had occasion, which they found they

---

[1] J. Scarlett, *The Stile of Exchanges* (1682). The latest treatment of the origins and development of the Stock Exchange is E. Victor Morgan and W. A. Thomas, *The Stock Exchange. Its History and Functions* (1962).

[2] K. G. Davies, 'Joint-Stock Investment in the later Seventeenth Century', *Econ. H.R.* New Series, iv (1951), p. 283.

could more easily do in Joint-Stock, than in laying out the same in Lands, Houses or Commodities, these [i.e. shares] being more easily shifted from Hand to Hand: This put them upon Contrivances, whereby some were encouraged to Buy, others to Sell, and this is it that is called Stock-Jobbing.[1]

By this date Houghton was quoting the shares of nearly sixty companies, most of them recently floated.[2] In addition to the activities of these new companies, a bitter struggle was being carried on to break open the monopoly of some of the older ones, especially the East India Company; though conducted to a free trade tune, this tended to the formation of rival vested interests like the English East India Company of 1698.[3] The effects of this situation on the security market were later summarised by Defoe as follows.

The Subject then was chiefly the East India Stock, tho' there were other Stocks on foot too, tho' since sunk to nothing; such as the Hudson's Bay Company, the Linnen Manufacture Stock, Paper Stock, Salt-Petre Stock and others, all at this Day worse than nothing, tho' some of them then Jobb'd up to 350 per Cent. as the two first in particular. But the East India Stock was the main Point.[4]

Defoe, like Houghton, implies that the market was principally in the shares and bonds of private companies. In his earlier pamphlets *An Essay upon Projects* (1697) and *The Villainy of Stock-Jobbers detected* (1701) he had, correctly, put equal emphasis on jobbing in Bank of England notes and government tallies created to finance the war with France. The evidence reviewed in earlier chapters shows that these securities were in fact fully as important in the market of the mid and later 1690s as private shares were during the boom of 1691–5. And besides the brisk traffic in the government's tallies, Navy bills, etc. there was a slower market in its long annuities, which changed hands rather more often than their cumbersome form of transfer would suggest. The market during King William's war was therefore one in both private shares and public securities, and this accounts for a good deal

---

[1] John Houghton, F.R.S., *A Collection for Improvement of Husbandry and Trade* (1692–1703), 15 June 1694. On 7 July 1693 he had stated that 'Actions signifie Shares in Companies . . . This buying and selling of Actions is one of the great Trades now on foot . . . I find a great many understand not this affair, therefore I write this.' The French 'action' soon gave way to 'share' in general usage.

[2] The number fell off sharply after 1695. Cf. the account of the boom in Scott, *Joint Stock Companies* I, ch. xvii.

[3] G. L. Cherry, 'The Development of the English Free-Trade Movement . . . 1689–1702', *J. Mod. Hist.* xxv (ii) (1953), 103.

[4] [Daniel Defoe], *The Anatomy of Exchange-Alley* (1719), pp. 13–14.

of the interest and bitterness it aroused, since jobbers could easily be accused not merely of desire for quick profits, but also of imperilling national security by driving down the price of the government's promises to pay.

In this early period it may well have seemed that the market would in future centre on company floatations, and that dealings in government securities would gradually decline once the war ended. In fact, the reverse occurred. The age of reason was also an age of war, and the English government's voracious demands for capital to finance it easily outpaced the requirements of private companies during the whole of the eighteenth century. This is reflected in the quotations in John Castaing's *Course of Exchange*, also started in the 1690s, which came to concentrate almost entirely on government loans. In 1699 he was quoting prices for Bank, East India and African Company stock, the Orphans' Chamber of the City of London, the Million Act and the Million Lottery, and the New East India Company, besides listing the sums lent, and the amounts so far repaid, on up to twenty short-term Exchequer loans.[1] In 1712 he was quoting prices for African, Bank, East India and South Sea stock, and in addition 'Irish Lands' and tickets in the 1710 lottery, as well as the state of short-term loans.[2] In 1720, even at the height of the South Sea Bubble, he contented himself with quotations for the South Sea subscriptions and the two new marine-insurance companies, and ignored the host of new short-lived share companies.[3] At the mid-century his list quoted twenty-one securities, and noted the state of repayments on four short-term Exchequer loans. Seven of these twenty-one securities were for the three monied companies, the two insurance corporations, the Million Bank and the Equivalent Corporation (all in their origin closely tied to the public debt); the rest were government long-term loans managed by the Bank and the Exchequer.[4] It is worth

---

[1] J. Castaing, *The Course of the Exchange, and other things* (1699) (Stock Exchange Reference Library). The earliest surviving copy of Castaing's list is for 1698, but he may have started it earlier. Castaing was a Huguenot immigrant, who became an English designer on 19 August 1688. His list was continued after his death and developed lineally into the present Official List.

[2] Ibid. 1712. Irish Lands were Army debentures 'sunk in Ireland', see above, p. 396.

[3] Ibid. 1720.

[4] Op. cit. 1753. The Equivalent Corporation had been formed in 1719–24 by holders of £248,550 debentures originally made out in Anne's reign to settle the part of the Equivalent not paid in cash. The Equivalent was compensation payable to Scotland at the Union to reimburse her for having to help pay the interest on English debts contracted before the Union. See Neil Munro, *The History of the Royal Bank of Scotland 1727–1927* (privately printed 1928), chs. 3 and 4, and P. W. J. Riley, *The English Ministers and Scotland 1707–1727* (1964), ch. xiv.

noting in this context that the number of shareholders of the finance companies was relatively small. The £200,000 capital of the Million Bank was originally put up by 305 subscribers.[1] The London Assurance had only 470 proprietors of the 32,000 Ship Charter shares in September 1753.[2] Another insurance office, the Sun Fire Office, had 4,800 shares; in 1740 these were owned by only 130 proprietors, and changed hands infrequently.[3] Adam Anderson writes that there was a number of other small companies like the New River Company and the London-Bridge Water Company whose shares rarely came on the market.[4]

The predominance of government securities in the eighteenth-century market has been conventionally explained in terms of the Bubble Act of 1720, which has been held to have impeded new company floatation, and thus arrested the flow of risk capital into industry. It is doubtful, however, whether the explanation can be accepted without serious qualifications. Professor Du Bois showed some years ago that the Act was less of an obstacle to company floatation than had previously been supposed.[5] More fundamentally, it seems from the evidence discussed in previous chapters that the saving classes of the community in the first half of the eighteenth century were primarily interested either in fixed-interest securities or in the purely speculative chances offered by government lotteries. The rudimentary state of contemporary business organization precluded the offer to the investing public of many safe shares or debentures, and speculative ambitions were an impracticable source of long-term finance for business purposes. In consequence, investors tended to put their money into land or government securities. The development of provincial capital resources, and the further growth of financial specialization and expertise in London, were to be needed before funds could be raised on a sufficient scale to finance the Industrial Revolution and the concurrent revolutions in transport, lighting and housing.

[1] P.R.O. Chancery Masters' Exhibits, c 46/1, list of subscribers to the Million Bank 1695.

[2] London Assurance, dividend books, dividend list, 29 September 1753. The ship charter shares were 91% of the total shares.

[3] Dickson, *Sun Insurance Office*, pp. 288, 290.

[4] Adam Anderson, *An Historical and Chronological Deduction of the Origin of Commerce* (2 vols., 1764), ii. 292.

[5] A. B. Du Bois, *The English Business Company after the Bubble Act* (New York, 1938).

II

The market in shares and bonds in the 1690s centred on Exchange Alley near the Royal Exchange. The whole of this district had been rebuilt after the Great Fire of 1666, including the Royal Exchange itself in 1669. Exchange Alley twisted between Cornhill, opposite the Exchange, to Lombard Street, and contained several coffee-houses, two of which in particular, Jonathan's and Garraway's, were already used by dealers in securities for business purposes. At Garraway's, according to Houghton writing in April 1692, could be seen 'what Prices the Actions bear of most Companies trading in Joynt-Stocks'.[1] Two years later he describes the brokers as being 'chiefly upon the Exchange, and at Jonathan's Coffee-house, sometimes at Garaway's, and at some other Coffee-Houses'.[2] Advertisements in his paper from the middle of 1695 reminded readers that at Jonathan's 'may be bought and sold . . . all Stocks and Shares'. Sam's Coffee House in Exchange Alley, and Powell's and the Rainbow in Cornhill, are also mentioned in contemporary sources, but the chief centres were evidently Jonathan's and Garraway's, both in Exchange Alley. Jonathan's was founded about 1680 by Jonathan Miles, and was from the start connected with financial business. The Garraways were a City family of the period, who were landlords of the Sun Fire Office in its early days. The coffee-house was started by Thomas Garraway in the early 1670s.[3] The trend to financial specialization, using coffee-houses as a place of business, is typical of the period: other examples are Edward Lloyd's Coffee House, a centre for marine insurance, and Tom's and Causey's Coffee Houses, used in their early days by the Hand in Hand Fire Office and the Sun Fire Office.[4] Jonathan's as a centre for dealers gradually superseded Garraway's (which was concentrating on auction sales by the 1750s), and developed lineally into the Stock Exchange of 1772.[5]

Houghton's description of market technique in the 1690s shows that securities could be purchased either by applying directly to their owner or by using a broker. Bargains were either for immediate transfer (if the transfer

---

[1] Houghton, *Collection*, 6 April 1692.   [2] Ibid., 22 June 1694.
[3] Bryant Lillywhite, *London Coffee Houses* (1963); Dickson, *Sun Insurance Office*, ch. 3. Garraway is also spelt Garaway, Garway, etc., in the records. For the ownership of Jonathan's in 1748 see below, p. 505.
[4] Dickson, op. cit.   [5] See below, p. 506.

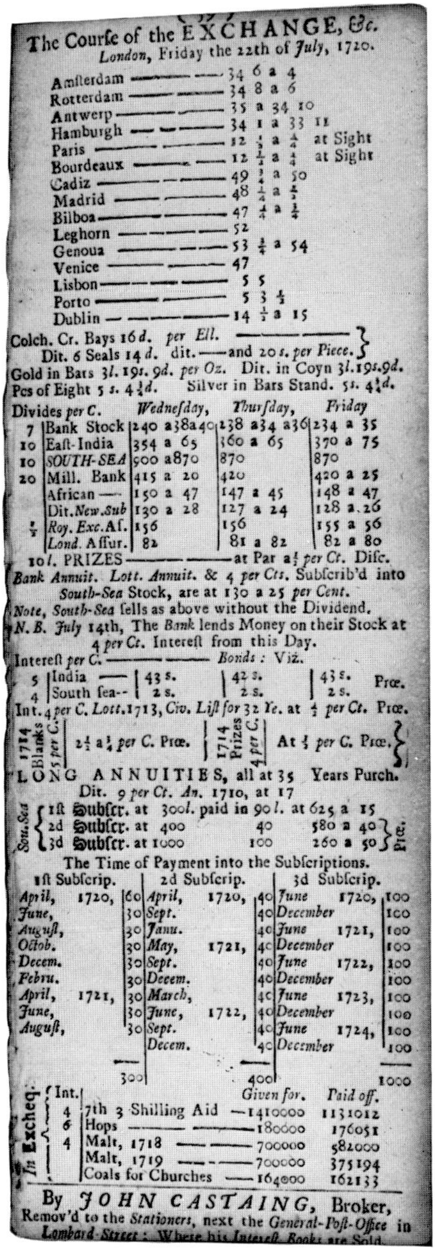

The Course of the EXCHANGE, &c.

London, Friday the 22th of *July*, 1720.

Amsterdam	34 6 a 4
Rotterdam	34 8 a 6
Antwerp	35 a 34 10
Hamburgh	34 1 a 33 11
Paris	32 $\frac{1}{2}$ a $\frac{1}{4}$ at Sight
Bourdeaux	12 $\frac{1}{2}$ a $\frac{1}{4}$ at Sight
Cadiz	49 $\frac{3}{4}$ a 50
Madrid	48 $\frac{1}{4}$ a $\frac{1}{2}$
Bilboa	47 $\frac{1}{4}$ a $\frac{3}{4}$
Leghorn	52
Genoua	53 $\frac{3}{4}$ a 54
Venice	47
Lisbon	5 5
Porto	5 3 $\frac{1}{2}$
Dublin	14 $\frac{1}{2}$ a 15

Colch. Cr. Bays 16 *d.* *per Ell.* }
Dit. 6 Seals 14 *d.* dit. — and 20 *s. per Piece.* }
Gold in Bars 3*l.* 19*s.* 9*d.* *per Oz.* Dit. in Coyn 3*l.* 19*s.* 9*d.*
Pcs of Eight 5 *s.* 4 $\frac{1}{4}$*d.* Silver in Bars Stand. 5*s.* 4 $\frac{1}{4}$*d.*

Divides *per C.*		*Wednesday,*	*Thursday,*	*Friday*
7	Bank Stock	240 a 38 a 40	238 a 34 a 36	234 a 35
10	East-India	354 a 65	360 a 65	370 a 75
10	*SOUTH-SEA*	900 a 870	870	870
20	Mill. Bank	415 a 20	420	420 a 25
	African —	150 a 47	147 a 45	148 a 47
	Dit. *New. Sub*	130 a 28	127 a 24	128 a 26
$\frac{1}{2}$	*Roy. Exc.* As.	156	156	155 a 56
	Lond. Assur.	82	81 a 82	82 a 80

10*l.* PRIZES — at Par a $\frac{1}{2}$ *per Ct.* Disc.
Bank Annuit. Lott. Annuit. & 4 *per Cts.* Subscrib'd into *South-Sea* Stock, are at 130 a 25 *per Cent.*
Note, South-Sea sells as above without the Dividend.
N. B. July 14th, The *Bank* lends Money on their Stock at 4 *per Ct.* Interest from this Day.

Interest *per C.* — *Bonds* : Viz.

5	India —	43 *s.*	42 *s.*	43 *s.*	Prœ.
4	South sea --	2 *s.*	2 *s.*	2 *s.*	

Int. 4 *per C. Lott.* 1713, *Civ. List for* 32 *Ye.* at $\frac{1}{2}$ *per Ct.* Prœ.

1714 Blanks 5 *per* C.	2 $\frac{1}{2}$ a $\frac{3}{4}$ *per* C. Prœ.	1714 Prizes 4 *per* C.	At $\frac{1}{2}$ *per* C. Prœ.

LONG ANNUITIES, all at 35 Years Purch.
Dit. 9 *per Ct. An.* 1710, at 17

Sou. Sea				
1st Subscr.	at 300*l.*	paid in 90 *l.*	at 625 a 15	
2d Subscr.	at 400	40	580 a 40	Prœ.
3d Subscr.	at 1000	100	260 a 50	Prœ.

The Time of Payment into the Subscriptions.

1st Subscrip.		2d Subscrip.		3d Subscrip.	
April, 1720,	60	*April,* 1720,	40	*June* 1720,	100
June,	30	*Sept.*	40	*December*	100
August,	30	*Janu.*	40	*June* 1721,	100
Octob.	30	*May,* 1721,	40	*December*	100
Decem.	30	*Sept.*	40	*June* 1722,	100
Febru.	30	*Decem.*	40	*December*	100
April, 1721,	30	*March,*	40	*June* 1723,	100
June,	30	*June,* 1722,	40	*December*	100
August,	30	*Sept.*	40	*June* 1724,	100
		Decem.	40	*December*	100
	300		400		1000

In Excheq. Int.		*Given for.*	*Paid off.*
4	7th 3 Shilling Aid	1410000	1131012
6	Hops	180000	176051
4	Malt, 1718	700000	582000
	Malt, 1719	700000	375194
	Coals for Churches	164000	162133

By *JOHN CASTAING*, Broker,
Remov'd to the *Stationers*, next the *General-Post-Office* in *Lombard-Street* : Where his *Interest Books* are Sold.

12. John Castaing's *Course of the Exchange*, showing prices at the height of the South Sea Bubble

books were not closed for making dividend payments) or for transfer at a future date. The right to buy at a future date was called a 'refusal' of stock and the right to sell at a future date a 'put'. There was still some uncertainty about the form of document used to record these option bargains. Houghton reproduces a form of printed contract (with suitable blanks) which was still in use in 1720, and specified the parties, the shares to be delivered or received, the date of delivery, and the premium paid, a receipt for which was put at the foot of the document.[1] But use was also made of covenants and indentures drawn up by scriveners. The earliest of this kind so far traced, dated 29 July 1687, is a covenant by Sir Bazill Firebrass (as he spelt himself) of Mark Lane to deliver £1,000 East India stock at 200 to Sir Thomas Davall on or before 1 March 1688, in return for a premium of 150 guineas.[2] Sir Stephen Evance, a leading banker, King's Jeweller, and Chairman of the Royal African Company, used both covenants like this and indentures (where the premium is not stated) to record a series of bargains in the summer of 1691, mostly in shares of the Company of White Paper Makers, but also in African and East India stock.[3] In each contract Evance was undertaking to deliver stock in six months' time at a given price; when the premium is stated it amounted to roughly 20% of this. He was, in effect, making a series of bets that the market would fall, with associates who thought it would rise, as it in fact did. These techniques were similar to those of the Amsterdam Bourse, then and for many years to come the leading European market in securities, and must have derived from them. Between 1650 and 1688 the Bourse had developed the further refinement of quarterly settlement days (*rescontre-dagen*) at which all bargains could be either adjusted or continued to the next settlement, but these were not introduced to the English market until the 1740s.[4]

The speculative nature of a good deal of share business at the turn of the seventeenth century is understandable in view of the contemporary addiction

---

[1] J. Houghton, *A Collection for Improvement of Husbandry and Trade* (1692–1703), 22 June 1694.

[2] P.R.O. C 111/50, Chancery Masters' Exhibits, Evance Papers.

[3] Ibid. Evance shot himself early in Anne's reign.

[4] J. G. van Dillen, 'Effekten Koersen aan de Amsterdamsche Beurs 1723–1794', *Economisch-Historisch Jaarboek*, xvii (1931), 1, and his chapter in the *Algemene Geschiedenis der Nederlanden* (Utrecht, 1954), vii, ch. x. For the introduction of quarterly settlement in England see below, p. 508. 'Rescontre' was a term used by Dutch merchants to indicate that a bill had been paid by changing it to a current account — 'solvit per rescontre' as distinct from 'per banco' 'per wissel' and so on (Mortimer, 5th ed., p. 28 n.). The transfer of the term to Stock Exchange business is understandable.

R   D.F.R.

to gambling and wagers, which took the form of bets not only on cards, dice and horses, but also on the issue of private and public events. For instance on 19 March 1693 Sir Cleave More, Bart., of Bankhall, Lancs., contracts with Whitfield Hayter, a London goldsmith-banker, to pay him £300 within twenty days of the death of his (More's) father-in-law Joseph Edmonds of Cumberlow Greene. On 6 May 1693 Samuel Day, of London, Fish-monger, binds himself to pay James Moyer thirty guineas in gold ten days after Moyer marries or dies. On 18 November 1695 Henry Shales contracts with Whitfield Hayter to pay the latter five guineas if he (Shales) drinks wine, ale or brandy before Michaelmas 1696. On 2 November 1700 Sir Stephen Evance bets James Folkingham 10 to 1 on a stake of twenty guineas that war will not be declared against the Empire, France or Spain by Christmas Day, and so on.[1] The combination of themes is well caught by Thomas Shadwell in his play *The Volunteers: or, the Stock-Jobbers*, first performed in 1693. Colonel Hackwell asks Welford, one of the other characters who has come to see him, 'Is it about the Linnen-Manufacture?' drawing from Welford the aside 'Ha! this Godly old Fellow is of the Voca-tion of Stock-jobbing'. Hackwell then asks if it is about the glass, the copper, the tin, the divers, the paper, or 'the Dippers; who will make Sarcenet keep out Rain like Drap de Berry?' Welford assures Hackwell and Mrs. Hackwell that he wants to see them about none of these, 'nor no Wager about retaking of Mons, Philipsburgh, Montmelian; Nor Invading of France by the first of August', and leads the disappointed pair off to discuss private business.[2]

The pure theory of the market at this date was that buyers and sellers dealt with each other either directly or through a broker. If a broker was employed to buy, he got in touch with a second broker with an order to sell. For example, George Guy, broker for Simon York, agrees in September 1699 with William Hatton, broker for Walter Kent, Esq., to transfer or cause to be transferred to Walter Kent £250 Bank Stock.[3] Here broker deals with broker, and stock is actually transferred. The broker's commission was at this date ½%, and according to Edward Hatton some 'have got 1000 or 1500*l*. per An.'[4] Brokerage, as distinct from commission, was (partially)

---

[1] All these contracts are among the Evance Papers previously referred to. Cf. 7 Anne, c. 16 (1708), 'An Act to prevent the laying of Wagers relating to the Publick' (the title is self-explanatory), and 9 Anne, c. 19 (1710), 'An Act for the better preventing of excessive and deceitful gaming' (this made pledges of land etc. by gamblers null).

[2] Act I, sc. ii.

[3] Bank of England Record Office, Register of Contracts in Bank Stock. For this register see below, p. 516.

[4] Edward Hatton, *The Merchant's Magazine* (1701), p. 208.

limited in 1697 to ⅛%. Both rates were the same in the 1740s.[1] By then, as will be seen later, brokers were extensively engaged in dealings on margin, where no stock changed hands but they were still entitled to brokerage.

A number of entries in one of the early (1696–1705) indexes to the Bank stock ledgers throw some light on the emergence of stockbrokers to join the existing ranks of corn-brokers, dyers-war-brokers, grocery-brokers, hemp-brokers, silk-brokers and exchange-brokers.[2]

TABLE 86

Some early stockbrokers

Name	Address	Description
James Causton	London	Merchant, now Broker
Phesaunt Crisp	London	Merchant (erased), Broker
George Guy	London	Merchant, now Broker
William Hatton	London	Merchant (erased), Broker (erased), now Esquire
Charles Torriano	London	Merchant (erased), Broker

Source: Bank stock, alphabet to ledgers 1696–1705.

All these appear as brokers in stock in the register of contracts in Bank stock just referred to. In 1697, owing to complaints about the activities in Exchange Alley at a time of national financial crisis, Parliament passed an Act limiting the number of brokers of all kinds including stockbrokers to 100 and forbidding them to deal in government securities without the Treasury's leave.[3] Those who petitioned the City of London (the admitting authority) to be Sworn Brokers under the Act included Henry Cotigno, Stephen Mahieu, Benjamin Nunes and Elias Paz.[4] David Avila, Abraham Cardel, Henry Cotigno, Thomas Lewes and Elias Paz were among those who also

---

[1] Brokerage was limited to ⅛% in sales of Exchequer orders and tallies by 8 & 9 Wm. III, c. 20, s. lx (1697). The same rate seems to have become general for other securities. For rates in the 1740s see Archief Brants, 1344, 28 February 1746, van Hemert & Co. in London to J. I. de Neufville in Amsterdam, ½% commission and ⅛% brokerage charged on a sale of securities. Cf. below, p. 516, for up to ½% brokerage still allowed in 1697.

[2] For a list of all these see Houghton, *Collection*, 3 August 1694.

[3] See below, p. 516.

[4] Corporation of London Records Office, Brokers' Petitions, 1633, 4534a., 5143, 5311.

petitioned the Treasury to be 'Treasury brokers'; according to Cotigno a grudging twenty were admitted.[1]

The letter of the law of 1697 forbade Sworn Brokers to deal in stock themselves, and in fact none of those mentioned, whether English like Guy, Hatton or Lewes, Huguenot like Mahieu, or Jewish like Avila, Nunes or Paz appears as a dealer in stock in the ledgers of the Bank and East India Company. But it would be unwise to deduce that Sworn Brokers were always so punctilious. One of the smaller dealers in Bank stock around 1700 was Moses Hart 'alias Hartig, merchant [erased] now Broker'.[2] Hart's dealing activities steadily increased, but this did not prevent him acting as a Sworn Broker from 1708 to 1738.[3] Other examples are Joseph Coysgarne, Stephen Daubuz, Samson Gideon and William Whitmore, all Sworn Brokers and large dealers. Of 818 English and 36 Jewish brokers of all kinds admitted by the City of London as Sworn Brokers between 1708 and 1755, at least 43 are identifiable as dealers in stock, though they had presumably been admitted as stockbrokers.[4] Similarly, it is doubtful whether the monopoly of admission of brokers given to the City of London in 1697 and confirmed in 1708 was treated with much respect. Mortimer in 1761 estimated that only one-third of those who acted as stockbrokers were Sworn Brokers.[5] In deference to this state of affairs, contemporaries in the 1690s and for half a century afterwards used broker and jobber as interchangeable terms. Jobbers themselves, however, always described themselves either as 'brokers' (or some other occupational label such as 'mercer') or simply as 'gent.' They evidently thought 'jobber' pejorative.[6] Thus, of six brokers in the 4%s of 1748, taken at random from the alphabets, four were Sworn Brokers, two were not; two were extensive dealers of whom one was and one was not a Sworn Broker. Yet all six described themselves as 'broker'.[7]

---

[1] *Cal. T. Papers 1697–1702*, pp. 39, 40, 41, 42. For Cotigno's statement, Guildhall Brokers' Petitions, 1633.

[2] Bank stock alphabet 1696–1705.

[3] Corporation of London Records Office, Brokers' Admissions 1708–1801.

[4] Ibid. Identification of dealers from the stock ledgers in the Bank of England Record Office.

[5] Thomas Mortimer, *Every Man his own Broker*, p. 161. For this monopoly see below, pp. 517 ff.

[6] For some occupational labels see below, pp. 498, 512.

[7] Bank of England Record Office, 4% (1748) stock, accounts for Alexander Bunyan, George Bennett, Robert Chambers, Stephen Gardes, Henry Longe, David Salomons. Bennett and Longe were not Sworn Brokers. The dealers were Bennett and Chambers.

The dealers or jobbers of the 1690s, about whom information is more easily available than it is about brokers — for the latter, by the nature of their office, tend not to appear in records — were a mixed bunch plying a mixed trade. It was seen earlier that the banker Evance dealt in futures in paper and linen shares, and in African and East India stock.[1] The surviving papers of Charles Blunt, who was setting up as a merchant in this period, show similar transactions.[2] More systematic information is available in the ledgers for East India and Bank stock. The first available for the former is dated 1706–8.[3] The number of accounts in it identifiable from their turnover as those of dealers is over eighty, twenty-seven of which were in Jewish names.[4] The majority of the dealers were London merchants and goldsmith bankers. For example, Peter Delmé and John Hopkins were later among the richest men of the day. Peter Henriquez jun. was a merchant, a lender to government and agent for correspondents in Amsterdam. George Caswall, Stephen Child, William Hamond, Richard Hoare, John Marke, Thomas Martin, John Mead, John Narbonne and Benjamin Tudman were goldsmith bankers. Both bankers and merchants dealt in short-dated securities too: thus Caswall, Hoare, Martin and Tudman, together with the merchants and East India stock dealers James Colebrooke, Edward Gibbon, John Lambert and Thomas Le Heup, were among the subscribers of Navy and other bills to the South Sea Company in 1711.[5]

East India stock was liable to marked variations in its price, owing to a number of different factors: the political battles preceding the union in 1709 of the English Company of 1698 and the Old Company; the return or loss of Indian cargoes; the issue of native wars; the smiles or frowns of princes. Basically it was a speculator's stock. Bank stock, leaving aside the exceptional circumstances of the Bank's early years, was in contrast essentially sober and respectable, with a narrower price range offering far less opening for killings. It is not therefore surprising to find that the number of dealers in it was much lower. The ledger for 1696–1705 contains accounts for about a dozen,

---

[1] See above, p. 491.

[2] P.R.O. C 114/164–5, Chancery Masters' Exhibits, papers of Charles Blunt. The latter was the brother-in-law of the barrister John Freke, who published a price list of securities only isolated copies of which survive, and a relative of the financier and South Sea Director John Blunt. Charles Blunt killed himself in September 1720, worth on paper £250,000 according to the newspapers.

[3] Bank of England Record Office.

[4] It is possible to identify the active accounts fairly accurately without adopting a precise number of transfers above which AB is a jobber and below which he is not.

The list of subscribers (B.M. Harl. MS. 7497) is discussed above, p. 449.

including Delmé, Henriquez and Hopkins. Others were William Sheppard, a goldsmith banker, and the great Huguenot merchant and exchange contractor Sir Theodore Janssen.

The dealer aimed at turning his balance over profitably, always retaining enough stock to meet orders promptly, but not so much that a sharp fall in prices caught him at a disadvantage. The monthly balances of Sheppard in Bank stock in 1700 and of a later dealer in Consols, William Cotsford, in 1754, were as follows:

TABLE 87

Dealers' balances of stock 1700 and 1754

	Sheppard	Cotsford
	£	£
J	1,959	4,186
F	7,018	3,457
M	9,783	5,195
A	7,458	5,519
M	2,094	4,034
J	4,103	858
J	6,233	2,374
A	1,602	2,872
S	7,209	151
O	12,756	2,099
N	17,686	2,783
D	5,271	610

Source: Ledgers for Bank stock and 3% Consols, Bank of England Record Office.

The dealers' accounts show transactions with each other and with non-professionals more or less indifferently. It may be presumed that with the latter, perhaps also with the former, they employed brokers. Already, willy-nilly, the dealer was becoming a stabilizer in the market, normally ready to buy and to sell, and professionally interested in adjusting demand and supply.

Owing to their greater numbers, the turnover of individual jobbers was smaller in East India Stock than in Bank stock. Between April 1706 and February 1707 William Atwill, a prominent East India jobber, made fifty purchases and sixty-five sales, amounting to just over £100,000. His 115 transfers were about 5% of the annual total. Between 2 January and 24

December 1700 the banker William Sheppard made 278 purchases and 371 sales of Bank stock totalling nearly £500,000. His 649 transfers were 22% of the annual total. A prominent East India jobber could thus only secure a twentieth of yearly business, while a prominent Bank stock-jobber could secure a fifth. None the less, the relatively limited number of transfers in both stocks, except in times of great excitement, set an upper limit to the amount of jobbing work available.[1] It was this which made it both possible and necessary for dealers to have some other occupation as well. The trend over the next fifty years was towards a reduction in the number of dealers and a growing professionalism in their ranks; and to the simultaneous development of a market in time-bargains which offered larger and more tempting opportunities than jobbing transfers of stock, and led to a great increase in the number of brokers.

A final point to be noticed is that by the end of the wars of 1689–1713 it had become common form for speculators to buy up batches of tickets in the government lotteries, and resell them by dividing each ticket into shares. This enabled the small man who could not afford a £10 ticket (yet alone a £100 one) to buy a piece of it; and the gambler to spread his risks by buying shares in a number of tickets, any one of which might draw a prize. Thus Mathew West, goldsmith at the Seven Stars in Clare Street near Clare Market, advertised in December 1713 that he had bought 200 tickets in each of the last two government lotteries and resold each ticket divided into twenty shares 'and thereby gave entire Satisfaction to the Persons concern'd therein'.[2] He now proposed to do the same for the 'considerable Number' of tickets in the Queen's Lottery which he had purchased. A twentieth part of a ticket was to cost 11s. 6d., running up to £2 17s. 6d. for a quarter-ticket. He pointed out that for £11 10s. 6d. it was possible to buy a twentieth part of twenty tickets, and so on.

III

The trends towards specialization and dealings on margin referred to in the previous section were already apparent by the time of the South Sea Bubble of 1720. In the period immediately preceding the crisis the number of active

---

[1] East India stock ledgers, Bank of England Record Office. For numbers of transfers see Appendix D.

[2] *The British Mercury,* 9 December 1713, p. 6.

accounts in East India stock was still higher than in any other, but not so high as in the early years of the century: the merger of the Old and New Companies in 1709, and the increase in the amount of other market securities, had tended to concentration of East India business in fewer hands. In the ledger for 1715–19 there are over sixty dealers, fourteen of whom are Jews; twenty-three had also been dealers in 1706–8. As at the earlier period, several were bankers, Edward Bowman, Nathaniel Brassey, Sir George Caswall, Thomas Greene, John Humphreys, William King, John Marke, Thomas Martin, Richard Nicholls, Thomas Snow, Elias Turner, George Wanley and Matthew Wymondesold.

In Bank stock, though the Bank's capital had quadrupled since the early 1700s, there were only about twenty dealers at this date, including six of these bankers (Brassey, Caswall, Marke, Martin, Snow and Wymondesold) and a number of brokers, either licensed, like Moses Hart — the only dealer to have survived from the group active in the 1690s — or unlicensed, like Edward Crull, 'of Exchange Alley, gent', and John Nodes, 'of Milk Street, Mercer', both named as brokers by the Commons' Committee of Secrecy in 1721.[1] The remaining Bank stock dealers were substantial merchants, like the Anglo-Dutch Sir Justus Beck (who went bankrupt during the Bubble to the tune of £347,000),[2] Anthony da Costa, Sir Matthew Decker, Sir Theodore Janssen the great South Sea director whose fortune was largely confiscated after the Bubble, Sir Randolph Knipe, and Francis Pereira. Beck, Decker and Pereira were also East India dealers.

Transfers of government stock, first handled by the Bank of England in 1715, had become an important business for it by 1720. By 1719 it managed six of these stocks, accounted for and transferred by the same methods as its own. The ledgers for the largest, the 5%s of 1717, show that in the period 1717–19 several goldsmith bankers, familiar from other stocks, were fairly extensive dealers: John Gladwin, John Marke, James and Thomas Martin, John Mead, Thomas Snow, Robert Surman (Deputy Cashier of the South Sea Company) and George Wanley. Humphreys, Snow and Wanley were all East India jobbers too. With the exception of their accounts, however, the others dealers were surpassed in turnover by the professional brokers and jobbers Edward Crull and John Nodes, by Christopher Whitmore 'of St. Andrews Holborn, Broker', and in particular by John Harvey 'of the Bank of England, gent.', who was a clerk in one of the government stock transfer offices. Dealing by transfer clerks, later to cause many headaches

---

[1] *HCJ* xix. 575–7.   [2] See above, p. 158.

for the directors of the Bank and other companies, had clearly already begun.[1]

The South Sea Bubble itself gave rise to a number of lawsuits, two of which throw further light on the working of the market and the relations between brokers and their clients. From a suit brought by Richard Child, Lord Castlemaine, M.P. for Essex, against the banker Matthew Wymondesold, it appears that the latter's business in 'Change Alley during the Bubble was of four kinds: jobbing in stock; dealing on margin for his own account; and doing both as a broker for others. His account books — a ledger, a journal, and a bought-and-sold book — show numerous transactions with other dealers such as Ephraim Abarbanel, Isaac Franks, William Lock, Gabriel Lopez, James Testard and Robert Westley.[2] Wymondesold explained that

all the time this Defendant was employed by the Complainant as aforesaid he this Defendant did deal very greatly in buying and selling Stocks on this Defendant's own account and believes the same was publickly known to all or most persons who were considerable dealers in stocks at that time and who frequented the coffee houses near Exchange Alley to one of which the Complainant during the time aforesaid resorted almost daily and on some days several times in a day and the said Mr. Fawke (Castlemaine's bookkeeper) during this time spent great part of his time in and about Exchange Alley in order on the Complainant's behalf . . . to observe the prices of and the transactions in stocks and to give the Complainant an account thereof from time to time . . . notwithstanding the suggestions in the Bill that a person acting by commission for others and dealing also on his own account may have opportunity of imposing on his principal.

Wymondesold was not a Sworn Broker, but says that he regarded himself as bound in honour to his client.

Tho' he was not a Broker he always thought himself obliged to buy and sell as well as he could for his employers and did so . . . He doth believe that when the Complainant at any time gave this Defendant directions to buy or sell stock or other publick securitys for or on behalf of the Complainant this Defendant went from the Complainant as he best remembers to Jonathan's Coffee House in Exchange Ally which was the principal market for stocks and where the markett prices of stocks could best be learnt to buy or sell or at least to know the true price of stocks and publick securitys.

---

[1] Cf. below, p. 512, for later developments.

[2] P.R.O. C 11/247/1, *Child* v. *Wymondesold*, catalogued as 'George I and II'. One large parchment (Wymondesold's answer to Child's case) with smaller ones containing copies of Wymondesold's accounts. Unless otherwise stated all the references in the text are to this source.

D.F.R.

He did not tell Castlemaine with whom bargains in stock on his account were made,

nor in this Defendant's judgement did it in any way concern the Complainant to know any such names by reason that in the transactions and dealings of this Defendant on the Complainant's behalf this Defendant was at stake and answerable to the Complainant to make good to him the performance of all bargains by this Defendant made upon his account.

A large number of the bargains for Castlemaine were for a future date, but were a good deal less formal than those involving the use of option contracts, and generally for much shorter periods — sometimes for as little as a week ahead.[1] When settlement-day arrived Castlemaine would normally not expect to transfer stock, but merely to pay the 'difference' or 'margin' between the price agreed to when the bargain was struck and the market price on the day named for settling. This is why Wymondesold refers to Castlemaine's transactions as 'chiefly in the nature of wagering than actually buying or selling of stock'. Why, if no actual transfer of stock was involved, should the broker with such fictitious orders to buy have needed to contact another broker with an (equally fictitious) order to sell the amount required? The answer seems to be that in this way the buying broker *AB* laid off the series of bets made with him by his client. For example, if when instructed to buy £10,000 South Sea stock at 88 for settlement in one month broker *AB* carries the risk himself, and at settlement-day stock has risen to 90, *AB* must pay the difference of £200 (£9,000—£8,800) himself. If, however, he has a claim on his fellow-broker *CD* for £10,000 stock at 88, which *CD*'s client has instructed him to sell at the same date, then the £200 due is now paid by *CD*'s client to *AB*'s client — less brokerage.

Bearing this in mind, and having regard to the form of Wymondesold's books, it is clear that buying and selling for time depended primarily on the brokers' bookkeeping entries: every 'purchase' in the book of broker *AB* was a 'sale' in that of broker *CD*. If *AB* and *CD* made a number of bargains, on behalf of different clients on a given day, they could adjust them when the day arrived by setting off the total of claims each had on the other. There was clearly already a strong case for extending the scope of this technique by replacing the existing multiplicity of settlement-days by a limited number, on the lines of those of the Amsterdam Bourse.

---

[1] The periods for which option contracts ran during the South Sea Bubble were, however, much shorter than usual, often for only two weeks or a month, see brokers' accounts in H.L.R.O., Parchment Coll., South Sea Company Papers, Box 167.

Castlemaine's case does not mention the use of formal contracts for making forward purchases but these options (puts and refusals) were evidently still in use. A surviving contract dated 14 September 1720 — when the peak of the South Sea boom had already passed — stipulates a premium of £630 for the right to buy £1,000 South Sea stock at 700 in three months' time.[1] Like Evance's contracts in the 1690s this is payment for the right to buy; assuming that a six months' rate would have been double (i.e. £1,260), the ratio of premium to purchase price — about one-fifth — is the same as in the earlier period. By this date forward purchases by written indentures or covenants were rarer but were still sometimes used.[2]

Though chiefly buying for Castlemaine on margin, Wymondesold also acted for him as a broker in the orthodox sense. For instance, on 16 March 1720 Castlemaine gave him an order to buy £2,000 South Sea stock 'as this Defendant believes not for any future day further than the next transfer day', and he accordingly bought £2,000 stock of Samson Gideon, to be transferred on 19 March. Gideon subsequently asked whether Wymondesold would accept a transfer of the stock to his account by Edward Harle, then thought to be of good standing, and Wymondesold agreed. Before any stock changed hands, however, Harle, who was the Secretary of the Million Bank, went bankrupt, through misfortune not dishonesty as he explained to his employers on 21 March 1720.[3] Wymondesold admitted that he himself was liable to pay Castlemaine £680 — the difference between the price of stock on the day the order was given and the price on the named transfer day. His liability, he explained, was due to his failure to name the vendor of the stock to Castlemaine. This was perhaps a misunderstanding of the City of London's regulations of 1708, which obliged Sworn Brokers to disclose the names of their principals 'either Buyer or Seller, if thereunto required'.[4] Wymondesold was not a Sworn Broker, nor is there evidence that Castlemaine had asked who the vendor was. In any case, he refused Wymondesold's offer, preferring to compound with Harle for £300. The incident shows that

[1] Add. MS. 22639, Papers relating to the Company of Mines Royal in Jamaica, f. 193.

[2] London University MS. 89, f. 30, printed indenture for sale by Edward Waller to William Soley of £2,000 South Sea stock, to be transferred before the books close at Christmas 1720 on payment of £22,000. Dated 1 August 1720. Possibly printed indentures were thought more likely to bind the parties at a time of exceptional conditions in the market.

[3] P.R.O. Chancery Masters' Exhibits, C 114/17, f. 258, Minutes of Directors of the Million Bank 1714–1724, 21 March 1720.

[4] See below, p. 518.

unsworn brokers had developed rules of professional conduct based partly at least on those of their licensed brethren.

Another broker who found himself in trouble as a result of the Bubble was David Shrimpton, who described himself later as having by 1720 been 'employed for some time as a broker in the buying and selling of stock in and about Exchange Alley'.[1] He was admitted as a Sworn Broker as 'David Shrimpton, Mason, in Aldermanbury' on 10 January, 1721; his bond was not discharged until March 1759, presumably on his death or retirement from business.[2] Two of his clients in 1720 were James Noke 'of London merchant' and Cave Wiseman, a financial shark who was 'abt: ye beginning of June 1720 and for some time after . . . Governor of ye Welsh Copper Company the Patent whereof he and al. had then lately purchased'. Noke's dealings in partnership with Wiseman during 1720 turned out — like those of so many other speculators — to be disastrous. In 1725, unable to stave off his creditors, he fled to Holland. In the following year he unwisely returned, was recognised, seized by his creditors, and adjudged bankrupt. The immensely complicated suit, which reopened transactions dating back before the Bubble, show that Noke and Wiseman were agreed — if on nothing else — that during 1720 Shrimpton had bought stock for his own account and was now trying to charge them with it. Shrimpton contended that he was only acting as their 'broker and Agent', but he had to explain away the awkward fact that he had personally signed a promissory note for stock, in consequence of which his creditors later threw him into gaol. Although it is not now possible to determine the rights and wrongs of the case it seems clear that Shrimpton, like Wymondesold, was dealing for himself as well as others, that he confused the two sets of transactions: and paid dearly for it. Besides broking and dealing he was evidently acting as an agent as well. Noke, examined about 160 Welsh Copper Company shares, explained to the Court that in June 1720

ye said 60 shares in ye name of ye said Norris Jeamson were . . . by ye said Wiseman's Directions transferred by him to David Shrimpton the said Wiseman's then Broker and that ye said David Shrimpton was by virtue of Lre of attorney . . . from ye said Andrew Richmond Impowered to Sell and Dispose of ye said 100 shares in his name.

The blurring of distinctions between brokers and jobbers, between sworn and unlicensed brokers, between personal bargains and those made for clients,

---

[1] P.R.O. C 103/134, *Noke* v. *Wiseman* (1727). Unless otherwise stated, all references in the text are to this source. The papers are so voluminous and confused that more specific references are impossible.

[2] Corporation of London Records Office, Brokers' Admissions 1708–1801.

noticed in the earlier period, were still characteristic of the market. The broker's lot, if sometimes hard, was certainly varied. His activities were also still sufficiently novel to be of interest to the amusement-seeking public. A scene from Mrs. Susannah Centlivre's *A Bold Stroke for a Wife*, first performed in 1718, takes us inside Jonathan's Coffee House in Exchange Alley, and illustrates several of the points made so far in this chapter.[1] Though clearly also acting as brokers, the denizens of Jonathan's are described as 'stock-jobbers' and as such are distinguished from Tradelove the 'Change-Broker', who is presumably a Sworn Broker. The stock-jobbers' jargon is very similar to that reproduced by Mortimer forty years later, without which 'it would be impossible for their lungs to hold out'.[2] They are each presumably carrying their order and bought-and-sold books, and, fortified by the new stimulants tea and coffee, are briskly buying, selling, and settling 'differences' on previous accounts. Options are referred to briefly: one of the jobbers has 'a good Putt for next Week'. 'The books' are presumably the transfer-books at the Bank, South Sea House, etc. A further point is that the terms 'Bull' and 'Bear' are already in use. Bulls (who drive things into the air) buy more stock for a given date than they have orders for, expecting the market to rise. If it has risen by settlement day they have claims against fellow brokers for stock at, say, 180, when the market price — partly owing to their demands — has risen to 190. The selling broker must provide stock (at a loss) at the lower price, which the buying broker can sell at a profit, or pay the difference between the two prices. The bear (probably an abbreviation for bearskin-seller, a reference to the proverb 'to sell the bearskin before killing the bear') thinks the market will fall, and sells more stock than he has orders to sell. When settlement-day arrives, if prices have indeed fallen — partly owing to his tactics — he has claims against the buying broker for so much stock at, say, 190, when prices are actually only 180. The buying broker must take delivery (the extra stock the bear needs to do this now being available at the lower price) or pay the difference. The price of South Sea stock is shown as highly dependent on good (or bad) news from Spain, the country with the power to control the company's trade and therefore its profits: just as Indian news was so dramatically to affect the price of East India stock in the 1760s. Foreign 'news' may, however, simply be made up in Exchange Alley. The prominent role of Jews in the market is evidently already a matter of note. Settlement of accounts is still very much a

---

[1] Susannah Centlivre, *A Bold Stroke for a Wife* (1718), Act IV, sc. I, reproduced below, pp. 504–5.

[2] Mortimer, op. cit., p. 73 n.

continuous process through the trading year, and there is no sign yet of fixed settlement-days.

Jonathan's Coffee-House in Exchange-Alley, Crowd of People with Rolls of Paper and Parchment in their Hands; a Bar, and Coffee-Boys waiting.

Enter TRADELOVE *['a Change-Broker'] and Stock-Jobbers with Rolls of Paper and Parchment*

1ST STOCK.	South-Sea at seven Eighths; who buys?
2ND STOCK.	South Sea Bonds due at Michaelmas, 1718. Class Lottery-Tickets.
3RD STOCK.	East-India Bonds?
4TH STOCK.	What, all Sellers and no Buyers? Gentlemen, I'll buy a thousand Pound for Tuesday next at 3 Fourths.
COFF. B.	Fresh Coffee, Gentlemen, fresh Coffee?
TRADE.	Hark ye, Gabriel, you'll pay the Difference of that Stock we transacted for t'other Day.
GABRIEL.	Ay, Mr. Tradelove, here's a Note for the Money upon the Sword-Blade Company. (*Gives him a Note.*)
COFF. B.	Bohea-Tea, Gentlemen?

Enter a Man.

MAN	Is Mr. Smuggle here?
1ST COFF. B.	Mr. Smuggle's not here, Sir, you'll find him at the Books.
2ND STOCK.	Ho! here comes two Sparks from the other End of the Town; what News bring they?

Enter Two Gentlemen.

TRADE.	I would fain bite[1] that Spark in the brown Coat, he comes very often into the Alley, but never employs a Broker.

Enter Colonel [Fainwell] and Freeman ['a Merchant'].

2ND STOCK.	Who does anything in the Civil List Lottery? or Caco[2]? Zounds, where are all the Jews this Afternoon? Are you a Bull or a Bear Today, Abraham?
3RD STOCK.	A Bull, faith — but I have a good Putt for next Week.

[*Colonel Fainwell is introduced as a Dutch merchant just come to England. Freeman has a letter 'from one that belongs to the Emperor's Minister' saying that the Spaniards have raised their siege of Cagliari. Freeman says that the news may be depended upon.*]

TRADE.	Sir, I am much oblig'd to you, 'Egad, 'tis rare News. — Who sells South-Sea for next Week.
STOCK JOB.	(*Altogether*). I sell; I, I, I, I, I sell.

[1] i.e. get the better of him in a business deal by not over-scrupulous means.

[2] Chocolate beans. Cf. Mortimer's later account of deals in green peas and mackerel, *Every Man his own Broker*, pp. 90–91.

1ST STOCK.   I'll sell 5000 for next Week, at five Eighths.

2ND STOCK.   I'll sell ten thousand, at five Eighths, for the same Time.

TRADE.   Nay, nay, hold, hold, not altogether, Gentlemen, I'll be no Bull, I'll buy no more than I can take: Will you sell ten thousand Pound at a half, for any Day next Week except Saturday?

1ST STOCK.   I'll sell it you, Mr. Tradelove.

[Freeman states that the Spaniards have raised the siege of Cagliari.]

A STOCK.   How's this? The Siege of Cagliari rais'd; — I wish it may be true, 'twill make Business stir, and Stocks rise.

1ST STOCK.   Tradelove's a cunning fat Bear; if this News proves true, I shall repent I sold him the five [*sic*, for ten] thousand Pounds.

IV

By the close of the War of Austrian Succession the market in securities had greatly increased both its scale and sophistication. It was now based firmly on Jonathan's Coffee House, Garraway's having become a centre for the sale of goods by auction.[1] A disastrous fire on 25 March 1748, which burned down the whole quarter around Exchange Alley, leaving in ruins Jonathan's, Garraway's, the Jerusalem and several other coffee-houses, the offices of the London Assurance, and 'upwards of a hundred' private houses, shops, etc., at first 'stirred the whole town' but imposed no more than a temporary check on the brokers and jobbers.[2] Heavy government borrowing during the Seven Years War further increased the volume of securities traded at Jonathan's, and in 1761 one of the brokers, Thomas Mortimer, published *Every Man his own Broker*, the first full-length description of what went on there. The

[1] *The Public Advertiser* carried regular notices of these sales, which were conducted by Sworn Brokers licensed to deal in the various commodities. Such sales were also carried out at the Royal Exchange Coffee House in Threadneedle Street and the Corn Exchange Coffee House in Mark Lane. Ships were auctioned at Lloyd's Coffee House in Lombard Street.

[2] For the fire, see *The London Evening Post*, 24–26 March 1748. The name of Jonathan's owner is given as Rebecca Price and of Garraway's as Joseph Wilson. The *General Advertiser*, 13, 14 and 15 September 1748, lists contributors to relieve the sufferers from the fire, and those relieved. Rebecca Price received £200 and Joseph Wilson £100. The total paid was £5,775. The phrase 'stirred the whole town' comes from Archief Brants, 1344, van Hemert & Co. in London to de Neufville & Co. in Amsterdam, 25 March 1748, 'om deese Zaak is de geheele Stadt in beweeging geweest'.

fact that his book ran into nine editions during the following twenty years is indicative of public interest in the market. Mortimer failed, however, in his avowed aim of eliminating the brokers' trade by educating the investing public in the niceties of market technique.[1] The brokers continued to increase in numbers and corporate spirit. Jonathan's grew cramped, and in 1773 its members raised a subscription to build a new house for their business at the corner of Threadneedle Street and Sweeting's Alley, just behind the Royal Exchange.[2] It was at first intended to call this 'infant college of iniquity' New Jonathan's, but when it was opened on Tuesday 13 July 1773 'the brokers and others . . . came to a resolution . . . it should be named the Stock Exchange, which is to be wrote over the door'.[3] In the late 1770s members acquired from the Bank of England 'spacious rooms . . . adjoining to the Transfer offices' for the preliminaries to transfer business.[4] In 1801, war having once again greatly increased the volume of trading, a new and much larger building was opened in Capel Court near Threadneedle Street, parts of which are incorporated in the present Stock Exchange.

The war loans of the 1740s resulted in the introduction of new and sophisticated types of speculation in Exchange Alley. The reappearance of public lotteries, for instance, which were held nearly every year during the war, led to the reintroduction of the sale of shares of tickets which had proved so popular during the War of the Spanish Succession.[5] Thus Weaver's state lottery office in Cornhill was selling shares of a half down to a sixteenth in all the prizes of the current lottery in September 1745.[6] New practices introduced in the 1740s were the hiring and insurance of tickets. The first, known as 'riding a Horse in the Lottery' or simply 'riding on Horse-back', consisted, as a contemporary explained, in

hiring the Chance of a Ticket at a certain Price per Day; shou'd that Number, so hir'd, come up a Prize, it then belongs to the Person that paid the Hire, upon his paying the Value of the Ticket.[7]

---

[1] Thomas Mortimer, *Every Man his own Broker*, 1st and 2nd eds., 1761; 3rd, 4th and 5th, 1762; 7th, 1769; 8th, 1775; 9th, 1782. The 6th edition is not listed in the B.M. catalogue. The first edition was published under the pseudonym 'Philanthropos'.

[2] *The Morning Chronicle*, 16 July 1773; *The London Evening Post*, 10–13 July 1773.

[3] *The Morning Chronicle*, loc. cit., and *The General Evening Post*, 13–15 July 1773.

[4] Mortimer, op. cit. (9th ed. (1782)), p. 162; the passage does not occur in the 8th ed. (1775).

[5] See above, p. 497.

[6] *The Penny London Post or Morning Advertiser*, 4–6 September 1745.

[7] *The Art of Stock-jobbing, a Poem. By a Gideonite* (1746), p. 18.

If the money used to 'hire' tickets had been used to buy them, it would of course have helped to keep their price up. Parliament, therefore, determined to monopolize the benefits of speculation for its own projects, forbade hiring of tickets in 1743 and 1744 under penalty of £500.[1] But the ingenuity of ticket-office keepers, and others who made block purchases of tickets, was not daunted. As the author previously quoted observes,

this is abolish'd by Act of Parliament, and as in all things (tho' in never so strong a manner drawn up) some Hole is found to creep out of, so they have found out a new Way that answers the same Purpose, which is insuring of Tickets. In Jonathan's you find many Puffs.[2]

The new practice, as described some years later by Mortimer, had three varieties. 'Insurance from blanks' could be obtained by paying a premium for, say, ten tickets. While the 'policy' lasted, the insured was given an undrawn ticket for any of the ten drawn blank. A variation was simply to hand the insurer a list of ticket numbers; he undertook while the policy lasted to pay the cash price of a new ticket for every one drawn blank. With the third procedure, 'insurance for prizes', the insured obtained £20 if any of the tickets whose numbers he had given to the insurer were drawn prizes while the policy lasted. Except for the first type of insurance actual possession of tickets was not necessary. This was one of a number of ways in which the circle of speculators, often men of little standing or property, was continually widening. Mortimer says that during the Seven Years War the clerks and waiters at Jonathan's bought policies every year, the insurers making profits of up to 25%.[3]

Riding on horseback and ticket insurance were new bubbles on the stream of speculation. A much more important innovation, probably dating from the early 1740s, was the introduction of quarterly settlement days for market bargains; these days were called Rescounter Days or Rescounters, in imitation of the *Rescontre-Dagen* of the Amsterdam Bourse. In the early 1720s the only fixed periods in the London market for the forward sale or purchase of securities were for 'puts' and 'refusals', which were normally for three or six months.[4] In 1734, however, after an attempt in the previous year had

---

[1] 16 Geo. II, c. 13 (1743), 17 Geo. II, c. 18 (1744).

[2] *The Art of Stock-jobbing*, loc. cit.

[3] Mortimer, op. cit. (5th ed. (1762)), pp. 85 ff.

[4] See the list of London security prices dated 5 January 1731 sent by Stephen Daubuz to Dutch clients in C. H. Wilson, *Anglo-Dutch Commerce and Finance*, facing p. 75. There are several of these lists in Archief Brants, 927. All the puts and refusals in them are for three and six months.

miscarried in the Lords, Parliament passed an Act forbidding these option dealings under heavy penalties, to which the broker and his client were both liable.[1] It was thought the measure was likely to be effective. 'The price of the Funds will be kept up', writes the merchant William Isaac Kops from London to Simon Bevel in Haarlem on 15 July 1734,

> by an Act that our Parliament made last session that there can be no more speculative dealing, which means that people can no longer make 1, 2 or 3% by buying or selling.[2]

A year later, on 18 June 1735, Robert Hennebo, an Amsterdam broker, writes to Bevel that

> the English cannot cause a fall by speculation in London, because a year ago a law was passed by which it is forbidden under heavy penalties to give premiums for a rise or fall of prices, or to deal in stocks for time. So in London only cash purchases and sales can be made.[3]

Thirty years after this date option dealings were so rare in London that they were referred to as 'Species of dealing in stocks in Holland scarcely known in England'.[4] According to William Hussey, speaking in a debate of 1771, the first object of the act of 1734, 'to prevent [puts and] refusal[s]' was 'immediately effected'.[5] The usual statement that the Act was a dead letter seems therefore to be quite untrue. However, by eliminating one type of market speculation it must have stimulated the other, dealing on margins, where the penalties on the broker were less severe, and harder to enforce, as Hussey pointed out. This would in turn have made the case for regular settlement days (like the Dutch Rescounters) increasingly urgent.

The date of their introduction has not been exactly traced, but may tentatively be put in the early 1740s.[6] In July 1737 the Sun Fire Office was

---

[1] For the details of this measure see below, p. 519.

[2] Archief Brants, 1649; Kops to Bevel, 15 July 1734, in Dutch.

[3] L. van Nierop, 'Brieven van den Amsterdamschen makelaar Robert Hennebo aan . . . Simon Bevel over Engelsche fondsen (1735–1736)', *Economisch-Historisch Jaarboek*, xvii (1931), 57, Hennebo to Bevel, 18 June 1735.

[4] Quoted in Dr. L. S. Sutherland, *The East India Company in Eighteenth Century Politics* (1952), p. 41 n.

[5] B. M. Egerton MS. 230, f. 19, Cavendish's Reports of Debates in the House of Commons, debate on a bill against stock-jobbing 23 April 1771. The words in square brackets in the text are omitted.

[6] Cf. the introduction of £1,000 Exchequer bills in 1742 (above, p. 384) and of assignable scrip in government loans in 1743 (above, p. 217).

still buying stock 'for the opening the 26th Instant', that is, for the day on which the transfer books reopened after being closed to pay a dividend.[1] On 9 November 1744 (O.S.) (20 November (N.S.)) John and Wolfgang van Hemert write from London to Jan Isaak de Neufville in Amsterdam that 'the funds here are very firm, so that people must wait to see if the coming rescounters will make any change'.[2] This must refer to English Rescounters, since the Dutch ones for November, held on 15th (N.S.), were already over by the time the letter was written. The later practice, described below, was for the English Rescounters to take place on the first transfer day after the Dutch ones, so that account could be taken in London of Dutch settlements. It seems likely that when first introduced the London Rescounters took place nominally on the same day as the Dutch ones — 15 February, 15 May, 15 August and 15 November — but in fact eleven days later, until England also adopted the Gregorian calendar in 1752.[3]

From the 1740s the London Rescounters — the word itself was obviously an adaptation of the Dutch 'rescontre' — were the chief occasions for settlement of market bargains, and are so described at the end of the Seven Years War by Mortimer, who, however, throws no light on the date of their introduction.[4] It would be easy to deduce from his account that bargains were only settled on Rescounter days, but this is inherently unlikely. Description of practice in the later 1760s shows that there were intermediate settling days as well, based (like the Sun Fire Office's purchase in 1737) on the opening and shutting of the transfer books. There is no reason to doubt that the two systems had co-existed since the introduction of the London Rescounters. The change of calendar in 1752 made one alteration necessary, however: the English Rescounters had to be held on the first transfer day after the Dutch Rescounters, which continued to be on the 15th of February,

---

[1] Sun Fire Office, Minutes of the Committee of Management 21 July 1737.

[2] Archief Brants, 1344: 'de fondsen Zyn hier heel willigh, Zoo dat men afwagten Moet of de verwagt wordende Resconters Eenige verandering Zullen geven'.

[3] Dealers' accounts — e.g. stock and Drawing Office accounts for the prominent dealers Abraham Craiesteyn, John Collman, William Cotsford (Bank of England Record Office) — are unhelpful in dating the origin of the London Rescounters. The transfers and payments in these accounts are not made at regular intervals.

[4] Mortimer, op. cit. (5th ed. (1762)), p. 26. He ascribes their introduction to the volume of foreign, particularly Dutch, buying and selling in the London market. For the origin of the Dutch word 'rescontre' see above, p. 491. English dealers sometimes spelt the London Rescounters 'rescontre', see note 1 on p. 510.

May, August and November. The results of Dutch settlements were sent over to London by the first mail packet.[1]

The Rescounter procedure described by Mortimer shows that something like a clearing house in Stock Exchange bargains had evolved, some years before the London bankers set up a clearing house for their own business. It seems at least plausible that the first development influenced the second. At the Rescounters brokers could set off a series of bargains, adjust their total indebtedness with each other, and note where actual delivery of stock rather than payment on margin was required. The buying broker might be referred by the selling broker to a third against whom the latter had a claim, by the third broker to a fourth, and perhaps 'all round the House' until he found one who could produce what he wanted.[2] Presumably it was never known until the Rescounters whether actual delivery of stock would be required by buyers or not. For this reason the broker always needed to be sure that his books balanced — that he had as many claims on his fellows as they had on him; for if not, he might find himself obliged to obtain a large amount of stock at short notice and at an unfavourable price. It seems clear, however, that the majority of bargains at the Rescounters were not for real purchases, but only for transactions on margin. The brokers, on behalf of their clients, paid the 'difference' between the price of the stock when ordered and its price on Rescounter day. Sellers might allow buyers unable or unwilling to settle to 'continue' to the next Rescounters, on paying a fee of from 1% to 4%, depending on the activity of the market. The decision whether to settle or continue (the cant term 'contango' was not used instead of 'continue' until the nineteenth century) turned on which was more expensive — that is, on assessment of the likelihood of prices rising or falling before the next settlement.[3] The reverse process, continuation by sellers, was called 'backwardation'.[4] The whole procedure, of course, facilitated extensive gambling. Mortimer recalls a case in the 1750s of a speculator whose holdings in the

---

[1] P.R.O. C 12/57/22, *Hobson v. de la Fontaine*, and C 12/1623/1, *André v. Verney and Burke*. Both cases arose out of dealings in East India stock in the late 1760s. The former contains a copy of de la Fontaine & Brymer's London jobbing account, which shows stock bought for John Hobson for 'Rescontre of August' and 'November Rescontre' and also for intermediate dates. The second case explains the use of intermediate settling-days and the connection between the London and Amsterdam markets. I am indebted to Dr. L. S. Sutherland for drawing my attention to this material.

[2] Mortimer, op. cit. (5th ed., 1762), pp. 82–84.

[3] [Isaac de Pinto], *Traité de la Circulation et du Crédit*, pp. 295–6.

[4] Ibid., p. 308. De Pinto says backwardation was introduced in the mid-1750s, but *The Art of Stockjobbing* (1746), p. 18 n., refers to it, though the account given of it is unintelligible.

funds amounted to no more than £100, while his fictitious turnover of stock at Jonathan's was £75,000 in a single quarter.[1]

Actual transfers of stock, which formed the solid base for the airy fabric of speculation, had increased during the war of 1739–48 from perhaps 15,000 to perhaps 35,000 a year.[2] (It would be interesting to know the ratio between real and speculative bargains.) It might be supposed that the jobbers would have increased accordingly. But the evidence is that their circle had contracted by the early 1750s as much as that of brokers had expanded. This can be illustrated from Bank stock, with a capital of £10,780,000, and 3% Consols, with a capital of £9,137,821. In the former, the two principal dealers were Joseph Caneo and John Castell, both described as 'of London, gent.' Between 1 January and 31 December 1754 Caneo made 124 purchases and 111 sales of stock totalling £140,826; Castell made 73 purchases and 79 sales, totalling £101,647. There were 1,539 transfers of Bank stock during the year, and assuming an average transfer of £1,000 the turnover was £1,539,000. Between them Caneo and Castell had handled 25% of this in terms of transfers and 15% in terms of stock. In 3% Consols, William Cotsford 'gent., the Post Office', had built up a dealer's empire. In the same year 1754 he handled 870 purchases and 868 sales of stock totalling £632,781. This was 36% of the total numbers of transfers and assuming an average transfer of £381, 34% of total turnover.[3]

The concentration of jobbing in a few hands was due, in the first place, to the normal trend of specialization. The work involved, after all, even for dealers like Cotsford, was not very large — his turnover in Consols did not amount to more than ten or a dozen transfers each transfer day, and the transfer books were closed for half the year.[4] His — and other jobbers' — business in other stocks was not extensive enough to change this picture. A relatively small number of jobbers could thus handle the major part of the work. Second, the development of dealings on margin in Exchange Alley, provided more fruitful opportunities for speculation and, unlike jobbing, required little working capital. But for this, competition in jobbing would have been stiffer, the number of jobbers larger, and annual turnover higher.

Being fairly constantly involved in transfers of stock, but unable normally to make a living from them, the jobber needed a salaried occupation which

---

[1] Mortimer, op. cit. (5th ed. (1762)), p. 34 n., 'a few years' since'.

[2] See above, p. 467.

[3] Ledgers for Bank stock and 3% Consols, Bank of England Record Office. For average units of stock transferred see above, p. 465.

[4] See above, p. 463.

kept him near the books without taking up too much of his time. The most obvious and convenient was a clerkship in one of the transfer offices of the three 'monied companies', where the greater part of the stock dealt in on the market was actually transferred from seller to buyer. John Harvey, the Bank of England clerk and dealer in 5% stock in the period shortly after the peace of 1713, is an early example of this combination of occupations.[1] During the next twenty or thirty years the number of such dealers grew. In the 1730s and 1740s John Apthorp, Peter Merrick and Benjamin Whichcote 'of the Bank', and Samuel Bull, Jeremiah Pratt, John Rice, and Benjamin Webb, all 'of South Sea House', were large-scale jobbers, whose accounts, together with those of other professional dealers like Joseph Caneo, Henry Carington, John Castell, John Collman, William Whitmore, extend over many folios at the back of the stock ledgers, and record a high proportion of the total annual transfers.[2] From 1798 the Bank of England found it convenient to separate dealers' accounts in 3% Consols, with their active turnover, into special jobbers' ledgers.

The dealers who were not transfer clerks followed a number of other occupations. Some acted as stockbrokers. John Castell and Richard Willoughby are both described in the 1730s as 'Broker, Exchange Alley'.[3] Neither was a Sworn Broker; another dealer, William Whitmore, was — he was admitted by the City as 'Draper, Exeter Court in the Strand' in November 1723, the bond not being discharged until September 1762.[4] Joseph Caneo is described at first as 'Fenchurch Street, merchant', later by a discreet 'London, gent.' Henry Carington was 'gent., Austin Friars', later 'Hoxton'. Another Hoxton dealer, John Collman, was a grocer in Hoxton Square. William Cotsford was a clerk in the General Post Office.[5] Dealers who started as transfer-office clerks might later set up on their own, like Benjamin Whichcote: his address in the mid-1740s was still 'the Bank of England'; this is scored through later and 'Exchange Alley' substituted.

The problem of the transfer clerks' jobbing activities was recurrently studied by the directors of the companies, without much effect. As early as

---

[1] See above, p. 498.

[2] Bank of England Record Office, ledgers for these stocks. After the first folios, active accounts tended to be put at the back of the ledger.

[3] Bank of England Record Office, alphabet books to the ledgers.

[4] Corporation of London Records Office, Brokers' Admissions 1708–1801.

[5] He appears in the earliest surviving G.P.O. Establishment Book as the second of ten Sorters at a salary of £50 p.a. By 1747 he had become Assistant and Sorter to the Clerk of the Yarmouth Road. In July 1765 he became Clerk of the Bristol Road. He died in November 1766.

1712 the Bank of England ruled that no servant should 'transact any business in buying, selling or transferring Stocks'.[1] In 1745 a further attempt was made by forbidding them from 'buying, selling or transferring any Annuities transferable at the Bank'.[2] In 1753 these rules were extended to cover lottery tickets, and all government securities.[3] The evidence already reviewed shows how ineffective these rules were. The South Sea Company's directors were equally unsuccessful. In 1745 they recorded their displeasure at the company's clerks dealing in stock. In September 1749, having learned that several clerks were extensive dealers, they 'referred to the Committee of Accounts to examine into the Transactions and Dealings in Stocks, of the Officers and Clerks in the Transfer Offices, and Report their Opinion whether the same interfere with their Business in the Office'.[4] But nothing seems to have come of these moves, and the clerks went on dealing as merrily as ever.

The pattern of jobbing in East India stock in the 1740s and early 1750s continued to differ in some important respects from that of jobbing in other securities. Though the fierce speculation of the 1760s lay in the future, the number of jobbing accounts was about fifty, a reduction since the earlier part of the century, but markedly higher than in other stocks.[5] Moreover, while the dealer in Bank stock, Consols, Reduced Threes and South Sea annuities — the biggest stocks in the market — was by the mid-eighteenth century essentially a professional, operating an account with a high turnover on a relatively small balance, the East India jobbers were still mostly men of substance, whose jobbing was largely confined to this stock, and clearly a sideline to other activities. The pattern of occupations resembles that of the early 1700s. Several dealers were bankers. These included William Belchier, Edward Ironside, George Lee and Richard Stone, all of Lombard Street; Philip Hollingworth, Fraser Honywood; John Lightfoot of Threadneedle Street, Thomas Snow of Temple Bar, and Robert Surman, the former Deputy Cashier of the South Sea Company, now senior partner of Surman, Dinely & Cliffe of Lombard Street.[6] Other East India jobbers were substantial merchants, like John Backer, Abraham and Francis Craiesteyn, Benjamin Mendes da Costa, John Edwards of Old Jewry and Henry

---

[1] W. Marston Acres, *The Bank of England from within* (1931), i. 227.   [2] Ibid.

[3] Ibid., p. 228.

[4] Add. MS. 25512, f. 63, South Sea D. Ct. Bk. 28 September 1749. For the order of 1745, ibid., f. 64.

[5] Bank of England Record Office, East India stock ledgers.

[6] The firm stopped payment in 1757. For a short period in the 1750s they were bankers to the Sun Fire Office, Dickson, *Sun Insurance Office*, p. 237.

Muilman. (Several of these had maintained close contact with friends and relatives in Holland.) There was also a certain number of professional dealers, including Abraham Atkins, John Boldero, John Castell (the large dealer in Bank stock and Consols), Gabriel Lopez, Gael Morris, and David Shrimpton — who had evidently recovered from his set-backs in the 1720s. The largest of all the East India jobbers at this date was the great financier and loan contractor Samson Gideon. Owing to the competition between individuals turnover was lower than in other stocks. Even Gideon was only turning over £80,000 to £100,000 a year in the 1740s; nearly all the other East India jobbers had less than half this amount of business.

V

Several trends are discernible in the development of the London market between the 1690s and the 1750s. It was primarily a market in government securities; transactions in the shares of private companies other than the three 'monied companies' were relatively small in scope and frequency after the 1690s. Besides government stock, brokers were prepared to take orders for the miscellany of short-term government obligations: Army debentures, Navy bills, Exchequer bills, and tallies of loan. The market fairly quickly developed considerable sophistication of technique. It introduced option dealing for forward sales and purchases, and, when these were forbidden, concentrated on margin transactions, and introduced quarterly settlement days for clearing all bargains. These were timed to take account of settlements on the Amsterdam Bourse, with which the London market had increasingly close connections from the 1720s. They were retained until made fortnightly in April 1885.[1] Already on the eve of the Seven Years War the London Stock Exchange could challenge comparison with the much older Bourse in Amsterdam and was evolving (despite backslidings and mistakes) into a technically perfect market; from which one of its members, David Ricardo, was to draw conclusions about the operation of the economy as a whole.

The operators in it were of mixed origins, and included bankers, merchants, government contractors, tradesmen, clerks. A substantial

[1] *The Times,* 14 April 1885, City column.

minority throughout the period, particularly in dealings in East India stock, were Jews. Others were English-domiciled Huguenots. Others, again, were of Dutch origin, and retained close connections with their homeland. Members of Nonconformist communities are harder to identify, but there is evidence that some prominent jobbers belonged to them. Four of the earliest brokers admitted by the City of London under the legislation of 1708 were Quakers.[1] Nathaniel Garland, a linendraper in Cornhill, and an East India jobber, was one of the London Dissenting Deputies Committee between 1735 and 1745. Abraham Craiesteyn was also chosen a member of this Committee in 1752. Samuel Lesingham, an East India jobber in the period 1715–19, served as a Dissenting Deputy from 1735 to 1737.[2] Abraham Atkins of Clapham, a big East India jobber in the 1740s, was a Particular Baptist.[3] No clear distinction between jobbers and brokers can be made, even at the end of the period; there are too many examples of the same person acting as both. A distinction of function is, however, observable, with the jobber tending more and more to become the main supplier of stock, and the broker to become more and more an agent in speculative transactions of considerable refinement, where no transfer was usually contemplated. Correspondingly, the circle of jobbers tended to shrink over the half-century and that of brokers to grow.

The main criticisms of these developments followed obvious lines: objections to Jews, foreigners and men of low origins; to novel ways of getting rich quickly; to new and outlandish techniques and vocabulary; to bearish manipulation of prices.[4] Against this, it could be argued that the evolution of the market was an essential counterpart to government borrowing, and that its operations helped provide a flow of new capital for war loans.[5] It could also be argued that the daily valuation of the government's credit on the floor of Jonathan's was, like the popular press, one of the features of England's 'open' form of government in the eighteenth century; and that this form, despite the risks it involved, was to prove more secure in the long run, because more firmly based on public discussion and evaluation,

---

[1] Corporation of London Records Office, Repertory 112, Minutes of the Court of Mayor and Aldermen 1707–8, ff. 259–60, 6 May 1708, admission of Robert Brasier, Walter Benthall, Abraham Coleman and John Timbrell on affirmation. It is not stated what sort of brokers they were to be, however; they may not have been stockbrokers. For the Act of 1708, below, p. 517.

[2] Guildhall Library, MS. 3083/1, Minutes of the Dissenting Deputies 1732–67.

[3] Walter Wilson, *The History and Antiquities of Dissenting Churches*, iv (1814), 231.

[4] For these criticisms see above.

[5] As de Pinto, op. cit. in particular, contended.

than the closed and supposedly more efficient bureaucratic governments of France and other European Powers.

VI

True to its tradition of frowning on new forms of economic enterprise — unless practised by landowners at the expense of tenants — Parliament made repeated attempts between the 1690s and the 1770s to check the growth of Exchange Alley, and the activities of its denizens. Most of these attempts, however, were ineffectual, owing to their time-honoured but futile identification of economic pressures with human wickedness or folly. The earliest steps were taken in 1697, a year of crisis at the end of a period in which government credit had steadily deteriorated. First, the Bank of England insisted that all contracts for the sale of its stock should be invalid unless registered at the Bank within seven days and transferred within fourteen. Its aim was to prevent bear operations on its stock at a time when an important new subscription was pending, but the method chosen was ineffective. The register was duly opened, but only 150 entries were ever made in it.[1] A second measure attempted to limit the number of brokers of all kinds, including stockbrokers, to 100.[2] The City, which was the admitting authority under the Act, decided that twelve of these were to be aliens and twelve Jewish.[3] According to the Act, brokers, who were to wear a badge signifying their admission, were not to deal in goods or securities on their own account, were to note all orders for purchase or sale in their books within three days of receiving them, and were not to take more than $\frac{1}{2}\%$ brokerage. Furthermore, until the end of the next session of Parliament none were to discount or deal in tallies 'struck on any Parliamentary Fund' unless licensed to do so

---

[1] 8 & 9 Wm. III, c. 20, s. xxxiv; Bank of England G. Ct. Bk. i, ff. 114, 121–2, 16 January 1697 and 1 February 1697; Bank of England Record Office, Register of Contracts in Bank stock, opened 13 April 1697. For the circumstances in which the statute was passed see above, pp. 344–55.

[2] 8 & 9 Wm. III, c. 32. Previous Bills in 1693 and 1696 to regulate stock-jobbing had been shelved, see *HCJ* xi, 116, 132; 535, 541.

[3] Corporation of London Records Office, Repertory 101 (1696–7), ff. 197–8, 26 April 1697, the Court of Aldermen decides that up to twelve of the hundred brokers shall be Jewish and up to twelve 'of other Nations'.

by the Treasury. All bargains turning on puts or refusals of stock were to be void. The statute was to be in force for only three years, but was later extended to 1708.[1]

Keeping government tallies and bills at par, and preventing heavy falls in prices, could not really be accomplished by coercing the dealers. During his Treasurership Lord Godolphin seems to have been well aware that the price level of securities depended on other factors, some controllable, like care over monetary policy, some not, like the fortunes of war. The renewal of the provisions of 1697 in another form in 1708 was therefore a sop to public opinion, rather than a serious attempt to regulate prices. It was also in part a mere expedient to reimburse the City of London for a small loss of revenue. Under the new statute, which abolished the office of Garbler of Spices, the Court of Mayor and Aldermen was granted the right to admit all brokers practising within the City liberties 'under such restrictions and limitations for their honest and good behaviour as that Court shall think fit and reasonable', for an entry fee of forty shillings, and an annual subscription of the same amount.[2] Unlike the Act of 1697, this therefore delegated most of the framing regulations for brokers to a subordinate authority.

On 23 March 1708 the Lord Mayor, Sir William Withers, eleven aldermen, and the Recorder and one of the Sheriffs of the City, met to consider the new statute.[3] They nominated a committee with a quorum of three 'to Peruse the said Act and Advise and Consider what Number of Persons may be requisite for this Court to admit as Brokers', whether their numbers should be limited, and how the entry fee was to be paid. On 30 March the committee tabled a report recommending the admission as brokers of twelve aliens of the Dutch and French congregations in the City and twelve aliens of other congregations, but evidently no limit to other admissions.[4] This was good sense if the City wanted a large revenue from fees, though the provision about the Dutch and French Churches was subsequently rejected, only twelve members of the Jewish congregations being allowed admission.[5] (This number was subsequently held constant, a new Jewish broker only being admitted on the death or retirement of an existing

---

[1] By 11 & 12 Wm. III, c. 13. Cf. Dudley Abrahams, 'Jew Brokers of the City of London', *Jewish Hist. Soc. of Eng. Miscellanies* (1937), p. 80. Abraham says that the Act of 1697 stipulated that there should be twelve Jewish brokers, but this is clearly incorrect.

[2] 6 Anne, c. 68.

[3] Corporation of London Records Office, Repertory 112 (1707–8), f. 112.

[4] Ibid., ff. 119–20.

[5] Ibid., f. 276, 1 June 1708.

one.) The Recorder, Sir Salathiel Lovell, was asked to draft a form of broker's bond, which was approved on 8 April but amended later in the month, and again early in May, in particular by making it optional, not compulsory, for the broker to disclose his principal.[1] The bond of 1697 was a short document requiring a broker on admission to exercise his office in accordance with the late statute, without 'Fraud, Covin, or any corrupt or crafty devices'. The new bond, since the statute of 1708 was uninformative, was longer and more complicated, requiring the registration of bargains in the broker's books within three days of making them, and the disclosure of principals if asked, and forbidding brokers to do business in Exchange Alley, or to deal in securities on their own account.[2]

On 6 May 1708 the Court of Aldermen decided to impose a fine of £25 on anyone acting as broker without being licensed,[3] and in the following month the Common Serjeant was consulted about the possibility of a suit after several Sworn Brokers had complained of 'one Mustaphia, a Jew, acting as a Broker not being admitted thereto'.[4] But there is no record of further action. The difficulties of prosecution, given the likely hostility of witnesses, would, indeed, have been formidable. Connivance was easier, particularly in the most rapidly growing of the broker's trades, broking in stock. From the evidence reviewed in this chapter it seems clear that the machinery of 1708, in so far as it was meant to curb speculation in securities, was soon regarded as an elaborate sham.

The subject of control of Exchange Alley was taken up again by Parliament in December 1720 in the first glow of righteous (if self-interested) indignation against the speculation during the South Sea Bubble, in which a majority of the Commons and a minority of the Lords had participated. On 20 December 1720 the Commons ordered a Bill 'for the better Establishment of publick Credit by preventing, for the future, the infamous Practise of Stock-Jobbing'.[5] It was shelved in the Lords, however, and after this nothing was done until 1733 when, as a result of another, though lesser, scandal, the exposure of the murky affairs of the Charitable Corporation and the York Buildings Company,[6] a further Bill against jobbing was drafted.

[1] Ibid., ff. 121–3, 215–18, 247.

[2] Corporation of London Records Office, Brokers' Bonds, bonds of 1697 and 1708. The form of the earlier bond was prescribed in the statute.

[3] Corporation of London Records Office, Repertory 112, ff. 260–1.   [4] Ibid., ff. 316–17.

[5] HCJ xix, 392. The Bill was ordered by the Commons on 20 December 1720, and passed the Lower House on 31 March 1721. For the parliamentary share in speculation in 1720 see above, p. 108.

[6] See above, p. 155.

Its sponsor in the House of Commons was Sir John Barnard, the chief apostle of financial purity, and it passed the Lower House by a narrow 55 votes to 49 on 30 April 1733.[1] Once more the Lords stood in the way: they amended the Bill so heavily that it had to be dropped. In the following year Barnard returned to the attack, and this time he was successful,[2] probably because the current expectation that Great Britain would enter the War of Polish Succession was causing security prices to fall. In 1737 'Sir John Barnard's Act', as it was to be known for the rest of the century, was made perpetual.[3] It aimed, first, at option contracts ('puts' and refusals); second, at dealings on margin. Premiums paid for puts and refusals were in future to be of no effect, and those who paid or received them, together with their brokers or agents, were subject to a penalty of £500. Those who sold for a future day stock they did not already possess also incurred a penalty of £500; their broker incurred a penalty of £100 if he knew that his principal held no stock when the sale was made. From 1 June 1734 it was to be compulsory for brokers to record all contracts in their books, including the names of their principals — the point insisted on in 1697, and waived in 1708. It is doubtful whether the Act of 1734 was any more successful in this respect than the earlier measures — Mortimer's examples of brokers' books show only the names of other brokers, not those of principals. As between options and margins the act was more lenient to the second, for the broker could presumably fairly easily plead ignorance of his client's stockholdings. This was the basis for Hussey's view in 1771 that the Act eliminated the first type of forward dealing but not the second.[4]

The difficulties of legislation against jobbing were numerous. An act might stimulate one practice by forbidding another; it was argued earlier that this was the main effect of Barnard's Act of 1734. The legislature was constantly left behind by the appearance of new speculative techniques: this was true of the provisions against 'riding on horseback' in the 1740s.[5] The attempts to separate broking from jobbing, and to license all brokers, were largely ineffectual. Similarly, the belief that sharp plunges of the market caused by external factors could be remedied by coercing jobbers was misplaced. This was shown in the crisis of 1745–6. Prices in Exchange Alley plummeted from September 1745 as Charles Edward Stuart's army moved south towards London. The fall was checked in December, but early in the new year there was still plenty of cause for alarm.[6] Charles Edward's

---

[1] *HCJ* xxii. 10, 133, 201; *Parl. Hist.* ix. 68.   [2] 7 Geo. II, c. 8.
[3] 10 Geo. II, c. 8.   [4] See above, p. 508.
[5] For these see above, p. 506.   [6] For the movement of prices see above, p. 223 n.

victory over Hawley at Falkirk in January 1746, and fears about French naval action to link up with the rebels, kept prices dull, and East India bonds were still at a discount. This seemed an apt moment for a further blow at 'rogues' who aimed at pushing prices lower still, and on 7 March 1746 the Commons appointed the indefatigable Barnard, together with Sir John Rushout and Horatio Walpole, to bring in a new Bill against them.[1] Their draft measure proposed a penalty, left blank, for conspiring 'to do any Act . . . with the Design and View of lowering the Price' of stock, and on those who sold forward at a price below the current one. Other clauses, like those of 1734, were all aimed at preventing a further fall in prices.[2] The effect of this coercion of the bears was not tested, owing to the rally of security prices after Cumberland's victory at Culloden on 16 April 1746. The conclusions which the whole episode might have suggested about the influence of external events on the market were not drawn at once, and further Bills against stock-jobbing were introduced in 1756 and 1771[3] — years of falling prices, like 1697, 1734 and 1746. By the seventies, however, the climate of opinion was changing. In the debate on the Bill of 1771 Sir George Colebrooke was able to argue at a theoretical level that 'the trading of Stock like every other thing ought to be free of interruption',[4] and at a practical level that market circulation was a prime condition of raising the year's supply. Henceforward, the failure of coercive legislation, the growing corporate self-consciousness of the brokers, and the belief that the wealth of nations could only increase if controls on enterprise were reduced, were all to favour the relinquishing of responsibility for professional conduct in the market, and the drawing up of rules for all forms of dealing there, to the members of the Stock Exchange themselves.

[1] 'Bull and Bear, is Honest Man and Rogue', *The Art of Stock-jobbing: a Poem* (1746), p. 17; for the committee see *HCJ* xxv. 88, 7 March 1746.

[2] *British Museum Collection of Parliamentary Papers 1731–1800*, i, no. 27, 'A Bill more effectually to prevent the infamous Practice of Stockjobbing.'

[3] *HCJ* xxvii. 546 (1756); xxxiii. 349 (1771).   [4] B.M. Egerton MS. 230, f. 21.

Appendixes

A. TENDERS FOR THE CONVERSION OF THE NATIONAL DEBT IN 1720 (SEE CHAPTER 5)

1. The first proposal was made by the Treasury to the South Sea Company, undoubtedly after prior consultation. It was dated 21 January 1720. The debts exchangeable were to be 'taken in' by 25 March 1721. The company was to make a certain payment to the Exchequer of £1.5m. It was to make a further payment of two years' purchase on the Irredeemable debts (annuities for terms of years) exchanged for new South Sea stock. It was not known in advance how large this sum would be: the maximum was computed as £1,578,752. The company was also to circulate (cash at sight) up to £800,000 Exchequer bills until midsummer 1727. It was to be paid nothing by the government for this.
Source: Add. MS. 25498, f. 156, South Sea D. Ct. Bk., 21 January 1720.

2. The next (and counter) proposal was made by the Bank of England, and dated 27 January 1720. The Bank offered to 'take in' the debts exchangeable by 24 June 1721, thus giving itself more time than its rival. It offered no certain payment. It offered the uncertain payments of three years' purchase on long annuities exchanged, three years' purchase on short annuities, and 20% on Redeemables (ordinary stock). The maximum payable was computed as £5,547,500. The new debts *could be paid off after midsummer 1724.* The Bank also agreed to circulate £800,000 Exchequer bills for four years, for an allowance of £4,000 a year.
Source: Cobbett, *Parl. Hist.* vii. 633–7. Neither this nor the second Bank proposal (no. 4, below) were entered in the *Commons Journals*. Both the South Sea proposals (nos. 3 and 5, below) were entered, as the references show.

3. The South Sea Company's amended proposal, also dated 27 January 1720 raised its certain payment to £3·5m., and the volume of Exchequer bills to be circulated to £1m. Further, the whole debt that the government owed to the South Sea Company *was to be reduced to 4% at midsummer 1727*, but not repaid before.
Source: HCJ xix. 246 and Cobbett, *Parl. Hist.* vii. 629–33. Cobbett says that this proposal was dated 22 January 1720; at col. 637, however, he shows the true date.

4. The Bank's next offer, dated 1 February 1720, retained 24 June 1721 as the closing date for taking in the public debts. But it undertook to give a fixed amount of new Bank stock in exchange for them. This was to be £1,700 Bank stock for each £100 p.a. long annuity, and an amount in proportion for short annuities. The Bank added that it had under-estimated the volume of the Redeemables in its first offer, and it therefore amended its maximum possible payment from £5,547,500 to

B

Debts exchanged for new South Sea stock in 1720

No.	Type of debt	Amount per annum or at par 1720 £	Amount exchanged for new South Sea stock £	Amount not exchanged £	Discharge of sums in previous col.	Amount added to South Sea Company capital for sums exchanged £	Interest on government's increased debt to company until midsummer 1727 %
	Long Annuities						
1	1693 ·	124,281	75,766	48,515	expired	1,515,319	5
2	1694 ·	15,237	8,871	6,366	25 January 1792	177,420	5
3	1704 ·	104,618	81,249	23,369	25 January 1792	1,624,971	5
4	1705 ·	46,000	38,970	7,030	5 April 1803	779,393	5
5	1706 ·	184,243	160,988	23,255	5 January 1805	3,219,763	5
6	1707 ·	72,187	64,411	7,776	5 April 1806	1,288,220	5
7	1708 (1) ·	40,000	35,289	4,711	5 April 1807	705,790	5
8	1708 (2) ·	80,000	69,819	10,181	5 July 1807	1,396,380	5
	TOTALS ·	666,566	535,363	131,203		10,707,256	
	Short Annuities				*expired*		
9	Balance of 1710 lottery tickets not exchanged for South Sea stock in 1719 ·	40,669	30,835	9,834	29 September 1742	431,690	5
10	Annuities of 32 years at 9% (1710) ·	81,000	66,500	14,500	29 September 1742	931,003	5
	TOTALS ·	121,669	97,335	24,334		1,362,693	

					discharged		
11	Lottery 1713 . . .	563,300	464,990	98,310	1721–8	464,990	4
12	Blanks 1714 . . .	1,055,990	865,250	190,740	1721–4	865,250	5
13	Prizes 1714 . . .	652,020	538,720	113,300	1721–4	538,720	4
14	5% 1715 (1)* . .	910,000	706,176	203,824	1724	706,176	5
15	5% 1715 (2)* . .	169,000	137,526	31,474	1724	137,526	5
16	5% 1717* . . .	9,534,077	8,329,291	1,204,786	1723	8,329,291	5
17	4% 1717* . . .	947,514	748,556	198,958	1727	748,556	4
18	Army debentures 4% 1718* . .	1,603,987	1,210,792	393,195	1727–8	1,210,792	4
19	5% (Navy) 1719* .	110,313	107,803	2,510	1724	107,803	5
20	Bank lottery 1719* .	500,000	441,700	58,300	1728	441,700	4
21	Exchequer lottery 1719	500,000	434,605	65,395	1721–5	434,605	4
	TOTALS . .	£16,546,202	£13,985,409	£2,560,792		£13,985,409	

* Managed by the Bank of England. All the other debts listed were managed by the Exchequer.

S

£5,667,500. It now also proposed (like the South Sea Company) that from mid-summer 1727 the whole state debt to it was to carry only 4% interest.
Source: Cobbett, *Parl. Hist.* vii. 639–40.

5. The South Sea Company's final — and winning — proposal was also dated 1 February 1720. It raised the company's certain payment to £4m.; and its uncertain payment to 4½ years' purchase on all Irredeemable debts exchanged, by 1 March 1722, plus one year's purchase on all *long* annuities *not* exchanged by then. The maximum payable to the state was computed as £7,567,503. The Exchequer bill clause was unaltered. The date at which the state could start to *pay off the debts* subscribed into the South Sea Company was brought back to midsummer 1724.
Source: HCJ xix. 247, and Cobbett, *Parl. Hist.* vii. 637–39.

6. The House of Commons accepted the fifth offer, but amended it, in consultation with the South Sea Company, while the Bill to incorporate it was being drafted. The date by which debts were to be exchanged was accepted (see 5) as 1 March 1722. The certain payment offered was raised to £4,156,306, probably because the company had over-estimated the volume of long annuities and would therefore pay less for their exchange. The date by which the whole state debt to the South Sea Company was to be lowered to 4% was extended to midsummer 1727, as in (3). The Act did not state the maximum sum payable by the company.
Source: South Sea Act, 1720 (6 Geo. I, c. 4).

NOTE TO APPENDIX B

The table is from the figures given in *BPP* (1898), lii. 278–81, which are in turn taken from *BPP* (1868–9), xxxv. 524. In neither case is any source quoted for them. Both reports were professedly based on original sources. H. W. Chisholm, Chief Clerk of the Exchequer, who prepared the earlier one, said that he incorporated in it the knowledge acquired from forty years' service in the department, op. cit. 326, while the second was 'compiled from original records of Income and Expenditure in the Public Record Offices of England and Ireland', *BPP* (1898), lii. 271.

Virtually the same figures occur in an 'Abstract of what Publick Debts and Incumbrances have been Subscribed to or Discharged by, ye South Sea Company . . . since ye 25th of December 1719', House of Lords Record Office, South Sea Company Papers, Box 167. Only five sums in this differ from those in the Parliamentary Papers, for small amounts. Other lists of all or part of the sums concerned, and the amounts of them exchanged, are in P.R.O. T 1/242 no. 58, Treasury Board Papers, a return from the Bank of England dated 7 September 1722, and T 1/237, no. 6, an account of the sums exchanged, probably based on the two other accounts. In all these there are only small variations in the figures.

Summary of the figures involved

	£	Of which ex-changed for new South Sea stock £
Total long annuities 1720 at 20 years' purchase	13,331,332	10,707,256
Total short annuities 1720 at 20 years' purchase	1,703,336	1,362,693
	15,034,688	12,069,948
Total redeemable stock at par	16,546,202	13,985,409
Total debts exchangeable	£31,580,890	£26,055,357

The South Sea Company's nominal capital at the start of 1720 was £11,746,844. As a result of the subscriptions of £26m. government debts in 1720 it increased to £37,802,201. £2m. of this was cancelled at midsummer 1722, and £4m. more sold to the Bank of England later in the same year, reducing the nominal capital to £31,802,201. The £2m. cancelled stock was, however, revived in 1723, making the total capital £33,802,201. This was then divided equally into 'trading stock' and fixed-interest 'annuities'.

NOTES TO APPENDIX C

It must be emphasized that for reasons discussed below the table is one of orders of magnitude rather than of strict accountancy. The totals, in particular, assume that all the individual amounts were outstanding at the same date in the year, which was not so. But it is probably worth while to have orders of magnitude rather than nothing.

1. The figures for tallies annually struck at the Exchequer for short-term loans are from *BPP* (1868-9), xxxv, which was compiled from the Treasury Annual Account Books. There are no reliable figures for tallies of fictitious loan before 1703. The Exchequer year in which tallies were issued ran from Michaelmas to Michaelmas. (For a recent discussion of the difficulties caused by variations in fiscal dating see R. C. Jarvis, 'Official Trade and Revenue Statistics', *Ec. H.R.*, 2nd series, xvii (1964), 43.

2. The annual balances of Exchequer bills standing out uncancelled are taken from *BPP* (1857-8), xxxiii, for the years 1696–1711 and 1723–5 inclusive. It appears, although it is not explicitly stated, that these are balances at Michaelmas each year. The remaining

C

Volume of short-dated securities annually outstanding 1688–1754

Year (see notes)	Exchequer tallies		Exchequer bills	Navy bills	Victualling bills	East India bonds	South Sea bonds	Totals
	For loans made in cash	Fictitious loans						
	£	£	£	£	£	£	£	£
1690	...	...	...	...	...	451,959	...	451,959
1691	...	...	...	...	...	330,242	...	330,242
1692	...	...	...	...	...	304,679	...	304,679
1693	...	...	...	...	...	272,790	...	272,790
1694	...	...	...	...	...	318,873	...	318,873
1695	...	...	...	...	...	637,297	...	637,297
1696	...	...	50,000	...	...	809,201	...	859,201
1697	...	...	1,881,475	222,258	182,114	596,525	...	2,882,372
1698	...	...	1,498,713	357,473	322,028	631,555	...	2,809,769
1699	...	...	1,051,707	237,244	118,884	964,394	...	2,372,229
1700	...	...	876,062	287,421	171,713	1,131,189	...	2,466,385
1701	...	...	651,092	364,955	316,341	1,112,483	...	2,444,871
1702	...	...	553,417	393,029	158,347	828,586	...	1,933,379
1703	1,906,690	1,200,000	539,497	...	...	1,171,112	...	4,817,299
1704	1,620,539	914,915	538,412	681,689	523,296	1,137,563	...	5,416,414
1705	2,520,142	824,526	535,312	865,804	747,369	701,460	...	6,194,613
1706	1,880,570	1,250,031	529,377	899,832	957,299	668,159	...	6,185,268
1707	2,633,697	537,002	1,879,409	1,018,960	1,041,110	882,633	...	7,992,811
1708	2,092,692	1,005,726	1,827,899	1,205,907	1,101,536	882,444	...	8,116,204
1709	1,552,833	1,573,711	2,631,785	1,576,128	1,345,894	3,303,157	...	11,983,508
1710	1,518,337	3,404,377	3,055,938	1,779,509	1,709,252	3,349,105	...	14,816,518
1711	645,127	1,814,689	3,193,433	2,088,106	1,984,331	2,920,387	...	12,646,073
1712	1,251,510	1,146,178	3,343,713	...	194,930	3,083,599	200,000	9,219,930
1713	896,127	497,629	4,492,697	...	143,681	2,872,154	400,000	9,302,288
1714	1,271,159	...	4,625,325	35,543	57,840	2,727,047	400,000	9,116,914
1715	1,022,922	473,379	4,561,025	137,027	128,698	2,718,881	500,000	9,541,932
1716	1,285,478	1,345,247	4,561,025	208,199	128,448	2,604,692	600,000	10,733,089
					181,...	2,050,226	700,000	8,345,971

Year								
1718	1,933,573	620,204		274,763	164,623	3,107,671	700,000	9,361,859
1719	953,377	1,098,357		314,800	191,113	2,972,317	700,000	7,509,702
1720	1,044,762	1,049,907	2,561,025	478,833	262,521	3,020,274	776,950	8,552,860
1721	1,064,016	479,352	1,279,738	571,351	360,540	2,989,484	4,415,950	11,800,606
1722	1,010,997	709,055	1,919,613	208,703	128,195	3,335,175	4,441,950	11,717,988
1723	1,034,109	759,336	1,919,913	318,988	196,041	3,443,175	4,171,140	11,724,702
1724	1,265,181	526,770	1,819,913	380,644	227,606	3,427,536	3,926,330	11,510,180
1725	825,835	700,000	1,756,113	272,183	204,047	3,425,210	3,681,520	10,578,808
1726	560,900	388,315	1,470,013	353,304	363,658	3,424,269	3,436,710	10,207,865
1727	975,000	300,000	1,680,709	477,859	498,176	3,424,291	3,191,900	10,934,946
1728	633,000	..	2,067,720	574,396	490,998	3,424,280	2,947,090	10,522,829
1729	594,396	67,000	1,892,124	580,036	453,137	3,399,056	2,702,280	9,688,029
1730	505,604	..	2,142,031	572,725	457,898	3,226,889	2,457,470	9,362,617
1731	466,000	..	1,615,202	611,228	513,666	3,085,287	2,212,660	8,504,043
1732	386,000		788,912	771,448	505,986	3,074,682	1,967,850	7,494,878
1733	304,000		1,545,278	955,171	576,727	3,068,148	1,011,650	7,460,974
1734	1,070,000		2,066,785	161,269	139,704	3,067,661	758,825	7,264,244
1735	100,000		2,140,346	157,336	79,505	3,013,154	482,800	5,973,141
1736	790,000		1,760,391	92,076	54,137	3,012,954	369,025	6,078,583
1737	243,572		2,369,175	82,161	40,203	3,360,553	209,675	6,305,339
1738	265,328		2,643,700	127,541	94,786	3,395,436	112,100	6,638,891
1739	262,400		2,168,555	174,777	152,541	3,422,986	107,000	6,288,259
1740	1,100,000		2,241,400	320,727	250,120	3,424,865	10,450	7,347,562
1741	2,310,000		2,263,347	339,010	273,404	3,427,595	6,550	8,619,906
1742	1,200,000		2,506,858	437,510	247,107	3,429,395	..	7,820,870
1743	1,000,000		3,057,510	328,145	172,626	3,430,845	..	7,989,126
1744	600,000		3,687,361	433,224	270,155	3,429,595	..	8,420,335
1745	1,749,000		3,179,805	675,554	422,623	4,130,295	..	10,157,247
1746	2,000,194		2,740,272	1,236,517	828,262	4,008,465	..	10,813,710
1747	508,000		2,649,163	1,510,532	658,781	4,010,441	..	9,336,917
1748	548,000		2,475,422	2,115,391	959,765	4,120,231	..	10,209,809
1749	1,094,345		3,160,316	191,615	104,461	4,242,456	..	8,793,193
1750	506,692		2,439,709	280,353	169,682	2,103,922	..	5,500,358
1751	500,000		2,864,121	463,405	311,687	900,000	..	5,039,213
1752	500,000		3,483,476	255,539	137,733	1,821,353	..	6,198,101
1753	495,500		2,093,062	475,296	157,728	2,000,000	..	5,221,586
1754	504,500		1,533,475	536,290	212,288	2,101,270	..	4,887,823

figures are from P.R.O. E 406/90–106 (Exchequer Bill Certificate Books), and are for the balance at Christmas each year. The books also give midsummer balances from 1714. It should be noted that the figures for years after 1725 in the Parliamentary Paper referred to are for Supply bills only and do not include those charged on the annual Malt and Land taxes. They are therefore artificially small.[1] The bulk of Exchequer bills was cancelled annually, and a new issue was made, charged on the following session's taxes. The annual balances shown in the table thus comprise old bills of Supply *plus* current bills in anticipation of taxes. A comparison of the end-of-year balances with those at midsummer and with the figures for the annual issue of bills shows that the first of these give a fairly accurate indication of the volume of bills in circulation during the preceding year.

3. The figures for Navy and Victualling bills in course of payment are only approximations, since each year's amount includes up to about 10% for accrued interest, see above pp. 403, 404. However, they are better than nothing. They are taken from the *House of Commons Journals*. The balances are for Michaelmas in the years 1697–1711 inclusive (except 1698 and 1701) 1717–21, 1724 and 1747. In the other years the balance is at Christmas. There are figures for various items of the Navy Debt 1686–1715 in P.R.O. Adm. 49/173, but it does not seem to be possible to extract a continuous series from this source.

4. The annual balance of East India bonds are taken from the company's General Ledgers, India Office Library. The figures are for midsummer each year. Before 1709 they are for the Old Company only.

5. The figures for South Sea bonds are conjectural before 1719–20 and during the 1720s. Those for 1712–18 derive from the South Sea Directors' Court Minutes, Add. MSS. 25494, f. 100; 25495, ff. 62, 248; 25496, f. 54. Those for the 1720s are arrived at by taking the known balances in 1720 and 1732 and apportioning the diminution equally between the intervening years. (The balances for 1720 and 1732 are shown in 'The Report of the Committee appointed to Inspect and Examine the Several Accounts of the South Sea Company' (1732), f. 19, Hse. Lds. Record Office, South Sea Company Papers, Box 167.) From 1732, annual balances at Lady Day and Michaelmas are given in South Sea General Court Minutes, vol. iii, Add. MS. 25545, ff. 7, 33, 47, 60, 70, 75, 86, 89, 92. The company's Register of Bonds (Add. MS. 25580) is not helpful, since it only covers the period 1720–34, and does not show the annual balances outstanding.

NOTES TO APPENDIX D

1. The table is from the transfer books kept at the Bank of England Record Office. No transfer books exist for South Sea Stock, or before 1791 for South Sea annuities. In addition, few figures are available for Exchequer annuities. The Table therefore relates to only part of the National Debt.

---

[1] This presumably vitiates some of the conclusions in E. B. Schumpeter, 'English Prices and Public Finance 1660–1822', *Rev. of Econ. Statistics*, February 1938, which relies on the figures in the Parliamentary Paper.

D

Annual numbers of transfers of stock

Year	Bank of England	East India Company	5% 1715	5% 1717	4% 1717	Army Debentures 4% 1718	Bank Lottery 1719	Civil List 1721	Bank 3% 1726	Totals
1694	369	850*	..	..	..	..	..	..	..	1,219
1695	1,371	..	..	..	..	..	..	..	..	1,371
1696	1,322	..	..	..	..	..	..	..	..	1,322
1697	2,082	..	..	..	..	..	..	..	..	2,082
1698	2,477	880	..	..	..	..	..	..	..	3,357
1699	2,365	880	..	..	..	..	..	..	..	3,245
1700	2,930	2,600	..	..	..	..	..	..	..	5,530
1701	1,692	..	..	..	..	..	..	..	..	1,692
1702	1,326	..	..	..	..	..	..	..	..	1,326
1703	1,049	..	..	..	..	..	..	..	..	1,049
1704	1,163	2,170	..	..	..	..	..	..	..	3,333
1705	1,077	2,170	..	..	..	..	..	..	..	3,247
1706	970	2,330	..	..	..	..	..	..	..	3,300
1707	1,538	2,330	..	..	..	..	..	..	..	3,863
1708	1,103	..	..	..	..	..	..	..	..	1,103
1709	1,731	..	..	..	..	..	..	..	..	1,731
1710	5,770	..	..	..	..	..	..	..	..	5,770
1711	5,484	..	..	..	..	..	..	..	..	5,484
1712	3,390	..	..	..	..	..	..	..	..	3,390
1713	2,632	..	..	..	..	..	..	..	..	2,632
1714	2,726	..	..	..	..	..	..	..	..	2,726
1715	1,653	..	..	..	..	..	..	..	..	1,653

1716	1,471	..	1,884	..	..	..	..	..	..	3,355
1717	2,102	..	1,495	1,081	536	..	..	..	..	5,214
1718	2,081	..	840	11,121	2,488	642	..	..	..	17,172
1719	2,181	..	866	8,357	962	1,374	..	..	..	13,740
1720	7,352†	..	845	10,880	1,017	1,717	..	..	..	21,811
1721	2,383	..	196	1,995	82	191	..	362	..	5,209
1722	1,746	..	136	670	94	157	47‡	1,071	..	3,921
1723	1,810	1,009	147	266	114	268	198	669	..	4,481
1724	2,814	1,473	21	..	157	157	89	364	..	5,075
1725	2,471	1,527	..	..	76	274	126	210	..	4,684
1726	2,586	1,596	..	..	122	144	70	..	..	4,518
1727	1,990	1,656	..	..	12	72	21	..	3,059	6,810

* See note 3.   † See note 5.   ‡ No earlier transfer books for this stock.

D (continued)

Year	Bank of England	East India Company	3% 1726	3% 1731	3% 1742	3% 1743	3% 1744	3% 1745	1% 1746
1728	2,197	1,759	2,805	..	..	..	..	..	..
1729	1,717	1,522	2,018	..	..	..	..	..	..
1730	1,851	1,696	1,209	..	..	..	..	..	..
1731	1,658	1,606	1,056	..	..	..	..	..	..
1732	1,794	1,410	985	2,962	..	..	..	..	..
1733	1,843	1,258	1,317	1,545	..	..	..	..	..
1734	1,772	1,082	1,116	1,149	..	..	..	..	..
1735	1,702	995	1,173	1,167	..	..	..	..	..
1736	1,783	1,497	945	723	..	..	..	..	..
1737	2,181	1,505	987	837	..	..	..	..	..
1738	1,970	1,223	760	764	..	..	..	..	..
1739	1,659	1,279	814	761	..	..	..	..	..
1740	1,470	1,035	760	739	..	..	..	..	..
1741	1,572	888	790	738	..	..	..	..	..
1742	1,578	1,068	855	713	1,388	..	..	..	..
1743	1,782	1,216	815	779	1,325	..	..	..	..
1744	1,489	1,076	623	582	582	3,177	117	..	..
1745	1,604	1,008	554	442	473	2,637	3,423	90	..
1746	2,457	891	562	414	476	1,651	1,850	3,030	549
1747	1,404	995	456	425	417	1,557	1,309	1,403	5,357
1748	1,296	862	513	465	417	753	1,229	1,007	2,799
1749	1,791	1,229	700	622	655	1,557	1,365	1,329	2,977
1750	1,827	1,407	646	673	747	1,092	1,280	1,331	2,024
1751	1,620	1,085	675	655	739	1,360	1,009	1,078	2,440
1752	1,740	1,107	695	367	422	773	1,172	630	1,364
1753	1,785	914	815	17	6	19	20	12	90
1754	1,539	940	1,242	..	..	..	..	..	..

D (continued)

4% 1747	4% Lottery 1747	4% 1748	4% Navy 1749	3% 1750	East India $3\frac{1}{2}$% 1750	Consols 3%	Reduced 3%	Totals
..	..	..	..	..	..	..	..	6,761
..	..	..	..	..	..	..	..	5,257
..	..	..	..	..	..	..	..	4,756
..	..	..	..	..	..	..	..	4,320
..	..	..	..	..	..	..	..	7,151
..	..	..	..	..	..	..	..	5,963
..	..	..	..	..	..	..	..	5,119
..	..	..	..	..	..	..	..	5,037
..	..	..	..	..	..	..	..	4,948
..	..	..	..	..	..	..	..	5,510
..	..	..	..	..	..	..	..	4,717
..	..	..	..	..	..	..	..	4,513
..	..	..	..	..	..	..	..	4,004
..	..	..	..	..	..	..	..	3,988
..	..	..	..	..	..	..	..	5,602
..	..	..	..	..	..	..	..	5,917
..	..	..	..	..	..	..	..	7,646
..	..	..	..	..	..	..	..	10,231
..	..	..	..	..	..	..	..	11,880
3,751	..	..	..	..	..	..	..	17,074
5,079	3,330	1,771	..	..	..	..	..	19,521
3,711	2,583	6,709	2,930	..	..	..	..	28,158
3,891	3,005	6,125	2,688	687	401	..	..	27,824
3,127	1,346	4,501	2,704	2,363	2,445	..	..	27,147
2,380	949	3,365	1,916	585	1,712	1,893	1,328	22,398
120	51	172	85	16	1,958	4,794	10,685	21,559
..	..	..	..	..	718	4,897	11,605	20,941

2. The figures were obtained by multiplying the number of pages for a given year in each transfer book by the uniform number of transfers per page, usually three or four. For East India and Bank stock, whose transfers bore stamp duty, the result is generally accurate, since spoiled transfers are rare. For other stocks 5% (an allowance reached by sampling) was deducted to allow for spoils.

3. The East India figures for before 1723 are for the Old Company, and are based on the six surviving transfer books for this period, none of which is for a period exceeding nine months. The monthly transfer rate appearing from these books was multiplied by ten, the number of months in the year in which the books were usually open. For the years 1698–9, 1699–1700, 1704–5 and 1706–7 the transfer books cover part of each calendar year. An equal number of transfers was assumed in each.

4. The Bank of England and East India Company kept separate volumes for transfers made by attorneys. The Bank series ends in 1711, and its attorney transfer books are missing for the years 1701– inclusive. The East India attorney transfer books exist for the whole period 1726–54. For the Bank the highest number of transfers by attorney 1694–1711 was 687, in 1711; the lowest was 39, in 1709. The corresponding figures for East India stock 1723–54 are 253, in 1743 and 96, in 1739. The figures in the table are the sum of ordinary and attorney transfers.

5. In addition to the 7,352 ordinary transfers of Bank stock in 1720 there were 966 transfers, and 522 re-transfers, of stock pledged as security for loans. The remainder of the re-transfers of pledged stock were made in the years 1721–9.

Bibliography

T H E bibliography is largely confined to sources referred to in the text, but adds some others that were consulted. Some references of only marginal significance are excluded from the bibliography, but are included in the index. The bibliography is divided into the following main sections:

A. Manuscript sources.
B. Printed sources published before 1757.
C. Printed sources published after 1757, and unpublished theses.

Places of publication are given only where they are outside London.

A. MANUSCRIPT SOURCES

Archives Nationales, Paris

G 7/722, Financial proposals of Sieurs Cazier and Marchal 1703–15.
G 7/1119, Contrôle général, miscellaneous memoranda and correspondence.

The Bank of England

(i) *Head Office*
Directors' Court Minutes, with indexes.
General Court Minutes, with indexes.
Subscription book for original stock 1694.
Collection of Bonds and counsel's opinions 1701–43, one volume.
Yearly accounts 1729–62.
Bank stock ledger no. 1.
General ledgers 1–12 (to 1760), with indexes.
Contracts for the circulation of Exchequer bills.

(ii) *Record Office, Roehampton*
Bank stock ledgers (except no. 1), with indexes.
Subscription books and journals for issues of Bank stock in 1697, 1709, 1722, 1742, 1746.
Subscription book for the circulation of Exchequer bills 1711, also containing an abstract of the terms of circulation contracts 1711–58.
Dividend books for certain years in the period 1697–1726 (the next book is for 1806).
Registers of deaths of proprietors of Bank stock.

Register of contracts for sale of Bank stock 1697–1721.

Bundles of powers of attorney (powers were bound in volumes after 1760).

Drawing Office ledgers for current accounts kept at the Bank, with indexes.

Ledgers for South Sea annuities from 1723. Without indexes, but the accounts are in roughly alphabetical order.

South Sea 3% (1751) stock ledgers.

Registers of deaths of proprietors of South Sea annuities from 1723.

> There are no ledgers for South Sea *stock*; the ledgers are noted in an old Bank of England Record Office catalogue as 'deposited with Bosanquet and Co. and ... supposed to be destroyed'. Lloyds Bank Ltd., which absorbed Bosanquet Salt & Co. in the nineteenth century, does not have these ledgers among its present records. There are no transfer books for South Sea stock or annuities for this period.

Stock ledgers for the East India Company, including those of the Old or London Company before 1709. Without indexes, but the accounts are in roughly alphabetical order.*

East India stock transfer books, not a continuous series before 1709.*

Book of East India proprietors' names and holdings at 31 March 1709.*

Box of cancelled East India dividend warrants 1709–1833.*

Ledgers and transfer books for all government stocks managed by the Bank of England, starting with the 5%s of 1715. With indexes. There are also registers of deceased proprietors for several government stocks.

* These records are now in the India Office Library, see p. xv.

Bodleian Library, Oxford

Estates of the South Sea Directors as Sold (2 vols., n.d., clearly 1720–30). Printed catalogues, with handwritten notes of prices, etc. The inventories of their estates compiled by the directors were published by order of parliament in 1721, see below, p. 546.

Firth b. 18 (54), Third Money Subscription receipt, 1720.

CHANDLER, R. (publ.), *Votes of the House of Commons* for 1726, containing three reports from the trustees for sale of South Sea directors' estates. These reports are not in the British Museum *Votes* for 1726–7.

The British Museum

(i) *Additional Manuscripts*

6116, letters from Bishop Nicolson of Carlisle, later of Londonderry, to Bishop, later Archbishop, Wake: f. 12, 21 April 1709, on the supplies for the year; ff. 113–14, 21 Oct. 1720, on the effects of the South Sea crisis in Ireland.

15898, f. 101, William Lowndes's paper 'The Course of the Exchequer on the Receipt Side'.

17477, Papers collected by Adam Anderson. At ff. 31–52, statement of Colin Campbell's debts, dated 1748–9; at ff. 118–21, state of the National Debt 1731–2.

20721, Revenue Accounts 1685–99, perhaps emanating from the parliamentary Committee of Accounts.

22265, Papers relating to the Navy, trade, etc., 1704–32. At ff. 116–17, 'An Account of the Disposition of the Stock and Annuities arising from the Late Directors' Estates', n.d., probably *c.* 1730.

22639, Papers relating to the Company of the Mines Royal in Jamaica 1720–7. At ff. 193, contract for refusal of South Sea stock in 1720.

25494–513, Minutes of the Court of Directors of the South Sea Company 7 September 1711–22 January 1754.

25544 and 25545, Minutes of the General Courts of the South Sea Company 31 January 1721–24 January 1760; vol. 1, which starts in 1711, is missing.

25559–61, Memorials, etc., presented by the South Sea Company 1711–85. No. 25561 at ff. 4 ff. contains a series of accounts which the company presented to the House of Lords in 1733, including statements of the sales of the ex-directors' estates. (Cf. p. 540 below.) At ff. 106 ff. there are statements about the reduction of interest on the government's debt to the company in 1750.

25568–70, Minutes of the South Sea Company's Committee of Lawsuits 1721–42. Volume 4 (for 1742–60) is missing.

25580, South Sea Company's Register of Bonds, 20 February 1720–3 March 1734, showing bonds issued but not repayments.

27871, Collection of powers of attorney and other papers relating to the South Sea Company, 1710–49.

31025, Collection of Exchequer bills, Exchequer bonds, etc., donated by the Comptroller and Auditor General in 1879.

32888, Newcastle Correspondence, ff. 428, report of House of Commons debate on the West Indian Sugar Bill, March 1759.

33038, Papers and memoranda of the Duke of Newcastle on taxation and finance 1688–1756.

34195, Collection of original letters, warrants and papers 1576–1763, containing Exchequer receipts, and Orders of Payment for short- and long-dated loans.

34355, Correspondence between Charles Montague and William Blathwait about Exchequer bills 1696–7.

34728, West Papers, vol. ii. Robert Knight's letter to James West dated Paris 10 Dec. 1742 (N.S.), asking West's favour in securing Knight's return to England, is at f. 7.

38330, Liverpool Papers, vol. cxli, 1715–45.

(ii) *Other MSS.*

Egerton 230, Cavendish's reports of Commons' debates. At ff. 19 ff. debate on stock-jobbing Bill, 23 April 1771.

Harleian 4959, Minutes of the Union Commissioners 1702–3.

Harleian 7497, List of those who have subscribed £3,000 or more to the South Sea Company, dated 8 August 1711.

Lansdowne 829, ff. 123–34, report to the Queen on the financial situation by the Commissioners of the Treasury, dated 31 August 1710.

Portland Loan 29/291, undated scheme for settling Army debts, *c.* 1700.

Ibid. 29/28, George Caswall to Robert Harley about the settling of floating debts, dated 6 October 1710.

Child's Bank, records now in possession of Glyn, Mills & Co.

Ledgers.

Posting Book 1717–56.

Balancing Book 1746–70.

Sir Francis Child's Posting Book 1700–13.

Samuel Child's Posting Book 1740–52.

Corporation of London Records Office

Card index of MSS. under 'loans' for amounts lent through the City Chamber on security of taxes 1660–1705 and 1713.

MS. 40/31 Register of loans totalling £100,000 on the Poll Tax (29 & 30 Ch. II, c. 1) 1678. One volume.

MS. 40/57 Register of loans totalling £244,340 on the first four shilling Aid (4 Wm. and M., c. 1) 1693–4. One volume.

MS. 40/92 Register of two loans made on the credit of the Exchequer in general under 10 Wm. III, c. 1 (1699), one volume. The first loan was for £392,000, the second for £116,900.

MR shelf 23, Register of £175,000 lent on the credit of £400,000 South Sea stock, 1713. This was lent for the Treasurer of the Navy, Charles Caesar.

In the same volume (there is no foliation) there is a list of buyers of 17,500 £10 tickets in the Civil List Lottery of 1713 (12 Anne, c. 11).

Assessments Box 1.2, Receipts for subscriptions to Exchequer bill circulation 1697.

Court of Mayor and Aldermen Papers, Brokers' Bonds 1697 and 1708.

Petitions from brokers to be admitted as Sworn Brokers, 1708, and Brokers' Bonds. (Stephen Mahieu, no. 4534 a., Henry Cotigno, no. 1633, Benjamin Nunes, no. 5143, Elias Paz, no. 5311.)

Register of Brokers admitted 1708–1801.

Repertories 101 and 112, Minutes of the Court of Mayor and Alderman 1696–7 and 1707–8.

Gemeente Archief, Amsterdam

(i) *Archief Brants*

There is an excellent catalogue of this collection by Dr. I. H. van Eeghen, *Inventaris van het Familie — Archief Brants* (Amsterdam, 1959).

565–7. Ledgers of Quirijn Brants en Zoon 1715–63.

927 (de Flines): 7 February 1727 (N.S.), stock held in trust; 11 May 1731, price lists from London showing three- and six-monthly Puts and Refusals for securities.

1344. Letters from London to J. I. de Neufville & Co. in Amsterdam 1730–53. The letters are in Dutch.

1649. Correspondence from London to Simon Bevel in Haarlem 1720–36. The letters are in either Dutch or English.

1736–42. Ledgers of Simon Bevel of Haarlem 1710–36.

(ii) *Notarial Archive*

(a) 3317/69; 3320/89, 310, 311; 3151/1171: all procurations by Dutch investors in English government securities in the 1690s.

(b) Card index covering 1700–10.

(c) *Registers van Schepenkennissen*. Loans recorded before the magistrates of Amsterdam.

Guildhall Library, London

MS. 3083/1, Minutes of the Dissenting Deputies 1732–67. Index at back of volume.

MS. 9579, Certificate book of establishment of Dissenting Meeting-houses in London 1689–1719. Certificates were signed by the minister and some members of the congregation.

House of Lords Record Office, Parchment Collection

(i) *South Sea Company Papers, Box 167*

'An Abstract of What Publick Debts and Incumbrances have been Subscribed to or Discharg'd by ye South Sea Company . . . since ye 25th: of December 1719. . . .'

'An Account of what Stock has been made out pursuant to Agreements made with the Subscribers to ye South Sea Company's Capital Stock and at what time.' (1720).

'An Account of what . . . Sums of Money have been taken up . . . on Accot. of the S.S. Co. . . . since the 25th of December 1719.'

'Copy of the Minutes of the Committee [of the South Sea Company] to treat with the Bank', 15 September 1720–10 November 1720.

'Copy of the Power Authorizing [three South Sea clerks] to Subscribe The Several Species of the Irredeemable Debts into the Capital Stock of the South Sea Company.' [The first subscription of annuities in 1720.]

'Copy of the Form and Preamble of the Subscriptions of the Several Species of the Irredeemable Debts into the Books directed by the Act.' (1720).

'Copy of the Power Authorizing [three South Sea clerks] to Subscribe the Several Species of the Redeemable Debts into the Capital Stock of the South Sea Company.' [The first subscription of Redeemables in 1720.]

'Copy of the Form and Preamble of the Subscription of the Several Species of the Redeemable Debts into the Books directed by the Act.' (1720).

'Copy of the Power Authorizing [three South Sea clerks] to Subscribe the Several Species of the Irredeemable Debts into the Capital Stock of the South Sea Company.' [The second subscription of Annuities in 1720.]

'Copy of the Form and Preamble of the Subscriptions of the Several Species of the Irredeemable Debts into the Books directed by the Act.'

Preambles to the four Money Subscriptions of 1720.

'An Abstract of the Ledgers of the Loan.'

Miscellaneous accounts of brokers who acted for John Aislabie and others in 1720.

'The Report of the Committee appointed to Inspect and Examine the Several Accounts of the South Sea Company, laid before the General Court of the said Company the 16th of June 1732.' Printed 1733, see below, p. 546. This report contains accounts showing the company's liabilities at the end of 1720, the amounts by which its capital increased in 1720, how the 'surplus' stock of 1720 was disposed of 1721–8, and the produce of the sales of the directors' estates.

(ii) *Other MSS.*

B.57–63, copy books of the four subscriptions for new South Sea stock in 1720.

India Office Library, Commonwealth Relations Office

East India General Court Minutes, vols. i and ii, 1702–66.
East India Directors' Court Minutes, vols. 39–63, 1702–50.
General ledgers 1682–1756.
General Cash Journal 1742–50.

The London Assurance

Ship Charter Ledger A 1720–63.
Balance sheets 1728–38 (the next is for 1762).
Dividend lists.

London University Library

MS. 89. Papers relating to the South Sea Company 1712–83.

Public Record Office

Adm. 20/107(i). Treasurer of the Navy's ledger 1711–12. This shows the General Mortgage tallies subscribed by him to the South Sea Company in July 1711.

Adm. 49/11. Navy bills 1672–1758. Contains forms of bills and of their assignment, and Interest warrants.

Adm. 49/13. Original victualling bills 1779–86.

Adm. 49/66, 67. Ledgers showing tickets in the Malt Lottery 1697 issued for the service of the Navy.

Adm. 49/173. Abstract of the Debt of the Navy 1686–1715.

AO 1/867/16. Declared Account for the period 22 June 1709–24 June 1710 of Lionel Herne and Samuel Edwards, Paymasters of Interest on Exchequer bills. (The last account declared by the Paymasters was for the half-year ending 5 July 1720.)

C 11/247 (1). *Child* v. *Wymondesold*, a case arising out of speculation in 1720. Catalogued 'Geo. 1st and 2nd'.

C 11/695/35. *Cortisois* et al. v. *da Costa*. Includes a schedule of accounts 1711–30 kept by da Costa for Lewis Fernandes Parfamo of Brussels.

C 12/57/22. *Hobson* v. *de la Fontaine*.

C 12/1623/1. *André* v. *Verney and Burke*.

The last two cases concern dealings in East India stock in the 1760s.

C 46/1. Documents relating to the Million Bank. This bundle contains (*a*) a list of subscribers to the society in 1695; (*b*) a list of reversionary annuities to which the Bank is entitled, dated 24 November 1702, and probably the original of the printed list (see p. 545 below); (*c*) a bundle of dividend warrants for Million Bank stock in 1712.

C 103/134. *Noke* v. *Wiseman* (1727). A case arising out of share dealings in 1720.

C 107/47. Book of tickets of the first class of the Groningen lottery of 1721.

C 111/50. Papers of Sir Stephen Evance, mostly relating to the 1690s. Many of the papers are in poor condition.

C 111/127. *Crow* v. *Phill*. Contains mercantile correspondence of the 1690s.

C 114/9–23 and 153. Minute books and ledgers of the Million Bank 1696–1796.

C 114/164–5, papers of Charles Blunt.

E 134/8 & 9 Geo. I, Trinity Term, no. 9, *Crossley* v. *Shadforth*. Speculation abroad by English merchants in 1720.

E 401/1987–92, 2018–20, 2044–5, 2064–5, 2090–1, 2103–4, Receipt Books, Pells' for 1691–3, 1707, 1720, 1730, 1743, 1750.

E 401/2594. Copy of subscription books to double the Bank of England's capital, February 1709.

E 401/2595. Register of loans on the Candle Act (8 Anne, c. 5), and repayments, 1710–17.

E 401/2599 and 2600 (1711–12). Books containing the names of prize-winners in the second lottery of 1711 (9 Anne, c. 19) and the second lottery of 1712 (10 Anne, c. 19). The first book is dated 20 December 1711, the second 25 March 1717.

E 403/1400. Issue Roll for the 14% long annuities, Michaelmas 1719–Lady Day 1720. This roll forms part of a series for these issues, starting 12 April 1696 and ending 27 March 1796.

E 403/1935–37. Issue Books, Pells', 1743.

E 404/520. A bundle of receipts for contributions to loans at the Exchequer.

E 406/51. Assignment Book, Auditor's, 1690–1697. This volume consists entirely of entries of powers of attorney to receive fees, interest of loans, etc.

E 406/89–106. Certificate Books for issue and discharge of Exchequer bills 1696–7 and 1712–57. The half-yearly balances of bills are given only from Christmas 1714.

E 406/208–210. Warrants relating to Exchequer bills, 1713–37. No. 208 contains the form of the 1713 bills and instructions for their issue. No. 209 contains contracts with the Bank of England from 1722 to circulate Exchequer bills, and notes of the establishment of the offices of Paymasters of Exchequer bills (ff. 36–37) and Comptroller of Exchequer Bills (f. 58).

E 407/16 and 17. Assignment Books 1705–17 for the Bankers' annuities created in 1705 under 12 Wm. III, c. 12 (1701).

E 407/18–25. Register of Powers of Attorney 1706–09.

E 407/90. Powers of Attorney and Debentures 1700–1800.

E 407/95–99. Miscellaneous assignments 1702–16.

E 407/104–5. Miscellaneous Powers of Attorney 1736–70. These last four series are unhelpful as a guide to the turnover of Exchequer securities, and confirm the superior clarity of the monied companies' records.

E 407/134, Pt. II. One bundle contains a series of Exchequer bills, partly fragments, dated 1697, 1701 and 1709.

E 407/165. Register of Tallies of Pro struck on the Hereditary and Temporary Excise 1684–91.

E 407/166. Entry book of tallies delivered for long-term loans 1708–10.

T 1/87. Treasury Papers 1703.

T 1/231 (3). Treasury Board Papers 1720. Various accounts, comparisons of the proposals of the Bank of England and the South Sea Company in 1720, suggested heads for the South Sea Act and the Bubble Act, and several returns from the South Sea directors of the sums subscribed into South Sea stock in 1720.

T 1/237, no. 6. Treasury Board Papers. Various papers about the South Sea Company, probably compiled for the Parliamentary inquiry in 1721; including an account of the debts subscribed into the company in 1720.

T 1/242. Treasury In-Letters 1722. At f. 58, return from the Bank of England dated 7 September 1722 of amounts of stock transferable at the Bank subscribed into the South Sea Company in 1720.

T 1/333–41. Treasury Board Papers 1748–50.

Index 4635. Memorials, etc., received by the Treasury Board 1719–21. This contains little of any importance about the South Sea crisis. Protests from annuitants at the subscription of their annuities are noted in November and December 1720 (ff. 187, 188, 192, 196, 200).

T 29/24 (i) and (ii). Treasury Board Minutes 22 March 1718–28 April 1722.

T 29/31. Treasury Board Minutes 1747–51.

T 29/627. Extracts from Treasury Board Minutes about discounts on government securities 1691–1702. Signed by Christopher Tilson [a Treasury Clerk], n.d., but probably 1702.

T 30/2 and 11–12. Treasury Annual Account Books 1700–5 and 1745–55. The 'Abstracts' show loans in cash on the annual tax funds.

T 38/668. Departmental Accounts. Subscription of Navy bills in the second Register Book to the South Sea Company; compiled by Robert Knight the company's Cashier, and dated 10 March 1715. The amount involved was only £12,529 with interest, and the bills were old ones made out in 1682–6 for half-pay and pensions.

T 38/796. Departmental Accounts. List of £203,916 in Army debentures made out to contractors and officers, September 1717–July 1718. Signed Thomas Mercer and dated 13 August 1718.

T 48/21. Lowndes Papers. Bundle no. 6 contains a copy of an Ordnance debenture dated 25 March 1711, and a return from the South Sea Company dated 10 December 1712 about the stock created 'for the use of the Publick' in the company.

T 54/19, f. 609. Opinion of Sir Edward Northey, dated 16 December 1706, about a stopped victualling bill.

WO 48/35. Ordnance Treasurer's ledger 1696–7.

WO 48/95. Ordnance Treasurer's ledger 1754.

WO 49/109. Entry Book for Army debentures 1689–91 and 1715. The debentures were made out for lands purchased at Portsmouth, Harwich and Chatham.

The Royal Exchange Assurance

'Doomsday Book' compiled in 1876 by the corporation's Accountant, J. A. Higham, to digest records surviving from the fire of 1838.

The Sun Fire Office

Minute Books for the 1730s.
Ledgers 1728–62.

B. PRINTED SOURCES PUBLISHED BEFORE 1757

Burney Newspaper Collection, British Museum.
Nichols Newspaper Collection, Bodleian Library.

Most of the remaining works in this section were consulted in the Goldsmiths' Library at London University. Identification of authorship in the period 1701–50 from L. N. Hanson, *Contemporary Printed Sources for British and Irish Economic History 1701–1750* (Cambridge, 1963). The titles given below are generally somewhat abbreviated.

J[OSIAH] C[HILD], *Brief Observations concerning Trade and Interest of Money* (1668).
Proposals for Subscriptions of Money &c. (1674).
YARRANTON, ANDREW, *England's Improvement by Sea and Land. To Out-do the Dutch without fighting* (1677).
SCARLETT, J., *The Stile of Exchanges* (1682).
[NORTH, Sir DUDLEY], *Discourses upon Trade* (1691).
A Plain and Easie Way for the Speedy Raising of Money . . . By a Divine of the Church of England (November 1691).
The Present War no Burthen to England (1692).
HOUGHTON, J., *A Collection for Improvement of Husbandry and Trade* (1692–1703).
Reasons for the Abatement of Interest to Four in the Hundred . . . By E.H. (1692).
The Clothiers Complaint: or, Reasons for Passing the Bill Against the Blackwell-Hall Factors . . . (1692).
SHADWELL, THOMAS, *The Volunteers; or, the Stock-Jobbers* (1693).
BRISCOE, JOHN, *A Discourse on the Late Funds of the Million-Act . . .* (1694).
[PATERSON, WILLIAM], *An Account of the Transactions of Mr. William Paterson in Relation to the Bank of England* (1695).
Some Thoughts Concerning the Better Security of our Trade and Navigation . . . (1695).
Angliae Tutamen: Or, The Safety of England . . . By a Person of Honour (1695).
BURNABY, A., *An Essay upon the excising of Malt: as also the present case of tallies consider'd. By A. Burnaby of the Middle Temple* (1696).
WHISTON, JAMES, *The Causes of our Present Calamities in reference to the Trade of the Nation . . .* (1696).
Proposals to Supply His Majesty with Twelve or Fourteen Millions of Money . . . for the Year 1697 . . . By A.D. of Greys Inn Esq., and some Others his Friends (1697).
DEFOE, DANIEL, *An Essay upon Projects* (1697).
CASTAING, J., *The Course of the Exchange and other things.* The earliest copy is for 1698, after which there are volumes for nearly all succeeding years. The most complete set is in the Stock Exchange Library, London.
[DAVENANT, CHARLES], *Discourses on the Publick Revenues and on the Trade of England* (2 vols., 1698).

[DAVENANT, CHARLES], *The True Picture of a Modern Whig* (1701).

DEFOE, DANIEL, *The Villainy of Stock-Jobbers detected* (1701).

HATTON, EDWARD, *The Merchant's Magazine* (1701).

Remarks by Way of Answer, Paragraph by Paragraph, To The Character of a Modern Whig (1701).

A List of the Several Reversionary Annuities To which The Million Bank are Intituled (n.d., prob. 1702, British Museum 8223.e.7).

Some Remarks on the Bill for Taking, Examining and Stating The Publick Accounts of the Kingdom (1702).

DEFOE, DANIEL, *The Consolidator: or, Memoirs of sundry transactions from the world in the moon* (1705).

[BROUGHTON, JOHN], *Remarks upon the Bank of England . . . By a Merchant of London, and a true Lover of our Constitution* (1705).

Reasons Against Charging Trade with Annuities (1707).

The Reasons of the Decay of Trade and Private Credit . . . By a Merchant of London (1707).

[TENCH, NATHANIEL], *A Defence of the Bank of England* (1707).

A Short View of the Apparent Dangers and Mischiefs from the Bank of England (1707).

Reasons Offer'd against the Continuance of the Bank. In a Letter to a Member of Parliament (1707).

JUSTICE, ALEXANDER, *A General Treatise of Monies and Exchanges* (1707).

A Letter to a Person of Quality, Relating to the Bank of England (1710).

[DEFOE, DANIEL], *An Essay upon Publick Credit* (1710).

[DEFOE, DANIEL], *Eleven Opinions about Mr. H—y : with Observations* (1711).

[WALPOLE, ROBERT], *A State of the Five and Thirty Millions* (1711).

[WALPOLE, ROBERT], *The Debts of the Nation Stated and Considered in four Papers* (1712).

WALPOLE, ROBERT, *A Short History of the Parliament* (1713).

EDGAR, WILLIAM, *Vectigalium Systema* (1714).

ASGILL, JOHN, *An Abstract of the Publick Funds* (1715).

HOLLAND, JOHN, *The Ruine of the Bank of England, and all Publick-Credit inevitable* (1715).

LEIGH, EDWARD, *An Essay upon Credit* (1715).

CENTLIVRE, SUSANNAH, *A Bold Stroke for a Wife* (1718).

[DEFOE, DANIEL], *The Anatomy of Exchange-Alley* (1719).

An Examination and Explanation of the South-Sea Company's Scheme for taking in the Publick Debts (17 February 1720).

[HUTCHESON, ARCHIBALD], *Some Calculations relating to the Proposals made by the South-Sea Company . . .* (31 March 1720).

An Argument to shew the Disadvantage That would Accrue to the Publick From obliging the South-Sea Company to fix what Capital Stock They will give for the Annuities (1720).

[TRENCHARD, JOHN], *A Comparison between the Proposals of the Bank and the South-Sea Company* (1720).

A visit to the South-Sea Company and the Bank [by James Milner, M.P.]. Published later in 1720 as *Three Letters Relating to the South Sea Company and the Bank.*

STEELE, Sir RICHARD, *A Nation a Family* (1720).

Some Remarks and Observations Relating to the Transactions of the Year 1720 (1720). [A defence of the South Sea Company.]

Reasons for making void and annulling those Fraudulent and Usurious Contracts, into which Multitudes of unhappy Persons have been drawn ... by the late directors of the South-Sea Company ... (n.d. [? 1721]).

[DEFOE, DANIEL], *A True State of the Contracts Relating to the Third Money Subscription* (1721).

The Case of the Borrowers on the South-Sea Loans (1721).

The Reports of the Honourable the Committee of Secrecy ... exactly set forth. By A[rchibald] H[utcheson] (n.d., clearly 1721).

The Proceedings of the Directors of the South Sea Company (1721).

The Case of Sir Theodore Janssen (n.d., clearly 1721).

Inventories of the estates of the South Sea directors of 1720 (2 vols., 1721).

The Pangs of Credit ... By an Orphan Annuitant (1722).

A letter to the Governor of the Bank of England (1722).

Index Rerum et Vocabulorum for the use of the Freeholders of Counties and Freemen of Corporations (1722).

The Accompts of the several Masters of the High Court of Chancery (1725).

ERASMUS PHILIPS, *The State of the Nation, in Respect to her Commerce, Debts and Money* (1726).

GOULD, Sir NATHANIEL, *An Essay on the Publick Debts of this Kingdom* (1726).

[PULTENEY, WILLIAM, later Earl of Bath], *Some Considerations on the National Debts, the Sinking Fund, and the State of Public Credit* (1729).

EDWARD LAURENCE, *The Duty and Office of a Land-Steward* (Dublin, 1731).

An Account of several Work-Houses for employing and maintaining the Poor (2nd ed., 1732).

The Report of the Committee appointed to Inspect and Examine the Several Accounts of the South Sea Company, laid before the General Court of the said Company the 16th. of June 1732 (1733, a printed version of the report referred to above, p. 540).

Observations on the Laws of Excise (n.d., clearly 1733).

A Letter from a Member of Parliament to his friends in the Country (1733).

An Appeal to the Landholders concerning the Reasonableness and General Benefit of an Excise upon Tobacco and Wine (1733).

[AMHURST, NICHOLAS], *An Argument against Excises, in several Essays, lately published in the Craftsman, and now collected together. By Caleb d'Anvers* (1733).

The Landed Interest consider'd ... By a Yeoman of Kent (1733).

A Letter from a Merchant of London to a Member of Parliament [in answer to the *Letter from a Member of Parliament*] (1733).

The Reply of a Member of Parliament to the Mayor of his Corporation (1733).

[WALPOLE, Sir ROBERT], *Some General Considerations concerning the Alteration and Improvement of Publick Revenues* (1733).

[PULTENEY, WILLIAM], *An Enquiry into the Conduct of our Domestick Affairs* (1734).

[WALPOLE, Sir ROBERT], *Some Considerations concerning the Publick Funds, the Publick Revenues and the Annual Supplies Granted by Parliament* (1735).

ALLEN, WILLIAM, *Ways and Means to Raise the Value of Land* (publ. 1736, written 1734).

Considerations Occasioned by a Proposal for Reducing Interest to Three per Cent. (1737).

Considerations upon a Proposal for Lowering the Interest of all the Redeemable National Debts to Three per Cent. per Ann. (1737).

Queries Relating to the Reduction of the National Redeemable Debts from Four to Three per Cent. per Ann. (1737).

Reasons Against Lowering the Interest of the Redeemable National Debt From 4 to 3 per Cent. shewing This Scheme to be Detrimental to the Public (1737).

[BARNARD, Sir JOHN], *Reasons for the more speedy Lessening the National Debt and Taking off the most Burthensome of the Taxes* (1737).

[BARNARD, Sir JOHN], *Reasons for the Representatives of the People of England to take advantage of the Present Rate of Interest for the more speedy Lessening of the National Debt* (1737). Another title for the preceding pamphlet.

A Speech Without-Doors Addressed to the National Creditors for the Redeemables at 4l. per Cent. (1737).

A true account of the rise and progress of the South Sea Company (1743).

An Essay . . . or a Method . . . To Pay the National Debts . . . by Reviving . . . the Woolen Exportation Trade (1744).

Proposals to raise Ten Millions and Five Hundred Thousand Pounds a Year . . . By an Officer of the Stamp-Duties (1744).

A Letter to Sir John Barnard upon his Proposals for raising three Millions of Money for the Service of the Year 1746. From a Member of the House of Commons (1746).

BARNARD, Sir JOHN, *A Defence of several Proposals for Raising of Three Millions for the Service of the Government for the year 1746* (1746).

Remarks on a Letter to Sir John Barnard (1746).

An Essay on the Inequality of our Present Taxes (1746).

The Art of Stock-jobbing, a Poem. By a Gideonite (1746).

TOLAND, JOHN, *Miscellaneous Works* (ed. des Maizeaux (2 vols., 1747)), i. 404 ff. 'The Secret History of the South Sea Scheme', a tract evidently written by one of the South Sea directors of 1720 and amplified by Toland.

A List of the Names of the Corporation of the Governor and Company of Merchants . . . Trading to the South-Seas . . . 25 December 1747, Goldsmith's Library Extra Size fol. xviii (49).

An Essay upon Publick Credit, in a Letter to a Friend (1748).

'A Letter from a Gentleman in Town to his Friend in the Country' and 'Thoughts on the same Subject' [i.e. the reduction of interest]. (*Gent. Mag.*, November 1749.)

[CREED, Sir JAMES], *Three Letters to the Proprietors of Stock in the East-India Company, Relative to the Question to be Ballotted for on Wednesday, January 3d., 1749. By a Director* (1749). (3 January 1749 means 3 January 1750.)

Considerations on the Proposal for the Reduction of Interest so far as it Relates to the East-India Company (dated at end 30 December 1749).

[BARNARD, Sir JOHN], *Considerations on the Proposal for Reducing the Interest on the National Debt* (6 February 1750).

Annotations on a Late Pamphlet Intituled Considerations on the Proposal for reducing the Interest on the National Debt (1750).

The Necessity of Lowering Interest and Continuing Taxes demonstrated in a Letter to G.B. (1750).

A Copy of a Letter Wrote to a Member of Parliament after The Proposals for reducing the Publick Debt were rejected at the last General Court of the Bank of England (1750).

An Essay on the National Debt and National Capital ... by Andrew Hooke, Esq. (1750).

[MASSIE, JOSEPH], *An Essay on the Governing Causes of the Natural Rate of Interest* (1750).

A Dispassionate Remonstrance of the Nature and Tendency of the Laws now in Force for the Reduction of Interest (1751).

[MAGENS, NICHOLAS], *The Universal Merchant* (1753).

[ELIBANK, PATRICK MURRAY, Lord], *An Inquiry into the Original and Consequences of the Publick Debt* (Edinburgh, 1753).

RANGER, CHARLES (pseud. for A. Murphy), *The Grays Inn Journal*, 3 November 1753 (description of Jonathan's Coffee House).

The Connoisseur. By Mr. Town, Critic and Censor-General, 7 February and 25 April 1754 (anti-Semitic sentiment).

BOLINGBROKE, HENRY, Viscount, *Works* (5 vols., 1754).

C. PRINTED SOURCES PUBLISHED AFTER 1757, AND UNPUBLISHED THESES

(I) *Calendars, Parliamentary Papers, Statutes, Journals*

Calendar of Treasury Papers 1557–1730 (7 vols., 1868–97). The first five volumes were published by Longmans, Green & Co., subsequent ones, and all the calendars below, by H.M.S.O. The first six of these volumes were edited by Joseph

Redington, the seventh, which came out in 1897 after a gap of eight years, by W. A. Shaw, who continued to edit this calendar and the subsequent *Calendar of Treasury Books* until his death in 1943.

Calendar of Treasury Books and Papers 1731–45 (ed. W. A. Shaw, 4 vols., H.M.S.O., 1898–1903). This calendar broadened the scope of the former one by including Treasury Books as well as Treasury Papers.

Calendar of Treasury Books 1660–1718 (ed. W. A. Shaw, 32 vols. in 64 H.M.S.O., 1904–61). This calendar was narrower than its predecessor because it excluded Treasury Papers, presumably on the ground that these had already been dealt with by Redington. What was really needed was a combined calendar of Books and Papers. In compensation, Shaw included lengthy introductions at intervals, in which he surveyed the financial and political history of the separate periods calendared. From 1689 he included the accounts in the new Treasury Annual Accounts series, and other material. Shaw's own views were curiously vehement and often based on inaccurate data, and must be treated with caution. There is an excellent obituary of Shaw by Sir John Clapham, 'William Arthur Shaw 1865–1943', *Proceedings of the British Academy*, xxix (1944).

British Museum Collection of Parliamentary Papers 1731–1800, vol. i, no. 27, Bill against stock-jobbing 1746.

Ibid., vol. xcvi, *Account of the Transactions of the Million Bank Society in the Grant, Purchasing, and Sale of Annuities, &c.* (1796).

British Museum Collection of Parliamentary Papers 1806 vol. xii, 447, 1806–7, vol. iv, p. 49, and British Parliamentary Papers 1810–11, vol. x, p. 483, for foreign holdings in the Funds in 1803, 1806, 1810 and 1811.

Reports from Committees of the House of Commons (15 vols., 1803), i (reports on the Charitable Corporation and the York Buildings Company 1732–5); ii. 73 ff. (Army organization); iv. 73–75 (East India Company dividends 1708–56).

BPP (1842), xviii, Report on Exchequer bills and forgeries of them.

BPP (1857–8), xxxiii, Return of the National Debt of Great Britain and Ireland 1691–1857.

BPP (1868–69), xxxv, Accounts of public income and expenditure of Great Britain 1688 ff.

BPP (1890–91), xlviii, Report of the proceedings of the commissioners for reducing the National Debt 1786–1890.

BPP (1898), lii, History of the earlier years of the Funded Debt from 1694 to 1786. The last four volumes are extremely informative. They are based on original materials, though these are not listed, and are accompanied by valuable historical notes. The reports of 1868–9 and 1890–1 are particularly useful in the latter respect. The report of 1898 contains sections on the debts due to the monied companies as well as listing all government long-term loans.

The Statutes of the Realm (9 vols., 1810–22), to and including 1713. This very useful series was never completed. References to statutes in the text are to this series up to and including 1713, and thereafter to Danby Pickering's much less satisfactory edition, *The Statutes at Large*.

The Journals of the House of Commons (vols. x–xxvi cover the years 1688–1754) and *Journals of the House of Lords* (vols. 14–28 cover the years 1685–1756) are extremely useful, and have been insufficiently used by historians of this period. They are accurate and carefully indexed. Cobbett's *Parliamentary History of England* (36 vols., 1806–20; vols. v–xv cover the years 1688–1765) is also informative, but is less accurate and needs to be checked against the first two series where possible. The debates in each of Cobbett's volumes are listed at the front of it, followed by an index of the principal speakers.

(II) *Articles, books and unpublished theses*

ABRAHAMS, DUDLEY, 'Jew Brokers of the City of London', *Jewish Hist. Soc. of England, Miscellanies* (1937), p. 80.

ACRES, W. MARSTON, *The Bank of England from within* (2 vols., 1931).

— 'The Directors of the Bank of England', *Notes and Queries*, 179 (1940). Valuable biographical notes. In vol. 196 (1951) Acres published a few corrections to his earlier list.

AMSINCK, C., 'Die ersten hamburgischen Assenuranz Compagnien und der Actiekhandel im Jahre 1720', *Zeitschrift des Vereins für Hamburgische Geschichte*, ix (1894), 465.

ANDERSON, A., *An Historical and Chronological Deduction of the Origin of Commerce* (2 vols., 1764; 4 vols., 1787–9).

ASHTON, J., *A History of English Lotteries* (1893).

ASHTON, R., *The Crown and the Money Market, 1603–1640* (Oxford, 1960).

ASHTON, T. S., *The Industrial Revolution in England* (H.U.L. 1947).

— *An Economic History of England. The 18th Century* (1955).

— *Economic Fluctuations in England 1700–1800* (Oxford, 1959).

BAASCH, E., *Holländische Wirtschaftsgeschichte* (Jena, 1927).

BANNISTER, SAXE, *The Writings of William Paterson, Founder of the Bank of England* (2 vols., 1858).

BEATSON, R., *Political Index* (2 vols., 1788).

— *Chronological register of the British Parliament ... 1708 to ... 1807* (3 vols., 1807).

BEBB, E. D., *Nonconformity and Social and Economic Life 1660–1800* (1935).

BEVERIDGE, Lord (ed.), *Prices and Wages in England from the 12th to the 19th Century* (1939).

BINNEY, J. E. D., *British Public Finance and Administration 1774–92* (Oxford, 1958). The definitive modern account of the machinery of public finance in the later eighteenth century. There is a good deal of additional miscellaneous informa-

tion in Dr. Binney's thesis, 'The public revenue and expenditure of Great Britain
... 1774–92' (Oxford University D.Phil. thesis, 1952).

BOUNIATIAN, M., *Studien zur Theorie und Geschichte der Wirtschaftskrisen* (2 vols.,
Munich, 1908), ii: *Geschichte der Handelskrisen in England 1640–1840.*

BRISCO, N., *The Economic Policy of Robert Walpole* (New York, 1907).

Letter-books of John ... Earl of Bristol (3 vols., Wells, 1894).

CAMPBELL, Miss S., 'Usury and Annuities of the Eighteenth Century', *LQR*, xliv
(1928), 473.

— 'The economic and social effect of the usury laws in the Eighteenth Century',
TRHS, 4th ser., xvi (1933), 197

CARSWELL, J. P., *The South Sea Bubble* (1960).

CARTER, Mrs. A. C., 'Analyses of Public Indebtedness in Eighteenth-Century
England', *BIHR* (1951), 173.

— 'The Dutch and the English Public Debt in 1777', *Economica*, New Series, xx
(1953), 159.

— 'Dutch Foreign Investment, 1738–1800', ibid., p. 322.

— 'The Huguenot contribution to the early years of the Funded Debt. 1694–1714',
Proc. Huguenot Soc. of London, xix (3) (1955), 21.

— 'Transfers of Certain Public Stocks ... 1st January to 31st March 1765',
BIHR xxviii (1955), 202.

CARTWRIGHT, J. J. (ed.), *Wentworth Papers 1705–1739* (1882).

CHANDAMAN, C. D., 'The English Public Revenue (1660–1688)', unpub. London
University Ph.D. thesis, 1954.

CHANDLER, G., *Four Centuries of Banking*, i (1964). The first part of the official
history of Martin's Bank.

CHERRY, G. L., 'The Development of the English Free-Trade Movement in
Parliament, 1689–1702', *J. Mod. Hist.* xxv (1953), 103.

CLAPHAM, Sir J. H., *The Bank of England, a history* (2 vols., Cambridge, 1944).

CLARK, D. M., 'The Office of Secretary to the Treasury in the Eighteenth Century',
AHR xlii (1936–7), 22.

COHEN, J., 'The Element of Lottery in British Government Bonds, 1694–1919',
Economica, New Series, xx (1953), 237.

COWLES, VIRGINIA, *The Great Swindle: The story of the South Sea Bubble*
(1960).

COXE, W., *Memoirs of ... Sir Robert Walpole* (3 vols. 1798).

COXE, W., *Memoirs of the administration of the Right Honourable Henry Pelham*
(2 vols., 1829).

DARWIN, K., 'John Aislabie 1670–1742', *Yorkshire Arch. Journal*, xxxvii (1950),
262.

DAVIES, K. G., 'Joint-Stock Investment in the later Seventeenth Century', *Econ.
H.R.*, 2nd ser., iv (1951–2), 283.

— *The Royal African Company* (1957).

DEFOE, DANIEL, *A Review of the State of the British Nation* (ed. A. W. Secord, New York, 1938).

DICKSON, P. G. M., *The Sun Insurance Office 1710–1960. The history of 250 years of British Insurance* (Oxford, 1960).

DILLEN, J. G. van, 'Effectenkoersen aan de Amsterdamsche Beurs 1723–1794', *Economisch-Historisch Jaarboek*, xvii (1931), 1.

DONNAN, E., 'The early days of the South Sea Company, 1711–1718', *J. Ec. and Business Hist.* ii (1929–30), 419.

DU BOIS, A. B., *The English Business Company after the Bubble Act 1720–1800* (New York, 1938).

ERLEIGH, Viscount, *The South Sea Bubble* (1933).

EWEN, C. L., *Lotteries and Sweepstakes in the British Isles* (1932).

FRANCIS, J., *Chronicles and Characters of the Stock Exchange* (1849).

GIBBON, E., *Miscellaneous Works* (1796).

GIUSEPPI, J. A., 'Sephardi Jews and the early years of the Bank of England', *Trans. Jewish Hist. Soc. of England*, xix (1953), 53. The lists of names discussed in this article are published in ibid., *Miscellanies* (1962).

GOWER, L.C. B., 'A South Sea Heresy ?', *LQR*, lxviii (1952), 214.

GRELLIER, J. J., *The Terms of all the loans for the last fifty years* (1799).

—— *The History of the National Debt from 1688 to the beginning of 1800* (1810).

GROENEVELD, F. P., *De Economische Crisis van het Jaar 1720* (Groningen and Batavia, 1940).

HAAFTEN, M. van, *Elementaire Levensverzekerings-wiskunde* (2 vols., Groningen and Batavia, 1947).

HAMILTON, E. J., 'Prices and Wages at Paris under John Law's system', *Quarterly Journ. Economics*, li (1936), 42.

—— 'Prices and Wages in Southern France under John Law's system', *Econ. History*, iii (1934–7), 441.

HANSON, L. N., *Contemporary Printed Sources for British and Irish Economic History 1701–1750* (Cambridge, 1963).

HARDWICKE, Earl of (ed.), *Miscellaneous State Papers* (2 vols., 1778).

HARGREAVES, E. L., *The National Debt* (1930).

HARRISS, G. L., 'Fictitious Loans', *Econ. H.R.* 2nd ser., viii (1955), 187.

HECKSCHER, E., 'A Note on South Sea Finance', *Journal of Economic and Business History*, iii (1930–1), 321.

HENDERSON, A. J., *London and the National Government 1721–1742* (Durham, North Carolina, 1945).

HOMER, SIDNEY, *A History of Interest Rates* (Rutgers University Press, 1963).

HORSEFIELD, J. K., *British Monetary Experiments 1650–1710* (1960).

HOUTZAGER, D., *Hollands Lijf-en Losrentleningen voór 1672* (Schiedam, 1950).

HUGHES, E., *Studies in Administration and Finance* (Manchester 1934).

—— *North Country Life in the Eighteenth Century* (I) *The North East* (Oxford, 1952).

INSH, G. P., *The Company of Scotland* (1932).

JARVIS, R. C., 'Official Trade and Revenue Statistics', *Econ. H.R.* 2nd ser., xvii (1964), 43.

JOHN, A. H., 'Insurance Investment and the London Money Market of the 18th Century', *Economica*, New Series, xx (1953), 137.

— 'War and the English Economy 1700–1763', *Econ. H.R.*, 2nd ser., vii (1954–5), 329.

— 'The Course of Agricultural Change 1660–1760', in L. S. Pressnell (ed.), *Studies in the Industrial Revolution presented to T. S. Ashton* (1960).

KENNEDY, WILLIAM, *English Taxation 1640–1799* (1913).

KING, WILLIAM (ed.), *Memoirs of Sarah, Duchess of Marlborough* (1930).

KING, W. T. C., *History of the London Discount Market* (1936).

KLAVEREN, J. VAN, 'Rue de Quincampoix und Exchange Alley. Die Spekulationsjahre 1719 und 1720 in Frankreich und England', *Vierteljahrschrift für Sozial-und-Wirtschaftsgeschichte*, vol. 48 (1961), p. 329.

LETWIN, WILLIAM, *The Origins of Scientific Economics* (1963).

LEVASSEUR, E., *Recherches historiques sur le système de Law* (Paris 1854).

LILLYWHITE, BRYANT, *London Coffee Houses* (1963).

LLOYD, A., *Quaker Social History 1669–1738* (1950).

LOW, J. M., 'The Rate of Interest: British Opinion in the Eighteenth Century', *Manchester School*, xxii (1954), 115.

LÜTHY, H., *La Banque Protestante en France de la Révocation de l'Edit de Nantes à la Révolution*, vol. i: *Dispersion et Regroupement (1685–1730)*; vol. ii: *De la Banque aux Finances (1730–1794)* (Paris, 1959, 1961).

McLACHLAN, J. O., *Trade and Peace with Old Spain, 1667–1750* (Cambridge, 1940).

MARTIN, J. B., *The Grasshopper in Lombard Street* (1892).

MELVILLE, LEWIS, *The South Sea Bubble* (1921).

Memoirs of the late Sir John Barnard, Knt. (1820, repr. 1885).

MICHAEL, W., 'Der Sudseeschwindel vom Jahre 1720', *Vierteljahrschrift für Sozial und Wirtschaftsgeschichte*, vi (1908), p. 549. His later account, in the third volume of his *Englische Geschichte im achzehnten Jahrhundert* (Berlin, 1934), adds little to the earlier one.

MIKOLETZKY, H. L., 'Die Grosse Anleihe von 1706', *Mitteilungen des Österreichischen Staatsarchivs*, vii (1954), 268.

MORGAN, E. VICTOR, and THOMAS, W. A., *The Stock Exchange. Its History and Functions* (1962).

MORGAN, W. T., 'The South Sea Company and the Canadian Expedition in the Reign of Queen Anne', *Hisp. Am. Hist. R.* viii (1928), 143.

— 'The Origins of the South Sea Company', *Pol. Sci. Q.* xliv (1929), 16.

MORTIMER, THOMAS, *Every Man his Own Broker* (1st and 2nd eds. 1761, 3rd, 4th, and 5th eds. 1762, 7th ed. 1769, 8th ed. 1775, 9th ed. 1782). The 6th ed. is not listed in the British Museum Catalogue. The first edition was published under the pseudonym 'Philanthropos'.

MUNRO, NEIL, *The History of the Royal Bank of Scotland 1727–1927* (privately printed 1928).

NIEROP, L. VAN, 'Brieven van den Amsterdamschen makelaar Robert Hennebo aan ... Simon Bevel over Engelsche fondsen (1735–6)', *Economisch-Historisch Jaarboek*, xvii (1931), 47.

PERRY, T. W., *Public Opinion, Propaganda and Politics in Eighteenth-Century England* (Camb., Mass., 1962). An interesting study of the Jewish Naturalization Act of 1753.

[PINTO, I. DE], *Traité de la Circulation et du Crédit* (Amsterdam, 1771).

PLUMB, J. H., *Sir Robert Walpole. The making of a statesman* (1956).

— *Sir Robert Walpole. The King's Minister* (1960).

POSTLETHWAYT, J., *History of the Public Revenue* (1759).

PRESSNELL, L. S., 'The Rate of Interest in the Eighteenth Century', in L. S. Pressnell (ed.), *Studies in the Industrial Revolution presented to T. S. Ashton* (1960).

PRICE, F. G. HILTON, *Temple Bar, or some account of 'Ye Marygold', no. 1 Fleet Street* (1875).

— *A Handbook of London Bankers* (1876, enlarged 1890–1).

PRIESTLEY, MARGARET, 'London Merchants and Opposition Politics in Charles II's reign', *BIHR*, xxix (1956), 205.

REALEY, C. B., *The Early Opposition to Sir Robert Walpole, 1720–1727* (Lawrence, Kansas, 1931).

Resolutions Proposed concerning [the] Bank of England (26 June 1815). This broadside, in the author's possession, seems to be an extract from a larger work. It is factual, but critical of the Bank.

RICHARDS, R. D., *The Early History of Banking in England* (1929).

— 'The Stop of the Exchequer', *Economic History*, ii (1929–33), 45.

— 'The Lottery in the history of English Government finance', ibid. 57.

— 'The Bank of England and the South Sea Company', ibid. 348.

— 'The Exchequer Bill in English Government Finance', ibid. iii (1934–7), 193.

— *The First Fifty Years of the Bank of England 1694–1744* (*History of the Principal Public Banks*, ed. J. G. van Dillen) (The Hague, 1934).

RILEY, P. W. J., *The English Ministers and Scotland 1707–1727* (1964).

ROGERS, J. E. T., *The First Nine Years of the Bank of England* (1887).

— *A History of Agriculture and Prices*, vii (Oxford, 1902).

SCHUMPETER, E. B., 'English Prices and Public Finance 1660–1822', *Rev. of Econ. Statistics*, Feb. 1938.

SCOTT, W. R., *The Constitution and Finance of ... Joint Stock Companies to 1720* (3 vols., Cambridge, 1910–12).

SHAW, W. A., 'The Beginnings of the National Debt', in *Historical Essays*, ed. T. F. Tout and J. Tait (1907).

— (ed.), 'Letters of Denization and Acts of Naturalization ... 1603–1700', *Publications of the Huguenot Society of London*, xviii (1911).

— (ed.), 'Letters of Denization and Acts of Naturalization ... 1701–1800', *Publications of the Huguenot Society of London*, xxvii (1923). Cf. the supplementary volume by William and Susan Minet, ibid. xxxv (1932).

For Shaw's edition of the *Calendar of Treasury Books* see p. 549 above.

SINCLAIR, Sir JOHN, *The History of the Public Revenue of the British Empire* (3rd ed., 3 vols., 1804).

SPERLING, J. G., 'Godolphin and the organisation of public credit, 1702 to 1710', unpub. Cambridge University Ph.D. thesis, 1955.

— 'The Division of 25 May 1711, on an amendment to the South Sea Bill', *Hist. J.* iv. 2 (1961), 191.

— *The South Sea Company. An Historical Essay and Bibliographical Finding List* (publ. 17, Kress Library of Business and Economics, Boston, Mass., 1962).

SUTHERLAND, Dr. L. S., *A London Merchant, 1695–1774* (Oxford, 1933, reissued 1962).

— 'Samson Gideon and the Reduction of Interest 1749–1750', *Econ. H.R.* xvi (1946), 15.

— 'Samson Gideon: Eighteenth Century Jewish Financier', *Trans. Jewish Hist. Soc. of England*, xvii (1951–2), 79.

— *The East India Company in Eighteenth Century Politics* (Oxford, 1952).

— 'The City of London and the Devonshire-Pitt Administration, 1756–7', Raleigh Lecture on History, British Academy, 1960.

— and BINNEY, J. E. D., 'Henry Fox as Paymaster of the Forces', *Eng. Hist. Rev.* lxx (1955), 229.

SWIFT, J., *The Conduct of the Allies* (1711); *The History of the Four Last Years of the Queen* (1713), *Works*, ed. H. Davis, vi and vii (Oxford, 1951).

THAYER, T., 'The Land-Bank System in the American Colonies', *J. Ec. Hist.* xiii (1953), 145.

VILAIN, J., 'Heurs et Malheurs de la Spéculation (1716–1722)', *Rev. d'histoire moderne et contemporaine*, 4 (1957), 121.

DE VRIES, J., *De economische Achteruitgang der Republick in de Achtiende Eeuw* (Amsterdam, 1959).

VÜHRER, A., *Histoire de la dette publique en France* (2 vols., Paris, 1886).

WILSON, C. H., *Anglo-Dutch Commerce and Finance in the Eighteenth Century* (Cambridge, 1941).

WILSON, WALTER, *The History and Antiquities of Dissenting Churches* (4 vols., 1808–14).

YOGEV, GEDALIA, *The Economic Activity of the Anglo-Jewish Patriciate in the eighteenth century international trade* (summary of unpub. Ph.D. thesis, Hebrew University of Jerusalem, 1962).

Index

Abarbanel, Ephraim, jobber, 499
Abbot, Mordecai, 52, 366, 366 n.
Abdy, Sir John, 444
Abingdon, Earl of, 443
Abney, Dame Mary, 294
Accountant-General of Chancery, 292–293, 293 n., 390, 434–5
Aggregate Fund, *see* Debt, National
Aislabie, John: Treasurer of Navy, then Chancellor of Exchequer, 85 n.; in touch with South Sea directors, 89, 94; character of, 95; purchases stock (1719–20), 96, 96 n.; suggests division of South Sea plan, 99; defends South Sea proposal in Parliament, 100; invests in South Sea subscriptions, 109; list of, in third Money Subscription, 126; implicated in corruption by committee of secrecy's report, 172; expelled from Parliament and retires to his Yorkshire estates, 173; death, 173; value of estate confiscated, 188 n.; owns Bank stock, 281
Aislabie, William, East India director, brother of John, 106 n.
Aislabie, William, son of John, 297
Allen, William, 476–7
Alphen, Hieronimus van, 315
America, North: holders of English government stock in, 317, 324, 330–1
Amicable Assurance Office, 292
Amsterdam: Bank of, 5, 43–44, 58; English investments of citizens of, 307, 315, 325–6, 326–7; Bourse, its links with England, 335–6, 491, 509–10
Annuities: earliest debts in form of, 21; redeemable debts to be turned into, 21, 22 n.; life, of 1693–4, 53–54; reversions to, sold, 57; used to finance War of Spanish Succession, 59–62;

technique of subscribing to, 76–77; proposal to exchange them for redeemable stock (1717) abandoned, 84–85; proposal to exchange them for new South Sea stock (1719–20), 97 ff. and App. A; amount of, and exchanges for South Sea stock, 132, 134 and App. B; procedure of exchanges, 131–3; terms, 135; former holders of, try to contest their bargains, 169–70; former holders of, affect South Sea Company's attitude to its trade, 181; and suffer losses of capital and income as result of South Sea Bubble, 181–6; used as *douceurs* in war-loans of 1740s, 219. *See also* Transfers of securities *and* Turnover of stock
Anson, Admiral Lord, 290, 295, 450
Apthorp, Charles, 330, 331
Apthorp, John, jobber, 512
Arbuthnot, Dr. John, 267
Argyll, Duke of, 109
Army credit: after King William's War, 393–7; debts of, partly exchanged for Irish lands, 394–6; debentures, 394–396; post-1713 debts, 397; Ordnance Board's system, 397–8; Transport Commissioners, 398; Clothing Assignments as part of, 399
Arnold, Christopher, goldsmith-banker, 295, 450
Arthur, Daniel, 443 n.
Arthur family, 152
Arundell, Richard, 297
Ashburnham, Lord, 265
Astell, William, South Sea Company director, 112 n., 113, 115, 119–20, 147, 187 n., 189
Athias, Simson da Costa, & Co., 308
Atkins, Abraham, jobber, 188, 412 n., 515

PRINTED IN GREAT BRITAIN
BY ROBERT MACLEHOSE AND CO. **LTD**
THE UNIVERSITY PRESS, GLASGOW